TRANSPORT CATEGORY
AIRCRAFT SYSTEMS

JEPPESEN

BY THOMAS W. WILD

Jeppesen Sanderson, Inc.

Published in the United States of America
Jeppesen Sanderson, Inc.
55 Inverness Drive East, Englewood, CO 80112-5498
www.jeppesen.com

ISBN-13: 978-0-88487-232-0
ISBN-10: 0-88487-232-7

Jeppesen Sanderson, Inc.
55 Inverness Dr. East
Englewood, CO 80112-5498
Web Site: www.jeppesen.com
Email: Captain@jeppesen.com
© Jeppesen Sanderson Inc.
All Rights Reserved. Published 1996
Printed in the United States of America

JS312631-002

PREFACE

This book has been written to provide a simple and self-contained description and familiarization of large transport category aircraft and their onboard systems. It would be impossible to cover every transport category aircraft's systems in detail. So an attempt has been made to familiarize the reader with the basics of aircraft systems that are common to all large aircraft.

This text is designed for the reader who has some basic knowledge of aeronautical terminology and aircraft systems. The emphasis of the information presented here will be on introducing the reader to aircraft systems through the use of example aircraft. The components and operation of a specific aircraft's systems will be explained and illustrated, and it is most important that the reader thoroughly study each illustration and diagram in detail.

By generalizing this information to other aircraft, the reader can gain an understanding of transport category aircraft systems. *At no time should the information contained in this text be used for actual operation or maintenance. The information contained in this text is for familiarization and training purposes only.*

Acknowledgments:
- Airbus Industrie
- AlliedSignal Aerospace
- American Trans Air
- Boeing Airliner Magazine
- Boeing Aircraft
- Lockheed Aeronautical Systems
- McDonnell Douglas Aircraft
- Northwest Airlines
- Pratt & Whitney

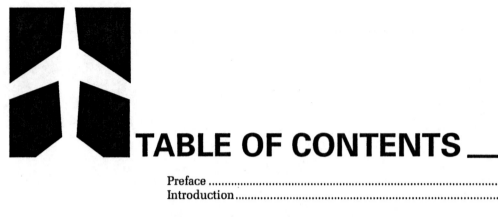

TABLE OF CONTENTS _____

Preface iii
Introduction vi

CHAPTER 1   Types Of Transport Aircraft
Boeing 727 Series 1-1
Boeing 737 Series 1-4
Boeing 747 Series 1-6
Boeing 757 Twin Jet Series 1-9
Boeing 767 Twin Jet Series 1-13
Boeing 777 Twin Jet Series 1-15
Douglas Aircraft Company...1-20
McDonnell Douglas DC-9 Series..1-20
McDonnell Douglas MD-80 Series..1-22
McDonnell Douglas MD-90 Series..1-25
Douglas DC-10 Series 1-26
McDonnell Douglas MD-11 1-29
Lockheed L-1011 Tristar Series 1-31
Airbus Industrie 1-34

CHAPTER 2   Auxiliary Power Units, Pneumatic, And Environmental Control Systems
APU Systems 2-1
Pneumatic Systems 2-8
Environmental Control Systems 2-10
Pressurization Systems 2-13

CHAPTER 3   Anti-icing Systems And Rain Protection
Aircraft Ground Deicing/Anti-icing 3-3
Boeing 757 Aircraft Anti-icing Systems..3-5
Lockheed L-1011 Anti-icing Systems...3-6

CHAPTER 4   Electrical Power Systems
Power Sources 4-1
System Components...4-1
Electrical System Configurations...4-2
Boeing 727 Electrical System 4-4
Boeing 737-300 Electrical Power System..4-7
Boeing 747 Electrical Power System 4-11
Boeing 777 Electrical Power System 4-15
DC-9 Electrical Power System 4-17
DC-10 Electrical Power System 4-19

CHAPTER 5   Flight Control Systems
Boeing 727 5-1
Lockheed L-1011 Flight Controls 5-7
A320 Flight Controls...5-22
Boeing 777 Flight Control (Fly-By-Wire) System 5-30
McDonnell Douglas DC-10...5-33

CHAPTER 6   Fuel Systems
Turbine Engine Fuels 6-1
Fuel System Contamination 6-1
Fuel Systems..6-2
Boeing 737-300 Fuel System 6-6

    L-1011 Fuel System..6-6
    McDonnell Douglas DC-9 Fuel System 6-21
    Boeing 747-400 Fuel System 6-21

CHAPTER 7   Hydraulic Systems
    Hydraulic Fluid 7-1
    Components Of Hydraulic Systems 7-2
    Boeing 737-300 Hydraulic System 7-4
    Boeing 757 Hydraulic System 7-7
    Boeing 757 Landing Gear System 7-13
    Boeing 747-400 Hydraulic Power System 7-23
    Boeing 747-400 Landing Gear 7-27
    Lockheed L-1011 Hydraulic System 7-29
    McDonnell Douglas DC-9 Hydraulic System 7-30
    McDonnell Douglas DC-10 Hydraulic System 7-31

CHAPTER 8   Oxygen Systems
    Lockheed L-1011 Oxygen System 8-2
    Boeing 737-300 Oxygen Systems..8-8
    Boeing 747-400 Oxygen Systems..8-10

CHAPTER 9   Warning And Fire Protection Systems
    Fire Protection Systems 9-1
    Lockheed L-1011 Fire Protection Systems......................................9-5
    Aircraft Warning Systems 9-10
    L-1011 Aural Warning Systems 9-10
    Boeing 737-300 Fire And Warning Systems 9-12
    Boeing 757 Fire Protection Systems..9-22
    Engine Indication And Crew Alerting System 9-29

CHAPTER 10   Communications, Instruments, And Navigational Systems
    Communications 10-1
    Navigation Equipment 10-4
    Boeing 737-300 Avionics 10-7
    Boeing 757 Avionics 10-14
    Boeing 767 Flight Management System 10-31
    Boeing 777 Avionics 10-31
    Boeing 777 Navigation Systems 10-34
    L-1011 Flight Management System 10-37

CHAPTER 11   Information And Auxiliary Systems
    Boeing 777 Airplane Information Management Systems.................11-1
    Boeing 747-400 Central Maintenance Computer System 11-4
    Potable Water Systems 11-9
    Waste Systems 11-14
    Lighting Systems 11-19
    Emergency Equipment 11-23
    Equipment Cooling Systems 11-27
    Maintenance Information..11-34

APPENDIX A A-1
APPENDIX B B-1
GLOSSARY G-1
INDEX..I-1

INTRODUCTION

Transport aircraft have undergone many changes with the advent of the electronic age. Modern aircraft depend highly on electronic controls. Onboard computers now control many of the functions that were controlled by pilots and flight engineers in the past.

Although many of the conventional types of aircraft are still being used, flight crew members and technicians will need knowledge of both the conventional and electronically controlled aircraft and their systems. New generation aircraft have most of the aircraft systems controlled by electronics and computers no longer require a flight engineer. A good understanding of the aircraft's systems is certainly a prerequisite to perform any type of aircraft operation or maintenance. A large transport aircraft, for the purposes of this text, is an aircraft that can transport approximately 100 passengers and their baggage, and utilizes multi-turbofan engines.

Large transport aircraft are manufactured by several companies around the world, such as The Boeing Commercial Airplane group, McDonnell Douglas, Lockheed, and Airbus Industries. Some of the aircraft that will be discussed are the Boeing models 727, 737, 747, 757, 767, 777, and McDonnell Douglas DC-9, MD-80, MD-90, DC-10, and the MD-11. Lockheed L-1011 and Airbus A300, A310, A319, A330, A340 will also be discussed. Almost every aircraft model has several dash number series that identifies a certain series within a model number. Each series number is the same basic model of the aircraft, but with each different dash number changes have been made to the design.

A large transport aircraft can be divided into several groups of components. A group of components that work together to perform a common aircraft function is generally referred to as an aircraft system. Large transport aircraft contain several systems. One method of classifying the aircraft's systems is as follows:

- APU system
- Pneumatic System
- Environmental Control (heating, cooling, pressurization) systems
- Anti-icing System
- Electrical power system
- Fuel system
- Hydraulic system
- Landing gear system
- Oxygen System
- Fire detection and protection system
- Warning systems
- Communication system
- Instrument system
- Navigation system
- Potable and waste water systems
- Equipment cooling system
- Lighting system
- Powerplant system
- Emergency systems

There are a number of ways to divide the aircraft into its many systems. The method used here is just an example. By dividing the aircraft into its systems, each area can be studied separately.

Transport aircraft systems all have major differences in design, yet many of the systems have functional similarities. For example, the normal function of the Auxiliary Power Unit (APU) is to supply compressed air and turn a generator. Although the function is very much the same, a particular APU's operation may be somewhat different from aircraft to aircraft. As each aircraft's system is studied, a specific aircraft will be explained, and information for the operation of each system can be generalized to other aircraft. Keep in mind that each aircraft system's specific operation is a little different according to the needs of that aircraft.

TYPES OF
TRANSPORT AIRCRAFT

Figure 1-1. A Boeing 727-200 aircraft. (Boeing)

BOEING 727 SERIES

A departure from basic aircraft design, the tri-jet 727, pictured in Figure 1-1, was developed as a modern short-to-medium range jet to replace the many piston and turboprop airplanes in such service. Three JT8D engines were chosen for reasons of economy and desired performance. Two of the engines (number 1 and 3) are mounted on each side of the aft fuselage, as can be seen in Figure 1-2. These engines are called the pod engines because they are mounted in nacelles that are attached to the fuselage by horizontal pylons. The center engine (number 2) is mounted in the aft center of the fuselage and gets its air through the use of a "S"

duct, as illustrated in Figure 1-2. The JT8D and its main components and systems is shown in Figure 1-3. The first 727 rolled out of the factory on November 27,1962. The 727 has two basic dash numbers (series); the -100 and -200 Series. The specifications and dimensions for the 727-200 Series aircraft are shown in Figure 1-4.

Design range was from 150 to more than 1,700 statute miles. The 727 requires two pilots and a flight engineer (FE) on the flight deck, with the FE controlling most of the aircraft's major systems. The 727C offered a convertible version, either passenger or cargo, which could

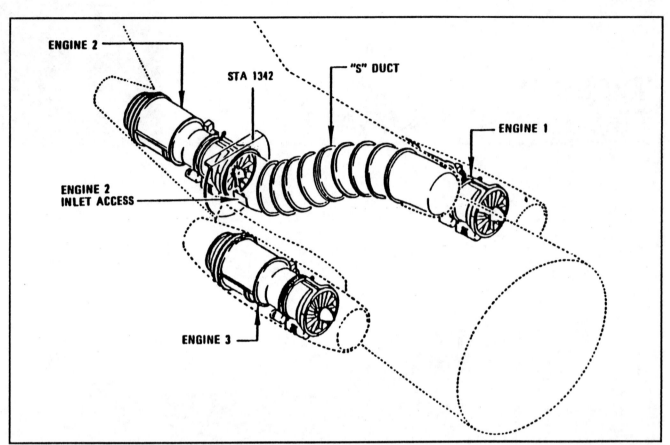

Figure 1-2. Boeing 727 engine location. (Boeing)

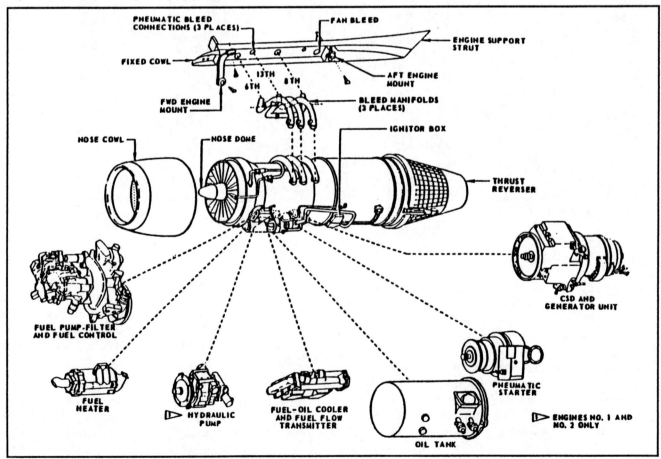

Figure 1-3. JT8D engine components. (Boeing)

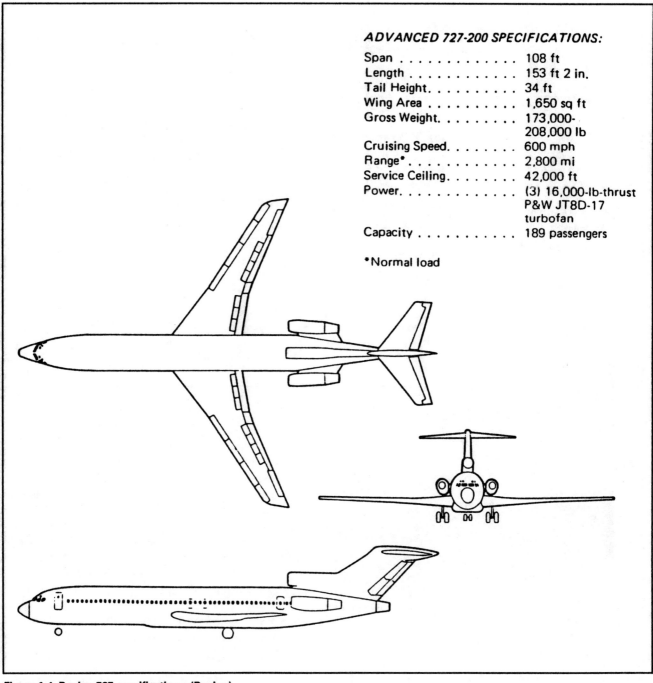

ADVANCED 727-200 SPECIFICATIONS:

Span . . . . 108 ft
Length . . . . 153 ft 2 in.
Tail Height. . . . . 34 ft
Wing Area . . . . 1,650 sq ft
Gross Weight. 173,000-
                            208,000 lb
Cruising Speed. . . . . . . 600 mph
Range*. . . . . 2,800 mi
Service Ceiling. . . . . . . 42,000 ft
Power. . . . . (3) 16,000-lb-thrust
                            P&W JT8D-17
                            turbofan
Capacity . . . . 189 passengers

*Normal load

Figure 1-4. Boeing 727 specifications. (Boeing)

be ready for operations in a few hours. The 727QC was a conversion which could be accomplished in a matter of minutes using palletized seats and galleys.

By late 1964, certain air routes had apparent need of a higher capacity medium-range jet transport. The 727-200 was created, which was a 727-100 with an additional 20 feet of cabin length and capable of ranges of 1,500 statute miles. Success of the 727-200 was immediate. The Advanced 727-200 featured higher gross weight, increased fuel capacity and range, more pow-

erful engines, and many other refinements. In 1973, the 1,000th 727 rolled from the factory, and by the end of 1977 almost 1,500 727s had been sold. The popular tri-jets were serving with some 80 operators worldwide.

727 POWERPLANT

The JT8D's initial rating of 14,000 pounds of takeoff thrust has been uprated over the years to permit significant increases in aircraft payload and range, shorter takeoff distance, and higher rate of climb. The Pratt &

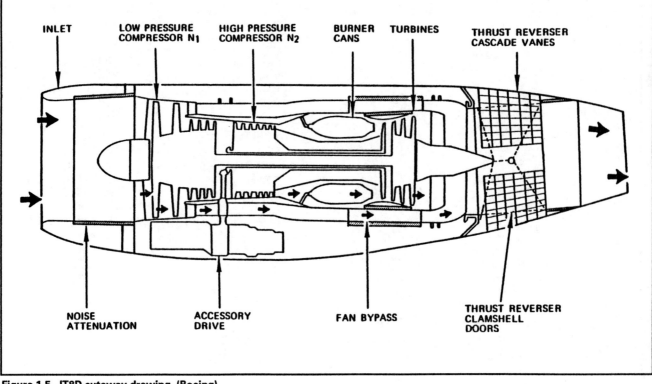

Figure 1-5. JT8D cutaway drawing. (Boeing)

Figure 1-6. Boeing 737-500 aircraft. (Boeing)

Whitney JT8D is a twin spool axial-flow gas turbine engine equipped with a secondary air duct which encases the full length of the engine. A simple diagram to illustrate the general configuration of the engine is shown in Figure 1-5.

BOEING 737 SERIES

The 737, shown in Figure 1-6, is the smallest member of the Boeing family of jet airliners. A short-range airplane, the twin-jet has the same body width and the same accommodations found in other Boeing jetliners. The 737-100 and -200 Series, powered by two wing-mounted Pratt & Whitney JT8D engines, are capable of flying routes of 100 to 2,000 statute miles.

The 737 was ordered into production in early 1965, and the first 737 completed its maiden flight in 1967. The 737-100 is 94 feet long overall and the 737-200 is 100 feet long. The basic dimensions and profile drawings of a 737-200 are illustrated in Figure 1-7. The high-lift system of the 737 uses triple-slotted trailing edge wing flaps , leading-edge slats outboard of the nacelles, and single-type flaps along the wing between the nacelles and fuselage. With these high-lift devices, the 737 can operate from runways as short as 4,000 feet.

The 737 was the first Boeing jetliner not requiring a flight engineer. It is operated by a pilot and copilot from a flight deck where simplicity is the keynote.

Because of its role as a short-range jetliner, the 737 is designed so that little ground support equipment and few servicing units are required. Baggage handling and most servicing and maintenance can be accomplished from ground level.

The newer members of the Boeing 737 jetliner "family" are the 737-300, -400, and -500. Designed to take advantage of more efficient engines and to carry more passengers than earlier 737s, the 737-300 was ordered into production in 1981.

Design changes resulted in lower direct operating costs and a 20% reduction in fuel burned per seat over the 737-200.

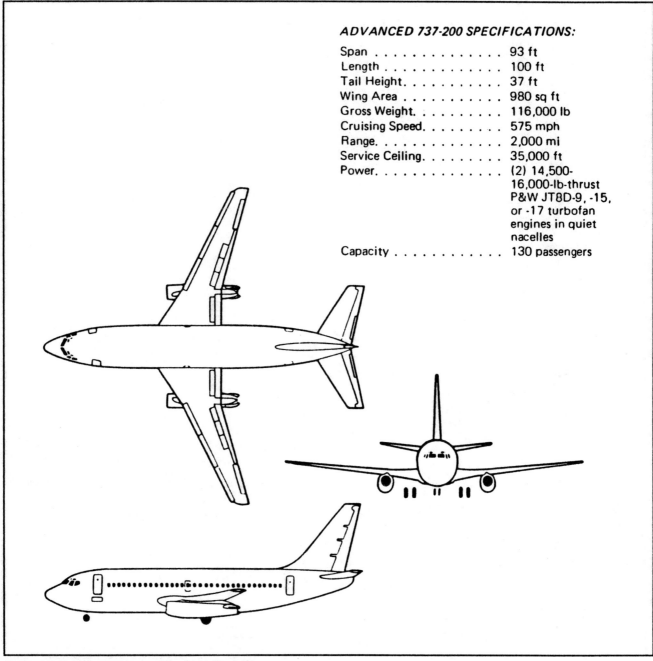

ADVANCED 737-200 SPECIFICATIONS:

Span . . . . 93 ft
Length . . . . 100 ft
Tail Height. . . . . 37 ft
Wing Area . . . . 980 sq ft
Gross Weight. . . . . 116,000 lb
Cruising Speed. . . . . 575 mph
Range. . . . . 2,000 mi
Service Ceiling. . . . . 35,000 ft
Power. . . . . (2) 14,500-
16,000-lb-thrust
P&W JT8D-9, -15,
or -17 turbofan
engines in quiet
nacelles
Capacity . . . . 130 passengers

Figure 1-7. Boeing 737-200 specifications. (Boeing)

BOEING 737-300, -400, -500 FEATURES AND POWERPLANTS

The 737-300 uses two wing-mounted CFM56-3 turbo-fan engines produced by CFM International, which is jointly owned by General Electric and SNECMA of France. These engines also provide greatly reduced noise levels and have thrust ratings of around 20,000 pounds.

Visible differences from the standard 737-200 are the 104 inch (2.6 m) fuselage extension, giving the airplane

an overall 9 foot 7 inch (33.4 m) greater length, and the larger engines mounted forward of the wing on struts (737-100 and -200 engines are tucked up directly under the wing). The new 737-300 also has 6 feet of span added to the horizontal tail and small wing-tip extensions. Specifications and a drawing of the 737-300 is shown in Figure 1-8.

The flight deck reflects digital technology instrumentation. This equipment provides 737 operators with substantial commonality benefits in equipment. The

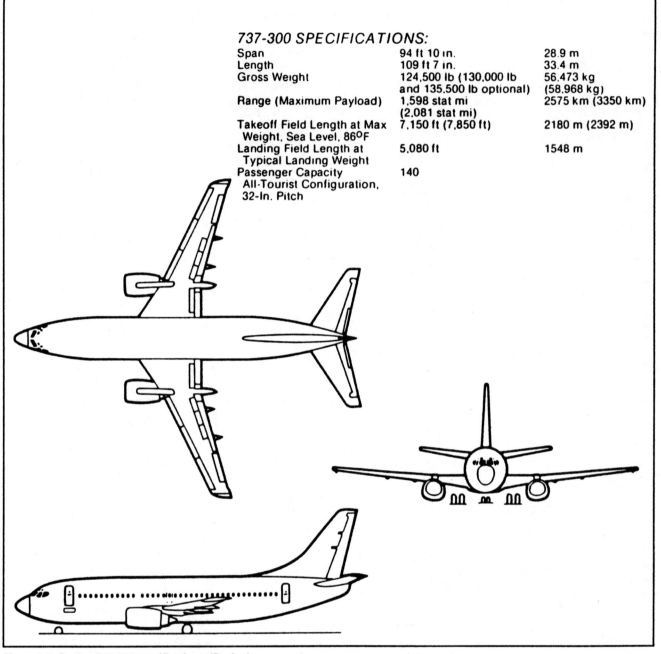

737-300 SPECIFICATIONS:

Span	94 ft 10 in.	28.9 m
Length	109 ft 7 in.	33.4 m
Gross Weight	124,500 lb (130,000 lb and 135,500 lb optional)	56,473 kg (58,968 kg)
Range (Maximum Payload)	1,598 stat mi (2,081 stat mi)	2575 km (3350 km)
Takeoff Field Length at Max Weight, Sea Level, 86°F	7,150 ft (7,850 ft)	2180 m (2392 m)
Landing Field Length at Typical Landing Weight	5,080 ft	1548 m
Passenger Capacity All-Tourist Configuration, 32-In. Pitch	140	

Figure 1-8. Boeing 737-300 specifications. (Boeing)

737-300 and up, although having 80% commonality with the present 737-200, is considered a new generation airliner because of the use of composite materials inside and out as well as the new engines and avionics.

The 737-400 is 120 inches longer than the 737-300 and has a maximum takeoff weight of 142,500 pounds, with increases in gross weight expected in the future. The engines are CFM56-3B-2s or C-1s rated at 22,000 pounds SLST (sea level static thrust). The aircraft will carry between 135 and 172 passengers, depending upon the seating arrangement. The 737-400 is the largest of the 737 family.

The 737-500 began service in 1990 for lower density short-to-medium range routes. The 737-500 incorporates the proven technology features of the 737-300, but in a 737-200 sized airframe. The 737-500 is offered in gross weights from 115,500 pounds up to 133,500 pounds, giving it the capability to carry 108 mixed class passengers 2,500 nautical miles. The engines are CFM56-3-B1s re-rated to 18,500 to 20,000 pounds SLST. Other than the length differences, the 737-300, -

400, -500, aircraft are very similar with regard to basic shape and engine location.

BOEING 737-600, -700, -800

The 737-600, 737-700 and 737-800, 128 to 149 passenger aircraft, are equipped with a larger wing, a higher output thrust CFM56-7 engine, and many updated systems. The 737-800 version is a stretched 737-400, with the 737-700 conforming to the size of the 737-300. The 737-600 is the same fuselage length as the 737-500.

The -600,-700,-800 have been called "double derivatives." The airplanes are derivatives of the current 737s and the design processes are derivatives of the highly successful 777 digital design process. Some of the improvements to the -600, -700, and -800 are as follows:

- A new engine.
- An aerodynamically new wing.
- An upgraded avionics system.
- An improved electrical power system.
- An upgraded auxiliary power unit (APU).

BOEING 737-600,-700, -800 POWERPLANTS

Primary design goals for the new CFM56-7 engine are to decrease noise, fuel burn, and maintenance cost, while increasing thrust and time on wing.

The engine features a new 61-inch diameter fan with wide-chord titanium blades and a high-flow booster, coupled to a CFM56-5B core and low-pressure turbine. The maximum thrust has been increased to over 26,400 lbs. Engine control is accomplished through a full authority electronic engine control.

BOEING 737-600, -700, -800 DESIGN FEATURES

The redesigned wing, with increased chord and span, increase takeoff performance, cruise speed, cruise altitude, and range. These design features have improved the cruise efficiency 16 percent while increasing the speed to .78 Mach. The larger wing also allowed for increased fuel volume. The combined effect of the improved wing performance, increased fuel volume, and more efficient engine has significantly increased each airplane's maximum range. The high-lift system has also been redesigned for improved performance and reduced maintenance. The flap system is double slotted, rather than triple slotted like the earlier dash number airplanes.

AVIONICS

When the 777 liquid crystal flat panel displays were shown to fit the 737 flight deck, they were installed on the new 737s. The display system:

- Allows for a common crew rating.

- Provides software-driven format changes between the standard format on the 737, 757, and 767, and the Primary Flight Display/Navigation Display (PFD/ND) format on the 747-400 and 777.

- Other upgrades to the avionics include the use of ARINC 700 equipment, the installation of a combined air data inertial reference unit, a digital yaw damper, digital antiskid, enhanced autothrottle, and upgrades to the flight management computer.

ELECTRICAL POWER

Electrical power has been increased from 50 to 90 KVA. Each engine powers an integrated drive generator (IDG) designed for high reliability through increased oil cooling and light loading during normal dual engine operation. If needed, either IDG can power the entire airplane with no reduction in cabin electrical capabilities. The AC bus is designed to allow all buses to be powered from any of four sources: IDG1, IDG2, APU, or external power. This allows simple and reliable bus transfer from any source. The DC power system uses many of the high-reliability components used on the present 737 fleet. The switching controls are improved by adding a standby power control unit. This replaces relay switching logic with redundant circuit cards, and provides built-in-test functionality for switching relays.

AUXILIARY POWER UNIT (APU)

The increased demands on the pneumatic system to start the engines and the 90 KVA engine electrical system required Boeing to upgrade the APU. The generator is used as a motor to start the APU, eliminating the DC starter motor, clutch, and extra battery. The APU cooling fan has been eliminated through the use of an eductor cooling system first used on the 777. APU maintenance has been greatly simplified by replacing the metal shroud around the engine with a thermal blanket fire protection design.

BOEING 747 SERIES

Design of the Boeing 747, first of the giant jetliners, began in the early 1960s, when market research indicated the need for a much larger capacity transport to cope with the growing passenger and cargo traffic. In 1968, the first 747 rolled from the world's largest building at the time. The first flight occurred in 1969 and

Figure 1-9. A Boeing 747-400 aircraft. (Boeing)

the first scheduled 747 service began in 1970. A 747-400 aircraft can be seen in Figure 1-9.

The 747 has been produced in several basic models, the -100 , -200, -300, -747SR, -747SP and -400 Series, with the -400 Series being the latest version. The different model series and the first flight dates are shown in Figure 1-10.

747 MODEL SERIES	FIRST FLIGHT DATE
747-400M	1989
747-400	1988
747-300M	1982
747-100B	1979
747-SP	1975
747-200B/C	1974
747-SR	1973
747-300	1973
747-200L	1973
747-200F	1971
747-200	1970
747-100	1969

Figure 1-10. First flight dates and Boeing 747 model series. (Boeing Airliner)

The 747 is offered in three basic configurations; all passenger, mixed passenger/cargo, and all freighter. In convertible or freighter versions, the 747's volume and upward hinged nose allow straight in loading of long and bulky articles. An optional main deck cargo side door is available on all three models.

An unusual feature of the 747 is the unique upper deck, immediately behind the cockpit. This area can be used as a luxurious first class lounge, or for standard passenger seating.

The wing flap system, and a 16-wheel, four-main-truck landing gear allow the 747 to operate from runways

normally used by 707s. As more powerful engines became available, new range and load capabilities were possible. The initial 747-100 had a 710,000 pound takeoff weight, which has been raised to 833,000 pounds for later 747s.

In 1972, the first 747F Freighter went into service, carrying loads of more than 200,000 pounds in regular service, with the first of three 747C Convertibles beginning service in 1973. The 747SR (Short Range) began service with Japan Air Lines, seating 498 passengers. Later, seating capacity of newly delivered 747SR's increased to 550. The 747 family has grown to include several different models. Specially equipped Advanced Airborne Command Post 747's, designated E-4, replaced US Air Force EC-135s. Boeing also modified several 747-100s as combined tanker transports, special freighters, and the vehicle to transport the Space Shuttle.

747-200B SPECIFICATIONS

Span . . . . 195 ft 8 in
Length . . . . 231 ft 10 in
Tail Height . . . . 63 ft 6 in
Wing Area . . . . 5,500 sq ft
Gross Weight . . . . 775,000-833,000 lb
Cruising Speed . . . . 600 mph plus
Range . . . . 6,000 nm
Design Ceiling . . . . 45,000 ft
Power . . . . P&W JT9D (46,950 to 54,750 lb thrust);

GE CF6-50E2 (52,000 lb. thrust);

Rolls-Royce RB211 (50,100-53,110 lb. thrust)

Typical Capacity . . . . 452 passengers
Fuel Volume . . . . 52,409/53,985 US gal

747 DESIGN FEATURES

The 747-400 is a wide body airplane with four wing-mounted engines and is designed for long range operation at high payloads. The maximum range is approximately 7,300 nautical miles (with horizontal stabilizer fuel tank). The aircraft is a derivative of the 747 family (-100, -200, -300) and includes major new features of:

• Two-crew flight deck (earlier models of the 747 required an FE to control aircraft systems).

• Crew rest area

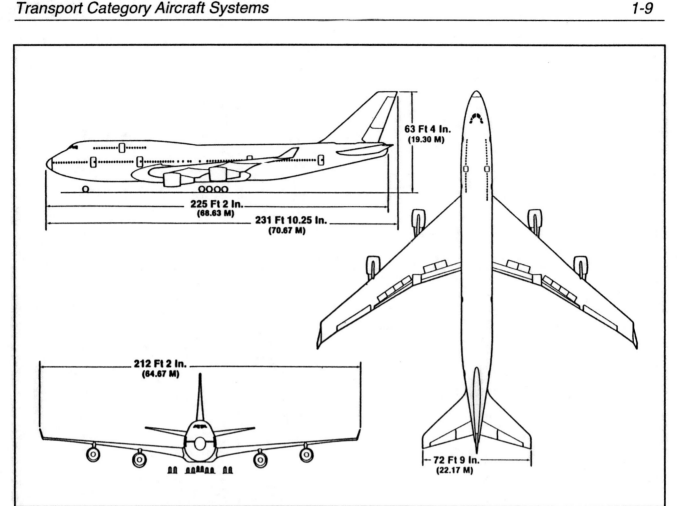

Figure 1-11. Dimensions of the Boeing 747-400. (Boeing)

- Advanced avionics and electronics

- High performance engines

- Advanced APU

- Wing tip extensions and winglets

- Advanced aluminum alloy wings

- Optional horizontal stabilizer fuel tank

- Increased gross weight

- Interior configuration flexibility

- Carbon brakes

The principle dimensions of the 747-400 airplane are shown in Figure 1-11 with a frontal and profile view. The maximum width of the airplane is the wing span of 212 feet nominal, maximum is 213 feet, which includes the winglets . The wing and horizontal stabilizer are set at a 7° dihedral. The wing dihedral affects engine mounting because the struts are attached perpendicular to the wing. The maximum height of the airplane, 63 feet 4 inches, is from the ground to the vertical stabilizer tip. The vertical stabilizer is swept back 45°. The maximum fuselage height of the airplane, 32 feet 2 inches, is from the ground to the upper deck skin. The maximum length of the airplane, 231 feet 10 inches, is from the radome to the vertical stabilizer tip. The general arrangement of the 747-400 is shown in Figure 1-12.

747 POWERPLANTS

Engines from General Electric, Pratt & Whitney, and Rolls-Royce are all available for the 747 and each manufacturer has met the challenge of developing powerplants with ever increasing thrust ratings. Engine certification evolution is shown in Figure 1-13. Most of the engines certificated for the 747 series of aircraft are in the area of 50,000 to 60,000 pounds of thrust. A cutaway picture of a typical high bypass engine used on the 747 is illustrated in Figure 1-14.

BOEING 757 TWIN JET SERIES

The Boeing 757 is a new-generation twin-engine, short-to-medium range jetliner which combines an efficient

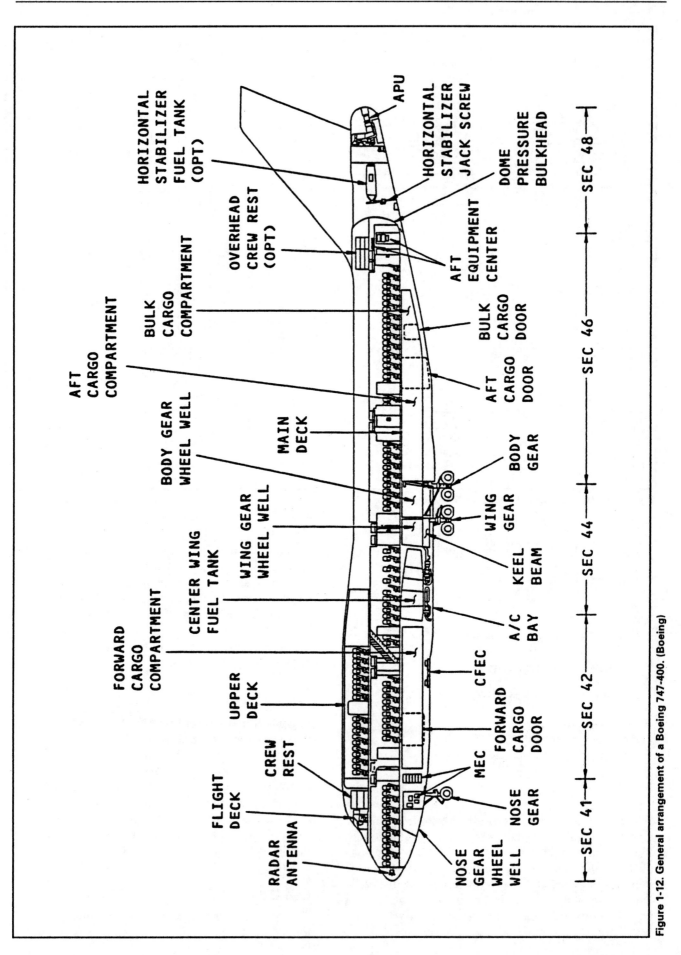

Figure 1-12. General arrangement of a Boeing 747-400. (Boeing)

MANUFACTURER	ENGINE	YEAR CERTIFIED
Rolls Royce	RB211-524G	1989
General Electric	CF6-80C2B1F	1989
Pratt & Whitney	PW4056	1988
General Electric	CF6-80C2B1	1987
Pratt & Whitney	JT9D-7R462	1983
Rolls Royce	RB211-524D4	1979
Pratt & Whitney	JT9D-7Q	1979
Rolls Royce	RB211-524B2	1979
General Electric	CF6-50E2	1979
General Electric	CF6-45A	1978
Rolls Royce	RB211-524	1977
Pratt & Whitney	JT9D-70A	1976
Pratt & Whitney	JT9D-7F	1975
General Electric	CF6-50	1974
Pratt & Whitney	JT9D-7	1971

Figure 1-13. Certification evolution for Boeing 747 engines. (Boeing Airliner)

six-abreast seating fuselage with new-technology wings and engines. The aircraft's principal dimensions can be seen in Figure 1-15. Its passenger capacity is between that of the 727-200 and the 767.

The 757 carries 186 passengers in a typical US airline first-class/tourist mixed-class configuration, or it can accommodate 224 passengers in a typical all-tourist arrangement. The 757 features spacious stowage bins that provide ample space for carry-on luggage. In fact, overhead stowage space per seat is equal to that in the 747.

Fuel efficiency of the new airliner was a very important design goal, and the 757 meets that objective. On a 500-mile flight, it burns about 48% less fuel per seat than the airplanes it displaces from airline fleets, such as the 727-100.

The 757 is operated by a two-person flight crew in a simplified glass cockpit. The 757 is powered by either a Pratt & Whitney PW2037 or a Rolls-Royce

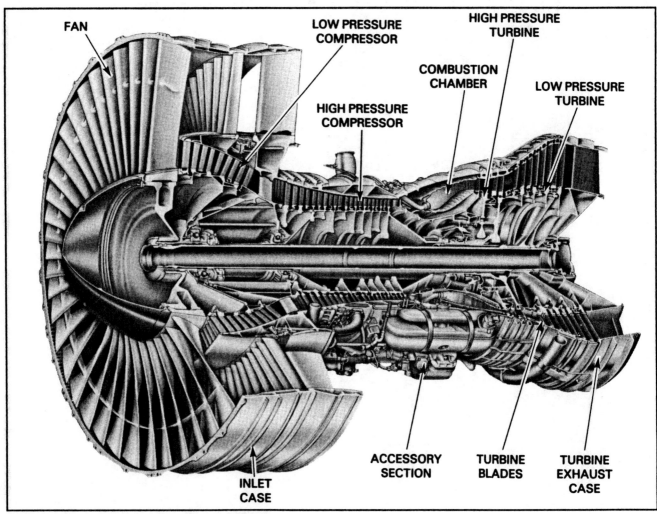

Figure 1-14. Cutaway JT9D engine. (Pratt & Whitney)

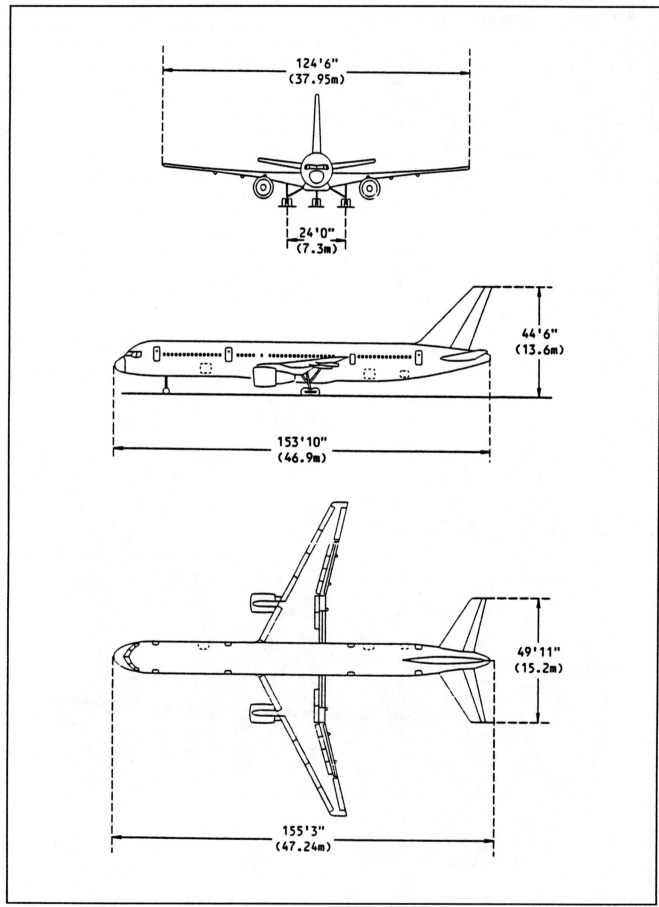

Figure 1-15. Boeing 757 principle dimensions. (Boeing)

Figure 1-16. Boeing 757 aircraft. (Boeing)

Figure 1-17. A Boeing 767 aircraft. (Boeing)

RB211-535. The engines are wing mounted on pylons (Figure 1-16).

757 POWERPLANT

The Pratt and Whitney 2037 is a twin spool, axial flow, high compression, high bypass ratio turbofan engine. The engine has a single stage fan, split 16 stage compressor, combustion chamber, and a split seven stage turbine.

The N_1, or low pressure spool, consists of the fan, four stage compressor and a five stage turbine. The N_2, or high pressure spool, consists of a twelve stage compressor and a two stage turbine. The two spools are mechanically independent. The N_2 spool drives the engine accessories. The air driven starter connects to the N_2 rotor.

The engine incorporates variable pitch stator vanes and automatic surge bleed valves to ensure good starting characteristics, plus surge and stall-free operation throughout the airplane's flight envelope.

757 SPECIFICATIONS

Length Overall . . . . 155 ft 3 in (47.32 m)

Wingspan . . . . 124 ft 6 in (37.9 m)

Tail Height . . . . 44 ft 6 in (13.56 m)

*Maximum Takeoff
   Gross Weight . . . . 240,000 lb (108,800 kg)

*Maximum Range. . . . . 3,500 mi (6,480 km)

Passengers. 186
                            170 tourist class
                            16 first class
                            224 all tourist

BOEING 767 TWIN JET SERIES

The Boeing 767, shown in Figure 1-17, is a new-generation commercial airplane whose design makes use of the latest in technology to provide maximum efficiency. It provides modern twin-aisle wide-body passenger cabin comfort.

Production of the new twin-jet began in 1978. The 767's design has been refined to give maximum performance per unit of fuel burned. Design achievements also include operational flexibility, low noise levels, advanced airplane systems, and growth potential. New structural material, including advanced composites, are also employed.

The 767 cabin, measuring more than 4 feet wider than the standard fuselage in Boeing jetliners, will seat 211 passengers in a typical mixed-class configuration (six-abreast in first class, seven-abreast in tourist class), or as many as 290 in the all-tourist configuration.

The first 767 was rolled from the factory in 1981 with Pratt & Whitney engines. A second 767 type, powered by General Electric CF6 engines, also received FAA certification. Another variation of the basic model, the 767-200ER (Extended Range) version was certified with a higher gross weight. A longer body version, the 767-300, was certified in 1983.

767-200 SPECIFICATIONS

Span . . . . 156 ft 1 in

Length. . . . . 159 ft 2 in

Tail Height . . . . 52 ft

Wing Area. . . . . 3,050 sq ft

Body Width. . . . . 16.5 ft

Passengers. . . . . 211 (mixed class);
                            up to 290 in charter
                            configuration

Cruising Speed . . . . Mach .80

Lower Deck Volume . . . . 3,102 cu ft

Gross Weight. . . . . 300,000 to 345,000 lb

Range. . . . . 3,200 to 5,600 statue mi.

Engine . . . . Two Pratt & Whitney
                            JT9-7R4 or General
                            Electric CF680A, at
                            airline option
                            (48,000-lb thrust)

First Delivery . . . . August 19, 1982

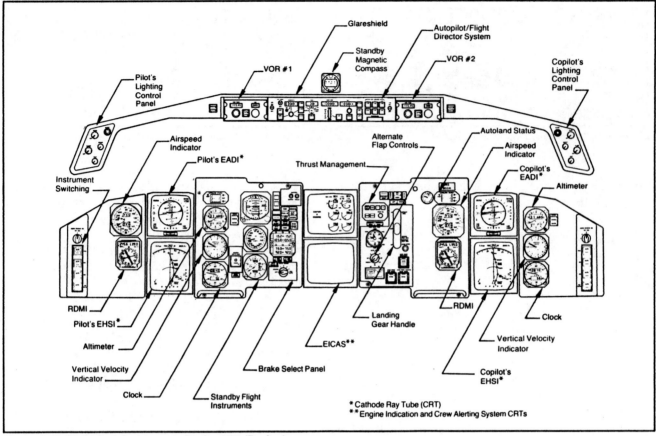

Figure 1-18. Flight deck instruments Boeing 767. (Boeing)

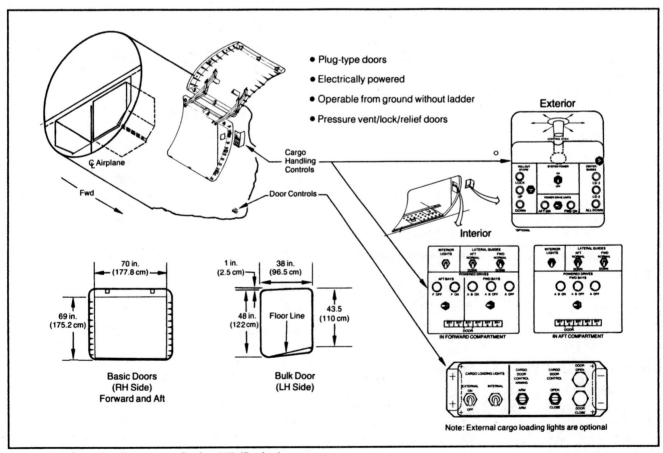

Figure 1-19. Cargo loading system Boeing 767. (Boeing)

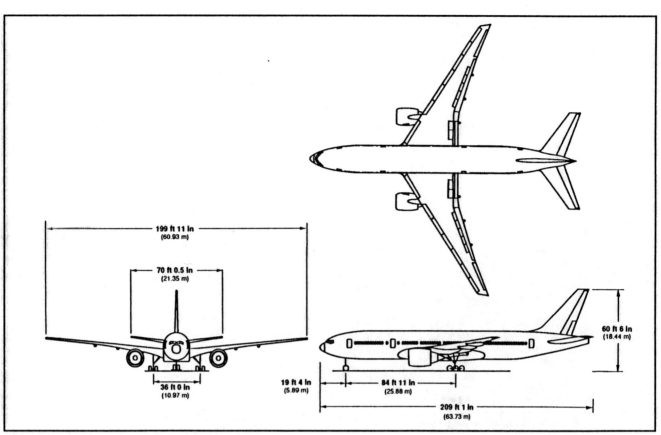

Figure 1-20. Boeing 777 general arrangement. (Boeing)

757-767 DESIGN FEATURES

The two crew member airliner flight deck, shown in Figure 1-18, is standard on the new-generation Boeing 757 and 767 twin-jets. The flight deck features digital electronics, including an Engine Indicating and Crew Alerting System (EICAS) that centralizes all engine displays and provides automatic monitoring of engine operation. Taking advantage of equipment commonality, the 757 and 767 flight decks feature the same elements. Forward windshields are identical, yielding downward visibility during landing approach. The flight decks employ digital electronic instruments, including color cathode ray tube displays. An all-digital electronic automatic flight management system not only reduces crew workload, but also contributes to lower fuel consumption. Use of digital electronics also makes possible upgrading in navigation capability as air traffic control systems change. The flight deck includes a low-profile control column designed to permit full view of the instrument panel. Design of the nose section and location of air-conditioning outlets means lower cockpit noise levels.

The cargo system consists of forward, aft and bulk cargo compartments. A complete cargo loading system is available for lower deck cargo as shown in Figure 1-19.

767 POWERPLANTS

The 767 can be equipped with a Pratt & Whitney JT9D-7R4 or a General Electric CF6-80 series engine, with other engine types also being produced. Takeoff thrust of these series of engines range from 48,000 to 61,500 pounds, allowing airline operators to select the appropriate thrust level for aircraft and route requirements.

Thrust of the new PW4000 series engine ranges from 50,000 to 60,000 pounds, with growth capability to around 100,000 pounds, making the engine ideal for all current and new versions of the Boeing 747, 767, and the 777.

BOEING 777 TWIN JET SERIES

Another Boeing airplane is the -777 series, shown in Figure 1-20. The 777's fuselage has a diameter of 20 feet 4 inches (6.2 meters) — a wider body than any other jetliner except the Boeing 747. The 777's interior cross-section is at least 5 inches (13 centimeters) greater than current wide-body tri-jets, affording more "comfort space" to trade between seat width, aisles, and seat pitch. The 777 can be configured in any combination of seating arrangements, ranging from six to ten seats abreast with two aisles.

With an overall length of about 209 feet (63.7 meters), the 777 offers two-class seating for 375 to 400 passengers, or three-class seating for 305 to 328 passengers. In an all economy configuration, the airplane can seat as many as 440 passengers.

The airplane, shown in Figure 1-21, has a standard maximum takeoff weight of 506,000 pounds (229,520 kilograms) and a range capability of up to 4,660 statute miles (4,050 nautical miles or 7,500 kilometers).

Figure 1-21. Boeing 777 aircraft. (Boeing)

The structural capability of the airplane allows two optional maximum takeoff weights of 515,000 pounds (233,600 kilograms) or 535,000 pounds (242,670 kilograms). The first option allows a range of up to 4,950 statute miles (4,300 nautical miles or 7,960 kilometers); the second option permits a range of up to 5,600 statute miles (4,900 nautical miles or 9,020 kilometers).

All of the initial 777s are sometimes referred to as "A-Market" models. The terms A-Market and B-Market generally refer to wide-body airplane range segments, with the A-Market considered from 3,000 to 5,000 - nautical miles to accommodate domestic or regional routes; and the B-Market designating ranges of between 5,000 to 7,000 nautical miles.

The company has committed to a longer-range, higher-weight version. This model, dubbed the "B-Market" model, has the same physical dimensions as the initial A-Market 777. However, the longer-range B-Market 777 is capable of a higher takeoff weight of 580,000 pounds (263,620 kilograms) as an option, and uses higher

engine-thrust ratings and carries more fuel. All of the 777 family members utilize common engines. The longer-range 777 accommodates 305 to 328 passengers in a three-class arrangement on routes of up to 7,600 statute miles (6,600 nautical miles or 12,200 kilometers).

WING DESIGN

The 777's wing uses the most aerodynamically efficient airfoil ever developed for subsonic commercial aviation. In a further refinement of designs introduced on the Boeing 757 and 767, the 777's wing features a long span with increased thickness while achieving higher cruise speeds. This advanced wing enhances the airplane's ability to climb quickly and cruise at higher altitudes than competing airplanes. It also allows the airplane to carry full passenger loads out of many high-elevation, high-temperature airfields.

Fuel volume requirements of the 777 is accommodated entirely within the wing and its structural center section. For the initial A-Market airplane, fuel capacity is 31,000 gallons (117,335 liters), while the longer-range B-Market model carrys up to 44,700 gallons (169,190 liters).

Airlines participating in the 777 design effort encouraged Boeing to commit to the performance capabilities of an optimum wing, which has a span of 199 feet 11 inches (60.9 meters).

777 POWERPLANTS

The three leading engine manufacturers developed more efficient and quieter turbofans to power the 777, and all three have been selected by 777 customers. United Airlines, ANA and Japan Air System selected Pratt & Whitney engines for their 777s, British Airways, Lauda Air, ILFC, Euralair, China Southern, Continental and Gulf Air chose General Electric engines, and Thai Airways International, Cathay Pacific and Emirates picked Rolls-Royce engines.

For the A-Market airplane, these engines are rated in the 74,000 to 77,000 pound thrust class. For the longer-range B-Market model, these same engines will be capable of thrust ratings in the 84,000 pound category. The engines could be developed to even higher thrust rating, depending on future payload and range requirements.

All three makes are more powerful than current engines, and offer excellent fuel efficiency while allowing the 777 to be as quiet as a 767, even though the 777 engines provides 40 percent more power. Key factors in this performance are new, larger-diameter fans with wide-chord fan blade designs and bypass ratios ranging from 6 to 1 to as high as 9 to 1. This compares to the typical 5 to 1 ratio for the engines of today's wide-body jets.

Pratt & Whitney is offering the PW4000 series of engines (see Figure 1-22), General Electric is offering its all-new GE-90 series (see Figure 1-23), and Rolls-Royce is offering the Trent 800 series of engines.

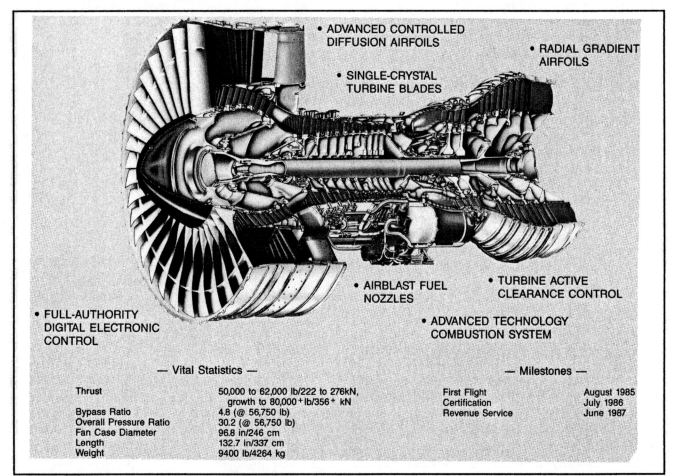

• ADVANCED CONTROLLED DIFFUSION AIRFOILS

• SINGLE-CRYSTAL TURBINE BLADES

• RADIAL GRADIENT AIRFOILS

• AIRBLAST FUEL NOZZLES

• TURBINE ACTIVE CLEARANCE CONTROL

• FULL-AUTHORITY DIGITAL ELECTRONIC CONTROL

• ADVANCED TECHNOLOGY COMBUSTION SYSTEM

— Vital Statistics —

Thrust	50,000 to 62,000 lb/222 to 276kN, growth to 80,000+ lb/356+ kN
Bypass Ratio	4.8 (@ 56,750 lb)
Overall Pressure Ratio	30.2 (@ 56,750 lb)
Fan Case Diameter	96.8 in/246 cm
Length	132.7 in/337 cm
Weight	9400 lb/4264 kg

— Milestones —

First Flight	August 1985
Certification	July 1986
Revenue Service	June 1987

Figure 1-22. UT Pratt & Whitney PW 4000 cutaway. (Pratt & Whitney)

Figure 1-23. GE 90 high bypass turbofan. (General Electric)

MATERIALS

New, lightweight, cost-effective structural materials are used in several 777 applications. For example, an improved aluminum alloy is used in the upper wing skin and stringers. Known as 7055, this alloy offers greater compression strength than current alloy, enabling designers to save weight and also improve corrosion and fatigue resistance.

Progress in the development and fabrication of weight-saving advanced composite materials are evident in the 777. Carbon fibers embedded in toughened resins are found in the vertical and horizontal tails. The floor beams of the passenger cabin also are made of these advanced composite materials.

Other composite applications include those on secondary structures such as aerodynamic fairings. Composites, including resins and adhesives, account for 9 percent of the 777's structural weight, compared to about 3 percent on other Boeing jets.

FLIGHT DECK AND CONTROL SYSTEM

In response to airline preference expressed during the planning and definition phase, the layout of the 777's flight deck is in a horizontal format similar to that of the 747-400. Principle flight, navigation and engine information is presented on six large display screens. As can be seen in Figure 1-24, they incorporate advanced liquid-crystal display technology. The depth of the new "flat panel" displays' are about half that of CRTs. In addition to saving space, the new displays weigh less and require less power. They also generate less heat, which contributes to greater reliability and a longer service life, and do not require the heavy, complex air conditioning apparatus needed to cool equipment on current flight decks. Pilots appreciate that flat panel displays remain clearly visible in all conditions, even direct sunlight.

Three multipurpose control display units, or CDUs, installed in the center aisle stand provide data display and entry capabilities for flight management functions and are the primary interface with an integrated Airplane Information Management System, known as AIMS. For the first time in a commercial application, the CDUs have color displays, again in response to market preferences. Adding color allows pilots to assimilate the information more quickly.

AIMS provides flight and maintenance crews with pertinent information concerning the overall condition of the airplane, its maintenance requirements and its key operating functions, including flight, thrust, and communications management.

Figure 1-24. Boeing 777 flight deck. (Boeing)

The flight crew transmits control and maneuvering commands through electrical wires, augmented by computers, directly to hydraulic actuators for the elevators, rudder, ailerons and other control surfaces. This three-axis "fly by wire" flight control system saves weight, simplifies factory assembly compared to conventional mechanical systems relying on steel cables, and requires fewer spares and less maintenance in airline service.

A key part of the 777's fly-by-wire system is a Boeing patented two-way digital data bus, which has been adopted as a new industry standard: ARINC 629. It permits airplane controls, actuation systems, and computers to communicate with one another through a common wire path (a twisted pair of wires) instead of through separate one-way wire connections. This further simplifies assembly and saves weight, while increasing reliability through a reduction in the amount of wires and connectors. Three of these pathways will be installed for redundancy.

INTERIOR

In addition to being one of the most spacious passenger cabins ever developed, the 777's interior offers operators unsurpassed configuration flexibility. Zones of flexibility have been designed into the cabin areas specified by the airlines, primarily at the airplane's

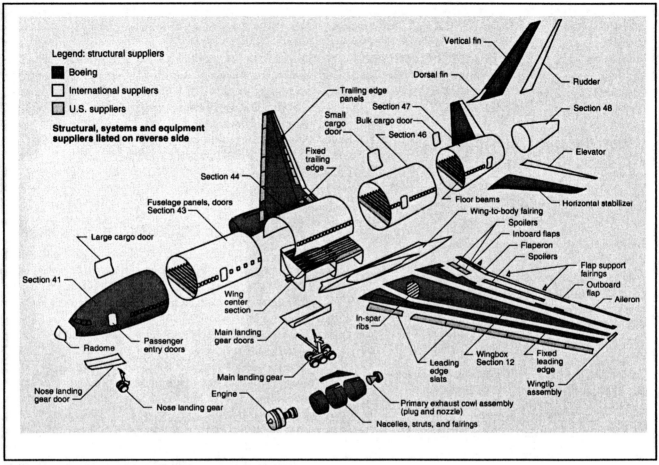

Figure 1-25. Boeing 777 International cooperation. (Boeing)

doors. In 1-inch increments, galleys and lavatories can be positioned anywhere within these zones, which are pre-engineered to accommodate wiring, plumbing and attachment fixtures. Passenger service units and over-head stowage compartments are designed for quick removal without disturbing ceiling panels, air condi-tioning ducts or support structure.

For more efficient in-flight service, the 777 is equipped with an advanced cabin management sys-tem. Linked to a computerized control console, the cabin management system assists the cabin crews with many tasks and allows the airlines to provide new ser-vices for passengers, including a digital sound system comparable to the most state-of-the-art home stereo or compact disc players.

CARGO CAPACITY

The fuselage cross-section of the 777 is circular and large enough to accommodate not only a spacious pas-senger cabin, but also excellent capacity in the lower hold. The lower hold's mechanized cargo handling system is compatible with all unit load devices (LD) and pallets. One of the container arrangements utilizes

LD-3s loaded side by side. All told, the 777 can accom-modate a maximum of 32 LD-3 containers plus 600 cubic feet (17 cubic meters) of bulk-loaded cargo for total lower hold volume of 5,645 cubic feet (160.1 cubic Meters).

LANDING GEAR

The main landing gear for the 777 is a standard two-post arrangement, but features a six-wheel truck instead of the conventional four-wheel units. This pro-vides the main landing gear with a total of 12 wheels for better weight distribution on runways and taxi areas, and avoids the need for a supplemental two-wheel gear under the center of the fuselage. Another advantage is that the six-wheel trucks allow for a more economical brake design.

INTERNATIONAL TEAM

The skills and resources of a number of international aerospace companies, as illustrated in Figure 1-25, contributed to the design and production of the 777. Firms in Europe, the Pacific Rim, and the United States provided components and portions of the struc-ture to Boeing.

The largest single overseas participant is the Japanese aerospace industry. Led by Mitsubishi Heavy Industries, Kawasaki Heavy Industries, and Fuji Heavy Industries, this group of companies is continuing its long-standing business relationship with Boeing. Together, these firms are helping design and build about 20 percent of the airframe structure.

777 EXTENDED-RANGE TWIN-ENGINE OPERATIONS

The new Boeing 777 jetliner was delivered service-ready — that means it was reliable and ready to fly all intended missions, including long-duration, over-water flights.

Included in this service-ready goal was a plan for special certification approval to fly extended range twin engine operations, or ETOPS, missions upon delivery. Specifically, ETOPS refers to a portion of the flight that is more than one hour from an alternate airport should the airplane have to divert and fly on only one engine or with an essential system problem.

Until the 777, twin-engine aircraft have been unable to fly ETOPS flights until they first have proven their capability in revenue service for at least two years. Special certification and in-service experience were required because existing twin-engine aircraft originally were designed for shorter flights and never intended to fly long distances over water. Also, engine technology had not advanced to a point where engine shutdown reliability had been proven for ETOPS missions at delivery.

Today, the 777 is the first twin-jet designed from the outset for long distances — anywhere from 4,600 to 7,600 statute miles, serving routes such as New York to London, Denver to Honolulu, or Tokyo to Sydney. To ensure reliability, the 777 was designed, tested and flown under all appropriate conditions to prove it is capable of flying up to 180-minute ETOPS missions before the airplane is delivered to its first customers.

DOUGLAS AIRCRAFT COMPANY

Douglas Aircraft Company is a division of the McDonnell Douglas Corporation. Douglas has delivered more than 45,600 commercial and military planes, including the long line of Douglas Commercial (DC) models.

Presently in production are the McDonnell Douglas MD-11 tri-jet liners, two-engine MD-80 short-to-mid range commercial transports, and military aircraft.

The Douglas Aircraft Company conducts research in support of its aircraft projects and is engaged in a number of advanced design studies aimed at development of future aircraft models. The following discussion will focus on Douglas aircraft that are in airline service, or soon will be. McDonnell Douglas has produced a complete line of aircraft in its DC series, such as the DC-3, DC-6, etc. but most of these aircraft are no longer in airline service. The DC-8 aircraft is used in some airline service, but its life as an airliner is probably somewhat limited. Some aircraft that are or soon will be used in airline service are the DC-9, DC-10, MD-80, MD-90, and MD-11 Series aircraft. When the Douglas Aircraft Company merged with McDonnell Douglas, the "DC" was changed to "MD" to designate the aircraft models.

MCDONNELL DOUGLAS DC-9 SERIES

The DC-9 was designed by Douglas to meet the airline's growing need of a short-to-medium range jet aircraft. The McDonnell Douglas DC-9 made its first flight and started airline operations in 1965. Since then, more than 1,000 aircraft have been built and are in service with airlines and private operators throughout the world. Both the DC-9 Series 10, and the DC-9 Series 20 (1968) (See Figure 1-26), are high performance models designed for short runways carrying up to 90 passengers. The DC-9 Series 30 (1967) accommodates up to 115 passengers, and the DC-9 Series 40 (1968), 125 passengers. The DC-9 Series 50 (Figure 1-27), introduced into service in 1975, has a maximum capacity of 139 passengers. The development of the DC-9 Series and the changes to the basic design are shown in Figure 1-28. The DC-9 Series was designed with a two-crew cockpit.

Figure 1-26. A DC-9-20 series aircraft. (McDonnell Douglas)

Figure 1-27. A DC-9-50 series aircraft. (McDonnell Douglas)

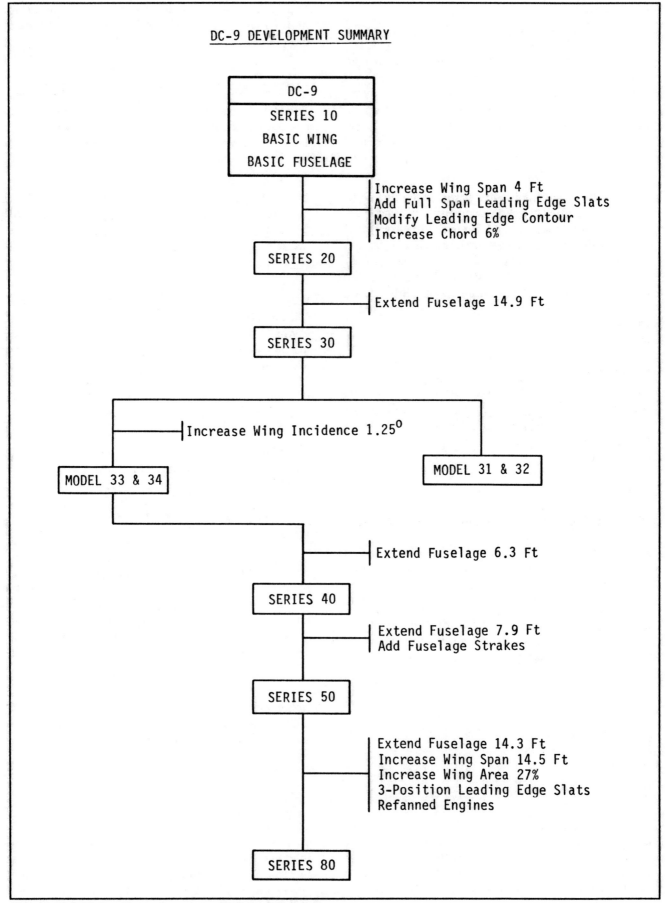

Figure 1-28. DC-9 development summary. (McDonnell Douglas)

DC-9 DESIGN FEATURES

The basic dimensions of each series and a profile view is presented in Figure 1-29. Extensive wing optimization studies and flight testing resulted in a wing configuration providing for a high cruise speed, yet retaining short-field performance. The DC-9 Series 10 wing had an aspect ratio of 8.546 and a sweepback of 24°. Growth versions of the DC-9 required modifications to the basic wing, such as a wing span increase of 2 feet per tip and leading edge slats.

The T-tail configuration was chosen as the most efficient compromise between weight and drag. Materials, minimum thickness, related frame section areas, and attaching details were chosen for tear-resistant strength within the frame bays. Accordingly, the fuselage shell in the pressurized area is designed for a dependable operation differential pressure of 7.46 PSID, which provides a cabin altitude of 8,000 feet while flying at 35,000 feet.

DC-9 POWERPLANT

The DC-9 is powered by two Pratt & Whitney JT8D axial-flow turbofan engines mounted on the fuselage aft of the wing. Fuselage mounted engines were important to the design configuration because:

- Lower stalling speeds resulted from clean wing design

- Elimination of wing pylon interference drag

- Better directional control in the event of an engine failure (reduced yawing moment arm due to engine thrust being closer to centerline).

There are many basic variations of the JT8D engine to fulfill the most diverse requirements of the short-to-medium range jet transport market.

The JT8D has a forward fan with an integral full-length fan discharge duct and a single mixed-exhaust nozzle. It has a 13-stage split compressor, a 9-can annular combustion chamber, and a split 4-stage reaction impulse turbine. The engine has a two-piece quick-opening split cowl which gives easy access to all components. The right and left units are demountable and are designed for maximum commonality. Engine accessories include an air turbine starter, a hydraulic pump, a constant-speed drive, and a 40 KVA generator. The accessories are grouped for maximum accessibility and can be removed for maintenance without disturbing adjacent units. The engine and its accessories can be seen in Figure 1-30.

The DC-9 can be started from a pneumatic ground cart, by its own self-contained APU, or by crossbleed air from the other engine.

MCDONNELL DOUGLAS MD-80 SERIES

The MD-80 was certified by the FAA and entered commercial service in 1980. The MD-80, shown in Figure 1-31, is an advanced-technology successor to the popular DC-9 twin-jet.

The McDonnell Douglas MD-80, a quiet and fuel-efficient twin-jet, uses advanced Pratt & Whitney JT8D-200 engines. The liberal use of sound-suppressing materials allows the MD-80 to meet stringent noise regulations.

Five MD-80 models, the MD-81, MD-82, MD-83, MD-87, and MD-88 are produced at the Douglas Aircraft Company's Long Beach, California facility. The MD-81, -82, -83, and -88 are 147 feet 10 inches (45.05 meters) long and accommodate a maximum of 172 passengers. The MD-87 is 130.4 feet (39.7m) in length, with a maximum passenger capacity of 139. Wingspan for all models is 107 feet 10 inches (32.86 m).

Technology advancements in the MD-80 include a digital flight guidance system with a nonstop range of 1,750 to 3,260 statute miles (2,815 to 5,246 kilometers), depending on the model. The MD-80's maximum takeoff weight ranges from 140,000 pounds (63,503 kg) to 160,000 pounds (72,576 kg).

The area of the MD-80 wing is 1,209 square feet (112.3 sq. m), approximately 21 percent greater than the 1,000.7 square feet (92.9 sq. m) of the DC-9. With the larger wing, MD-80 fuel capacity totals 5,779 gallons (21,873.5 L), an increase of 2,100 gallons (7,949 L) over the standard capacity of the DC-9 Series 30. In the MD-83, fuel capacity is 7,000 gallons (26,500 L).

Height of the MD-80's distinctive T-tail is 29 feet 8 inches (9.02 m). The horizontal stabilizer has a span of 40 feet 2 inches (12.2 m). The MD-87 has a higher vertical tail, 30.5 feet (9.29 m).

A typical cabin arrangement in the MD-80 is 142 seats, with a first class section of 12 seats and a coach area of 130. Other interior arrangements include 155 all economy-class seats and up to 172 seats in MD-80's intended for short route service. On the MD-87's, seating capacity ranges from 100 to 130. Seats are in a four-abreast pattern in first class and five-abreast in coach and economy sections.

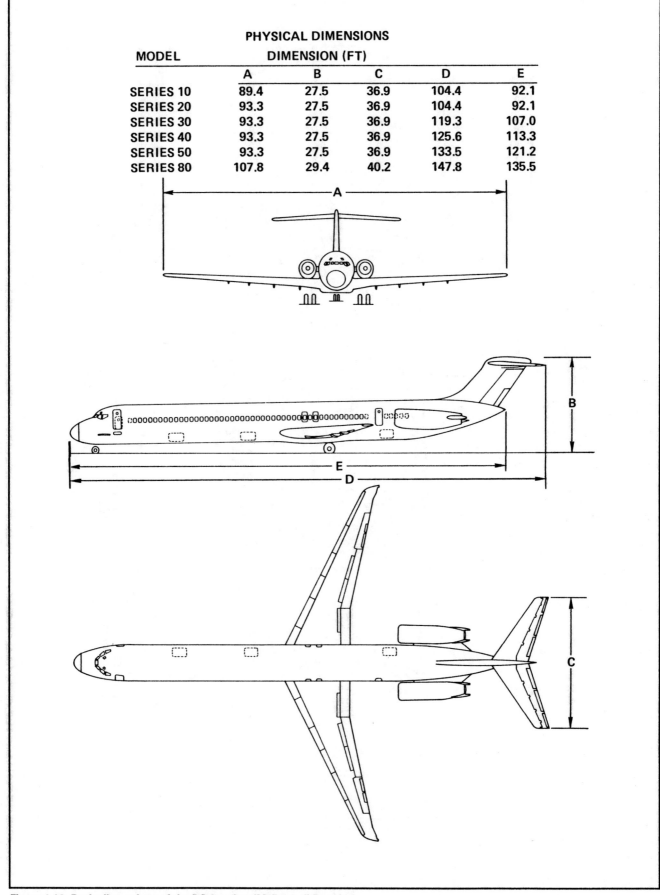

PHYSICAL DIMENSIONS

MODEL	DIMENSION (FT)				
	A	B	C	D	E
SERIES 10	89.4	27.5	36.9	104.4	92.1
SERIES 20	93.3	27.5	36.9	104.4	92.1
SERIES 30	93.3	27.5	36.9	119.3	107.0
SERIES 40	93.3	27.5	36.9	125.6	113.3
SERIES 50	93.3	27.5	36.9	133.5	121.2
SERIES 80	107.8	29.4	40.2	147.8	135.5

Figure 1-29. Basic dimensions of the DC-9 series. (McDonnell Douglas)

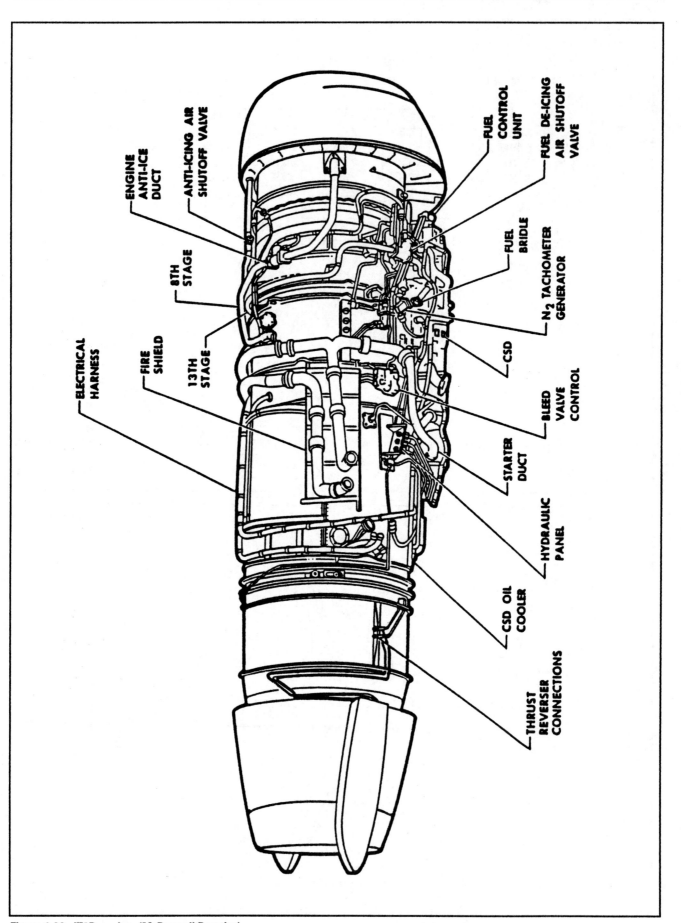

Figure 1-30. JT8D engine. (McDonnell Douglas)

Figure 1-31. McDonnell Douglas MD-80 aircraft. (McDonnell Douglas)

The three below-deck cargo compartments on MD-81, MD-82, and MD-88 models have a total volume of 1,253 cubic feet (35.48 cu m). Cargo is loaded into the compartments through three doors (two forward, one aft), each 50 x 53 inches (127 x 134.6 cu m).

MD-80 POWERPLANTS

Power for the MD-80 is generated by two Pratt & Whitney Aircraft JT8D-200 series turbofans, mounted one on each side of the aft fuselage. The MD-81 was certified with the JT8D-209 engine. Higher thrust JT8D-217A and -217C engines for operations from high altitude, high-temperature airports are available. The JT8D-219 engines are the most powerful and fuel efficient of JT8D family and are frequently used for long-range operations. The smaller MD-87 uses the JT8D-217C or the JT8D-219 engines for performance from short airfields over extended ranges. The JT8D-219 is rated at 21,000 pounds (79,493 kg) plus 700 pounds (317.5 kg) in reserve. Both the -217C (MD-88) and the -219 engines offer fuel burn reductions of about two percent through use of advanced technology hardware. The larger fan increases the bypass ratio from about 1.00 for earlier JT8D engines to about 1.7, resulting in lower specific fuel consumption and noise emission.

MD-80 DESIGN FEATURES

The two-person flight crew allows for advanced technology systems which are designed into the MD-80. Electronic flight instrumentation (EFIS), wind shear detection capability, advanced flight management systems for improved navigation, and more fuel efficient flight profiles are offered on the MD-80 Series. In addition, structural life has been extended to more than 50,000 landings with added protection against corrosion. The MD-80's integrated digital cockpit improves aircraft performance and reduces fuel consumption. For example, the auto-throttles can be engaged prior to takeoff, and the autopilot engaged shortly after takeoff. Once these systems are engaged, the pilot is not required to touch the manual flight controls and throttles until rolling out on the ground after landing.

The MD-80 is equipped with two identical Sperry digital computers to direct seven digital flight control subsystems: the automatic pilot, speed control system, automatic throttles, thrust rating system, altitude alert, flight director control function, and the automatic reserve thrust system. Either computer has the capacity to independently manage the subsystems. The MD-80 is equipped with an automatic reserve thrust system that functions during takeoff in case one of the two engines should fail. Detecting the loss of thrust, the flight guidance computer automatically signals the other engine to increase its thrust to compensate for the decrease in takeoff power.

MD-83

The MD-83 carries 155 passengers and their baggage 2,900 statute miles (4,670 km) with a maximum seating capacity of 172 passengers. Maximum takeoff gross weight is 160,000 pounds (72,576 kg). The extra range of the MD-83 comes from the takeoff weight increase and installation of two fuel tanks in the belly of the aircraft, increasing the fuel capacity by 1,160 gallons (4,290 L). This gives the MD-83 a total fuel capacity of 7,000 gallons (26,495 L).

MD-88

Development of the MD-88, newest of the popular McDonnell Douglas MD-80 series of twin-jets, began in January 1986. Featuring advanced interior design and cockpit systems, the MD-88's first flight and certification was in 1987. Standard powerplants for the MD-88 are two Pratt & Whitney JT8D-217C engines, each of which develops 20,000 pounds (9,072 kg) of takeoff thrust. With a full load of passengers and baggage, range of the MD-88 is more than 2,360 statute miles (3,800 km).

MCDONNELL DOUGLAS MD-90 SERIES

The MD-90 series of twin-jets are offered by McDonnell Douglas as a family of advanced mid-size, medium range airliners. The aircraft offers capacity growth with maximum commonality for present operators of McDonnell Douglas MD-80s. The twin-jets are available in three sizes: the MD-90-30, the MD-90-40, and the MD-90-10. The flight crew consists of the pilot and co-pilot.

MD-90-30

The aircraft uses two V2500 engines, shown in Figure 1-32, with 25,000 pounds (11,363.6 kg) of takeoff thrust. The MD-90-30, as currently configured, is 152.6 feet (46.5 m) long to accommodate 153 passengers in a standard mixed-class configuration. Maximum takeoff weight will be 156,000 pounds (70,760 kg) with a full payload range of 2,750 statute miles (4,415 km).

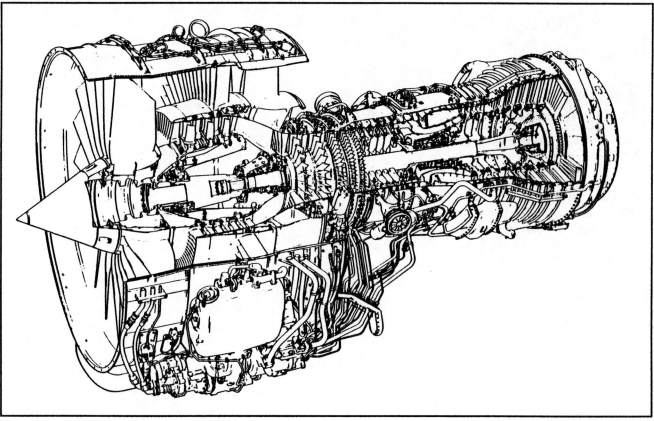

Figure 1-32. IAE V2500 engine cutaway. (Airbus)

MD-90-40

The MD-90-40, as currently configured, uses two V2500 engines which develop 28,000 pounds (12,727 kg) of takeoff thrust and will accommodate between 170 and 180 passengers in a standard mixed-class configuration. Maximum takeoff weight will be 163,500 pounds (74,150 kg). The MD-90-40 will have a cruise speed of 0.76 Mach.

MD-90-10

The MD-90-10, with 114 seats in a typical mixed-class arrangement, will have a fuselage length of 130.4 feet (39.7 m). Using its V2500 engines with a takeoff thrust rating of 22,000 pounds (10,000 kg), it will have a maximum takeoff gross weight of 139,000 pounds (63,050 kg) and an operating empty weight of 81,500 pounds (36,968 kg).

MD80-MD90 DESIGN FEATURES

The aircraft are manufactured by using a novel modular concept for production of major fuselage sections. Interchangeable, standardized fuselage sections common to different models of the MD-80 or MD-90 are built up as major subassemblies, then brought together with other segments to make the unique MD-80 or MD-90 transports, as they move down the shared assembly line.

In addition to providing a more efficient production line to reduce costs and lead times, the new modular approach offers a degree of flexibility that assures quick incorporation of new technologies and innovations.

MD-90 POWERPLANTS

The internationally developed and manufactured V2500 turbofan engines for the MD-90s represent today's most advanced design for fuel efficiency, low noise, and high reliability in jet powerplants.

Blending the technology of five nations, the V2500 is the product of Pratt & Whitney division of United Technologies in the United States; Rolls-Royce in the United Kingdom; MTU of the Federal Republic of Germany; Fiat of Italy, and Japanese Aero Engines Corp. of Japan.

The engine is a high-bypass ratio turbofan with a fan diameter of 5.25 feet (1.6 m), approximately 10.5 feet (3.2 m) in length. It is offered at thrust levels ranging from 22,000 pounds (10,000 kg) up to 28,000 pounds (12,727 kg).

DOUGLAS DC-10 SERIES

The excellent performance of the DC-10 tri-jet, pictured in Figure 1-33, is demonstrated by its operational statistics. Since its introduction into scheduled airline service in 1971, the DC-10 has flown more than 7.1 billion statute miles (10.94 billion km) in revenue service.

Figure 1-33. DC-10 aircraft. (McDonnell Douglas)

Five versions of the DC-10 are in airline service. The Series 10, equipped with General Electric CF6-6 turbofan engines, has a maximum range of 4,400 statute miles (7,079 km). The Series 15, similar to the Series 10, offers additional thrust for takeoffs from hot climate, high-altitude airports. Two intercontinental models are the Series 30, (Figure 1-34) powered by General Electric CF6 50 engines, and the Series 40, with Pratt & Whitney Aircraft JT9D engines. The fifth model of the tri-jet is the DC-10CF (convertible freighter) which can be arranged to carry all-cargo, all-passengers, or a combination of the two. All models of the DC-10 will carry up to 380 passengers, but most airlines arrange the interior for 250 to 275 seats in the first class and coach arrangement. The DC-10 has an almost 19-foot-wide (5.7 m) cabin.

Figure 1-34. McDonnell Douglas DC-10-30 aircraft. (McDonnell Douglas)

SERIES 10

The DC-10 Series 10 model, with transcontinental US non-stop range, was the first of the McDonnell Douglas wide-cabin tri-jet series. Designed for service on routes of 300 to 4000 statute miles (480 to 6,436 km), the Series 10 is powered by General Electric CF6-6 engines, each rated at 40,000 pounds (17,144 kg) takeoff thrust.

SERIES 15

The Series 15 model of the DC-10 combines the basic smaller airframe of the Series 10 with a version of the more powerful engines used on the longer range Series 30s. The combination gives the Series 15 outstanding performance with full loads from high altitude airports in warm climates.

It is powered by three General Electric CF6-50C2-F engines, each with a takeoff thrust of 46,500 pounds (21,092 kg). Range of the Series 15, with full payload, is about 3,600 statute miles (5,792 km).

SERIES 30

The Series 30, an intercontinental version with a range of approximately 5,900 statute miles (9,493 km), was the third DC-10 model to be committed to production. It is equipped with advanced General Electric CF6-50 fanjets. The Series 30 began its flight test program on June 21, 1972.

SERIES 30F

The DC-10 Series 30F, which is a pure freighter version, will carry palletized payloads of up to 175,000 pounds (79,380 kg) more than 3,800 statute miles (6,115 km). It can be operated up to 460 statute miles (741 km) farther with the addition of auxiliary fuel tanks in the aft end of the lower cargo compartment.

SERIES 40

The second DC-10 model launched was the intercontinental range Series 40, built in two versions. One, with a range of 5,350 statute miles (8,608 km) is powered by Pratt & Whitney Aircraft JT9D-20 turbofan engines. The other, equipped with the more powerful Pratt & Whitney JT9D-59A engines, has a range of approximately 5,800 statute miles (9,322 km).

DC-10CF AND DC-10F

The fourth basic DC-10 version is the DC-10CF (convertible freighter). Available in the basic Series 10, Series 30, or Series 40, the DC-10CF uses either the P&W or GE engines, and is capable of overnight conversion from a passenger configuration to an all-cargo arrangement and vice versa.

All versions of the DC-10CF convertible transport have a total available cargo space of more than 16,000 cubic feet (452.8 cu m), or as much as four 40-foot-class (12.19 m) railroad freight cars.

The main cabin will accommodate 30 standard 88 × 108 inch (223.5 × 274.3 cm) pallets or 22 standard 88 ×

125 inch (223.5 × 317.5 cm) pallets. A cargo door, 8.5 feet 11.5 feet (2.6m × 3.5 m), swings upward from the side of the forward fuselage.

DC-10 POWERPLANTS

The DC-10's General Electric and Pratt & Whitney Aircraft powerplants represent significant advances in engine performance and technology. The high bypass ratio turbofans yield such improvements as lower specific fuel consumption, lower noise levels, smokeless exhaust, easier maintenance and design for high reliability. Thrust ratings range from 40,000 to 54,000 pounds (17,144 to 24,494 kg).

Two of the engines are mounted conventionally on pylons beneath the wings, and the third is installed above the aft fuselage at the base of the vertical stabilizer. This arrangement offers both aerodynamic and operating advantages. All three engines are interchangeable with only minor adjustments; and the installations are designed to provide easy access for inspection and maintenance of each.

DC-10 DESIGN FEATURES

Overall length of all DC-10 versions is approximately 182 feet (55.47 m). Wingspan is 155 feet 4 inches (47.37 m) on the Series 10 and Series 15 aircraft and 165 feet 4 inches (50.42 m) on the Series 30 and 40. Wings are swept at an angle of 35°. Gross takeoff weight ranges from 440,000 pounds (195,048 kg) for the Series 10, to 580,000 pounds (251,748 kg) for the Series 30 and Series 40.

INTERIOR

The DC-10 cabin interior is 18 feet 9 inches (571.5 cm) wide at passenger seat level. A broad ceiling, approximately eight feet (240 cm) high, gives room-like spaciousness. Rapid and easy entrance and exit are provided through eight passenger doors. Six doors measuring 76 x 42 inches (193 x 106.7 cm) are wide enough to admit two persons side-by-side with the remaining two doors measuring 76 x 32 inches (193 x 81.3 cm). In some coach configurations (see Figure 1-35) seats are arranged in nine-abreast rows with a 2-5-2 configuration, or in 10-abreast arrangements of 3-4-3. Airlines have the option of using a lower-deck galley system or a conventional arrangement of galleys in the main cabin to allow more space on the lower deck for cargo.

ENVIRONMENTAL SYSTEMS

An advanced air conditioning and cabin pressurization system provides separate automatic temperature controls for the three main cabin sections and for the

cockpit and lower galley, assuring optimum comfort for all passengers, regardless of variations in load density in the different areas. The cabin pressurization system maintains sea level pressure in the DC-10 at

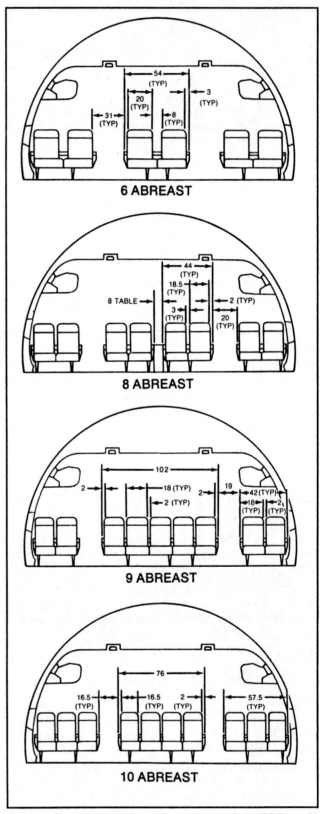

Figure 1-35. DC-10 main cabin cross section. (McDonnell Douglas)

flight altitudes up to 22,000 feet (6,705.6 m) and a cabin altitude of less than 7,000 feet (2,133.6 m) at flight altitudes up to 40,000 feet (12,190 m). Automatic controls prevent sudden changes in pressure as the aircraft climbs or descends.

FLIGHT DECK

Large windshields provide exceptional visibility, particularly during approaches and landings and for ground maneuvering. The DC-10 has been certified for automatic landing operation under Category IIIA weather conditions, providing capability for operation in near zero visibility.

MCDONNELL DOUGLAS MD-11 SERIES

The MD-11, shown in Figure 1-36, is an advanced wide-cabin, tri-jet aircraft which is an advanced version of the DC-10. The MD-11 is produced by the Douglas Aircraft Company. The standard MD-11 is available in three models; passenger, all-freighter and "combi", where passengers and freight are carried on the main deck. Advances in aerodynamics, propulsion, aircraft systems, cockpit avionics and interior design have greatly improved performance and operating economy of all MD-11 models. A wide variety of interior arrangements is available with seating capacities on the standard airplane ranging from 250 in a three-class arrangement to more than 400 in an all-economy configuration. Below deck, the MD-11 provides combined containerized or palletized cargo capability. Maximum range carrying 323 passengers is up to 8,039 statute miles (12,938 km) nonstop, an improvement of 27 percent compared to the DC-10 Series 30 configured in a comparable two class arrangement.

MD-11 POWERPLANTS

Three General Electric CF6-80C2, Pratt & Whitney 4460, or Rolls-Royce RB211-524L engines power the standard MD-11. These engines provide maximum efficiency in their thrust class with substantial fuel burn reductions. The engines are located in much the same manner as on the DC-10 aircraft.

MD-11 DESIGN FEATURES

The addition of winglets at the wing tips, redesigned wing airfoils with more camber near the trailing edge, and a smaller horizontal tail with an extended tail cone, help reduce drag. Together with the advanced engines, the aerodynamic improvements lower fuel burn by about 20 percent per trip, compared to the DC-10 Series.

The MD-11's all new flight deck, with advanced systems, makes it possible for operation with a two-pilot crew, compared to the three crew members required for earlier tri-jets (DC-10). The flight deck features six cathode ray tube displays, digital instrumentation, wind shear detection, guidance devices, and a dual flight management system that helps conserve fuel. The flight deck also has a dual digital automatic flight control system (autopilot). The navigation and display systems have double backups for maximum safety. The MD-11 flight deck operates on the "dark cockpit" philosophy — 99 percent of the time all lights for switches, warnings, and other devices are off. A light goes on only as an alert, assuring prompt pilot attention.

Status of the aircraft and all its systems is provided to the crew without need for looking up at overhead panels. All alert information is displayed on the engine CRT. The normal, abnormal and emergency checklist functions are performed automatically rather than simply annunciated to the crew, as on previous aircraft.

COMBI, FREIGHTER INTERIORS

The longer fuselage of the standard MD-11 has enabled McDonnell Douglas to design an efficient "combi" aircraft (see Figure 1-37) that permits a variety of cargo/passenger configurations on the main deck. A typical combi interior, seen in Figure 1-38, provides for three-class seating for 176 passengers and six pallets, with 14 LD3 containers and six additional pallets below-deck. A large, main deck rear cargo door for the combi is another MD-11 feature. The MD-11 also can be configured as an all-freighter. Weight limited pay-

Figure 1-36. MD-11 aircraft. (McDonnell Douglas)

Figure 1-37. MD-11 combi aircraft. (McDonnell Douglas)

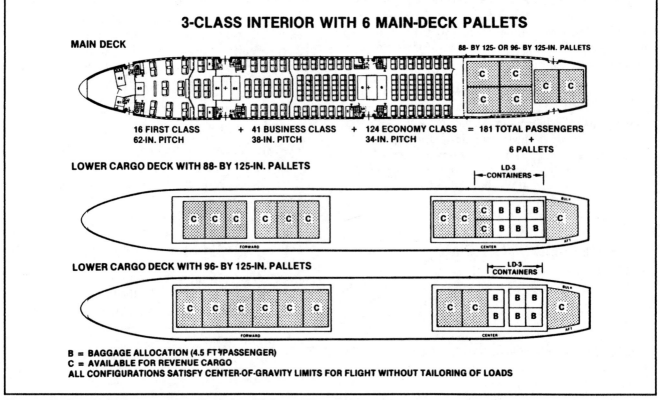

Figure 1-38. A typical MD-11 combi configuration. (McDonnell Douglas)

load is 205,700 lb. (93,304 kg) and non-stop range is 4,076 statute miles (6,560 km) at maximum payload and landing weight.

AUTOMATIC SYSTEM CONTROLLERS (ASC)

Automatic system controllers (ASC) are used to control the four basic systems—hydraulic, electrical, environmental, and fuel. The ASCs have replaced the flight engineer. The ASCs are contained in the overhead panel, viewable and reachable by either of the two pilots. The ASC contains four segregated panels, each of which is controlled by two redundant computers and is independent of the other systems. There is manual backup in case of dual computer failures.

The overhead panel is designed so that a logical sequence of aircraft items—hydraulic, electrical, environmental and fuel, are arranged with each engine's systems grouped vertically under its fire shutoff handle. Thus, it is simple to check or operate any system function.

Automated checklists for all four major systems are completed simultaneously, rather than in series.

FLIGHT CONTROL COMPUTER (FCC)

The flight control computer (FCC), formerly called automatic pilot and flight director, now includes auto-matic throttles and the longitudinal stability augmentation system (LSAS). LSAS enhances the pitch stability of the aircraft. An automatic landing system that meets FAA Category IIIB all-weather requirements, including rollout, further reduces crew workload and enhances the operational reliability of the MD-11.

The digital FCC interfaces with the full authority digital electronic control (FADEC) engine system, making engine operation precise and smooth. Wind shear detection and guidance data to assist flight crews in escaping shears also are provided by the flight control computer.

DUAL FLIGHT MANAGEMENT SYSTEM (FMS)

The dual flight management system (FMS) is derived from earlier first generation FMS designs. It includes a larger memory, faster response time and makes management of the flight considerably simpler for the pilot. Designed for optimum efficiency, the FMS guides the aircraft in vertical and lateral flight.

One major workload reduction is the automation of navigational radio management by FMS. The pilot no longer needs to set a variety of headings and radio frequencies during the flight. The FCS and FMS have been functionally integrated so that pilots essentially control speed, heading, and pitch on one set of controls that provide maximum capabilities for aircraft operation with minimum workload.

Two multi-function display units for the FMS are on the pilots' console. They also can be used for standby navigational displays. A third display on the console unit provides readouts for such functions as ground-to-air and air-to-ground communication and a display of gates available at the destination airport. It also interfaces with the aircraft's centralized fault-display system, thus providing a single point for maintenance crews to check systems following a flight.

LOCKHEED L-1011 TRISTAR SERIES

The L-1011, shown in Figure 1-39, has four basic models: the L-1011-1, L-1011-100, L-1011-200, and the L-1011-500. Each model uses three Rolls-Royce RB-211 engines, which range in thrust from 42,000 pounds to 51,000 pounds.

Figure 1-39. A Lockheed L-1011 aircraft. (Lockheed)

DESIGN FEATURES

The fuselage is of semi-monocoque construction, consisting of the flight station, a number of barrel sections, and an afterbody which supports the No. 2 engine and empennage. The fuselage also encloses a center wing box which, on some aircraft, contains sealed compartments that act as fuel tanks. The basic L-1011 structure can be seen in Figure 1-40.

Outer wings are attached to the center wing box by permanent fasteners to form a single unit. The wings are tapered and swept back from the center wing box. Outer wing boxes are compartmented and sealed to serve as integral fuel tanks.

The empennage consists of a vertical fin, a one piece rudder, a horizontal stabilizer, and a hinged elevator. The horizontal stabilizer is a one piece assembly consisting of a center box section joined to two outer stabilizer sections by permanent fasteners. The stabilizer is attached to the afterbody by rear mounted pivots. Airgate fairings are attached to the inboard side of each

outer stabilizer section to seal the opening in the fuselage which accommodates the stabilizer movement.

The L-1011 TriStar uses the "service center" concept of placing all possible equipment of a system in one area to simplify servicing and maintenance. Access to the Forward Electronics Service Center (FESC) is from either the flight station or an external panel, as can be seen in Figure 1-41. Access to the Mid Electrical Service Center (MESC) is from the galley or an external panel. All other compartments can only be entered externally.

The Environmental Control System (ECS), hydraulics and auxiliary power unit (APU) compartments are not pressurized. The forward and center cargo compartments, while pressurized, are not life-sustaining in terms of ventilation, as only containerized cargo is placed in these compartments. The aft cargo compartment is ventilated for the bulk cargo which includes pets and other livestock.

FLIGHT DECK

The flight deck requires three flight crew members: the Captain, First Officer, and Flight Engineer/Second Officer. There is also seating for two observers in the aft area of the flight deck.

CABIN

The cabin configuration allows for 250 or more revenue producing seats, depending on the amount of coach class seating. Seven lavatories are provided for passenger convenience. Cabin seating provides for 8 in-flight cabin attendants, and two (2) galley food preparation attendants during takeoff and landing.

CARGO COMPARTMENT

The forward and center cargo compartments are configured for containerized cargo, while the aft cargo compartment is utilized for bulk cargo as shown in Figure 1-42. The forward cargo compartment is equipped to handle preloaded (containerized) cargo containers. Normally the maximum allowable load is 18,000 pounds. The compartment access door opens outward and provides a clear opening of 70 by 68 inches. The compartment can be adapted for continuous use of bulk loading, or for continuous or occasional use of part bulk and part containerized cargo. The cargo doorway has barrier-net attachment provisions to prevent bulk cargo from shifting. The compartment walls, ceilings, and floors will restrain a full compliment of eight containers, as can be seen in Figure 1-42. Manually engaged empty-space stop-locks provide positive container location when carrying less than a full compliment of containers. Remotely controlled

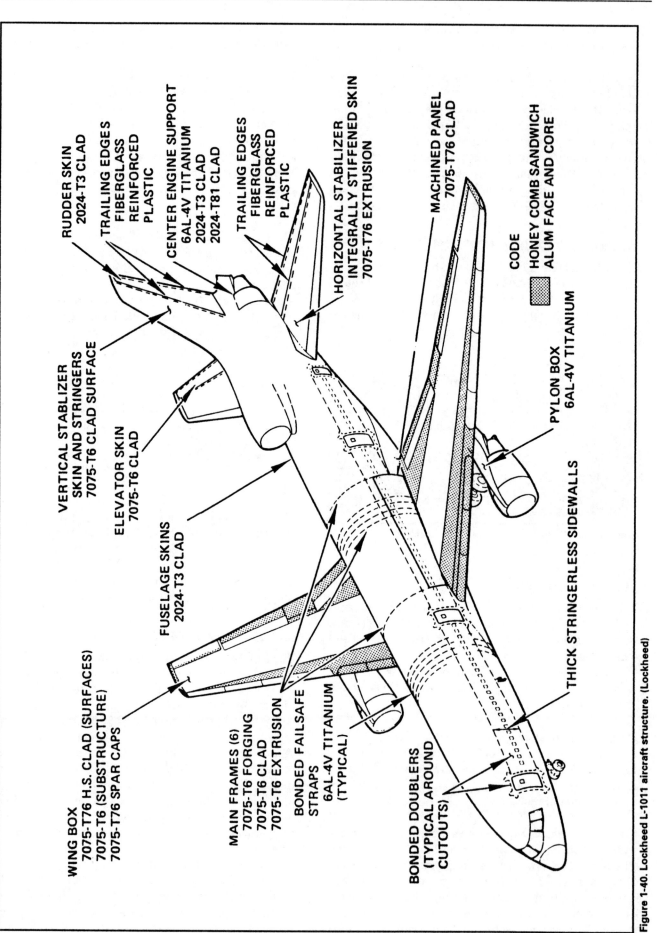

Figure 1-40. Lockheed L-1011 aircraft structure. (Lockheed)

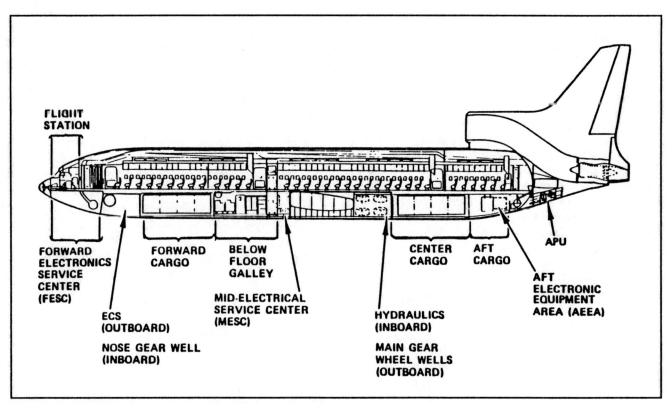

Figure 1-41. L-1011 internal compartment locations. (Lockheed)

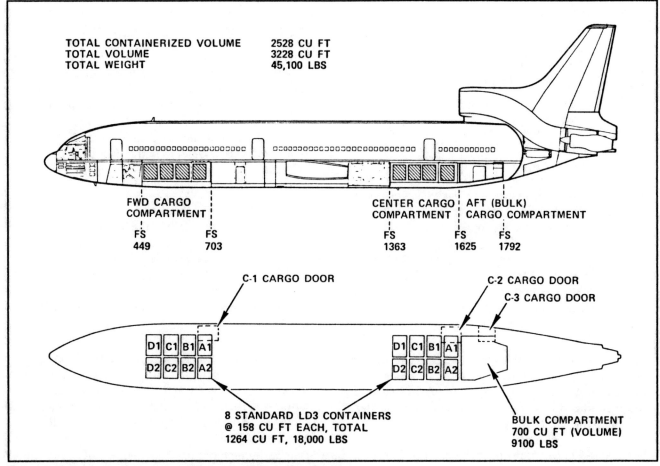

Figure 1-42. Cargo compartment system configurations. (Lockheed)

floor-mounted stops, for longitudinal and lateral container movement, are installed at the cargo compartment door. Fixed container stops are installed at the forward end of the compartment.

L-1011 POWERPLANTS

The three RB-211 Series engines are located on the left and right wings, and on the fuselage afterbody. The wing engines are pylon mounted (Figure 1-43), and the center engine is mounted at the rear of the afterbody. A fixed air inlet is connected to No. 2 engine by an S duct. Both inlet and S duct are faired into the fuselage afterbody. The basic outline of the RB211 engine is illustrated in Figure 1-44. The engine incorporates a three spool compressor which includes the fan (N_1), intermediate pressure compressor (N_2), and the high pressure compressor (N_3). Each compressor section has a matching turbine section which drives its corresponding compressor section.

THE AIRBUS INDUSTRIE PRODUCT LINE

The heart of the new Airbus product line, the A310 and A300-600 have been developed from the original A300, the world's first twin-engine widebody. The Airbus widebody fuselage allows flexible passenger accommodation and side-by-side LD3 containers underfloor.

FAMILY COMMONALITY

The advanced Airbus product line incorporates a high degree of commonality between family group members (A320 family, A300/A310 and A330/A340). This can give valuable savings in parts inventory and training, as well as large benefits in operational flexibility.

The benefits of commonality are particularly evident when considering the A319/A320/A321 and A330/A340 families. Fly-by-wire flight controls, besides giving full flight envelope protection, enable aircraft of radically different weights and sizes to be given virtually identical handling characteristics. In conjunction with cockpit commonality and systems similarities, this permits Cross-Crew Qualification across the whole A319/A320/A321/A330/A340 spectrum. This benefit, stemming from the logical use of modern technology, is unique to Airbus Industrie and produces substantial improvements in total operating costs and flexibility.

A310

The A310 is 20% smaller than the A300 and uses the same fuselage cross-section. The A310 incorporates significant advances in aerodynamics and structure and introduced a new generation of two-man "glass" cockpits with cathode ray tube presentations.

The A310-300 introduced the concept of fuel in the horizontal tail whereby range is increased through increased fuel capacity and reduced drag. In the course of development, range has been continually increased to well over 5000 nautical miles.

A300-600

This aircraft was developed by incorporating A310 systems and technology in the original A300. With a slightly higher passenger and cargo capacity than the A300, the A300-600 benefits from all the advances in technology made during the production lifetime of the original A300. Thus the A310 and A300-600 share a common two-man "glass" cockpit and have extensive systems and engine commonality.

With the same Type Rating these two aircraft form the basis of the Airbus Industrie widebody family.

AIRBUS A320

The A320 is a short/medium range twin-engine subsonic commercial transport aircraft introduced as the first single aisle aircraft to the Airbus family. The seating capacity varies between about 120 and 179 passengers. The design combines the high technology available today with the wide experience gained by Airbus Industries from the A300 and A310. The A320, shown in Figure 1-45, with a second-generation, two-man "glass" cockpit with sidestick controllers, is the first subsonic civil aircraft with fly-by-wire flight controls, giving full flight envelope protection. Being the only non-derivative aircraft in its category, it is able to take full advantage of all advances in avionics, aerodynamics, and materials made during the previous decade. Its wider fuselage improves passenger accommodation, gives greater layout flexibility and enables the A320 to offer an optional, standard-based, containerized cargo system for the first time in a single-aisle aircraft.

DESIGN FEATURES

The A320-200 series general dimensions and engine locations are shown in Figure 1-46. The aircraft features a two-person crew flight deck, along with CRT displays and electrically signaled flight controls. The centralized maintenance system and the use of composites in the structure are also advanced features of the A320.

The structure of the A320 is generally of conventional design and construction, similar to that employed on the earlier Airbus aircraft. Conventional materials are employed for much of the airframe structure, with more extensive use of improved aluminum alloys.

Composite material has been employed in many areas of the A320 structure, as can be seen in Figure 1-47.

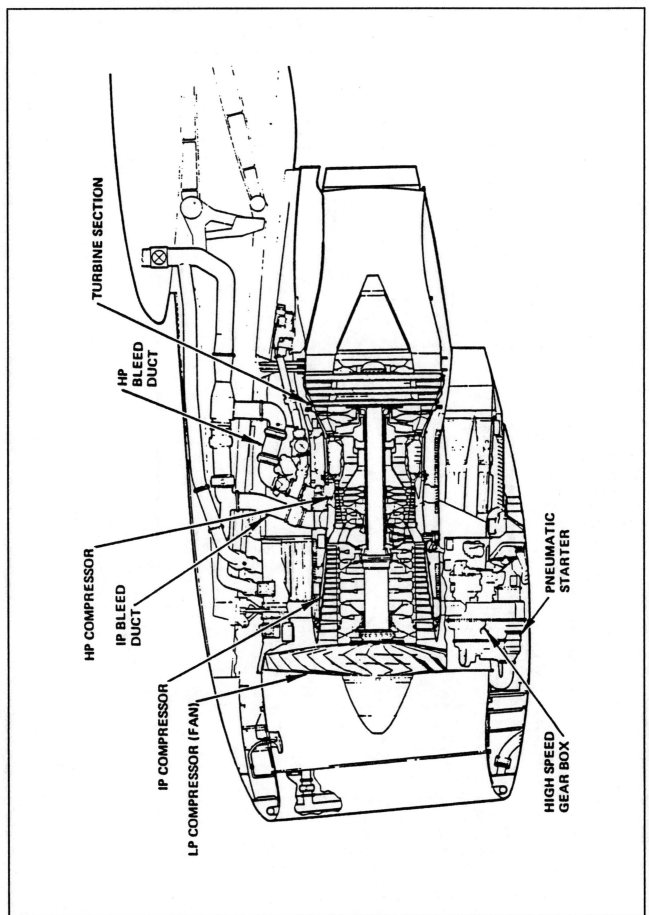

TURBINE SECTION

HP BLEED DUCT

HP COMPRESSOR

IP BLEED DUCT

IP COMPRESSOR

LP COMPRESSOR (FAN)

PNEUMATIC STARTER

HIGH SPEED GEAR BOX

Figure 1-43. L-1011 wing mounted engine installation. (Lockheed)

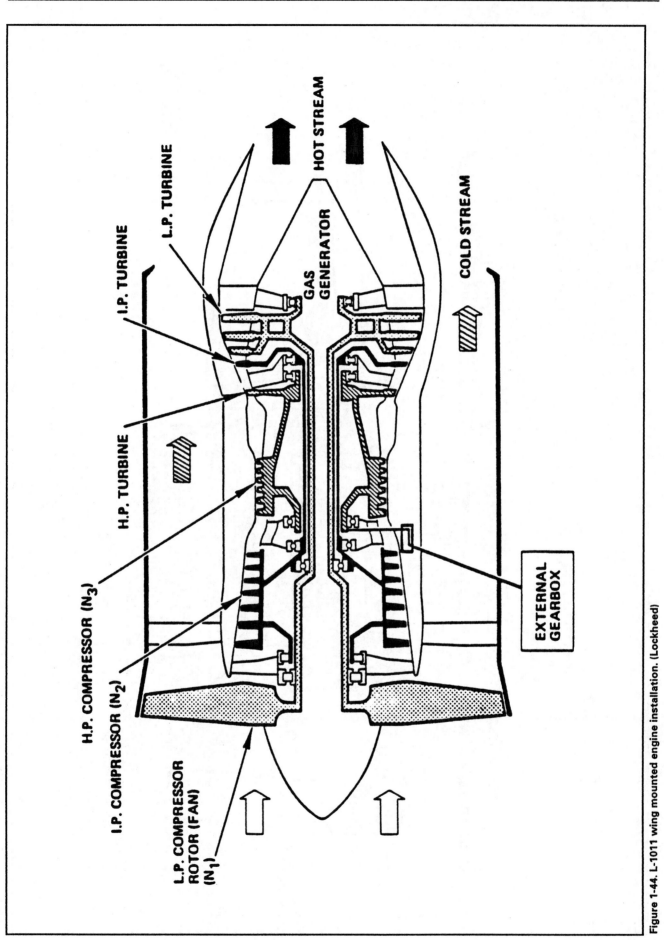

Figure 1-44. L-1011 wing mounted engine installation. (Lockheed)

Figure 1-45. Airbus Industrie A320. (Airbus)

The fuselage employs a conventional type of skin, stringer, and frame construction, except in the nose section where frames are used without stringers. Skin thickness variations are produced by chemical or mechanical machining and the stringers are attached by rivets. All areas of the fuselage are pressurized except for the radome, the rear fuselage section, the nose landing gear bay, and the lower segment of the center section.

The wing, which is of conventional structure and material, consists of three main components: a center wing box integral to the center fuselage to which are attached the left and right cantilevered outer wing sections, thus providing a continuous wing structure. Each outer wing section has five slats, two flaps, five spoilers and an aileron. All moving surfaces, except slats, are made of composite materials.

The flight compartment arrangement includes stations for the Captain, First Officer, and a third occupant (observer) facing forward. Controls and indications for systems are provided on the main instrument panels, center pedestal and overhead panel.

The passenger cabin, shown in Figure 1-48, has a maximum width of 145.5 in (3.70 m) and a height of 84 in (3.95 m). However, the cabin height is reduced in the forward and aft entrance areas for technical purposes. The A320 cabin interior has been designed according to the latest industrial design concepts to create an air of spaciousness.

The four seat tracks running the length of the cabin allow 4 or 6 abreast seating. Standard and optional lavatory and galley positions are provided at each end of the cabin on either side of the entrance areas. The seat tracks are spaced apart so as to give approximately equal space under each seat for carry-on baggage.

Galleys and lavatories are attached to the aircraft structure and are manufactured as pre-assembled cells with an integrated floor panel. This design helps protect against corrosion caused by leakage in these areas.

The main components of the semi-automatic cargo loading system, which are shown in Figure 1-49, are available as a standard option. The system is based on a new container derived from the widely used LD3 container by reducing its height from 64 inches to 46 inches. The base plate is identical to that of the LD3 container and hence existing container loaders, ground support equipment and warehouse facilities are compatible with the A320 container. In addition, this container can be used in wide body aircraft, providing their system has adequate restraints. The containers are supported on a single roller track along the cargo compartment center line, and on their outer edges, by rollers built into the restraint fittings. Power drives are incorporated into the center roller track with the doorway areas controlled by ball mat and transverse drive systems. The Control Panel, located at the Cargo Loading Door (LD), uses a joystick to activate the Power Drive Units (PDU).

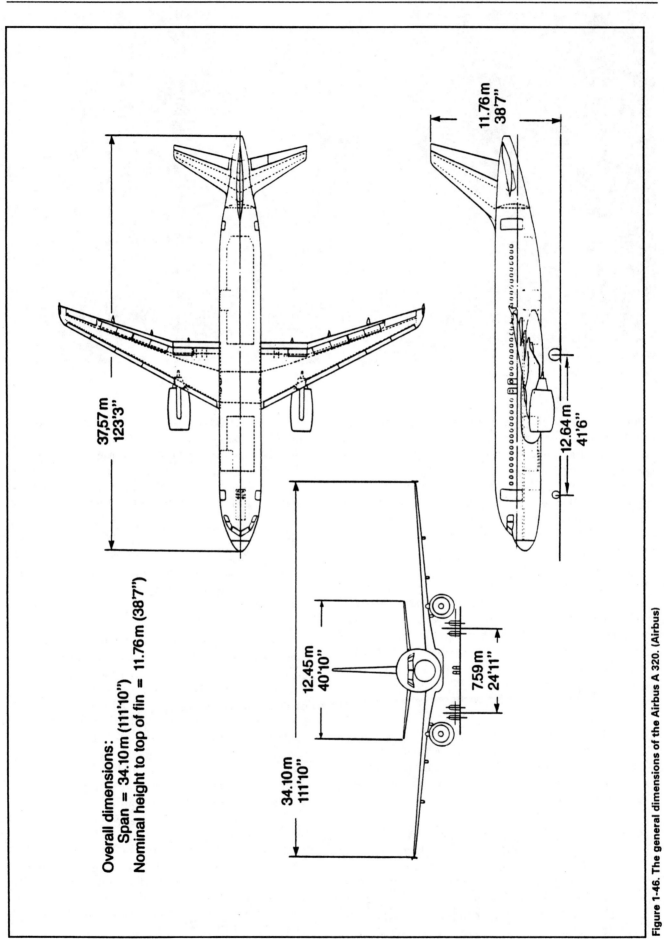

Overall dimensions:
Span = 34.10 m (111'10")
Nominal height to top of fin = 11.76 m (38'7")

37,57 m
123'3"

11.76 m
38'7"

12.64 m
4'1'6"

12.45 m
40'10"

7.59 m
24'11"

34.10 m
111'10"

Figure 1-46. The general dimensions of the Airbus A 320. (Airbus)

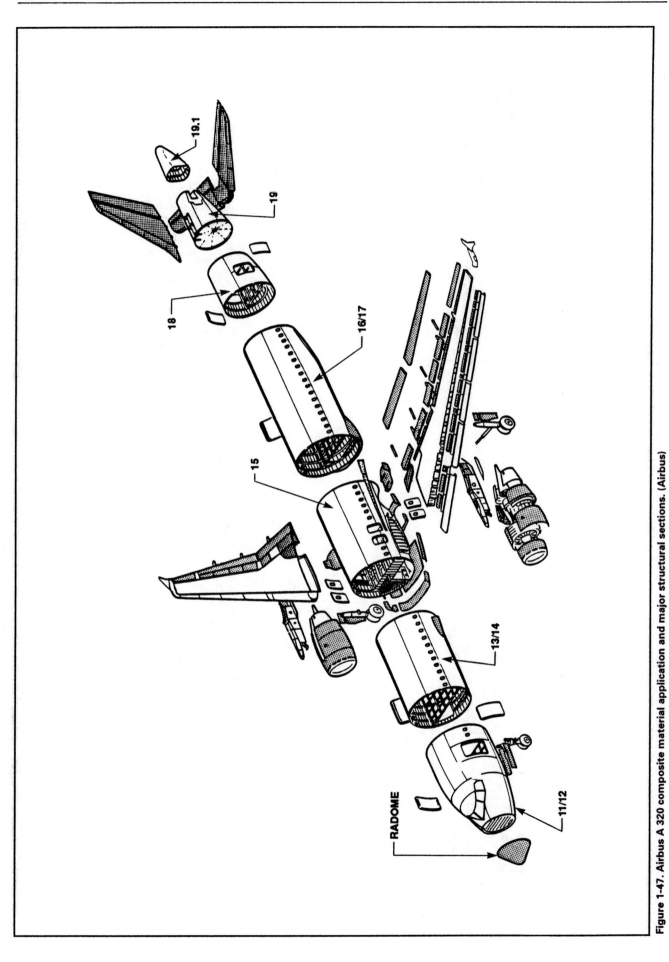

19.1

19

18

16/17

15

13/14

RADOME

11/12

Figure 1-47. Airbus A 320 composite material application and major structural sections. (Airbus)

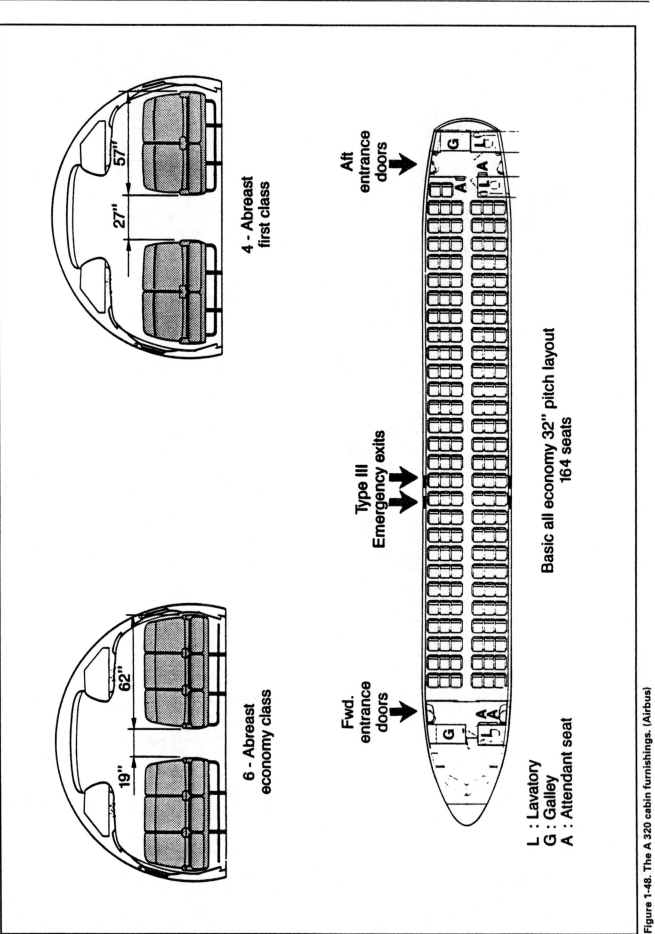

Figure 1-48. The A 320 cabin furnishings. (Airbus)

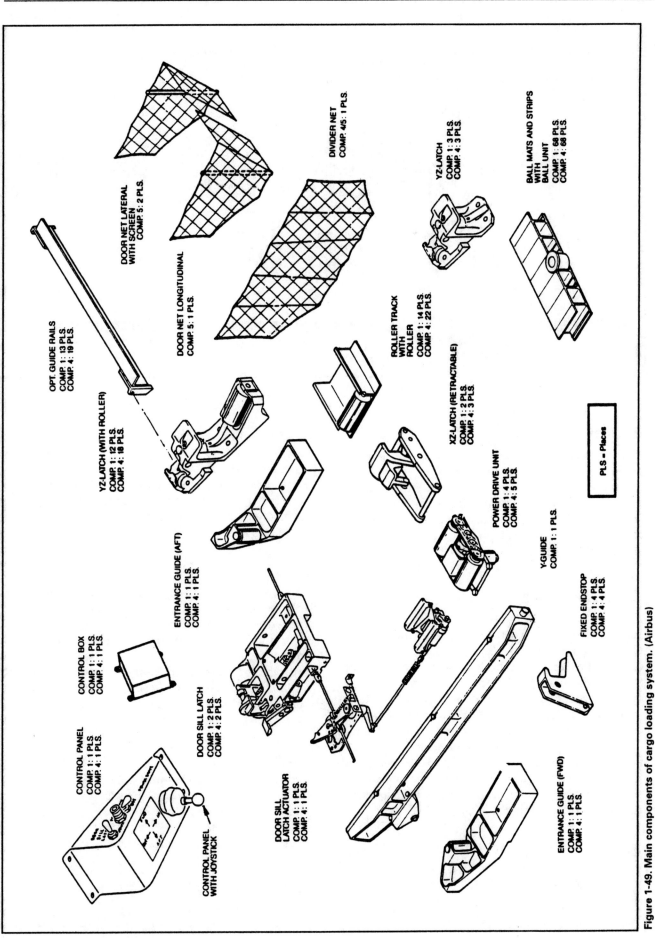

Figure 1-49. Main components of cargo loading system. (Airbus)

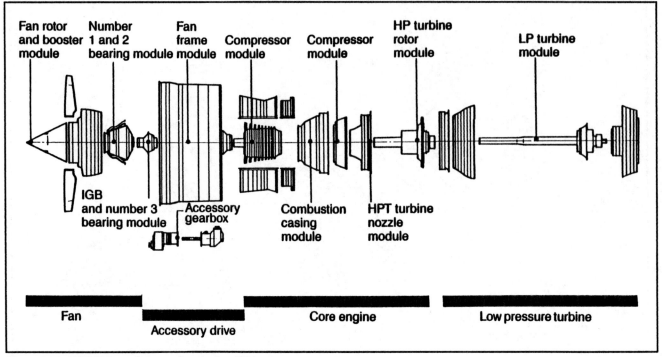

Figure 1-50. CFM 56-5 modular engine design. (Airbus)

A320 POWERPLANTS

The Airbus A320-210 use two CFM56-5A1 engines, while the A320-230 uses two V2500-A1 engines. Both of these engines are equipped with a Full Authority Digital Engine Control (FADEC) system. The engines are wing mounted and are attached by an engine pylon consisting of a main frame which can be converted to accept either of the engine types available for the A320.

A320 POWERPLANTS

The CFM56-5-A1 engine is a derivative of the CFM56 family certified at 25,000 pounds take off thrust. The FADEC allows "custom tailored" thrust ratings for the optimization of aircraft performance. Fuel consumption versus flight profile and aircraft weight allows optimum functional integration with the A320 Fly-by-wire Control System. The CFM56-5 engine's modular construction is illustrated in Figure 1-50. The modules have provided for the use of a reduced number of parts, improved sub-assembly designs, and better repairability. To achieve a high degree of modular interchangeability, all engine mating points are dimensionally controlled and modular balancing is used.

The main engine panel is located on the center pedestal in line with the engine throttle levers, as shown in Figure 1-51. A320 main engine starting is normally performed using the FADEC automatic start sequencing logic. The rotating selector is positioned in the "IGNITION" position, then the master lever of the

corresponding engine is moved to "ON". The FADEC then automatically, through its start command logic, sequences the starter valve operation, ignition, and high pressure (HP) fuel valve. The FADEC then monitors N_1, N_2, and EGT and ensures the appropriate limit protection. A manual override function allows start sequence to be controlled by the pilot via FADEC.

A321

The A321, shown in Figure1-52, is a maximum commonality, minimum change, stretch of the A320, produced in response to market demand for an aircraft with the technological efficiency of the A320 to serve on routes with higher traffic densities. The A321 has 40 percent more underfloor hold volume than the A320 and 25 percent more seats, giving exceptionally low seat-mile costs. The A321 entered service in early 1994.

A319

The A319, shown in Figure 1-53, is a reduced capacity version of the A320 with 124 seats in a two-class configuration. It offers more range potential and lower operating cost than any competitor in this category. Entry into service of the A319 was in mid-1996.

AIRBUS A330/A340 SERIES

The A330/A340, launched in 1987, is one aircraft produced initially in three versions: one twin and two

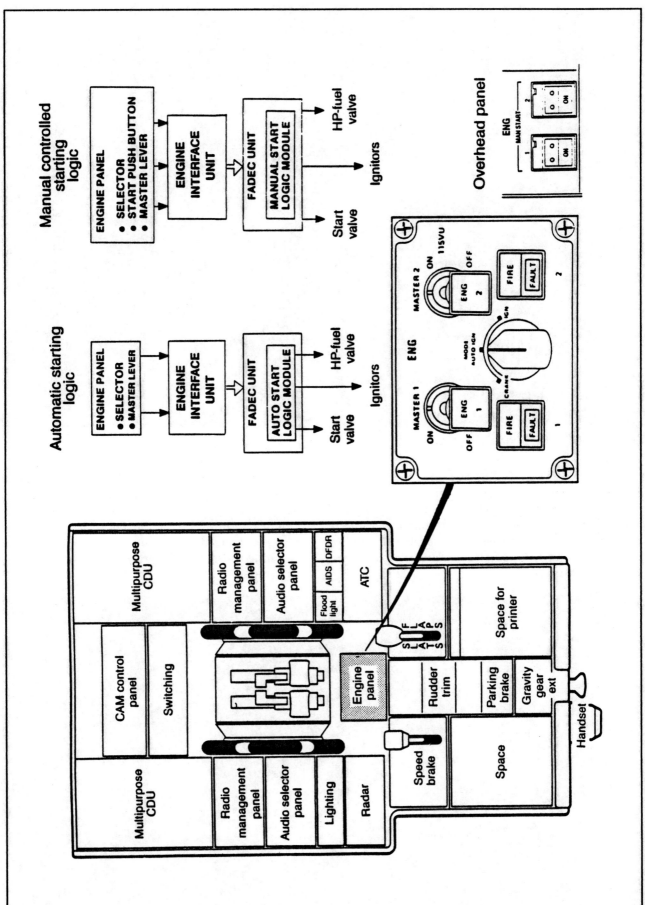

Figure 1-51. Airbus A 320 main engine starting. (Airbus)

Figure 1-52. Airbus Industrie 321 (Airbus)

four-engine models. Seating capacity ranges from about 260 to 440. The aircraft share the same airframe, the differences being engines, engine-related systems and fuselage length. Thus, for the first time, airlines are offered a twin for routes where a four-engine aircraft is needed, without the penalties normally associated with two distinct fleets.

The A330 (see Figure 1-54), is a third-generation, twin-engine widebody aircraft with typically 335 seats in a two-class arrangement. It offers a range of 4,850 nautical miles with a full complement of passengers and baggage. It is ideal as a direct replacement for earlier-generation tri-jets and as a growth replacement for earlier twin-jets.

Figure 1-53. Airbus Industrie A319. (Airbus)

Figure 1-54. Airbus Industrie A330. (Airbus)

Figure 1-55. Airbus Industrie A340. (Airbus)

The four-engine A340, shown in Figure 1-55, is offered in two sizes, allowing operators to tailor capacity and capability to demand. The larger A340-311 has seat-mile costs on a level with those of the largest four-engine airliner, while the smaller A340-200 has as long of range of any commercial airliner available.

Both the A330 and A340 represent the first steps towards new aircraft families and developments are already foreseen. For the immediate future, market demand is already showing a need for a version of the A340-300 with even greater range capability, a need which will be met by a higher design weight and a higher engine thrust.

CHAPTER 1
STUDY QUESTIONS

1. List the different aircraft systems.

   _____

   _____

   _____

2. Define the term "aircraft systems" as it pertains to this text.

   _____

   _____

   _____

3. List the types of aircraft in Chapter 1, and tell the number and location of the powerplants.

   _____

   _____

   _____

4. Explain the difference between an aircraft model number and its dash number.

   _____

   _____

   _____

5. What is the purpose of an "S" duct?

   _____

   _____

   _____

6. List the basic series for the Boeing 737.

   _____

   _____

7. What is the initial takeoff thrust rating of the JT8D on the 727 aircraft?

   _____

   _____

8. List the basic series (dash numbers) of the 747.

   _____

   _____

9. What thrust ratings are certified for the 747 series of aircraft?

   _____

   _____

10. List the basic series for the following models of aircraft: DC9, DC10, MD80, and MD 90.

   _____

   _____

11.   Define a "combi" aircraft.

     _____

     _____

     _____

12.   List the powerplants used on the MD11.

     _____

     _____

     _____

13.   List the powerplants and their thrust ratings for the Boeing 777.

     _____

     _____

     _____

14.   Define the term ETOPS.

     _____

     _____

     _____

AUXILIARY POWER UNITS, PNEUMATIC, AND ENVIRONMENTAL CONTROL SYSTEMS

CHAPTER 2

APU SYSTEMS

An auxiliary power unit (APU), shown in Figure 2-1, is a compact, self-contained unit that provides electrical power and compressed air during periods of airplane ground activity, or in flight if needed. In some cases, operation is limited to ground use only. The unit con-

Figure 2-1. AlliedSignal 36-150 gas turbine APU. (AlliedSignal)

sists of a small gas turbine engine with engine controls, mountings and enclosures necessary for safe and continuous operation. The APU gas turbine compressor bleed system, or a load compressor, is connected to the airplane's pneumatic system and supplies pneumatic power for main engine starting and other airplane functions. The APU also frees the aircraft from dependence on ground power equipment by supplying electrical power to energize the airplane's electrical systems.

The APU is installed in the tail cone of most airplanes, isolated from flight critical structure and control surfaces by a firewall shroud, as shown in Figure 2-2. The APU provides power for systems operation, generally when the main engines are not running.

A 24-volt battery is provided for APU starting. The main airplane battery switch must be ON to operate the APU. This battery is provided with a battery

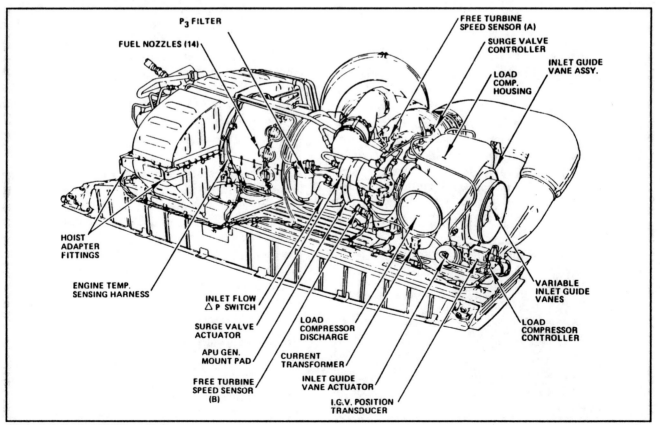

Figure 2-2. Typical APU installation.

charger which is disconnected during APU starter engagement. Power for normal APU battery charging is provided by the aircraft's electrical system.

Depending upon the aircraft, the APU drives one or two generators that are generally identical to the engine driven generators. The APU generators are usually capable of supplying all or most of the electrical load needed by the airplane. If maximum shaft output power is being used in conjunction with pneumatic power, pneumatic loading will be modulated to maintain a safe APU exhaust gas temperature. The electrical load has priority over the pneumatic load.

Fuel is normally supplied to the APU from one of the airplane's main tanks.

The APU oil system is a self-contained system consisting of independent supply, pumps, regulator, cooler, filters, and indicator. Switches on the APU control panel in the cockpit operate the APU. Sometimes the APU can be controlled from a ground accessible control panel. Fire detection and extinguishing systems are installed to provide fire protection for the APU.

Although many types and manufacturers of APUs are used on transport aircraft, many similarities exist in their basic operation. The description and operation of some examples are covered in the following information.

ALLIEDSIGNAL GTCP85 SERIES APU

The GTCP 85-98 APU proved to be an instant success. The airlines no longer had to depend on ground power availability to maintain electrical power, start engines or operate the ECS systems. With the advent of self-contained onboard APUs, the APU soon become standard equipment on most commercial transport aircraft. Figure 2-3 illustrates the two-bearing GTCP85 APU. The design was simplified by combining the rotating group assembly into a

Figure 2-3. AlliedSignal 85 series APU cutaway. (AlliedSignal)

single-piece. The first stage impeller, the second stage impeller, and the simplified turbine wheel are all mounted close to each other.

This same basic APU model is installed on the MD-80, Boeing 727 and the 737. The unit was externally modified to fit the new tail installation on the 737 and designated the GTCP85-129. Unlike the Boeing 727 APU, which is fuselage mounted and is ground operable only, the Boeing 737 APU can be started in flight and operated to 35,000 feet.

As airplanes grew in size, the need for additional bleed air for Environmental Control Systems (ECS) and starting large turbofan engines required two to three times the pneumatic energy from the APU. An increased output compressor provided enough pneumatic power for starting these larger engines. Faster, cooler, main engine starts were required, which extracts even more pneumatic power from the APU.

With the introduction of the Boeing 737-400 aircraft, AlliedSignal incorporated another growth version of the GTCP85-129 Series. The GTCP85-129(H) utilizes the latest technology in hot section materials and an Electronic Temperature Control (ETC) system that limits hot section temperatures based on aircraft need and ambient conditions. The Electronic Temperature Control provides engine operating temperature limits for two operating modes, Main Engine Start (MES) and Environmental Control System (ECS) operation. Under the original design, Exhaust Gas Temperature (EGT) was limited at a constant 1,200°F. In the dual mode electronic design, the EGT limit can increase from 1,150°F for environmental control systems operation to 1,275°F for main engine starting. Main Engine Starting typically constitutes only 5% of the operating time.

A cast one-piece turbine design helped to effectively lower the EGT temperatures. This more aerodynamically efficient turbine design produces the same power with less work, allowing a reduction in exhaust gas temperature for the same power. The fuel control was modified to provide fuel to the engine by using a Timed Acceleration Fuel Control Unit (TAFCU), which resulted in a 50% increase in cast turbine wheel life.

GTCP85 APU ENGINE SYSTEMS DESCRIPTION

The GTCP85-129 APU engine, used with the 737 series aircraft, is a single shaft gas turbine engine utilizing two centrifugal compressors and one centrifugal turbine. It is a self-contained unit consisting of an air inlet door with a door open switch on the right side of the aft fuselage. The air inlet supplies air for the engine and for accessory cooling. After the air enters the APU compartment, the airflow splits into two paths. The engine intake airflow and the cooling airflow. The accessories are cooled by the accessory cooling air using a fan driven by the engine gear box. The flow of cooling air is controlled by a shutoff valve that is pneumatically operated and then exhausted overboard through a hole in the lower shroud.

The fuel control unit, consisting of a fuel pump, acceleration control and governor, is supplied from a main tank through the fuel shutoff valve. Fuel from the fuel control unit enters the combustion chamber through the fuel solenoid valve and fuel nozzle. The Oil system consists of an oil pressure and oil return scavenge pump, two oil pressure switches, high oil temperature switch and an oil cooler. The starter, which uses 28VDC from the aircraft battery, APU battery, or an external DC supply, is used to turn the engine during the start cycle. A centrifugal switch controls the starting sequence for many of the systems used on the APU. The exhaust gas temperature probe for the EGT indicator and the control thermostat are mounted in the exhaust section. The control thermostat is used during acceleration and during normal operation to control the APU bleed valve's output. The exhaust ducting is cooled by four air inlets around the exhaust pipe.

OPERATION OF THE GTCP 85 APU

A typical GTCP85 APU starting procedure is as follows: The battery switch is placed to the ON position, which allows battery bus power to the control circuits and master switch. By placing the master switch momentarily to START and releasing it to the ON position, the start sequence is initiated. The fuel shutoff valve opens fully, followed by the air inlet door. When the door is fully open, the battery (or external DC if used) is connected to the starter and the APU begins to rotate. At approximately 10% RPM, the oil pressure increases to 4 psig, low oil pressure switch No. 1 (LOP 1) closes, sequencing power to the ignition exciter unit and the fuel solenoid valve. The oil pressure then reaches 55 psig (at approximately 37% RPM), as the engine rotation increases, allowing low oil pressure switch No. 2 (LOP 2) to open, extinguishing the amber LOW OIL PRESSURE light on the forward overhead panel.

The APU accelerates, being assisted by the starter. At 50% RPM, the speed switch operates and the power to starter is disconnected. At 95% RPM, the speed switch operates and the APU is ready to supply electrical and pneumatic power. The load control valve, shown in Figure 2-4, serves to limit bleed air flow to the aircraft pneumatic systems. The load control valve is mounted

on the turbine plenum and is actuated pneumatically. The air is derived from a probe protruding into the airstream from the compressor housing. It is directed into the inlet of a pressure regulator fitted with a filter. After the pressure regulator reduces the pressure of the air to a constant level (approximately 19-1/2 psi), it passes to the load control valve. The effects of the loading are monitored thermostatically in the exhaust. In some APUs, a single thermostat controls both the load control valve and the acceleration limiter; others have separate thermostats. In either case, the thermostat limits the load control valve as necessary to limit EGT.

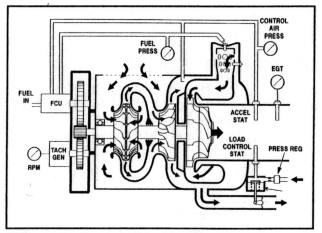

Figure 2-4. Load control valve—85 series.

APU OPERATION—BOEING 757

The APU system control panel for the Boeing 757 is shown in Figure 2-5. An APU start requires both the aircraft and APU batteries. The APU battery supplies power to the starter, the air inlet door, and the APU control circuitry. The aircraft battery supplies power for fire protection, the APU fuel valve, and the direct current (DC) fuel pump. It also supplies control circuitry power when the APU battery voltage drops because of heavy starter motor load.

Positioning the APU Selector momentarily to START, as shown in Figure 2-5, begins the start sequence. The APU fuel valve opens and at the same time the APU inlet door starts to open. A fuel pump in the left main tank also starts.

When the inlet door is fully open, an electric starter engages and the APU accelerates to its normal operating speed.

The starter duty cycle is a maximum of 3 consecutive starts or attempted starts within a 60-minute period, with a 5-minute cooling down period between attempts.

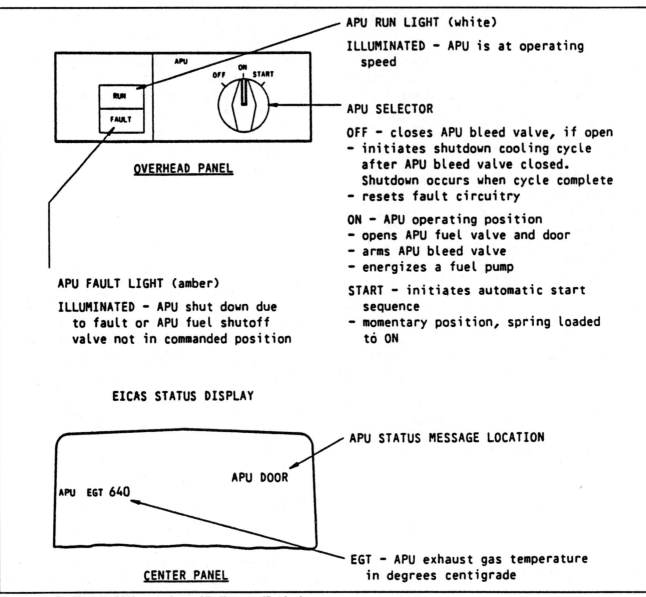

APU RUN LIGHT (white)

ILLUMINATED - APU is at operating
    speed

APU SELECTOR

OFF - closes APU bleed valve, if open
  - initiates shutdown cooling cycle
    after APU bleed valve closed.
    Shutdown occurs when cycle complete
  - resets fault circuitry

ON - APU operating position
  - opens APU fuel valve and door
  - arms APU bleed valve
  - energizes a fuel pump

START - initiates automatic start
    sequence
  - momentary position, spring loaded
    to ON

APU FAULT LIGHT (amber)

ILLUMINATED - APU shut down due
    to fault or APU fuel shutoff
    valve not in commanded position

EICAS STATUS DISPLAY

APU STATUS MESSAGE LOCATION

APU DOOR

APU EGT 640

EGT - APU exhaust gas temperature
    in degrees centigrade

Figure 2-5. Boeing 757 APU control panel/indicators. (Boeing)

When the APU RUN light illuminates, as shown in Figure 2-5, the APU is used to supply electrical power and pneumatic system bleed air.

Fuel for APU operation normally comes from the left main tank. A DC fuel pump supplies the fuel when alternating current (AC) power is not available. When AC power is available, the left forward AC fuel pump is signaled to start regardless of its switch position. It then supplies fuel to the APU and the DC pump remains off.

The APU, shown in Figure 2-6, has a system which incorporates a time-delay feature to permit APU cooling before shutdown. Closing the bleed valve will remove most of the load on the APU, therefore reducing APU engine temperatures. This protects the unit from thermal shock. If the APU is supplying pneumatic power, moving the selector OFF closes the bleed valve before shutting down the APU. The time-delay is

variable from 0 to 120 seconds. It is nominally set at 60 seconds. If the APU bleed valve has been closed for more than 60 seconds when the selector is moved OFF, the APU shuts down with no delay.

Figure 2-6. AlliedSignal 331-200 series APU. (AlliedSignal)

Figure 2-7. AlliedSignal 331-500 series APU. (AlliedSignal)

APU OPERATION—BOEING 777 ALLIEDSIGNAL GTCP331-500

The GTCP331-500 APU, available for the Boeing 777, is shown in Figure 2-7.

It is a constant speed gas turbine engine that features rugged, economical state of the art design. The basic APU is comprised of three major sections; the power section, load compressor section, and the accessory gearbox section.

The power section utilizes a single shaft with a dual centrifugal compressor impeller, a triple stage axial turbine with containment ring, a nozzle, and a reverse flow annular combustor. The power section drives the load compressor and accessory gearbox.

In Figure 2-8, air enters the inlet plenum on the top side of the engine, then splits to provide the requirements of the load and power section compressors. The air entering the power section compressor passes through the second stage diffuser into the combustor where fuel is added. After being burnt, the hot gases pass through the turbine wheels and nozzles and finally out the exhaust. Some air enters through the

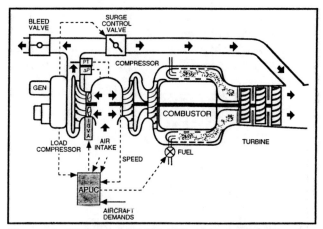

Figure 2-9. AlliedSignal 331-500 APU systems. (AlliedSignal)

IGVs and load compressor. This air is then discharged through the scroll to service the aircraft.

The load compressor consists of a single centrifugal impeller and a diffuser. The load compressor is connected by a quill shaft to the power section and compressor. Inlet air is controlled by inlet guide vanes as can be seen in Figure 2-9. The power section and load section impellers share the same inlet plenum duct.

The accessory gearbox provides gear reduction for the high speed torque of the power section and the APU accessories. Accessories installed on the gearbox are the oil cooled generator, oil pump, fuel control, air turbine starter, and electrical starter motor. The gearbox also serves as a reservoir for the lubrication system.

The APU is suspended in the tail cone. Air enters through an opening covered by an air intake door at the top of the fuselage skin. The door is opened by an electric actuator when a command to run is given to the APU from the flight deck controls. Both the intake and exhaust systems are acoustically treated to reduce noise.

The load compressor, shown in Figure 2-10, must be sized to provide the maximum amount of air flow that

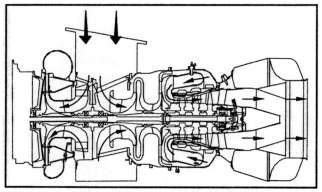

Figure 2-8. AlliedSignal 331-500 airflow. (AlliedSignal)

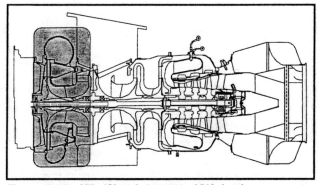

Figure 2-10. AlliedSignal 331-500 APU load compressor. (AlliedSignal)

the aircraft will require. If there were no controls over airflow, it would impose full load on the turbine and require a very high fuel flow, whether or not the aircraft demanded air. Inlet guide vanes between the compressor and the air inlet match compressor flow to the demand. Inlet guide vane (IGV) position is changed by an actuator, using fuel from the fuel control unit as a hydraulic fluid, controlled by the APU Controller

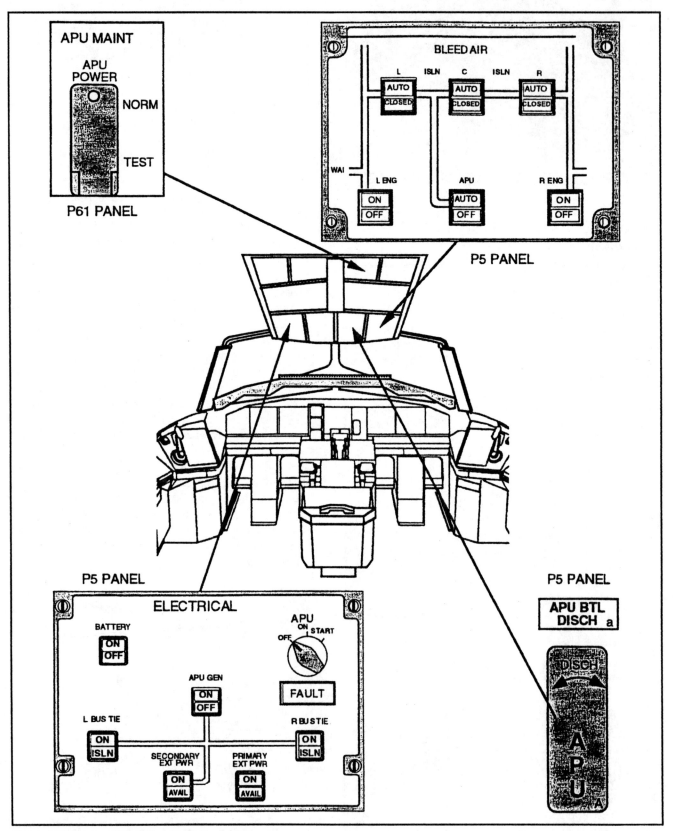

Figure 2-11. Boeing 777 APU control. (Boeing)

(APUC) in response to signals from the aircraft control circuits. As the IGVs open, the power required to drive the load compressor increases. The fuel flow and EGT also increase. When there is no demand, the APUC commands the IGVs to the minimum close position so that the load compressor imposes almost no load on the power section. When the IGVs are at the minimum closed position (76%), the condition under which the unit is running (that is, full speed with no load) is called "idle".

The B777 flight deck controls are shown in Figure 2-11. Illustrated are the switches and indicators that control and monitor the APU. The APU control selector is used to start and stop the APU. The APU fire handle is used for emergency purposes to stop the APU. After an APU fire handle shutdown, the fire handle must be pushed back in to reset the system.

The APU maintenance switch in the TEST position powers the APUC when the APU control selector is OFF. This permits the APU data to show on the status and maintenance page formats. If EICAS is powered, as shown in Figure 2-12, and the status page for the APU is selected, the operator will be able to see RPM rise during an attempted start cycle. When the APU reaches 7% speed, the APUC turns on the ignition and commands open the fuel shutoff valve which allows metered fuel flow. A "pre-lightoff" flow for the given ambient condition is commanded until lightoff is achieved, detected by a rise in EGT. After lightoff, the speed is controlled and will follow a prescribed reference by modulating the fuel flow command. The fuel flow command is subject to limits that prevent excessive turbine inlet temperature, power section surge, lean blowout, and poor atomization. The RPM rises smoothly, the exhaust gas temperature approaches but does not exceed the limit. The electric starter will be de-energized at 50% speed (if used) and the air turbine starter control valve (ATSCV) closed at 55% (if a pneumatic start). The ignitor unit is deenergized at 50%.

The APU continues to accelerate at a steady rate. The rate of acceleration is a timed function based on P_4 altitude and T_2 inlet temperature with T_4 trim control, (T_4, or TIT, is turbine inlet temperature).

If a fault occurs during acceleration, the starter motor is disengaged and the fuel shut-off valve is closed, forcing the APU to shutdown. When the APU speed reaches 95%, the APUC switches from the starting mode to speed governing mode. Two seconds later, the APU RUNNING signal is sent, triggering a message on the upper EICAS screen and allowing the generator control unit (GCU) to load the generator, if switched on

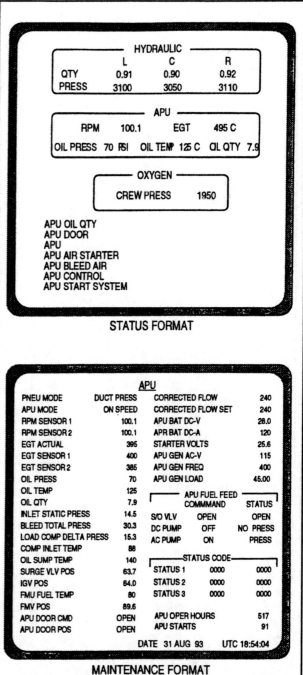

Figure 2-12. Boeing 777 APU systems page display. (Boeing)

by the flight deck. Pneumatic loading would also be possible at this time. The unit has reached its idle (no load) speed of 100% and the EGT will stabilize at the engines idle value. The idle EGT is a good indication of the internal condition of the APU unit.

APU OPERATION—LOCKHEED L-1011

The APU used in the Lockheed L-1011 is basically a turboshaft jet engine. The power turbine (free turbine) drives the APU load system consisting of the APU

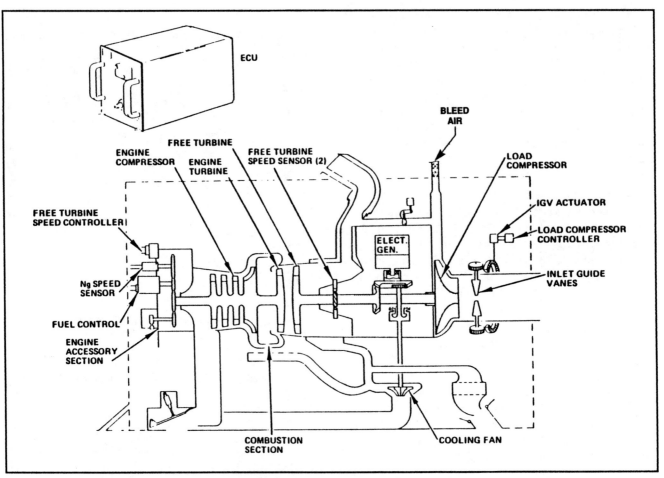

Figure 2-13. APU power system schematic. (Lockheed)

generator, the load compressor, and a cooling fan (Figure 2-13).

Since the APU generator must be driven at a constant speed, the free turbine speed must be maintained at a constant rate of 33,000 RPM. To achieve this constant rate there must be a balance between engine power output and total load on the generator, load compressor, and cooling fan. To achieve this balance, the electronic control unit (ECU) controls engine speed (power output) by controlling fuel flow and controls load by controlling a set of inlet guide vanes on the inlet of the load compressor.

The ECU senses free turbine speed through two free turbine speed sensors. The ECU controls engine power output by controlling fuel flow through the free turbine speed controller and the fuel control. The ECU also controls inlet guide vane position through the load compressor controller.

PNEUMATIC SYSTEMS

Compressed air for the pneumatic system can be supplied by the engines, APU, or a high pressure ground air source. The APU or ground source would supply the pneumatic system prior to engine start. The engines supply bleed air for pneumatics after engine start. The following systems normally rely on, or are examples of, systems that use pneumatics for operation:

- Air conditioning/pressurization

- Wing and engine anti-ice

- Engine cross starting

- Hydraulic reservoir pressure

- Air driven hydraulic pumps

ENGINE BLEED AIR

Air is generally bled from an intermediate stage (IP stage) or the low pressure stage (LP stage) of the engine's compressor to provide pressure air for the pneumatic system. At low engine speeds, when the pressure from the IP or LP bleed air is insufficient to meet pneumatic system needs, air is automatically bled from the high pressure (HP) stage bleed.

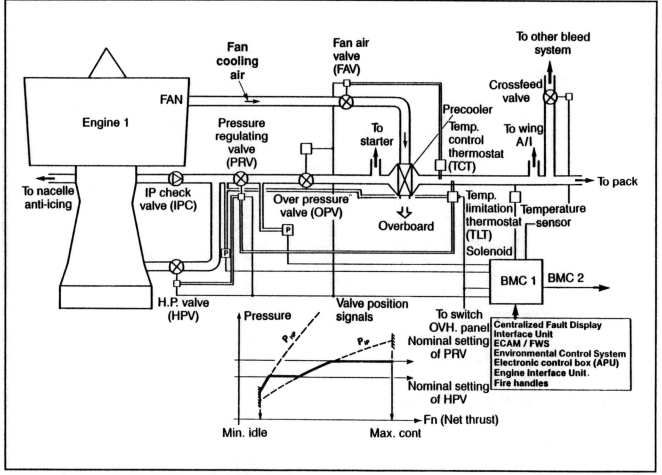

Figure 2-14. Airbus A320 bleed system schematic. (Airbus)

The transfer from the low pressure bleed to the high pressure bleed is achieved by means of a pneumatically operated high pressure regulating valve at the HP stage outlet, as shown in Figure 2-14.

Downstream of the junction of the IP and HP ducting, air is admitted into the duct by a pneumatically controlled butterfly valve, which acts as a shut-off and a pressure regulator valve. The IP check valve prevents reverse flow of the high pressure bleed air from entering the IP bleed stage of the engine.

Cooling air is directed from the fan stage of the engine, through a heat exchanger, to regulate pre-cooling of the hot bleed air from the engine's compressors. When the engine is started and delivery of hot bleed air is initiated, the pre-cooler modulating valve (fan air valve) modulates the flow of fan cooling air through the heat exchanger and regulates the duct air temperature. (See Figure 2-14). Some engine bleed systems use an air cleaner in the air bleed system to filter the air used for air conditioning before it enters the pneumatic system.

BOEING 757 ENGINE BLEED AIR SUPPLY SYSTEM

Engine bleed air for the pneumatic system comes from either the high pressure (HP) or the low pressure (LP) engine compressor section as illustrated in Figure 2-15. During low engine thrust operation, the HP valve is open allowing high pressure air to power the system. As thrust is increased, the HP valve automatically closes and the LP check valve opens to supply bleed air.

The bleed air flows through the engine bleed air valve for pressure control and then into the pneumatic ducting for distribution to the pneumatic system, as shown in Figure 2-15. Engine bleed air valves are electrically controlled by the bleed air switches. They are pressure actuated and therefore, even though the valves are signaled open prior to the engine start, they will remain closed until the engine is running. The engine bleed air OFF lights track the position of the engine bleed air valves. A light is illuminated any time the associated valve is closed and will extinguish when bleed air pressure opens the valve.

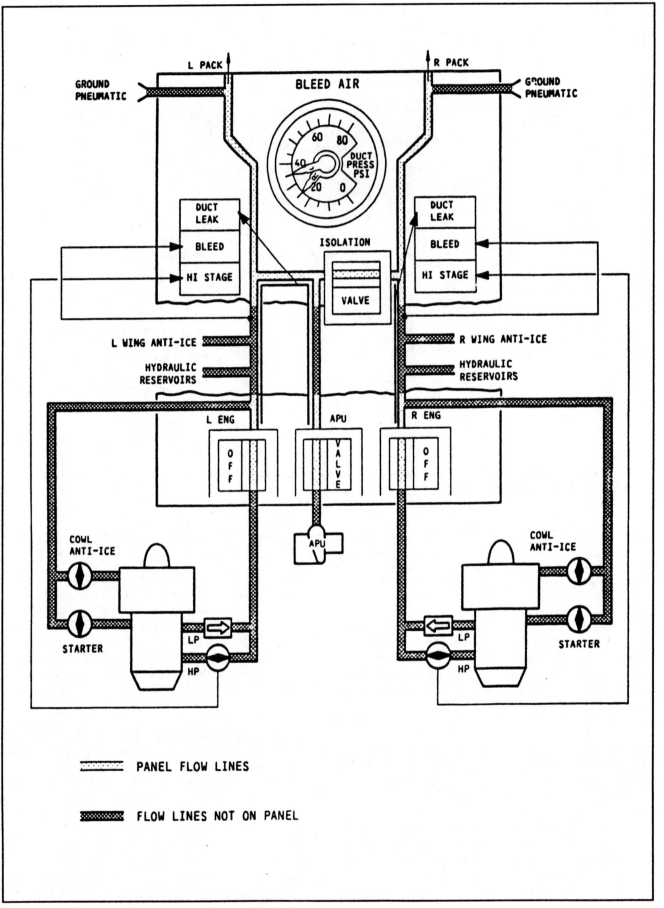

Figure 2-15. Boeing 757 bleed air system diagram. (Boeing)

PNEUMATIC DUCTING

Engine bleed air flows through the left and right pneumatic ducts to the using systems. Normal flight procedures require isolating the engine bleed air supply into left and right systems after engine start. Each engine supplies air to its corresponding air conditioning package, wing anti-ice ducting, and to a common manifold for the hydraulic reservoirs. The two sides are connected by a manifold. Separation of the sides is controlled by the operation of the isolation valve in the manifold. This valve is controlled by the isolation switch.

DUCT PRESSURE

The pneumatic duct pressure indicator, shown in Figure 2-15, shows the pressure in the left and right pneumatic ducts. These pressures should be approximately equal when the load on each system is equal. Pneumatic duct pressure is also read out on the EICAS display in the flight deck.

ENVIRONMENTAL CONTROL SYSTEMS

A large transport aircraft must provide a cabin environment that is comfortable for the crew and passengers. The aircraft operates at altitudes where temperature and pressure extremes would make the cabin unbearably cold and normal breathing would be impossible. On the other hand, the aircraft must also be comfortable when its on the ground on a hot day. This will require a system of heating and cooling the cabin air and a system for maintaining cabin pressure with enough oxygen to breathe.

The environmental control system's function is to control the cabin temperature and pressure. It accomplishes this by using two systems: an air conditioning system and a pressurization system. The air conditioning and pressurization systems normally use engine bleed air. Engine bleed air is hot and under pressure, as mentioned earlier. By passing this bleed air through the air conditioning packages (packs), the cabin air temperature is adjusted to the levels called for by the cockpit controls.

The APU bleed air, or ground high pressure air source, may be used to supply high pressure pneumatic air to the packs for normal usage of the air conditioning system on the ground. In some cases, ground conditioned air is used to cool or heat the aircraft cabin on the ground before flight. This air should not be confused with ground high pressure air mentioned previously. Ground conditioned air is conditioned by a unit separate of the aircraft. It does not pass through the packs, passing instead directly into the cabin distribution system. Control of the cabin pressure will be discussed later in this chapter.

Air is directed from the pneumatic manifold through the pack valve which controls the air entering the packs. Most aircraft have either two or three air conditioning packs. In Figure 2-16, an air conditioning pack is illustrated to show the main components of a pack. Some of these components are the heat exchangers, air cycle machine, ram air cooling doors, water separator, anti-ice valve, and the mixing valve. The terminology for these components might differ from airplane to airplane, but these basic components are used in almost every air-conditioning pack. The heat exchangers are air-to-air radiators which are used to cool the hot bleed air by passing ambient air through them. The ram air doors control the air flow through the heat exchangers.

The air cycle machine is an air cooling device that is made up of a compressor and an expansion turbine connected together by a common shaft. The air cycle machine changes the hot pneumatic system air to cold air for air conditioning by transforming heat into mechanical energy, as the air is expanded by the turbine.

Water that has condensed out of the air by the operation of the air cycle machine is removed by the water separator. To prevent icing in the water separator, a temperature sensor will signal the water separator anti-ice valve to provide warming air automatically. This will provide a temperature above freezing in the water separator.

The air mixing valve regulates the mixture of cold and hot air for distribution into the passenger and crew cabins. It is a combination of two or more interconnected valves in one body, and is controlled from the temperature control panel. As one valve opens, the other is driven closed, which allows hot or cold air to mix providing the proper temperature.

When the pack valve is turned on, as shown in Figure 2-16, air enters the pack and is split, with some of the air going to the hot air mix valve and the rest entering the pack. It passes through the primary heat exchanger where it is cooled to become warm air. It then passes through the compressor of the air cycle machine and is compressed and reheated. The air then passes through the secondary heat exchanger and is cooled again. Part of the air can then go to the cool air mix valve. The other part of the air passes through the air cycle machine expansion turbine where it is cooled even further. The air that has passed through the air cycle machine turbine, then passes through the water separator, and then on into the cold air mix valve.

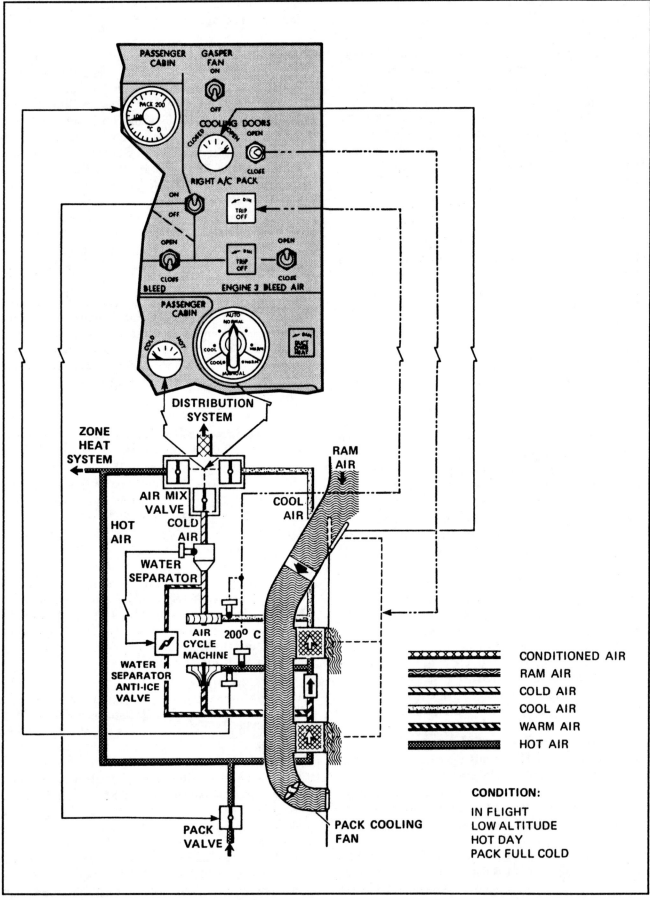

Figure 2-16. Boeing 727 air conditioning pack. (Boeing)

By controlling the mixing valves, the temperature called for can be supplied to the distribution system. The temperature sensor in the water separator will control the anti-ice valve to allow enough warm air to mix with the air exiting the expansion turbine to keep the air temperature above freezing.

The cooling door positions are controlled either automatically or manually in the cockpit to adjust the volume of the air passing through the heat exchangers. On the ground, or in slow flight modes, there is generally an auxiliary method of passing air through the heat exchangers, such as an electric pack cooling fan or a fan attached directly to the air cycle machine. Although each aircraft system works somewhat differently, they all use these basic components and principles for their operation.

BOEING 757 AIR CONDITIONING SYSTEMS

Conditioned air for the cabin comes from either the airplane air conditioning system or a pre-conditioned ground source. Air from the ground source enters the air conditioning manifolds and is routed through the mix manifold to the cabin distribution ducts.

The air conditioning system provides temperature controlled air by processing bleed air from the engines, APU, or high pressure air from a ground source. This temperature controlled air is mixed with recirculated cabin air in the mix manifold for distribution to the cabin.

757 AIR CONDITIONING PACKS

Airplane air conditioning, illustrated in Figure 2-17, is achieved by two identical packs (left and right), each of which is controlled by a pack control selector. Positioning the selector to AUTO or STBY sends an open signal to the pack valve.

The pack valve is a flow control valve and requires air pressure to open. When open, the valve limits air flow to a scheduled rate based on airplane altitude.

Pack temperature control is automatic when AUTO is selected. STBY N sets the pack to produce a constant moderate temperature. STBY C sets the pack to full cold operation. STBY W sets the pack so the outlet temperature is controlled by ram air flowing across the pack heat exchangers.

Conditioned air from the packs flow into a common manifold where it mixes with air from two recirculating fans. The mixed air is then ducted into the passenger cabin. Conditioned air, from the left pack duct

upstream of the mix manifold, is supplied to the flight deck.

747 AIR CONDITIONING SYSTEM

Air is directed from the pneumatic manifold to three air conditioning packs, as seen in Figure 2-18. The output from the packs enters a common conditioned air manifold. From this manifold, air is directed to the four zones of the pressurized area of the airplane. The temperature of the air delivered by the packs is determined by the zone requiring the coolest air input.

Conditioned air temperature is achieved by cooling the air from the pneumatic system by means of heat exchangers and, when required, regulating the flow of air through the air cycle machines (ACMs). Individual zone temperature requirements are satisfied by adding hot trim air to the output of the packs. However, trim air is not added to the zone controlling the output of the packs. Air for the upper deck area is tapped off a zone supply duct upstream of where trim air is added. Upper deck heat is added, as required, by electric heaters in the upper deck supply ducts. Gasper air is tapped from one of the zone supply ducts upstream of where the trim air is added. The gasper fan provides a positive supply of conditioned air to all zones. Recirculating fans in zones 1, 2, 3, and 4 increase ventilation rates in these areas.

There are both automatic and manual modes of operation for the air conditioning system. The automatic mode is the normal mode for all operations, with manual used only if automatic operation cannot be maintained. All three packs are normally utilized.

The air conditioning packs will shut down automatically (trip off) for conditions of excessive temperature, or for improper bypass valve and inlet/exit door sequencing. Since the pack valves are pneumatically operated, they will close as a result of low duct pressure.

Supplemental heating of the cargo areas is provided by air circulated around the individual cargo compartments. The aft cargo compartment heating system utilizes air from the pneumatic system for this purpose. Airflow through the system is automatically controlled by compartment temperature. The forward cargo compartment is heated by air exhausted from the equipment cooling system.

PRESSURIZATION SYSTEMS

Engine bleed air is utilized for cabin pressurization. Air from the compressors of the engines, which is pressurized and temperature conditioned by the air condi-

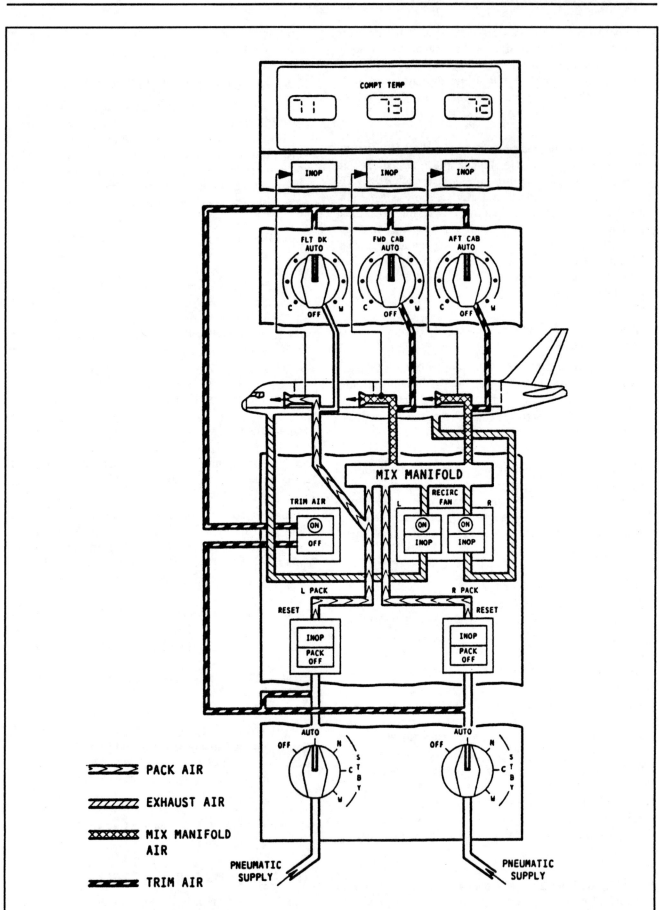

Figure 2-17. Boeing 757 air conditioning system. (Boeing)

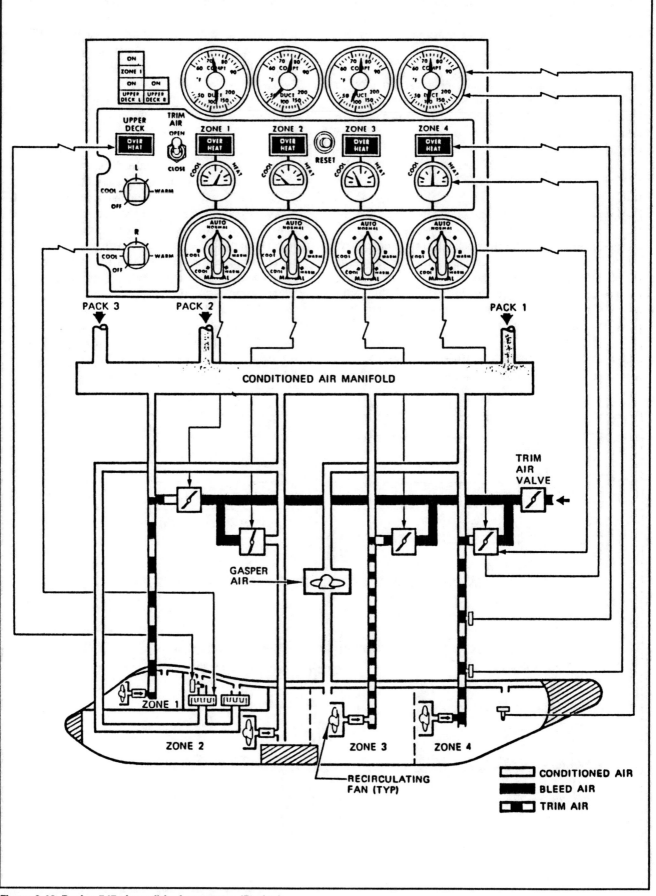

Figure 2-18. Boeing 747 airconditioning system. (Boeing)

tioning packages (packs), is distributed into the cabin and flight deck, as shown in Figure 2-19. Air is continually blown into the cabin to maintain proper pressure at altitude.

As mentioned earlier, the air pressure and oxygen level at high altitudes is insufficient to provide a suitable environment for the crew and passengers. To compensate for this, the amount of pack air that can escape from the cabin area is controlled by the outflow valve, as shown in Figure 2-19. By closing the outflow valve, the cabin will be pressurized more, thus lowering the cabin altitude. If the outflow valve is opened, it will allow more air to escape, thus increasing cabin altitude. As the pressure in the pressurized area of the aircraft increases, the atmospheric altitude inside the cabin decreases. And conversely, as the cabin pressure decreases, the cabin altitude increases. Instruments in the cockpit read the cabin altitude, cabin rate of climb, and pressure differential, illustrated in Figure 2-20.

The cabin altitude (inside pressure) cannot be held at sea level at high altitudes because of the pressure differential between the inside of the cabin and the outside of the cabin. The structure of the airplane is limited by a maximum differential pressure (PSID). Most maximum pressure differentials range from about 8.0 PSID to 8.9 PSID. This means the pressure in the aircraft cabin is 8.9 PSI higher than the outside of the cabin. If the pressure inside the aircraft was allowed to build up beyond the maximum pressure differential, the cabin structure could fail.

When the maximum pressure differential is reached, the cabin altitude must be increased (inside pressure decreased). This will cause the cabin altitude to climb, but at a much slower rate and at a much lower altitude than the aircraft. Safety valves (outflow valves) can open if the maximum pressure differential is exceeded and allow air in the cabin to escape. This will decrease the pressure differential and prevent any structural damage from occurring.

The outflow valve position is normally controlled by the system's pressure controller. Most aircraft have an indicator in the cockpit which informs the flight crew of the outflow valve position (see Figure 2-21).

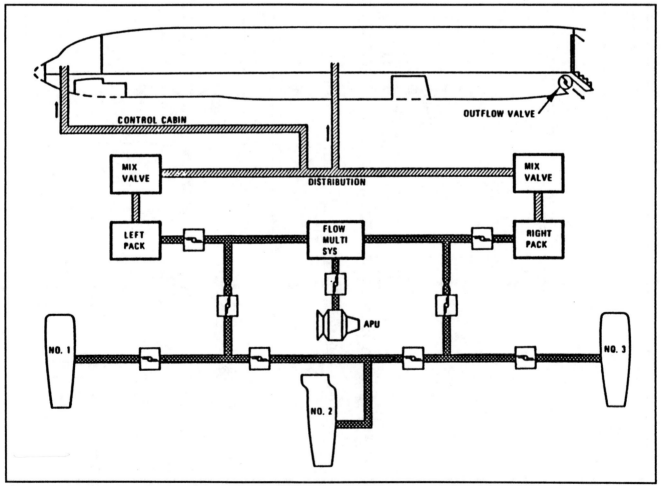

Figure 2-19. Pressurized pack air distributed to cabin. (Boeing)

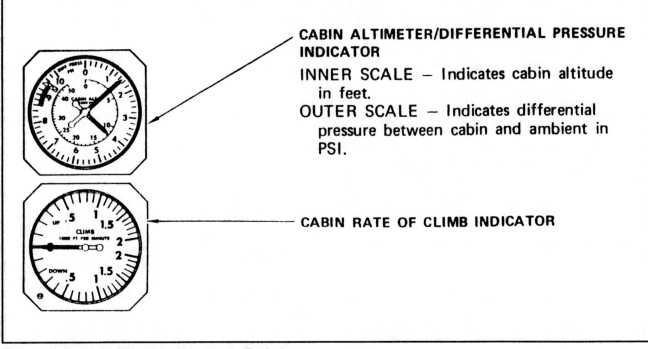

CABIN ALTIMETER/DIFFERENTIAL PRESSURE INDICATOR

INNER SCALE – Indicates cabin altitude in feet.

OUTER SCALE – Indicates differential pressure between cabin and ambient in PSI.

CABIN RATE OF CLIMB INDICATOR

Figure 2-20. Pressurization system instruments. (Boeing)

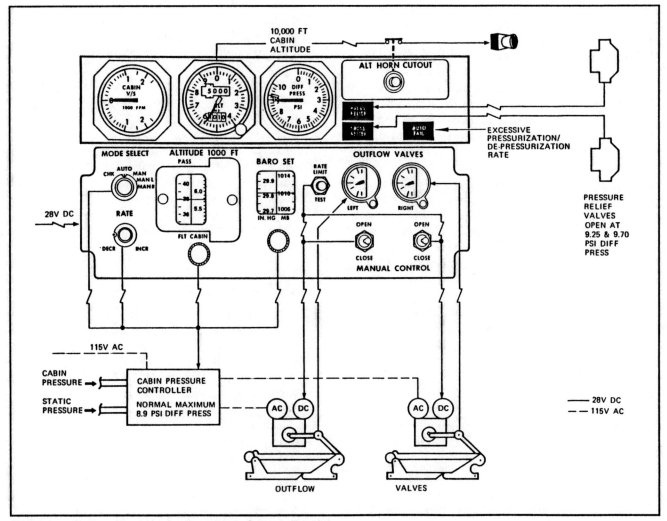

Figure 2-21. Boeing 747 pressurization system diagram. (Boeing)

Pressurization systems generally have two different modes of operation; automatic or manual. The automatic mode normally controls the system unless there is a malfunction, then the manual mode is selected and the outflow valve is controlled by the flight crew.

The pressurization system also allows the aircraft cabin pressure to climb and descend at a much slower rate than the aircraft is actually climbing or descending. On early pneumatic systems the rate of climb indicator is used to adjust the cabin pressure to a comfortable rate while climbing or descending the cabin. Most new style pressurization systems use electronic controllers and alternating current (AC) and/or direct current (DC) motors to open or close the outflow valve. Some of the larger aircraft are equipped with two outflow valves.

BOEING 747 PRESSURIZATION SYSTEM

The pneumatic system supplies engine compressor bleed air to the air conditioning and pressurization systems. The pneumatic system automatically selects either high or low stage bleed air from the engine compressor and delivers pressure regulated and temperature limited air to the pneumatic duct.

Normally during takeoff, climb, cruise, and most holding conditions, the system draws low stage air. For descent and other low engine thrust conditions, the high stage is required to provide for system demand. Bleed air temperature is normally controlled by a "precooler" which utilizes engine fan air to cool the hot bleed air.

Pressurization is maintained and controlled by governing the rate of air flow through two outflow valves (see Figure 2-21). Each outflow valve can be actuated by either an AC or DC motor. AUTO mode utilizes 115 volts alternating current (VAC) power. The outflow valves may be controlled by any one of the following example modes of operation.

- AUTO—Automatic is the normal operating mode. Both outflow valves are controlled automatically by the pressurization controller to maintain the selected cabin altitude. Both valves modulate together and maintain approximately the same relative position.

- MAN—Each outflow valve is controlled by its respective outflow valve control switch.

AUTOMATIC OPERATION

Cruise cabin altitude is normally set on the flight/cabin altitude selector prior to takeoff. After takeoff, the cabin altitude will climb to the altitude corresponding to the cruise cabin altitude setting at a controlled rate, as selected on the pressurization rate selector.

The cabin pressure selector switch allows selection of two differential pressure operating modes. The 8.9 PSI position provides a maximum differential pressure of 8.9 PSID for all normal high altitude operation. The 8.0 PSI position provides a differential pressure of 8.0 PSID for low altitude operation. When using the 8.0 PSI position, the reduced differential pressure imposes less stress on the fuselage structure, which provides an increased service life to the airplane.

There is an automatic differential pressure limiter set to 8.0/8.9 PSID which is operative in AUTO and MANUAL modes. Setting a cabin altitude on the flight/cabin altitude selector will result in a differential pressure of 8.0/8.9 PSI when the airplane reaches the corresponding flight altitude shown on the flight/cabin altitude selector (see Figure 2-21).

In AUTO and MANUAL modes, the system has a protective feature called "rate limit control". This feature is armed when cabin altitude is below 10,000 feet and is activated by cabin vertical speed rates above 3,100 feet per minute ascending or 2,000 feet per minute descending. Activation of this feature is indicated by illumination of the RATE LIMIT light. The rate limit control feature is deactivated and the RATE LIMIT light is extinguished if cabin altitude exceeds 10,000 feet.

There is an additional protective feature called maximum cabin altitude override which is activated when the cabin altitude exceeds 10,000 feet. This feature, utilizing 115 VAC power (high speed), will drive the outflow valve(s) toward the closed position limiting the cabin altitude between 10,250 and 14,000 feet.

PRESSURIZATION SAFETY RELIEF VALVES

Two cabin pressurization relief valves, shown in Figure 2-21, are installed to prevent excessive pressure within the airplane. If the cabin differential pressure reaches 9.25 PSID (or 9.7 PSID as a back-up), one or both valves will modulate OPEN. The operating valve(s) will close when the pressure returns below the activating pressure differential. A PRESS RELIEF light for each relief valve will illuminate whenever its respective valve is open and will extinguish when the valve(s) closes.

The NO. 2 air conditioning pack will automatically trip to assist in relieving excess cabin pressure if either cabin pressure relief valve opens. The pack

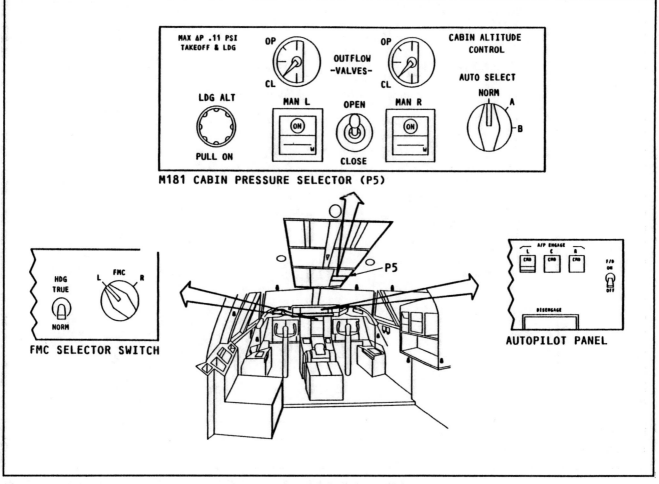

Figure 2-22. Cabin pressurization control system controls and indications. (Boeing)

cannot be reset until both cabin pressure relief valves are closed.

Negative pressure relief valves are installed in the forward and aft cargo doors. These valves open to prevent external atmospheric pressure from exceeding cabin pressure. The pressure negative relief valves are activated by differential pressure and are activated in any mode of pressurization system operation.

At touchdown, a signal from the landing gear ground safety relay causes the outflow valve to modulate towards OPEN, depressurizing the cabin at the rate set on the pressurization rate selector. The outflow valves will remain OPEN while the airplane is on the ground.

BOEING 747-400 CABIN PRESSURIZATION CONTROL SYSTEM

System mode of operation is by a cabin pressure selector panel which provides automatic and manual modes of operation (see Figure 2-22). Output from the panel is supplied to the two cabin pressure controllers,

(shown in Figure 2-23) together with data from the ADCs (air data computers), the FMC (flight management computer) and the autopilot system. The controllers alternate control of the system with every flight. The controller not in control will provide backup control as required. Thus, controller A will control both the ICU (interface control unit) left and the ICU right during one flight. On the next flight, controller B will control both ICU left and ICU right.

The ICUs integrate controller outputs and provide the operating signals for the two outflow valves. ICU right provides the operating signals to the right outflow valve. ICU left provides the operating signals to the left outflow valve.

The outflow valves can be operated manually from the selector panel through auxiliary panels P212 and P213, bypassing the controllers and interface control units. The outflow valve position is supplied to the interface units, controllers and selector panel. The locations of the pressurization system's major components are shown in Figure 2-24.

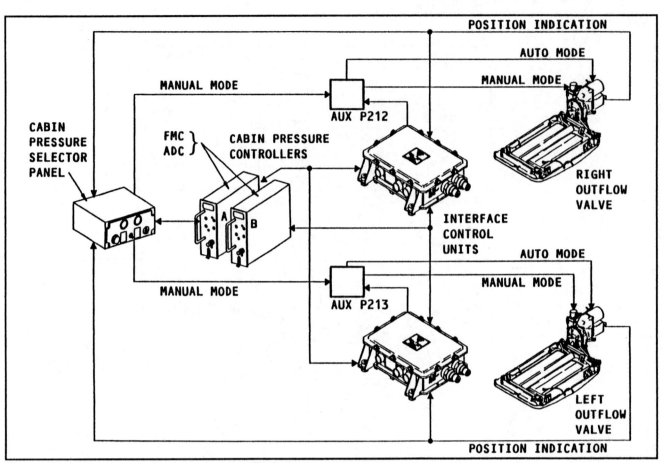

Figure 2-23. Cabin pressurization control system. (Boeing)

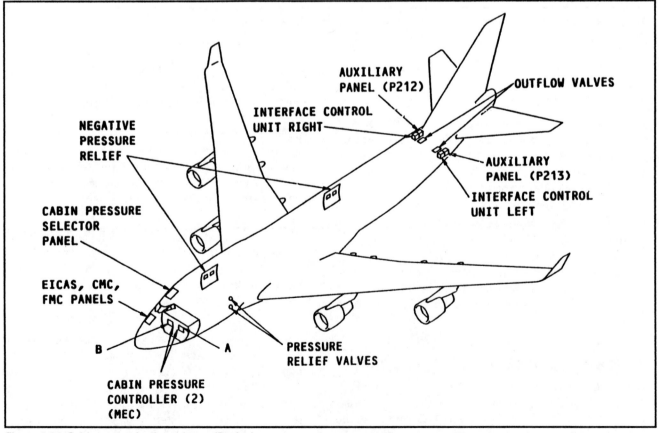

Figure 2-24. Cabin pressurization system. (Boeing)

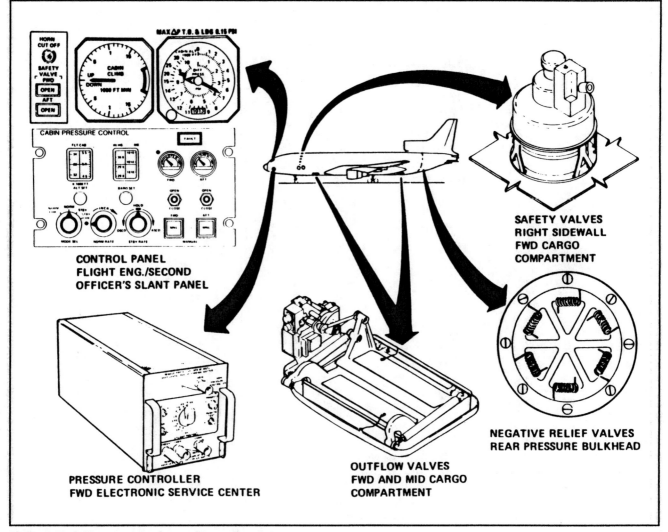

Figure 2-25. Cabin pressurization equipment location.

LOCKHEED L-1011 PRESSURIZATION SYSTEM

The pneumatically operated cabin pressurization system, which can be seen in Figure 2-25, meters the exhaust of cabin ventilating air to pressurize the entire fuselage area between the forward and aft pressure bulkheads. Areas that are not pressurized are:

• The nose gear wheel well and air conditioning service areas on each side.

• The area below the wing center section.

• The main landing gear wheel wells and the hydraulic service center between them.

Cabin pressure is controlled by a selective, automatic system with manual override control. Major components include the cabin pressure control panel, the cabin pressure controller, the negative pressure relief valve, two safety valves, and two electrically operated cabin outflow valves.

Pressurization control is normally operated in the automatic mode. In this mode, the flight crew selects the desired cabin or aircraft cruise altitude prior to takeoff, and sets barometric correction and landing field altitude prior to descent. The pressurization system is fast responding and pressure transients are controlled below normal threshold of detection.

In the automatic mode, cabin altitude is controlled at a fixed rate of change until the selected altitude is reached. For increasing altitude the rate is 500 feet per minute, and for decreasing altitude it is 300 feet per minute. Other fixed rates of change may be selected by the flight crew with complete automatic operation. The selectable range for increasing altitude is 200 to 1,500 feet per minute and for decreasing altitude the range is 120 to 900 feet per minute. The selectable

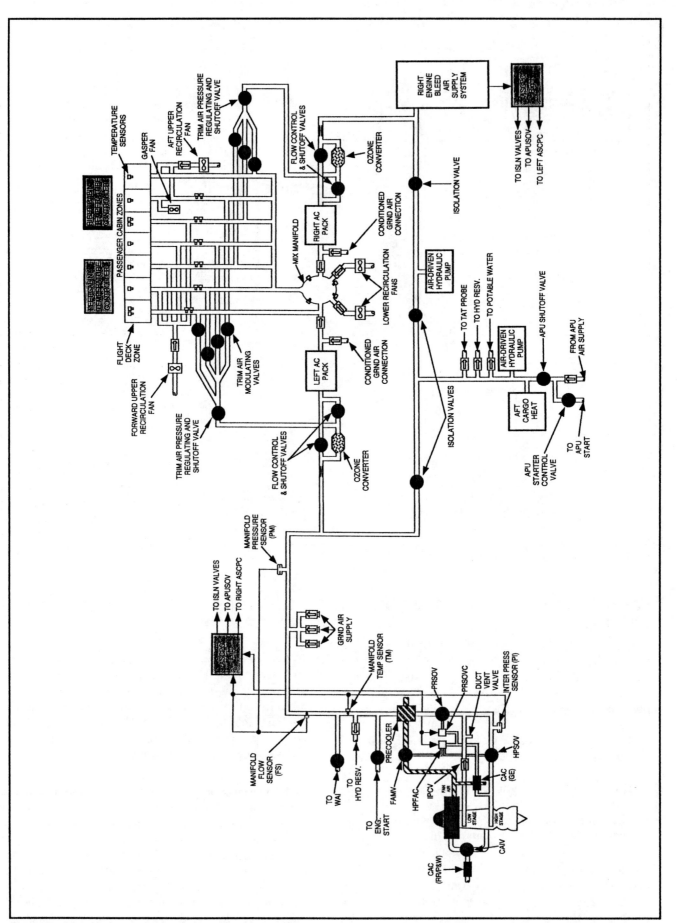

Figure 2-26. Boeing 777 environmental control system. (Boeing)

range for cabin altitude is from 1,000 feet below sea level to 10,000 feet above sea level.

The controller automatically controls the outflow valves to limit cabin pressure differential to a nominal 8.44 PSID. This provides a cabin altitude of 8,000 feet at an aircraft altitude of 42,000 feet. A sea level cabin altitude can be maintained up to an aircraft altitude of 22,000 feet without exceeding the maximum pressure differential.

The outflow valves, located in the bottom of the fuselage, exhaust air overboard at a rate to maintain the desired pressurization schedule. The actuators are driven automatically by AC motors and manually by DC motors to position the valves.

In the manual mode, the outflow valves are controlled by switches located on the selector panel. Manual control of the valves are completely independent of the automatic system. Pressurization control can be maintained in this mode with complete loss of AC power since the DC motor actuators are powered from the standby battery bus.

SAFETY RELIEF SYSTEM

The safety relief system includes both positive and negative pressure relief valves. The two positive pressure cabin safety valves are completely independent, pneumatically operated units, requiring only cabin and ambient pressure references. If the cabin pressure control system fails, these valves will operate to maintain cabin differential pressure below the maximum limit.

The two negative pressure relief valves are simple flapper type valves that open inward. They prevent cabin pressure from becoming less than ambient. This could occur during an extremely rapid descent from altitude. On the ground, the valves open to allow cabin pressure to change with ambient pressure when all other openings in the fuselage (doors, valves, etc.) are closed.

BOEING 777 ENVIRONMENTAL CONTROL SYSTEMS

The Boeing 777 environmental control systems, shown in Figure 2-26, consists of the air supply control system (ASCS), cabin air-conditioning temperature control system (CACTCS) and the cabin pressure control system (CPCS). The air control system manages the pressure, temperature, flow control, engine bleed air cooling and isolation valve control. The ASCS will gather the temperature, pressure and flow data and confirm that the information is within limits prior to use by the system controllers. The flight deck indica-

tion, and built-in-test (BIT) functions are also part of this validated information. This control of the temperature, pressure, and flow will be accomplished by the air supply and cabin pressure controller (ASCPC) which will control the air supply from both engines and the auxiliary power unit. It will also provide a backup function to the cabin air conditioning temperature control system (CACTCS) in the event of power loss to the cabin temperature controller (CTC). The cabin air conditioning temperature control system provides a mixture of fresh and cabin recirculated air to the cabin and fresh air only to the flight deck.

This study of the system will be directed to the interface of the CTC with the ASCPCs in the event of loss of all normal backup electrical power to the CTCs. In this case the CTCs will become inactive and the ASCPCs will control the flow of air through the cooling packs.

The cabin pressure control system provides for the comfort and safety of the passengers and crew by regulating the amount of air flow that exits through the aircraft fuselage. The ASCPCs will control the pressure automatically with automatic backup and manual override if necessary.

ASCPC INTERFACE WITH CACTCS

The cabin air conditioning and temperature control system (CACTCS) provides mixed fresh and cabin recirculated air to the cabin and fresh air to the flight deck to maintain the ventilation and temperature control requirements of the aircraft. Two air conditioning packs cool engine bleed or APU air to the temperature needed to maintain the temperature requirement of the cabin or flight deck zone requiring the coldest air. All other zones are trimmed, as necessary, by engine bleed or APU air. Fresh air from the air conditioning packs is supplied to a mix manifold where it combines with cabin recirculated air. One of the two flow control valves provides the required bleed air flow to each air conditioning pack. The air conditioning pack incorporates components as required to meet the demands of the systems. Four recirculation fans supplement the fresh air delivered to the cabin. Two fans are located in the crown zone and two in the mix bay. A diagram of the system can be seen in Figure 2-26.

The ASCPCs monitor the CACTCS activity from the ARINC 629 data bus, and serve as alternative control of supply and trim air. The ASCPC will also control the flow control valves for system shutdown if the CTC loses electrical power.

The cabin temperature controllers (CTCs) purpose is to adjust the flow control and pertinent components to attain the necessary temperature at the pack output.

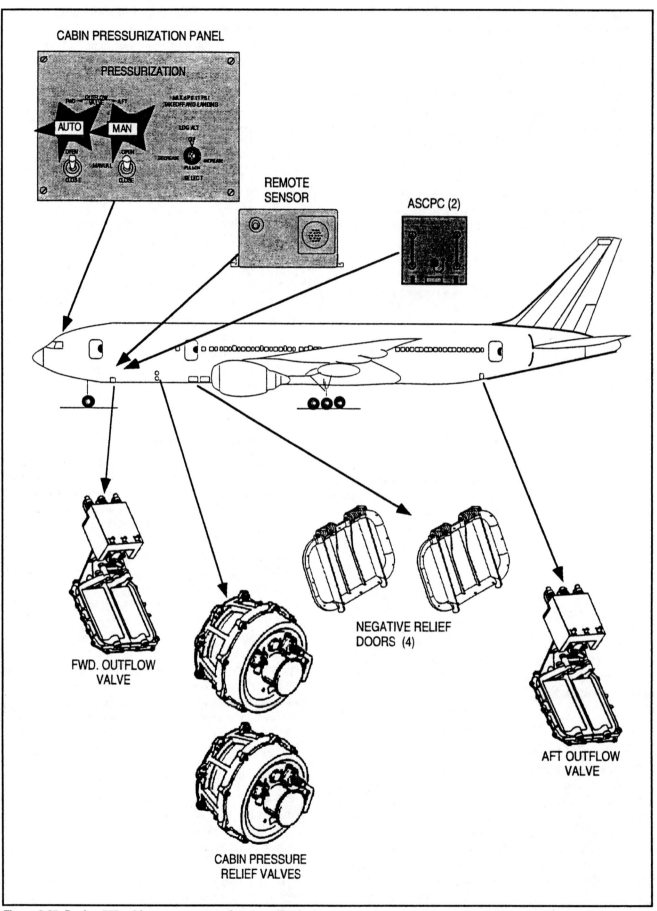

Figure 2-27. Boeing 777 cabin pressure control system. (Boeing)

The left and right CTCs operate independently of each other, and have a normal and backup channel. The cabin temperature controller (CTC) and the ASCPC control the flow of air to the air conditioning pack by adjusting the flow control and shutoff valves. The ASCPC sets the flow schedule that the CTC uses to control the flow limits. It also controls the valves during a system shutdown, emergency flow control and if the CTC loses electrical power.

The cabin pressure control system (CPCS), (Figure 2-27), regulates the cabin pressure within the pressurized areas of the airplane by regulating the airflow out of the aircraft. The system also provides positive pressure relief protection. The CPCS includes one cabin pressure control panel, two air supply cabin pressure controllers (left/right ASCPC), remote sensor unit (RSU), two outflow valves (forward and aft OFV), valve actuators, and pressure relief valves.

Each OFV can be independently placed under manual control. Control of each OFV is provided by two OFV channels. The left OFV channel communicates with the left ASCPC and is comprised of the left valve control unit (VCU) channel, the left motor unit and the gearbox assembly. The right VCU channel communicates with the right ASCPC and is comprised of the right VCU channel, the right motor unit and the gearbox assembly. When manual operation of the OFVs are selected, both OFV control channels will receive identical and independent control signals from the flight deck for manual control of the OFV, and will drive the gearbox simultaneously. When the automatic operation for the OFV is selected, only one OFV control channel will be allowed to drive the gearbox assembly, opening or closing the valve at any time.

Each CPCS channel will receive airplane performance and ambient data via the ARINC 629 system data bus to optimize performance of the cabin pressure control system.

There are two positive pressure relief valves in the cabin pressure control system. If the internal pressure rises above a preset pressure, the safety relief valves will open to bleed off the excess pressure.

There are four (4) negative pressure relief vents in the cabin pressure control system. If the external pressure is higher than the internal pressure of the aircraft, the negative pressure relief vents will open allowing ambient air to equalize the internal pressure.

When the outflow valve push switch is IN, the CPCS is in the automatic mode. The overhead panel avionics system (OPAS) sends a discrete signal via the ARINC 629 buses to the ASCPC. This will set the OFV for automatic operation. The left ASCPC is the preferred channel and will now set the proper flow rate. The ASCPC sends the command control signals by way of the ARINC 429 buses. If a failure of the automatic mode arises, the right ASCPC (standby channel) will assume control of the OFVs. A remote cabin pressure sensor also sends pressure data to the AIMS and the electrical management system (ELMS).

CHAPTER 2 STUDY QUESTIONS

1. Where is the APU located on most airplanes?

   _____
   _____
   _____

2. What is generally used to start an APU?

   _____
   _____
   _____

3. What are the main functions of an APU?

   _____
   _____
   _____

4. Describe the starting procedure for the 757's APU.

   _____
   _____
   _____

5. What are the sources for compressed air for the pneumatic system?

   _____
   _____
   _____

6. What are some of the systems that use pneumatics for their operation?

   _____
   _____
   _____

7. Describe the operation of the air conditioning packs.

   _____
   _____
   _____

8. What is used as source air for the pressurization system?

   _____
   _____
   _____

9. At high altitudes, what must be provided for a suitable cabin environment for the crew and passengers?

   _____
   _____

10. What controls the outflow valve in the manual mode of operation?

_____

_____

_____

11. Explain the term "cabin differential pressure".

_____

_____

_____

12. What is the purpose of the pressurization safety relief valves and the negative pressure relief valves?

_____

_____

_____

13. What AlliedSignal series APU can be used in the Boeing 777?

_____

_____

14. Describe the use of an APU load control valve.

_____

_____

_____

15. What is the purpose of a load compressor used in an APU?

_____

_____

_____

ANTI-ICING SYSTEMS AND RAIN PROTECTION

Ice build-up on certain aircraft areas and components can cause serious problems for aircraft operation. Ice can form on aircraft surfaces when the outside air temperature (OAT) on the ground and total air temperature (TAT) in flight is 10°C or below, and visible moisture in any form is present. Visible moisture can be in the form of clouds, fog with visibility of one mile or less, rain, snow, sleet, and ice crystals. Icing conditions also exist when: the OAT on the ground and for takeoff is 10°C or below, when operating on ramps, taxiways or runways where surface snow, ice, standing water, or slush may be ingested by the engines or freeze on engines, nacelles, or engine sensor probes. The icing conditions listed here are for example purposes only. The specific icing condition parameters may vary from air carrier to air carrier.

The anti-icing systems on large aircraft generally use hot engine bleed air and electrical heating elements to anti-ice certain areas of the aircraft. Bleed air anti-icing is provided for engines, wings, and sometimes antennas. Operation of the nacelle engine anti-ice and wing anti-ice systems impose a heavy demand on the engine's pneumatic air supply. When bleed air is being used, the engine's power (EPR) is adjusted either manually or automatically to compensate. The parts of the

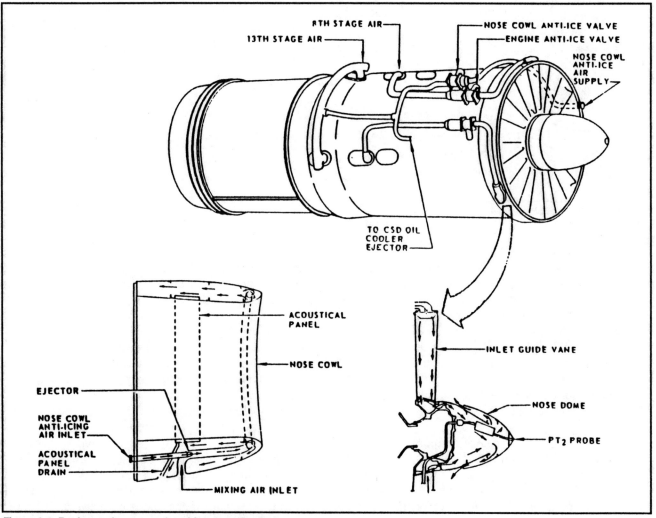

Figure 3-1. Engine and nose cowl anti-ice ring. (Boeing)

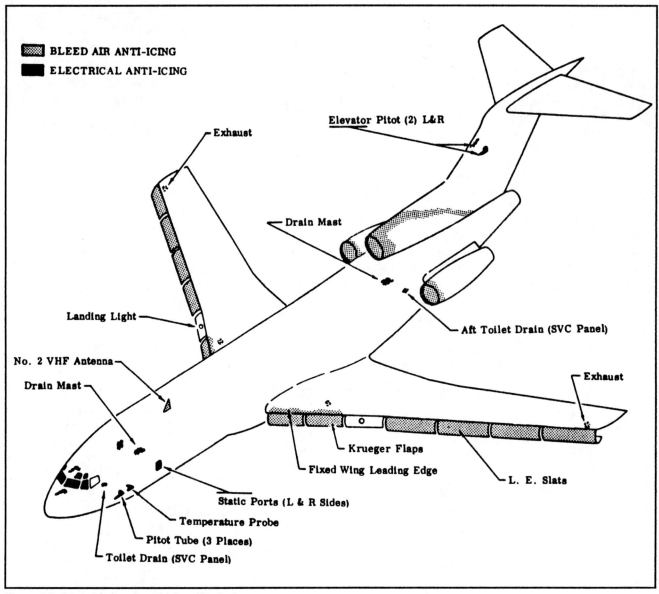

BLEED AIR ANTI-ICING
ELECTRICAL ANTI-ICING

Exhaust

Elevator Pitot (2) L&R

Drain Mast

Landing Light

Aft Toilet Drain (SVC Panel)

No. 2 VHF Antenna

Drain Mast

Exhaust

Krueger Flaps

Fixed Wing Leading Edge

L. E. Slats

Static Ports (L & R Sides)

Temperature Probe

Pitot Tube (3 Places)

Toilet Drain (SVC Panel)

Figure 3-2. Areas of aircraft anti-icing. (Boeing)

engine that are anti-iced (shown in Figure 3-1), may include the inlet guide vanes, the engine nose dome (including Pt$_2$ (EPR) Probe), the inlet duct, and the nose cowl leading edges. The areas of the aircraft that are electrically anti-iced can be the air data probes (pitot tubes, static ports, TAT probe), cockpit windows, stall warning, water drain masts, and toilet drain receptacles as shown in Figure 3-2. Heating of the cockpit windows is for anti-icing, anti-fogging, and bird impact protection.

Rain protection of the cockpit windows is accomplished normally by windshield wipers and rain repellent. Windshield wipers generally have two speeds, and a park position which will stow the wipers. The cockpit windows (windshields) can also have a windshield washer system and a fan driven defogger system.

Ice detectors (see Figure 3-5) are sometimes used on the outside of the aircraft to warn the pilots that icing is occurring on the aircraft in flight. An annunciator light in the cockpit is generally used to inform the flight crew of icing. The ice detector consists of a probe mounted near the front of the aircraft that vibrates at a set frequency. If ice starts to build up on the probe, the ice will change the probe's frequency and light the cockpit light, which will stay illuminated for one minute. This also turns on the probe heater which is connected to a five second timer that will heat up and deice the probe. If the icing condition is continuous, the probe will re-ice and re-energize the timer before the one minute delay expires, and the light will stay on continuously. If the icing condition is temporary, the heater will melt the ice and if no more ice is present, the icing light will go out after one minute.

AIRCRAFT GROUND DEICING/ANTI-ICING

Aircraft ground deicing/anti-icing plays a vital role in cold weather procedures to ensure that an aircraft is free of ice, frost, and snow contamination before takeoff. The equipment most commonly used by airlines for deicing and anti-icing airplanes is the truck-mounted mobile de-icer/anti-icer. These units generally consist of one or more fluid tanks, a heater to bring the fluid to the desired application temperature, an aerial device (boom and basket) to reach the areas that require deicing and/or anti-icing, and a fluid dispensing system (including pumps, piping and a spray nozzle). The dispensing system is generally capable of supplying the fluid at various pressures and flow rates, and the spray pattern can be adjusted at the nozzle.

There are two basic types of aircraft ground deicing/anti-icing fluids: Type 1 (unthickened) fluids and Type 2 (thickened) fluids. Type 1 fluids have a high glycol content (minimum 80%) and a relatively low viscosity, except at very cold temperatures. Viscosity is a measure of a fluid's ability to flow freely. For example, water has low viscosity, and honey has relatively high viscosity. Because the rate at which fluid flows off of the wing depends on the fluid viscosity, a high viscosity fluid is likely to have larger aerodynamic effects than a low viscosity fluid. The viscosity of Type 1 fluids depends only on temperature.

The holdover time, which is the length of time that they will protect the wing from ice, frost, and snow, is relatively short for Type 1 fluids. Because taxi times are often much longer than the holdover times provided by Type 1 fluids, Type 2 (thickened) deicing/anti-icing fluids were developed by fluid manufacturers in cooperation with the airlines. These fluids have significantly longer holdover times than Type 1 fluids. Type 2 fluids have a minimum glycol content of 50%, with 45% to 50% water plus thickeners (which increase the viscosity) and inhibitors.

In general, there are two methods for deicing/anti-icing an airplane with a mobile unit; a one-step and a two-step process. The former consists of applying heated fluid onto the airplane surfaces to remove accumulated ice, snow, or frost and prevent their subsequent buildup. The primary advantage of this method is that it is quick and uncomplicated, both procedurally and in terms of equipment requirements.

However, in conditions where large deposits of ice and snow must be flushed off of airplane surfaces, the total fluid usage will be greater than for a two-step process, where a more diluted fluid would be used for deicing.

Also, if Type 2 fluid is used, it may be somewhat degraded if applied at typical deicing temperatures.

The two-step process consists of separate deicing and anti-icing steps. In the deicing step, a diluted fluid, usually heated, is applied to the airplane surfaces to remove accumulated ice, snow, or frost. The dilution must be such that protection from refreezing is provided long enough for the second step (anti-icing) to be completed.

During the anti-icing step, a more concentrated fluid (either 100% or diluted appropriately, depending upon weather conditions), usually cold, is applied to the uncontaminated surfaces. Type 1 or Type 2 fluids can be used for both steps, or Type 1 can be used for the first step and Type 2 for the second. This choice would depend upon weather conditions, required holdover time, availability of fluids at a particular station, and equipment capability.

Specific deicing/anti-icing procedures are determined by a combination of common sense and airplane considerations. Maintenance manuals for each type of airplane provide specific procedures. General precautions include:

- Do not spray deicing/anti-icing fluid directly at or into pitot inlets, TAT probes, or static ports.

- Do not spray heated deicing/anti-icing fluid or water directly on cold windows.

- Do not spray deicing/anti-icing fluid directly into engine or APU inlets, air scoops, vents, or drains.

- Check that ice and/or snow is not forced into areas around flight controls during ice and snow removal.

- Remove all ice and snow from door and girt bar areas before closing any door.

Cargo doors should be opened only when necessary. Cargo containers should be cleared of ice or snow prior to loading. Apply deicing/anti-icing fluid on pressure relief doors, lower door sills, and bottom edges of doors prior to closing doors for flight.

Do not use hard or sharp tools to scrape or chip ice from an airplane's surface.

It is not recommended to deice/anti-ice an airplane with the engines or APU operating. Air conditioning pack valves should be closed to prevent fumes from entering the cabin.

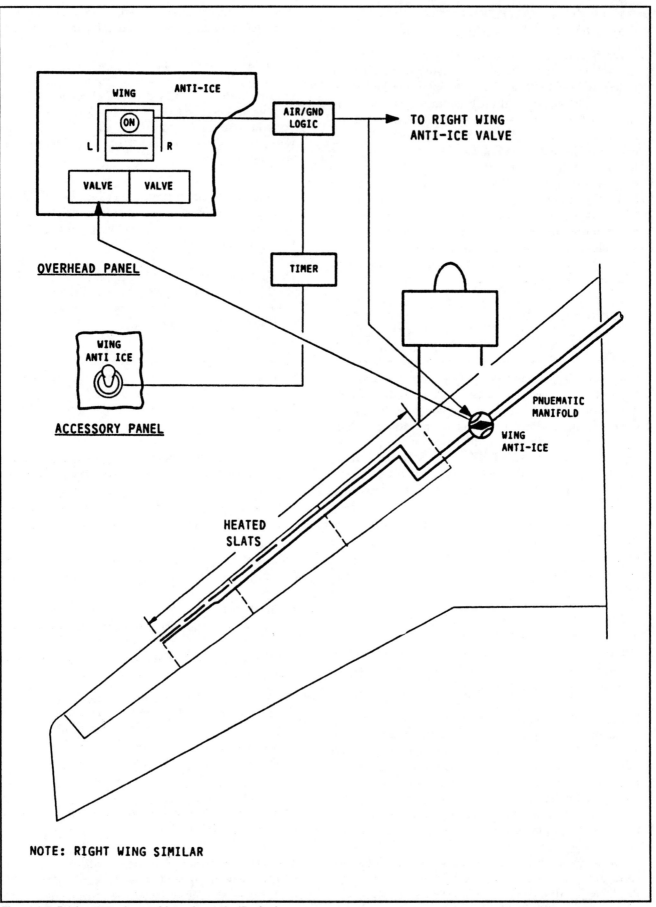

Figure 3-3. Boeing 757 wing anti-ice schematic. (Boeing)

BOEING 757 AIRCRAFT ANTI-ICING SYSTEMS

WING ANTI-ICE

Wing anti-ice operation is controlled from the cockpit by a single wing anti-ice switch. Turning on the wing anti-ice switch sends an open signal through the air/ground logic relay to the L and R wing anti-ice valves (Figure 3-3). The wing anti-ice valves are electrically controlled and pressure actuated. An open wing anti-ice valve permits bleed air to flow to the three leading edge slats, outboard of the engines, on each wing. The air/ground logic prevents wing anti-ice valve operation during ground operation. If a landing is made with the switch on, the wing anti-ice valves automatically close at touchdown. If there is disagreement between the switch and the valve position, an amber VALVE light for each wing illuminates. In the event of valve failure, an EICAS (Engine Indication and Crew Alerting System) advisory message, L or R WING ANTI-ICE, appears.

Due to air being bled from the engine for anti-icing, it is necessary to reduce the maximum EPR . Corrections to reduce maximum EPR limits when wing anti-ice is being used are made automatically. The anti-ice valve position is used to determine the EPR corrections.

An operational check of the valves can be conducted on the ground by pushing the wing anti-ice test switch. The test switch signal bypasses the wing anti-ice switch and opens the valves if air pressure is available. A timed delay automatically closes the valves to protect the wing structure from overheating. The VALVE lights illuminate when the valves are open and extinguish when the valves are closed.

ENGINE ANTI-ICE

Engine anti-ice operation for the engine cowl is controlled from the cockpit by individual engine anti-ice switches, as illustrated in Figure 3-4. The engine anti-ice system may be operated on the ground and in flight. To ensure prevention against flame-out caused by ice ingestion, engine ignition is automatically activated when the engine anti-ice switch is turned on, provided the engine start selector is in AUTOMATIC. Engine anti-ice must be on during all ground and flight operations when icing conditions exist or are anticipated. Turning on the engine anti-ice switches sends an open signal to the engine cowl anti-ice valves. This permits the cowl leading edge to be anti-iced by engine bleed air. Disagreement between the anti-ice switch and the cowl anti-ice valve position illuminates an amber VALVE light on each engine anti-ice switch.

Corrections to reduce maximum EPR limits when engine anti-ice is being used are also made automati-

cally. On older aircraft this reduction had to be calculated and set manually. The engine anti-ice switch position is used to determine the EPR corrections. The position of the valves are not considered.

ICE DETECTION

Ice is detected by a sensor on the nose of the airplane. The amber ICING light on the anti-ice panel illuminates and an EICAS advisory message is displayed when ice is detected. After ice is no longer present, the ICING light is extinguished. The ICING light and EICAS messages are inhibited when the ice detection system is inoperative.

COCKPIT WINDOW HEAT

The windshields are electrically heated for anti-icing and anti-fogging. When the cockpit switches are on, power is regulated to the windshields so they are continuously heated. The side windows are electrically heated for anti-fogging only. Overheat protection is provided for the windshields and side windows.

In addition to electrical heating of the windshields, conditioned air is ducted to the top of the windshield and then flows along the inside surface to provide supplemental anti-fogging. The anti-fogging airflow takes place continuously and is independent of window heat.

Windshield wipers may be used when the flight crew's visibility is impaired by moisture on the windshields. Scratching of the outer windshield surface may occur if the wipers are used on a dry windshield. A three-position windshield wiper selector controls the speed of the electric windshield wipers: LOW and HIGH are two selectable speeds, and OFF stows the wiper in the park position.

RAIN REPELLENT

Rain repellent may be used any time rain intensity requires the use of windshield wipers. It should be applied to one windshield at a time to allow the fluid to spread and visibility to improve before application is made to the other windshield. Rain repellent should not be used to clean a windshield. It smears and obscures forward visibility if applied to a dry windshield. If rain repellent is inadvertently applied, do not use the windshield wipers until required for rain removal.

One rain repellent can with a sight gauge, pressure gauge, and a manual shutoff valve is located in the cockpit. Its application is controlled by individual push-button switches on the overhead panel. Each push of the rain repellent switch provides a measured amount of fluid to the associated windshield. Each windshield has independent components to apply the rain repellent, so failure of any component in one system does not affect the operation of the other.

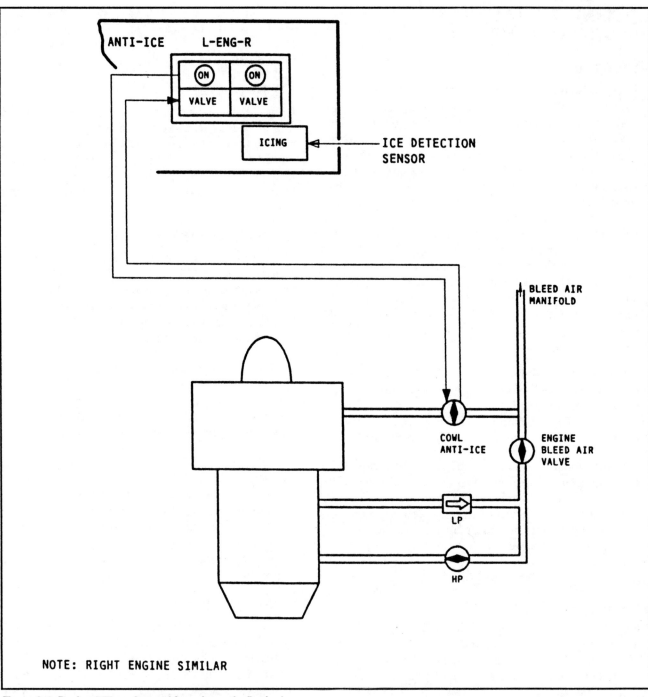

Figure 3-4. Boeing 757 engine anti-ice schematic. Boeing)

LOCKHEED L-1011 ANTI-ICING SYSTEMS

Pneumatic anti-icing is provided for the outboard wing slats, engine inlets, and VHF-1 antenna as shown in Figure 3-5. An ice detector on the lower forward fuselage senses icing conditions and controls an icing light on the pilots' caution and warning panel in the flight station. All pneumatic anti-icing systems are controlled and monitored in the flight station. The wing anti-ice system uses hot air from the pneumatic mani-

fold which is admitted by the pressure regulating shut-off valve to slats No. 5, 6, and 7. The wing engine inlet anti-icing system uses engine intermediate pressure air (engine bleed air) to anti-ice the engine inlet as can be seen in Figure 3-6.

Electrically heated air data sensors include four pitot probes (a primary and secondary pair for the captain and first officer), two total air temperature probes (left and right), and two angle of attack sensors (left and right). Each pitot probe contains two heating elements

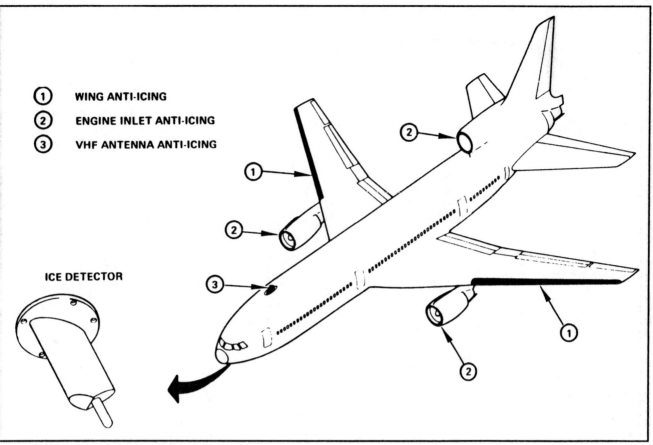

① WING ANTI-ICING

② ENGINE INLET ANTI-ICING

③ VHF ANTENNA ANTI-ICING

ICE DETECTOR

Figure 3-5. Lockheed L-1011 anti-ice systems. (Lockheed)

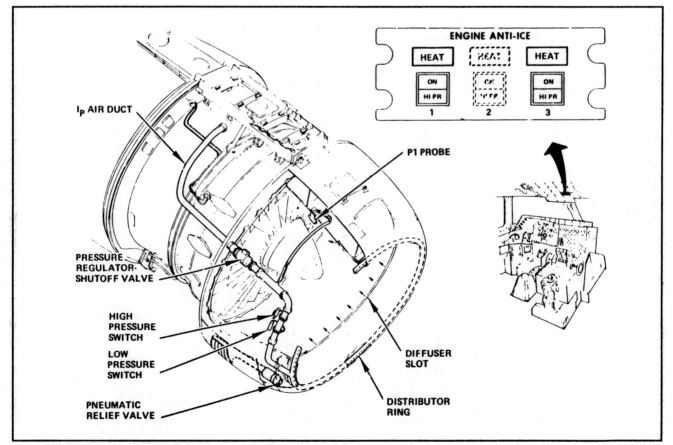

I_P AIR DUCT

PRESSURE REGULATOR-SHUTOFF VALVE

HIGH PRESSURE SWITCH

LOW PRESSURE SWITCH

PNEUMATIC RELIEF VALVE

P1 PROBE

DIFFUSER SLOT

DISTRIBUTOR RING

ENGINE ANTI-ICE

HEAT	HEAT	HEAT
ON HI PR	ON HI PR	ON HI PR
1	2	3

Figure 3-6. L-1011 wing engine inlet anti-icing. (Lockheed)

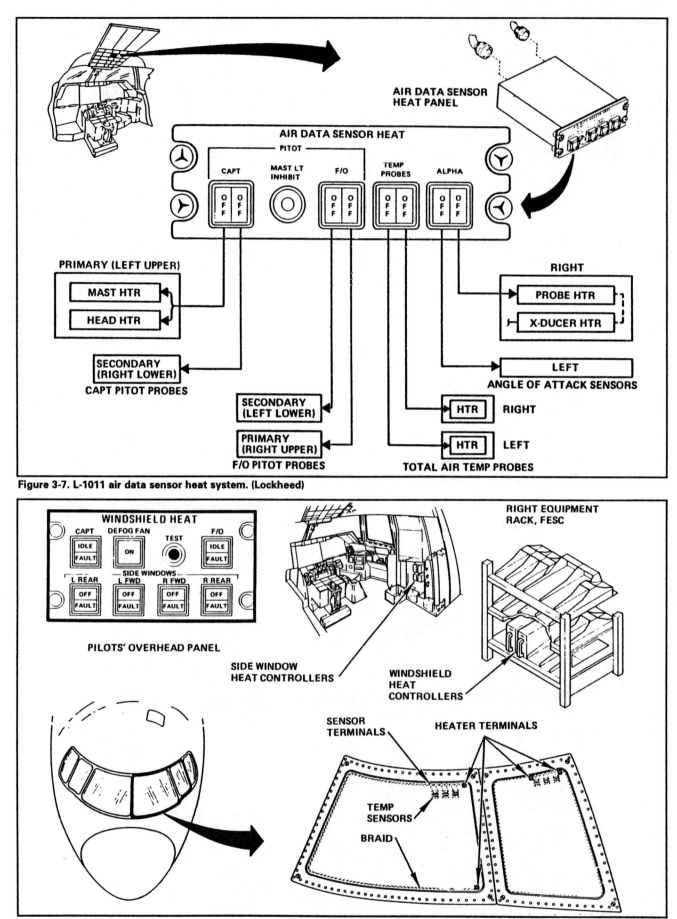

Figure 3-7. L-1011 air data sensor heat system. (Lockheed)

Figure 3-8. Windshield and side window heating. (Lockheed)

(see Figure 3-7), one for the mast and one for the head. Total air temperature probes have a single element. Each angle of attack sensor contains two heating elements, one for the probe and one for the transducer. Although the transducer in an angle of attack sensor is not exposed to icing atmosphere, it is heated to prevent condensation of moisture when the probe heater is operating.

Electrical power (115 VAC) to heating elements is controlled by switchlights on the air data sensor heat panel, shown in Figure 3-7, located on the pilots' overhead panel. Each switchlight controls power to two sensors and contains two OFF legends, one for each sensor. Each OFF light is controlled by a solid state modular circuit in the control panel which senses heater current. An OFF legend illuminates when heater current is not sensed, such as when the heater fails or the switchlight is unlatched.

In the ALPHA switchlight, an illuminated OFF legend may indicate failure of either the probe or transducer heater in the associated angle of attack sensor. When the switchlight is initially latched in, both OFF lights will remain illuminated for a brief period until normal operating temperature is reached.

WINDSHIELD AND SIDE WINDOW HEATING

The major components of the windshield and side window heating systems (see Figure 3-8) include: the windshield heat panel located on the pilots' overhead panel; a controller for each windshield, located in the FESC (Forward Electrical Service Center); a controller for each side window, located behind the kickplate of the flight engineer/second officer's console; a 6 KW, 200 VAC heating element in each windshield; and a 1.5 KW, 115 VAC heating element in each side window. Each heating element consists of a metallic braid and transparent conductive film, which are encased between windshield plies. The AC output of a controller is applied to the associated heating element braid at two heater terminals. Each windshield and side window contains three identical sensors located between the glass abrasion shield and the outer acrylic ply. One sensor is a spare. The outer two function in control circuits, one for normal mode temperature control and one for overheat mode temperature control. Sensor and heater terminals extend through the inner acrylic ply for connection to aircraft wiring. Switchlights on the windshield heat panel provide for separate control and monitoring of each windshield and side window heating circuit.

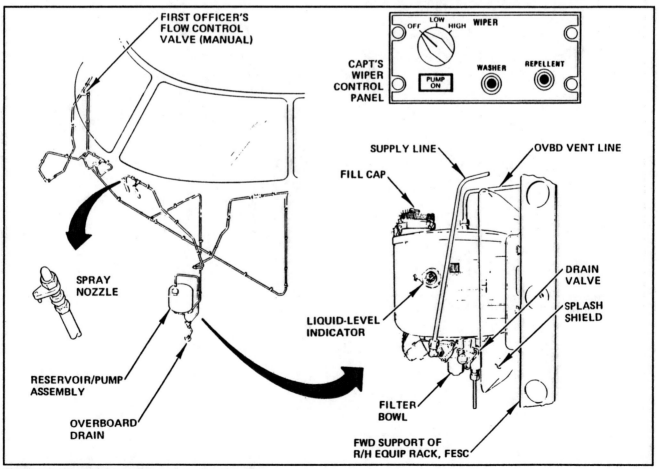

Figure 3-9. Windshield washer system. (Lockheed)

WINDSHIELD WASHER SYSTEM

Windshield washer fluid is supplied from a reservoir/pump assembly through four spray nozzles; two for each windshield. The system, shown in Figure 3-9, is controlled by a latching-type push-button switch on the captain's wiper control panel. A PUMP ON light adjacent to the switch is illuminated when the pump is powered. The motor/pump assembly, submersed in washer fluid, consists of a 3-phase AC motor and centrifugal pump. The pump provides a fluid flow rate of 10 GPH at 30+5 PSIG. The flow rate to each pair of spray nozzles can be adjusted with a manually operated flow control valve in the left/right side console. Each spray nozzle head has two outlets which direct fluid to each side of the associated windshield.

Separate wiper systems are provided for the left and right windshields. Major components of each windshield system include a control panel and wiper control assembly. The control panels, one each for the captain and first officer, are located on the pilots' overhead panel. Each wiper control assembly is mounted to the fuselage through an adapter and is accessible through a door in the forward pressure bulkhead. Major components of the control assembly include a reversible park motor, a two-speed wiper motor, and a gearbox as shown in Figure 3-10.

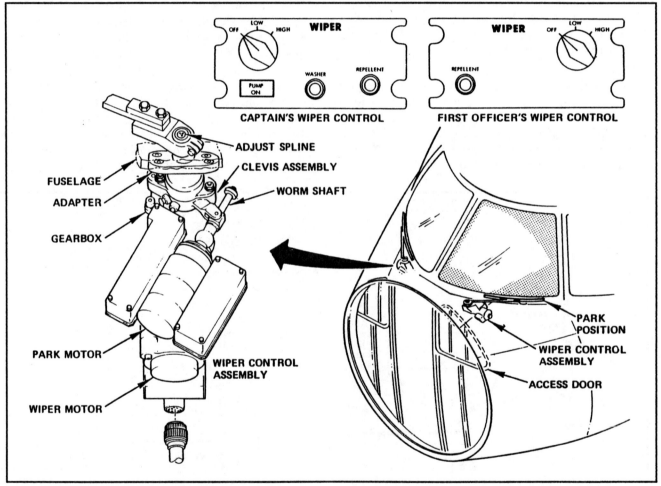

Figure 3-10. Windshield washer system. (Lockheed)

CHAPTER 3 STUDY QUESTIONS

1. Describe the basic weather conditions in which icing can occur.

    _____

    _____

    _____

2. What areas of the aircraft are anti-icing used with?

    _____

    _____

3. What is the purpose of engine anti-ice?

    _____

    _____

4. What are the purposes for heating the cockpit windows?

    _____

    _____

5. Explain the operation of an ice detector.

    _____

    _____

    _____

6. List the general precautions when deicing/anti-icing an airplane.

    _____

    _____

7. What problem can occur if wing anti-ice is used too long on the ground?

    _____

    _____

8. What must be reduced due to air being bled from the engines during use of anti-ice?

    _____

    _____

9. When can the engine anti-ice system be operated?

    _____

    _____

10. What rule should be followed when applying rain repellent to the windshield?

    _____

    _____

11. In what position are the windshield wipers stowed?

    _____

ELECTRICAL POWER SYSTEMS

CHAPTER 4

INTRODUCTION

The function of the electrical system on a large transport aircraft is to generate, regulate, and distribute electrical power throughout the aircraft. Electrical power is used to operate aircraft flight instruments, essential systems, and passenger services. New-generation aircraft are very dependent on electrical power because of the wide use of electronic flight instrument systems.

Essential power is, just as the name implies, power that is essential to the safe operation of the aircraft. Power for passenger services is provided to light the cabin, to operate the entertainment system, and to prepare food. It is obvious that transport aircraft need a self-contained, dependable, and adequate power generating system.

Most large aircraft use both direct current (DC) and alternating current (AC). Although many different voltages can be used, most large aircraft use 28 volts DC and three phase 115 volts AC at 400 Hz to power the aircraft.

By the use of transformer rectifier units (TRU), which change 115 VAC into 28 volts DC, the DC buses and DC components are powered through the aircraft AC generators. Some aircraft also change the 115 VAC to 26 VAC for lighting circuits.

Emergency or standby power can be supplied to the electrical system in the event of complete electrical generator failure from an onboard 28 VDC battery. Essential AC power can be obtained during standby power use from a static inverter. The static inverter changes 28 VDC to 115 VAC to power essential flight instruments that operate on 115 VAC. Aircraft power is time limited in the standby mode because of battery limits.

POWER SOURCES

Some power sources are engine driven AC generators, auxiliary power units (APU), external power, and ram air-driven generators.

Each engine drives an AC generator, shown in Figure 4-1, which provides normal inflight power for the entire aircraft. The APU can be used in flight as a backup power source. (One exception is the Boeing 727 aircraft, where the APU can only be operated on the ground.)

External power is used on the ground only, with power being provided by a ground power unit (GPU). GPUs can be portable or stationary units and generally provide AC power through an external plug on the nose area of the aircraft.

A ram air turbine can be used as an emergency source of power. If power from the engine driven generators and the APU is not available in flight, some aircraft incorporate a ram air turbine generator which can be deployed to provide AC power. The aircraft nickel cadmium battery can be used as a power source for standby or emergency power. The battery provides 28 VDC directly and 115 VAC 400 Hz by use of the static inverter.

SYSTEM COMPONENTS

The basic functions of the electrical system's components are to generate power, control electrical power, protect the electrical system, and distribute electrical power throughout the aircraft. The aircraft generators (engine driven and APU) change mechanical energy into electrical energy by using a constant speed drive (CSD) to turn the generator at a set speed. The speed at which the generator turns determines its output frequency. Since most electronic components on the aircraft need 400 cycles per second (Hz), the generator's speed must be held constant. The constant speed drive (CSD), turned by the engine, uses a differential assembly and hydraulic pumps to turn the generator at a constant speed.

The CSD can be mounted on the engine by an external, co-axial, integrated drive generator (IDG), or side-by-side arrangement. The IDG has the CSD drive and generator integrated together as shown in Figure 4-1.

Another common method of CSD mounting is where the generator and drive are mounted side by side,

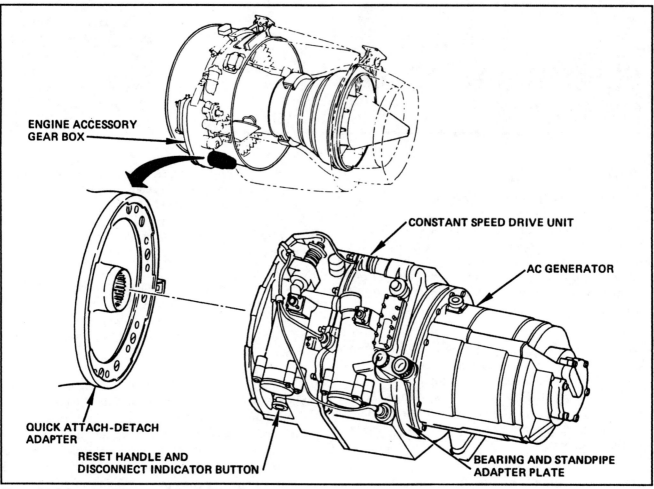

ENGINE ACCESSORY
GEAR BOX

CONSTANT SPEED DRIVE UNIT

AC GENERATOR

QUICK ATTACH-DETACH
ADAPTER

RESET HANDLE AND
DISCONNECT INDICATOR BUTTON

BEARING AND STANDPIPE
ADAPTER PLATE

Figure 4-1. Integrated drive generator. (Lockheed)

which reduces its size and weight. Most CSDs can be disconnected if a problem is experienced during operation. This also disconnects the generator, and a CSD cannot be reconnected in flight.

Transformer rectifier units (TRUs) are used to change 115 VAC, 400 Hz to 28 VDC as mentioned earlier. To do this, the TRU must use a transformer to reduce the voltage from 115 volts to 28 volts. The rectifier then changes the AC to DC current. Generally, each aircraft AC bus will feed a TRU which feeds each DC bus. Both AC and DC currents are used by the aircraft during operation.

Each generator has a voltage regulator or a generator control unit (GCU) which controls the generator output. Generator circuit protection monitors the various electrical system parameters such as voltage, frequency, overcurrent, undercurrent, and a differential fault. Load controls sense real system load to provide a control signal to the CSDs for frequency control. Current transformers are used for current load sensing and protection of a differential fault (feeder line short). The electrical system control panel is either

located on the pilot's overhead panel or the flight engineer's panel.

ELECTRICAL SYSTEM CONFIGURATIONS

There are basically three different electrical system configurations used on large transport aircraft: the parallel, the split bus, and the split system parallel type.

PARALLEL TYPE

The parallel type is used on the Boeing 727, 747 (early series), DC-10, and the L-1011 aircraft. The total aircraft electrical system load is shared equally by all active generators in the parallel system. One advantage of this system is that if one generator fails, the other generators will pick up the load from the failed generator without interrupting primary electrical service. The system also has the capability to automatically redistribute the load among the other active generators.

A basic diagram of the Lockheed L-1011's power distribution system is shown in Figure 4-2. The AC tie bus

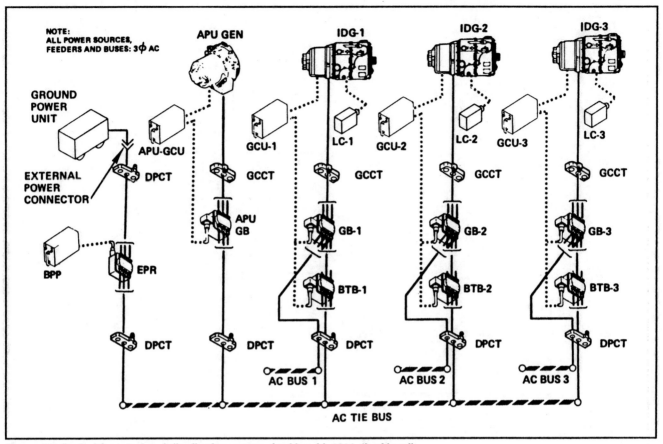

Figure 4-2. Basic AC control and distribution system, Lockheed L-1011. (Lockheed)

enables paralleled generator operation. Bus tie breakers permit paralleled or isolated generator operation, and prevent the paralleling of external power with operating generators.

Each of the four generators is controlled and protected by its own generator control unit (GCU) which also controls the generator breaker in its channel. Bus tie breakers 1, 2, and 3 are controlled by GCUs 1, 2, and 3 respectively. Generator control current transformers (GCCTs) monitor line current and supply signals to the GCUs for control and protective functions, and to load controllers (LCs) during paralleled generator operation. The load controllers control IDG speed to maintain equal real load division between paralleled generators. Differential protection current transformers (DPCTs) monitor feeder cables for open and shorted conditions.

SPLIT BUS SYSTEMS

Some examples of aircraft that utilize the split bus electrical system configuration are the Boeing 737, 757, 767, 777, and McDonnell Douglas DC-9. In the split bus system, illustrated in Figure 4-3, the generators are not operated in parallel. Each generator supplies power separately from the other generator to its respective aircraft bus. The only time the two generator channels are connected is when the aircraft is on external power, APU power, or if one generator fails. The generator channels are electrically connected by bus tie breakers (BTBs) which open and close automatically, depending upon the source of power. When external power or APU power is being used to supply power, the BTBs are closed, connecting both generator channels together.

When an engine driven generator (number 1) comes on line, the number 1 BTB opens as the generator accepts the system load. As the other engine driven generator comes on line, the number 2 BTB opens and now each generator channel is independent in its operation. A more thorough discussion of this type of electrical system configuration is contained later in this chapter.

SPLIT PARALLEL SYSTEMS

The split parallel type electrical system configuration can operate with all generators in parallel, or it can be split or electrically disconnected by a split system breaker. The split system breaker, when closed, connects both halves of the synchronous bus. When open, it splits the synchronous bus into two separate halves,

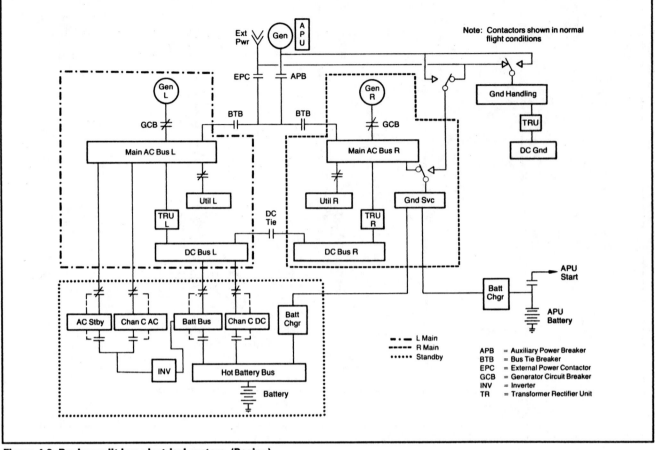

Figure 4-3. Boeing split bus electrical system. (Boeing)

or systems. The split system parallel type is used on the Boeing 747-400 aircraft.

BOEING 727 ELECTRICAL SYSTEM

The Boeing 727 uses a parallel electrical generating system as mentioned earlier. The electrical main power distribution system is shown in Figure 4-4. Each engine driven generator uses a constant speed drive (CSD) mechanism. The CSD oil is cooled by engine fan air ducted through an air-oil heat exchanger. The cooling effectiveness of the heat exchanger is measured by a temperature comparator which measures the rise in oil temperature through the CSD, as illustrated in Figure 4-5.

The load on each generator is automatically regulated by a load controller when the generators are paralleled. Individual frequency control knobs (Figure 4-5) signal the load controllers, which in turn can bias the CSD's output. When a generator is operating isolated, rotating its frequency control will result in minor changes in the output speed of the CSD. This speed change is reflected on the frequency meter. When a generator is paralleled, its frequency control can affect minor changes in the load being carried by the CSD. The load change is indicated on the generator's kilowatts (KW) meter.

When any generator is being paralleled by connecting it to a load bus that is being powered from another generator, an automatic paralleling circuit delays closing of the generator breaker until the generator's output is in phase with that of the other generator. The automatic paralleling protection circuit is not available when generators are being paralleled by closing a bus tie breaker. When this is done, the frequency of the generator to be paralleled must be adjusted manually with the frequency control.

The voltage regulator automatically controls the generator field strength. The field strength is reflected in one of two indications. When the generator is operating isolated, a change in field strength results in a voltage change. When operating in parallel, a change in field strength results in a KVAR (kilovolt-amps-reactive) load change for the generator. A malfunction of a voltage regulator would result in variations of the voltage (isolated) or KVAR load (reactive load, paralleled).

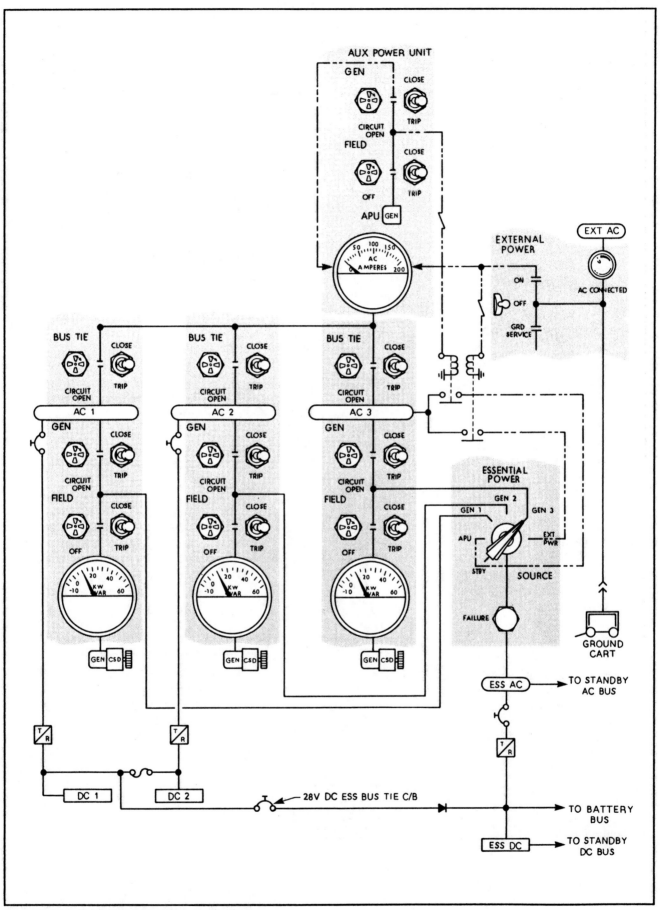

Figure 4-4. Boeing 727 electrical system. (Boeing)

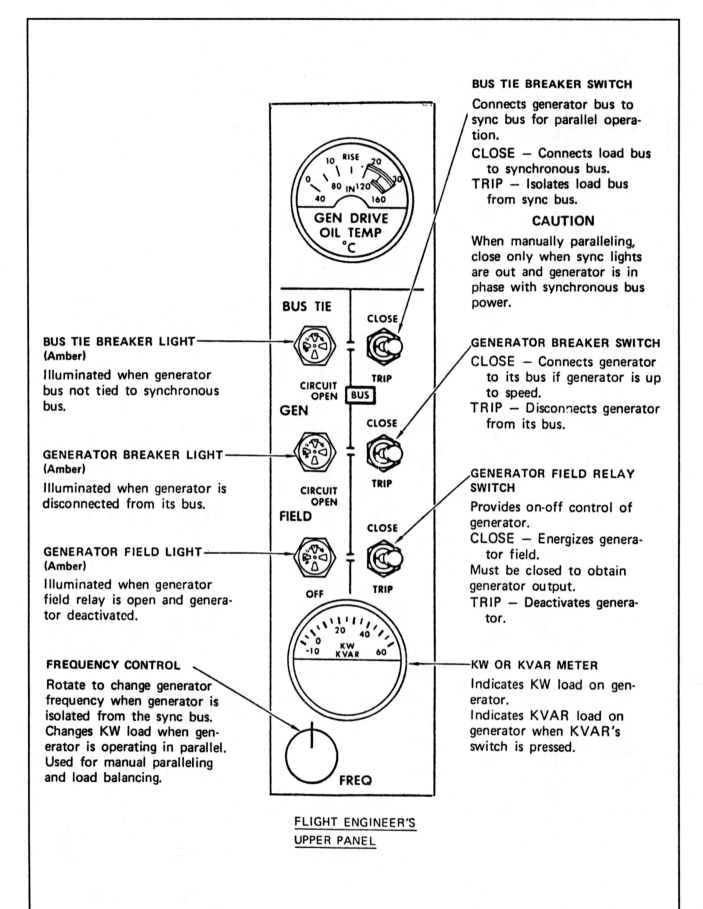

BUS TIE BREAKER SWITCH

Connects generator bus to sync bus for parallel operation.

CLOSE — Connects load bus to synchronous bus.

TRIP — Isolates load bus from sync bus.

CAUTION

When manually paralleling, close only when sync lights are out and generator is in phase with synchronous bus power.

GENERATOR BREAKER SWITCH

CLOSE — Connects generator to its bus if generator is up to speed.

TRIP — Disconnects generator from its bus.

GENERATOR FIELD RELAY SWITCH

Provides on-off control of generator.

CLOSE — Energizes generator field.

Must be closed to obtain generator output.

TRIP — Deactivates generator.

BUS TIE BREAKER LIGHT (Amber)

Illuminated when generator bus not tied to synchronous bus.

GENERATOR BREAKER LIGHT (Amber)

Illuminated when generator is disconnected from its bus.

GENERATOR FIELD LIGHT (Amber)

Illuminated when generator field relay is open and generator deactivated.

FREQUENCY CONTROL

Rotate to change generator frequency when generator is isolated from the sync bus. Changes KW load when generator is operating in parallel. Used for manual paralleling and load balancing.

KW OR KVAR METER

Indicates KW load on generator.

Indicates KVAR load on generator when KVAR's switch is pressed.

Figure 4-5. Boeing 727 generator controls. (Boeing)

Transformer rectifier units convert 115 volts three phase AC to 28 volts DC. When the DC meter selector is placed in the ESS TR, TR1, or TR2 position, the voltage is measured at the load bus. The ammeter indicates current leaving the transformer rectifier. With the selector in the BATTERY position, voltage is measured at the battery. The ammeter indicates current leaving the battery (minus indication) or charging current (plus indication).

MAIN POWER DISTRIBUTION

AC power developed by three generators is fed to their respective load buses (see Figure 4-4). The synchronous bus provides the means for connecting the load buses and operating all generators in parallel. This provides a means for powering all buses if one or two generators are inoperative. When APU or external power is utilized, power is supplied to the synchronous bus, and thus all the load buses.

APU ELECTRICAL POWER

When the APU is operating, placing the APU generator breaker switch to CLOSE will provide power to the synchronous bus. The amount of load being carried by the APU or external power source is indicated on the AC ammeter on the APU panel. The electrical system will not accept power of incorrect voltage or frequency and gives priority to the power system being selected.

ESSENTIAL POWER

The essential AC bus can receive power from any generator. The essential DC bus is normally powered by the essential AC bus via a TR unit. Certain items which are essential to the operation of the airplane are powered by these buses. Essential power is obtained at a point between the generator and the generator breaker. With the No. 3 bus tie breaker CLOSED, the APU or external power will furnish essential power through the synchronous bus to load bus No. 3. For ground operation, normal power transfers from the APU to other sources can be made without tripping essential power because of a holding relay. DC power is developed by TR units that are fed by AC load buses No. 1 and 2, or by the essential AC bus. The essential AC and DC buses normally feed the standby AC and DC buses.

BATTERY AND STANDBY POWER

The standby and battery power system, shown in Figure 4-6, are used to power critical communication and navigation equipment required to maintain safe flight when no other AC power is available on the airplane. The standby power system contains an AC and a DC bus.

Under normal operating conditions, the standby AC and DC buses receive power from essential AC and DC.

However, whenever the essential power selector is placed in the STANDBY position, the standby buses are disconnected from the essential buses and the battery bus supplies standby DC directly and standby AC through the static inverter. If essential AC power is lost in flight, the auto standby power system will shift to the standby mode automatically powering standby AC and DC from the battery bus. In the event of complete loss of AC power, the battery could supply the battery bus and standby buses for approximately 25 minutes.

BATTERY CHARGER

The battery charger will be operative anytime AC power is available to it. The charging rate will slowly decrease until the battery becomes fully charged. Then a pulsing charge occurs for about two minutes. After pulsing, the charge rate will drop to zero until the battery discharges enough to require recharging. The battery charger receives AC power from the AC transfer bus.

BOEING 737-300 ELECTRICAL POWER SYSTEM

The Boeing 737-300 electrical system, illustrated in Figure 4-7, is an example of a split bus system in which there is no paralleling of the AC sources of power during normal operation. All generator bus sources must be manually connected through the movement of a switch. The source of power being switched onto the generator bus will automatically disconnect an existing source.

Electrical power is generated by one 45 KVA generator on each engine and by an APU generator rated at 45 KVAs in flight and 55 KVAs on the ground. Each engine generator is connected to its respective engine through a CSD (constant speed drive) which converts variable engine RPM to the constant speed needed to produce 400 Hz used by the electrical system components.

In flight each generator normally powers its own generator bus, as shown in Figure 4-8. If one generator is inoperative, the APU generator may be used to power the inoperative generator's bus. Since the rest of the electrical system is initially powered from the two generator buses, all electrical components can be powered with any two operating generators.

Each generator system consists of a generator bus, a main bus, and a transfer bus. If there is a failure of a generator bus, the associated transfer bus can be supplied automatically from the powered generator bus. Each transfer bus has an associated transfer relay which automatically selects the opposite generator bus as a power supply if its normal generator bus fails and the transfer switch is in AUTO.

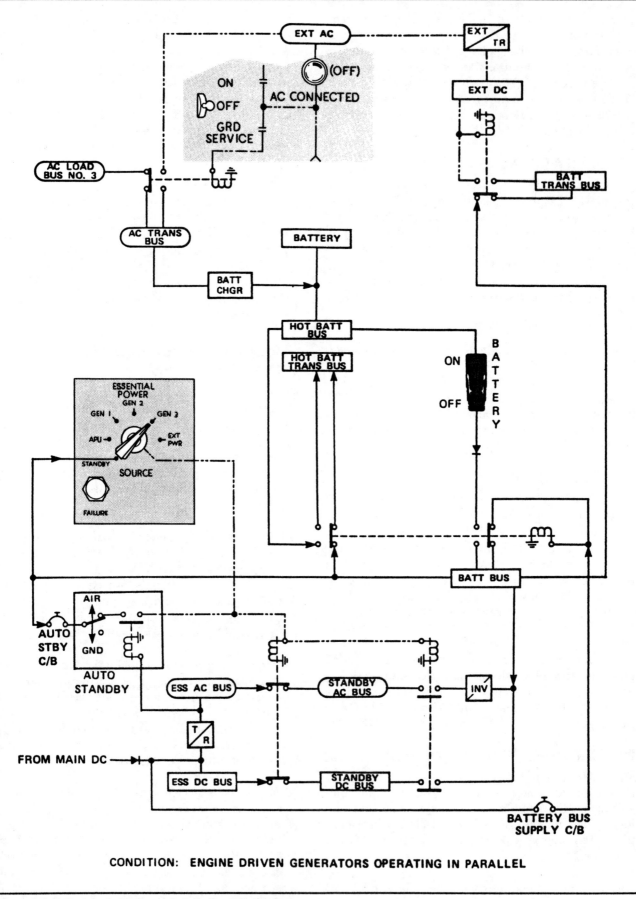

Figure 4-6. Battery and standby power, Boeing 727. (Boeing)

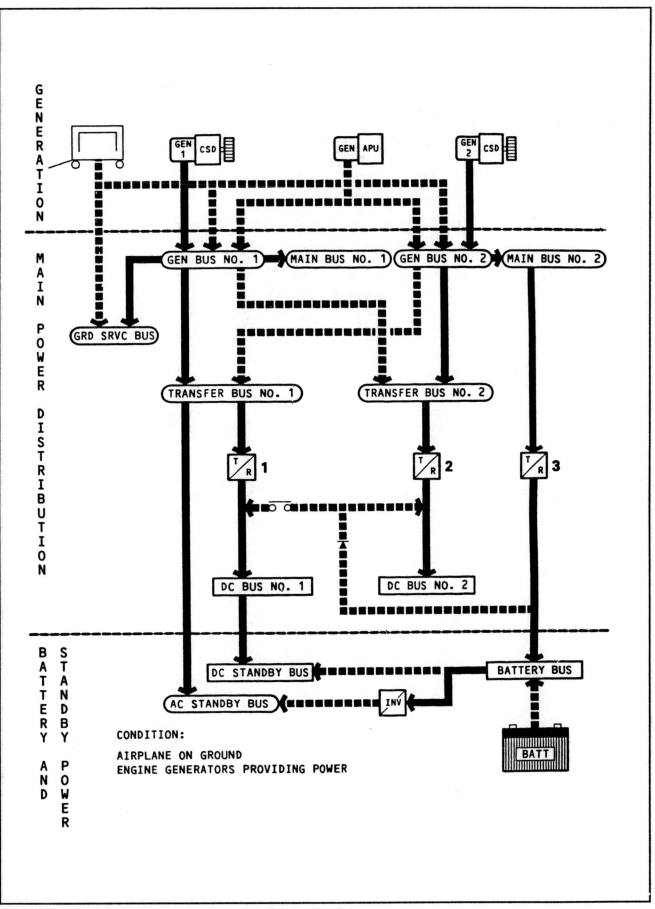

Figure 4-7. Boeing 737-300 electrical system concept diagram. (Boeing)

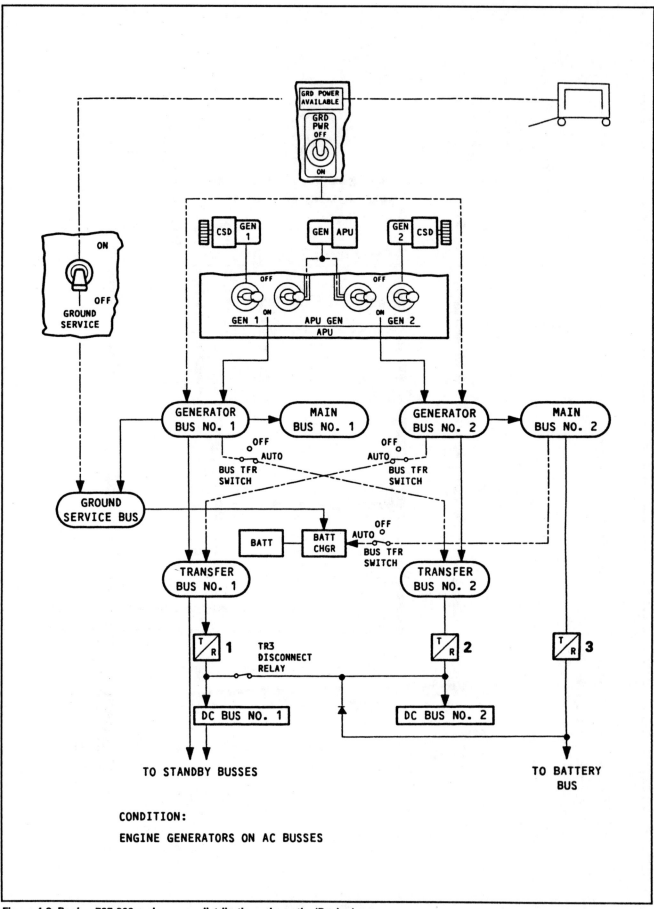

Figure 4-8. Boeing 737-300 main power distribution schematic. (Boeing)

The No. 1 and No. 2 transfer buses provide power for two transformer rectifier (TR) units that convert 115 VAC power to 28 VDC power for the No. 1 and No. 2 DC buses. The No. 2 main bus provides power for TR 3, which normally supplies power to the battery bus. A 36-ampere hour nickel cadmium battery supplies secondary (standby) DC power.

The standby power system is provided to supply power to the captain's primary instruments, communications, and navigation equipment. Normally, the standby AC and DC buses receive power from the airplane's AC and DC buses. In the event of complete generator power failure, the battery supplies power to the battery bus, connects the standby AC bus to the standby inverter, and connects the DC standby bus to the battery bus.

A fully charged battery has sufficient capacity to provide power to essential flight instruments, communication, and navigation equipment for a minimum of 30 minutes.

For ground operation, the APU generator can be connected to either one or both generator buses. External power can also be used to power both generator buses in lieu of power from the APU generator. Connecting an external power source to the airplane and closing the ground service switch located at the forward attendant's panel provides power for servicing and cleaning without powering all airplane electrical buses.

ELECTRICAL CONTROL AND MONITORING

Operating conditions of the CSD can be observed on the generator drive oil temperature indicator, as seen in Figure 4-9. Oil temperature is measured as it enters and leaves the CSD. Temperature differential between outlet and inlet temperature is determined electronically and indicated as RISE (out temperature minus in temperature). Two amber caution lights indicate CSD malfunctions, such as excessive oil temperature or falling oil pressure.

The generators are activated by closing the associated generator switch which connects the voltage regulator to the generator and connects the generator to its associated generator bus. The voltage regulator automatically controls the generator output voltage which can be observed on the AC voltmeter.

The frequency of the generator is dependent on the speed of the CSD and can be observed on the frequency meter. An advisory light will illuminate any time the generator is not connected to its respective bus.

Both the generator bus and the transfer bus have associated lights which illuminate when electrical power is

lost on the respective bus. An automatic feature of the transfer bus allows it to seek power from the opposite generator bus if its normal power source is lost. A bus transfer switch permits this feature to be deactivated.

When the DC meter selector is positioned to TR 1 or TR 2, the voltage is measured at the load bus. When the DC meter selector is positioned to TR 3, voltage is measured directly. The DC ammeter indicates the current leaving the transformer rectifier. There are no warning lights for a power loss of a DC bus.

BATTERY CHARGER

The battery charger is normally powered from the ground service bus. If this bus loses power, it automatically transfers its power source to main bus No. 2. The battery charger functions as long as one generator is on line and the bus transfer switch is in the AUTO position.

BOEING 747 ELECTRICAL POWER SYSTEM

The 747-400 electrical power system, shown in Figure 4-10, is an example of a split system parallel type. The system includes:

- External/APU power

- Engine powered generators

- DC power

- Standby power

- Load distribution

- Indicating system.

External APU power supplies electrical power during ground operations. It includes two external power sources and two APU generators. Electrical power supplied by the engines is used for all normal flight operations. Engine power consists of four integrated drive generators (IDG). The DC power system supplies those loads requiring DC power. It includes the batteries and transformer rectifier units.

Standby power supplies power to selected loads when the primary power sources have failed. The load distribution system is used to control and distribute AC and DC power throughout the airplane. The indicating system includes the electrical power interfaces with EICAS and the central maintenance computer and related displays. Electrical power is distributed in the airplane through the AC and DC distribution systems, which are illustrated in Figure 4-11. The AC distribution system is made up of four main buses and several auxiliary buses.

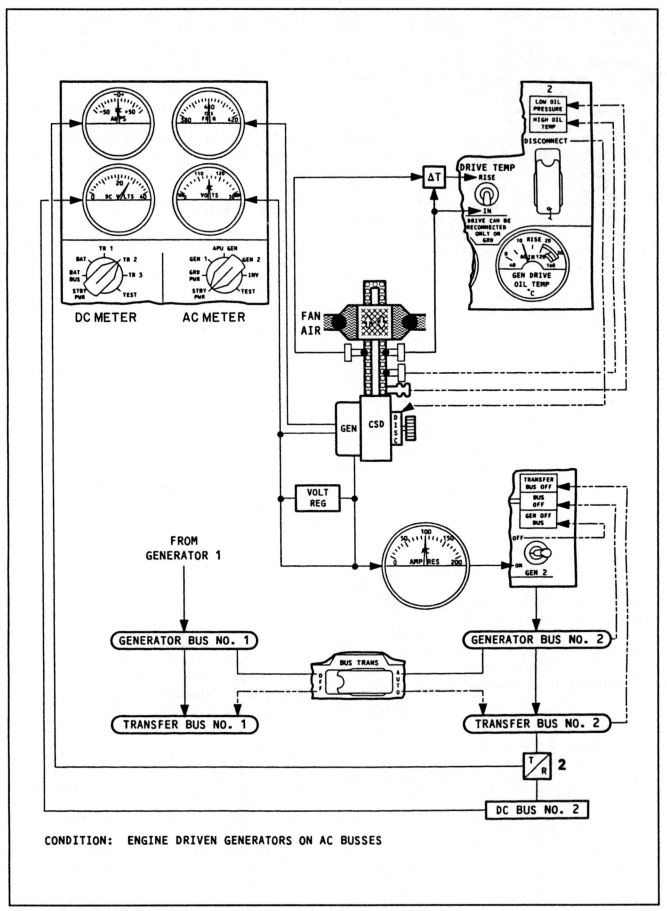

Figure 4-9. Boeing 737-300 electrical power controls and monitoring schematic. (Boeing)

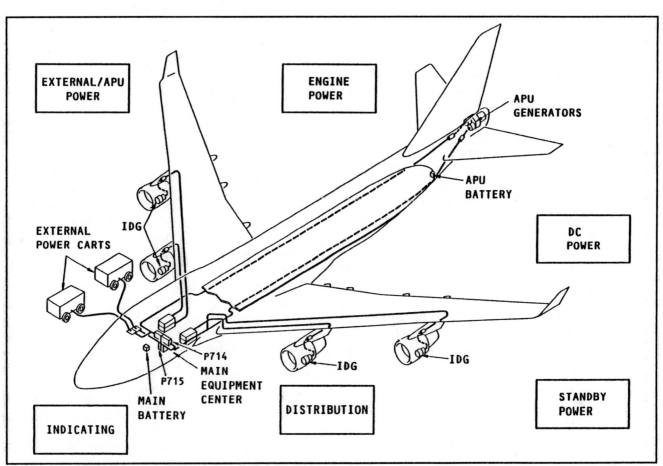

Figure 4-10. 747-400 electrical power system. (Boeing)

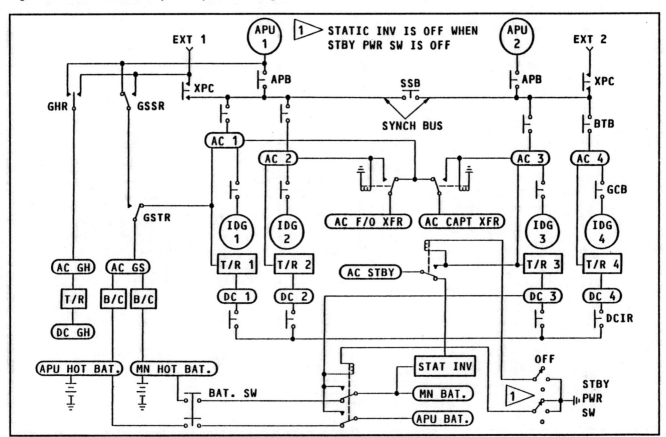

Figure 4-11. Boeing 747-400 electrical power system schematic. (Boeing)

The AC buses are powered by the IDGs, APU generators, or external power carts. An IDG is connected to its respective bus by closing the associated generator circuit breaker (GCB). Parallel operation of the IDGs is accomplished when the associated bus tie breakers (BTBs) and GCBs are closed. The synchronizing (synch) bus is divided into two sections by a split system breaker (SSB). With proper use of the breakers (See Figure 4-11), any generator can supply power to any load bus and any combination of the IDGs can be operated in parallel. The power output of the APU generators or external (APBs) power carts can also be connected to the load buses by closing the auxiliary power breakers or external power contactors (XPC).

There are two transfer buses: the captain's and the first officer's. The captain's transfer bus is normally powered from AC bus 3. If AC bus 3 is not powered, the transfer bus will transfer to AC bus 1 for power. The first officer's transfer bus is normally powered from AC bus 2, but will transfer to AC bus 1 if AC bus 2 should lose power. The standby AC bus is normally powered, but will switch to the static inverter if the AC bus is not powered.

The ground handling bus is powered from either an APU generator or external power through the ground handling relay (GHR). The bus is powered automatically whenever external power or APU power is available. The ground handling bus is not powered in flight.

Power to DC buses 1, 2, 3, and 4 is supplied by transformer rectifier units (TRUs). The DC buses parallel through the DC isolation relays (DCIR). The DC ground handling bus is powered when the AC ground handling bus is powered.

EXTERNAL POWER OPERATION

Three-phase, 400 Hz, 115 volt AC power is supplied to the airplane by two external power carts through the external power receptacles. Before the power is connected to the airplane systems, two bus control units (BCUs) sample it. The BCUs check for proper seating of the plugs, voltage, frequency, phase rotation, and that the plug interlock system is not shorted to the main feeder wires. When the BCUs are satisfied that all of these conditions are met, they turn on the external power AVAIL lights on the electrical system control panel in the flight deck, shown in Figure 4-12.

There are two momentary switches labeled EXT PWR 1 and EXT PWR 2 on the electrical system control panel. Pressing EXT PWR 1 signals BCU 1 to close its associated external power contactor (XPC). BCU 2

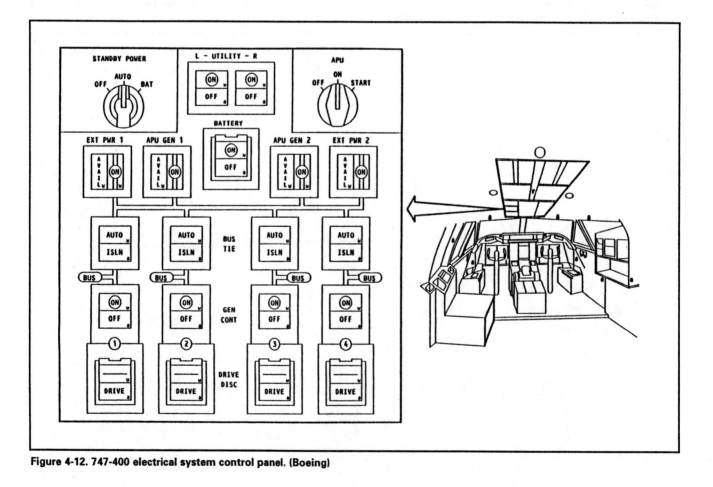

Figure 4-12. 747-400 electrical system control panel. (Boeing)

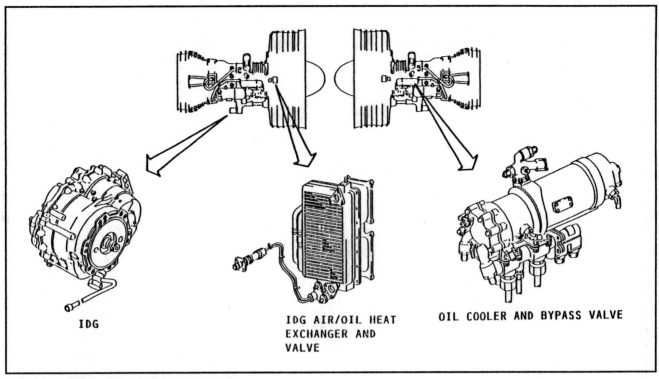

Figure 4-13. IDG system components. (Boeing)

closes the split system breaker (SSB) at this time if no other power is on the synch bus. Power is now on the airplane and is being supplied by the aft power cord. Pressing EXT PWR 2 signals BCU 2 to trip the SSB and close its associated external power contactor. Now EXT PWR 1 is powering the left side of the synchronizing (synch) bus and EXT PWR 2 is powering the right side of the synch bus.

APU POWER

Three phase 400 Hz AC power is supplied to the airplane by the APU driven generators. Before the power is connected to the airplane systems, two auxiliary generator control units (AGCU) monitor the power to ensure that it is at the proper voltage and frequency. When the AGCUs are satisfied that the power requirements are met, they signal the BCUs to turn on the two APU generator AVAIL lights on the electrical system control panel in the flight deck. Closing these switches will allow the aircraft to be powered by the APU generators in a similar manner as external power.

INTEGRATED DRIVE GENERATOR

The IDG portion of the engine power system, shown in Figure 4-13, involves the mechanical aspects of the IDG and its oil cooling components. The constant speed drive (CSD) portion of the IDG is a hydromechanical device. It adds or subtracts speed from the variable input of the engine gearbox to maintain the IDG generator at 12,000 RPM.

IDG oil is used for speed control, lubrication, and cooling. Heat generated by the IDG is cooled by passing the oil through an air/oil heat exchanger and a fuel cooled oil cooler. The cooled oil is then returned to the IDG. The oil cooler is the primary means of cooling the oil, but is assisted by the air/oil heat exchanger under certain operating conditions. Four generator control units (GCUs) are used to provide control, protection, and built-in test equipment (BITE) for their respective generator channels.

The GCU receives oil temperature, oil pressure, and IDG speed signals, as can be seen in Figure 4-14. It sends speed commands to the IDG governor and control signals to the air/oil heat exchanger valve.

Speed commands from the GCU to the IDG are used to control IDG speed to maintain a reference frequency. Air/oil heat exchanger valve control signals are sent to the valve to control its position. BITE circuitry is provided in the GCU to identify a malfunction or failure of the electrical system. The BITE mode of operation is initiated under two conditions: anytime a protective trip occurs and periodically (automatically).

BOEING 777 ELECTRICAL POWER SYSTEM

The 777 electrical power system is very much like the split bus systems used on the other two-engine Boeing aircraft (737, 757, 767). Most of the 777 electrical

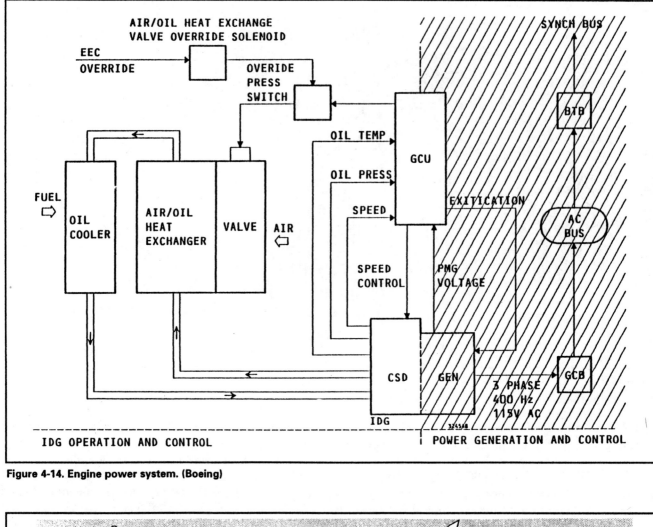

Figure 4-14. Engine power system. (Boeing)

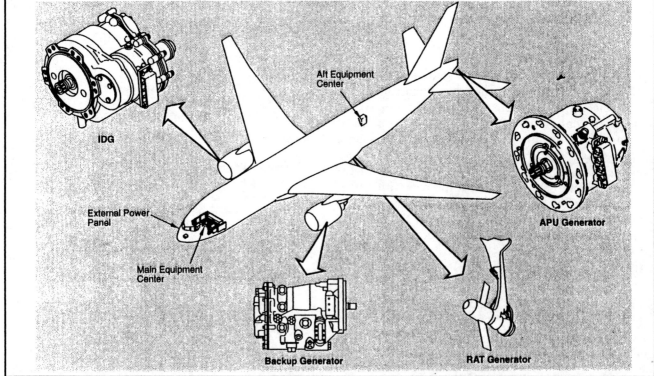

Figure 4-15. Boeing 777 electrical power system components.

power system was developed with proven technology, with new improved features which increase its reliability to support the fly-by-wire flight control system. The system also has an efficient load management system which can control electrical distribution. The electrical system supplies 115 VAC and 28 VDC by the use of two integrated drive generators (IDG), APU generator, two backup generators, ram air turbine (RAT), main and APU batteries, and external power. These components can be seen in Figure 4-15.

There is one IDG on each engine which serves as the primary source of AC power with the APU generator available during flight. These generators provide 120 KVAs of power each. There is also one backup generator per engine which can supply 20 KVAs of AC power. Each backup generator also contains two permanent magnet generators (PMG) that supply power to three flight control DC (FCDC) power supply assemblies. A RAT generator is another source of backup AC power which can supply up to 7 KVA. For ground operations, there are two external power connectors on the bottom forward side of the fuselage. Each external power source supplies 90 KVA of AC power. The main battery is in the main equipment center. The APU battery and charger are in the aft equipment center. Both of the batteries can supply 28 VDC power.

ELECTRICAL LOAD MANAGEMENT SYSTEM (ELMS)

The ELMS distributes, monitors, and protects electrical power. It also supplies control logic for some airplane systems. This makes it possible for the ELMS to replace complex relay logic and circuit cards used on previous airplanes. ELMS components are shown in Figure 4-16. The left, right, and auxiliary power panels contain the buses and breakers to control switching to the main buses. The panels supply power directly to loads that use 20 amps or more. They also supply power to the power management panels and to the ground handling/service distribution panel. The main breakers and contactors are in the power panels. However, the GCUs and BPCU control these breakers and contactors. The left, right, and standby power management panels contain the buses, breakers, and relays to control switching to smaller electrical loads. These panels supply power to loads that draw 20 amps or less. The power management panels have processors that monitor loads and control most switching components in the ELMS panels. The ground service/handling distribution panels contain the components for switching power to the ground handling and ground service buses. The backup converter monitors, protects, and controls the backup generators and power switching for the transfer buses.

DC-9 ELECTRICAL POWER SYSTEM

The electrical power system, illustrated in Figure 4-17, consists of both a primary and a secondary electrical system which satisfy the requirements for aircraft self-sufficiency over the entire DC-9 ground and flight operation.

PRIMARY ELECTRICAL SYSTEM

The primary electrical system is composed of alternating current (AC) and direct current (DC) electrical power derived from two engine-driven AC generators, one auxiliary power unit (APU) driven AC generator, four DC unregulated transformer rectifiers and their associated control equipment and mechanical interface.

The engine-driven generators, rated at 40 kilo-volt ampere (KVA), are 120/208 volts alternating current, 3-phase, 400 Hz brushless units and are direct coupled through axial gear constant speed drives. The APU-driven generator is exactly the same except that it is mounted directly to the APU drive. The generators are blast air cooled and contain integral permanent magnet generators for excitation and power contractor control.

The engine generator channels are normally operated unparalleled at 115/200 VAC, 400 Hz while using the APU generator as a backup for redundancy and greater flexibility in aircraft dispatchability. An automatic cross-tie network with in flight galley load shedding is provided to allow single-generator system operation in case of a generator failure. The APU generator may also be used for ground operation and maintenance.

Four solid-state unregulated transformer-rectifier units convert 3-phase, 115/200 volt alternating current to 28 volt direct current used for all direct current system loads normally required in operation.

Two of the transformer-rectifier units are normally operated in parallel for each two direct current system channels. These channels may be operated in parallel by closing a manually controlled direct current cross-tie switch.

SECONDARY ELECTRICAL SYSTEM (STANDBY SYSTEM)

The secondary electrical system is composed of a 35 ampere hour nickel-cadmium battery, a solid-state battery charger, a 410 volt-ampere static inverter and their associated control and protection equipment.

The battery system provides emergency capability for certain navigational and communications equipment in the event of an all-generator failure. The battery is sized sufficiently to accommodate the high current

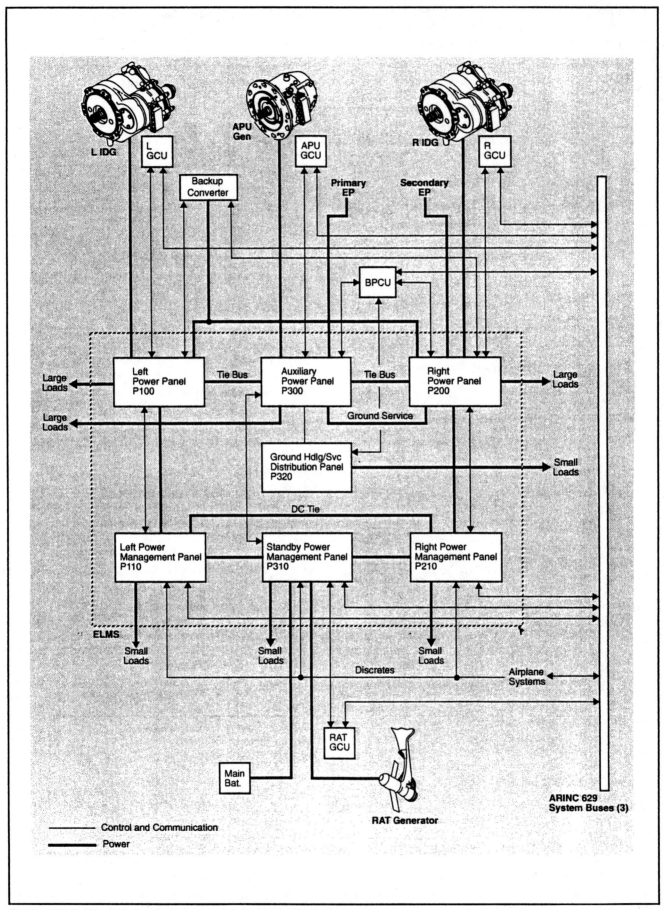

Figure 4-16. Boeing 777 electrical power control system. (Boeing)

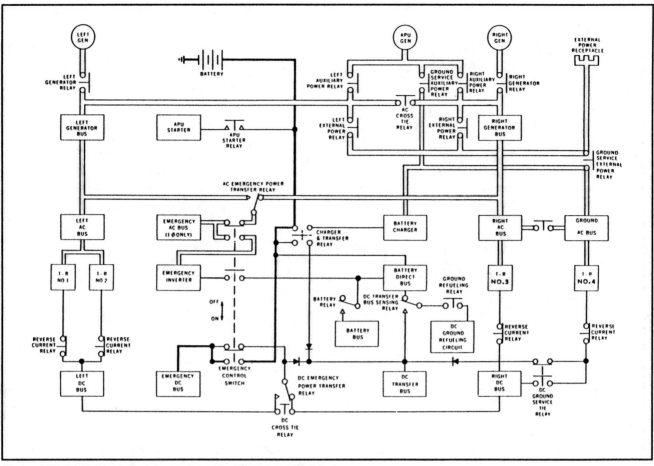

Figure 4-17. DC-9 electrical system schematic. (McDonnell Douglas)

APU start requirements, as well as to provide a full 45 minute emergency load capability.

The battery consists of cell assemblies connected in series for 28 volts direct current. Quick-disconnect connectors facilitate maintenance and removal. The battery is electrically connected so that it can be charged during ground operation, as well as in flight.

The static inverter is normally used with the battery to supply emergency alternating current loads. It can also be used for refueling. A special ground service bus arrangement is provided to facilitate ground handling functions.

DC-10 ELECTRICAL POWER SYSTEM

The three engine generators and one APU generator, shown in Figure 4-18, each with 90 KVA capacity, along with the power distribution network, allow for automatic or manual selection of alternate AC power sources. In the event of a loss of the primary power sources in flight, two emergency sources of power are available. The aircraft battery with a static inverter will provide at least 30 minutes of critical system power for safe flight and landing. An air driven generator is installed primarily for emergency electrical power to provide up to 20 KVA of long term emergency power for critical systems.

A self contained auxiliary power unit (APU) is installed as standard equipment on all DC-10 series aircraft. The APU is located in an unpressurized section of the lower fuselage, aft of the cabin pressure bulkhead. While on the ground, it can supply electrical power and compressed air for operation of the air conditioning systems and power for starting the main engines, thus eliminating dependence on external power equipment for normal ground operation of the aircraft systems. However, external provisions are available on the aircraft which allow ground support units to be utilized as needed. The APU may be used in flight as an auxiliary source of electrical and pneumatic power. However, dispatchability and safe operation of the aircraft are not dependent on the APU.

LOAD SHEDDING SYSTEM

Most newer large aircraft incorporate an automatic load shedding system. This system reduces the electrical

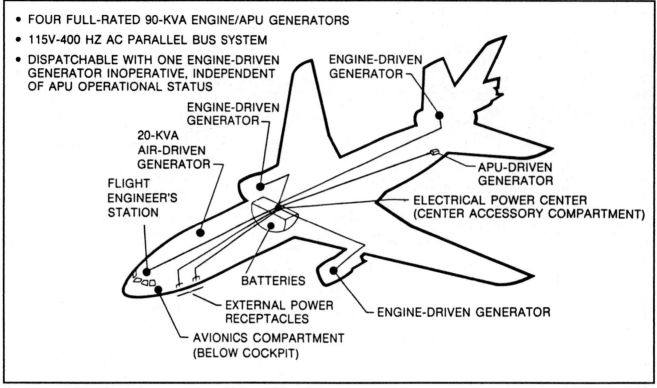

- FOUR FULL-RATED 90-KVA ENGINE/APU GENERATORS
- 115V-400 HZ AC PARALLEL BUS SYSTEM
- DISPATCHABLE WITH ONE ENGINE-DRIVEN GENERATOR INOPERATIVE, INDEPENDENT OF APU OPERATIONAL STATUS

ENGINE-DRIVEN GENERATOR

ENGINE-DRIVEN GENERATOR

20-KVA AIR-DRIVEN GENERATOR

FLIGHT ENGINEER'S STATION

APU-DRIVEN GENERATOR

ELECTRICAL POWER CENTER (CENTER ACCESSORY COMPARTMENT)

BATTERIES

EXTERNAL POWER RECEPTACLES

ENGINE-DRIVEN GENERATOR

AVIONICS COMPARTMENT (BELOW COCKPIT)

Figure 4-18. DC-10 electrical power system. (McDonnell Douglas)

load on the generating system. An example of an aircraft that uses a load shedding system is the Boeing 757. The Boeing 757 has three conditions which result in load shedding: generator loss, overload, and engine start.

During takeoff or in flight, the loss of one generator causes both utility buses and all galley buses to trip off. As a result, both UTILITY BUS OFF lights illuminate. In flight, they can only be reset by re-establishing a second generator. When a second generator comes on line, the utility and galley buses reset automatically.

Arming of this load shed protection requires that the air/ground logic be in the flight mode, or that the thrust levers both be moved into the takeoff range. Consequently, advancing both thrust levers before engine start or after engine shutdown can cause a trip off of the utility and galley buses. Additional loads are automatically shed if an engine is shut down in flight.

On the ground prior to engine start, the overload protection operates in two phases. When the APU or

external power exceeds its load limit, the galleys trip off. The utility buses trip off if the overload continues, illuminating the UTILITY BUS OFF lights.

If only the galleys trip off, they reset automatically as soon as the respective bus tie breaker opens or when all electric hydraulic pumps are selected OFF. For example, during engine start, as the generator comes on line and its bus tie opens, the galleys connected to it automatically reset. A manual reset is required if the utility buses also trip off. If a separate generator is supplying each main AC bus, only the utility and galley buses associated with the overloaded generator are shed.

Engine start load shedding occurs when the APU is used for both electrical and pneumatic power during engine start. This load shed trips the utility and galley buses, illuminating both UTILITY BUS OFF lights. By unloading the APU electrically, ample APU pneumatic power is assured for the engine start.

CHAPTER 4 STUDY QUESTIONS

1. What type of electrical power is used on large aircraft?

   _____

   _____

2. List the typical aircraft power sources.

   _____

   _____

   _____

3. What is the function of a CSD?

   _____

   _____

4. What controls the output frequency of a generator?

   _____

   _____

5. List the basic electrical system configurations.

   _____

   _____

   _____

6. Define the term GPU.

   _____

   _____

   _____

7. What electrical system configuration is used on the 727 aircraft?

   _____

   _____

8. How are CSDs cooled?

   _____

   _____

   _____

9. What is special, if anything, about essential power?

   _____

   _____

   _____

10. Define a split bus system.

   _____

   _____

11. Define a split system parallel system.

_____

_____

_____

12. What is used on the 727 aircraft to monitor electrical power?

_____

_____

13. What is the purpose of standby power?

_____

_____

FLIGHT CONTROL SYSTEMS

BOEING 727 FLIGHT CONTROLS

Large aircraft control systems are very similar to small aircraft in that they control the aircraft around three axes. The longitudinal, vertical, and lateral axes use controls which allow movement of the aircraft so it can revolve to change flight directions.

Motion about the longitudinal axis, which runs through the nose and out the tail parallel to the fuselage, is the axis that produces roll.

Motion about the lateral axis, which is wing tip to wing tip, produces pitch.

Movement of the aircraft around the vertical axis produces yaw.

Flight controls that control the aircraft about these axes are the primary flight controls which consist of the ailerons (longitudinal axis, roll), the elevators (lateral axis, pitch), and the rudder (vertical axis, yaw). The primary flight controls for a Boeing 727 are shown in Figure 5-1.

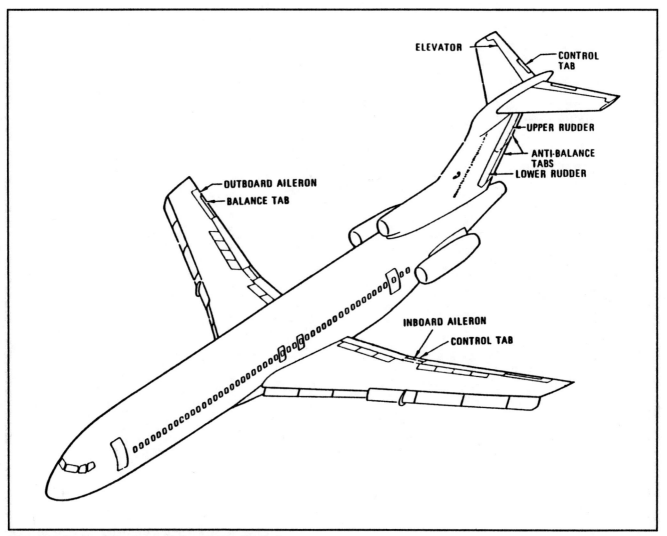

Figure 5-1. Boeing 727 primary flight controls. (Boeing)

Most large aircraft primary flight control surfaces are hydraulically powered. The hydraulic power sources are divided between multiple hydraulic systems to minimize the impact of the loss of any one of the aircraft's hydraulic systems.

Each hydraulic system uses its own individual actuating cylinders, in case of a hydraulic fluid leak in that system. Each control surface uses two or more hydraulic systems with each system having individual actuating cylinders connected to the flight controls.

Primary pitch control is provided by elevators mounted on the trailing edge of the horizontal stabilizer. Elevator movement is normally controlled by the elevator power control units. Each unit on the Boeing 727 is powered by both hydraulic systems as shown in

Figure 5-2. If one system fails, either system will power both elevators. If both hydraulic systems are lost, the control tabs unlock and allow mechanical control of the elevators.

Pitch trim is sometimes provided by moving the leading edge of the horizontal stabilizer up or down. The Boeing 727's horizontal stabilizer is operated electrically by either a main trim motor or an autopilot/cruise trim motor as shown in Figure 5-3. A mechanical stabilizer brake will stop stabilizer movement any time control column movement is in the opposite direction to the trim wheel rotation. If the trim motors fail, the stabilizer trim can be operated manually.

Yaw control is provided by the rudder, or rudders, generally mounted on the trailing edge of the vertical sta-

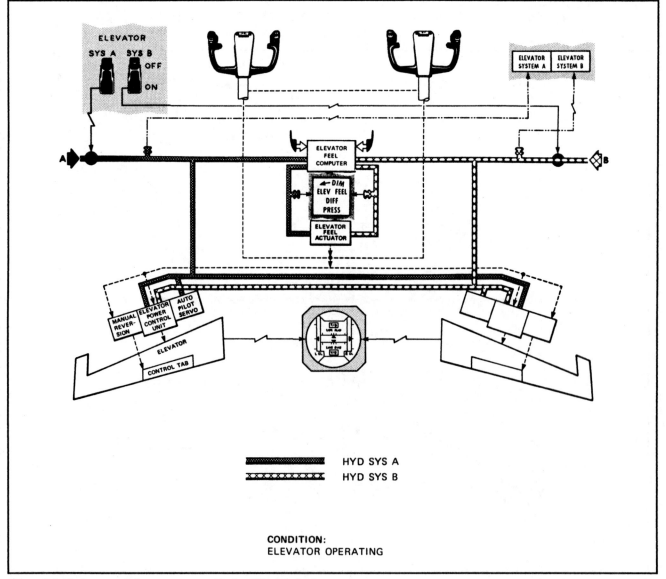

Figure 5-2. Pitch control elevator system, Boeing 727. (Boeing)

bilizer or fin. The Boeing 727 yaw control system, illustrated in Figure 5-4, uses two full time yaw dampers to move the rudders to oppose airplane yaw.

Yaw damper operation is controlled by yaw damper rate gyros which augment rudder pedal inputs. Sometimes anti-balance tabs are used on each rudder which move in the direction of rudder displacement, providing the effect of a larger rudder. Rudder pedal feel is supplied by a feel and centering mechanism. The lower rudder can be operated by the standby hydraulic system in the event of normal hydraulic pressure loss.

If hydraulic pressure is lost to the primary controls, the 727 aircraft uses manual reversion which incorporates control tabs mounted on the ailerons and on the elevator. These controls are unlocked from their actuating cylinders and manual inputs are provided to the control tabs from the cockpit.

The wings on large transport aircraft are generally swept back at an angle of about 30° to 35° to reduce high speed drag (see Figure 5-1). The lateral control of the aircraft involves creation of differential lift between the two wings which is accomplished on most aircraft by the use of ailerons mounted on the wing's trailing edge.

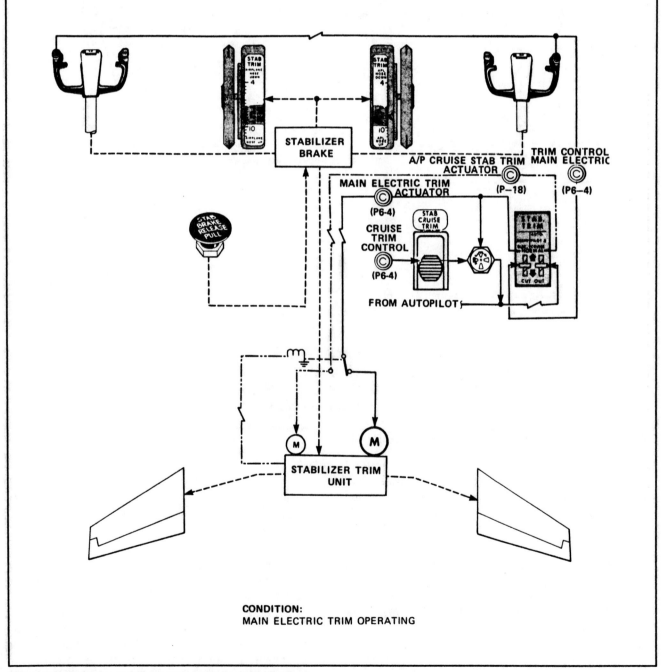

Figure 5-3. Pitch trim stabilizer system, Boeing 727. (Boeing)

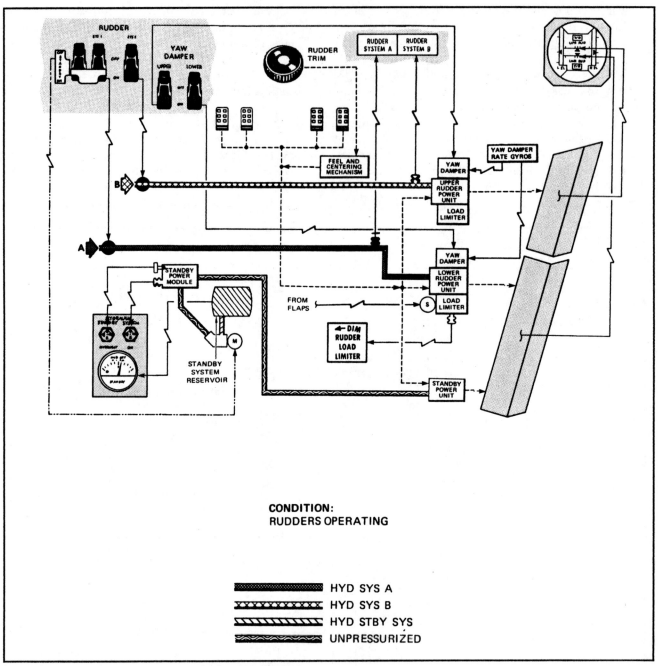

Figure 5-4. Yaw control rudder system, Boeing 727. (Boeing)

Some large aircraft use two sets of ailerons, an inboard and outboard set. As the aircraft's speed is increased, the aerodynamic loads on the ailerons tend to twist the wings because the wing is more flexible near the tip.

To overcome this problem, some aircraft use the technique of locking out the outboard ailerons during high speed flight. The outboard ailerons are locked in the faired (neutral) position when the trailing edge flaps are fully retracted.

Secondary flight controls, shown in Figure 5-5, are used to aid primary controls, relieve control pres-

sure, and increase or decrease the wing's lift. Some secondary controls are spoilers, wing flaps (trailing edge), leading edge devices (slats), and control trim systems.

Spoilers can be used in conjunction with the ailerons to create a wing lift differential. Spoilers are installed on the upper wing surfaces directly forward of the flaps, and consist of panels that assist the ailerons when maximum roll rates are required. Spoilers reduce the lift on the wing which moves down as the aircraft rolls (banks). Aileron control is supplemented by the flight spoilers which are controlled by the

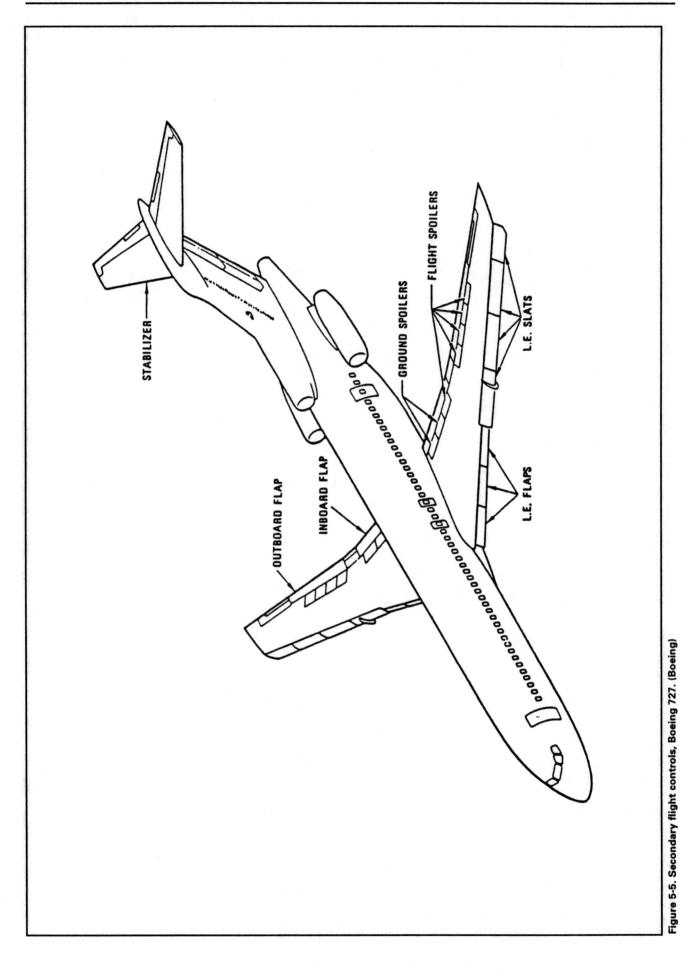

Figure 5-5. Secondary flight controls, Boeing 727. (Boeing)

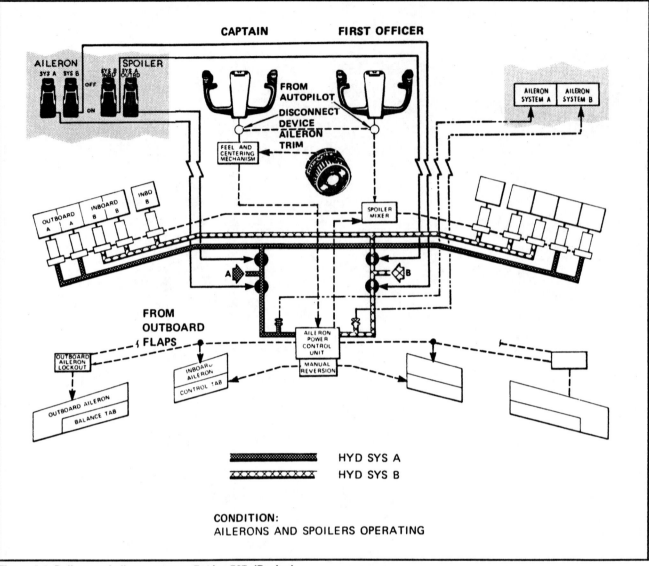

Figure 5-6. Roll control aileron system, Boeing 727. (Boeing)

spoiler mixer. The aileron and spoiler system for the Boeing 727 aircraft is illustrated in Figure 5-6.

The spoiler mixer senses aileron movement and automatically provides the correct amount of spoiler deflection. Spoilers can also be used as a backup if aileron control is lost. Spoilers, when used as landing speed brakes, extend upward about 60° during landing, which reduces the wing's lift. This increases drag with a resultant increase in weight on the wheels of the aircraft. This can shorten the landing roll by increasing the brake effectiveness.

Flight spoilers or speed brakes can also be used in flight to reduce the aircraft's speed. Ground spoilers, as the name implies, can only be used on the ground after landing to decrease lift and increase drag.

Wing flaps are employed to increase lift for takeoff and landing operations. Generally two pairs of flaps are

located on the wing trailing edge, an inboard and an outboard pair.

On many aircraft, the flaps are powered by the hydraulic system for normal operation with electric motors used for alternate operation.

On the Boeing 727 airplane two pairs of triple slotted trailing edge flaps, outboard and inboard, are normally operated by hydraulic pressure. The 727's flap position determines the availability of the outboard ailerons and controls the normal operation of the leading edge devices. The flap system for the 727 can be seen in Figure 5-7.

Leading edge devices are installed on the wing's leading edge to increase lift during takeoff and landing. Leading edge devices on the 727 consist of slats or flaps and are normally operated by hydraulic pressure.

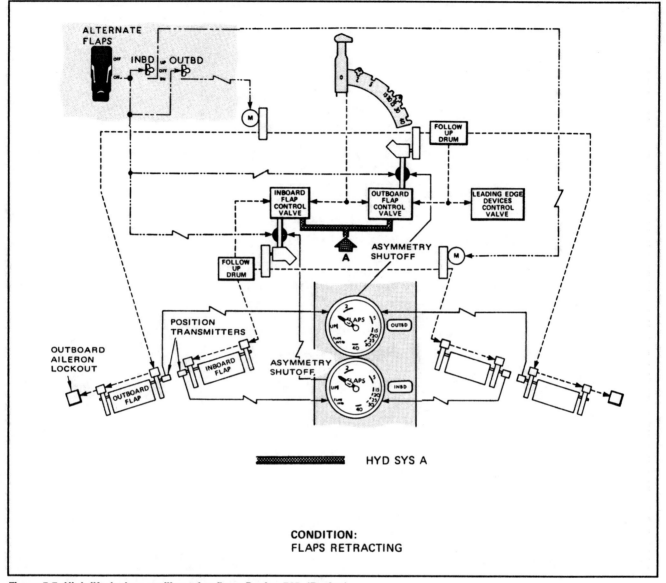

Figure 5-7. High lift devices, trailing edge flaps, Boeing 727. (Boeing)

The leading edge devices (flaps and slats) for a 727, shown in Figure 5-8, are controlled by the outboard trailing edge flap position. When the trailing edge flaps reach position 2, two leading edge slats on each wing are extended. With the flaps in position 5 or greater, all leading edge devices are fully extended. When the flaps are retracted, this sequence is reversed.

A back-up or standby system is generally provided for operation of the leading edge devices if the primary means of operation is lost. Trim systems are provided for most aircraft primary controls by changing the control system's power unit input.

The control feel system provides a variable control force which closely simulates forces a pilot would feel

if the controls were operating with only aerodynamic forces on the control surfaces.

The 727 aircraft system uses two major components, the feel computer and the feel control unit. The computer determines the correct control force from airspeed and stabilizer position data which provides a variable hydraulic force to the elevator feel unit.

LOCKHEED L-1011 FLIGHT CONTROLS

All flight controls, shown in Figure 5-9, are fully hydraulic powered utilizing multiple independent hydraulic pressure sources. Surface trim is accomplished by repositioning the control surface, therefore, there are no trim tabs.

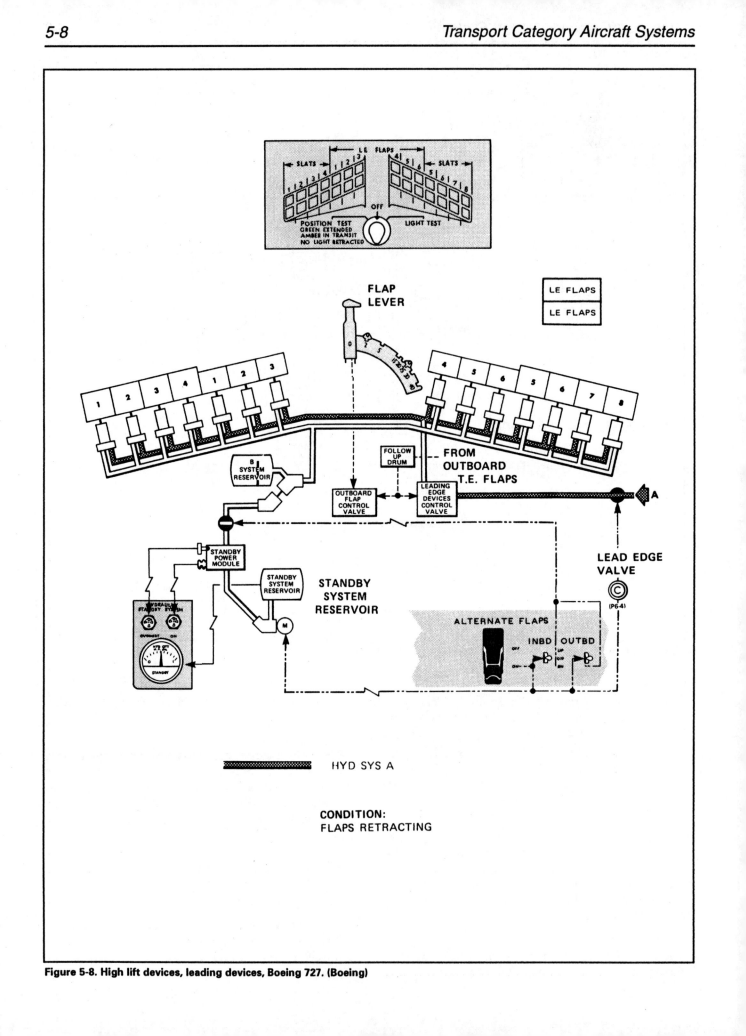

Figure 5-8. High lift devices, leading devices, Boeing 727. (Boeing)

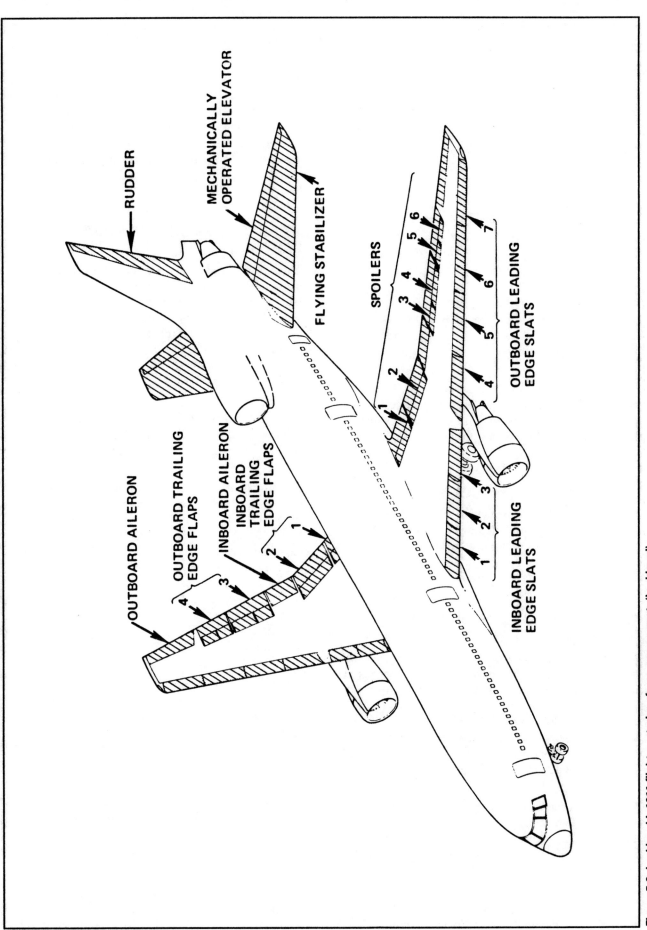

Figure 5-9. Lockheed L-1011 flight control surface arrangement. (Lockheed)

PRIMARY FLIGHT CONTROLS

There are four full time ailerons and, when flaps are extended, specific spoiler panels are deployed for roll augmentation. Under this condition the spoiler panel deflection control is derived from inboard aileron position.

Pitch control is accomplished by a flying stabilizer and elevators. The elevators are mechanically actuated as a function of stabilizer movement.

Yaw control is accomplished by a conventional powered rudder surface. Rudder travel and applied movement force (hydraulic pressure) is restricted as a function of airspeed.

There are several spoiler functions, such as speed brakes, roll augmentation, direct lift control (DLC), and automatic and modulated deployment to control wing lift during final approach.

Automatic ground spoilers deploy specific spoiler panels at landing touchdown or during a rejected take-off. This action reduces wing lift and ensures positive tire contact with the runway, thus providing best possible braking action.

SECONDARY FLIGHT CONTROLS

Secondary flight controls consist of eight Fowler type trailing edge flaps which deploy incrementally from 0° to 42°. The aircraft also uses fourteen leading edge slats which can be fully deployed when flaps are extended beyond the 4° position.

FLIGHT CONTROLS HYDRAULIC POWER DISTRIBUTION

The primary flight controls are powered by hydraulic systems A, B, C, and D. Secondary flight controls are powered by hydraulic systems A and C. Automatic pilot servos and the direct lift control servos are powered by hydraulic systems A and B, as seen in Figure 5-10. A hydraulic fuse in the rudder system A supply and return lines protects against loss of system A hydraulic fluid in the event of a No. 2 engine fan failure.

When an excessive hydraulic system demand occurs, secondary flight controls are isolated from the power source by priority valves, thus giving priority to primary flight controls. The slat hydraulic C isolation valve protects system C against No. 1 engine fan failure.

The flight control panels are used to direct operation of the flight servo-actuators and power drive units. They also control the fault monitoring system and certain avionic functions.

The normal condition of the control panels is that there are no lights illuminated when there are no faults within the systems. In the presence of faults, appropriate advisories will be annunciated to the pilots, giving instructions to bypass the fault condition. There are also surface position indicators that display the position of the primary and secondary flight control surfaces to the flight crew.

AILERON CONTROL SYSTEM SCHEMATIC

The aileron system (see Figure 5-11) is normally controlled from either of the control wheels through the left hand captain's control path. This control path consists of a combination of cables and pushrods, terminating at the left hand inboard aileron servo. In normal operation, the left hand inboard aileron is the master aileron and all other aileron servos receive their inputs from the master aileron.

The left hand inboard aileron servo also includes the roll autopilot servo. Therefore, all autopilot inputs are supplied through the master aileron.

A control path is also incorporated from the first officer's control wheel and terminates at the right hand inboard aileron servo. The two control paths are interfaced together at the interconnect over-ride bungee (stretchable rubber cord) and through the roll disconnect mechanism. However, simultaneous motion in the two paths is isolated by the lost motion device in the first officer's control path. This lost motion device ensures that, in normal operation, movement of either control wheel will be transmitted to the left inboard aileron servo.

Subsequent motion of the master aileron will then be supplied into not only the right hand aileron servo, but also into the right hand control path. For roll augmentation purposes, interface between the aileron control and spoiler control systems is provided by two spoiler mixers and two outboard spoiler control selectors.

Artificial feel/trim is accomplished by a trim actuator and spring bungee which provides a force acting on the captain's control path.

AILERON TORQUE LIMITER

The torque limiter functions as a control cable input bellcrank in the pilot's roll control system. If a jam occurs in the control path, the torque limiter will break

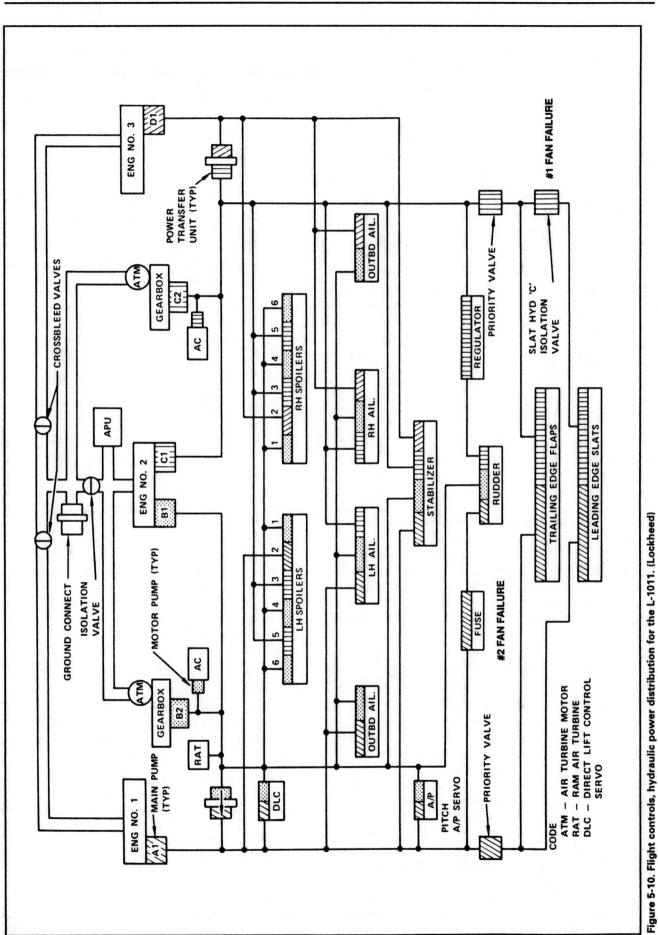

Figure 5-10. Flight controls, hydraulic power distribution for the L-1011. (Lockheed)

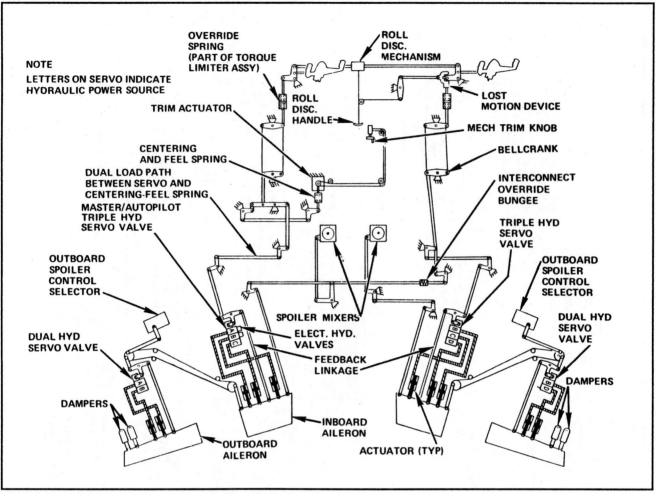

Figure 5-11. L-1011 aileron control system schematic. (Lockheed)

out at 28 pounds of control wheel force to allow continued control to the opposite side. This breakout against a jam will actuate the warning switch and send a logic signal to the roll monitor to warn the pilots of the malfunction location.

During roll system operation, the torque limiter converts the pilot's control pushrod motion to cable motion, as illustrated in Figure 5-12.

If a malfunction occurs, such as a jam in the control path, the pilot would break out the torque limiter with a 28 pound force on the control wheel. This action will effectively uncouple him from the jam and allow continued roll control through the opposite control path. The breakout will cause the cam to rotate relative to the output arm, by forcing the spring-loaded follower arm rollers out of the cam detents. One degree of relative motion between the cam and output arm actuates the warning switch.

The left inboard aileron servo is the master servo for the roll control system. All other aileron servos are

slaved to this aileron actuation. Manual inputs through the dual input pushrods, or avionic inputs, drive the three actuators which in turn move the aileron surface. Dual surface position feedback rods, shown in Figure 5-11, null the servo control valves.

The outboard spring bungee and the pushrod linkage control the left outboard aileron servo. The inboard spring bungee and the pushrod system lead back along the wing, through the fuselage, and terminate at the right hand inboard aileron servo in the right wing.

Flight control surface dampers prevent flutter of the outboard ailerons (see Figure 5-11) or rudder in the event of servo shutdown during flight. Dampers prevent elevator flutter in the event of drive cable failure. On the ground they serve as gust locks. The dampers are identical and interchangeable.

Aileron trim is accomplished by rotating the aileron trim control wheel mounted on the pilots' center console. A torque tube transmits the output to the cable

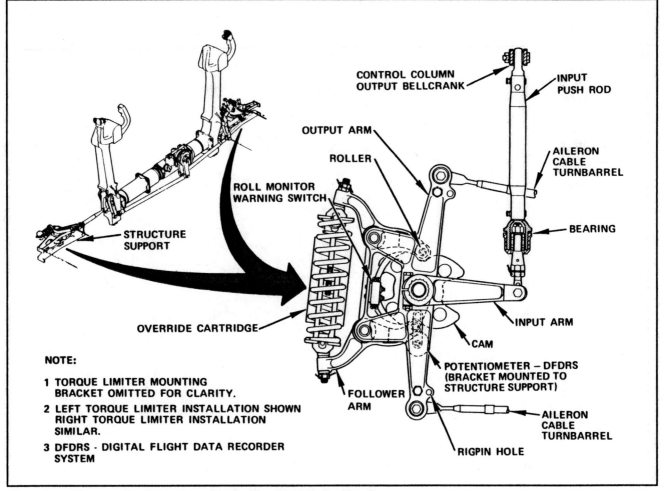

Figure 5-12. Aileron torque limiter assembly, Lockheed L-1011. (Lockheed)

drum. From the cable drum, cables run beneath the cabin floor to the trim actuator (see Figure 5-11).

SURFACE POSITION INDICATOR

The surface position indicator (SPI) monitors the position of the primary flight control surfaces, as shown in Figure 5-13. All roll, pitch, and yaw control surfaces are monitored, but monitoring is only performed for four of the spoiler panels. The inboard ailerons are monitored constantly.

To check the outboard ailerons, the momentary outboard aileron switch, located on the SPI, is pressed. The indicators are driven by synchro transmitters attached to the control surfaces. The trim flags annunciate a position discrepancy in the autotrim system.

SPOILER CONTROL SYSTEM

The spoiler and speed brake control system, illustrated in Figure 5-14, improves roll control, modulates spoiler deflection for direct lift control during approach and landing, and provides aerodynamic braking during flight and after touchdown. Six pairs of spoilers are hydraulically operated by spoiler servo control assemblies.

The primary component of the system is the direct lift control servo (DLCS). It receives inputs from the speed brake control lever or electro-hydraulically from signals in the flight control electronic system. The DLCS is a dual hydraulic unit which drives an output lever and linkages to the left and right mixers and controlex cable to the No. 1 spoiler servo control assemblies. Jam protection bungees are installed in the linkages. The left hand mixer controls both No. 4 spoiler servo control assemblies and also provides inputs into both outboard control selectors. These control the spoiler servo control assemblies for both No. 5 and 6 spoilers. The right hand mixer controls both No. 2 and 3 spoiler servo control assemblies.

STABILIZER CONTROL SYSTEM

The stabilizer is actuated by four separate hydraulic actuators, each powered by a separate hydraulic sys-

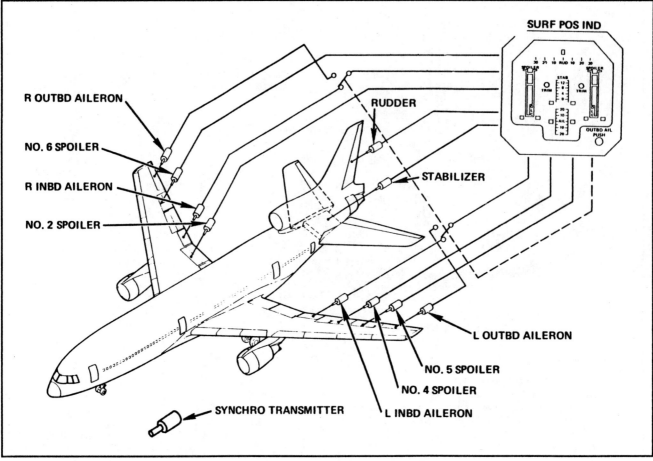

Figure 5-13. Control surface position indicator, functional diagram, L-1011. (Lockheed)

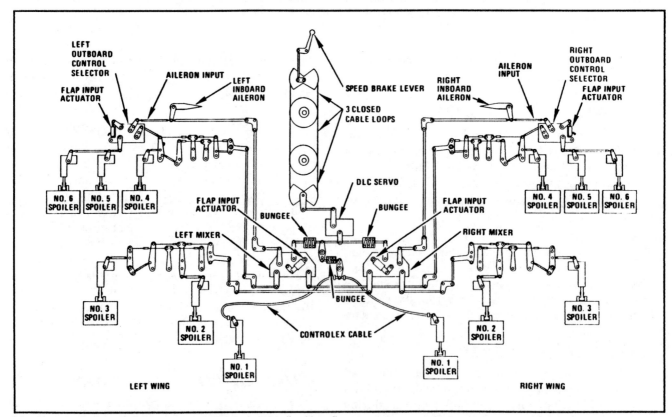

Figure 5-14. Spoiler control system schematic, L-1011. (Lockheed)

tem. Two dual servos, each controlling two separate hydraulic systems, control the pressure to the appropriate stabilizer actuators (see Figure 5-15).

Stabilizer movement is around the two hinges mounted at the stabilizer rear spar. Movement of the stabilizer is transmitted by the elevator drive cables, and moves the elevators in response to stabilizer movement.

Manual control inputs, initiated from the control columns, are transmitted through dual control cable/push rod paths to related dual servos. The override bungees permit movement of the serviceable control path in event the opposite path should jam. Switches mounted at each over-ride bungee, aft disconnect coupler, and cable break detectors, provide advisory indications in the event a control path should jam or break. In addition, in the captain's control path, a rotary damper is provided to dampen feedback oscillations in the control paths.

Stabilizer movement is transmitted back to each dual servo by dual feedback linkages. Each feedback linkage incorporates a self-healing breakout mechanism, which will open should stabilizer movement be transmitted into a jammed control path or servo.

Hydraulic pressure is supplied by systems A, B, C, and D. Systems A and B pressurize the left hand (LH) dual servo and related actuators, with systems C and D pressurizing the right hand (RH) dual servo and related actuators. Autopilot inputs are supplied to the mechanical control paths by a separate autopilot servo utilizing hydraulic systems A and B as pressure sources.

In the event of a pitch system jam, the captain's and first officer's control columns can be disconnected from each other to allow independent motion by pulling the pitch disconnect handle (see Figure 5-15). The handle is mounted forward on the left side of the center console. Pulling the handle up and turning it 90° counterclockwise locks the clutch in the disengaged position and illuminates the PITCH DISC light in the handle.

CABLE TENSION REGULATOR

The cable tension regulator, Figure 5-16, is used to maintain constant tension on the control cables, compensating for length changes resulting from temperature variations, pressurization, and structural deflection. The tension regulator is composed of two cable quadrants, bearing mounted to an output torque shaft.

Splined to the torque shaft is a spindle assembly, which provides a bearing surface for a sliding crosshead. The crosshead assembly can slide on the spindle bearing surface. Each end of the crosshead is link connected to one of the cable quadrants. Two compression springs extend from the spindle pivot link to the crosshead, exerting an outward force.

This force maintains 100-120 pounds of tension on each cable, as long as no control force is applied and the crosshead is free to slide on the spindle shaft. Slack take-up units are incorporated in the links between the crosshead and the cable quadrants.

ELEVATOR CONTROL SYSTEM

The elevators are actuated by horizontal stabilizer movement through a cable system, as shown in Figure 5-17. The cable system consists of a nylon covered drive cable attached to the aircraft structure and the aft side of the aft drive quadrant. A nylon covered return cable is also attached to the structure and aft drive quadrant.

The forward cable quadrants are located inside the horizontal stabilizer center section. The aft drive quadrant is located just outside the center section in the horizontal stabilizer trailing edge area. A pushrod on top of the aft drive quadrant connects the elevator with the cable control system.

The elevator is hinged, with the cable control system, to the horizontal stabilizer by nine hinges, and balanced by thirteen balance weights to prevent flutter in case of a free elevator. Horizontal stabilizer motion moves the forward cable quadrants which change the cable position rotating the aft drive quadrant. The pushrod thereby deflects the elevator.

RUDDER SYSTEM

Manual rudder control inputs are initiated by either the captain's or the first officer's rudder pedals, and are transmitted by a single cable loop to a quadrant located in the afterbody, as can be seen in Figure 5-18.

At the quadrant, the motion is transmitted by pushrod to the rudder control bellcrank and from that point by pushrod to the rudder servo and the rudder feel/trim bungee. The rudder servo supplies pressure from hydraulic systems A, B, and C to a pair of dual tandem actuators.

Autopilot inputs from the avionic flight control system (AFCS) are supplied to a pair of servo-mounted electro-hydraulic control valves for driving the rudder in

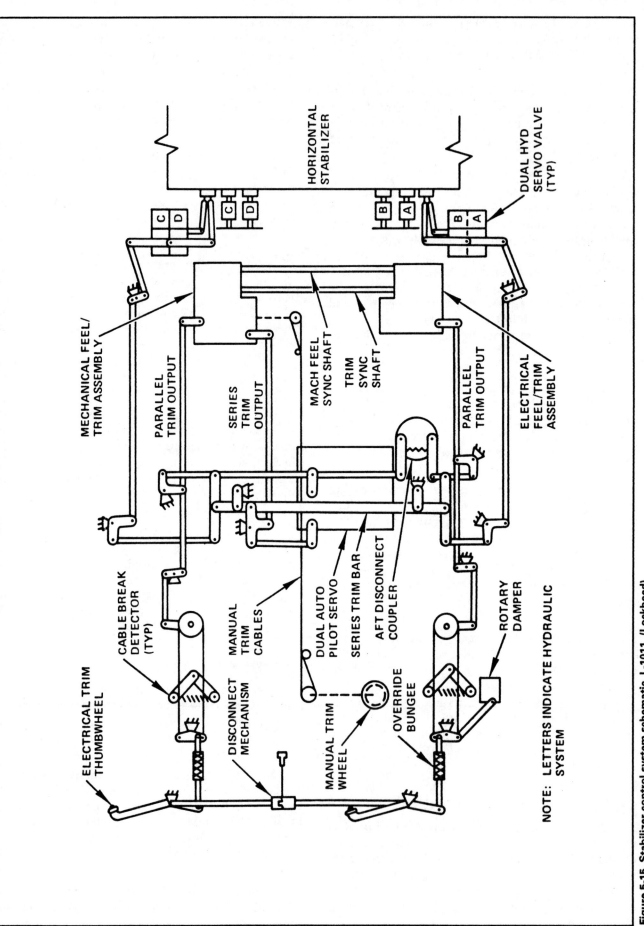

Figure 5-15. Stabilizer control system schematic, L-1011. (Lockheed)

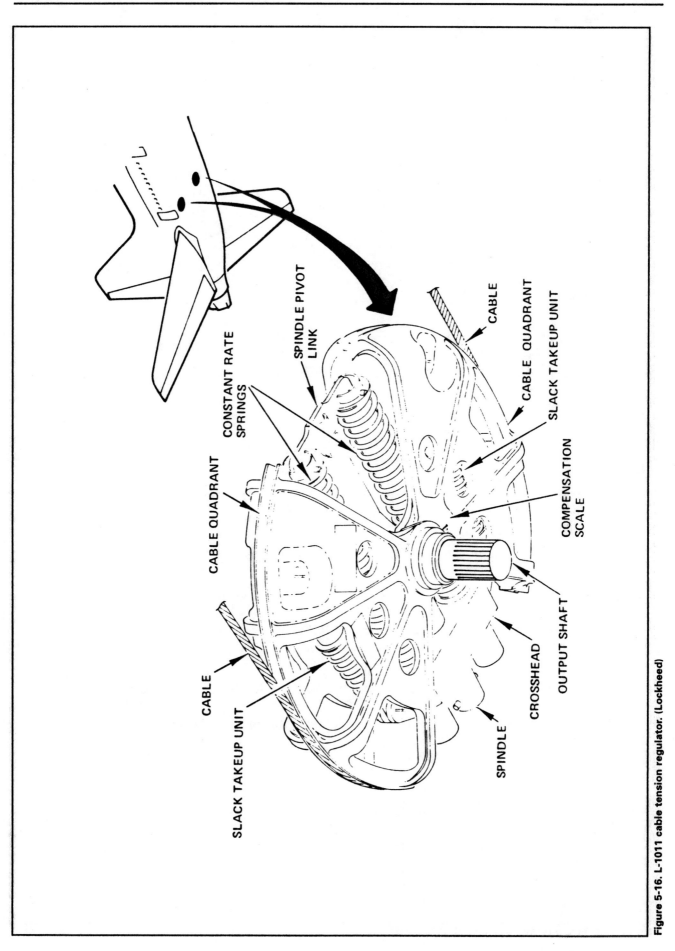

Figure 5-16. L-1011 cable tension regulator. (Lockheed)

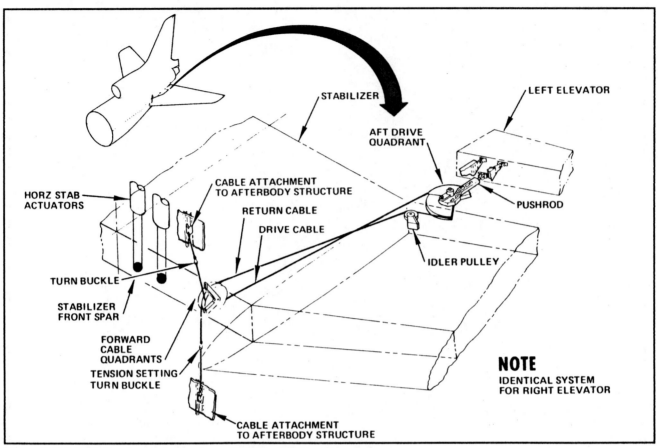

Figure 5-17. L-1011 elevator control system schematic. (Lockheed)

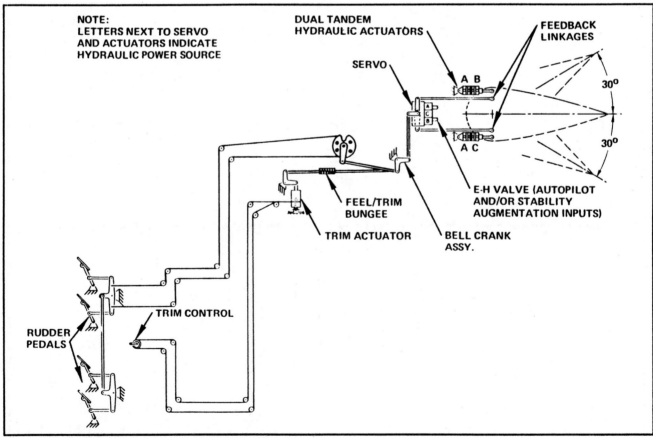

Figure 5-18. Rudder system schematic, L-1011. (Lockheed)

autopilot modes. Rudder travel is limited by a hydraulic pressure limiting system which decreases the effective force being applied to the rudder. Hydraulic limiting is achieved automatically as a function of airspeed.

Rudder trim is initiated from the rudder trim control at the flight station and is transmitted by a cable loop to the rudder trim actuator. Movement of the trim actuator changes the neutral position of the rudder feel/trim bungee and thus transmits motions into the rudder control path.

FLAP SYSTEM

Manual control of the flaps is initiated from the flap control handle, as shown in Figure 5-19. Motion is transmitted by cable loops and dual pushrods to the load relieving actuator.

Cable break detectors are installed on the cable loop and should a cable break, the detection switches will shut off hydraulic pressure at the power drive unit, thus stopping the flaps.

The load relieving actuator, in conjunction with inputs from the load relieving system (LRS) computer, functions to limit flap extension to 28° when airspeed is greater than 164 knots, regardless of flap position selected.

The flaps are driven by a dual hydraulic motor power drive unit (PDU). The PDU receives hydraulic power from hydraulic systems A and C. Initial input to the flap PDU is by mechanical linkage from the flight station flap control handle to the PDU input lever.

The start-up switches de-energize the hydraulic shut-off valves to port fluid to release the brake and to operate the motors. As the output shaft reaches the selected position, the feedback mechanism gradually repositions the control spool to the null position, causing the motors to stop and the brake to be applied.

From the PDU the flaps are driven by a series of torque shafts and actuator jackscrews. Initially the torque is applied through the aft angle gearboxes which incorporates a torque limiting brake. The brake will stall the PDU if applied torque is 20% greater than normal operating torque. Each actuator (two for each flap segment) drives the actuator jackscrews, actuating the flap and flap vane.

A position transmitter, an asymmetry brake, and an asymmetry transducer are installed on the outboard end of each drive train. Their purpose is to provide flap position inputs to the flap position indicator at the pilots' center instrument panel.

The asymmetry brake is used to stop drive train rotation in case of a drive train overspeed, or if a flap asymmetry condition is detected by the flap asymmetry comparator. The asymmetry transducers provide flap position inputs to the flap asymmetry comparator.

Should an asymmetrical flap condition occur (split flaps), the comparator will shut down the PDU and stop drive train rotation by applying the asymmetry brakes.

SLAT SYSTEM

The leading edge slat system comprises seven slats on each wing (see Figure 5-20). Three slats are located inboard of the engine pylon, and four slats are located outboard of the pylon.

Manual control of the slats is initiated from the flap control lever. Motion is transmitted through the cable loop, shared by the flap control system, to the flap/slat quadrant.

From the quadrant, motion is transmitted by the slat cable loop/pushrod to the slat PDU. The cable loops incorporate break detectors performing the same functions as those described in the flap system. If a cable should break, the slat PDU would be shut down.

The slat PDU is driven by dual hydraulic motors receiving hydraulic pressure from systems A and C. Each slat is operated by a single jack-screw type actuator as seen in Figure 5-21. The inboards extend 28° while the outboards travel 30°.

All the actuators are driven through a common torque tube drive train by the PDU located in the left wing root forward edge. The torque brakes on the left side absorb initial start torque. Angle gearboxes direct the torque tube drive from the fuselage to the wings.

An asymmetry control system is provided to shut down the PDU and hold the panels in position when an asymmetrical condition develops. The asymmetry brake, located at the outboard end of each torque drive, uses a rotary transducer to limit slat asymmetry to approximately 6°. The asymmetry comparator is located in the mid electrical service center (MESC).

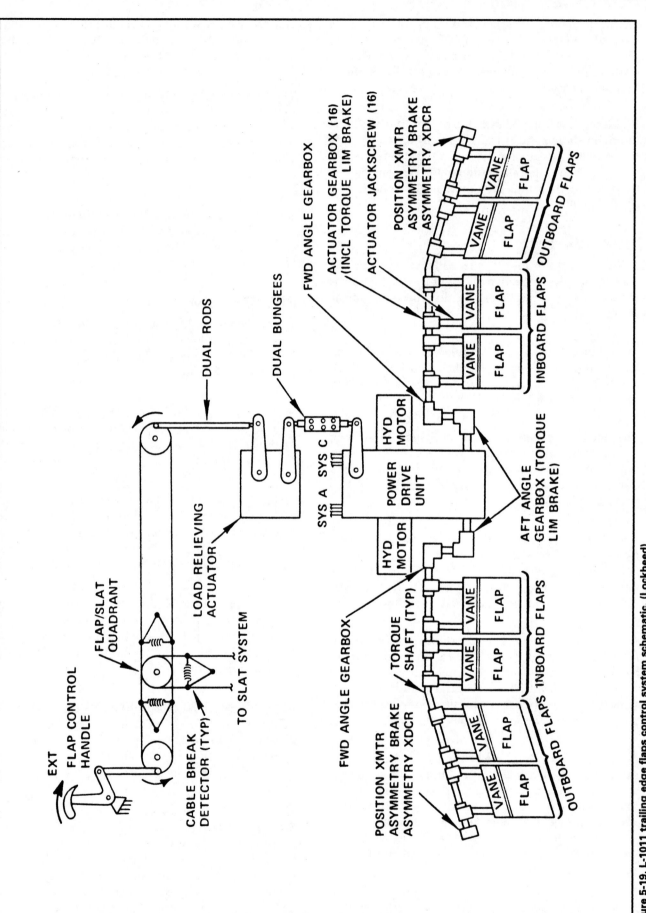

Figure 5-19. L-1011 trailing edge flaps control system schematic. (Lockheed)

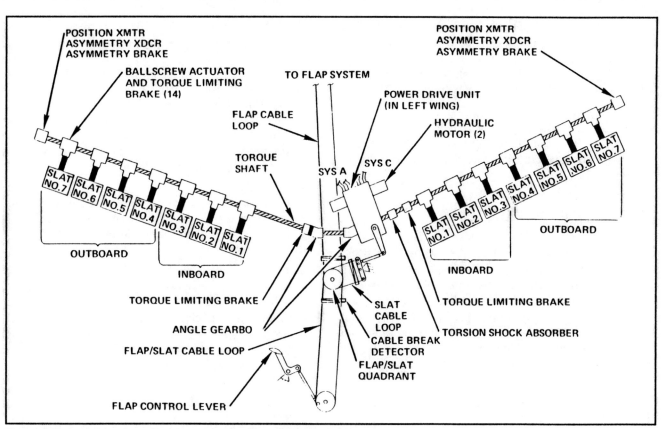

Figure 5-20. L-1011 leading edge slat control system schematic. (Lockheed)

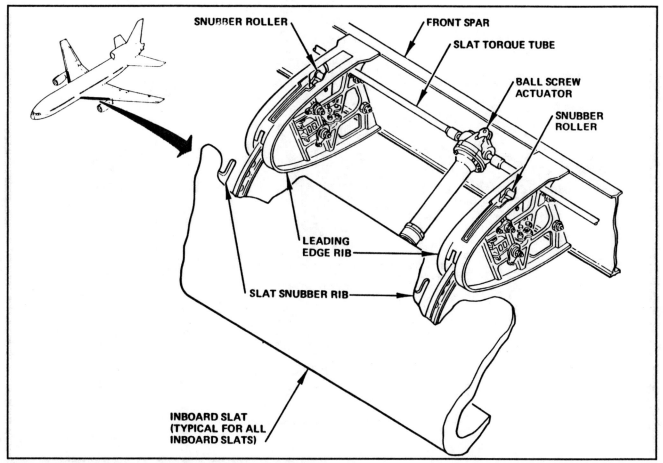

Figure 5-21. Inboard leading edge slat installation. (Lockheed)

Control of the slat PDU is by cable path from the flap control handle at the flight station through the flap/slat quadrant located in the MESC. Movement of the flap control handle will allow the slat quadrant to move during the first 4° of handle movement.

The slats are normally fully extended or retracted. When the slats reach their full travel, switches in the PDU energize the shutoff valves which close and shut down the PDU.

SLAT MONITOR PANELS

The slat position indicator, shown in Figure 5-22, is mounted in the slat monitor panel at the FE station. The left wing transmitter drives the pointer marked L; the right wing transmitter drives the pointer marked R. Leading edge slat proximity switches sense individual slat extension and illuminate the slat monitor panel extend lights. The proximity logic box controls the operation of the LE TRANS and the LE EXT lights on the flap position indicator.

AIRBUS A320 FLIGHT CONTROL (FLY-BY-WIRE) SYSTEM

The flight control surfaces of the Airbus Industrie A320 aircraft are shown in Figure 5-23. The A320 incorporates a fly-by-wire flight control system. A fly-by-wire system uses electrical signals instead of cables to cause the flight control surfaces to move. A series of redundant electrical flight control computers control the aircraft flight control surfaces.

Two types of electrical flight control computers installed are the elevator and aileron computer (ELAC) and the spoiler and elevator computer (SEC).

The primary functions of the two computers are to control the aileron, the elevator and the trimmable horizontal stabilizer (THS), and to provide spoiler control and alternate control of elevators and the THS. The two computers of the ELAC are installed, each of them achieving control and monitoring of one servojack (actuator) on each aileron and elevator, as well as control and

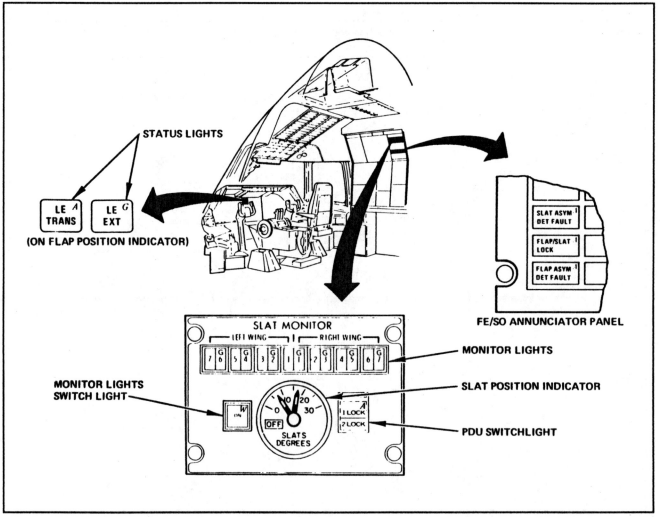

Figure 5-22. L-1011 slat monitor panels. (Lockheed)

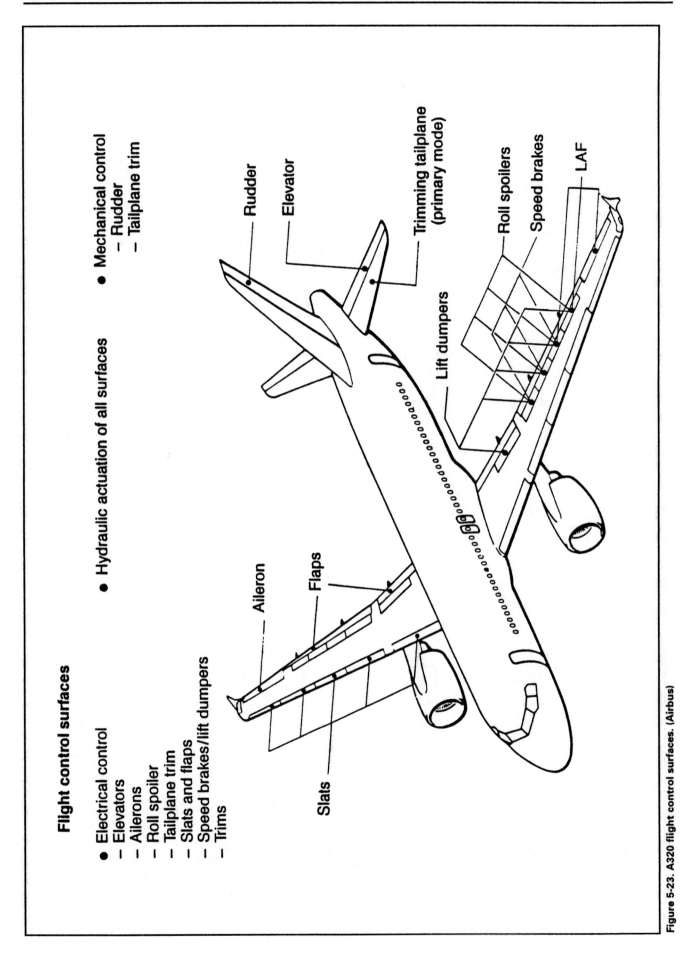

Flight control surfaces

- **Electrical control**
  - Elevators
  - Ailerons
  - Roll spoiler
  - Tailplane trim
  - Slats and flaps
  - Speed brakes/lift dumpers
  - Trims

- **Hydraulic actuation of all surfaces**

- **Mechanical control**
  - Rudder
  - Tailplane trim

Rudder

Elevator

Trimming tailplane (primary mode)

Roll spoilers

Speed brakes

LAF

Lift dumpers

Aileron

Flaps

Slats

Figure 5-23. A320 flight control surfaces. (Airbus)

monitoring of one of the three electric motors of the THS actuator in normal (electrical) operating mode.

Three computers of the SEC type achieve control and monitoring of the spoiler servojacks (actuators). In addition, the SECs provide alternate control for the elevators and the electric motors of the THS actuator.

Two flight control data concentrators (FCDC) are installed, achieving maintenance and data concentration functions. On the cockpit overhead panel, one OFF/ON reset push-button for each ELAC and SEC is installed.

HYDRAULIC AND ELECTRICAL POWER SUPPLY

Hydraulic power to the flight control system is simultaneously provided by three independent hydraulic systems identified by the colors blue, green and yellow, as shown in Figure 5-24. Priority valves are fitted within common hydraulic lines supplying large actuators to give priority to the primary flight controls. This eliminates any operational reduction after a single hydraulic failure in flight.

EFCS electrical supply is ensured in normal operation from 28 VDC. EFCS electrical emergency supply is ensured by the essential bus supplied from an emergency generator which is driven from the blue hydraulic circuit.

The blue hydraulic circuit is pressurized by the ram air turbine (RAT) in emergency conditions. Batteries are provided to maintain 28 VDC on the essential bus during transients. In the event of a total loss of the main electrical generation system, the emergency generator will automatically supply the emergency equipment. Batteries will take over and supply power when the landing gear is selected to the down position.

ROLL CONTROL

Roll control is provided on each wing by one aileron augmented by four roll spoilers mounted on the upper wing surfaces, as mentioned earlier.

Surface controls are actuated by independently supplied, electrically signaled, hydraulic servojacks. Surface position is based on signals from the sidestick controllers processed by the electrical flight control computers, illustrated in Figure 5-25.

Each upper wing surface is powered by one servojack. Servojacks are controlled by biased servo valves which use a monitoring system to detect any system failure.

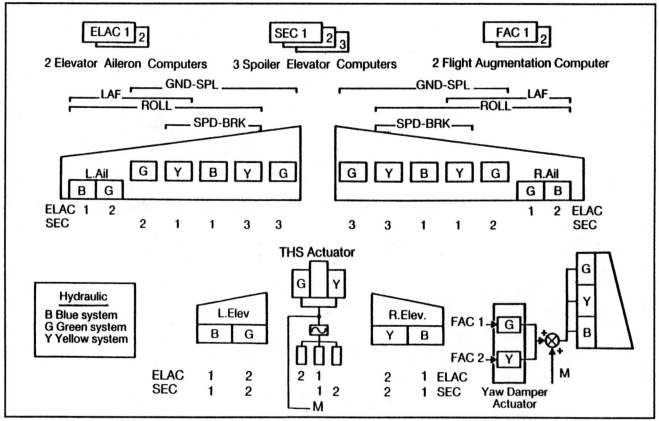

Figure 5-24. Electrical flight control system power, A320. (Airbus)

A detected system failure will cause the servojack to fully retract.

Two servojacks are installed on each aileron. In normal operation only one servojack is in active mode; the other one being in dampening mode. If the active servojack fails, the dampened one becomes active and the failed jack is switched automatically to the dampening mode.

Servojack position for feedback and monitoring purposes is provided by a linear variable differential transducer (LVDT), which is integrated in the power stage of the servojack.

Autopilot orders received from the two flight management and guidance computers (FMGC) are automatically integrated via the electrical flight control system. Wing gust load alleviation is achieved by aileron and spoiler deflections. The load alleviation function (LAF), which will be described later, is accomplished by the electrical flight control computers.

PITCH CONTROL

Pitch control is provided by the trimmable horizontal stabilizer (THS) and two elevators hinged on the stabilizer. Each elevator is actuated by independently supplied, electrically signaled, hydraulic servojacks, shown in Figure 5-26.

Surface position is based on signals from the sidestick controllers processed by the electrical flight control computers. Two servojacks are installed on each elevator. As with roll control, one servojack is in the active mode with the other one being in the dampening mode.

In case of a servojack failure, functions reverse. In the event of total electrical control loss, the servojacks are automatically switched to a centering mode and will hold the surface in the neutral position.

Servojack position feedback and monitoring is provided in much the same manner as the ailerons except for the use of the rotary variable differential transducers (RVDT) installed on the servojack and on the surfaces.

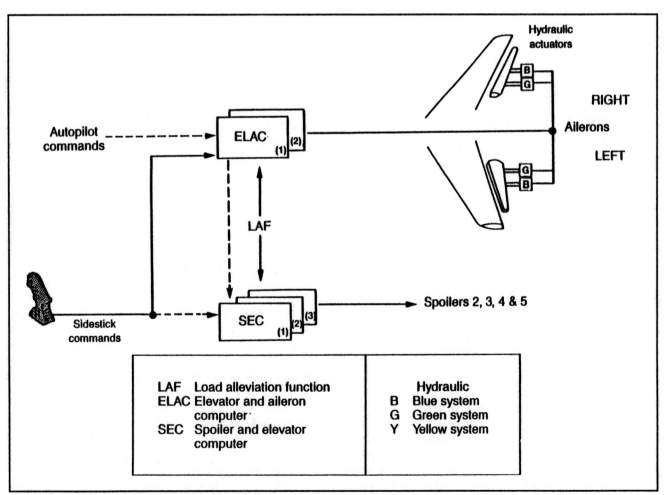

Figure 5-25. A320 roll control aileron system. (Airbus)

Autopilot orders received from the two FMGSs are automatically integrated via the electrical flight control computers into the electrical flight control system.

Pitch trim is provided by adjustment of the THS. Pitch trim is signaled automatically in the normal operating mode. Manual means of controlling the THS are provided from interconnected handwheels located on the center pedestal. The mechanical control is capable of overriding the electrical control.

The THS is actuated by a fail-safe ball screw-jack driven by two independently supplied hydraulic motors and coupled by a dual load path differential gear. Electrical and automatic trim signals are processed by the electrical flight control computers and control three electric motors (in normal operation only one motor is active). The electric motors drive the control linkage to the hydraulic valves which control the hydraulic motors.

The single mechanical trim wheel run is connected to the same linkage. On the center pedestal, adjacent to each trim wheel, trimmable horizontal stabilizer position is indicated by an index on a scale.

YAW CONTROL

Yaw control is provided by a single piece rudder actuated by three independently supplied hydraulic servojacks. They are signaled via interconnected pedals by a single cable run up to a spring loaded artificial feel unit connected to the trim screw-jacks. The commands are transmitted by a single load path linkage fitted with a centering spring device. This holds the servojack inputs in the neutral position should a disconnect occur. Rudder travel is limited as a function of air speed (CAS).

Orders are delivered by the flight augmentation computer (FAC) controlling electric motors coupled to a variable mechanical stop, as illustrated in Figure 5-27.

Yaw dampening is operative throughout the whole flight envelope. Yaw damper commands are transmitted via a differential unit. Yaw stability augmentation orders are delivered by the FACs.

Artificial feel is provided by a spring rod, the zero force position of which being controlled by an electrical trim actuator. An automatic reset function initiated by pressing the RESET push-button allows the rudder trim position to be nulled through the FACs. Rudder trim position is displayed on an indicator adjacent to the trim switch.

SPEED BRAKE/GROUND SPOILER CONTROL

There are three speed brakes located on the upper surface of each wing. The basic arrangement of the speed brakes, ground spoilers, and roll augmentation spoilers is shown in Figure 5-24. The speed brakes are selected by a lever situated on the center pedestal.

Each speed brake surface is powered by one servojack controlled by the corresponding electrical flight control computer, which is also used for roll spoiler. All upper wing surfaces are used as ground spoilers during landing. They are automatically extended after touchdown when specific ground conditions are fulfilled.

Example conditions are the selection of one engine thrust reverser or the speed brake lever being armed to the deploy position. This condition is also dependent on both engines' thrust levers being below idle and the aircraft must be on the ground.

ELECTRICAL FLIGHT CONTROL SYSTEM (EFCS)

The electrical flight control computers are designed to ensure a high degree of safety. This is accomplished by using a high level of redundancy, which consists of five EFCS computers installed in the aircraft. The use of dissimilar redundancy which consists of two types of computers, with each being capable of achieving pitch and roll control along with other redundant features assuring aircraft control.

Each computer is also composed of one control unit and one monitoring unit. Control and monitoring software are different and the control and monitoring units are physically separated.

MONITORING

In each computer, one monitoring channel is associated to a control channel by use of self monitored channels. Each computer is able to detect its own failures (microprocessor test, electrical power monitoring, input and output test). Input monitoring by comparison of signals of the same type, but sent by different sources, and checking of the signal coherence along with permanent cross talk between associated control and monitoring channels, consolidate, and validate information received. This allows permanent monitoring of each channel by its associated one. Automatic test sequences can be performed on the ground when electric and hydraulic power are applied (no surface deflection during test).

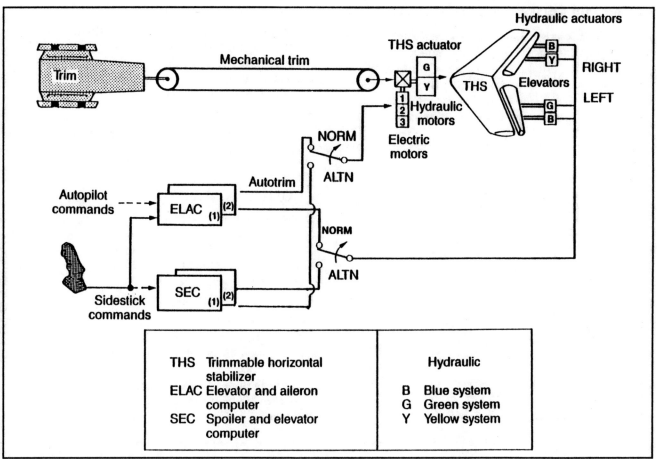

Figure 5-26. A320 pitch control elevator system, A320. (Airbus)

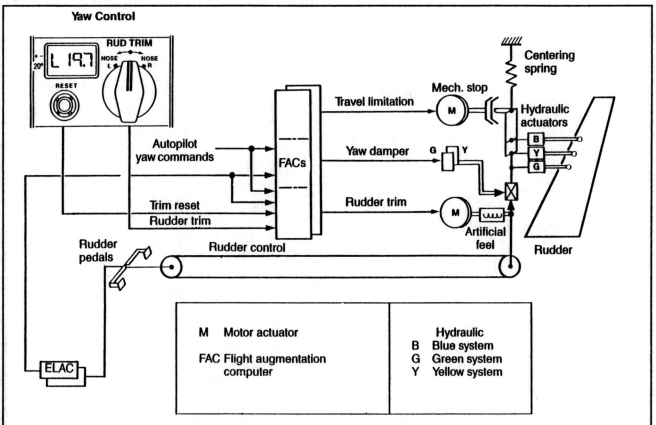

Figure 5-27. A320 yaw control rudder system. (Airbus)

SIDESTICK CONTROLLER

The sidestick controllers are used for pitch and roll manual control (see Figure 5-28). The sidestick controllers are installed on the captain's and first officer's forward lateral consoles. An adjustable arm rest is fitted on each seat to facilitate the sidestick control. The sidestick controllers are electrically coupled.

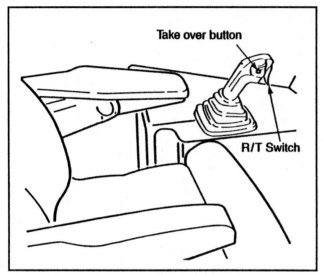

Figure 5-28. Sidestick controller, A320. (Airbus)

In the case of one pilot wanting to take control of the aircraft (priority), the autopilot instinctive disconnect button is used to signal the priority system. A visual indication is given to the pilots to indicate left or right sidestick priority. In autopilot operation the sidestick controllers remain in neutral position.

The autopilot function can be overridden by the pilots and the autopilot then disengages.

CONTROL LAWS

Normal control laws selected for A320 pitch and lateral control are maneuver command laws with normal acceleration and roll rates used as basic parameters. Inside the normal flight envelope, the main features are a neutral static stability, short term attitude stability, along with automatic longitudinal trimming.

The flight characteristics that can be controlled are the automatic elevator in a turn, lateral attitude hold in a turn, Dutch roll dampening, turn coordination, and engine failure compensation. In addition, protections are provided against extreme attitudes (pitch and roll), excessive load factors, overspeed, and stall.

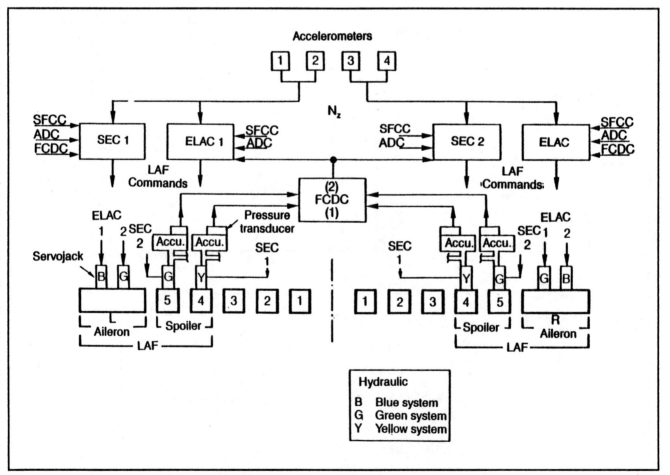

Figure 5-29. Load alleviation function, A320. (Airbus)

LOAD ALLEVIATION FUNCTION (LAF)

The load alleviation function is accomplished by the electrical flight control system (EFCS). The LAF is implemented in the elevator and aileron computer (ELAC) and the spoiler elevator computer (SEC). The control surfaces used are both ailerons as well as spoilers 4 and 5 (i.e. the outboard pair on both sides) for up gusts.

There are four specific accelerometers that are installed in the forward fuselage station to provide the electrical flight control computers (FCU) with vertical acceleration values. These sense the up gust and deploy the spoilers to smooth out the normal result of an up gust of wind as described in the before mentioned example.

Four hydraulic accumulators are installed to provide the extra hydraulic flow needed to achieve the surface rates and duration of movement required for load alleviation as illustrated in Figure 5-29.

HIGH LIFT CONTROL SYSTEM

High lift augmentation is achieved on each wing by the five leading edge slats, in conjunction with the two single element Fowler flaps, as shown in Figure 5-30. The slats and flaps are electrically signaled.

The position of the slat and flap control lever is signaled via a command sensor unit (CSU) to two identical digital computers (slat flap control computer, SFCC). The slat and flap drive systems are controlled and monitored by the SFCC, each of which controls one slat and one flap hydraulic motor. Position feedback, instrumentation, and recording is provided by position pick-off units (PPU) located at the power control unit (PCU) of each drive system, illustrated in Figure 5-30.

The slat and flap drive system consists of two similar hydromechanical systems, each comprising two hydraulic motors, differential gear and transverse torque shafts operating the slats and flaps through

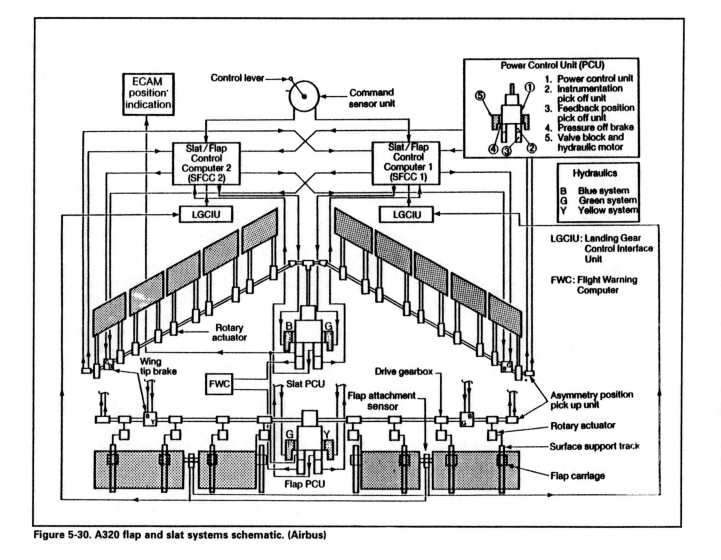

Figure 5-30. A320 flap and slat systems schematic. (Airbus)

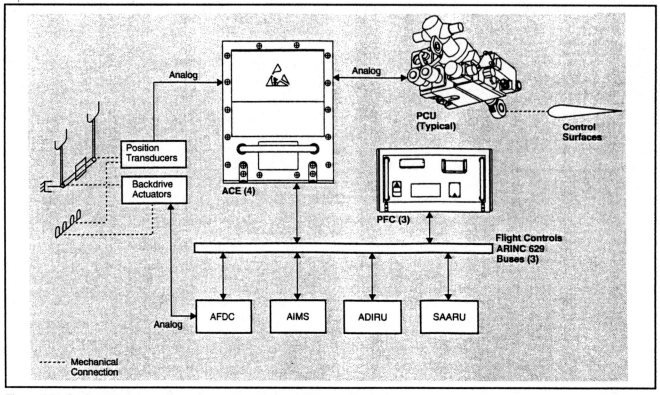

Figure 5-31. Boeing 777 primary control system operational diagram. (Boeing)

rotary actuators. Wing tip brakes (WTB) installed within the torque shaft system, controlled by the SFCCs prevent asymmetric operation, blow back, runaway, or overspeed. A pressure off brake is provided between each hydraulic motor of the PCU and the differential gear to lock the transmission system when the slat or flap system is static.

Position pick-off units (PPUs) at each end of the torque shafts are used for both detection of asymmetric operation of the surfaces and for system monitoring.

BOEING 777 FLIGHT CONTROL (FLY-BY-WIRE) SYSTEM

Two separate flight control systems control the airplane; the primary flight control system (PFC) and the high lift control system (HLCS). The PFC and the HLCS are electronic "fly-by-wire" systems. The PFC supplies roll, pitch, and yaw control through ailerons, flappers, elevators, rudder, and horizontal stabilizer while the HLCS uses inboard and outboard trailing edge flaps, leading edge slats, and Krueger flaps.

The PFC is a modern, three-axis, fly-by-wire system which permits a more efficient aircraft structural design. The PFCS supplies manual and automatic airplane control and flight control law envelope protection in all three axes. There is stability augmentation in the roll, pitch, and yaw axis. The PFCS calculates

commands to position the control surfaces using sensor inputs from the control wheel, control column, rudder pedals, speed-brake lever, and pitch trim switches.

The control surfaces include two ailerons, two flaperons, and fourteen spoilers for roll control. There are two elevators and a moveable horizontal stabilizer for pitch trim control, and a tabbed rudder for yaw control. Position transducers (see Figure 5-31) convert the flight crew commands of the control wheels, the control columns, the rudder pedals, and the speed-brake lever to analog electrical signals. These signals go to the actuator control electronics (ACEs). The ACEs convert the signals to digital format and send them to the primary flight computers (PFCs). The PFCs communicate with the airplane systems through the three flight controls ARINC 629 buses. The PFCs use mid-value evaluation to reject a hard or passive failure of input signals.

In addition to command signals from the ACEs, the PFCs also receive data from the aircraft information management system (AIMS), air data inertial reference unit (ADIRU) and secondary attitude air data reference unit (SAARU). These signals are airspeed data, inertial reference data, angle of attack and flap position. The PFCs calculate the flight control commands based on control laws, augmentation and envelope protections. The digital command signals from the PFCs go to the

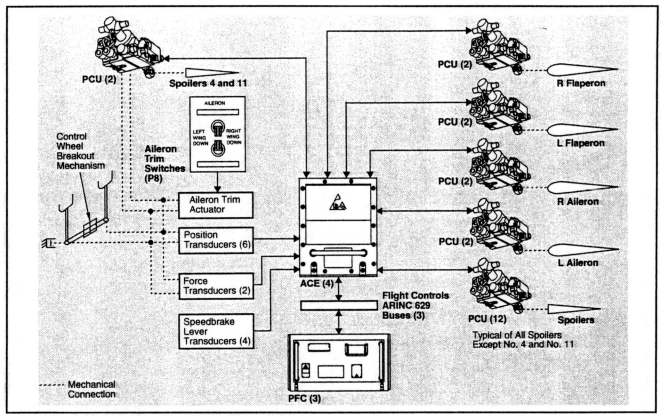

Figure 5-32. Boeing 777 PFCS roll control system. (Boeing)

ACEs. The ACEs change these command signals to analog format before sending them to the power control units (PCUs). One, two, or three PCUs operate each control surface. The PCUs contain a hydraulic actuator, and electro-hydraulic servo-valve, and a position feedback transducer.

When commanded, the servo-valve causes the hydraulic actuator to move the control surface. The position transducer sends a position feedback signal to the ACEs. After conversion to digital format, the ACEs send the signal to the PFCs. The PFCs stop the PCU command when the position feedback signal equals the commanded position. The PFCs receive autopilot commands from the three autopilot flight director computers (AFDCs). The PFCs calculate and output the flight control commands in the same manner as explained before. In addition, the PFCs supply the backdrive signals to the backdrive actuators through the AFDCs. The backdrive actuators move the control wheels, control columns and rudder pedals in synchronization with the autopilot commands. The movement of the flight deck controls provides visual cues to the flight crew.

The PFCS has three modes of operation: normal, secondary, and direct. All control laws and protection functions are active in the normal mode. The control laws calculate commands for roll, yaw, and pitch con-

trol. The protection functions include stall warning, overspeed, overyaw, and bank angle. The autopilot operates only in the normal mode. It cannot be engaged in the secondary or direct mode. The PFCS switches automatically to the secondary mode if the PFCS detects a loss of important sensor data. The secondary mode operates the same as the normal mode except that some of the protection functions are not available. In the direct mode, position transducer signals (pilot commands) go directly to the ACEs and to the PCUs. The PFCs do not operate in this mode.

A cable system connects the two control wheels through a breakout mechanism. Each control wheel moves three independent position transducers. There are force transducers to detect a pilot override during autopilot operation. A mechanical feel and centering mechanism supplies feel forces to the control wheels.

When the flaps extend, the ailerons and flaperons move down (droop) to increase lift. When drooped, the ailerons and flaperons continue to supply roll control, as shown in Figure 5-32. During high speed flight, the PFCs fair the ailerons to the wing and lock out their operation. At low speed, the PFCs unlock the ailerons and command their operation.

The speed-brake lever on the control stand moves a multiple channel speed-brake transducer. In flight, the

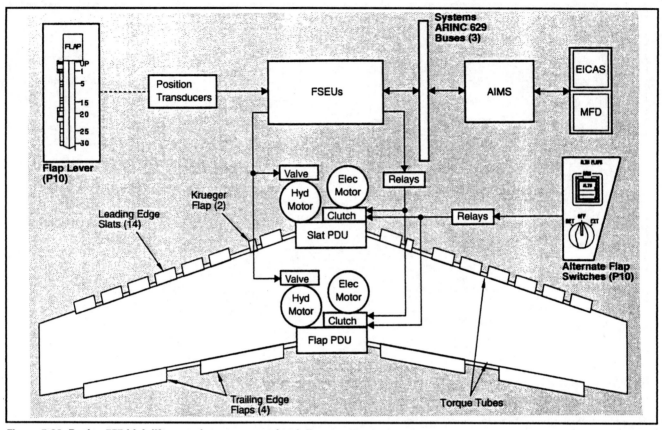

Figure 5-33. Boeing 777 high lift control system operational diagram. (Boeing)

PFCs command the speed-brakes to extend based on the speed-brake lever movement, airspeed and altitude. At high speed, the PFCs prevent the operation of some spoilers. When the airplane lands, the auto speed-brake actuator automatically moves the speed-brake lever to cause the spoilers to fully deploy.

The rudder controls the yaw attitude of the airplane. Linkages connect the two pairs of rudder pedals. Each pair of pedals moves two independent position transducers. The PFCs calculate the rudder authority based on airspeed. At low airspeed, the rudder has full authority. As airspeed increases, the PFCs gradually reduce the rudder authority. In flight, the PFCs send command signals to the ACEs and the PCUs for Dutch roll damping and turn coordination. There is no separate yaw damper unit.

The gust suppression function increases passenger comfort. When a side gust hits the vertical tail, the gust suppression pressure transducers send signals to the ACEs. The ACEs send this data to the PFCs to adjust the rudder PCU commands to dampen the force of the side gust.

The horizontal stabilizer is a one piece airfoil. It pivots at its rear spar. A ball-screw actuator, attached to the front spar, moves the stabilizer leading edge to a maximum of 4° up and 11° down. Two hydraulic motors, powered by different hydraulic power sources, cause the ball-screw actuator to move. Two stabilizer trim control modules (STCMs) receive commands from the ACEs to control the hydraulic pressure to the motors and brakes. A shutoff valve, on each STCM, stops hydraulic power when the appropriate cutout switch is moved. A cable driven system is installed that controls two spoilers and the stabilizer. The pilots use two alternate pitch trim levers and a set of cables to mechanically control the stabilizer. Two alternate pitch trim levers on the control stand connect to valves on each stabilizer trim control module (STCM). Moving both levers in the same direction at the same time sets valves in the STCM. This sends hydraulic fluid to the hydraulic motors to move the stabilizer.

The PFCs do a self-test and a test of the ACEs each time power is applied to the system. The flight controls synoptic page gives the flight crew a graphical overview of the flight control system. The display includes primary flight control surface positions, failures, and the current flight control mode. Trim position of the stabilizer and rudder are shown in degrees. The synoptic page helps the flight crew understand the impact of flight control

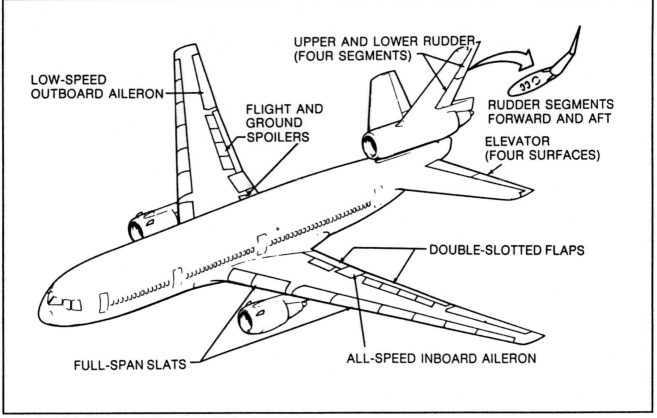

LOW-SPEED OUTBOARD AILERON

UPPER AND LOWER RUDDER (FOUR SEGMENTS)

RUDDER SEGMENTS FORWARD AND AFT

FLIGHT AND GROUND SPOILERS

ELEVATOR (FOUR SURFACES)

DOUBLE-SLOTTED FLAPS

ALL-SPEED INBOARD AILERON

FULL-SPAN SLATS

Figure 5-34. DC-10 flight control surfaces. (McDonnell Douglas)

system failures. There are three maintenance pages provided. Maintenance personnel can access the maintenance pages for functions, such as rigging, and checking the discrete outputs from the PFCS components.

The high lift control system (HLCS), shown in Figure 5-33, extends and retracts the leading and trailing edge devices. The leading edge slat system has seven slats and one Krueger flap on each wing. The slats have three positions: cruise (retracted), takeoff (sealed), and landing (gapped). The Krueger flap has only two positions: retracted and deployed.

Hydraulic or electric motors on the slat power drive unit (PDU) turn the slat torque tubes which drive the slat rotary actuators to extend and retract the slats. The trailing edge flaps have an inboard double slotted flap and an outboard single slotted flap on each wing. Hydraulic or electric motors on the flap PDU turn the flap torque tubes which drive the flap ball-screw transmissions. Two identical and interchangeable flap/slat electronic units (FSEUs), in the main equipment center, process the high lift commands. There are also two position transducers at each end of the slat torque tube drive lines and on each side of the flap PDU. These transducers supply the flap/slat positions to the FSEUs for control and monitoring.

MCDONNELL DOUGLAS DC-10

The aerodynamic configuration of the DC-10 (see Figure 5-34) uses a two position, full span, leading edge slat and a large chord, double slotted, trailing edge flap for optimum climb lift-to-drag ratios and low approach speeds.

The wing sweep of 35° and the airfoil section characteristics are the primary factors which produce efficient cruise characteristics at high Mach numbers.

The DC-10 has large chord trailing edge flaps coupled with full span leading edge slats to form the high lift system. The large chord, double slotted, trailing edge flaps provide a vane/flap shape and wing/vane flap for both takeoff and landing.

The flaps incorporate a nesting vane feature to provide a large chord when the flaps are extended. An example of a slotted flap is shown in Figure 5-35. The flap on each wing is separated by an all speed inboard aileron, located behind the engine, permitting separation of the inboard and outboard flaps.

The full span leading edge slats provide good stall characteristics and stall progression by proper tailor-

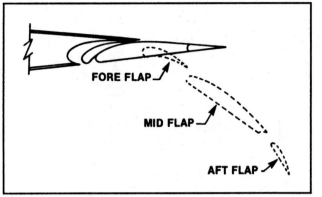

Figure 5-35. A triple-slotted flap.

ing of the slat configuration. The outboard slats extend automatically during a stall warning to provide good stall characteristics in the clean wing configuration.

For the high lift configurations, two extended slat positions are provided. The intermediate position is used for best climb performance in the takeoff configuration. The fully extended flap position is used to provide maximum lift in the landing configuration.

CHAPTER 5 STUDY QUESTIONS

1. List the axes that an aircraft moves around.

    _____

    _____

2. List the primary flight controls and their functions.

    _____

    _____

    _____

3. How are most large aircraft primary flight controls powered?

    _____

    _____

    _____

4. List and tell the functions of each secondary flight control on the Boeing 727 aircraft.

    _____

    _____

5. Describe how the pilots can monitor the aircrafts control surface position.

    _____

    _____

    _____

6. Explain the various uses of the spoiler system during the different flight and landing modes.

    _____

    _____

    _____

7. What is the purpose of a cable tension regulator?

    _____

    _____

    _____

8. Why is a cable tension regulator needed on some large aircraft?

    _____

    _____

9. Describe the term "fly-by-wire" as it applies to the Airbus A320 aircraft.

    _____

    _____

    _____

10. List the flight controls that are considered to be high lift devices.

    _____

    _____

11. Describe the operation of a triple-slotted trailing edge flap.

   _____

   _____

12. When and for what purpose are the leading-edge devices (slats) used?

   _____

   _____

13. What happens if an asymmetrical trailing edge flap condition occurs?

   _____

   _____

14. Describe the operation of the PFCS on the Boeing 777.

   _____

   _____

   _____

15. What do the terms ACEs and PFCs refer to on the Boeing 777?

   _____

   _____

   _____

CHAPTER 6

FUEL SYSTEMS

TURBINE ENGINE FUELS

Large transport aircraft use turbofan gas turbine engines which are designed to operate on a distillate fuel, commonly called jet fuel. Jet fuels are also composed of hydrocarbons with a little more carbon and usually a higher sulfur content than gasoline. Inhibitors may be added to reduce corrosion and oxidation. Anti-icing additives are also being blended to prevent fuel icing.

Three types of jet fuel in use today are: (1) Kerosene grade turbine fuel, now named Jet A; and (2) a blend of gasoline and kerosene fractions, designated Jet B. (3) A third type, called Jet A-1, made for operation at extremely low temperatures. Jet A and Jet B are the most common.

Both Jet A and Jet B fuels are blends of heavy distillates and tend to absorb water. The specific gravity of jet fuels, especially kerosene, is closer to water than aviation gasoline; thus, any water introduced into the fuel, either through refueling or condensation, will take an appreciable time to settle out. At high altitudes, where low temperatures are encountered, water droplets combine with the fuel to form a frozen substance referred to as gel. The mass of gel, or icing, that may be generated from moisture held in suspension in jet fuel can be much greater than in gasoline.

Because jet fuels are not dyed, there is no on-sight identification for them. They range in color from a colorless liquid to a straw-colored (amber) liquid, depending on age or the crude petroleum source. Jet fuel numbers are type numbers and have no relation to the fuel's performance in the aircraft engine.

FUEL SYSTEM CONTAMINATION

There are several forms of contamination in aviation fuel. The higher the viscosity of the fuel, the greater is its ability to hold contaminants in suspension. For this reason, jet fuels having a high viscosity are more susceptible to contamination than aviation gasoline. The principle contaminants that reduce the quality of turbine fuels are other petroleum products, water, rust or scale, and dirt.

WATER

Water can be present in the fuel in two forms: (1) Dissolved in the fuel or (2) entrained or suspended in the fuel. Entrained water can be detected with the naked eye. The finely divided droplets reflect light and in high concentrations give the fuel a dull, hazy, or cloudy appearance. Particles of entrained water may unite to form droplets of free water.

Fuel can be cloudy for a number of reasons. If the fuel is cloudy and the cloud disappears at the bottom, air is present. If the cloud disappears at the top, water is present. A cloud usually indicates a water-in-fuel suspension. Free water can cause icing of the aircraft fuel system, usually in the aircraft boost pump screens and low pressure filters. Large amounts of water can cause engine stoppage.

MICROBIAL GROWTH

Microbial growth is produced by various forms of micro-organisms that live and multiply in the water interfaces of jet fuels. These organisms may form a slime similar in appearance to the deposits found in stagnant water. The color of this slime growth may be red, brown, gray, or black. If not properly controlled by frequent removal of free water, the growth of these organisms can become extensive. The organisms feed on the hydrocarbons that are found in fuels, but they need free water in order to multiply. The buildup of micro-organisms not only can interfere with fuel flow and quantity indication, but, more important, it can start electrolytic corrosive action.

CONTAMINATION DETECTION

Coarse fuel contamination can be detected visually. The major criterion for contamination detection is that the fuel be clean, bright, and contain no perceptible free water. Clean means the absence of any readily visible sediment or entrained water. Bright refers to the shiny appearance of clean, dry fuels. Free water is indicated by a cloud, haze, or a water slug. A cloud may or may not be present when the fuel is saturated with water. Perfectly clear fuel can contain as much as three times the volume of water considered to be tolerable. Since fuel drained from tank sumps may have been cold-soaked, it should be realized that no method of water detection can be accurate while the fuel entrained water is frozen into ice crystals.

There is a good chance that water will not be drained or detected if the sumps are drained while the fuel is below 32°F after being cooled in flight. Draining will be more effective if it is done after the fuel has been undisturbed for a period of time, during which the free water can precipitate and settle to the drain point. The benefits of a settling period will be lost, however, unless the accumulated water is removed from the drains before the fuel is disturbed by internal pumps.

FUEL SYSTEMS

The aircraft fuel system stores fuel and delivers the proper amount of clean fuel at the right pressure to meet the demands of the engine or engines. A well designed fuel system ensures positive and reliable fuel flow throughout all phases of flight, which include changes in altitude, violent maneuvers and sudden acceleration and deceleration. Such indicators as fuel pressure, fuel flow, warning signals, and tank quantity are provided to give continuous indications of how the system is functioning.

FUEL SYSTEM COMPONENTS AND SUBSYSTEMS

The basic components of a transport aircraft fuel system include tanks, lines, valves, flow indicators, filters, fuel quantity, and miscellaneous warning components. The fuel systems of large aircraft can also be subdi-

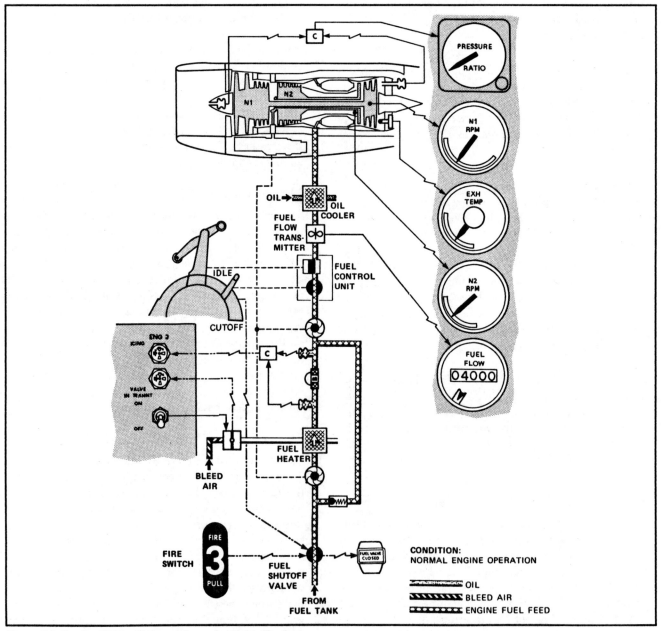

Figure 6-1. Boeing 727 fuel icing and warning light. (Boeing)

vided into several subsystems, which have provisions for fuel jettison (dumping), fuel heating, cross feeding fuel, tank ventilation, and central refueling.

FUEL TANKS

The location, size, shape, and construction of fuel tanks vary with the type and intended use of the aircraft. In most large aircraft, the fuel tanks are integral with the wing or other structural portions of the aircraft. Since integral fuel cells are built into the wings of the aircraft structure, they are not removable. An integral cell is a part of the aircraft structure, which has been so built that after the seams, structural fasteners, and access doors have been properly sealed, the cell will hold fuel without leaking. This type of construction is usually referred to as a wet wing.

Each tank is vented to the outside air through a ventilation system, in order to maintain atmospheric pressure within the fuel tanks. In order to permit rapid changes in internal air pressure, the size of the vent is proportional to the size of the tank. Most tanks are fitted with internal baffles to resist fuel surging caused by changes in the attitude of the aircraft. Usually an expansion space is provided in fuel tanks to allow for an increase in fuel volume due to expansion.

FUEL LINES AND FITTINGS

In an aircraft fuel system, the various tanks and other components are usually joined together by fuel lines made of metal tubing. Where flexibility is necessary, lengths of flexible hose are used. The metal tubing is usually made of aluminum alloy, and the flexible hose is made of synthetic rubber or Teflon®. The diameter of the tubing is governed by the fuel flow requirements of the engine.

Strainers or filters are used in the fuel system to trap water and other contaminants. Many filters incorporate a bypass in the event that the filter becomes completely or partially clogged. If ice is mixed with the fuel, the ice can collect in the filter until it begins to stop the flow of fuel. When this happens, a differential pressure switch will illuminate a warning light in the cockpit. This warning light, as shown in Figure 6-1, will alert the flight crew to the situation. By using fuel heat (a process of heating the fuel with engine bleed air), the ice crystals can be melted and the water will be consumed through the engine. If the blockage in the filter was not ice crystals, then the filter blockage is from fuel contamination and use of fuel heat will not correct the problem.

AUXILIARY FUEL PUMPS

The electrically driven centrifugal booster pump, shown in Figure 6-2, supplies fuel under pressure to

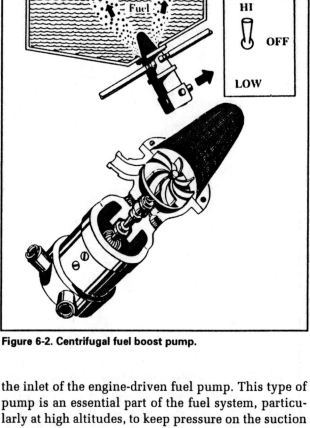

Figure 6-2. Centrifugal fuel boost pump.

the inlet of the engine-driven fuel pump. This type of pump is an essential part of the fuel system, particularly at high altitudes, to keep pressure on the suction side of the engine-driven pump from becoming too low. Most transport aircraft use two or more boost pumps per fuel tank. Each boost pump generally has an associated low pressure light that illuminates when the pump is switched off. This is illustrated in Figure 6-3.

ENGINE-DRIVEN FUEL PUMP

The purpose of the engine-driven fuel pump is to deliver a continuous supply of fuel at the proper pressure at all times during engine operation. The type of pump most used is the positive displacement, rotary vane type pump.

A schematic diagram of a typical engine-driven pump (vane type) is shown in Figure 6-4. Regardless of variations in design, the operating principle of all vane type fuel pumps is the same.

VALVES

Selector valves are installed in the fuel system to provide a means for shutting off the fuel flow, for tank and engine selection, for crossfeed, and for fuel transfer. The size and number of ports (openings) vary with the type of installation.

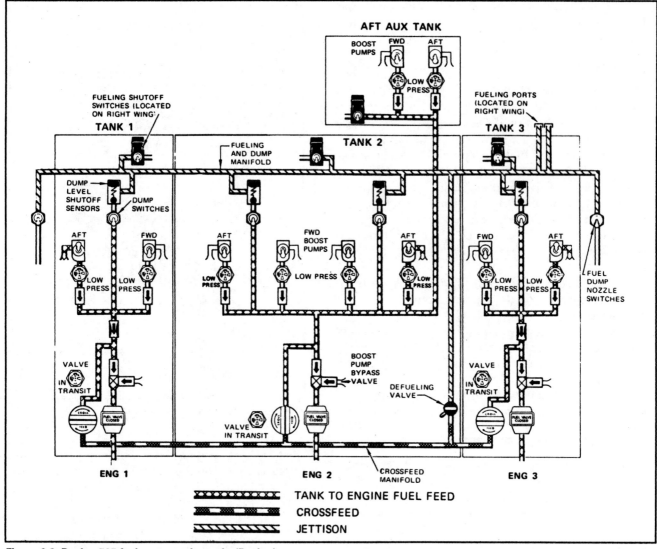

Figure 6-3. Boeing 727 fuel system schematic. (Boeing)

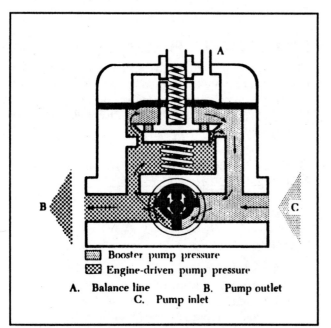

Figure 6-4. Engine driven fuel pump.

Selector valves may be operated either manually or electrically. Electrically operated valves have an actuator, or motor, which opens or closes the valve.

FUEL QUANTITY INDICATORS

Large transport aircraft generally use an electronic type (capacitance) fuel quantity indicating system. This system differs from smaller aircraft types in that it has no movable devices in the fuel tank. The dielectric qualities of fuel and air furnish a measurement of fuel quantity. Essentially, the tank transmitter is a simple electric condenser. The dielectric (or nonconducting material) of the condenser is fuel and the conducting material, air (vapor) above the fuel. The capacitance of the tank unit at any one time will depend on the existing proportion of fuel and vapors (air) in the tank.

FUEL FLOWMETER

The fuel flow transmitter used with many turbine engines is the mass flow type, having a range of 500 to

2,500 pounds per hour. It consists of two cylinders placed in the fuel stream so that the direction of fuel flow is parallel to the axis of the cylinders (see Figure 6-5). The cylinders have small vanes in the outer periphery. The upstream cylinder, called the impeller, is driven at a constant angular velocity by the power supply. This velocity imparts an angular momentum to the fuel. The fuel then transmits this angular velocity to the turbine (the downstream cylinder), causing the turbine to rotate until a restraining spring force balances the force due to the angular momentum of the fuel. The deflection of the turbine positions a magnet in the second harmonic transmitter to a position corresponding to the fuel flow. The turbine position is transmitted to the flight station indicator by means of a selsyn system.

FUEL PRESSURE GAUGE

On aircraft where the fuel pressure gauge is located some distance from the engine, a transmitter is usually installed. The pressure transmitter may be a simple cast metal cell that is divided into two chambers by a flexible diaphragm or by electrical transmitters which register fuel pressure on the gauge.

PRESSURE WARNING SIGNAL

In an aircraft with several tanks, there is always the possible danger of allowing the fuel supply in one tank to become exhausted. To prevent this, pressure warning lights are installed in the aircraft as shown in Figure 6-3.

Normal fuel pressure against the power surface of the diaphragm holds the electrical contacts apart. When the fuel pressure drops below specified limits, the contacts close and the warning light is turned on. This alerts the flight crew to take whatever action is necessary to boost the fuel pressure.

VALVE-IN-TRANSIT INDICATOR LIGHTS

On large transport aircraft, each of the fuel crossfeed and line valves may be provided with a valve-in-transit indicator light. This light is on only during the time the valve is in motion and is off when movement is complete.

FUEL TEMPERATURE INDICATOR

A means for checking the fuel temperature of the fuel in the tanks and at the engine is provided on most large turbine powered aircraft. During extreme cold, especially at altitude, the gauge can be checked to determine when fuel temperatures are approaching those at which there may be danger of ice crystals forming in the fuel

CROSSFEED SYSTEM

The main feature of the crossfeed system, shown in Figure 6-3, is its fuel manifold. As shown, fuel is being

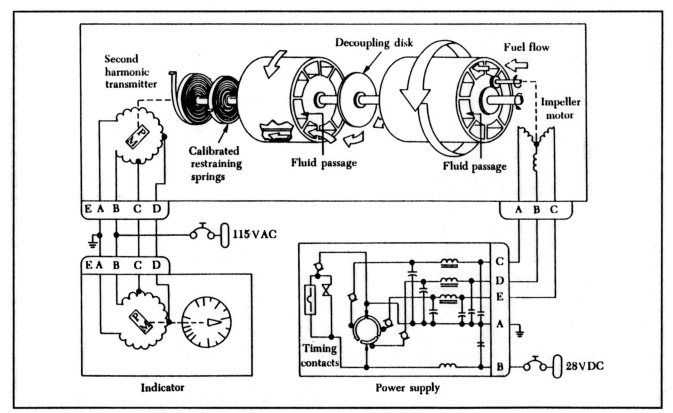

Figure 6-5. Schematic of a turbine engine fuel flow indicating system.

supplied from the main tanks directly to the engines. The crossfeed valves can be set so that all tanks feed into the fuel manifold and each engine receives its fuel supply from this line.

The auxiliary fuel supply can be delivered to the engines only through the manifold. The main advantage of this system is its flexibility. Should an engine fail, its fuel is immediately available to the other engines. If a tank is damaged, the corresponding engine can be supplied with fuel from the manifold.

CENTRAL REFUELING SYSTEMS

An advantage of the central refueling system is that all fuel tanks can be refueled at the same time through a single line manifold connection. This method of refueling has greatly reduced servicing time on large aircraft because fuel can be introduced into the fueling manifold under high pressure to fill each tank to the proper level.

FUEL JETTISON SYSTEMS

A fuel jettison (dump) system, illustrated in Figure 6-3, is required for transport category aircraft if the maximum take off weight exceeds the maximum landing weight. The maximum take off and landing weights are design specifications and may be found in the Aircraft Type Certificate data sheets.

A fuel jettison system must be able to jettison enough fuel within 15 minutes for transport category aircraft to meet the requirements of the Federal Aviation Regulations. It must be operable under the conditions encountered during all operations of the aircraft.

Design requirements are that fuel jettisoning must be stopped with a minimum of fuel remaining on a turbine powered aircraft for take off and landing and 45 minutes cruising time. The fuel jettison system for an example aircraft will be discussed later in more detail.

BOEING 737-300 FUEL SYSTEM

Fuel is contained in three tanks located within the wings and wing center section as illustrated in Figure 6-6. Tank No. 1 and No. 2 are integral with the wing structure, while the center tank lies between the wing roots within the fuselage area. Each tank is equipped with electrical fuel boost pumps which supply fuel directly to the respective engine through the engine fuel shutoff valve. Mechanical engine driven fuel pumps can also provide suction fuel feed from the two wing tanks. Fuel for APU operation is normally supplied from the left side of the fuel manifold.

Each fuel tank contains two AC powered fuel pumps which are fuel cooled and lubricated. A single failure

in the electrical system will not affect more than one pump in each tank. Individual pressure sensors monitor the output pressure of each pump.

FUEL FEED

Engine fuel shutoff valves are located at each engine mounting wing station. The valves are DC motor operated from the hot battery bus. They will close whenever the respective fire switch is pulled or the engine start lever is placed to CUTOFF.

The engine fuel manifolds are interconnected by use of the crossfeed valve. The crossfeed valve is DC motor operated from the battery bus. This valve provides the means of directing fuel to both engines from any tank.

Check valves are located throughout the fuel system to ensure the proper direction of fuel flow and to prevent transfer of fuel between tanks. Center tank check valves open at a lower differential pressure than the check valves in the No. 1 and No. 2 main tanks. This ensures that center tank fuel is used before main tank fuel, even though all fuel pumps are operating.

The purpose of the fuel vent system is to prevent damage to wings, to prevent fuel starvation due to excessive buildup of positive or negative pressures inside the fuel tanks, and to provide ram air pressure within the tanks. The tanks are vented into surge tanks which vent through a single opening at each wing tip. A sensor in the No. 1 tank allows monitoring of fuel system temperature.

FUELING/DEFUELING/ GROUND TRANSFER

Rapid fueling and defueling is accomplished at the single-point pressure fueling station in the right wing as shown in Figure 6-7. The fueling station is also used for the ground transfer of fuel between tanks.

Standard overwing fueling receptacles for No. 1 and No. 2 tanks are provided for gravity fueling in the absence of underwing pressure fueling facilities. A shutoff system is used during pressure fueling to automatically close the fueling valve in each fuel tank when the tank is full.

L-1011 FUEL SYSTEM

Fuel tanks on the L-1011, shown in Figure 6-8, are located in the wings and are of the integral type. The wing tank boundaries are defined by the forward and aft wing spars and by the wing ribs. Numbered from left to right, the tanks are: No. 2L outboard and inboard, No. 1, No. 3, and No. 2R inboard and outboard.

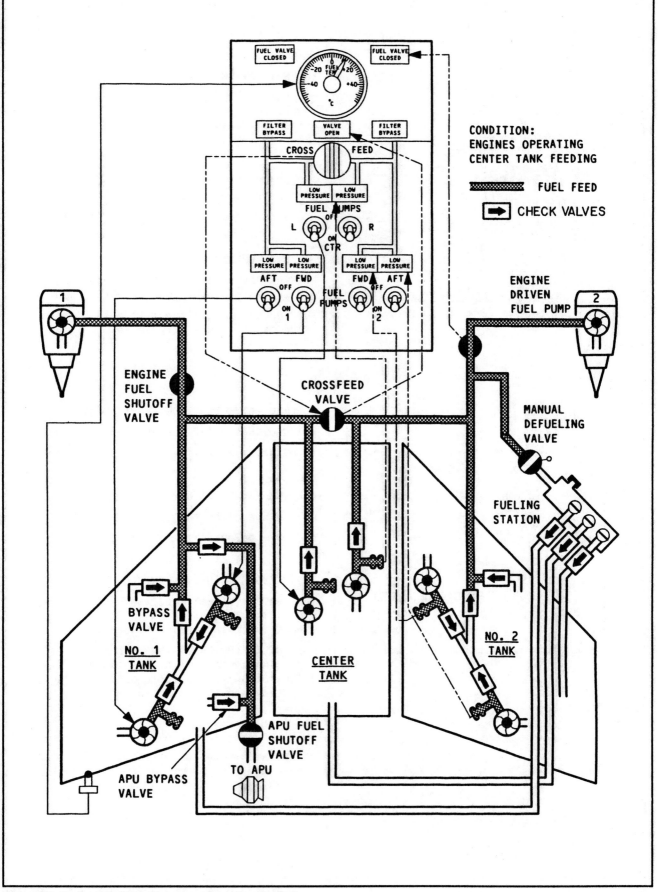

Figure 6-6. Boeing 737-300 fuel system schematic. (Boeing)

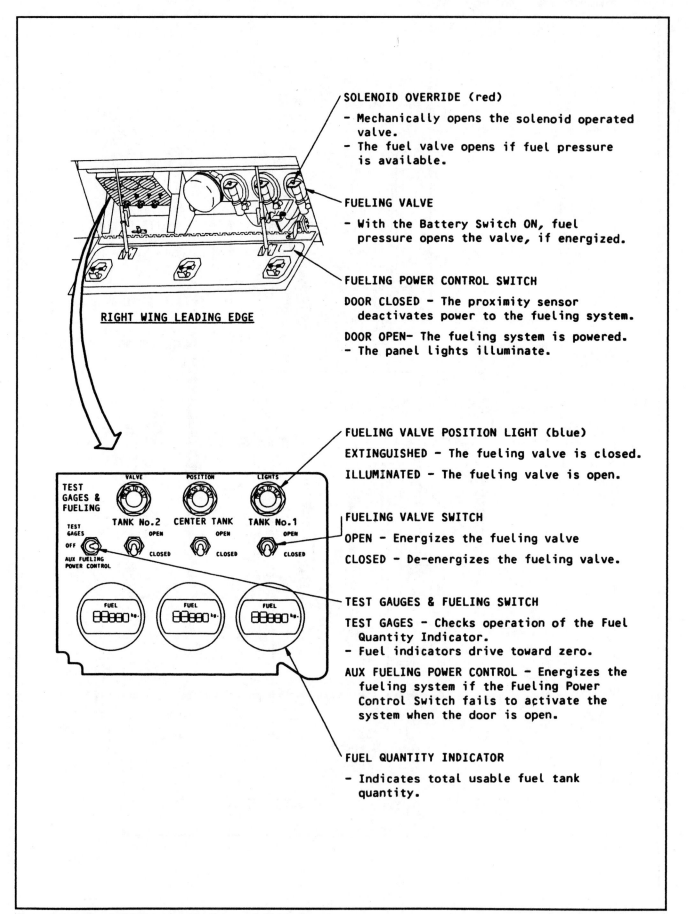

SOLENOID OVERRIDE (red)

- Mechanically opens the solenoid operated valve.
- The fuel valve opens if fuel pressure is available.

FUELING VALVE

- With the Battery Switch ON, fuel pressure opens the valve, if energized.

FUELING POWER CONTROL SWITCH

DOOR CLOSED - The proximity sensor deactivates power to the fueling system.

DOOR OPEN- The fueling system is powered.
- The panel lights illuminate.

RIGHT WING LEADING EDGE

FUELING VALVE POSITION LIGHT (blue)

EXTINGUISHED - The fueling valve is closed.

ILLUMINATED - The fueling valve is open.

FUELING VALVE SWITCH

OPEN - Energizes the fueling valve

CLOSED - De-energizes the fueling valve.

TEST GAUGES & FUELING SWITCH

TEST GAGES - Checks operation of the Fuel Quantity Indicator.
- Fuel indicators drive toward zero.

AUX FUELING POWER CONTROL - Energizes the fueling system if the Fueling Power Control Switch fails to activate the system when the door is open.

FUEL QUANTITY INDICATOR

- Indicates total usable fuel tank quantity.

Figure 6-7. Boeing 737-300 external fueling panel. (Boeing)

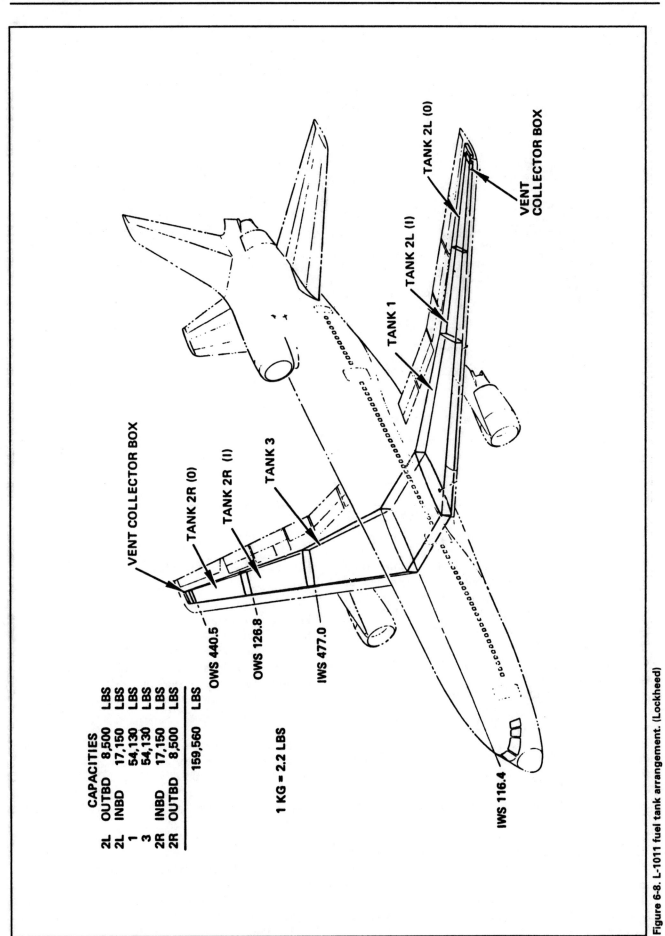

CAPACITIES

2L	OUTBD	8,500	LBS
2L	INBD	17,150	LBS
1		54,130	LBS
3		54,130	LBS
2R	INBD	17,150	LBS
2R	OUTBD	8,500	LBS
		159,560	LBS

1 KG = 2.2 LBS

Figure 6-8. L-1011 fuel tank arrangement. (Lockheed)

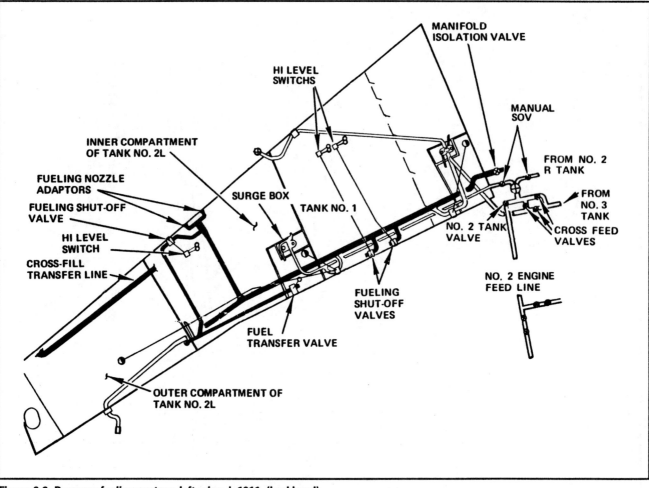

Figure 6-9. Pressure fueling system, left wing, L-1011. (Lockheed)

The six separate tank compartments function as three tanks. The inboard and outboard compartments of tanks 2L and 2R normally supply fuel to engine No. 2 and the APU. Tanks No. 1 and No. 3 normally supply fuel to engines No. 1 and No. 3, respectively. However, fuel from any tank or combination of tanks can be selected to supply fuel to any engine or combination of engines through the crossfeed system. The No. 2 left and right tanks are divided into inboard and outboard compartments by a sealed rib with tanks No. 1 and 3 separated from tanks 2L and 2R also by a sealed rib.

A vent collector box (surge tank) in each wing tip provides for pressure equalization during flight and during fueling and/or defueling operations; it also provides a trap for fuel that may enter the vent system.

Each tank has a fuel scavenge system which continually scavenges fuel and/or water from low points throughout the tanks and delivers the scavenged fuel into the boost pump surge boxes. The scavenge system also removes fuel that is trapped in the vent collector boxes and delivers the fuel to the fuel tanks for use by the engines.

PRESSURE FUELING/DEFUELING

The pressure fueling system is identical in both wings, only the left wing is shown in Figure 6-9. The pressure fueling system consists of fueling shutoff valves (SOV), fueling nozzle adapters, and the fueling manifold (shown in Figure 6-9 by the darkened lines). Associated with each SOV is a hi-level switch that is mounted in the top of the tank and will automatically close the fueling SOV when the tank is full.

Each fueling SOV has three separate ways of being controlled. One control is the HI-LEVEL switch. The second control is the OPEN-CLOSE switch on the fueling/defueling panel and the third control is the PRESELECT control also on the fueling/defueling panel.

The manifold isolation valve permits cross-ship fueling, allowing the tanks in both wings to be fueled with the fueling facility connected to either wing. The manifold isolation valve should be closed when pressure fueling from both wings simultaneously.

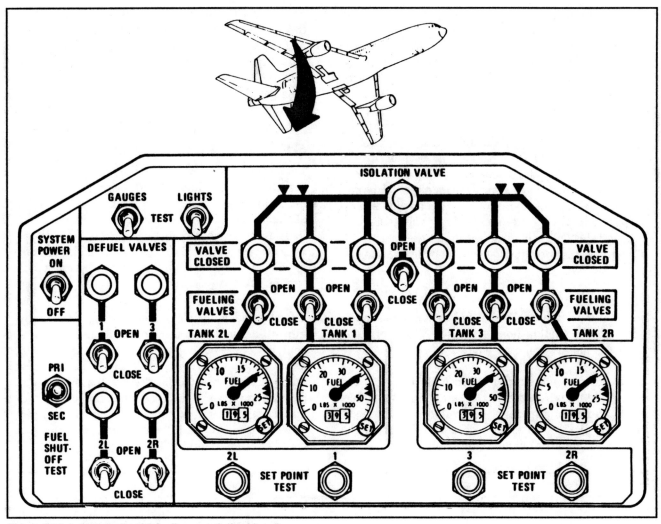

Figure 6-10. L-1011 fueling/defueling panel. (Lockheed)

Should pressure fueling capabilities not be available, the L-1011 may be fueled using the overwing fillers. The fillers are located in the No. 2 tanks; one filler in the outboard compartment, the other in the inboard. Fuel would have to be transferred inboard to either tanks No. 1 or 3.

The fueling/defueling panel, illustrated in Figure 6-10, is designed as a refuel/defuel schematic. The two sets of triangles represent the two sets of nozzle adapters on each wing. The four quantity indicators represent the fuel tanks. The heavy lines represent the fueling/defueling manifold. The valve closed indicator lights represent the fueling shutoff valves in each tank. The fueling valves toggle switches are used to control the fueling shutoff valves.

The isolation valve indicator light represents the manifold isolation valve (cross-ship valve). The solenoid hold switch below the indicator controls the valve. Imagine that the fueling valve control switches and valve closed indicator lights are replaced by the appro-

priate defuel valve indicator lights and solenoid-held control switch. The panel now schematically represents the defueling operation. When fueling or defueling from both wing stations simultaneously, the manifold isolation valve (cross-ship valve) should be closed to prevent fuel transfer from one fueling or defueling facility to the other.

The system power switch is a solenoid-held switch which provides electrical power to the panel. The set knob on the lower right corner of each quantity indicator is used to pre-select the desired quantity in each tank during the fueling operation. The set knob is rotated until the set bug on the face of the indicator is positioned to the desired amount of fuel to be contained in that tank. When the desired, or pre-selected, fuel quantity has been reached, the appropriate set point test light at the bottom of the panel will extinguish and the appropriate fueling shutoff valve will automatically close. The appropriate valve closed indicator light will also illuminate.

Two fueling hose adapters, shown in Figure 6-11, are located at the left and right wing fueling stations. Each adapter consists of an elbow shaped housing, a spring loaded poppet check valve, a protective cap, and a bayonet flange which will accept and retain a standard fueling/defueling hose nozzle. The bayonet flange is designed to break away to prevent damaging the adapter assembly if an excessive force is inadvertently applied to the fueling/defueling hose. The bayonet flange is easily replaced without disassembly of the adapter. Also, the poppet assembly will prevent loss of fuel from the manifold; a spring loaded seal in the cap prevents leakage of fuel into the wing leading edge if seepage occurs past the poppet check valve. Pressure fueling is accomplished by pumping fuel from a refueling truck into the aircraft's tanks at a maximum pressure of 50 PSI.

The defueling system consists of defueling valves, boost pumps (optional), the fueling/defueling manifold and the fueling nozzle adapters. The defueling system is identical in both wings.

Boost pump operation is not necessary to defuel the aircraft, but it will increase the defueling rate if operating. The boost pumps are controlled from the flight engineer panel, and cannot be controlled from the wing station control panel. When defueling from one wing only, the manifold isolation valve will allow the tanks in the opposite wing to be defueled. The manifold isolation valve should be closed when defueling from both wing stations simultaneously. The defueling valves (when opened) connect the associated engine supply manifold to the fueling/defueling manifold.

FUEL TANK VENT SYSTEM

The purpose of the vent system is to equalize air pressure during flight, fueling, and defueling. The vent system consists of a vent collector box (surge tanks), vent channels, and vent inlets as shown in Figure 6-12. All fuel tanks are vented to the vent collector boxes by vent channels. Inlets to the vent channels are through open vent inlets, through float operated vent valves, or suction relief valves.

The purpose of the vent collector box (surge tank) is to trap spilled fuel from the tank vent channels and prevent it from escaping overboard. The vent collector boxes are vented overboard through the standpipe and flame arrestor. An auxiliary vent valve is incorporated to provide pressure equalization if the main vent ices up. In flight, air flowing through the scoop carries away fumes at velocities exceeding flame propagation speeds as illustrated in Figure 6-13.

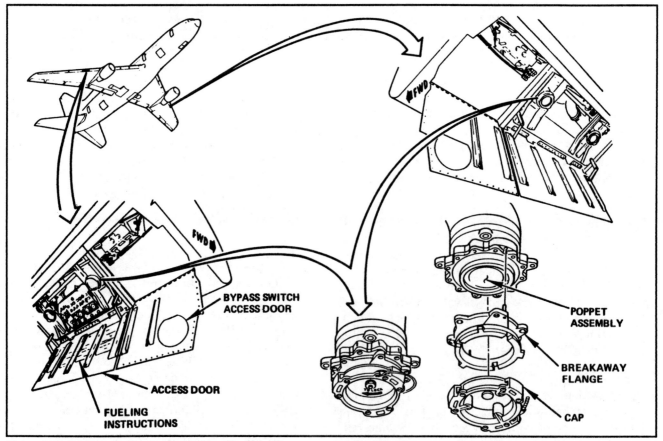

Figure 6-11. Pressure fueling hose adapters. (Lockheed)

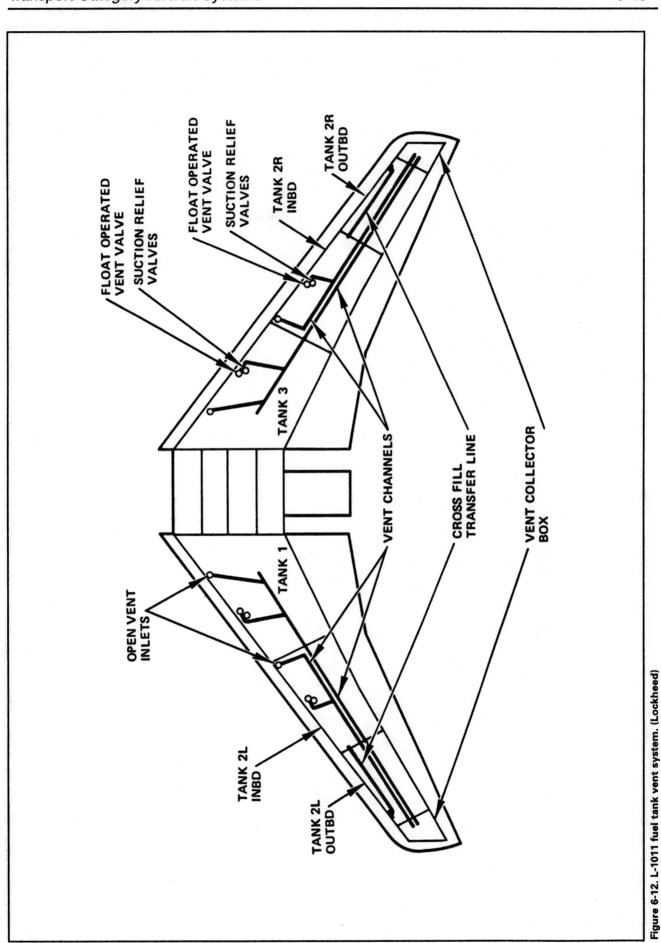

Figure 6-12. L-1011 fuel tank vent system. (Lockheed)

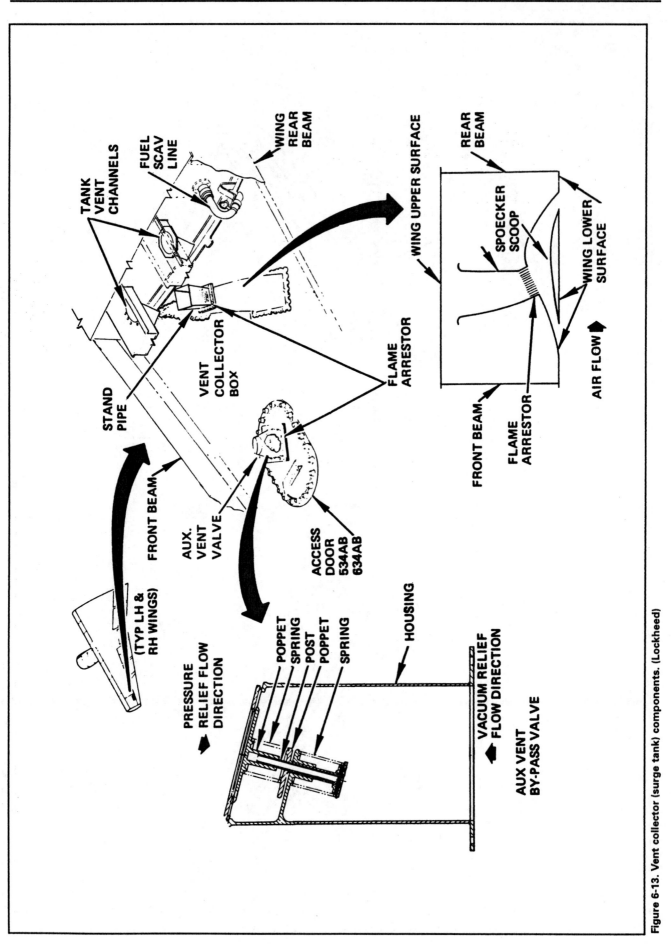

Figure 6-13. Vent collector (surge tank) components. (Lockheed)

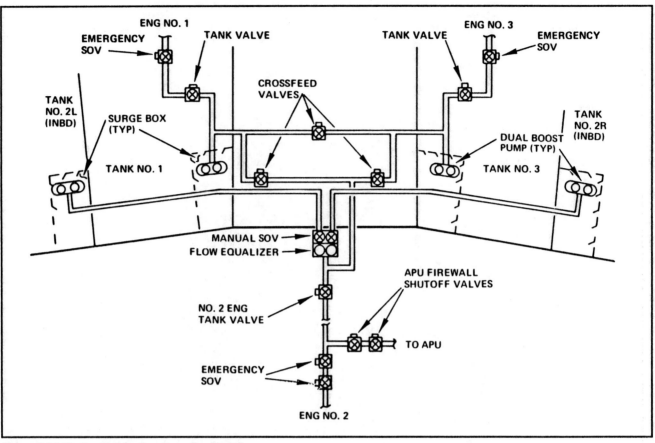

Figure 6-14. Engine fuel feed system. (Lockheed)

Jet scavenge pumps in tanks No. 2L and 2R, activated by boost pump motive flow, remove and return scavenged fuel from the vent collector boxes to their respective supply tanks.

ENGINE FUEL FEED SYSTEM

In normal engine feed operation, each tank supplies its respective engine. The boost pumps normally provide fuel, under pressure, to the engines through the associated tank valve and emergency shutoff valve (SOV) as shown in Figure 6-14. However, any engine driven pump can draw fuel from the tanks if the boost pumps are inoperative.

The flow equalizer ensures that the same amount of fuel is supplied from the No. 2L and 2R tanks, thus preventing lateral imbalance. On some aircraft, other than the L-1011, preventing a lateral imbalance must be done manually by monitoring the amount of fuel used from the outboard tanks. The APU receives fuel from the NO. 2 engine supply line, through the two APU firewall shutoff valves.

In the event of a No. 1 or No. 3 engine fire, pulling the appropriate fire handle will close the appropriate tank valve and emergency SOV. In the event of a No. 2

engine fire, pulling the No. 2 engine fire handle will close the two engine No. 2 emergency SOVs. The No. 2 engine tank valve will not be closed by the fire handle. This ensures that the APU can receive fuel when the No. 2 engine fire handle is pulled. The APU fire handle will close the APU firewall shutoff valves. All three tank valves can be controlled by switchlights at the flight engineer's fuel system panel.

The three crossfeed valves provide the capability of supplying fuel to any engine or combination of engines from any tank or combination of tanks. The engine feed system is identical in both wings.

Each main tank has a surge box, shown in Figure 6-15, which is where the fuel is drawn from the tank. The surge box prevents fuel from sloshing away from the intake of the boost pumps. Each surge box contains a single boost pump housing.

The boost pump housing contains two identical and interchangeable boost pumps. The pumps, operating individually and/or in parallel, provide fuel to the engine, and to the associated crossfeed and defuel (dump) valves.

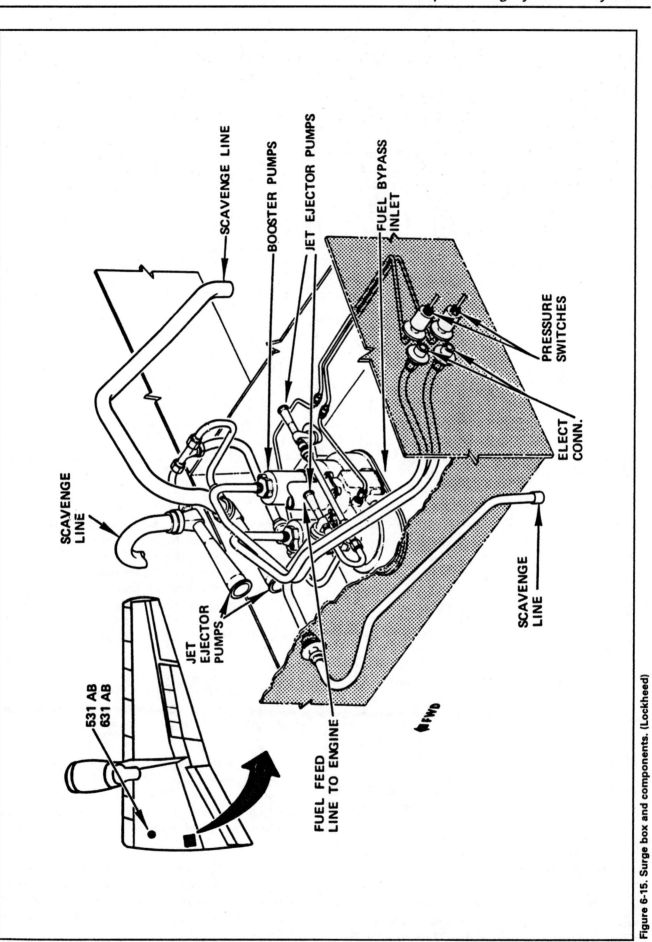

SCAVENGE LINE

BOOSTER PUMPS

JET EJECTOR PUMPS

FUEL BYPASS INLET

PRESSURE SWITCHES

ELECT CONN.

SCAVENGE LINE

SCAVENGE LINE

JET EJECTOR PUMPS

531 AB
631 AB

FUEL FEED LINE TO ENGINE

FWD

Figure 6-15. Surge box and components. (Lockheed)

The boost pumps also provide a second fuel output (motive flow) to operate the scavenge system jet ejector pumps. A third fuel pressure output is from each individual pump to its associated low pressure lights.

A bypass check valve is incorporated in the pump housing. This bypass valve allows fuel to be drawn from the tank (bypassing the boost pumps in the event the pumps fail or are clogged) and prevents fuel from being forced into the tanks.

SCAVENGE SYSTEM

The purpose of the scavenge system is to prevent water stratification in the fuel and to prevent or retard the growth of micro-organisms in the fuel tanks. The scavenge system continuously circulates the fuel and/or water in the fuel tanks.

There are two basic types of fuel scavenging pumps in the fuel system: the single jet ejector and the compound. The jet ejector pumps (single and compound) are used to scavenge fuel from several areas in the fuel tank. A cross section of the typical single jet pump is shown in Figure 6-16. The compound jet pump is simply five single jet pumps whose inlets are connected together and whose outlets are connected together.

Fuel is forced through the jet pump orifice at a high velocity. This creates a negative pressure or suction at the suction inlet. Fuel and/or water is picked up from low areas throughout the tanks by this suction and is pumped back to the surge box areas through the ejector pump outlets, as shown in Figure 6-15.

FUEL QUANTITY

The fuel quantity system has a two-fold function. First, it provides a combination counter/pointer indicator display of fuel quantity, and second, it provides low level signals for the fuel jettison control circuits and/or sump low level warning signals.

The fuel quantity function is a capacitance type system for tank quantity measurements. It consists of 30 full height density compensated tank probes (15 in each wing), one variable capacitor trimmer unit, four signal conditioners, eight fuel quantity indicators, and one total quantity indicator.

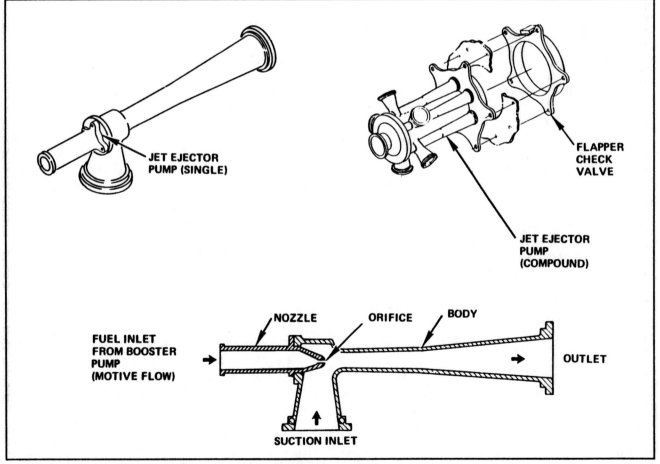

Figure 6-16. Single and compound jet ejector pumps. (Lockheed)

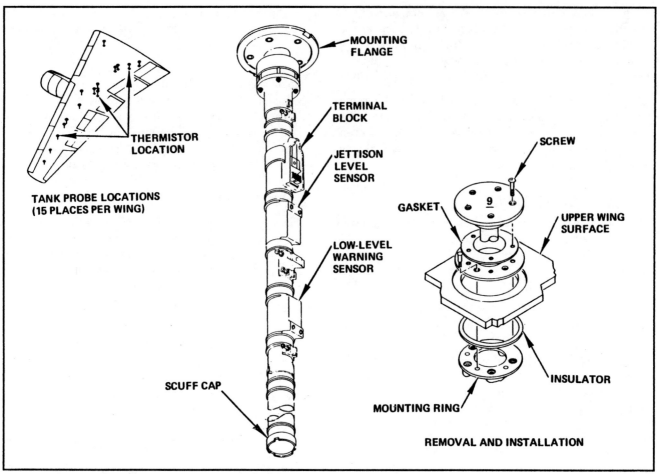

Figure 6-17. Capacitance fuel quantity probe. (Lockheed)

The fuel quantity tank probes are capacitance type devices which consist of two metal tubes, a removable flange, a scuff cap, and a terminal block. A typical fuel quantity tank probe is shown in Figure 6-17. The two metal tubes are mounted one inside the other. Concentricity of the tubes is controlled by Teflon insulating spacers.

When installed in the fuel tank, the probe becomes a capacitor with the fuel as the dielectric. The metal tubes are the two plates of the capacitor and the value of the capacitance varies with the height of fuel in the tank. The capacitance of each probe is sensed at the applicable signal conditioner, then converted to DC current to drive the appropriate quantity indicators.

Fuel capacitance signals "Q," shown in Figure 6-18, are fed from the tank probes to the variable capacitor trimmer unit, where they are adjusted to a proper level during system calibration. The adjusted signal "QA" is fed from the trimmer unit to its associated signal conditioner, where it is changed to a DC signal proportional to the capacitance input. The DC signal "QDC" is then fed to its respective indicator, where it

drives the indicator stepper motor to position the counter/pointer on the indicator.

The second function of the quantity system is to provide low level signals for the fuel jettison operation and/or for the low level warning. The low level thermistors are located on various tank probes throughout the tanks. The thermistor is basically a resistor having a high negative temperature coefficient and is very sensitive to the cooling fuel surrounding the unit. When immersed in fuel, the thermistor is cooled and its resistance is high. When uncovered and exposed to air-fuel vapors, its resistance is low.

The two levels of resistance exhibited by the thermistor, when immersed in fuel or uncovered, is applied to the respective signal conditioner which produces an ON or OFF low fuel level warning indication. These low level signals, "L," sent directly to their associated signal conditioner units, trigger an output from the signal conditioner "L" that will turn on the LOW warning light and/or close one or more of the dump (defuel) valves during the fuel jettison operation. During fuel jettisoning (fuel dumping), this function prevents the fuel from being dumped below a certain level.

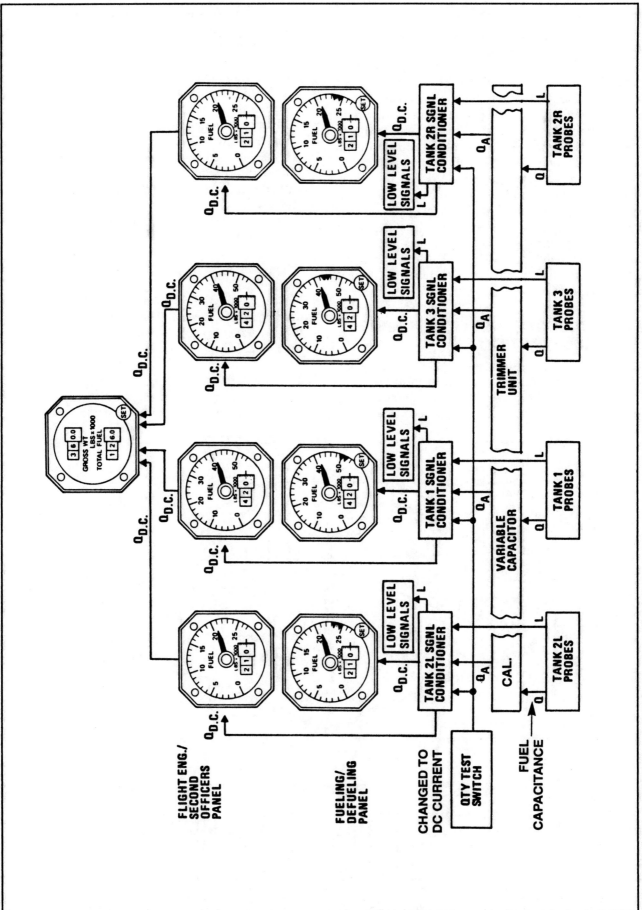

Figure 6-18. Fuel and indicating system block diagram. (Lockheed)

FUEL SYSTEM JETTISON

When fuel jettison is selected, as illustrated in Figure 6-19, the jettison valves, the manifold isolation valve, and the tank dump valves are opened. Fuel from the tanks is pumped through the opened tank dump valve into the fueling/defueling manifold and is pumped overboard through the opened left or right jettison valve and flame arrestor. If the left jettison valve failed to open, fuel could be jettisoned through the manifold isolation valve and right jettison valve. Fuel jettison can be terminated at any time by closing the dump valve, or automatic termination will result when the thermistor in the tank surge box is no longer submerged in fuel. The thermistor is located at the 8,000 pound level (3,629 kilograms), and when the fuel is depleted to this level, the dump valve closes automatically and jettison function in that tank is terminated.

MAGNETIC TYPE FUEL LEVEL GAUGE (DRIPLESS DIP STICK)

Six fuel level sight gauges are located in each wing lower surface to display fuel tank quantity levels as shown in Figure 6-20. The outer tubular housing provides a support for the float which is free to rise or fall with the tank fuel level. The float contains embedded permanent magnets which slide along the surface of the outer housing.

A stick, calibrated to indicate fuel quantity, is located within the housing. This stick is secured in the fully retracted position by a bayonet lock. When the bayonet lock is released, the stick extends by gravity from beneath the wing. The upper end of the stick contains a ferrous metal armature. When the stick is extended to the point where the armature is aligned with the magnets embedded in the float, magnetic latching occurs. The stick is then magnetically coupled to the float, rising or falling as the float follows the fuel level.

When fuel measurement is completed, the stick is pushed back to the fully retracted position and locked. As the stick is locked, the magnetic latch with the float is disengaged. The float then seeks the fuel level, where it remains until the next measurement operation.

To measure the fuel level by the use of a dripless stick, unlock the sight gauge, pull it all the way down, then push it back up until the detent is felt. The detent is

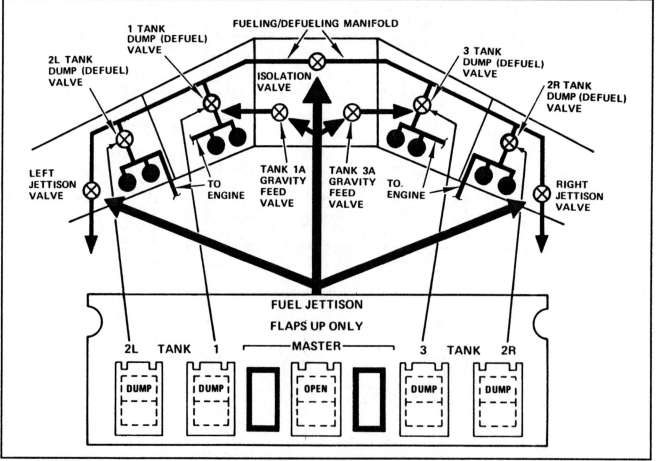

Figure 6-19. Fuel jettison (dump) operations. (Lockheed)

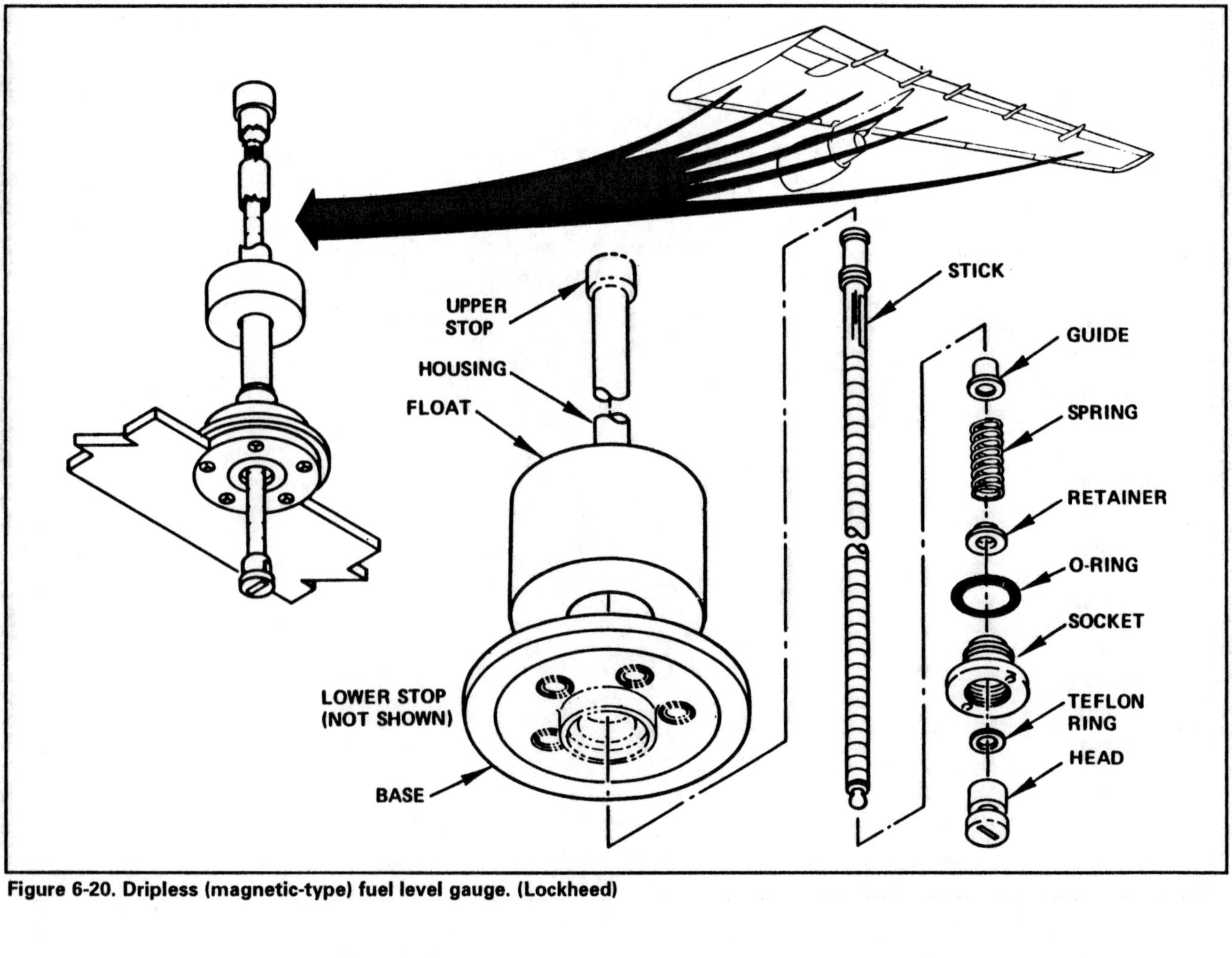

Figure 6-20. Dripless (magnetic-type) fuel level gauge. (Lockheed)

actually the stick being magnetically coupled to the float. The stick is calibrated for its particular location. The reading flush with the bottom edge of the socket should be used. When the readings are completed, push the stick back up and lock it in place. Dip sticks can be used to determine the tank quantity if the fuel quantity system is not operating.

MCDONNELL DOUGLAS DC-9 FUEL SYSTEM

A feature of the DC-9 fuel system (see Figure 6-21) is single point fueling. A single point fueling adapter, with integral regulator, is located on the right wing leading edge at approximately midspan. A fill control panel is located adjacent to the fill adapter. This control panel eliminates the need for personnel in the

Fuel distribution is accomplished by means of two boost pumps in each tank. Fuel is pumped from a tank into a feed manifold through a fire control actuated fuel shutoff valve, then into a shrouded fuel line in the fuselage running aft to the engine. A crossfeed valve permits fuel to be supplied to both engines from either main tank. The APU fuel line is connected to the right engine feed manifold inside the right main tank.

cockpit during fueling operations. In the main tanks, automatic shutoff is provided by two float switches in each tank. Overwing filling points are also provided for each main tank.

In addition to the automatic system, each fill valve can be operated by a switch on the fill panel or manually by an over-ride lever on the valve. These alternates permit manual filling to any level, even when the automatic system is inoperative. Defueling is accomplished through the fueling adapter by opening a manual defueling valve and operating a booster pump in the tank. This system also expedites transfer of fuel from one tank to another while the aircraft is on the ground.

BOEING 747-400 FUEL SYSTEM

Fuel storage tanks, shown in Figure 6-22, are used to store all fuel within vented areas of the wing, the wing center section, and the horizontal stabilizer.

The fuel storage areas are divided into two reserve tanks, four main tanks, the center wing tank, and the horizontal stabilizer tank (HST). These tank sections are integral units using the sealed structure of the airplane to store fuel and vent air.

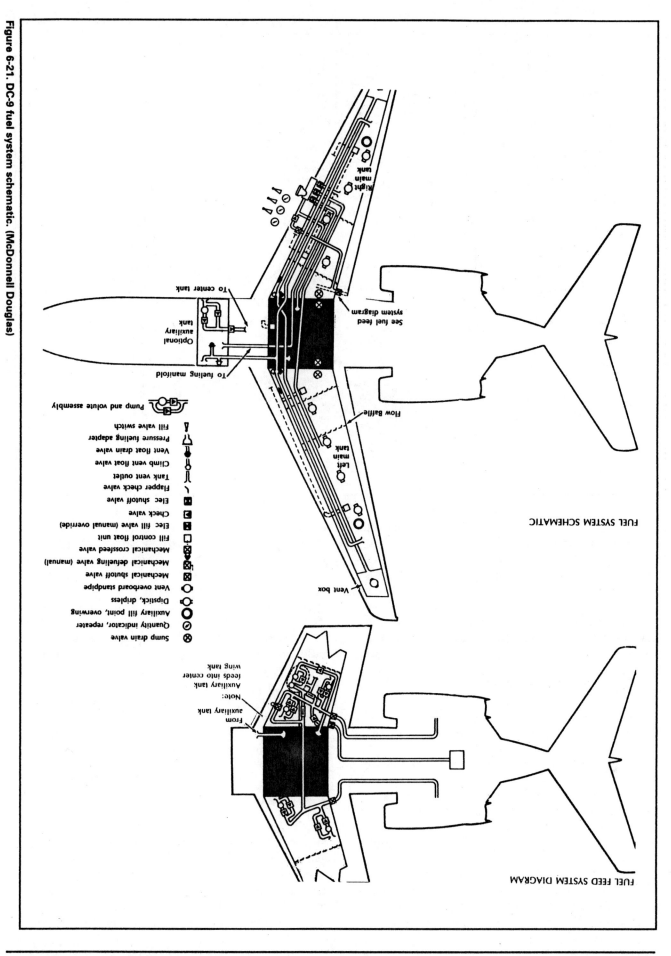

Figure 6-21. DC-9 fuel system schematic. (McDonnell Douglas)

FUEL SYSTEM SCHEMATIC

FUEL FEED SYSTEM DIAGRAM

Note:
Auxiliary tank feeds into center wing tank

From auxiliary tank

To center tank

Optional auxiliary tank

To fueling manifold

See fuel feed system diagram

Right main tank

Flow Baffle

Left main tank

Vent box

Sump drain valve
Quantity indicator, repeater
Auxiliary fill point, overwing
Dipstick, dripless
Vent overboard standpipe
Mechanical shutoff valve
Mechanical defueling valve (manual)
Mechanical crossfeed valve
Fill control float unit
Elec fill valve (manual override)
Check valve
Elec shutoff valve
Flapper check valve
Tank vent outlet
Climb vent float valve
Vent float drain valve
Pressure fueling adapter
Fill valve switch
Pump and volute assembly

Each wing has additional surge tanks located at the tips. These tanks are not used to store fuel but act as containers for overflow from the fuel tanks. The horizontal stabilizer also has a surge tank, but only in the right wing section. These tanks were described as the vent collector tanks on the L-1011 aircraft. Even though the terms used to describe the tanks are different, they serve basically the same function.

The wing center section is both a primary wing structure and a fuel storage tank. Spanwise beams divide the entire box section into five compartments for structural reasons. The compartments are not sealed or fluid tight from each other. The entire upper and front spar surfaces of the wing center box are coated to provide a secondary fuel barrier.

Fuel is supplied to the airplane through the fueling receptacles in either wing leading edge, as illustrated in Figure 6-23. The fueling system is controlled with the fueling control panel located in the left wing leading edge only. Electrical power for the system is auto-

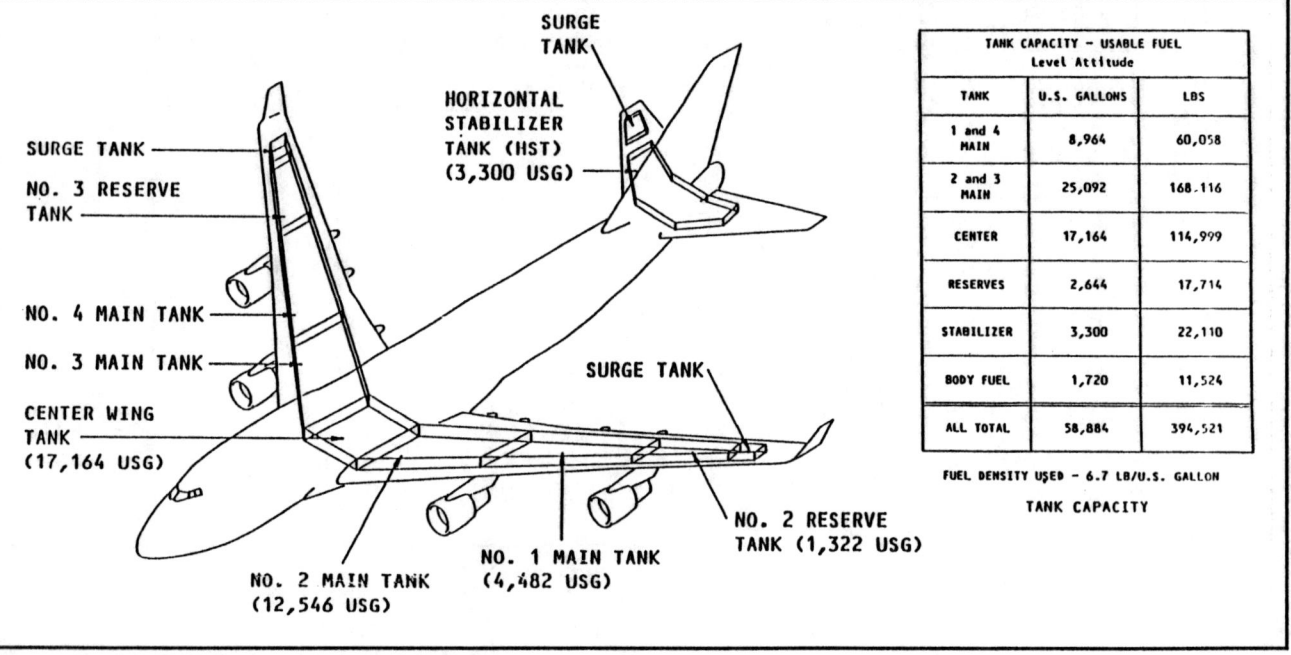

TANK CAPACITY – USABLE FUEL Level Attitude		
TANK	U.S. GALLONS	LBS
1 and 4 MAIN	8,964	60,058
2 and 3 MAIN	25,092	168.116
CENTER	17,164	114,999
RESERVES	2,644	17,714
STABILIZER	3,300	22,110
BODY FUEL	1,720	11,524
ALL TOTAL	58,884	394,521

FUEL DENSITY USED – 6.7 LB/U.S. GALLON

TANK CAPACITY

Figure 6-22. 747-400 fuel system schematic. (Boeing)

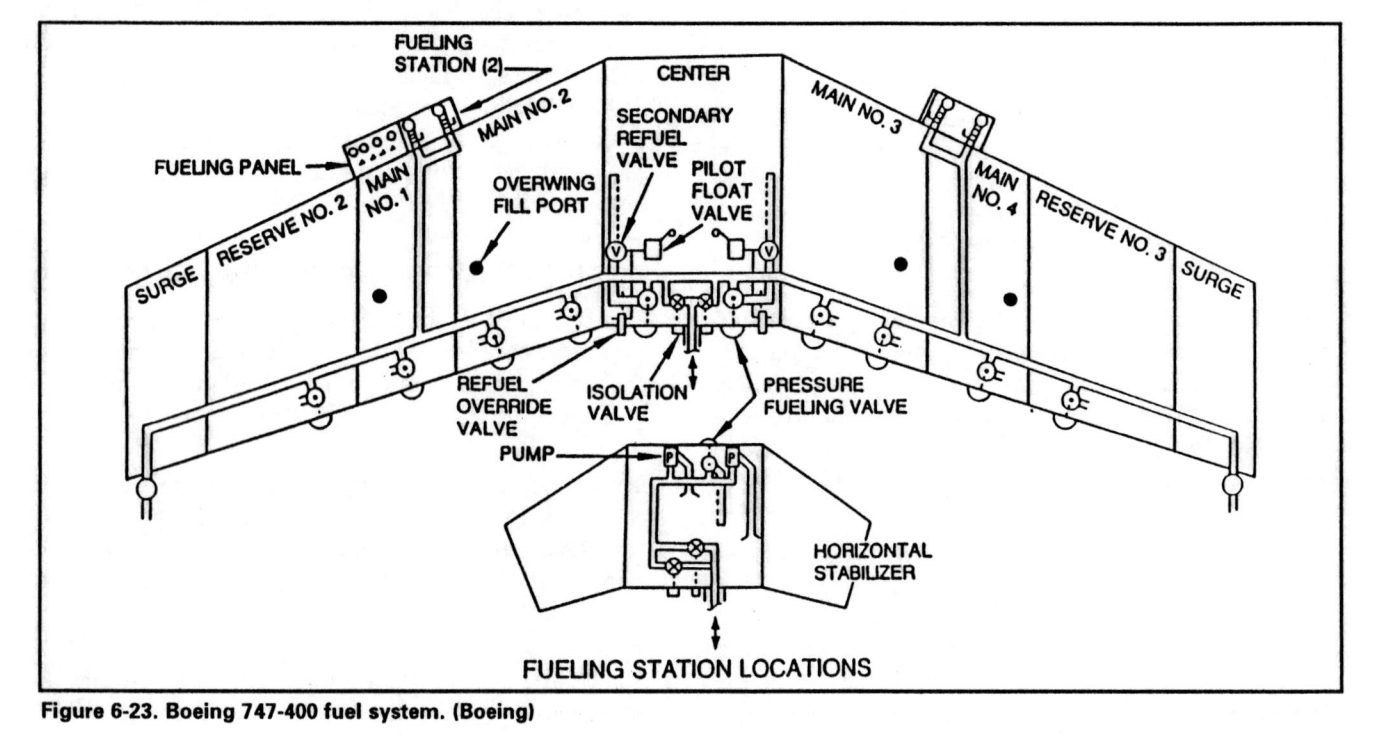

FUELING STATION LOCATIONS

Figure 6-23. Boeing 747-400 fuel system. (Boeing)

...matically connected when the fueling panel door is opened.

Fuel is supplied to the airplane from an external source with hoses that connect to any of the four fueling receptacles. Once connected, the fueling system is pressurized by opening the manual shutoff valves located at each fueling receptacle. The maximum allowable fueling pressure is 65 PSI.

Once fuel pressure is applied to the fueling system and the power supply selected, three types of fueling control are available: manual, top-off, and preselect. Manual fueling is accomplished by opening the desired refuel valve control switch. Once the desired fuel level is reached, the refuel valve control switch is closed.

Top-off fueling is similar to manual fueling except that the closing of the refuel valve is controlled by the fuel quantity indicating system (FQIS) processor. When a fuel tank is full, the processor closes the refuel valve.

Preselect fueling is also controlled by the FQIS processor. The desired fuel level is selected with the refuel select quantity switches and stored into the FQIS processor memory with the preselect switch. The FQIS processor closes the refuel valve for each tank according to the preselected fuel quantity and a programmed loading schedule in the FQIS processor software.

FUEL QUANTITY INDICATING SYSTEM

The fuel quantity indicating system (FQIS), shown in Figure 6-24, computes the quantity of fuel contained in each airplane fuel tank. The calculating function is performed by the fuel quantity processor.

Inputs to the processor come from the fuel sensors in each tank. Fuel quantity calculations for the horizontal stabilizer tank (HST) are performed by the remote electronics unit (REU). The quantity information is transmitted to the FQIS processor.

The fuel quantity information is presented on the engine indicating and crew alerting system (EICAS)

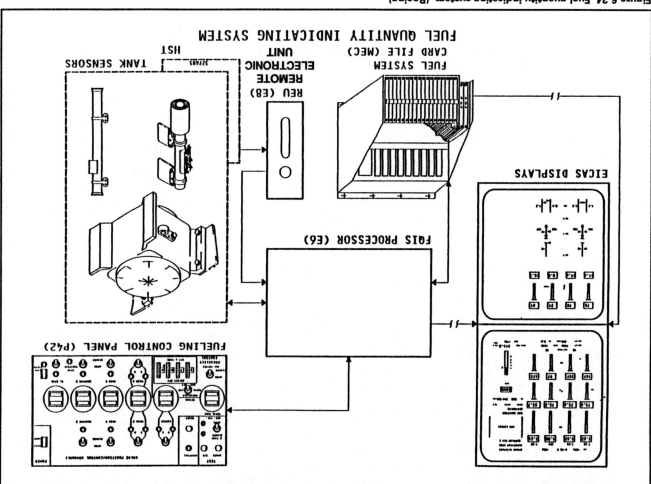

Figure 6-24. Fuel quantity indicating system. (Boeing)

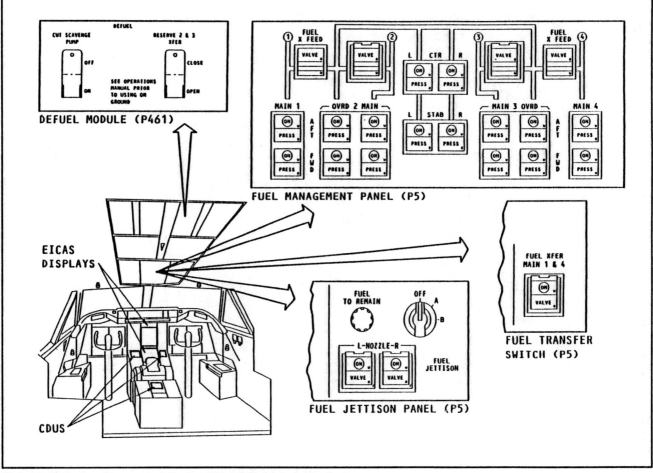

Figure 6-25. Fuel system control, Boeing 747-400 flight deck. (Boeing)

displays in the flight deck. During fueling operations, this information is also shown on the fueling indicators on the fueling control panel.

The FQIS processor basically consists of circuit cards, a volumetric top off (VTO) over-ride switch and connectors. The FQIS processor contains seven fuel quantity circuit cards which monitor the fuel tank components and calculate the fuel quantity in each tank.

Individual tank circuitry is isolated by using only one card for each tank. Tank position is determined by pin locations in the processor card connectors. Several other circuit cards are used in the FQIS processor for interfacing with other fuel system components, control of the refuel valve relay, and the volumetric top off adjustment cards.

Several of the fuel system electronic controls are circuit cards housed in the fuel system card file, shown in Figure 6-24. Each circuit card is mounted in one of the slots along the bottom shelf of the card file.

Interfaces between the fuel system and these cards are made through connectors above the circuit card shelf. A system access panel provides direct access to some of these interfaces.

Each of the circuit cards are line replaceable units (LRUs). Removal and replacement of these circuit cards requires observance of standard practices regarding the handling of electrostatic sensitive devices.

FLIGHT DECK FUEL SYSTEM CONTROLS

The fuel management panel, shown in Figure 6-25, provides either direct or arming control of the crossfeed valves, boost pumps, and override/jettison pump. Lights or mechanical bars in the panel switches provide display of system configuration. The panel is arranged as a schematic of the fuel system. Engines are noted by number with fuel feed pathways shown interconnecting the tanks with the engines.

Manual operation of a crossfeed valve is accomplished by pressing the respective fuel crossfeed valve switch.

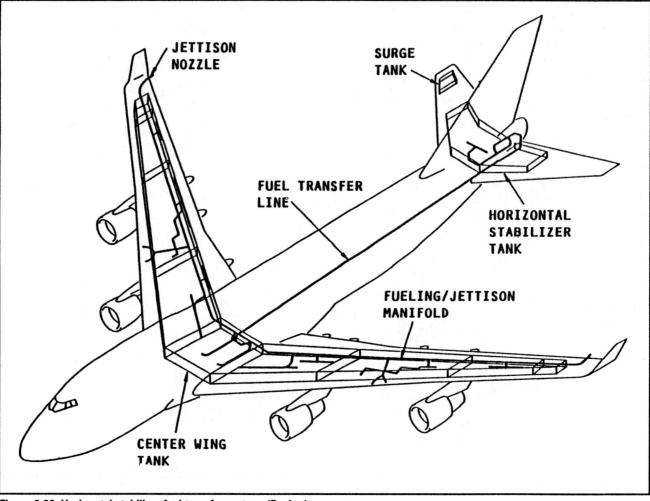

Figure 6-26. Horizontal stabilizer fuel transfer system. (Boeing)

When pressed, the switch displays a bar which connects the fuel pathways on the panel schematic. When pressed again, the bar disappears. The amber crossfeed valve light in the switch comes on when the switch and valve positions disagree. Crossfeed valve switches No. 2 and 3 are guarded.

The other switches on the fuel management panel command operation of either boost pumps or override/jettison pumps. Switch action for both types is the same. When the switch is pressed, an ON symbol appears on the switch. When the switch is pressed again, the ON symbol disappears. Low discharge pressure is sensed at each pump outlet by a pressure switch. Low pressure indication is shown by an amber light on the corresponding pump switch.

The fuel transfer switch provides manual control of the fuel transfer valve between the outboard main fuel tanks and the inboard main fuel tanks. The fuel jettison panel provides controls for activation of the auto-

mated jettison sequence. An adjustable control is included for setting the amount of fuel to remain.

The defuel panel provides manual control of the center wing tank (CWT) scavenge pump and the reserve tank transfer valves for defueling. During normal operation, electronic controls activate these components. The EICAS displays provide fuel system indications and messages. Access to the central maintenance computer system (CMCS) is provided through the control display units (CDU).

Fuel transfer from the 3,300 gallon horizontal stabilizer tank to the center wing tank is semi-automatic in operation. The basic transfer system is shown in Figure 6-26. The transfer pumps are armed by the flight crew during preflight from switches on the overhead panel. The pumps are turned on with a signal from the fuel system management cards when fuel in the center wing tank is reduced to 10,000 gallons. At that time, the isolation valves automatically

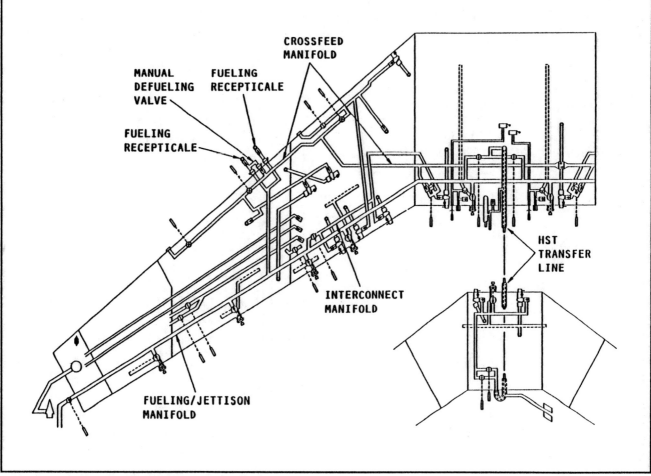

Figure 6-27. Boeing 747-400 defueling system. (Boeing)

open. Fuel is then pumped from the stabilizer to the center wing tank.

DEFUELING

The defueling system schematic, shown in Figure 6-27, shows the various paths the fuel can flow during selected operations, including defueling, and how the systems interface, allowing crossfeed and transfer. It should be noted that the fuel need not be pumped overboard to empty a specific tank. In many cases, fuel may be transferred into tanks with available space.

Fuel in the reserve tanks can only be transferred into the inboard main tanks (2 & 3). This transfer is accomplished by gravity. The flow of fuel is controlled by two transfer valves installed in parallel. To defuel or transfer fuel from the main tanks, the boost pumps are used to pump the tanks down to sump level.

FUEL SYNOPTIC DISPLAY

The EICAS fuel synoptic is presented on the auxiliary EICAS display. It is selected from the EICAS display select panel. This synoptic presents a real-time graphic representation of the fuel system along with digital values for tank and total fuel quantities.

Fuel flow is normally shown as selected green segments appropriate to the system configuration. Engine symbols are normally shown as white. During suction feeding, the engine symbol and the flow segments between the engine symbol and related tank are shown as amber.

FUEL GROUND TESTS

Selection of the ground tests systems menu is made from the central maintenance computer (CMC) menu. The ground tests systems menu lists each system in order by ATA chapter. The fuel system is displayed on this menu by using the next page key (on CDU). The CMC is described in more detail in Chapter 11.

With the fuel system selected for ground test, the ground tests menu displays the system components which may be tested. Pressing the line select key next to the system component initiates the ground test. A pass/fail indication is presented on the same line on the right side of the display as shown in Figure 6-28.

Pressing the line select key next to a fail indication brings up a display of the ground tests result. This page provides component level failure information. Included on this page are the identification of the failed component, the ATA chapter/section designation, the equipment number, and the flight deck effect.

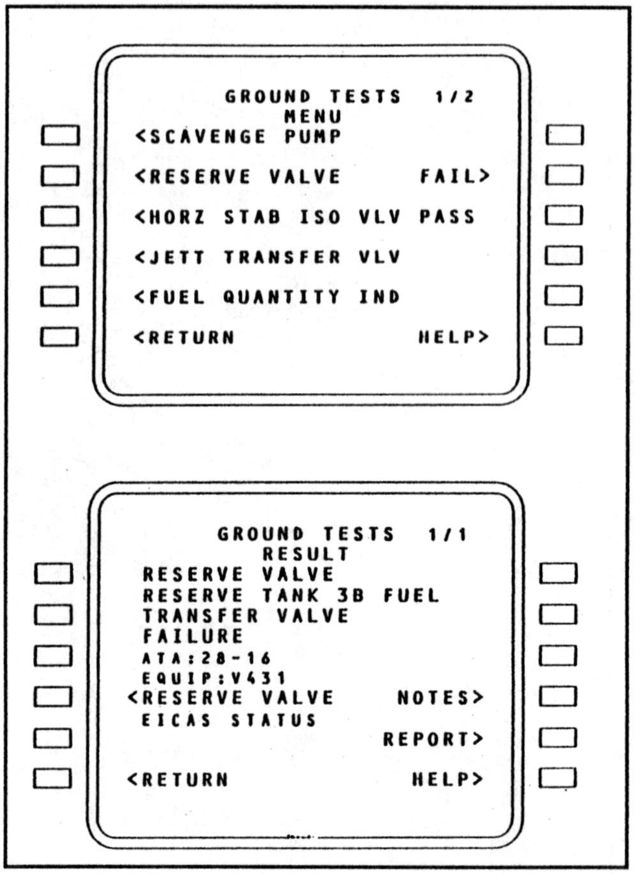

```
        GROUND TESTS  1/2
             MENU
    <SCAVENGE PUMP

    <RESERVE VALVE      FAIL>

    <HORZ STAB ISO VLV PASS

    <JETT TRANSFER VLV

    <FUEL QUANTITY IND

    <RETURN            HELP>
```

```
        GROUND TESTS  1/1
             RESULT
    RESERVE VALVE
    RESERVE TANK 3B FUEL
    TRANSFER VALVE
    FAILURE
    ATA:28-16
    EQUIP:V431
    <RESERVE VALVE      NOTES>
    EICAS STATUS
                       REPORT>
    <RETURN            HELP>
```

Figure 6-28. EICAS display, fuel system ground test. (Boeing)

CHAPTER 6 STUDY QUESTIONS

1. What types of turbine fuel are in common use?

    _____

    _____

2. What type of turbine fuel is used for extremely low temperatures?

    _____

    _____

3. What color, if any, is turbine fuel?

    _____

4. List some of the principal contaminates found in turbine fuel.

    _____

    _____

    _____

5. If the turbine fuel temperature is below 32°F, can the water collected in the sumps be drained? Why?

    _____

    _____

    _____

6. List the components used in the fuel system and subsystems of the fuel system.

    _____

    _____

    _____

7. What is the purpose of the fueling system's manifold isolation valve on the L1011?

    _____

    _____

    _____

8. What is the basic function of the fuel scavenge system?

    _____

    _____

    _____

9. What is the purpose of the magnetic type fuel level gauge (dripless dip stick)?

    _____

    _____

    _____

10. List the fuel tanks used on the 747-400.

    _____

    _____

    _____

11. What type of fueling controls are available on the 747-400 fueling system?

    _____

    _____

    _____

12. Describe the fuel system synoptic display.

    _____

    _____

    _____

HYDRAULIC SYSTEMS

Although some aircraft manufacturers make greater use of hydraulic systems than others, the hydraulic system of the average modern large transport aircraft performs many functions. Among the units commonly operated by hydraulic systems are landing gear, leading edge devices, flaps, speedbrakes, wheel brakes, and flight control surfaces.

Hydraulic systems have many advantages as a power source for operating various aircraft units. Most hydraulic systems are similar, regardless of their function. Much of the information learned about a particular system can be generalized to study other systems.

HYDRAULIC FLUID

Hydraulic system liquids are used primarily to transmit and distribute forces to various units to be actuated. Liquids are able to do this because they are almost incompressible. Thus, if a number of passages exist in a system, pressure can be distributed through all of them by means of hydraulic fluid.

Manufacturers of hydraulic devices usually specify the type of hydraulic fluid to be used. Some of the properties and characteristics that must be considered when selecting a satisfactory liquid for a particular system are viscosity, chemical stability, fire and flash point.

VISCOSITY

One of the most important properties of any hydraulic fluid is its viscosity. Viscosity is internal resistance to flow. A liquid such as gasoline flows easily (has a low viscosity) while a liquid such as tar flows slowly (has a high viscosity). Viscosity increases with temperature decreases.

Chemical stability is another property which is exceedingly important in selecting a hydraulic liquid. It is the liquid's ability to resist oxidation and deterioration for long periods. All liquids tend to undergo unfavorable chemical changes under severe operating conditions. This is the case, for example, when a system operates for a considerable period of time at high temperatures.

Flash point is the temperature at which a liquid gives off vapor in sufficient quantity to ignite momentarily or flash when a flame is applied. A high flash point is desirable for hydraulic liquids because it indicates good resistance to combustion and a low degree of evaporation at normal temperatures.

Fire point is the temperature at which a substance gives off vapor in sufficient quantity to ignite and continue to burn when exposed to a spark or flame. Like flash point, a high fire point is required of desirable hydraulic liquids.

PHOSPHATE ESTER BASE FLUIDS

Currently used in many large aircraft is Skydrol® 500B, a clear purple liquid having good low temperature operating characteristics and low corrosive side effects; and Skydrol® LD, a clear purple low weight fluid formulated for use in large transport aircraft.

Testing proved non-petroleum base fluids (Skydrol®) would not support combustion. Even though they might flash at exceedingly high temperatures, Skydrol® fluids could not spread a fire because burning was localized at the source of heat. Once the heat source was removed, or the fluid flowed away from the source, no further flashing or burning occurred.

INTERMIXING OF FLUIDS

Due to the difference in composition, hydraulic fluids will not mix. Neither are the seals for any one fluid useable with, or tolerant of, any of the other fluids. Should an aircraft hydraulic system be serviced with the wrong type fluid, immediately drain and flush the system and maintain the seals according to the manufacturer's specifications.

HEALTH AND HANDLING

Skydrol® fluid has a very low order of toxicity when applied to the skin in liquid form, but it will cause pain on contact with eye tissue. First aid treatment for eye contact includes flushing the eyes immediately with large volumes of water and the application of any anesthetic solution. The individual should be referred to a physician.

In mist or fog form, Skydrol® is quite irritating to nasal or respiratory passages and generally produces coughing and sneezing.

Silicone ointments, rubber gloves, and careful washing procedures should be utilized to avoid excessive repeated contact with Skydrol® in order to avoid solvent effect on skin.

COMPONENTS OF HYDRAULIC SYSTEMS

Figure 7-1 shows a basic hydraulic system. The first of the components, the reservoir, stores the supply of hydraulic fluid for operation of the system. It replenishes the system fluid when needed and provides a means for bleeding air from the system.

BASIC HYDRAULIC SYSTEM

A pump is necessary to create a flow of fluid. This basic system utilizes a hand pump to provide pressure. Large aircraft systems are, in most instances, equipped with engine-driven, electric motor-driven, engine

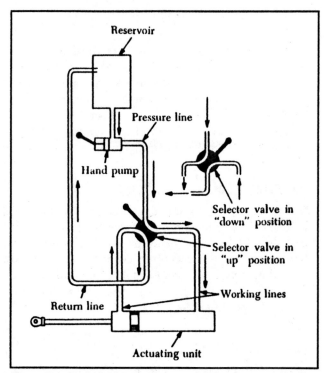

Figure 7-1. Basic hydraulic system with hand pump and four way selector valve.

bleed air-driven, or ram air turbine driven pumps. One system can also power another onboard system by using a power transfer unit.

The selector valve, shown in Figure 7-1, is used to direct the flow of fluid. These valves are actuated by solenoids or manually operated, either directly or indirectly through use of mechanical linkage. An actuating cylinder converts fluid pressure into useful work by linear or reciprocating mechanical motion, whereas a hydraulic motor converts fluid pressure into useful work by rotary mechanical motion.

FILTERS

A filter is a screening or straining device used to clean the hydraulic fluid, thus preventing foreign particles and contaminating substances from remaining in the system. If such objectionable material is not removed, it may cause the hydraulic system to fail through the breakdown or malfunctioning of a single unit of the system.

There are many models and styles of filters. Their position in the aircraft and design requirements determine their shape and size. Most filters used are generally of the inline type. The inline filter assembly is comprised of three basic units: head assembly, bowl, and element. The head assembly is that part which is secured to the aircraft structure and connecting lines.

Within the head there is a bypass valve which routes the hydraulic fluid directly from the inlet to the outlet port if the filter element becomes clogged with foreign matter. The bowl is the housing which holds the element to the filter head and is that part which is removed when element removal is required.

The element may be either a micronic, porous metal, or magnetic type. A typical micronic type filter is shown in Figure 7-2. This filter utilizes an element made of specially treated paper which is formed in vertical convolutions (folds). An internal spring holds the elements in shape.

POWER-DRIVEN PUMPS

Many of the hydraulic pumps used in aircraft are of the variable-delivery, or constant-delivery, type. A constant-delivery pump, regardless of pump RPM, forces a fixed, or unvarying, quantity of fluid through the outlet port during each revolution of the pump. Constant-delivery pumps are sometimes called constant-volume or fixed-delivery pumps.

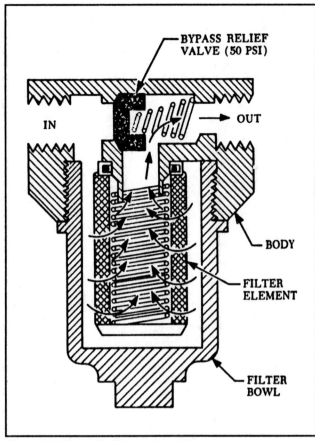

Figure 7-2. Hydraulic filter, micronic type.

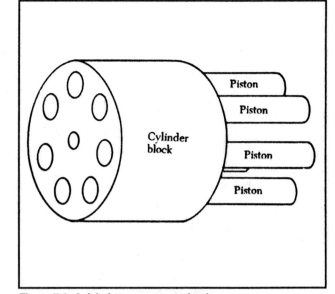

Figure 7-3. Axial-piston pump mechanism.

A variable-delivery pump has a fluid output that is varied to meet the pressure demands of the system by varying its fluid output. The pump output is changed automatically by a pump compensator within the pump.

Various types of pumping mechanisms are used in hydraulic pumps, such as gears, gerotors, vanes, and pistons. The piston-type mechanism is commonly used in power-driven pumps because of its durability and capability to develop high pressure. In 3,000 PSI hydraulic systems, piston-type pumps are widely used.

The basic pumping mechanism of piston-type pump (see Figure 7-3) consists of a multiple-bore cylinder block, a piston for each bore, and a valving arrangement for each bore. The purpose of the valving arrangement is to let fluid into and out of the bores as the pump operates.

Hydraulic pumps, as mentioned earlier, can be driven by the engines, electric motors, air turbine motors, ram air turbines, or a power transfer unit. Engine-driven pumps are mechanically linked and mounted on the engine accessory case.

Most electric motor driven pumps use alternating current to power the electric motor which drives the hydraulic pump. Switches in the cockpit control power to the electric motor-driven pumps.

Another method of powering hydraulic pumps can originate as pneumatic power (APU, ground connection, engine bleed air) which is used to drive an air turbine that turns the hydraulic pump.

In case all other methods of powering the hydraulic systems are lost, a ram air turbine (RAT) can be deployed into the air stream to drive a hydraulic pump. Ram air turbines are generally used only in emergency situations. The RAT, shown in Figure 7-4, drops down and the turbine (propeller) begins to windmill and turns a hydraulic pump to pressurize one of the hydraulic systems.

Power transfer units are basically two hydraulic pumps mounted back to back with one pump functioning as a motor. For example, with one system pressurized, half the unit acts as a motor, and the other half of the unit acts as a pump. Power transfer units (PTUs) are used to pressurize one system to another. The transfer of power is mechanical, as no fluid passes between systems. PTUs can be used to power hydraulic systems during ground operations, or in flight if needed.

PRESSURE RELIEF VALVES

A pressure relief valve is used to limit the amount of pressure being exerted on a confined liquid. This is necessary to prevent failure of components or rupture

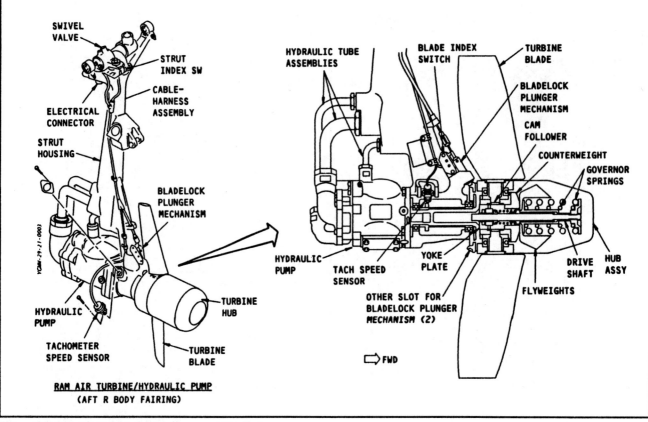

Figure 7-4. Ram air turbine/hydraulic pump. (Boeing)

of hydraulic lines under excessive pressures. The purpose of the system pressure gauge is to measure the pressure in the hydraulic system.

ACCUMULATOR

The accumulator is a steel sphere divided into two chambers by a synthetic rubber diaphragm. The upper chamber contains fluid at system pressure, while the lower chamber is charged with air. The main functions of an accumulator are to dampen pressure surges, to supplement the power pump, and to store power for limited operation of a hydraulic unit when the pump is not operating.

ACTUATING CYLINDERS

An actuating cylinder transforms energy in the form of fluid pressure into mechanical force, or action, to perform work. It is used to impart powered linear motion to some movable object or mechanism. Actuating cylinders are generally of the single-action or double-action type. In a single-action actuating cylinder, fluid under pressure enters the inlet port and pushes against the face of the piston, forcing the piston to move. As the piston moves, air is forced out of the spring chamber through the vent hole, compressing the spring.

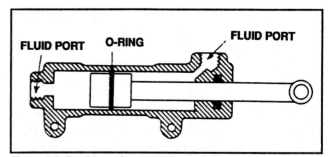

Figure 7-5. Double-action actuating cylinder.

A double-action (two-port) actuating cylinder is illustrated in Figure 7-5. The operation of a double-action actuating cylinder is usually controlled by a four way selector valve. By allowing pressurized fluid to enter one of the ports, the piston and rod will be moved in the direction of the force being applied against the piston. In this case, the piston can be moved under pressure right or left, depending upon which fluid port is pressurized.

BOEING 737-300 HYDRAULIC SYSTEM

Hydraulic power is provided by three independent sources: system A, system B, and the standby system,

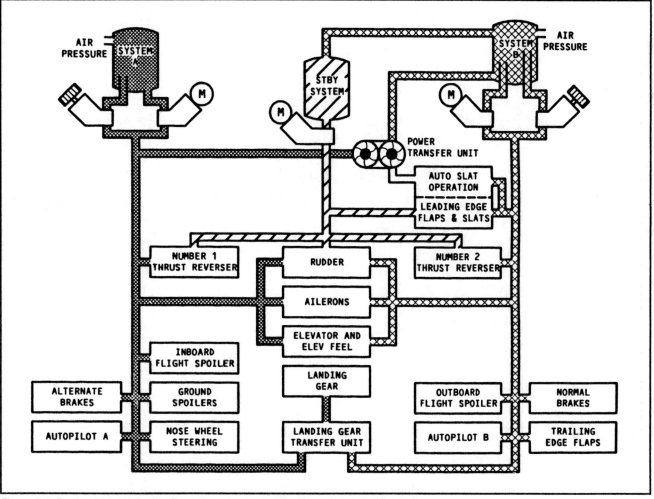

Figure 7-6. Boeing 737-300 hydraulic system power distribution schematic. (Boeing)

as shown in Figure 7-6. System A pressure is provided by engine No. 1 pump and an electric pump powered by engine No. 2 generator. System B pressure is provided by engine No. 2 pump and an electric pump powered by engine No. 1 generator. The standby system is used in the event of loss of either system A or System B pressure. Standby pressure is provided by one electric motor driven pump. Nominal operating pressure for each hydraulic system is 3,000 PSI. Each hydraulic system has a fluid reservoir located in the main wheel well area. The System A and System B reservoirs are pressurized by air from the pneumatic manifold. The standby reservoir is pressurized, and the fluid is maintained at the full level, by an interconnecting balance line to the System B reservoir. Pressurization of any type of reservoir ensures a positive fluid flow to the hydraulic pumps.

A power transfer unit provides a back up source of hydraulic power to operate the autoslats, should the System B engine driven pump pressure drop below limits. System A pressure drives a hydraulic motor,

which in turn drives a pump, pressurizing System B fluid from the reservoir to drive the autoslat system.

HYDRAULIC SYSTEM A

The fluid flow to the engine driven pump passes through a valve controlled by a fire switch. Pulling the fire switch shuts off the fluid flow to the pump.

The engine-driven hydraulic pump output pressure is controlled by the ENG pump ON/OFF switch, as shown in Figure 7-7. Positioning the switch to OFF activates the solenoid held blocking valve and isolates fluid flow from the using units. The electric motor pump is controlled by the ELEC pump ON/OFF switch. Temperature sensors are located in the case drain line and the pump housing. If the fluid or pump becomes overheated, the OVERHEAT light illuminates.

Hydraulic fluid used for cooling and lubrication of the pumps passes through a heat exchanger before returning to the reservoir. The heat exchanger is located in

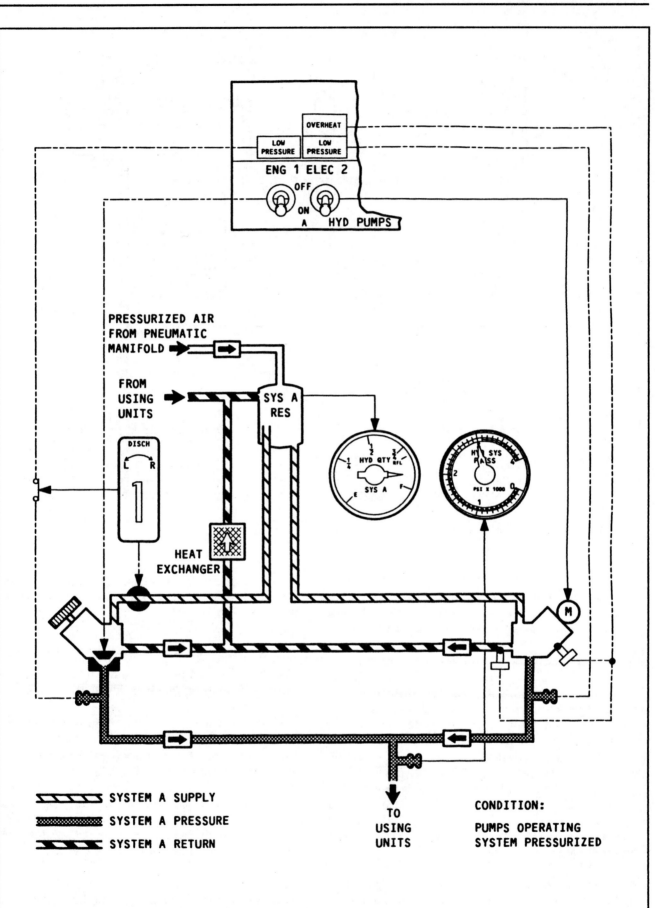

Figure 7-7. 737-300 hydraulic system A schematic. (Boeing)

the No. 1 main fuel tank and uses fuel to cool the hydraulic fluid.

Pressure transmitters, located in the engine driven and electric motor pump output lines, send signals to illuminate the appropriate LOW PRESSURE light if pump output pressure is below acceptable limits. Check valves, valves which allow flow in only one direction, isolate the two pumps. A system pressure transmitter sends the combined pressure of the pumps to the hydraulic system pressure indicator. System A fluid quantity is displayed on indicators at the reservoir and the first officer panel.

If a leak develops in the engine-driven pump or its associated lines, a standpipe in the reservoir prevents a total system fluid loss. With fluid level at the top of the standpipe, the reservoir indicates approximately 1/4 full. System A pressure is maintained by the electric motor driven pump.

Should a leak occur in any other system A components or lines, the quantity in the reservoir steadily decreases to zero.

HYDRAULIC SYSTEM B

System B operates very similar to system A, except the system B reservoir has two standpipes. One supplies fluid to the engine-driven pump; the other to the electric motor pump, as shown in Figure 7-8. If a leak should develop in the engine-driven pump or its associated lines, the system B quantity gauge reading decreases until it indicates approximately 1/2 full.

System pressure is maintained by the electric motor pump. If the leak is in the electric motor pump or associated lines, system B pressure is lost. However, sufficient fluid will be retained in the reservoir for operation of the power transfer unit.

HYDRAULIC STANDBY SYSTEM

The standby hydraulic system, shown in Figure 7-9, is provided as a backup in the event normal system A and/or B pressure is lost. The standby system reservoir is connected to the system B reservoir through a balance line for pressurization and servicing.

The single electric motor driven hydraulic standby pump is activated by positioning either flight control switch to its STBY RUD position, or by positioning the alternate flaps master switch to ARM. In the event of a loss of system A or B hydraulic pressure

during takeoff or landing, the standby system is activated automatically to provide power to the standby rudder actuator.

Positioning either flight control switch to STBY RUD also shuts off the corresponding hydraulic system pressure to ailerons, elevators, and rudder. With either switch in the STBY RUD position, the associated flight control LOW PRESSURE light is deactivated as the standby rudder shutoff valve opens.

In the event of system B pressure loss, the leading edge devices may be extended by positioning the alternate flaps master switch to ARM and momentarily positioning the alternate flaps position switch to DOWN. The leading edge devices are fully extended hydraulically, but cannot be retracted by the standby hydraulic system. The trailing edge flaps may be extended or retracted electrically. With the loss of system A and/or system B, the standby system provides pressure to operate the respective thrust reverser.

Hydraulic quantity indications, for any hydraulic system, may vary considerably during normal flight. The quantity of fluid indicated on the cockpit gauges represents only a small percentage of the total hydraulic fluid in the system. Consequently, the loss of a gallon or more of fluid may be quite impressive when viewed on the gauges, but generally has little or no effect on the operations of the systems.

During normal operations, hydraulic quantity indications vary when: the system becomes pressurized after engine start; raising or lowering the landing gear or leading edge devices; or when cold soaking occurs during long periods of cruise flight.

BOEING 757 HYDRAULIC SYSTEM

Three independent, full-time, 3,000 PSI systems, using a synthetic BMS 3-11 type IV fluid, provide power for operation of landing gear, flight control, and thrust reverser systems.

Each system is normally powered by two hydraulic pumps which are driven from independent power sources. Distribution of pressure from the three systems is such that the failure of one system will not result in loss of any flight control functions and the airplane can be safely operated in the event of loss of two hydraulic systems. An emergency hydraulic pump provides flight control operation in event of dual engine failure.

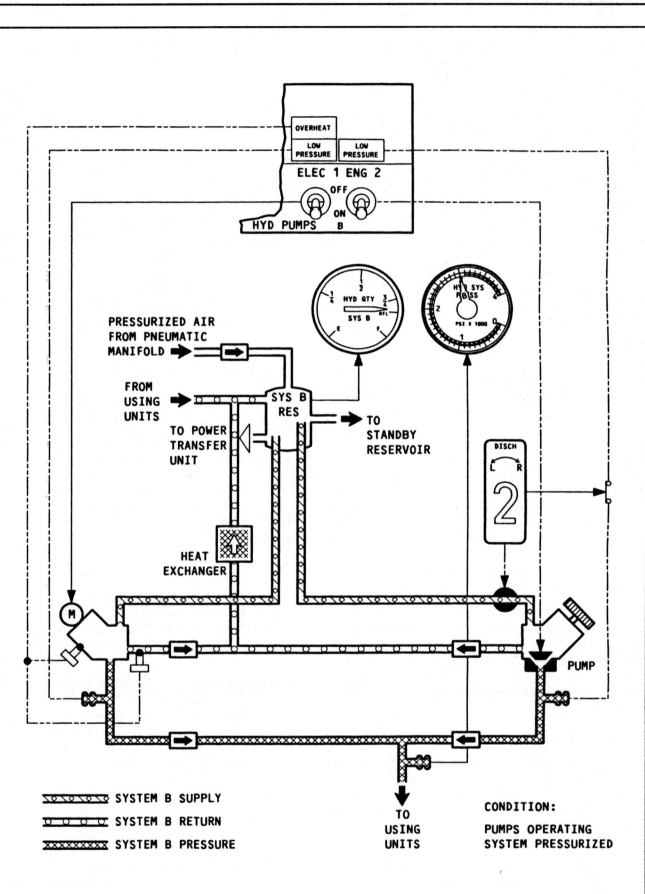

Figure 7-8. 737-300 hydraulic system B schematic. (Boeing)

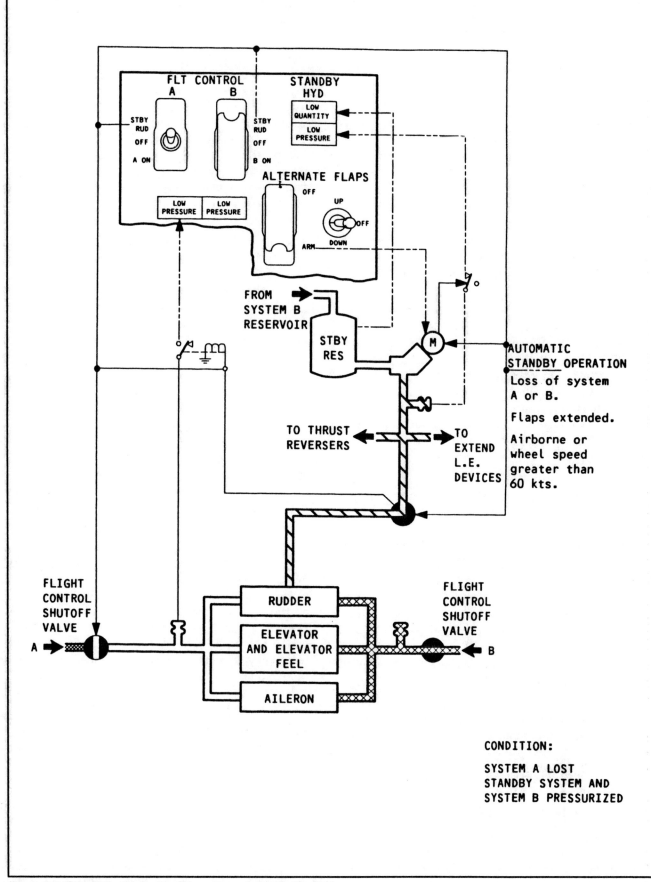

Figure 7-9. 737-300 hydraulic standby system schematic. (Boeing)

An electric motor pump is available in each system for ground maintenance. A central fill point facilitates fluid servicing of all three systems. Reservoir pressurization is obtained from the airplane pneumatic system and is available whenever the pneumatic ducts are pressurized. External hydraulic power can be connected to each system.

The three systems are color-coded to facilitate identification of tubing and components. Left system — red, center system — blue, and right system — green.

HYDRAULIC POWER DISTRIBUTION

The three hydraulic systems take their names from their locations: left, right and center. The systems are powered by a total of 7 pumps. Multiple pumps in each system ensure reliability, as illustrated in Figure 7-10.

The left and right are similar, with each system containing one engine-driven pump (EDP) and one alternating current motor pump (ACMP). A power transfer unit (PTU) connects the L & R systems mechanically. A hydraulic motor in the right system powers a hydraulic pump in the left system to provide sufficient flow to retract the landing gear and lift devices in the event of loss of the left engine or left engine-driven pump. The ram air turbine (RAT) retract actuator is powered by the right system.

The center system has two ACMPs for primary pumps, and a ram air turbine (RAT) for emergency power. The components of the system are located in the wheel wells and body fairings. There is no hydraulic interconnection between the three systems.

The hydraulic indicator and control panel is located on the left side of the overhead panel. Controls and indicators include amber system low pressure lights, reservoir low quantity/pressure lights, pump low pressure lights, pump control switches and pump overheat lights as shown in Figure 7-11.

The ram air turbine (RAT) control switch, containing green pressure and amber unlocked lights, is located on the engine START/RAT control panel in the center of the overhead panel.

SYSTEM OPERATION

Each reservoir is pressurized from the pneumatic system by regulated air which is ported to the reservoirs. This air pressure is used to provide a positive head of pressure at the suction inlet of all the pumps.

A dual pressure switch on the reservoir provides an engine indicating and crew alerting system (EICAS) advisory annunciation for low pressure indications.

Heat exchangers in each system cool fluid returning to the reservoir. A fin-type heat exchanger, shown in Figure 7-12, is installed in the main fuel tanks. The hydraulic flow from the case drain of the pumps within each system is cooled in the heat exchanger by thermal transfer between the hot hydraulic fluid and the cool fuel. The cooled hydraulic fluid is then returned to the system's reservoir. The heat exchangers must be completely immersed in fuel to provide adequate cooling.

Since the left and right hydraulic systems are very similar, only the right system's operation will be described. Both pumps, in the right system, shown in Figure 7-13, receive fluid from the reservoir standpipe and the ACMP can also receive fluid from the bottom of the reservoir when the reservoir isolation valve is operated. Both pumps are serviced by filter modules containing filters, pressure switches and check valves (see Figure 7-14).

The case drain (CD) flow from the pumps passes through the heat exchanger mentioned earlier and returns to the reservoir. Return fluid from the systems is routed through a return filter. The return filter, shown in Figure 7-15, incorporates a removable shut-off valve to facilitate replacement of the 15 micron paper filter, and a bypass valve to permit bypassing a clogged filter.

A system relief valve prevents over-pressure from the EDP and ACMP, which also powers the power transfer unit (PTU) motor. The power transfer unit (PTU) powers the left hydraulic system landing gear and flap/slat systems, utilizing the right hydraulic system engine driven pump (EDP), to provide operation of these systems when the left hydraulic system EDP is off or inoperative.

A pressure isolation valve operates to dedicate ACMP pressure output to the brakes, if needed. Each system contains pressure and return ground service connections.

The center hydraulic system, shown in Figure 7-16, uses a pressurized reservoir to provide fluid to two alternating current motor pumps and a ram air turbine pump. The ACMPs receive fluid from the reservoir standpipe and the RAT pump receives fluid from the bottom of the reservoir. The ACMPs and the RAT

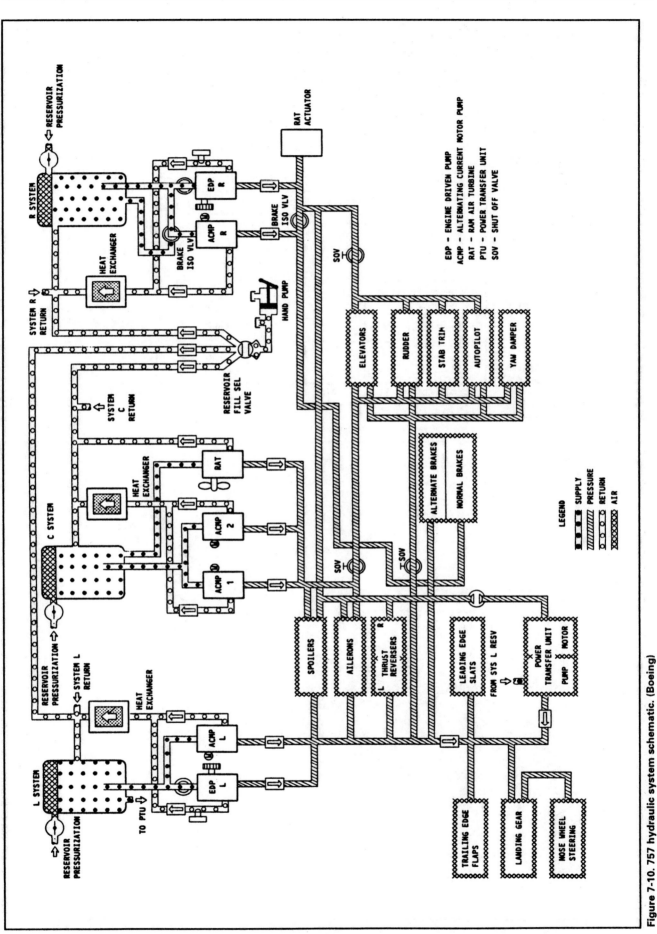

Figure 7-10. 757 hydraulic system schematic. (Boeing)

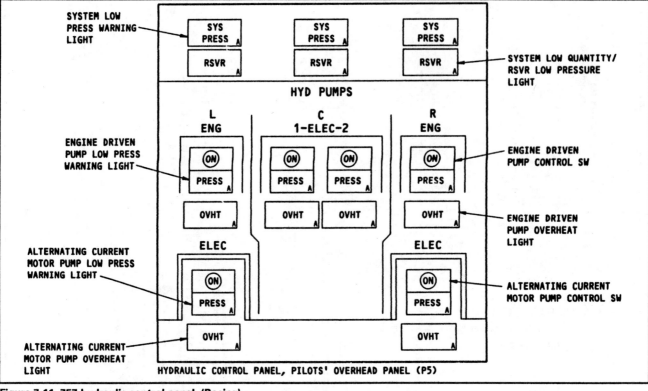

Figure 7-11. 757 hydraulic control panel. (Boeing)

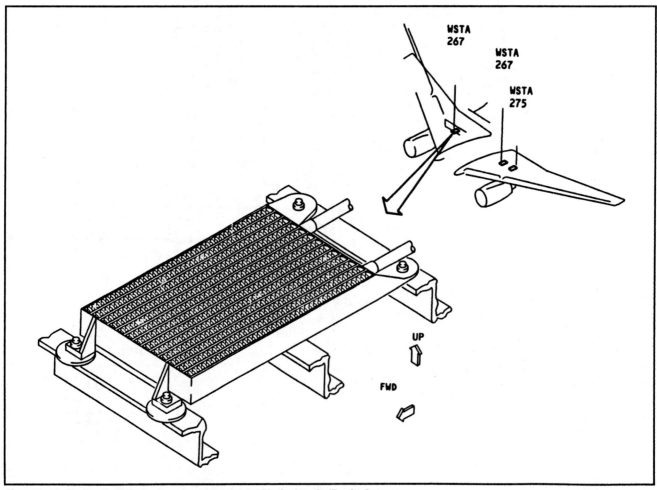

Figure 7-12. Hydraulic fluid heat exchanger mounted in fuel tank. (Boeing)

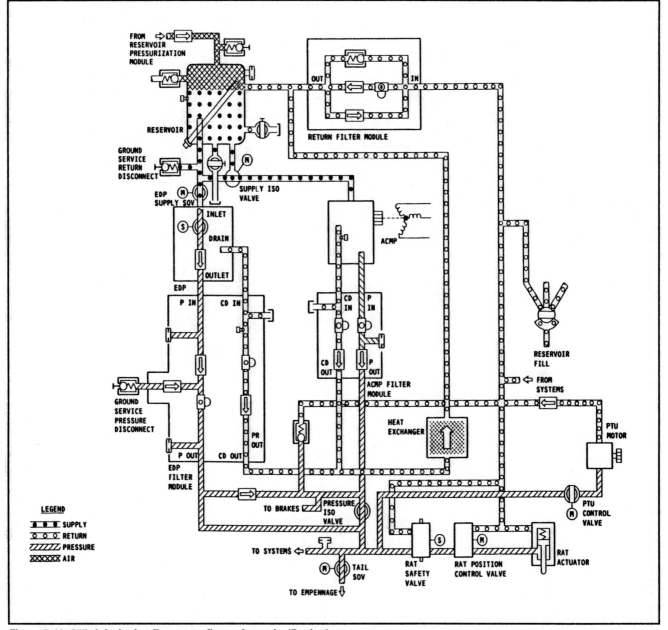

Figure 7-13. 757 right hydraulic system flow schematic. (Boeing)

are serviced by modules containing filters. The fluid from the pumps passes through a heat exchanger and joins system return fluid flowing back to the reservoir. Any one of the pumps can pressurize the center hydraulic system.

BOEING 757 LANDING GEAR SYSTEM

MAIN GEAR

The main gear and nose gear incorporate a standard air-oil strut for shock absorption and for supporting the airplane's weight. Each gear is hydraulically

extended and retracted and incorporates a hydraulically operated main gear door. The main gear is hydraulically tilted aft to fit into the wheel well structure on gear retraction and to provide air/ground sensing.

The main gear is held up and locked by an uplock hook engaging a roller on the shock strut, and held down and locked by overcenter locking of a downlock link. The main gear door actuator locks the main gear door closed.

Each gear has four wheels and brakes on a dual axle truck. The bearing mounted brakes are hydraulically actuated with antiskid protection provided.

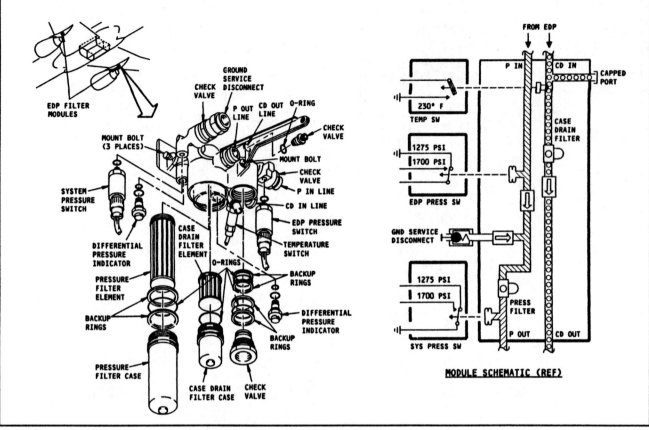

Figure 7-14. 757 engine driven pump filter module. (Boeing)

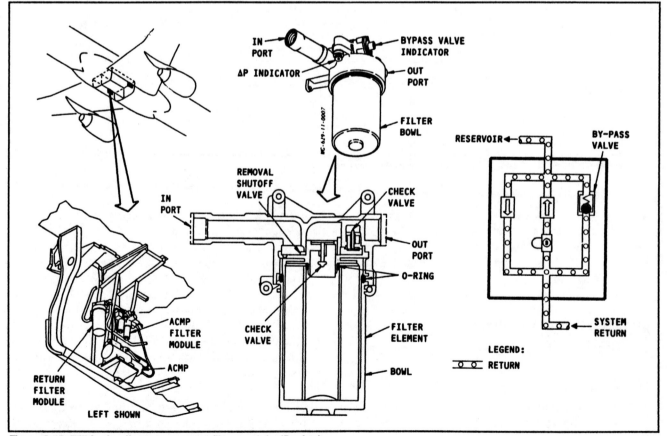

Figure 7-15. 757 hydraulic system return filter module. (Boeing)

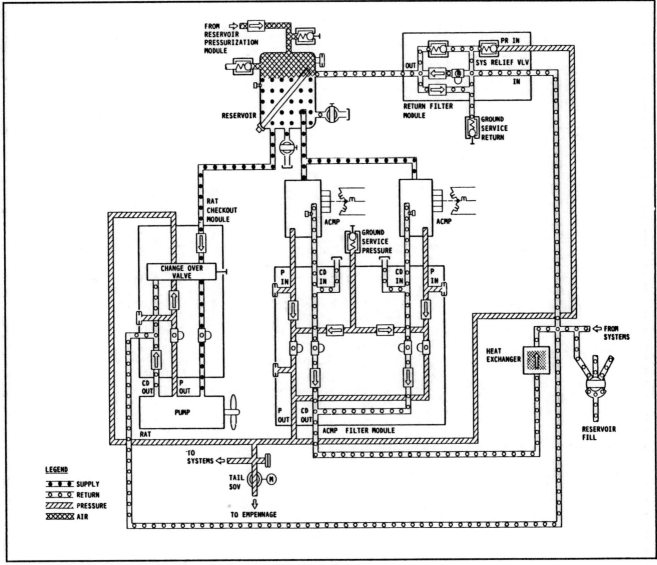

Figure 7-16. Center hydraulic system flow schematic, 757. (Boeing)

Alternate extension (emergency) is accomplished by an electric/hydraulic system which unlocks the main gear and doors to allow free fall extension. Gear position indication is provided by a dual proximity switch system controlled by the proximity switch electronics unit.

NOSE GEAR

The nose gear is hydraulically retracted, free falls to extend, and incorporates hydraulically sequenced forward doors for aerodynamic seal. Overcenter locking of a lock link, hydraulically actuated and aided by a pair of bungee springs, locks the gear in both the extended and the retracted positions.

Hydraulically powered nose wheel steering for ground directional control is provided with tiller or rudder control. Friction pads brake the nose wheels

on retraction. Alternate extension and gear position indication is accomplished in much the same manner as the main gear.

LANDING GEAR CONTROLS AND INDICATORS

A three position (UP, OFF, DN) landing gear lever is used to control landing gear extension and retraction, as shown in Figure 7-17. A lock solenoid in the landing gear lever prevents moving the lever to the up position when the main gear trucks are not tilted. A lock override button is provided. A guarded alternate EXTEND switch controls an electric motor-hydraulic pump which will unlock the gear doors and gear to allow free fall extension. Position indicators above the landing gear lever include three green gear down and locked lights, a gear door open amber light, and a gear disagreement amber light.

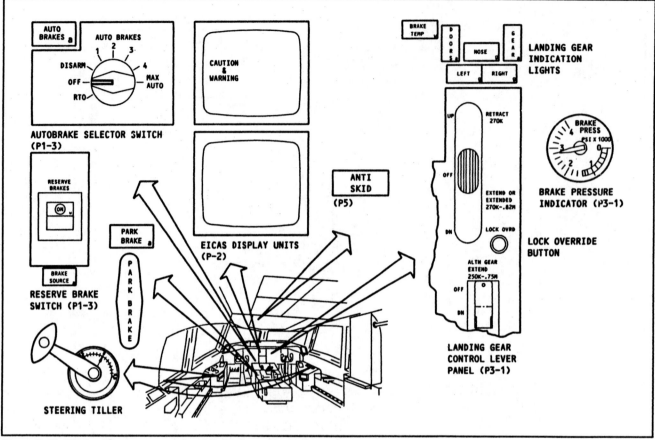

Figure 7-17. 757 landing gear control and indications. (Boeing)

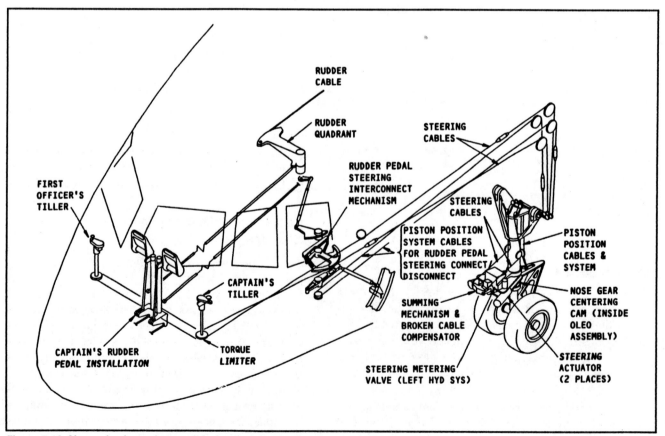

Figure 7-18. Nose wheel steering system description. (Boeing)

Eight hydraulic brake assemblies are operated by either the captain's or first officer's brake pedals. The autobrake system is controlled by a rotary selector switch, with an amber light above the switch to indicate a disarm condition. Brake pressure is indicated by a gauge handle on the quadrant stand. Indication of parking brake operation is provided by an amber light forward of the handle.

A reserve brakes switch will isolate the right hydraulic system alternating current motor-pump to the brakes. An amber BRAKE SOURCE light, below the reserve brake switch, provides indication of loss of normal and alternate hydraulic brake sources. Thermocouple devices on the brakes provide brake temperature sensing for display on EICAS. Another amber light indicates antiskid faults, with all amber lights having associated EICAS messages.

NOSE GEAR STEERING

The Boeing 757 nosewheel steering system, shown in Figure 7-18, is designed to achieve airplane directional control for ground operations. The nosewheel steering is controlled by two steering tillers, located on the left and right side of the flight compartment, or by the rudder pedals. Using the tillers provides for turns up to 65° left or right of center. The rudder pedals will give 7° left or right.

Whether the steering command is from the tillers or rudder system, the command signal is transmitted by cables to a hydraulic metering valve located on the nose gear. The metering valve directs hydraulic pressure to two steering actuators to steer the nose gear wheels. Internal centering cams in the nose gear shock strut center the wheels when the strut is extended after takeoff, and keep the gear centered when it is retracted and unpressurized during flight.

MAIN LANDING GEAR STRUCTURE

The main landing gear structure consists of a shock strut, torsion links, truck assembly, trunnion link, drag strut, side strut and down lock assembly, as can be seen in Figure 7-19. The shock strut inner and outer cylinders perform standard air-oil shock absorption and are serviced with dry air or nitrogen through a gas charging valve on the top of the strut, and with oil through an oil charging valve on the aft side of the strut. Torsion links connect the shock strut inner and outer cylinders. The truck assembly consists of a truck beam, axles, brake rods, and a protective shield. The truck beam attaches to the bottom of the inner cylinder, providing the pivot and attach point for the truck assembly.

NOSE LANDING GEAR STRUCTURE

The nose gear structure, shown in Figure 7-20, consists of a shock strut, torsion links, drag brace, and lock links. The shock strut is trunnion mounted in the nose gear wheel well and is supported by a two piece folding drag brace.

The upper drag brace is trunnion mounted to the wheel well structure and the lower brace attaches to a forging on the shock strut outer cylinder. The drag brace is held locked in both the extended and retracted positions by overcenter locking of lock links; the forward link attached to the apex of the drag brace and the aft link to a fitting on the aft nose wheel well bulkhead.

Bungee springs and a hydraulic actuator provide sequencing and overcenter locking of the lock links, which are responsible for locking the gear in the extended and retracted positions.

PROXIMITY SWITCH SYSTEM

The system monitors the position of the landing gear and other aircraft components. The proximity switch electronic unit (PSEU) contains the microprocessor and circuit cards to provide position indication and fault annunciation for the monitored systems by utilizing the feedback from proximity sensors.

The proximity switch electronics unit (PSEU) is a digital control unit containing four different types of circuit cards; proximity, logic, driver, and BITE cards. There are six interchangeable proximity cards. Each card contains 16 channels which pulse the sensors, determine target near or far, and switch voltage to the logic cards to a high or low output.

The logic cards receive the high and low voltage signals from the proximity cards and provide outputs to the driver cards which provide grounds (completed circuits) to lights, relays, switches, EICAS, etc. Two microprocessor based, built-in test equipment (BITE) cards provide fault isolation and system test capability.

Sensors provide position information to the proximity switch electronics unit (PSEU). Each sensor is a two-wire magnetic field producing coil-core device with wires connected to the PSEU proximity switch circuit card. The sensor operates in conjunction with a steel (magnetic) target. This action can be seen in Figure 7-21. The change in inductance as the proximity of sensor and target vary, provides a high or low output signal from the proximity switch cards to the appropriate logic card.

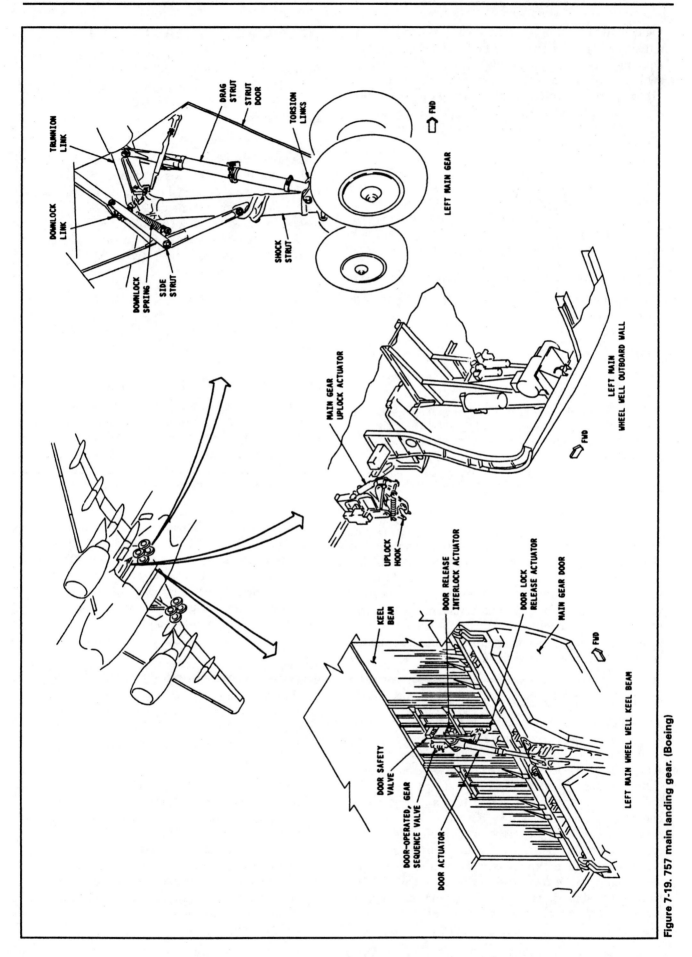

Figure 7-19. 757 main landing gear. (Boeing)

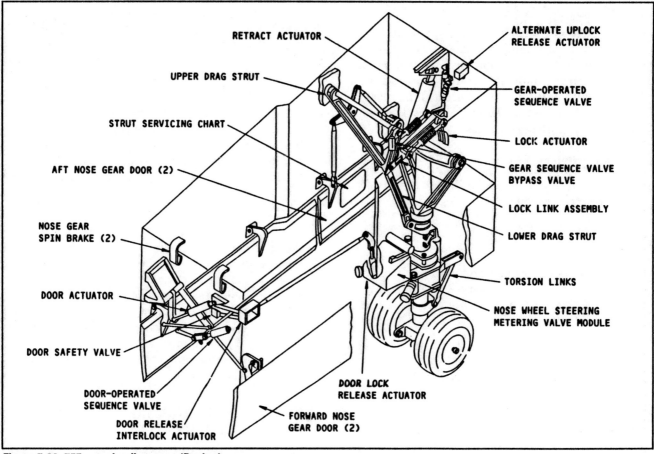

Figure 7-20. 757 nose landing gear. (Boeing)

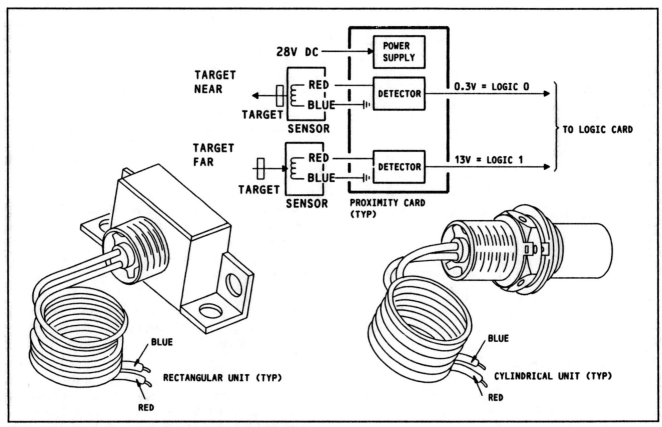

Figure 7-21. Proximity system sensors and targets. (Boeing)

AIR/GROUND SYSTEM

Air/ground relays switch various airplane system control circuits from ground to air mode, and air to ground mode. The relays are controlled by the proximity switch electronic unit (PSEU) using inputs from the main gear truck tilt proximity sensors, the nose gear compressed proximity sensors, and truck positioner shuttle valve pressure switches.

Two sensors on each main gear truck provide dual system truck tilt inputs to the PSEU. Two sensors on the nose gear strut provide dual nose gear strut compression inputs to the PSEU.

The sensor inputs are processed in the PSEU logic to provide inputs to drive air/ground relays which control various air/ground critical systems. PSEU and air/ground relay outputs are provided to the EICAS computers for air/ground system fault detection and annunciation.

GEAR POSITION AND INDICATION

Position indication for the landing gear system is provided by green and amber lights and EICAS caution, advisory, status and maintenance messages. The proximity switch electronic unit (PSEU) controls the lights and messages, using inputs from dual proximity sensor systems (system 1 and system 2).

An amber GEAR light illuminates when the landing gear position is not in agreement with the landing gear lever position, as sensed by both system 1 and system 2. Three green lights, NOSE, LEFT and RIGHT, illuminate when the respective landing gear is down and locked. An amber GEAR DOORS light illuminates when a landing gear door is not closed as sensed by both system 1 and system 2.

WHEELS AND BRAKE ASSEMBLIES

The main landing gear consists of dual tandem trucks, four wheels per truck. Each of the eight main gear wheels is provided with a hydraulically actuated, multiple disc brake. The nose landing gear is a single strut with dual wheels. The nose gear wheels do not incorporate brakes.

The normal brake system, shown in Figure 7-22, is powered by the right hydraulic system. The alternate system is powered by the left hydraulic system and is automatically selected upon loss of the right hydraulic system pressure. An accumulator in the right (normal) system is automatically selected when both normal and alternate system pressure is lost.

A reserve braking system is included in the normal brake system. The normal brake metering valves control brake pressure to the autobrake shuttle valves and the normal antiskid valves. The alternate brake metering valves meter hydraulic system pressure directly to the alternate antiskid valves.

Landing gear up line pressure is ported to actuators on the alternate antiskid valves to stop wheel rotation during landing gear retraction. Hydraulic pressure from the antiskid valves passes through a shuttle valve module which selects the pressurized system to the wheel brake assemblies.

When the right hydraulic system is pressurized, the accumulator is charged and the accumulator isolation valve (AIV) is open. A control line directs pressure to close the alternate brake selector valve (ABSV). Brake pedal operation meters right system pressure through the autobrake shuttle valves to the normal antiskid modules. The normal antiskid modules control hydraulic pressure individually to each brake through a shuttle valve module.

BRAKE TEMPERATURE MONITORING SYSTEM

The purpose of the monitoring system is to provide an indication of brake overheat by providing a color-coded number and box on the EICAS status page which represents the temperature of each brake and a white brake temperature light to indicate brake overheat.

ANTISKID/AUTOBRAKE

The purpose of the antiskid system is to monitor wheel deceleration and provide brake release to achieve optimum braking action under varying braking conditions. Normal and alternate antiskid valves receive pilot metered brake pressure from normal or alternate brake metering valves, depending on which brake system is pressurized. The antiskid valves are controlled by the antiskid/autobrake control unit to provide brake release if excessive wheel deceleration is detected. This brake release signal is developed by the control unit from the individual wheel speed transducer inputs.

The control unit also provides touchdown and hydroplane protection using inertial reference system (IRS) ground speed inputs.

There is no control switch for the antiskid system, therefore it is operational whenever the electrical systems are powered. An amber ANTISKID light indicates a fault in the antiskid system.

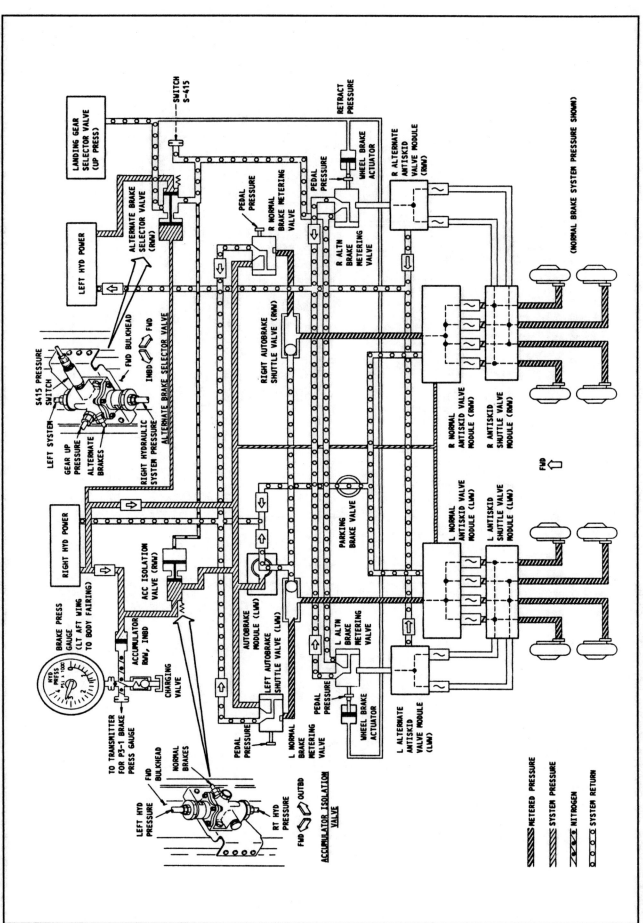

Figure 7-22. Brake hydraulic system, normal condition, 757. (Boeing)

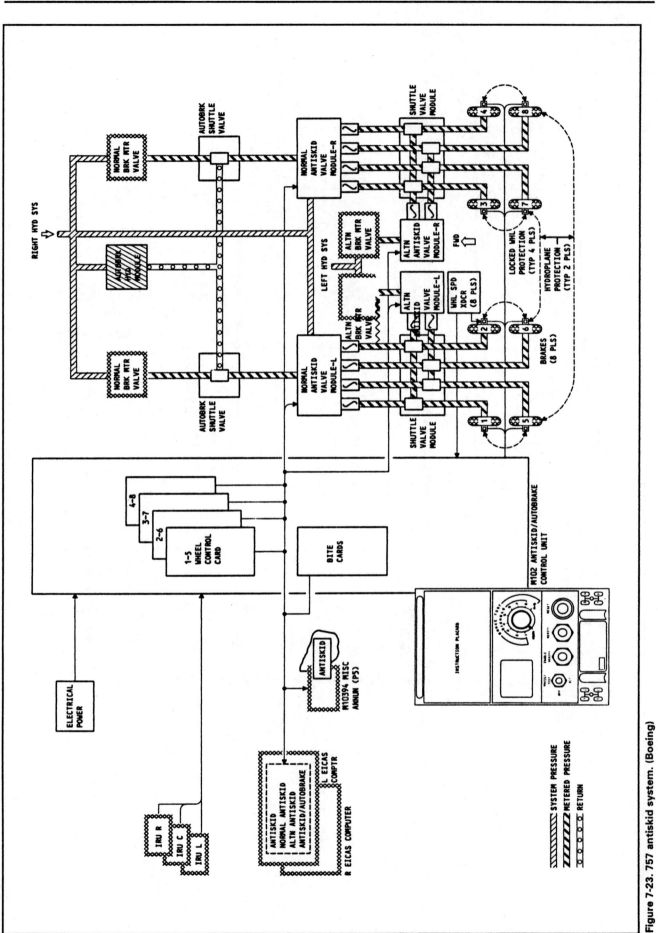

Figure 7-23. 757 antiskid system. (Boeing)

The antiskid function is controlled by four wheel control cards within the antiskid/autobrake control unit. Each card controls a fore/aft pair of wheels through individual wheel circuits, as can be seen in Figure 7-23.

The antiskid valve modules receive metered pressure from the brake metering valves or autobrake module. If a skid condition is detected, the control unit will reduce brake pressure to that wheel by providing signals to the normal and alternate antiskid valves.

The autobrake system automatically applies and controls brake pressure in an attempt to achieve an airplane rate of deceleration, as selected by the flight crew. The antiskid/autobrake control unit operates an autobrake module to provide metered pressure to the brakes through the normal antiskid valves.

Brake pressure varies according to the rate of airplane deceleration selected and the actual rate of deceleration obtained through braking, thrust reverser and ground speedbrake operation.

The autobrakes are controlled through an autobrake selector, shown in Figure 7-24. The switch allows deceleration selections for landing, autobrakes, one selection for rejected takeoff (RTO), an OFF position

and a disarm fault position. The amber AUTOBRAKE light indicates the system has faulted to a disarm mode.

BOEING 747-400 HYDRAULIC POWER SYSTEM

Four separate and independent main hydraulic supply systems, illustrated in Figure 7-25, are provided in the airplane to meet the power requirements of the flight control and other aircraft control systems. Each main supply system is associated with its respective engine with most of its components located in the nacelle area above and aft of the engine. The hydraulic supply system is identified by the same number as the corresponding engine.

The four main hydraulic supply systems are functionally identical. The systems differ only in reservoir capacity and the location of some components.

Hydraulic power for each system is provided by two pumps installed in parallel. An engine-driven pump is in operation at all times when the airplane engine is running. This pump is supplemented by an engine bleed air driven demand pump on system No. 1 and No. 4 and an AC motor driven demand pump on system No. 2 and No. 3. The demand pumps can be turned

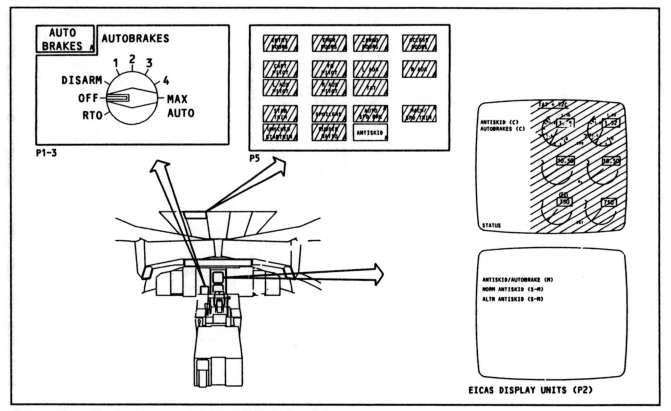

Figure 7-24. Autobrakes flight deck controls and indicators. (Boeing)

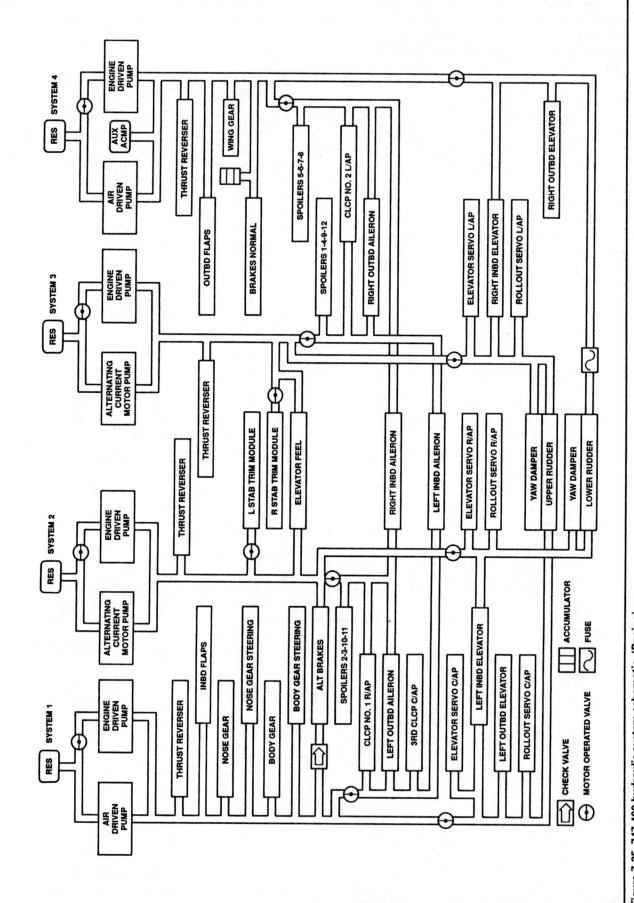

Figure 7-25. 747-400 hydraulic system schematic. (Boeing)

off, run continuously, or operated in the automatic mode where they will remain off until the demand exceeds the capacity of the engine driven pump.

Most of the components of the supply system are grouped in modules identified as pressure, return, and case drain. Ground service connections are provided at each of the pressure and return modules to permit the attachment of an external hydraulic supply source. Reservoir pressurization and central reservoir servicing connections are provided to support the hydraulic supply systems.

An auxiliary AC hydraulic system is installed in hydraulic supply system No. 4 to provide brake pressure during towing operations. Indicating and warning systems are provided to inform the pilots of operating conditions within each main hydraulic supply system. The indication and warning devices are located in the control cabin.

The engine hydraulic pump switch, shown in Figure 7-26, is an alternate action switch (push-on, push-off). Selecting the pump switch to ON allows the pump on the engine selected to pressurize its respective hydraulic components when the engine rotates. When selected to ON, a white ON is displayed on the face of the switch.

The engine hydraulic pump low pressure light illuminates whenever pump output pressure is below 1400 PSI and the fire handle has not been pulled.

The demand hydraulic pump switch has three position selections on system No. 1, 2, and 3. The demand pumps are the air driven pumps on system No. 1 and No. 4, and the AC motor driven pumps on system No. 2 and No. 3, as mentioned earlier.

System No. 4's switch has an additional position for the auxiliary AC motor pump (ACMP) control. The switch positions are ON: demand pumps operate continuously, AUTO; system No. 1 and 4 demand pumps (air driven) and the No. 2 and 3 demand pumps (ACMP) operate under the following conditions; when the engine driven pump pressure drops to 1,400 PSI, and when the fuel cut-off switch is in the cutoff position for that system.

Only the No. 1 and 4 demand pumps operate under the following conditions: when the trailing edge flaps are in transit, or when the trailing edge flap position is greater than zero degrees and air mode is sensed.

The third switch position: OFF shuts down selected demand pump operation.

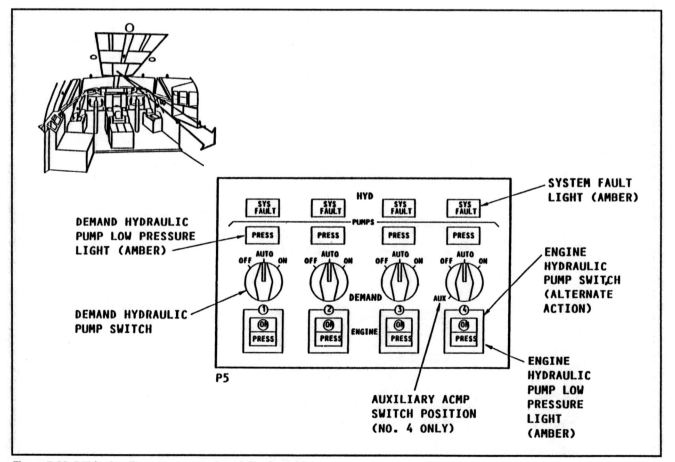

Figure 7-26. 747 hydraulic system control module. (Boeing)

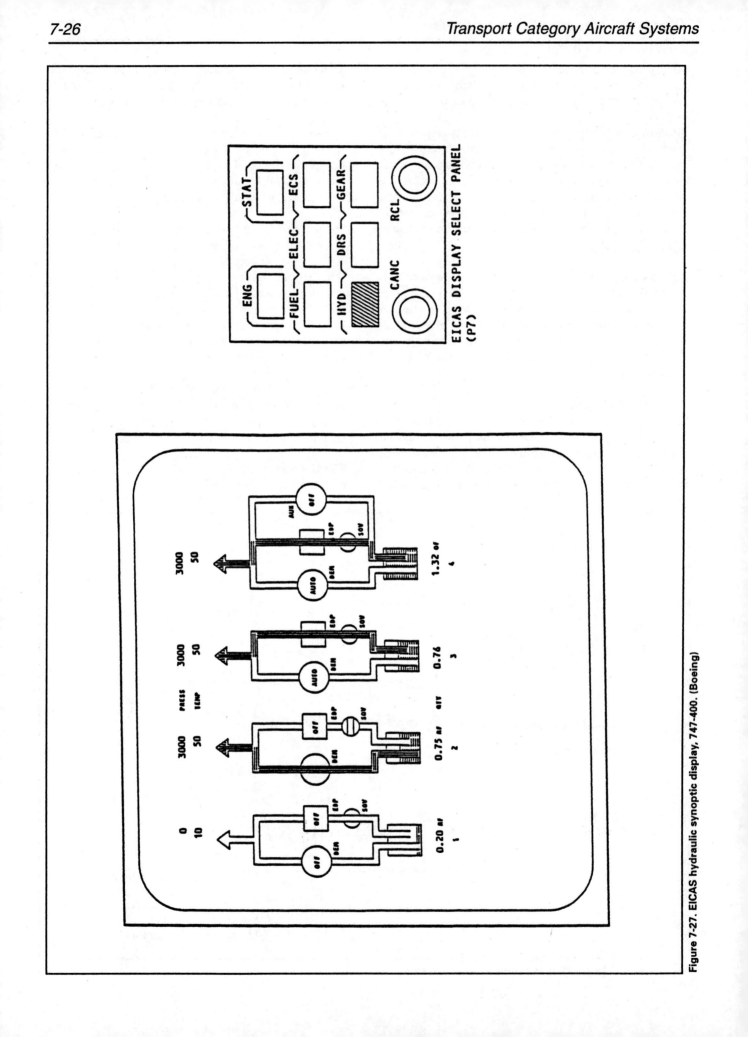

Figure 7-27. EICAS hydraulic synoptic display, 747-400. (Boeing)

The last switch position, AUXILIARY (system No. 4 only); the auxiliary ACMP operates continuously while the airplane is on the ground until system No. 4 engine driven pump or demand pressure rises above 1,400 PSI; Auxiliary ACMP pressurizes the entire hydraulic system No. 4. Primary use of the auxiliary ACMP is for wheel braking when the aircraft is being towed as described previously.

The amber system fault light will illuminate whenever system pressure is low, hydraulic fluid quantity is low, or hydraulic fluid temperature is excessive. The associated fault description will also appear on the PRIMARY EICAS display.

By depressing the hydraulic button on the EICAS select panel, the synoptic display is displayed as shown in Figure 7-27. The following hydraulic system information is available on the synoptic page: pump operation information; shutoff valve position; hydraulic quantity information; hydraulic fluid temperature; and hydraulic pressure.

BOEING 747-400 LANDING GEAR

The basic operating principles of the 747 landing gear are somewhat similar to the 757 system described previously. One main difference is the landing gear arrangement which uses two sets of main landing gear consisting of the wing and the body gear. Sixteen main gear wheels, tires, and brakes are mounted on four four-wheel trucks that support most of the aircraft's weight.

The wing and body gear, shown in Figure 7-28, are mounted with the wing gear attached to the inboard section of the wing, while the steerable body gear is mounted to the fuselage.

The nose landing gear, which incorporates two wheels and tires, is steerable when the shock strut is compressed and the centering cams are disengaged. After squat switches sense ground mode and input to the proximity switch electronic unit (PSEU), the rudder pedal steering mechanism is engaged. Steering from the rudder pedals is limited to 7° left and right. Input from the tillers will move the nose gear a maximum of 70° left and right. Autopilot inputs from the rollout control system, if engaged, will also steer the gear up to the rudder pedal limit.

Moving the tillers or pedals, as shown in Figure 7-29, drives two cable loops which are connected through a cable compensator and pivot links. The lower loop moves a steering metering valve, which directs hydraulic fluid from system No. 1 to the steering cylinders, causing the torsion links to move the inner strut and wheels.

Arming and control inputs to the body gear steering system are made when there is sufficient movement of the nose steering cables, and the aircraft is on the ground. The wheel speeds must also be less than 15 knots.

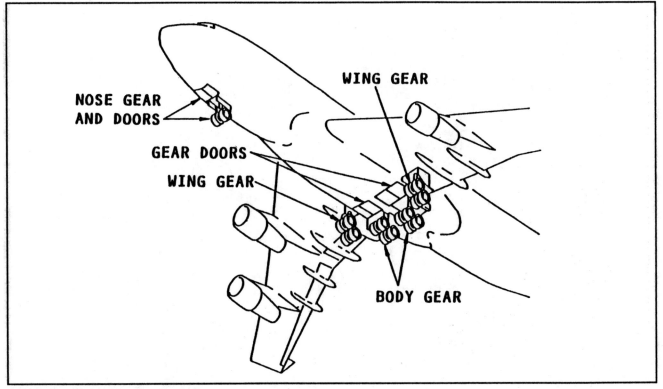

Figure 7-28. 747 landing gear. (Boeing)

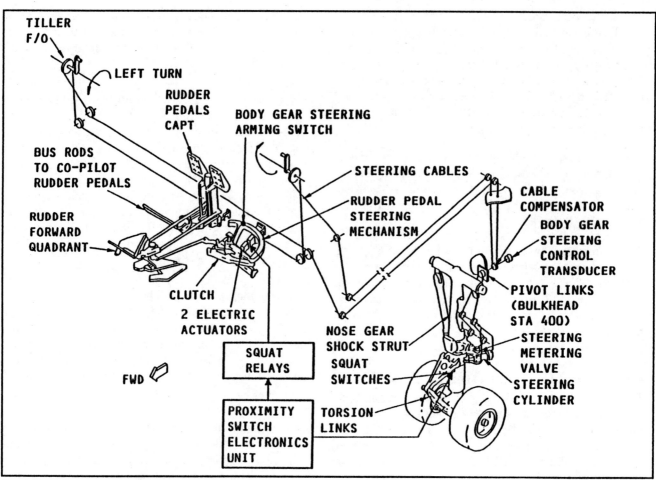

Figure 7-29. Nose gear steering system, 747. (Boeing)

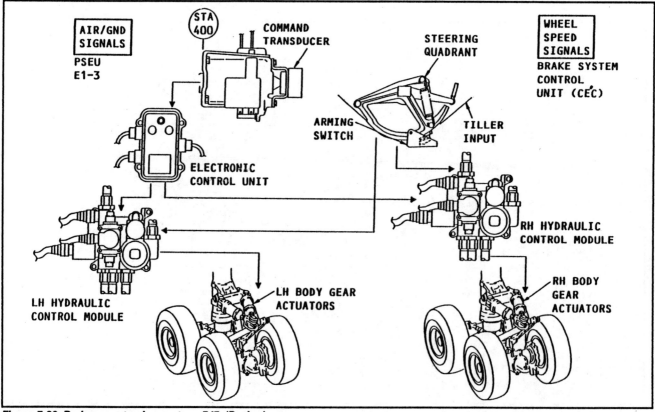

Figure 7-30. Body gear steering system, 747. (Boeing)

With the system armed, movement of the command transducer beyond 20° causes the transducer to generate an electrical signal proportional to the angle of nose wheel steering. This signal is processed in the electronic control unit and operates the servo in the hydraulic control modules, as shown in Figure 7-30. The modules control hydraulic pressure to the body gear steering actuators. The actuators are capable of turning the trucks to a maximum of 13°. Maximum body gear truck turning occurs at about 70° of nose wheel steering.

The brake, antiskid, autobrake, and proximity/gear position systems operate, for these discussions, somewhat similar to the 757 systems described earlier. The brake torque limiting system protects the landing gear from exerting excessive structural loads due to high brake torque. The system limits individual brake torque to a fixed maximum limit.

LOCKHEED L-1011 HYDRAULIC SYSTEM

The Lockheed L-1011 hydraulic systems (A, B, C, and D, shown in Figure 7-31), are used to pressurize the flight controls, landing gear, brakes, nose steering, and tail skid. Each of the systems has multiple pressure sources. System A can be pressurized by engine No. 1 engine-driven pump (A1) or a power transfer unit driven by system B. System B can be pressurized by engine No. 2 engine driven pump (B1), an identical air turbine motor (ATM) driven pump (B2), an AC electric motor driven pump (B3), or a pump driven by a ram air turbine. System C has identical sources as system B, except it has no ram air turbine. System D is pressurized by an engine No. 3 engine driven pump (D1) and a power transfer unit driven by system C.

All pressure sources for a given system are parallel and can individually or simultaneously pressurize that system. For example, pump C1 and C3 in system C can be operating at the same time.

All engine driven pumps (A1, B1, C1, D1) are driven by the engine high speed gear box. The ATMs can be driven by any source of air available from the pneumatic manifold. Each of the engines, the APU, or a ground air cart, can pressurize the pneumatic manifold. The routing of air to the ATMs is accomplished from the pneumatic control panel; then ATM operation is initiated from the hydraulic control panel. The AC motor driven pumps are operated by three-phase AC electrical power. They are low volume pumps for

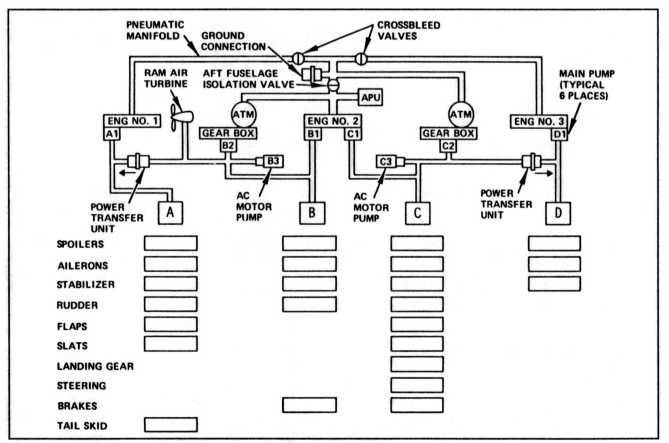

Figure 7-31. L-1011 hydraulic pressure sources and distribution, (Lockheed)

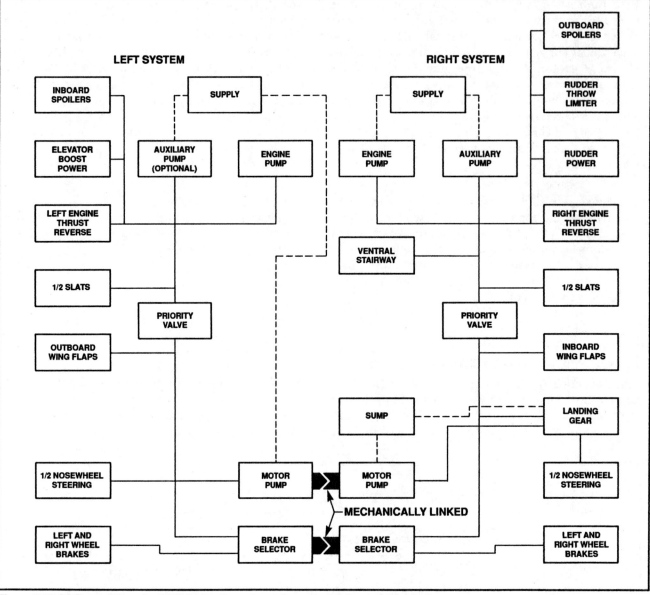

Figure 7-32. McDonnell Douglas DC-9 hydraulic system schematic. (McDonnell Douglas)

ground maintenance checks and pressurizing the reservoirs prior to engine start.

Each system will furnish hydraulic pressure to the various aircraft systems, as shown in Figure 7-31. For example, all four systems furnish pressure to the primary flight controls (spoilers, ailerons, and stabilizer). Therefore, any one system is capable of controlling flight.

MCDONNELL DOUGLAS DC-9 HYDRAULIC SYSTEM

The DC-9 uses two independent, continuously operating hydraulic systems, as shown in Figure 7-32. The primary power source for each system is an engine driven variable-displacement pump. As an alternate

power source, a reversible hydraulic motor pump (power transfer unit) can supply pressure to either system. When one system is pressurized, the alternate pump can supply pressure to the other without fluid exchange between systems. Both systems, the left and the right, use fire-resistant Skydrol® hydraulic fluid. The right hand system has an additional backup by an electric motor pump, which is powered from either engine's alternating current bus.

Each system develops an operating pressure of 3,000 PSI. To lengthen the service life of the components, flight operational control surfaces (such as rudder and spoiler) in both of the systems is reduced from 3,000 PSI to 1,500 PSI in flight; non-flight operational components, such as the wing flaps and landing gear, reduce to zero pressure in flight.

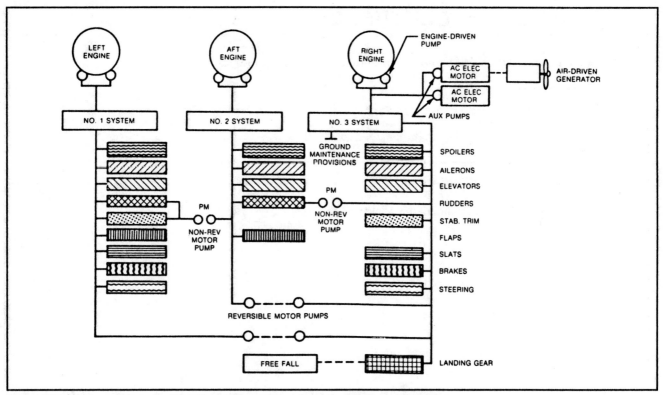

Figure 7-33. McDonnell Douglas DC-10 hydraulic system schematic. (McDonnell Douglas)

Although the left and right hydraulic systems are completely separate, almost all components, such as pumps, cylinders, reservoir assemblies, accumulators, filters, gauges, and valves, are identical.

The DC-9's tricycle landing gear is fully retractable. The dual wheel main gears, located at each inboard wing rear spar, retract up and into the wing and fuselage. The dual wheel nose gear retracts forward and up into the fuselage nose section. The landing gear is retracted and extended hydraulically by the right hand system, which also powers the gears and door latches.

For emergency operations, an alternate control lever releases the gear and lets it free-fall to the down-and-lock position. The inboard main gear doors and the forward gear door close after gear extension.

The hydraulically powered multiple disc brake on each main gear wheel is controlled by foot-pedal-operated valves. An electrically controlled antiskid system prevents locked wheels.

Dual steering cylinders are directly coupled to the shock strut support housing. Each cylinder is supplied by a separate hydraulic system and is controlled through separate, coordinated steering valves that are monitored by a mechanical follow-up linkage. Steering inputs are fed through the rudder control system for turns up to 17° in each direction; for turns up to 82° in

each direction, inputs are through the nose-wheel steering system.

MCDONNELL DOUGLAS DC-10 HYDRAULIC SYSTEM

The DC-10 is equipped with three separate, parallel, continuously operating closed circuit hydraulic systems shown in Figure 7-33. All systems operate at 3,000 PSI and utilize DMS 2014 fluid. The primary flight control surfaces are divided into segments and hydraulically powered in such a manner that loss of any one system does not significantly effect aircraft control during any phase of flight, including approach and landing.

Maintenance test and subsystem safety isolation provisions are incorporated in the hydraulic system, which monitor the system to provide fault and leakage detection of the individual component.

Maintenance and inspection techniques are simplified by the use of parallel, nearly identical, hydraulic systems, allowing troubleshooting and fault finding procedures developed for any single system to be used in the same way on all systems. The loads of the three hydraulic systems are balanced. Identical components such as pumps, reservoirs, filters, valves, and manifolds are installed in each system, thus reducing the number of spare parts required.

CHAPTER 7 STUDY QUESTIONS

1. What are characteristics that should be considered with regard to hydraulic fluids?

2. What should be done if hydraulic fluids are intermixed?

3. Sketch a simple hydraulic system and label the components.

4. What would happen if a hydraulic filter becomes clogged?

5. List the methods used to turn hydraulic pumps.

6. What is the normal pressure range of the hydraulic systems on transport aircraft?

7. Describe the hydraulic systems on the Boeing 737-300 aircraft.

8. How are the hydraulic systems identified on the 757?

9. Describe the method used to cool the hydraulic fluid on the 757.

10.   Describe the operation of the proximity switch system.

_____

_____

_____

11.   What is an on-demand pump and how does it operate?

_____

_____

12.   Describe the operation of the center body gear with regard to directional control of the aircraft.

_____

_____

_____

13.   List and describe the hydraulic systems on the L-1011 aircraft.

_____

_____

_____

_____

OXYGEN SYSTEMS

Without oxygen, people lose consciousness and can die in a short period of time. But, before this extreme state is reached, reduction in normal oxygen supplies to the tissues of the body can produce important changes in body functions and thought processes.

The sluggish condition of mind and body caused by a deficiency or lack of oxygen is called hypoxia. There are several causes of hypoxia, but the one which most concerns aircraft operations is the decrease in partial pressure of the oxygen in the lungs which occurs at high altitudes.

The rate at which the lungs absorb oxygen depends upon the oxygen pressure. The pressure that oxygen exerts is about one-fifth of the total air pressure at any one given level. At sea level, this pressure value is sufficient to saturate the blood. However, if the oxygen pressure is reduced, either from the reduced atmospheric pressure at altitude, or because the percentage of oxygen in the air breathed decreases, then the quantity of oxygen in the blood leaving the lungs drops, and hypoxia follows.

At high altitude there is decreased barometric pressure, resulting in decreased oxygen content of the inhaled air. Consequently, the oxygen content of the blood is reduced.

The low partial pressure of oxygen, low ambient air pressure, and temperature at high altitude make it necessary to create the proper environment for passenger and crew comfort. The most difficult problem is maintaining the correct partial pressure of oxygen in the inhaled air. This environment can be achieved by using a pressurized cabin.

Pressurization of the aircraft cabin is now the accepted method of protecting persons against the effects of hypoxia. Within a pressurized cabin, people can be transported comfortably and safely for long periods of time, particularly if the cabin altitude is maintained at 8,000 feet or below, where the use of oxygen equipment is not required. However, the flight crew in a transport aircraft must be aware of the danger of accidental loss of cabin pressure (explosive or rapid decompression) and must be prepared to meet such an emergency, should it occur.

Transport aircraft are equipped with supplemental, or emergency, oxygen systems in case of cabin decompression for both the flight crew and the passengers. Emergency supplemented oxygen is a necessity in any pressurized aircraft flying above 25,000 feet. The flight crew and passenger oxygen systems are generally separate and independent of each other in their operation.

The flight crew oxygen system is supplied from cylinders of compressed oxygen that flows through shutoff valves, regulators, lines, and masks to the flight crew. Under certain operating situations and decompression, the flight crew uses the oxygen mask for breathing. The flight crew oxygen system is usually a pressure-demand (on-demand) system.

The system provides either 100% pure oxygen or diluted oxygen (a mixture of oxygen and air from the flight deck environment), to the flight crew's oxygen mask. When one of the flight crew members inhales, oxygen is provided, but only when a breath is drawn in. The amount the oxygen is diluted with flight deck air will depend upon the flight deck altitude. This type of system is sometimes referred to as a diluter-demand system. Flight crew oxygen systems will be discussed in more detail later in this chapter.

Passenger emergency oxygen systems are generally of the continuous flow type which provides a steady flow of oxygen to the mask. Passenger oxygen systems have oxygen masks that drop from the ceiling of the cabin in case of cabin decompression. There are generally two types of systems, the compressed oxygen cylinder, or the solid state oxygen system (chemical oxygen generator).

The chemical oxygen generator differs from the compressed oxygen cylinder, in that the oxygen is actually produced at the time of delivery. Sodium chlorate, when heated to 478°F, releases up to 45% of its weight as gaseous oxygen. The necessary heat for decomposition of the sodium chlorate is supplied by iron which is mixed with the chlorate. The sodium chlorate and iron powder make up the oxygen generator chemical core. The initiator assembly starts the burning of the chemical core, and the oxygen produced is filtered before leaving the oxygen generator through the outlet

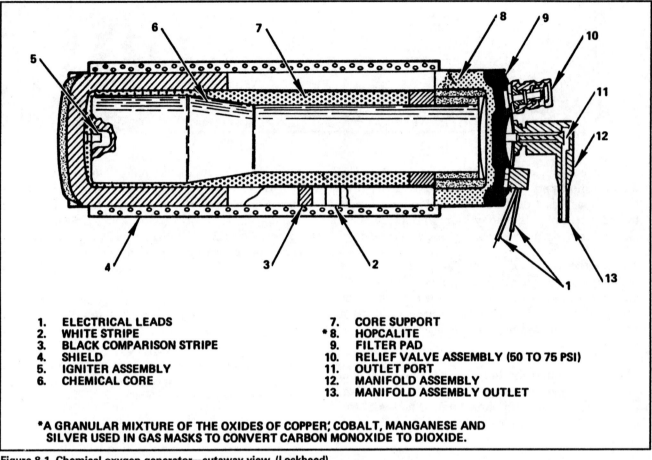

1. ELECTRICAL LEADS
2. WHITE STRIPE
3. BLACK COMPARISON STRIPE
4. SHIELD
5. IGNITER ASSEMBLY
6. CHEMICAL CORE
7. CORE SUPPORT
*8. HOPCALITE
9. FILTER PAD
10. RELIEF VALVE ASSEMBLY (50 TO 75 PSI)
11. OUTLET PORT
12. MANIFOLD ASSEMBLY
13. MANIFOLD ASSEMBLY OUTLET

*A GRANULAR MIXTURE OF THE OXIDES OF COPPER, COBALT, MANGANESE AND
SILVER USED IN GAS MASKS TO CONVERT CARBON MONOXIDE TO DIOXIDE.

Figure 8-1. Chemical oxygen generator—cutaway view. (Lockheed)

port. A cutaway view of an oxygen generator is shown in Figure 8-1.

Oxygen furnished at the mask is odorless, tasteless, and has a temperature of approximately 80°F. The oxygen generator case temperature reaches approximately 400°F. The white stripe will darken to show that the oxygen generator has been used. Normal operating pressure is below 50 PSI before being reduced for the mask.

The chemical generator can be initiated, or ignited, by activating the squib (electrically as on the L-1011) or by a percussion device. When a percussion device is used, passengers pulling the mask down for use releases a firing pin which starts the generator. The generators provide oxygen flow for about 12 to 18 minutes.

LOCKHEED L-1011 OXYGEN SYSTEM

FLIGHT CREW OXYGEN SYSTEM

The crew system, shown in Figure 8-2, will last a 5-man crew approximately 4 hours using diluted oxygen. An overpressure relief fitting will release all cylinder contents overboard if cylinder pressure

exceeds a certain limit. If this happens, the overboard discharge indicator, a green plastic disc mounted at the skin line on the right hand side of the flight station, will blow out.

If the oxygen cylinder's temperature is not excessive, an overpressure of the oxygen cylinder would normally be very rare. A slow-opening on-off valve releases cylinder pressure to the pressure reducer. The pressure reducer decreases cylinder pressure (1850 PSI at 70°F.) to 50-90 PSI. It also contains a relief valve that will safely relieve momentary overpressure.

On a panel near the cylinder is a quick disconnect fitting for maintenance checks. Corrosion-resistant steel tubing distributes the reduced pressure oxygen to five panel-mounted diluter-demand regulators, which further reduce oxygen pressure to breathing-pressure level.

These regulators indicate distribution line pressure, and contain a flow indicator and toggle control valves for oxygen pressure and dilution control. Aneroids within the regulators lessen oxygen dilution with increasing altitude and provide undiluted oxygen at positive pressure above 28,000 feet flight station altitude.

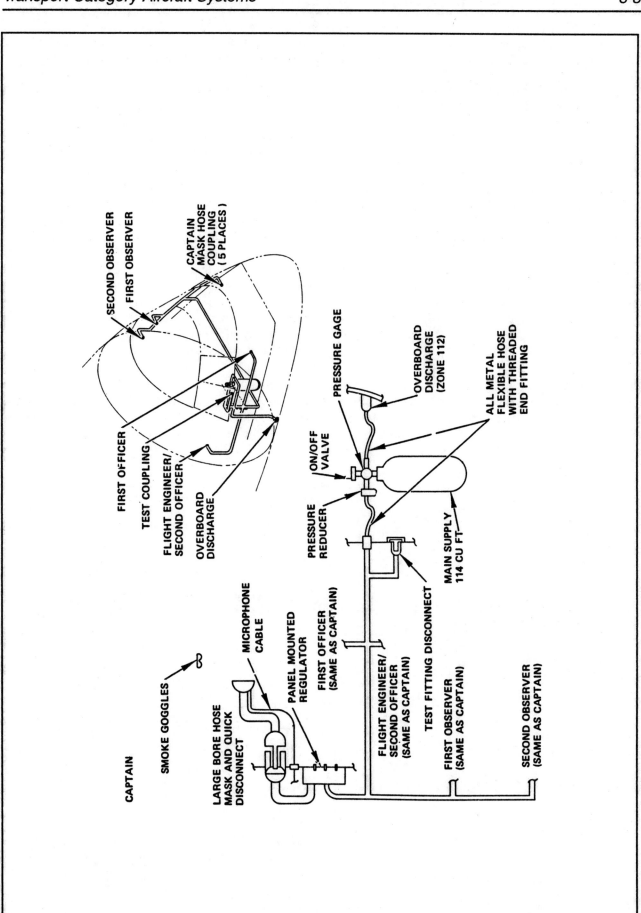

Figure 8-2. L-1011 crew oxygen system schematic diagram. (Lockheed)

Near the panel-mounted regulators are mask hose quick disconnects (QDs) and microphone cable jacks. These hose QDs will also accept the hose with a full-face smoke mask supplied with the flight station portable oxygen cylinder. To determine the oxygen level in the cylinder, it is weighed.

The flight crew oxygen mask, hose, and diluter-demand regulator are shown in Figure 8-3. A panel-mounted oxygen regulator and a mic/oxy panel are located near each of five flight station crew seats. On the front of the oxygen regulator are controls for oxygen dilution and pressure. On the back of the oxygen regulator are oxygen inlet and outlet ports, and an electrical connector for the 5 VAC panel light. On the bottom of the oxygen regulator is an ambient air inlet. The end of the mask hose that connects to the mic/oxy panel has a warning type connector that will not allow oxygen to flow through it if the connector is not fully seated in the hose coupling.

The regulated oxygen pressure gauge shows pressure entering the oxygen regulator. Oxygen will not flow from the oxygen regulator to the masks unless the on-off selector is in the ON position shown on the right side of the oxygen regulator panel in Figure 8-3.

With the 100% oxygen-normal oxygen selector in the 100% position, undiluted oxygen will be supplied to the mask regardless of flight station altitude. With this selector in the normal oxygen position, oxygen to the mask will be diluted with flight station ambient air in proportion to flight station air pressure. Dilution decreases with increasing altitude. At a flight station altitude of 28,000 feet or higher, oxygen to the masks will not be diluted at all. Normal flight station altitude (pressurized) is 8,000 feet.

With the emergency-normal-test mask selector in the normal position, flow to the mask is on demand (inhalation). In the emergency position, flow to the mask is continuous, and at positive pressure. The emergency position mechanically overrides the normal position. In the test mask position, flow to the mask is continuous, and at a pressure higher than in emergency position. The selector is spring-loaded out of the test mask position to the normal position.

The flight crew is required to have a portable breathing oxygen cylinder equipped with a full face smoke mask that operates in much the same manner as the crew oxygen system. It also operates with an undiluted on-demand regulator as shown in Figure 8-4. The mask

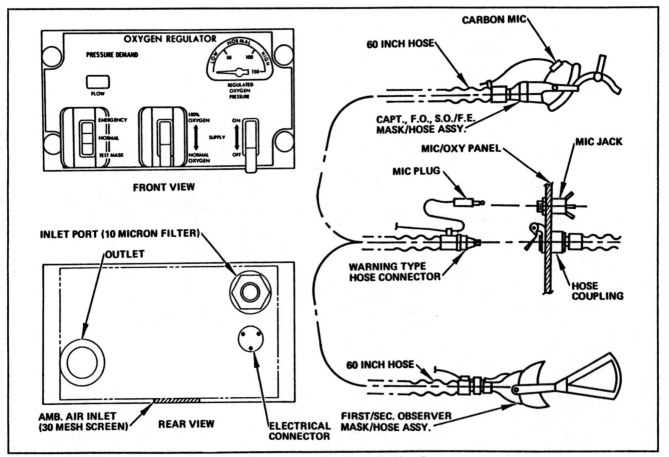

Figure 8-3. Flight crew oxygen mask, hose, and diluter-demand regulator. (Lockheed)

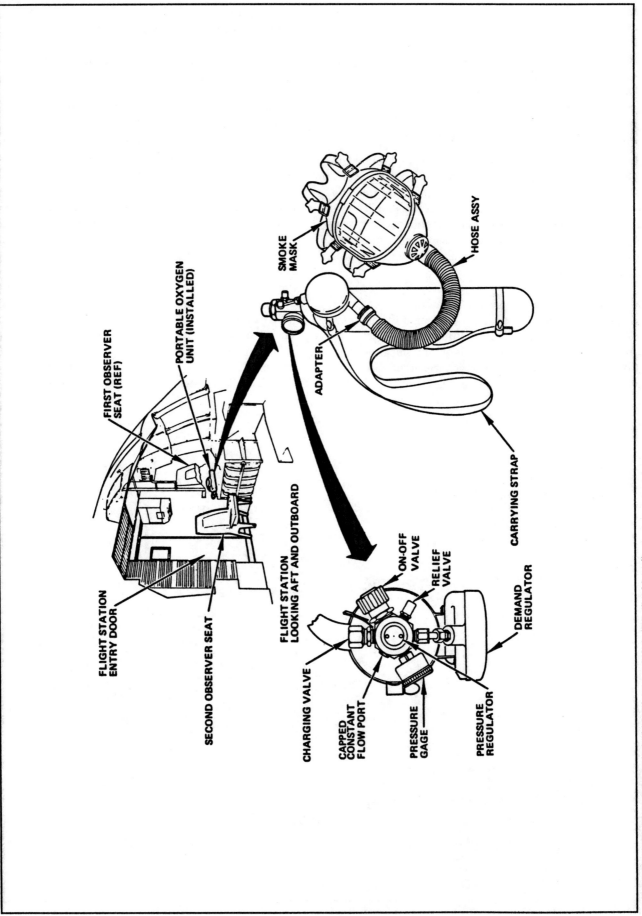

Figure 8-4. Flight crew portable breathing oxygen cylinder. (Lockheed)

hose can be connected to any crew station quick disconnect. Likewise, any crew mask can be connected to the portable cylinder. A pressure regulator at the top of the cylinder has a slow opening on-off valve, a charging valve, a pressure gauge, a relief valve, an overpressure safety plug, and a capped constant flow outlet, which is not used.

PASSENGER OXYGEN SYSTEM

Emergency oxygen for passengers is supplied from chemical oxygen generators through conventional face-cup masks. The generators, which are initiated by an electrical pulse, burn the two chemicals and produce oxygen for 15 to 18 minutes. Generators and associated rack-mounted mask(s) are secured in modules, one about each passenger seat group, attendant seat, and in each lavatory ceiling.

Oxygen masks, with associated supply tubes, are nested in a clear plastic rack and secured in the module by a hinged door. The door is magnetically latched, and for mask deployment, is electromagnetically unlatched by a solenoid. Oxygen generators and the masks associated with them, are divided into fifteen

groups; each group being identified numerically and composed of sectionally-situated modules.

System control components, shown in Figure 8-5, include a passenger oxygen controller, located at the Flight engineer's panel, and a sequence timer, located in the center cabin ceiling. The controller, through aneroid switching, automatically activates the system if cabin altitude rises to 13,000 feet. A manual switch on the controller provides for manual activation of the system if the aneroid switching circuits fail.

The sequence timer, when signaled automatically or manually, sequentially develops fifteen paired, timed, and synchronized output pulses, each pair consisting of a generator initiation pulse and a mask drop pulse. The 15 paired outputs are completed in about 7 seconds, then are redundantly repeated. The fifteenth output of the first cycle illuminates the OXYGEN FLOW light on the controller. Aircraft wiring connects the 15 output pulse pairs to the modules in each sequence group, initiating each generator in the group and energizing the solenoid for unlatching the mask rack door. The passenger oxygen controller incorpo-

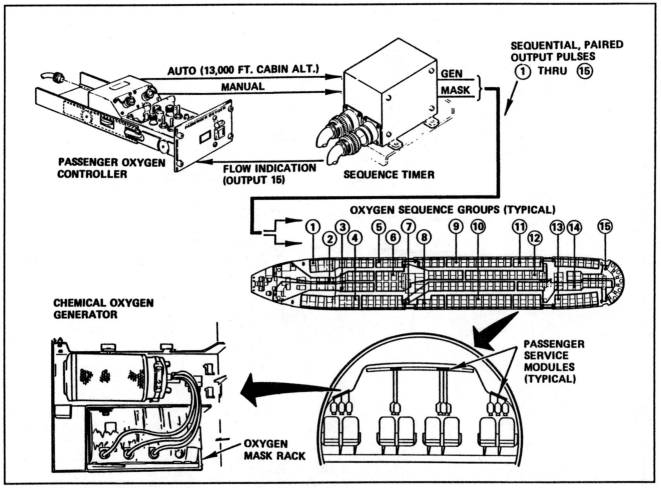

Figure 8-5. Lockheed L-1011 passenger oxygen system. (Lockheed)

rates a test panel which contains provisions for testing the system.

CHEMICAL OXYGEN GENERATOR

Oxygen generators are available in three sizes to supply oxygen to one, two, or three masks, as shown in Figure 8-6. They are approximately 7 inches long and 3 inches in diameter. Hermetically sealed cases have a shelf life of 10 years. Date of manufacture is indicated on the nameplate.

The case exterior contains black and white comparison stripes. The white stripe is heat-sensitive and will darken when the generator is used.

Oxygen from all masks constitutes about 1 percent of the cabin atmosphere, so there is no fire hazard due to oxygen from unused masks. Oxygen flow is continuous until the generator is expended.

PASSENGER SERVICE MODULES

An example passenger service module (PSM), shown in Figure 8-7, is ceiling mounted above each set of two passenger seats on the left and right sides of the cabin centerline. Oxygen masks are rack mounted in a mask compartment in the passenger service module (PSM) and are retained by a latched door.

A chemical oxygen generator, mounted adjacent to the mask compartment, is manifolded by clear plastic tubes to each oxygen mask. When the passenger oxygen system is activated, the door solenoid is energized; the door unlatches and springs open; the masks drop and are suspended by their supply tubes. Simultaneously, the chemical oxygen generator is actuated and supplies oxygen to each mask through its supply tube.

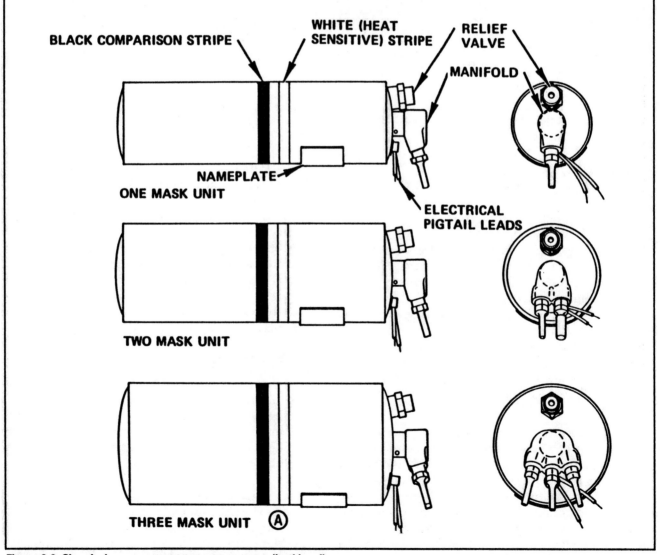

Figure 8-6. Chemical oxygen generator arrangement. (Lockheed)

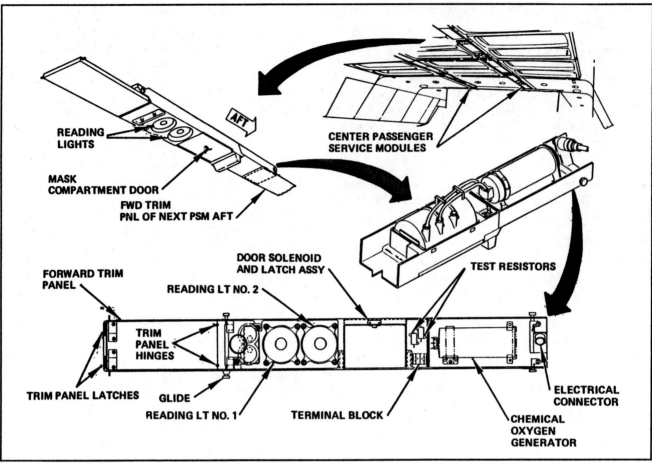

Figure 8-7. L-1011 typical passenger service module. (Lockheed)

BOEING 737-300 OXYGEN SYSTEMS

FLIGHT CREW OXYGEN

The flight crew and passenger oxygen systems, shown in Figure 8-8, are completely separate from each other. The flight crew oxygen system uses quick-donning diluter demand mask/regulators located at each crew station. Oxygen is supplied by a single cylinder. Pressure is read on the indicator located on the aft overhead panel when the battery switch is on. Oxygen flow is controlled through a pressure-reducing regulator to supply low pressure oxygen to a shut-off valve located behind the first officer's seat.

The mask/regulator is stored in a box immediately adjacent to each crew station. When the flight crew uses the mask, they squeeze the red release levers with the thumb and forefinger and remove it from stowage. Squeezing the release levers inflates the mask harness. The flow indicator will show a yellow cross momentarily as the harness pneumatically inflates. The Flight crew then places the mask over their head while releasing the levers. The harness will contract to fit the

mask to the crew members head and face. A microphone is contained in the mask for communication.

Oxygen flow is controlled by a regulator that is mounted on the oxygen mask. The regulator may be adjusted to supply 100% oxygen by pushing the normal/100% selector. The observer oxygen mask, regulator, and harness unit is the same as the pilots. Oxygen is available to the regulator when the cockpit shut-off valve is open. There is no flow indicator or reset-test lever.

PASSENGER OXYGEN

The passenger oxygen system is supplied by individual chemical oxygen generators located at each passenger service unit (PSU). Four continuous flow masks are connected to each generator. A generator with two masks is located above each attendant station and in each lavatory.

The system is activated automatically by a pressure switch at a cabin altitude of 14,000 feet or when the passenger oxygen switch on the aft overhead panel is positioned to the ON position. When the system is activated, the PASS OXY ON light will illuminate.

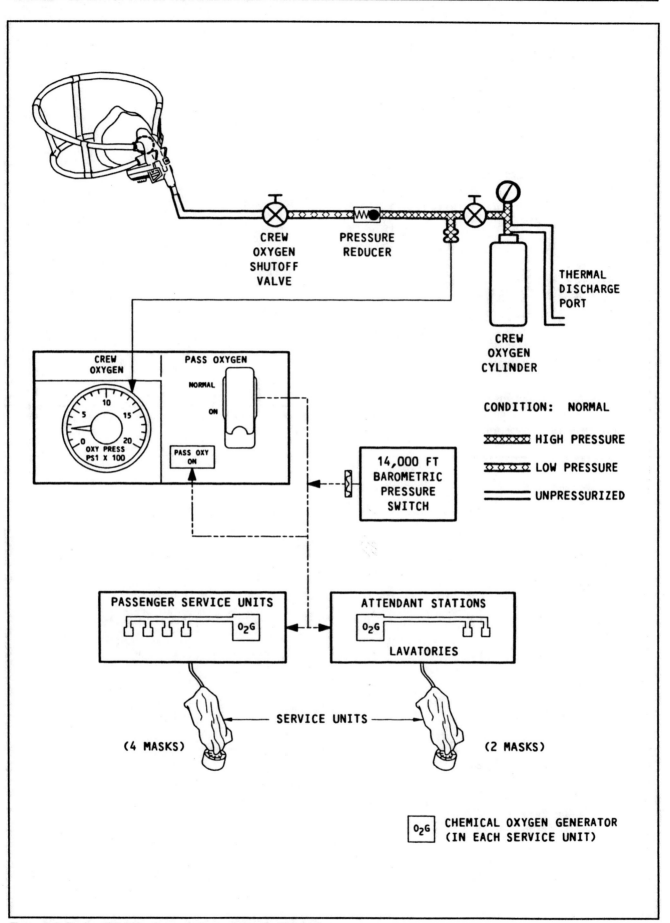

Figure 8-8. Boeing 737-300 oxygen system schematic. (Boeing)

Activating the system causes the masks to drop from the stowage compartments. The oxygen generators are activated when any mask in the unit is pulled down, releasing the firing pin attached to the oxygen mask hose. This action can be seen in Figure 8-9. Pulling one mask down causes all masks in that unit to come down and 100% oxygen flows to all masks.

A green in-line flow indicator is visible in the transparent oxygen hose whenever oxygen is flowing to the mask. Oxygen flows for approximately 12 minutes and cannot be shutoff. This same basic type of passenger oxygen system is also used on the 757, 767, and the A320 with some changes.

BOEING 747-400 OXYGEN SYSTEMS

The flight crew and passenger oxygen systems use oxygen cylinders to supply oxygen if needed. Several passenger oxygen systems have used chemical oxygen generators to supply the passengers in an emergency.

The 747 uses nine high pressure oxygen cylinders to store the passenger emergency oxygen. Each cylinder is equipped with a pressure gauge, shutoff valve and

frangible disc as shown in Figure 8-10. The frangible disc provides over-pressure relief through an overboard discharge port and manifold common to the crew system.

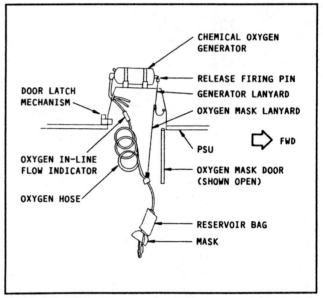

Figure 8-9. 737 pressure service unit oxygen mask compartment. (Boeing)

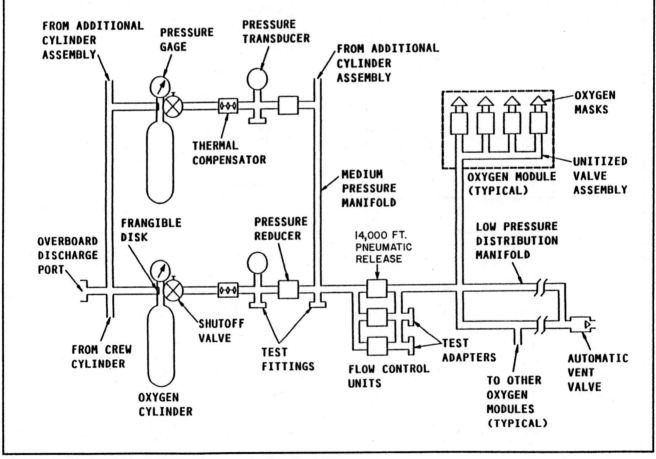

Figure 8-10. 747-400 passenger oxygen system operation. (Boeing)

A coupling with an integral thermal compensator connects the cylinder to a pressure reducer. A medium pressure manifold carries oxygen from the pressure reducers to the flow control units.

In the OFF (reset) condition, the flow control units prevent oxygen flow into the low pressure distribution manifold by closing the flow control units. Any small amount of oxygen leakage through the flow control units is discharged by the automatic vent valve to prevent unscheduled mask deployment.

When the flow control units are actuated, the resulting pressure surge unlatches the oxygen module doors, causing the masks to deploy. The surge also closes the automatic vent valve. Within several seconds of actuation, the pressure surge decays. While oxygen continues to flow to the masks, pressure in the manifold is sufficient to hold the automatic vent valve closed.

In some continuous flow systems using compressed oxygen cylinders, a valve is kept closed by an actuating pin. The valve is opened when the mask is pulled toward the passenger's face; a lanyard attached to the mask hose pulls the actuating pin out of the valve, allowing the valve to open and oxygen to flow to the mask. When oxygen is no longer required, the flow control units are reset by the flight crew, stopping the flow of oxygen to the distribution manifold. Residual pressure in the manifold is depleted through the masks allowing the automatic vent valve to open. Test fittings allow connection of an external pressure source and gauge for system testing.

A guarded three-position switch (see Figure 8-11) controls operation of the passenger oxygen system through the flow control units. With the switch in NORM, the system will activate one of the flow control units automatically at 14,000 feet cabin altitude. Momentarily placing the switch to ON activates the two other flow

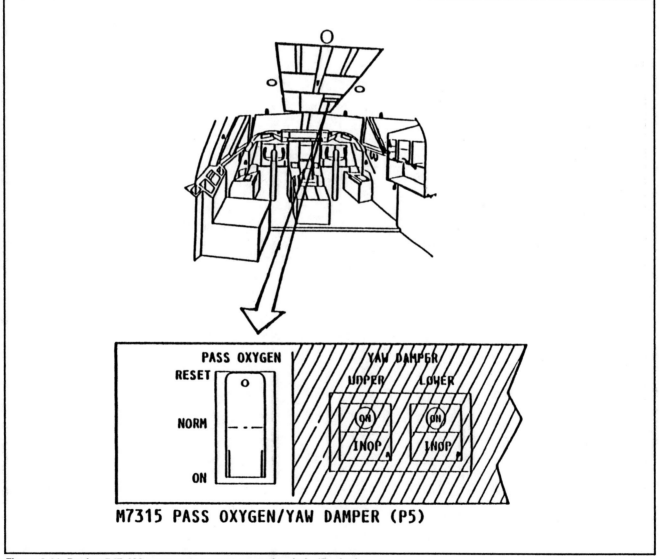

Figure 8-11. Boeing 747-400 passenger oxygen control switch. (Boeing)

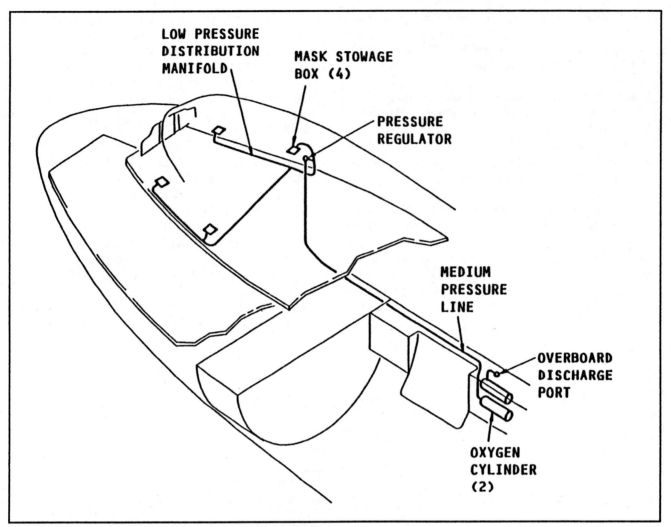

Figure 8-12. Flight crew oxygen system, Boeing 747-400. (Boeing)

control units. When oxygen is no longer required, the system is turned off by placing the switch momentarily to the RESET position. The switch is guarded to prevent unintentional system activation. Placing the switch to ON deploys all the passenger oxygen masks throughout the main and upper deck passenger cabins.

The flight crew emergency oxygen system operates in generally the same manner as the other Boeing aircraft already discussed in this chapter. The basic flight crew system is shown in Figure 8-12.

CHAPTER 8 STUDY QUESTIONS

1. What factors make it necessary to provide oxygen at high altitudes?

    _____

    _____

2. What normal method is used to protect the crew and passengers while operating at high altitudes?

    _____

    _____

3. Describe the operation of a chemical oxygen generator.

    _____

    _____

    _____

4. How is the passenger oxygen system initiated on an L-1011?

    _____

    _____

5. How can you tell if a chemical oxygen generator has been used?

    _____

    _____

6. If the flight crew selects normal on the 100%/normal oxygen lever at 12,000 ft cabin altitude, what is available from the mask?

    _____

    _____

7. The L-1011 crew's oxygen panel levers are set as follows: (on/off) set on; (100%/normal) set normal; (emergency/normal) set normal. What is available at the oxygen mask?

    _____

    _____

8. How is the passenger oxygen system oxygen generator activated?

    _____

    _____

9. At what altitude will the emergency oxygen system automatically activate on the 747-400 aircraft?

    _____

10. What is the source of oxygen in the passenger oxygen system on the 747-400?

    _____

    _____

WARNING AND FIRE PROTECTION SYSTEMS

Large transport aircraft have many on-board warning systems used to alert the flight crew to unsafe operational conditions. Some of these systems include fire and overheat, unsafe takeoff, unsafe landing, overspeed, cabin pressure, altitude alert, and ground proximity warning systems. Other warning systems used to provide information to the pilots or the flight engineer can be doors, flight controls, slat position, auto-pilot disconnect, and others.

Warning systems have generally the same basic function on most aircraft, although some warning systems do differ in configuration and operation. The particular warning systems used can also vary from aircraft to aircraft.

On newer generation aircraft, most of the warning systems are fed into the Engine Indicating and Crew Alerting System (EICAS), which provides messages or warnings to the flight crew on cathode-ray-tubes (TV screen) in the cockpit.

Along with fire detection warning systems, fire extinguishing systems also have a major role in protecting the aircraft against the threat of an onboard fire.

FIRE PROTECTION SYSTEMS

Because fire is one of the most dangerous threats to an aircraft, transport aircraft are protected by overheat, smoke, and fire protection systems. A complete fire protection system includes both a fire detection and a fire extinguishing system.

To detect fires or overheat conditions, detectors are placed in the various zones being monitored. A fire zone is an area or region of an aircraft which requires fire detection and/or fire extinguishing equipment and a high degree of inherent fire resistance. Some fire zone areas are the engine nacelles, APU areas, cargo compartments, and main landing gear wheel wells.

A fire detection system should signal the presence of a fire or overheating. Units of the system are installed in locations where there are greater possibilities of fire.

Detector systems in common use are the thermal switch system and the continuous-loop detector system.

Thermal switches are heat sensitive units that complete electrical circuits at a certain temperature. They are connected in parallel with each other, but in series with the indicator lights. If the temperature rises above a set value in any one section of the circuit, the thermal switch will close, completing the light circuit to indicate the presence of a fire or overheat condition. The thermal switch system uses a bimetallic thermostat switch or spot detector, similar to that shown in Figure 9-1. Each detector unit consists of a bimetallic thermoswitch. Most spot detectors are dual terminal thermoswitches.

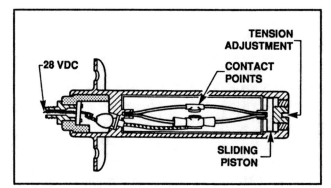

Figure 9-1. Fenwal spot detector.

A continuous-loop detector or sensing system permits more complete coverage of a fire hazard area than any type of spot-type temperature detectors. Continuous-loop systems are versions of the thermal switch system. They are overheat systems; heat sensitive units that complete electrical circuits at a certain temperature. Two widely used types of continuous-loop systems are the Kidde and the Fenwal systems.

In the Kidde continuous-loop system (Figure 9-2), two wires are imbedded in a special ceramic core within an inconel tube. One of the two wires in the Kidde sensing system is welded to the case at each end and acts as an internal ground. The second wire is a hot lead that provides a current signal when the ceramic

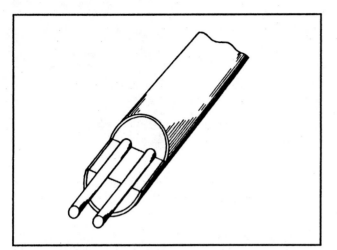

Figure 9-2. Kidde sensing element.

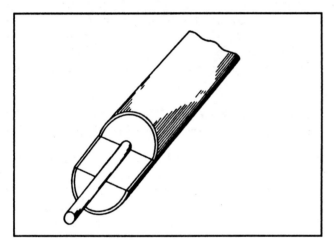

Figure 9-3. Fenwal sensing element.

core material changes its resistance with a change in temperature.

Another continuous-loop system, the Fenwal system (Figure 9-3), uses a single wire surrounded by a continuous string of ceramic beads in an inconel tube.

The beads in the Fenwal detector are wetted with a eutectic salt which possesses the characteristic of suddenly lowering its electrical resistance as the sensing element reaches its alarm temperature.

In both the Kidde and the Fenwal systems, the resistance of the ceramic or eutectic salt core material prevents electrical current from flowing at normal temperatures. In case of a fire or overheat condition, the core resistance drops and current flows between the signal wire and ground, energizing the alarm system.

Overheat warning systems are used on some transport aircraft to indicate high temperature areas that could lead to a fire if a malfunction occurs. The number of overheat warning systems varies from aircraft to air-

craft. On some aircraft, they are provided for each engine nacelle, wheel well area and for the area surrounding the pneumatic engine bleed air manifold. When an overheat condition occurs in the detector area, the system causes a light on the fire control panels to warn the flight crew.

A smoke detection system is generally used to monitor the cargo and baggage compartments for the presence of smoke, which is indicative of a fire condition. Smoke detection instruments, which collect air for sampling, are mounted in the compartments in strategic locations. A smoke detection system is used where the type of fire anticipated is expected to generate a substantial amount of smoke before temperature changes are sufficient to actuate a heat detection system. Smoke detection instruments are classified by their method of detection.

One type of detector consists of a photoelectric cell, a beacon lamp, a test lamp, and a light trap, all mounted on a labyrinth. An accumulation of 10% smoke in the air causes the photoelectric cell to conduct electric current. Figure 9-4 shows the details of the smoke detector, and indicates how the smoke particles refract the light to the photoelectric cell. When activated by smoke, the detector supplies a signal to the smoke detector amplifier. The amplifier signal activates a warning light and bell.

On some aircraft visual smoke detectors provide the only means of smoke detection. Indication is provided by drawing smoke through a line into the indicator, using either a suitable suction device or cabin pressurization. When smoke is present, a lamp within the indicator is illuminated automatically by the smoke detector. The light is scattered so that the smoke is rendered visible in the appropriate window of the indicator. If no smoke is present, the lamp will not be illuminated. A switch is provided to illuminate the lamp for test purposes. A device is also provided in the

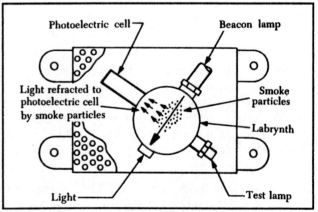

Figure 9-4. Photoelectric smoke detector.

indicator to show that the necessary airflow is passing through the indicator.

TYPES OF FIRES

The National Fire Protection Association has classified fires in three basic types. One type is the Class A fire, defined as fire in ordinary combustible materials such as wood, cloth, paper, upholstery materials, etc. Class B fires are defined as fires in flammable petroleum products or other flammable or combustible liquids, greases, solvents, paints, etc. The third type of fire is the Class C fire which is defined as fire involving energized electrical equipment where the electrical non-conductivity of the extinguishing media is of great importance.

AIRCRAFT COMPARTMENT FIRE CLASSIFICATIONS

The location of a fire is also identified by a letter designator. The cockpit and passenger cabin are designated Class A compartments, meaning that a fire may be visually detected, reached, and combated by a crewmember. The engines are generally Class C fire compartments, and fire warning is provided by fire detectors. There are two basic types of cargo compartments, Class B, in which a crewmember may reach and combat a source of fire. The other types of compartments are Class E or D, in which a crewmember cannot reach the source of fire.

Compartments are classified Class A when they provide for visual detection of smoke and have an accessible inflight fire extinguisher available.

The cargo and baggage compartments are classified "B" if they have sufficient access to enable a member of the crew to move all contents by hand, and to reach effectively all parts of the compartment with a hand fire extinguisher, while in flight.

When the access provisions are being used, no hazardous quantity of smoke, flames, or extinguishing agent can enter any compartment occupied by the crew or passengers. Each compartment should be equipped with an approved type smoke detector or fire detector to give a warning to the flight deck. Hand fire extinguishers must be readily available for use in all compartments of this category.

Compartments are classified Class C when they have smoke or fire detectors installed and a built-in fire extinguisher system controlled from the cockpit.

Cargo and baggage compartments are classified "D" if they are designed and constructed so that a fire occurring therein will be completely confined without endangering the safety of the airplane or the occupants. Ventilation and drafts controlled within each compartment must be configured so that any fire likely to occur in the compartment will not progress beyond safe limits. The compartment must be completely lined with fire resistant material.

On airplanes used to carry cargo only, the cabin area can be classified as a Class E compartment, if the window shades are closed and they are lined with fire-resistant material. A Class E compartment must also be equipped with a separate system of an approved type smoke or fire detector with a means provided to shut off the ventilating air flow to, or within, the compartment. Controls for such means shall be accessible to the flight crew in the cockpit. A means of excluding hazardous quantities of smoke, flames or noxious gases from the cockpit must also be provided. The required crew emergency exits must be accessible under all cargo loading conditions.

EXTINGUISHING AGENTS

Aircraft fire extinguishing agents have some common characteristics which make them compatible to aircraft fire extinguishing systems. All agents must be able to be stored for long periods of time without adversely affecting the system components or agent quality. The extinguishing agents must not freeze at normally expected atmospheric temperatures. The nature of the devices inside a powerplant compartment require agents that are not only useful against flammable fluid fires, but also effective on electrically caused fires. Agents are classified into two general categories based on the mechanics of extinguishing action: the halogenated hydrocarbon agents and the inert cold gas agents.

The probable extinguishing mechanism of halogenated agents is a chemical interference in the combustion process between fuel and oxidizer. Experimental evidence indicates that the most likely method of transferring energy in the combustion process is by molecule fragments resulting from the chemical reaction of the constituents. If these fragments are blocked from transferring their energy to the unburned fuel molecules, the combustion process may be slowed, or stopped completely (extinguished). It is believed that the halogenated agents react with the molecular fragments, thus preventing the energy transfer. This may be termed chemical cooling or energy transfer blocking. This extinguishing mechanism is much more effective than oxygen dilution and cooling.

Both carbon dioxide (CO_2) and Nitrogen (N_1) are effective cold gas extinguishing agents. Carbon dioxide, CO_2, has been used for many years to extinguish flammable fluid fires and fires involving electrical equipment. It is non-combustible and does not react with most substances. It provides its own pressure for discharge from the storage vessel.

Normally, CO_2 is a gas, but it is easily liquefied by compression and cooling. After liquification, CO_2 will remain in a closed container as both liquid and gas. When CO_2 is then discharged to the atmosphere, most of the liquid expands to gas. Heat absorbed by the gas during vaporization cools and becomes a finely divided white solid, dry ice snow. CO_2 is about 1 1/2 times as heavy as air, which gives it the ability to replace air above burning surfaces and maintain a smothering atmosphere. CO_2 is effective as an extinguishant primarily because it dilutes the air and reduces the oxygen content so that the air will no longer support combustion. Nitrogen, N_1, is an even more effective extinguishing agent. Like CO_2, N_1 is an inert gas of low toxicity. N_1 extinguishes by oxygen dilution and smothering. Freon® gas is also used as a cold gas extinguishing agent.

FIRE EXTINGUISHING SYSTEMS

A high-rate-of-discharge system (HRD) provides high discharge rates through high pressurization, short feed lines, large discharge valves, and outlets. Because the

agent and pressurizing gas of a HRD system are released into the zone in one second or less, the zone is temporarily pressurized, and interrupts the ventilating air flow. The few, large sized outlets are carefully located to produce high velocity swirl effects for best distribution.

The fire protection system of most large transport aircraft consists of two subsystems: a fire detection system and a fire extinguishing system. These two subsystems provide fire protection not only to the engine and nacelle areas but also to such areas as the baggage compartments and wheel wells as mentioned earlier.

The typical fire extinguishing portion of a complete fire protection system includes a cylinder, or cylinders, of extinguishing agent for each engine and nacelle area. This type of system uses an extinguishing agent container similar to the type shown in Figure 9-5.

The container is equipped with two discharge valves which are operated by electrically discharged cartridges. These two valves are the main and the reserve controls, which release and route the extinguishing

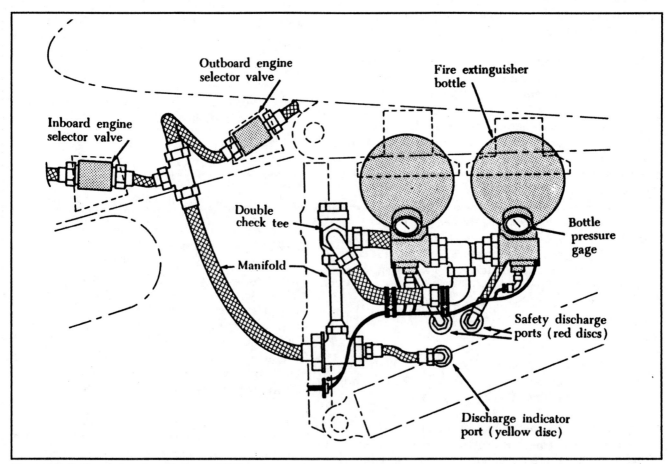

Figure 9-5. Dual container installation and fittings.

agent to the engine. A pressure gauge, a discharge manifold, and a safety discharge connection are provided for each container as shown in Figure 9-5.

The safety discharge connection is capped with a red indicating disk. If the temperature rises beyond a predetermined safe value, the disk will rupture, dumping the agent overboard. A missing red disk in the safety discharge ports indicates a thermal (overpressure) discharge. A yellow disk discharge indicator port is used to indicate that the system was fired from the cockpit. If the system was fired (activated) by the flight crew, this yellow disk will be missing.

LOCKHEED L-1011 FIRE PROTECTION SYSTEMS

The L-1011 has both fire detection and fire extinguishing capabilities for the three engines and the APU, as can be seen in Figure 9-6. It has a fire (overheat) detection system for the main landing gear wheel wells, but no fire extinguishing capability in these locations. The galley is equipped with a smoke detection system, and the galley oven ventilation system is equipped with a duct overheat detector. Portable fire extinguishers are located at strategic points throughout the flight station, passenger compartments, and the galley.

Fire detection is accomplished by dual loop sensors located at strategic points on the engines, in the APU compartment, and in the main landing gear wheel wells. Each loop is a continuous system with the sections of the sensors connected to each other by aircraft wiring. The sensors are identified as loop A and loop B. A sensor section consists of both loops parallel to each other and attached to a support tube by quick-release clamps. A Teflon®-asbestos grommet around the sensor is located at each clamp. The sensor support tube is attached to the structure by a quick-release fastener as shown in Figure 9-7. The location of the engine fire detection sensors and interconnect wiring is illustrated in Figure 9-8.

GALLEY/LOUNGE SMOKE DETECTOR

The detector unit, illustrated in Figure 9-9, consists of a test lamp, a beacon lamp, a labyrinth, and a light sensitive resistor. The labyrinth is located between the beacon lamp and the light sensitive resistor so that very little light from the beacon lamp can reach the resistor during normal conditions. However, when smoke is drawn through the labyrinth, the smoke becomes a medium by reflecting or scattering the light so that more light can reach the resistor, reducing the resistance value of the light sensitive resistor. The light

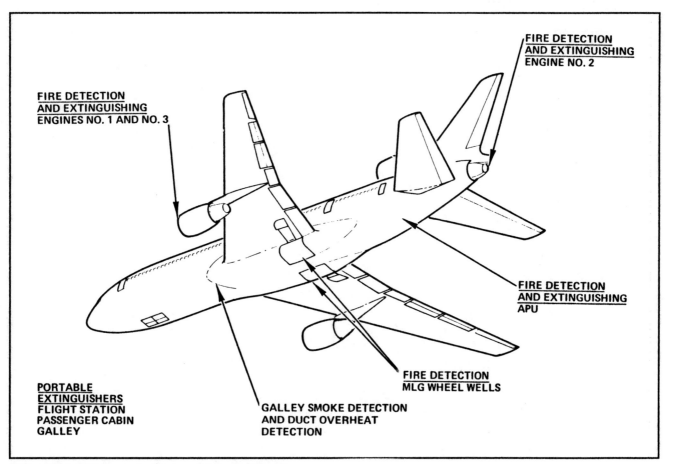

FIRE DETECTION AND EXTINGUISHING ENGINE NO. 2

FIRE DETECTION AND EXTINGUISHING ENGINES NO. 1 AND NO. 3

FIRE DETECTION AND EXTINGUISHING APU

FIRE DETECTION MLG WHEEL WELLS

PORTABLE EXTINGUISHERS FLIGHT STATION PASSENGER CABIN GALLEY

GALLEY SMOKE DETECTION AND DUCT OVERHEAT DETECTION

Figure 9-6. L-1011 fire protection provisions. (Lockheed)

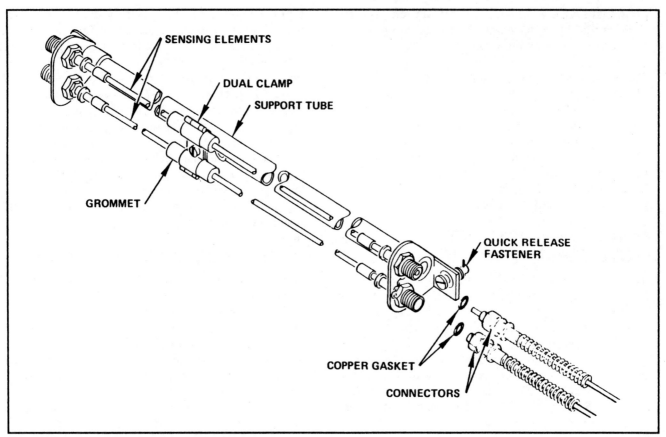

Figure 9-7. Dual fire detection sensors. (Lockheed)

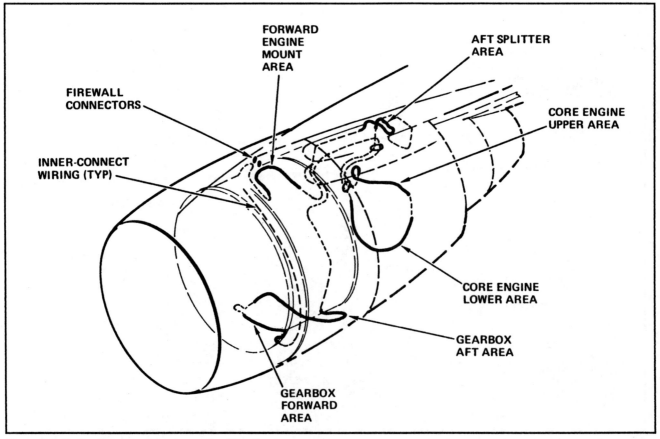

Figure 9-8. Engine fire detector sensors. (Lockheed)

sensitive resistor is connected to the smoke warning circuits. When the value of the resistance is reduced sufficiently due to the increased light intensity, the smoke warning circuits will be activated.

During a smoke detection system test, the test lamp is connected in series with the beacon lamp, and light from the test lamp shines directly on the light sensitive resistor. Therefore, performing a system test checks the integrity of the smoke detector system and the continuity of the beacon lamp.

FIRE EXTINGUISHER SYSTEM

The engines have two fire bottles located in the left hand side of the nose cowl of each pylon mounted engine, as illustrated in Figure 9-10. Bottle pressure gauges are mounted on each bottle and can be viewed through a Plexiglas window mounted in the bottle access panels. A thermal discharge indicator is located adjacent to the viewing windows. A 3/4 inch tube carries the fire extinguishing agent to a discharge nozzle located in the nose cowl to fan case mating point. The nozzle discharges the agent into the fan case and accessory sections of the engine.

The engine No. 2/APU fire bottles serve both engine No. 2 and/or the APU. Pressure gauges and thermal discharge indicators can be viewed from ground level in much the same manner as pylon mounted engines.

A tube carries the fire extinguishing agent to a discharge nozzle located in the forward end of the APU compartment. Another tube carries the fire extinguishing agent to two discharge nozzles for engine No. 2. The engine No. 2 nozzles are located on the engine No. 2 firewall and discharge the fire extinguishing agent into the fan case and accessory section of the engine. The engine/APU fire bottles use Freon® 1301, which is nitrogen pressurized.

WING ENGINE FIRE EXTINGUISHER

The wing engine fire extinguisher bottles, shown in Figure 9-11, are corrosion resistant steel spheres, with a volume of 224 cubic inches each. They contain 4.3 pounds of monobromotrifluoromethane and are charged with nitrogen to a pressure of 600 ± 25 PSI at 70°F. Each bottle assembly includes a pressure gauge and pressure switch, an initiator cartridge, a discharge port, and a thermal discharge safety.

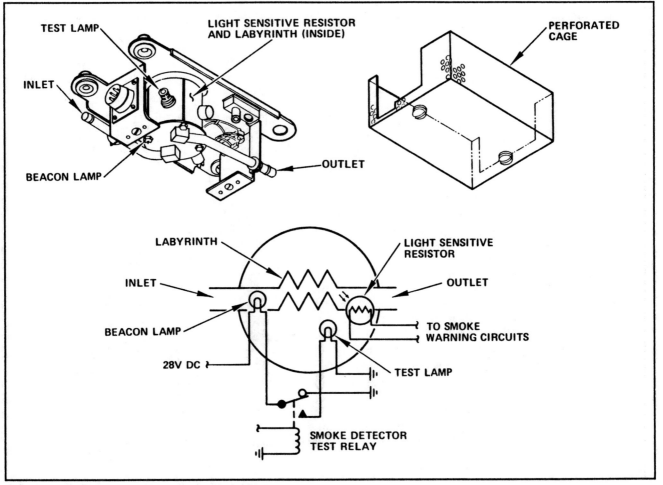

Figure 9-9. Galley/lounge smoke detector. (Lockheed)

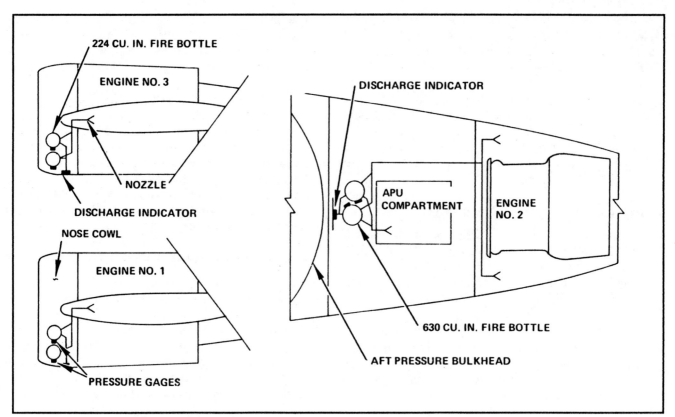

Figure 9-10. Fire extinguisher layout. (Lockheed)

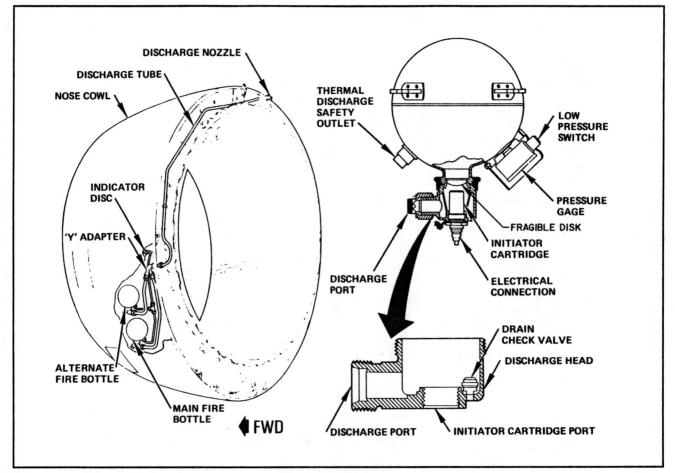

Figure 9-11. L-1011 wing engine fire extinguisher installation. (Lockheed)

The pressure gauge indicates internal pressure of the bottle. A pressure switch closes when pressure decreases and illuminates the appropriate discharge light adjacent to the fire pull handle at the flight station. The pressure switch is an integral part of the pressure gauge and therefore cannot be replaced without replacing the complete bottle assembly. The pressure gauge reads from 0 to 1500 PSI.

The fire extinguishing agent is released from the bottle by utilizing an initiator cartridge, or squib, to rupture a frangible disc. A strainer retains the pieces of the ruptured disc and prevents them from entering the discharge line. The initiator is an electrically fired cartridge.

Each cartridge assembly consists of two squibs, electrically connected in parallel. A DC voltage of 10-29 volts, at a minimum of 3 amps, is required to fire each squib. The cartridges are fired by actuation of a switch located adjacent to the applicable fire pull handle.

There is a drain check valve installed in each discharge head. The valve is spring loaded open which allows moisture to drain overboard and not accumu-

late around the initiator cartridge. This helps prevent misfire. When the bottle is fired, pressure buildup in the head will close the valve at 35 PSI and prevent loss of agent.

The thermal discharge outlet is designed to open if the pressure in the bottle should exceed its maximum limit. Rupture of the thermal discharge will be indicated by a missing red thermal discharge disk indicator and by the appropriate DISCH (discharge) light in the flight station.

Engine No. 2 and the APU share two fire bottles. Each bottle has two sets of initiator cartridges. One cartridge, when fired, will direct the agent to engine No. 2, and the other cartridge, when fired, directs it to the APU compartment. The bottles are larger than those mounted on the pylon engines.

A fire pull handle is provided for each of the three engines and the APU, as shown in Figure 9-12. Pulling the handle exposes a discharge switch. Moving the switch to the right discharges the main bottle and moving the switch to the left discharges the alternate bottle. When a bottle is discharged, the appropriate

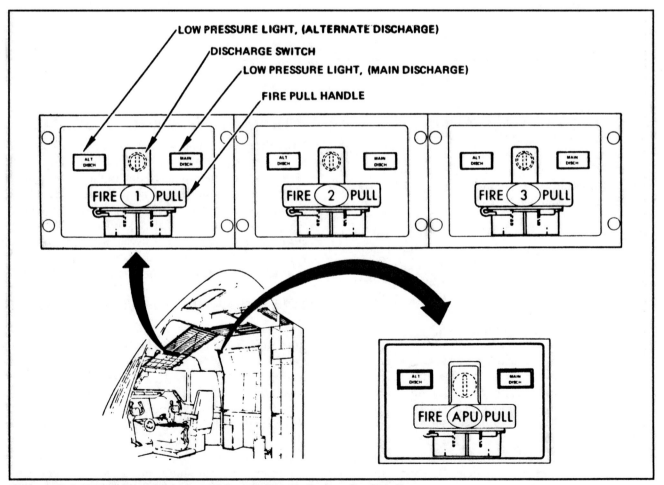

Figure 9-12. L-1011 flight station extinguisher control and indication. (Lockheed)

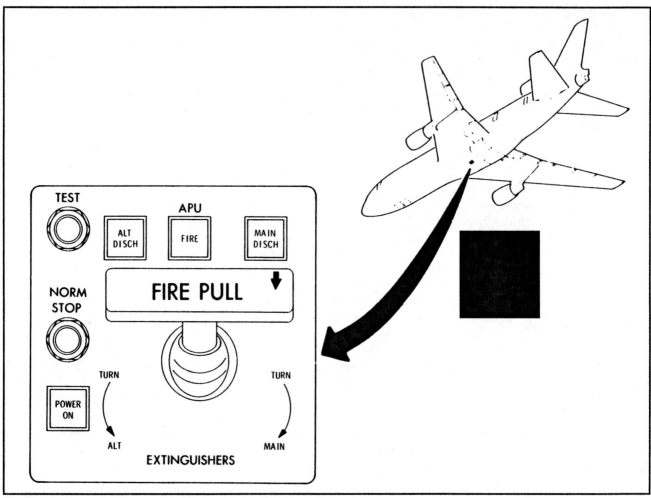

Figure 9-13. L-1011 APU external control panel. (Lockheed)

(MAIN or ALT) light adjacent to the fire pull handle is illuminated. Since the NO. 2 engine and the APU share the same bottles, both sets of discharge lights will be illuminated. If a fire bottle is discharged due to a bottle overpressure (thermal) condition, the DISCH light will also be illuminated.

The fire extinguisher test panel is located at the flight engineer station. Main and alternate test lights for each of the engines and the APU system determine the integrity of the electrical cartridge firing circuit during test. The test switch verifies continuity to the cartridges and the short switch checks the circuits for a short or grounded condition.

The APU fire extinguishing system is similar to the engine extinguishing systems. The APU fire extinguishing system contains two additional discharge indicators and an additional fire handle on the APU external control panel, as illustrated in Figure 9-13. The APU extinguishing system also includes an auto APU extinguishing relay which, when energized, will automatically discharge the main fire bottle into the APU compartment.

AIRCRAFT WARNING SYSTEMS

Most aircraft warning systems are either visual and/or aural warnings. Steady or flashing lights and EICAS messages are used to alert the flight crew visually. Aural warnings can make several different sounds. For example, the aircraft overspeed system makes a clacking sound, while the unsafe takeoff or unsafe landing system uses a horn. Each different sound represents a particular warning. Warning systems, as they pertain to specific aircraft, will be discussed with each aircraft.

L-1011 AURAL WARNING SYSTEMS

The L-1011 uses several aural warning systems, as illustrated in Figure 9-14. The cabin pressure warning system is fairly typical of other aircraft in that at 10,000 feet cabin altitude, an intermittent horn will sound to alert the flight crew of an unsafe cabin pressure. The aircraft's overspeed warning system is activated any time the aircraft's speed exceeds the maximum allowable airspeed. It will remain activated until the speed is reduced to safe limits. The aural warning system condition and sounds for other unsafe aircraft conditions are described in Figure 9-14. Other

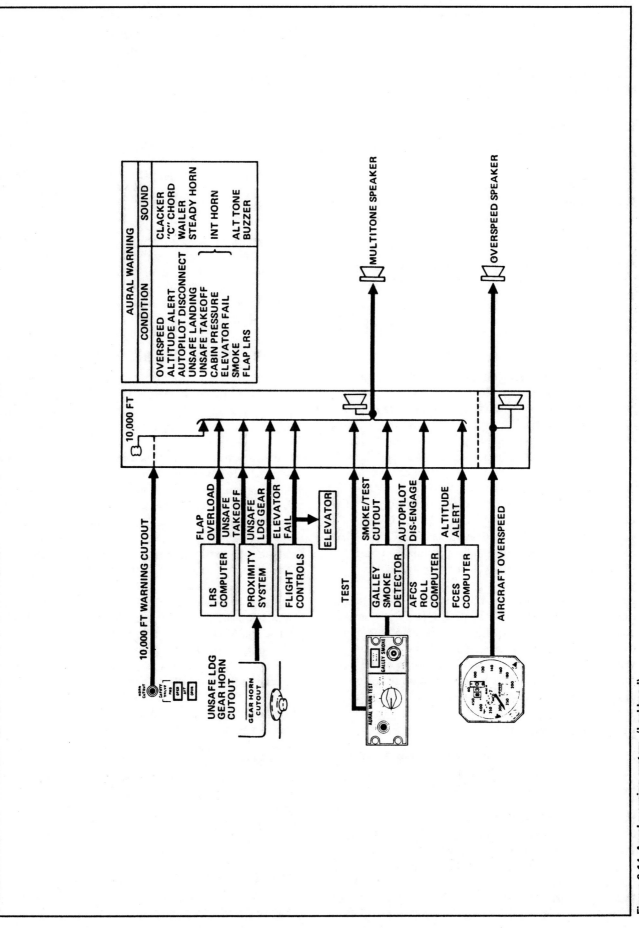

Figure 9-14. Aural warning system. (Lockheed)

warning systems will be discussed in more detail in the section on Boeing 737-300.

BOEING 737-300 FIRE AND WARNING SYSTEMS

FIRE PROTECTION

Fire protection consists of overheat and fire detection sensors and fire extinguishers. Detection provides visual and aural indications of overheat and fire conditions in the engines and main wheel well areas. The extinguishers provide a means of extinguishing engine and APU fires.

Four dual element overheat/fire detection loops are installed in each engine nacelle. The detectors are the Kidde sensor element type. At a predetermined temperature, the sensor activates the overheat warning system. At a higher temperature, the fire warning system is activated.

The dual element detectors are labeled A and B. An OVHT DET (overheat detection) switch for each engine, labeled A, B, and NORMAL, permits selection of loop A, B, or both A and B as the active detecting element(s). Normally operating as a dual-loop system, an alert is initiated only if both loops detect an overheat or fire condition.

An engine overheat condition is indicated by the illumination of the MASTER CAUTION light, OVHT/DET annunciator and the associated engine OVERHEAT light. The overheat light remains illuminated until the temperature drops below the onset temperature.

An engine fire condition is indicated by the illumination of the master FIRE WARNING and associated engine fire switch light and the sound of the alarm bell. The bell may be silenced and the master FIRE WARNING lights extinguished by pressing either master FIRE WARNING light or the bell cutout switch on the fire panel, as shown in Figure 9-15.

FIRE DETECTION

A Kidde sensor element fire detector loop is installed on the APU. At a predetermined alarm temperature, the sensor activates the warning signals.

If a fire is present, the FIRE WARNING lights illuminate, the bell sounds, the APU fire switch illuminates, and the APU shuts down. The warning horn in the main wheel well also sounds if the airplane is on the ground (see Figure 9-16). When the FIRE WARNING lights are illuminated, a fire is assumed and should be extinguished. The fire switch remains illu-

minated until the temperature surrounding the sensor/responder has decreased below the alarm temperature. Illumination of the amber APU DET INOP light, located on the fire panel, indicates a failure in the APU fire detector loop.

A fire detection loop is also installed in the main wheel well. The detector is a Fenwall metallic type. Testing the system checks the continuity of the loop by sending an artificial electronic signal to the fire warning system. The overheat and fire warning systems for the engines, APU, and wheel wells are shown in Figure 9-17.

The lavatory smoke detection system monitors air for the presence of smoke and provides an aural warning if smoke is detected. Pressing the INTERRUPT switch silences the aural warning. If smoke is still present when the switch is released, the alarm will sound again.

ENGINE FIRE EXTINGUISHER SYSTEM

The engine fire extinguisher system (see Figure 9-18) consists of two Freon® bottles with their associated plumbing to each engine, plus the fire warning switch, test, and bottle discharge lights.

The fire warning switch is normally locked down to prevent inadvertent shutdown of an engine. Illumination of an engine fire warning light, or engine overheat light, causes a solenoid to activate, which unlocks the fire warning switch. Pulling the engine fire warning switch up arms one discharge squib on each engine fire extinguisher bottle; closes the fuel tank shutoff valve; trips the generator control relay and breaker; and closes the hydraulic fluid shutoff valve. The engine driven hydraulic pump LOW PRESSURE light is deactivated. It also closes the engine bleed air valve resulting in loss of wing anti-ice to the affected wing and closure of the bleed air operated pack valve. Then the engine fire warning switch can be rotated to discharge the fire extinguisher bottle.

Rotation of the engine fire warning switch electrically fires a squib, puncturing the seal of the extinguisher bottle, discharging the extinguishing agent into the associated engine. One or both bottles may be discharged into either engine. Rotating the switch the other way discharges the remaining bottle. A BOTTLE DISCHARGE light illuminates a few seconds after the fire warning switch is rotated, indicating the bottle has discharged.

APU FIRE EXTINGUISHER SYSTEM

The APU fire extinguisher system consists of one Freon® bottle with its associated plumbing to the APU,

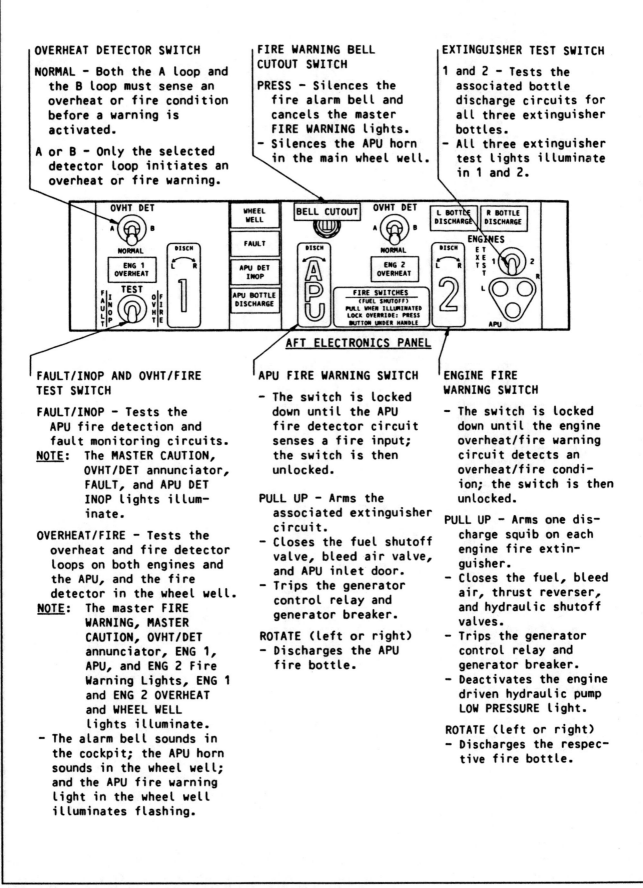

OVERHEAT DETECTOR SWITCH

NORMAL – Both the A loop and the B loop must sense an overheat or fire condition before a warning is activated.

A or B – Only the selected detector loop initiates an overheat or fire warning.

FIRE WARNING BELL CUTOUT SWITCH

PRESS – Silences the fire alarm bell and cancels the master FIRE WARNING lights.
– Silences the APU horn in the main wheel well.

EXTINGUISHER TEST SWITCH

1 and 2 – Tests the associated bottle discharge circuits for all three extinguisher bottles.
– All three extinguisher test lights illuminate in 1 and 2.

AFT ELECTRONICS PANEL

FAULT/INOP AND OVHT/FIRE TEST SWITCH

FAULT/INOP – Tests the APU fire detection and fault monitoring circuits.
NOTE: The MASTER CAUTION, OVHT/DET annunciator, FAULT, and APU DET INOP lights illuminate.

OVERHEAT/FIRE – Tests the overheat and fire detector loops on both engines and the APU, and the fire detector in the wheel well.
NOTE: The master FIRE WARNING, MASTER CAUTION, OVHT/DET annunciator, ENG 1, APU, and ENG 2 Fire Warning Lights, ENG 1 and ENG 2 OVERHEAT and WHEEL WELL lights illuminate.
– The alarm bell sounds in the cockpit; the APU horn sounds in the wheel well; and the APU fire warning light in the wheel well illuminates flashing.

APU FIRE WARNING SWITCH

– The switch is locked down until the APU fire detector circuit senses a fire input; the switch is then unlocked.

PULL UP – Arms the associated extinguisher circuit.
– Closes the fuel shutoff valve, bleed air valve, and APU inlet door.
– Trips the generator control relay and generator breaker.

ROTATE (left or right)
– Discharges the APU fire bottle.

ENGINE FIRE WARNING SWITCH

– The switch is locked down until the engine overheat/fire warning circuit detects an overheat/fire condition; the switch is then unlocked.

PULL UP – Arms one discharge squib on each engine fire extinguisher.
– Closes the fuel, bleed air, thrust reverser, and hydraulic shutoff valves.
– Trips the generator control relay and generator breaker.
– Deactivates the engine driven hydraulic pump LOW PRESSURE light.

ROTATE (left or right)
– Discharges the respective fire bottle.

Figure 9-15. Boeing 737 overheat/fire protection panel switches. (Boeing)

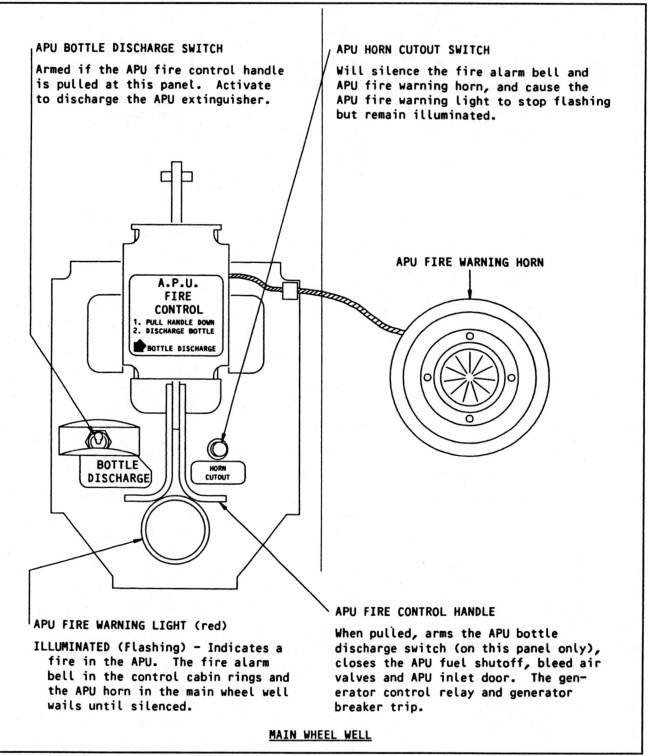

APU BOTTLE DISCHARGE SWITCH

Armed if the APU fire control handle is pulled at this panel. Activate to discharge the APU extinguisher.

APU HORN CUTOUT SWITCH

Will silence the fire alarm bell and APU fire warning horn, and cause the APU fire warning light to stop flashing but remain illuminated.

APU FIRE WARNING HORN

A.P.U. FIRE CONTROL
1. PULL HANDLE DOWN
2. DISCHARGE BOTTLE
BOTTLE DISCHARGE

BOTTLE DISCHARGE

HORN CUTOUT

APU FIRE WARNING LIGHT (red)

ILLUMINATED (Flashing) - Indicates a fire in the APU. The fire alarm bell in the control cabin rings and the APU horn in the main wheel well wails until silenced.

APU FIRE CONTROL HANDLE

When pulled, arms the APU bottle discharge switch (on this panel only), closes the APU fuel shutoff, bleed air valves and APU inlet door. The generator control relay and generator breaker trip.

MAIN WHEEL WELL

Figure 9-16. Boeing 737 APU ground control panel. (Boeing)

plus a fire warning switch, test, and bottle discharge light. Pulling the fire warning switch up, shown in Figure 9-15, provides backup for the automatic shutdown feature, arms the extinguisher circuit, shuts down the APU by deactivating the fuel solenoid, and closes the fuel tank shutoff valve. The APU bleed air valve and APU inlet door also close. The generator

control relay and generator breaker trip off line. The APU BOTTLE DISCHARGE light illuminates, indicating the bottle has discharged.

LAVATORY FIRE EXTINGUISHER SYSTEM

An automatic fire extinguisher system, shown in Figure 9-19, is located beneath the sink area in each

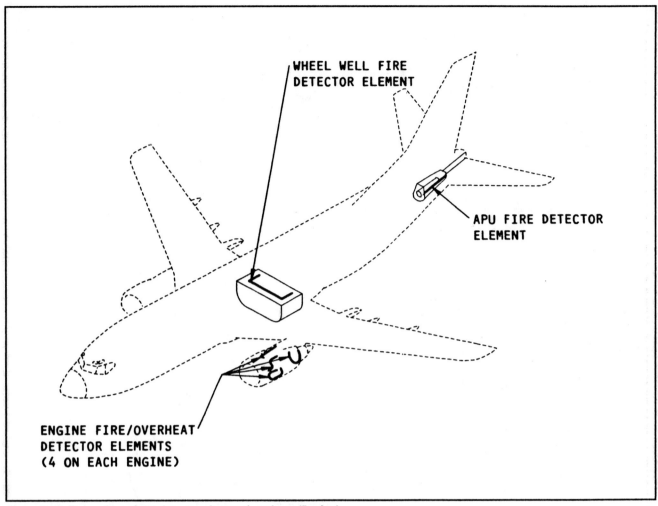

Figure 9-17. Fire and overheat detector element locations. (Boeing)

lavatory. The extinguisher discharges non-toxic Freon® gas through one, or both, of two heat-activated nozzles. One nozzle discharges toward the towel disposal container; the other directly under the sink. The color of the nozzle tips will change to an aluminum color when the extinguisher has discharged.

A temperature-indicator placard is located on the inside of the access door below each sink. White dots on the placard will turn black when exposed to high temperatures. If an indicator has turned black, or a nozzle tip has changed color, it should be assumed that the extinguisher has discharged. An inspection for fire damage should be made, the extinguisher replaced, and the temperature-indicator placard replaced before the next flight.

WARNING SYSTEMS

The aural and visual warnings alert the flight crew to conditions that require action or caution in the operation of the airplane. The character of the signal used varies, depending upon the degree of urgency or haz-

ards involved. Aural, visual, and tactile signals are used singularly, or in combinations, to provide simultaneously, both warning and information regarding the nature of the condition.

Red warning lights located in the area of the pilots' primary forward field of vision are used to indicate engine, wheel well, or APU fires, autopilot disconnect (flashing), and landing gear unsafe conditions. Conditions which require timely corrective action by the flight crew are indicated by means of amber caution lights.

Various aural warnings call attention to warnings and cautions. An aural warning for airspeed limits is given by a clacker, the autopilot disconnect by a warning tone, cabin altitude by an intermittent horn, landing gear positions by a steady horn. The unsafe takeoff warning is given by an intermittent horn, and the fire warning by a fire warning bell. Ground proximity warnings and alerts are indicated by voice warnings. Generally, aurals automatically silence when the associated non-normal condition no longer exists.

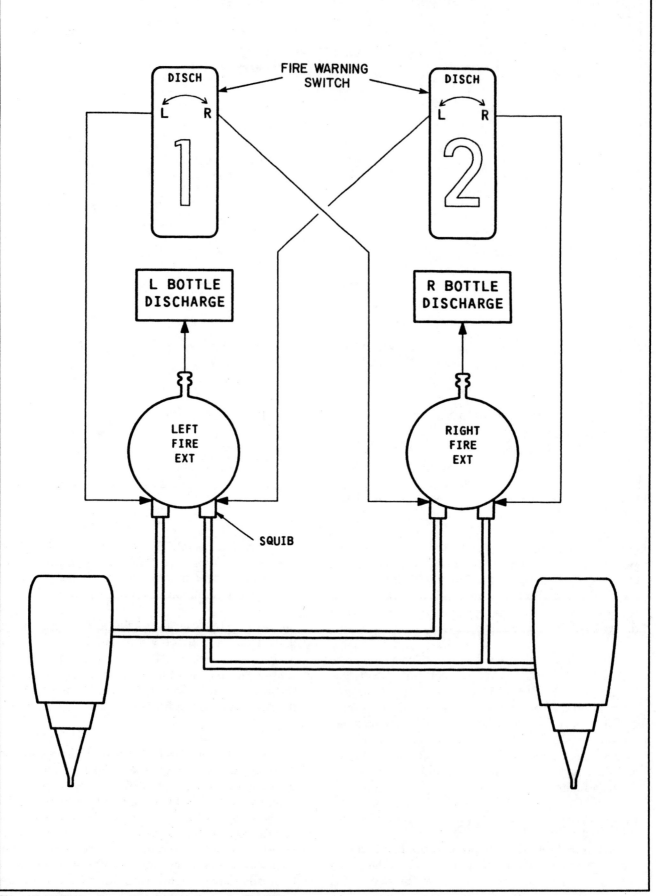

Figure 9-18. Engine fire extinguishing schematic. (Boeing)

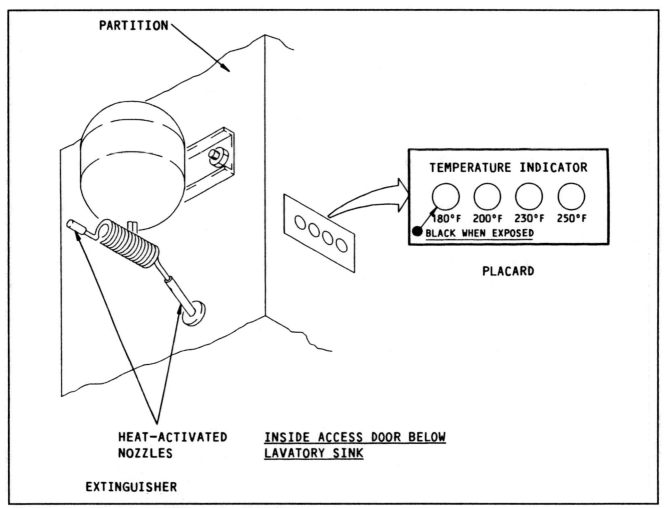

Figure 9-19. Lavatory fire extinguisher system. (Boeing)

TAKEOFF CONFIGURATION WARNING

The takeoff configuration warning is armed when the airplane is on the ground and either, or both, forward thrust levers are advanced for takeoff. An intermittent takeoff warning horn sounds if stabilizer trim is not in the green band range; or trailing edge flaps are not in the takeoff range; or leading edge devices are not in the correct position for takeoff; or speed brake lever is not in the down (stowed) position. The warning indication is canceled when the configuration error is corrected.

LANDING GEAR CONFIGURATION WARNINGS

Visual indications and aural warnings of landing gear position are provided by the landing gear indicator lights and landing gear warning horn. The landing gear indication lights (visual indication) are activated by signals from each gear, the landing gear lever, and the forward thrust lever position switches. If the green light for each gear is illuminated, the landing gear is down and locked. When the red light is illuminated,

the landing gear is in disagreement with the landing gear lever position (in transit or unsafe). When all of the lights are extinguished, the landing gear is in the up and locked position with the landing gear lever UP, or OFF.

A steady warning horn is provided to alert the pilots whenever the airplane is in a landing configuration and any gear is not down and locked. The landing gear warning horn is also activated by flap and thrust lever position.

Generally, when either thrust lever is retarded and the landing gear is in an unsafe condition, the landing gear warning horn will sound, but can be silenced using the warning horn cutout switch. Under certain conditions, the landing gear warning horn cannot be silenced. Although the actual flap settings and thrust lever positions will vary from one aircraft type to another, generally some provision is made to deactivate the horn cutout switch when the aircraft is in an actual landing configuration and the landing gear is not down and locked.

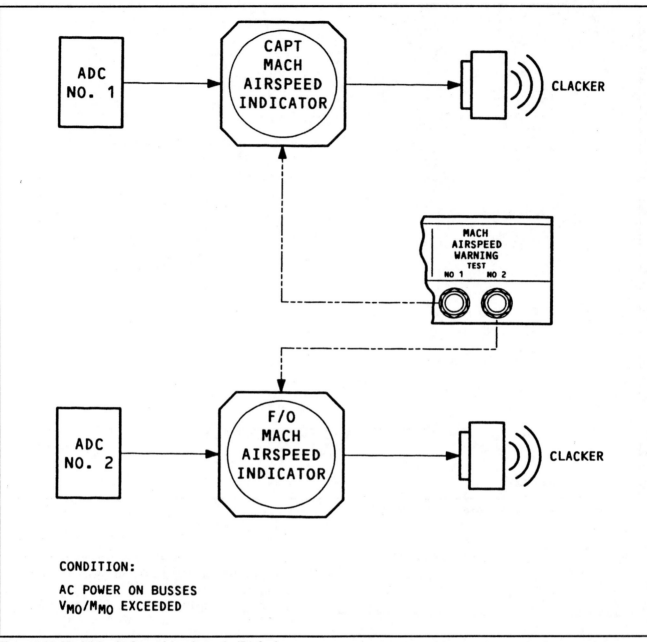

Figure 9-20. Mach/airspeed warning schematic. (Boeing)

MACH/AIRSPEED WARNING SYSTEM

Two independent mach/airspeed warning systems, shown in Figure 9-20, provide a distinct aural warning any time the maximum operating airspeed is exceeded. The warning clackers can be silenced only by reducing airspeed below maximum operating speed.

The systems operate from a mechanism internal to each pilot's mach/airspeed indicator. Test switches allow a system operation check at any time. Maximum operating airspeeds exist primarily due to airplane structural limitations at lower altitudes and airplane handling characteristics at higher altitudes.

STALL WARNING SYSTEM

Warning of an impending stall is required to occur a minimum of seven percent above actual stall speed. Natural stall warning (buffet) usually occurs at a speed prior to stall. In some configurations, the margin between stall and stall warning (buffet) is less than the required seven percent. Therefore, an artificial stall warning device, a stick shaker, is utilized to provide the required warning.

The stall warning, or stick shaker, shown in Figure 9-21, consists of two eccentric weight motors, one on each control column. It is designed to alert the pilots before a stall develops. The warning is given by vibrat-

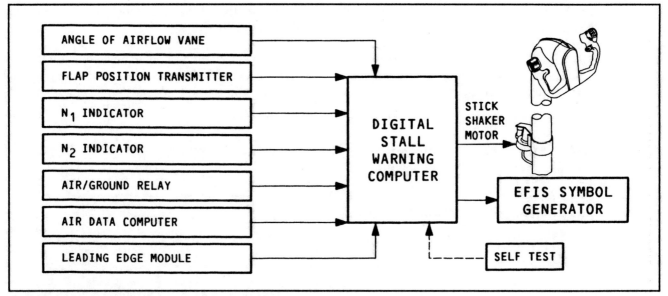

Figure 9-21. Boeing 737 stall warning system. (Boeing)

ing both control columns. The system is energized in flight at all times. The system is deactivated on the ground by the air/ground safety sensor.

Two independent digital computers are installed which compute the proper stall warning based on angle of attack, flap configuration, and thrust. In addition, the stall warning occurs when the airspeed falls below a specified value for the selected flap setting, this is referred to as the speed floor. The computers receive inputs from the angle of airflow vanes, the flap position transmitter, the N_1 and N_2 indicators, the air/ground relay, the air data computers, and the leading edge module, as can be seen in Figure 9-21.

GROUND PROXIMITY WARNING SYSTEM (GPWS)

The ground proximity warning system (GPWS) provides warnings and/or alerts to the flight crew when one of the following conditions exist:

Mode 1 — Excessive descent rate

Mode 2 — Excessive terrain closure rate

Mode 3 — Altitude loss after takeoff or go-around

Mode 4 — Unsafe terrain clearance when not in the landing configuration

Mode 5 — Excessive deviation below an ILS (Instrument Landing System) glide slope

Mode 6 — Descent below the selected minimum radio altitude

Mode 7 — Windshear condition encountered

Warnings for Modes 1 and 2 consist of red PULL UP lights and the aural "WHOOP WHOOP PULL UP."

Alerts for Modes 1, 2, 3, and 4 consist of the red PULL UP lights and one of the following aurals: "SINK RATE," "TERRAIN," "DON'T SINK," "TOO LOW GEAR," "TOO LOW FLAPS," "TOO LOW TERRAIN."

Alerting for Mode 5 consists of amber BELOW G/S (Glide Slope) sights and the aural "GLIDE SLOPE."

Windshear warnings consist of red WINDSHEAR lights and a siren followed by the aural "WINDSHEAR."

Windshear warnings take priority over all other modes. A warning and/or alert continues until the flight condition(s) is corrected. The ground proximity warning system adjusts the warning and alert envelopes to avoid nuisance warnings or alerts at airports with unique terrain conditions.

Mode 1 has two boundaries (see Figure 9-22) and is independent of airplane configuration. Penetration of the first boundary activates the PULL UP lights and generates a repeated aural alert of "SINK RATE." Penetrating the second boundary causes the repeated aural warning of "WHOOP WHOOP PULL UP."

Mode 2 monitors airspeed, radio altitude and radio altitude rate of change, barometric altitude rate of change, and airplane configuration. Mode 2 has two boundaries. Penetrating the first boundary causes an aural alert of "TERRAIN" repeated twice, followed by the repeated aural warning "WHOOP WHOOP PULL UP." After leaving the PULL UP area, the repeating "TERRAIN" message will again be heard while in the terrain portion of the envelope (see Figure 9-23).

Mode 3 (see Figure 9-24) provides an alert if a descent is made during the initial takeoff climb or during a go-around. Entering the envelope causes a repeated aural alert of "DON'T SINK." The alert continues until a positive rate of climb is established. If the airplane descends again before climbing to the original descent altitude, another alert is generated based on the original descent altitude.

The unsafe terrain clearance mode (4A) with gear retracted is armed after takeoff upon climbing through 700 feet radio altitude. When this envelope is pene-

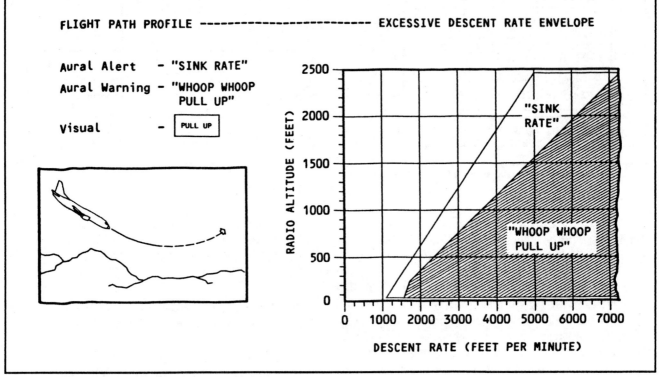

Figure 9-22. Mode1—excessive descent rate. (Boeing)

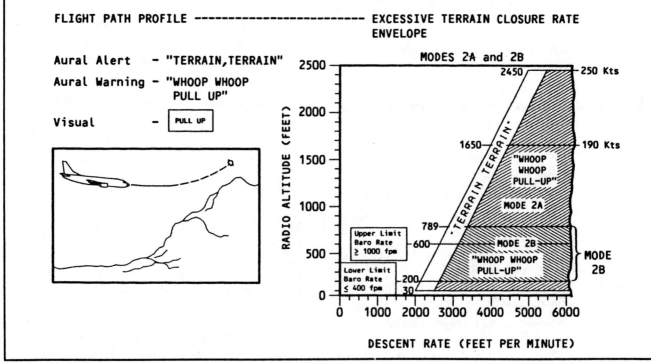

Figure 9-23. Mode 2—excessive terrain closure rate. (Boeing)

trated below 190 knots, the aural alert "TOO LOW GEAR" is sounded. Above 190 knots, the aural alert "TOO LOW TERRAIN" sounds.

Mode 4B provides an alert when the landing gear is down and flaps are not in the landing position. When the envelope is penetrated below 159 knots, the aural alert "TOO LOW FLAPS" is repeated. Above 159 knots, the aural alert "TOO LOW TERRAIN" sounds.

Mode 5 alerts the flight crew of an excessive descent as shown in Figure 9-25. The envelope has two areas of alerting, soft and loud. In both areas, the alert is a repeated voice message of "GLIDE SLOPE" and illumination of both pilots' BELOW G/S lights. The voice message amplitude is increased when entering the loud alerting area. In both areas, the voice message repetition rate is increased as glide slope deviation increases and radio altitude decreases.

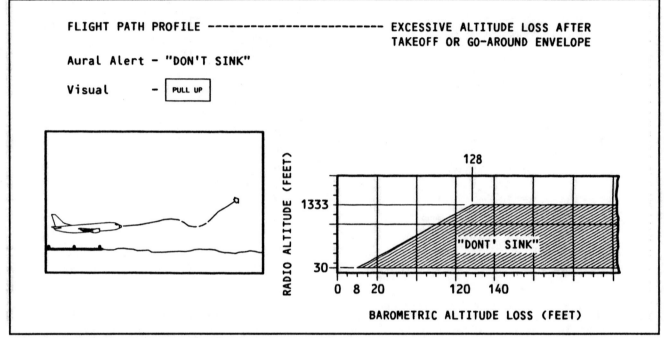

Figure 9-24. Mode 3—altitude loss after takeoff or go-around. (Boeing)

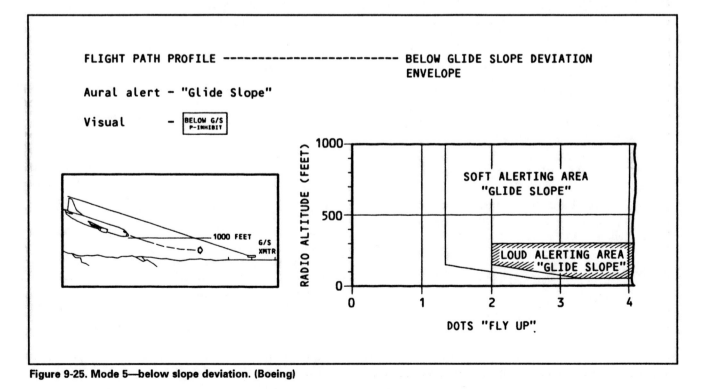

Figure 9-25. Mode 5—below slope deviation. (Boeing)

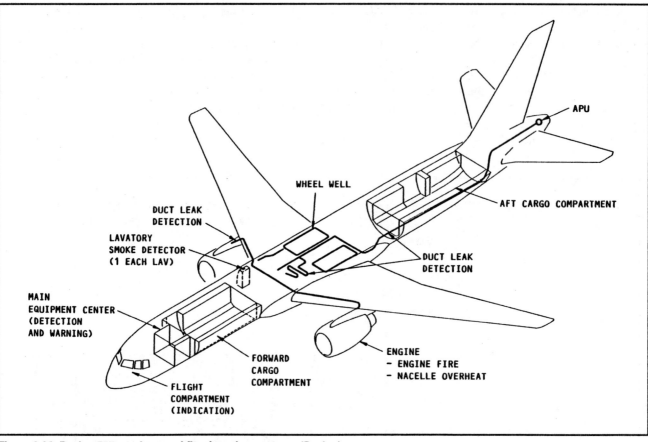

Figure 9-26. Boeing 757 overheat and fire detection systems. (Boeing)

Mode 6 is operated between 50 and 1000 feet radio altitude. It provides an aural alert as the airplane descends through the minimum decision altitude (MDA) set on the captain's radio altimeter. The alert is aural only and consists of "MINIMUMS, MINIMUMS" sounded one time.

The GPWS (ground proximity warning system) provides aural and visual warnings of windshear conditions (Mode 7). The aural warning consists of a two-tone siren followed by the words "WINDSHEAR WINDSHEAR." The aural warning is activated only once during a windshear encounter. The visual warning is provided by illumination of the WINDSHEAR lights on the captain's and first officer's instrument panels. The light remains illuminated until a safe airspeed has been re-established after the windshear has dissipated.

BOEING 757 FIRE PROTECTION SYSTEMS

FIRE DETECTION

The 757 fire detection systems, shown in Figure 9-26, monitor airplane components for fire, overheat, or smoke conditions, with each protected area being annunciated in the cockpit. Engine fire detection is provided by a four part, dual loop, Systron Donner-type fire detector system, with elements located in likely areas of fire initiation.

A Systron Donner detector, shown in Figure 9-27, consists of a sensor and a responder. The sensor tube contains a gas charged core material and helium under pressure. One end of the tube is sealed. The other end is mated through a ceramic isolator and hermetically sealed to the responder. The responder contains 2 pressure switches, a resistor, and is fitted with a 5 pin male connector. The two snap-over pressure switches are actuated independently by gas pressure in the sensor tube acting on small metal diaphragms within each switch. One switch, called the integrity switch, is normally held closed by the helium pressure and serves as a monitor of the detector integrity. Should the sensor lose pressure, the diaphragm would snap-over, opening the integrity circuit. The other switch, called the alarm switch, closes when heat increases the gas pressure in the sensor and causes its diaphragm to snap-over. The closed switch then signals an alarm to the system.

The sensors are able to respond in two modes: A localized flame or heat causing a discrete temperature rise,

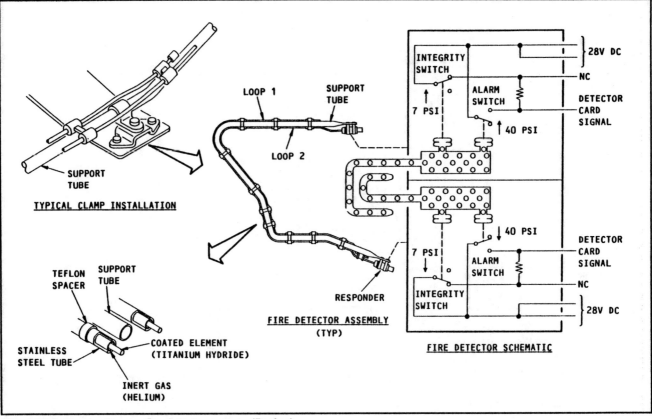

Figure 9-27. Systron Donner fire detector system. (Boeing)

which causes the core material to release gas to increase the pressure. The central core material has the unique property of releasing an extremely large volume of gas whenever any finite section is heated above a certain temperature. The other mode is a general increase in temperature over a large area, causing an average temperature rise, increasing overall gas pressure. Either of these modes are completely reversible. Should the temperature decrease, the gas pressure will decrease and the system will return to normal.

Each detector assembly consists of a support tube assembly, Teflon® liners, clamps, and two detector elements. The support tube establishes routing configuration of the detector element and provides attach points to the airplane. Engine overheat detection is provided by a one part, dual loop overheat detector element located in the pneumatic ducting areas.

The 757 uses a dual loop fire detection system for the APU. One detector is located above the APU, in the area of the APU air inlet, and the other detector is located on the right clamshell APU access door, located beneath the APU.

The forward and aft cargo compartments have dual smoke detectors installed in each compartment. The detectors are a flow through type, with air drawn from

the compartment by redundant blowers through sampling tubes. The air is then drawn through the detection chamber. This chamber is illuminated by a pilot lamp as the air passes through. The light ends up being absorbed by the light trap. Any smoke in the airstream will scatter the light rays and some will reflect on to the photo cell. A smoke concentration will activate the light sensitive relay within the electronic circuit and energize the smoke alarm.

The wheel wells are monitored for overheats caused by landing gear brake fires. The detector is a single loop, Fenwal type, mounted on the ceiling of each wheel well bay.

The wing and body pneumatic ducting is monitored by a Fenwal designed detection system. It is divided into left and right systems, (as shown in Figure 9-28) that provide an indication if there is a pneumatic ducting rupture inboard of the wing valves to their common connection in the air conditioning bay. The left system also extends aft along the APU pneumatic duct. It covers the wheel well area, the aft cargo compartment area, and the area aft of the pressure bulkhead back to the APU firewall.

Each lavatory has one smoke detector installed that will provide a visual/aural warning to the passenger

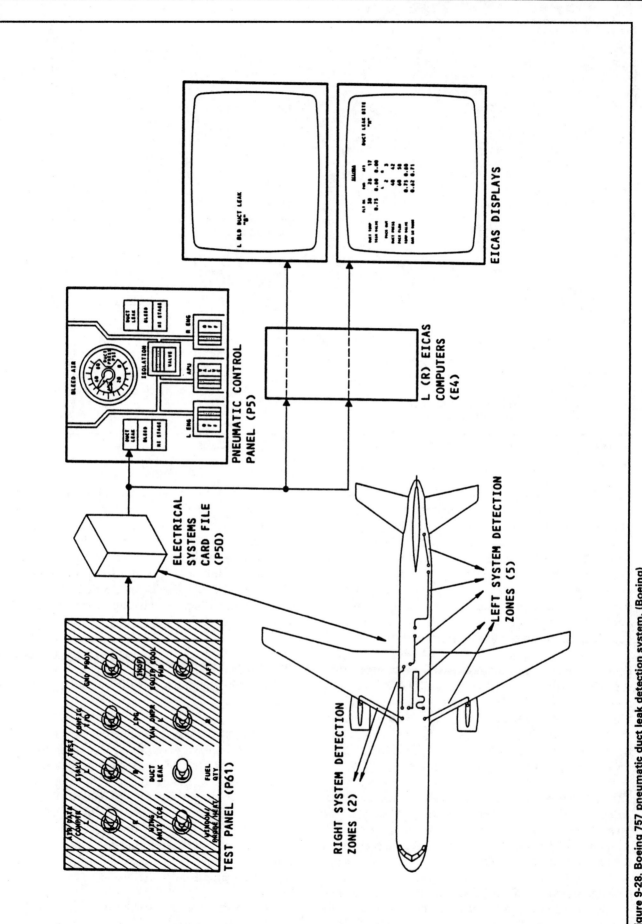

Figure 9-28. Boeing 757 pneumatic duct leak detection system. (Boeing)

cabin crew when smoke is detected in the lavatory. Sampling for smoke begins immediately after power is provided to the detector, indicated by the illumination of the green power indicator. When there is smoke present, the smoke outputs two alarm signals. One activates the sensor unit red alarm light and the second activates the detector horn. The red alarm light and the alarm horn provide a steady alarm indication after smoke has been detected. They may be reset only after the smoke condition no longer exists and the POWER/RESET switch has been pushed. If the POWER/RESET switch is pushed before smoke has cleared, the alarms (light & horn) will stop and the green power indicator light will go out; when released, the alarms will activate again.

FIRE EXTINGUISHING

The engine fire extinguishing system (see Figure 9-29) use two identical bottles located forward of the aft cargo compartment. The bottles can discharge to either engine. They are plumbed to each engine through separate discharge ports, each with its own electric firing squib.

Pulling the fire handle arms the squib detonating system, as shown in Figure 9-30, on both bottles for the respective engine. Rotating the fire handle in one direction electrically detonates the squib, discharging the extinguishing agent from one bottle. Rotating the fire handle in the other direction releases the second bottle into the same engine. A pressure switch installed in each bottle illuminates a bottle discharge light in the flight deck when the bottle is discharged.

The bottles weigh 25.25 pounds (11.48 kg) when full. They are filled with 19 pounds (8.6 kg) of Halon® and kept under pressure with a charge of nitrogen at 625 ± 25 PSIG. The bottles incorporate a low pressure switch which closes when bottle pressure decreases.

The switch and the bottle discharge indication circuit may be checked by using a ground checkout feature. The ground checkout feature is a push-button which forces the switch contacts closed, forcing a bottle discharged indication in the cockpit. This check insures integrity of the low pressure switch operation.

Overpressure relief is through the same valve that is used for refill, and is set to discharge at a maximum pressure. The bottle contents will discharge through the filler port into the bottle compartment. Four

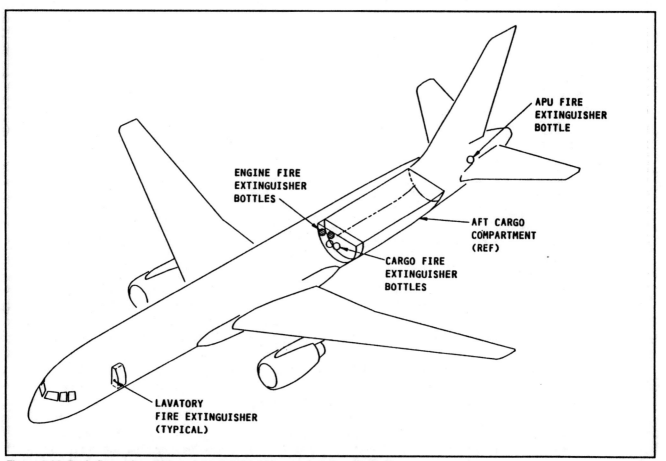

Figure 9-29. Basic fire extinguishing system and component location. (Boeing)

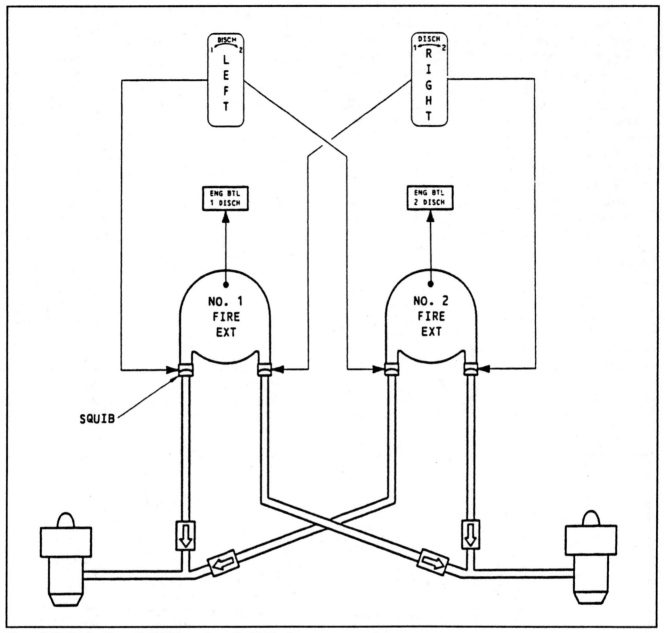

Figure 9-30. Engine fire extinguishing schematic. (Boeing)

mounting lugs are incorporated on each bottle and the two bottles are interchangeable.

The single APU bottle is located forward of the APU firewall. It can be discharged automatically, or may be manually discharged from the flight compartment, or from the nose wheel well area. The fire switch on the P8 panel, see Figure 9-31, is normally locked in position. With an APU fire signal, the fire switch is automatically unlocked. The switch can be unlocked manually at any time by pressing the manual override button beneath the handle. The bottle low pressure switch turns on the APU BTL DISCH light on the APU fire control panel. It also triggers the EICAS advisory display with the same message.

The two cargo compartments are protected by two bottles. They are located forward of the aft cargo compartment. Either or both bottles can be discharged to the selected compartment, as shown in Figure 9-32. The forward and aft compartments each have three nozzles in the ceiling. The spray hole pattern is designed to give maximum extinguishing agent coverage to the compartment areas. The APU/CARGO fire control panel provides the needed controls for the extinguisher system. The arming switches arm the appropriate squib circuits for the cargo compartment selected. The extinguisher bottle discharge switches release the extinguisher agent. The squib test panel provides a means for checking the continuity of the cargo bottle discharge squibs.

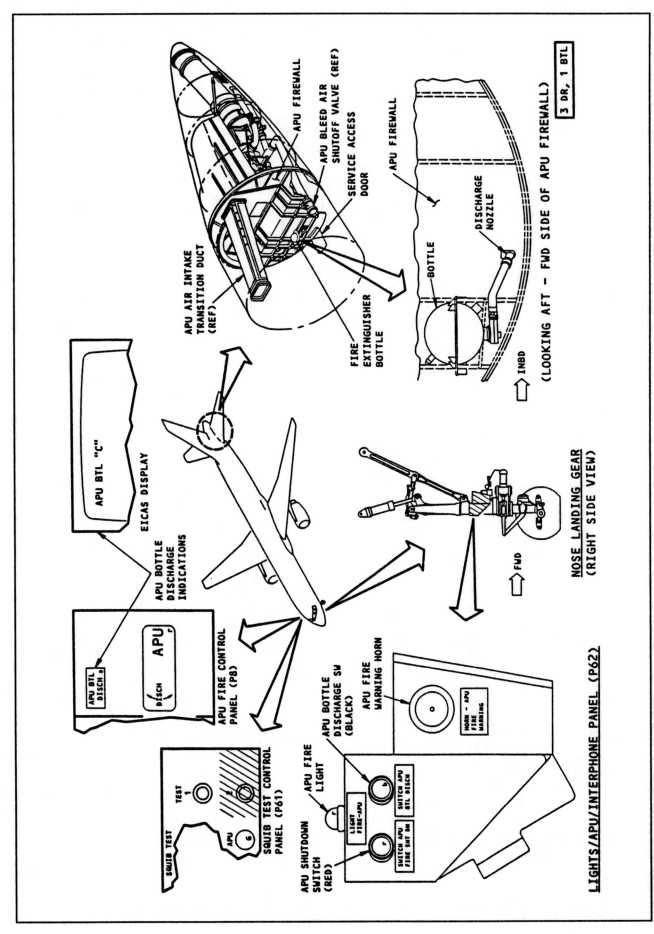

Figure 9-31. Boeing 757 APU fire extinguishing system. (Boeing)

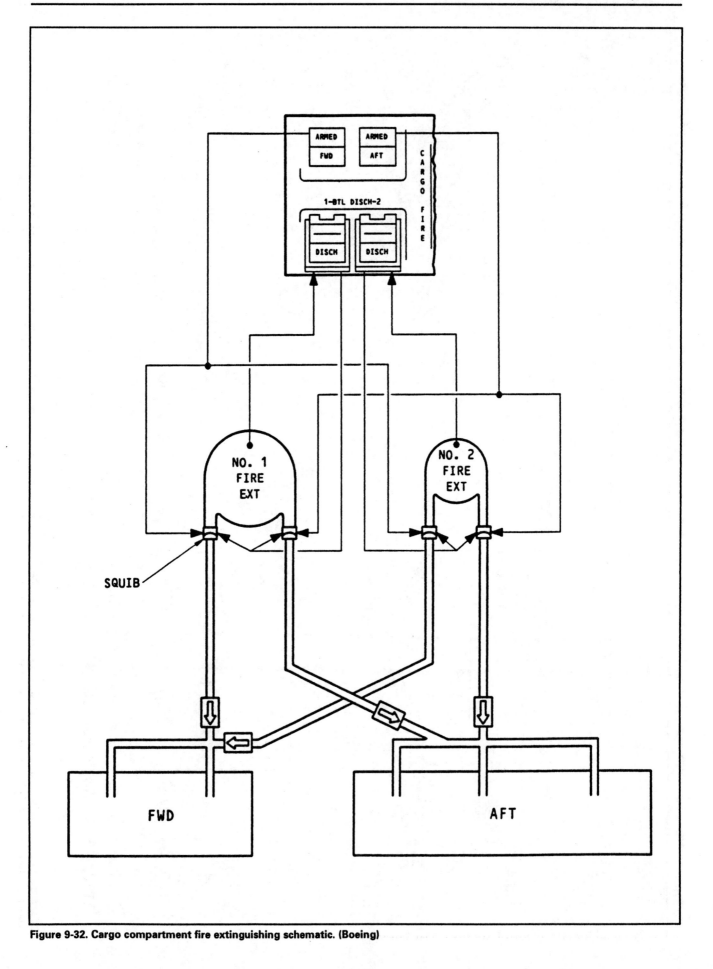

Figure 9-32. Cargo compartment fire extinguishing schematic. (Boeing)

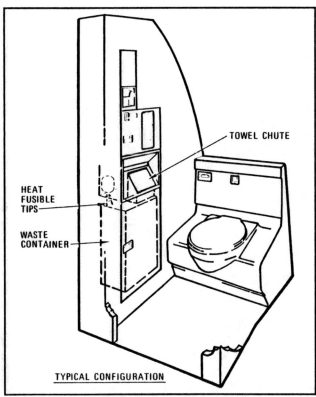

HEAT
FUSIBLE
TIPS

WASTE
CONTAINER

TOWEL CHUTE

TYPICAL CONFIGURATION

Figure 9-33. Lavatory fire extinguishing. (Boeing)

Each lavatory paper towel disposal bin is protected by a fire extinguisher bottle. The bottle is self-discharging and has no controls or indications in the flight compartment. Figure 9-33 shows this arrangement.

ENGINE INDICATION AND CREW ALERTING SYSTEM (ECAS)

Historically, commercial airplanes have utilized electromechanical system indicators that use multiple visual and aural cautions and warnings. These indicators did not offer the versatility and redundancy available with modern digital technology. Furthermore, they required considerable panel space. Systems that are monitored by a comprehensive caution and warning system require no monitoring by the crew, and they promote quick and accurate identification of problems.

In a significant advancement, several new generation Boeing aircraft, including the Boeing 757, utilize electronic displays and a sophisticated full-time monitoring systems. This system is known as EICAS, an acronym meaning — Engine Indication and Crew Alerting System.

EICAS offers improved flight operations by reducing flight crew workload through an effective automatic monitoring of engine parameters and alerting system through all phases of flight, from power-up through postflight maintenance. Only the parameters required to set and monitor engine thrust are displayed full time.

EICAS monitors the remaining parameters and automatically displays any out-of-tolerance parameter on a cathode-ray-tube display in the appropriate color. The alerting system's colored messages are designed to communicate both the failure and the urgency for responding to the failure, so that crew attention is only diverted to the extent appropriate to the malfunction. By utilizing cathode-ray-tube (CRT) displays, EICAS provides reduced panel space required for engine instrument displays, as well as status and maintenance indications.

EICAS has been designed to provide an improved level of maintenance data for the ground crew, without affecting the flight crews with extra workload. This improvement has been achieved by designing a system that will automatically record subsystem parameters when malfunctions are detected, as well as provide the capability for manual data recording with a single pushbutton by the flight crew. This eliminates the need for extensive hand recording of systems and performance data. These features not only increase the quality and accuracy of maintenance data recordings, but also improve the communications between the flight and the ground crews.

The EICAS system, shown in Figure 9-34, includes two multicolor cathode-ray-rube (CRT) display units, two computers, and two control panels. These components, together with two display-switching modules, the cancel/recall switches, and the captain's and first officer's master caution lights, jointly perform the various EICAS functions.

The EICAS computer processes and formats for display all engine and airplane system information required by the crew. Only one computer at a time is used for displaying the data on both display units. Computer selection is done on the display select panel.

Primary engine parameters and crew alerting messages are displayed on the upper display unit, and secondary engine parameters are displayed on the lower display unit, as illustrated in Figure 9-35.

EICAS monitors over 400 analog discrete inputs from airplane subsystems and sensors. When any abnormal condition is detected, an EICAS message is generated. This message will be an alert, status, or maintenance message.

Alert messages are automatically displayed in the upper left side of the primary engine display format. These alert messages are further divided into three levels of urgency. They are: level A — warning messages; level B — caution messages; and, level C — advisory messages. These messages require crew attention as shown in Figure 9-36.

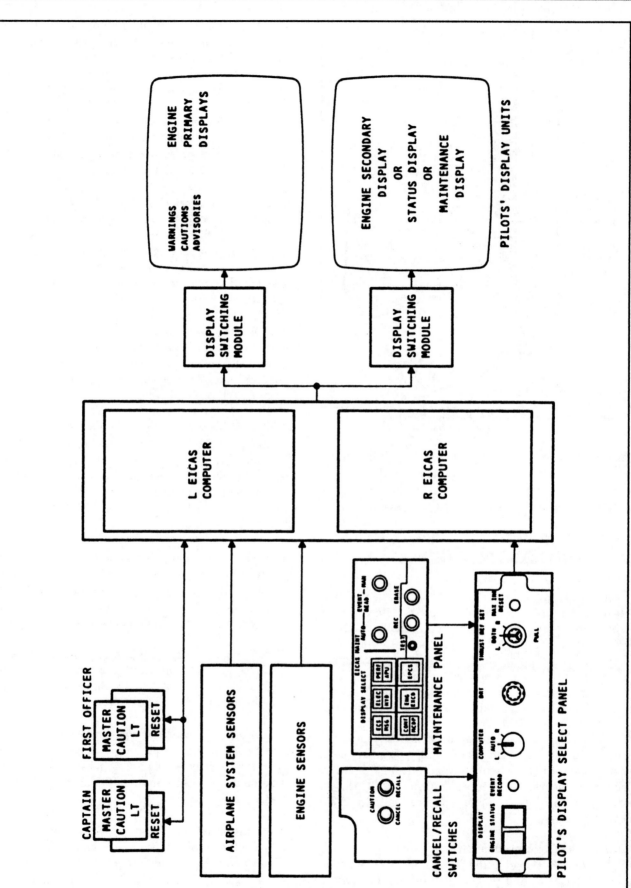

Figure 9-34. Boeing 757 EICAS—simplified system diagram. (Boeing)

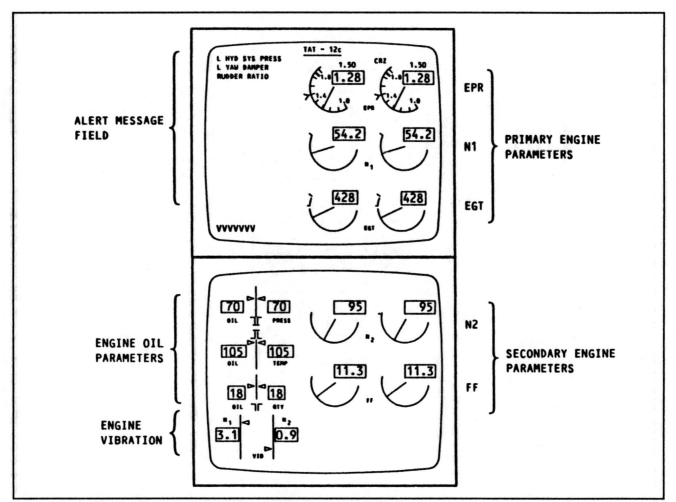

Figure 9-35. EICAS operational mode displays and engine parameters. (Boeing)

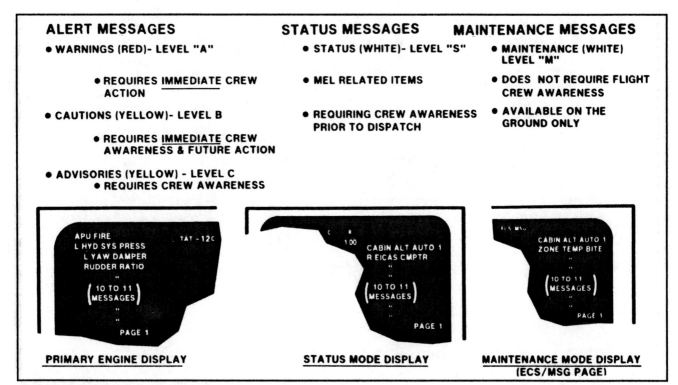

ALERT MESSAGES
- WARNINGS (RED)- LEVEL "A"

  - REQUIRES IMMEDIATE CREW ACTION

- CAUTIONS (YELLOW)- LEVEL B

  - REQUIRES IMMEDIATE CREW AWARENESS & FUTURE ACTION

- ADVISORIES (YELLOW) - LEVEL C
  - REQUIRES CREW AWARENESS

STATUS MESSAGES
- STATUS (WHITE)- LEVEL "S"

- MEL RELATED ITEMS

- REQUIRING CREW AWARENESS PRIOR TO DISPATCH

MAINTENANCE MESSAGES
- MAINTENANCE (WHITE) LEVEL "M"

- DOES NOT REQUIRE FLIGHT CREW AWARENESS

- AVAILABLE ON THE GROUND ONLY

PRIMARY ENGINE DISPLAY

STATUS MODE DISPLAY

MAINTENANCE MODE DISPLAY (ECS/MSG PAGE)

Figure 9-36. EICAS messages. (Boeing)

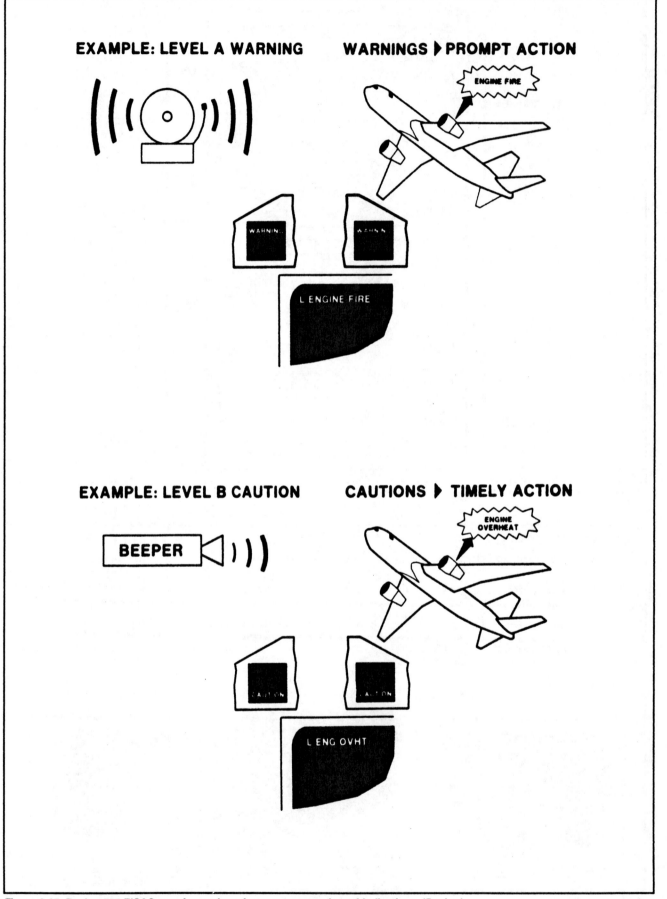

Figure 9-37. Boeing 757 EICAS warning and caution messages and aural indications. (Boeing)

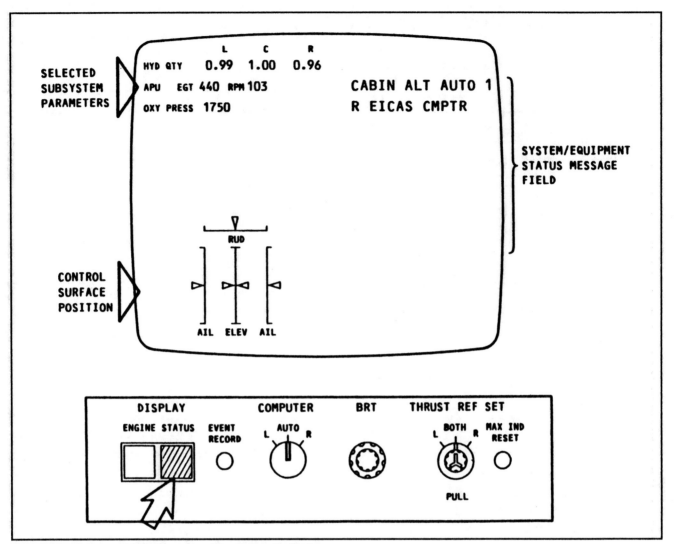

Figure 9-38. Boeing 757 EICAS status mode display. (Boeing)

WARNING AND CAUTION MESSAGES

Any time a level A warning is generated, shown in Figure 9-37, one of the EICAS display units displays a red warning message. Also, warning system signals simultaneously cause the master WARNING lights to illuminate and the fire bell or siren aural to sound.

Pressing either master warning light resets the warning system's circuitry for the master warning lights and the associated level A aurals. This action causes the WARNING light to extinguish and the warning aural to cease.

When a level B caution is generated, the EICAS displays a yellow message. It illuminates both master caution lights and sounds a beeper tone.

System status and status messages, shown in Figure 9-38, or maintenance data and maintenance messages, can also be displayed on the lower display unit on demand by using the appropriate display switches on the display select panel or maintenance panel.

CHAPTER 9 STUDY QUESTIONS

1. What is the basic function of a fire detection system?

    _____

    _____

    _____

2. What does EICAS stand for?

    _____

3. Explain the basic operation of a Fenwal continuous loop fire detector system.

    _____

    _____

    _____

4. Describe the operation of a smoke detection system.

    _____

    _____

    _____

5. List the types of classes of fires and what they involve.

    _____

    _____

    _____

    _____

6. What basic categories are fire extinguishing agents classified?

    _____

    _____

    _____

    _____

7. Describe the operation of a high-rate-discharge fire extinguishing system.

    _____

    _____

    _____

8. What condition is indicated if the red indicating disk is missing from the fire extinguishing system?

    _____

    _____

    _____

9. Explain the procedure in discharging an engine fire extinguishing system (both bottles).

    _____

    _____

    _____

10. What forewarning systems indications are used if a fire is present?

    _____

    _____

11. List the different onboard aircraft warning systems.

    _____

    _____

    _____

    _____

12. List the modes and warnings provided by the ground proximity warning system.

    _____

    _____

    _____

COMMUNICATIONS, INSTRUMENTS, AND NAVIGATIONAL SYSTEMS

COMMUNICATIONS

External communication systems primarily involve voice transmission and reception between aircraft or aircraft and ground stations. Some of the external communication systems that are used on large aircraft are high frequency system (HF), very high frequency systems (VHF), and selective calling systems (SELCAL).

Internal communication systems, or systems used to communicate within or around the aircraft, can consist of a flight interphone, service interphone, cabin interphone, and passenger address system. Each interphone system is similar in operation and will be described later in this chapter.

Another communication system, the aircraft communications addressing and reporting system (ACARS) is a data-link system which sends information between an aircraft and the airline ground base.

Some of the communication applications of ACARS that are common to many airlines are:

• Crew identification
• Out of gate time
• Off the ground time
• On the ground time
• In the gate time
• Dispatch and weather updates
• Engine performance
• Fuel status
• Passenger services
• Maintenance information
• ATIS (automatic terminal information service)

Radios are also used as navigational aids in a number of applications. They range from a simple radio direction finder, to navigational systems which use computers and other advanced electronic techniques to automatically solve the navigational problems for an entire flight.

Marker beacon receivers, instrument landing systems, distance measuring equipment, radar, area navigation systems, and omnidirectional radio receivers are but a few basic applications of airborne radio navigation systems available for use in aircraft. Other systems used to navigate and control the aircraft in flight can include autopilots (automatic flight), flight directors, flight management, and autothrottle systems.

The most common communication system in use is the VHF (very high frequency) system. In addition to VHF equipment, large long range aircraft are usually equipped with HF (high frequency) communication systems. VHF airborne communication sets operate in the frequency range from 108.0 MHz to 135.95 MHz.

In general, the VHF radio waves follow approximately straight lines. Theoretically, the range of contact is the distance to the horizon and this distance is determined by the heights of the transmitting and receiving antennas. However, communication is sometimes possible many hundreds of miles beyond the assumed horizon range.

A high frequency communication system (Figure 10-1) is used for long-range communication. HF systems operate essentially the same as a VHF system, but operate in the frequency range from 3 MHz to 30 MHz. Communications over long distances are possible with HF radio because of the longer transmission range. HF transmitters have higher power outputs than VHF transmitters.

AIRCRAFT COMMUNICATION ADDRESSING AND REPORTING SYSTEM (ACARS)

ACARS messages, mentioned earlier, are sent from the airplane via a VHF communication transceiver and a ground network to the airline ground operations base, and vice versa.

There is nothing new about sending messages between the airplane and the ground. What makes ACARS unique is that messages concerning everything from the contents of the fuel tanks and maintenance problems to food and liquor supplies can be sent by ACARS in a fraction of the time it takes using voice communications, in many cases without involving the flight crew.

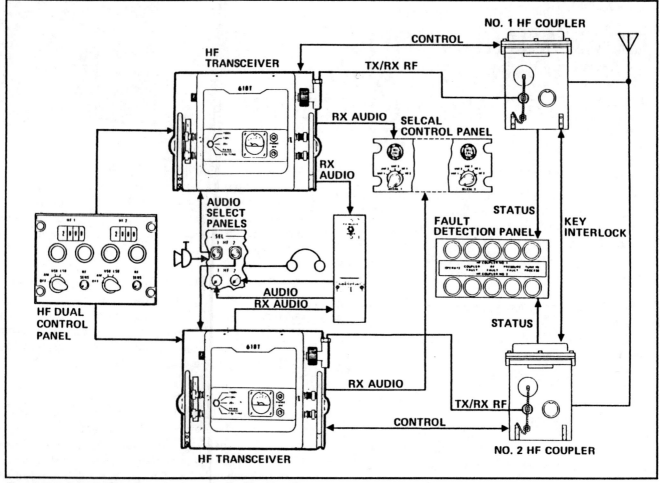

Figure 10-1. L-1011 HF communications system. (Lockheed)

Each ACARS message is compressed and takes about one second of air time to transmit. Sending and receiving data over the ACARS network reduces the number of voice contacts required on any one flight, thereby reducing communication workload. ACARS messages are limited to a length of 220 characters which is adequate for routine messages. Longer messages, known as multi-block messages, can be sent as a series of separate ACARS messages.

The ACARS network is made up of three sections: the airborne system; the service provider ground network; and the airline operations center (see Figure 10-2). The airborne system (see Figure 10-3) has an ACARS management unit (MU) which manages the incoming and outgoing messages, and a control unit (CU) which is used by the crew to interface with the system. A printer may be installed to print incoming messages.

ACARS may be connected to other airplane systems such as the digital flight data acquisition unit (DFDAU). The DFDAU collects data from many of the airplane systems such as air data, navigation, and engine instruments, and in turn makes the data available to the ACARS . More recent ACARS installations

have been connected to the flight management computer, permitting flight plan updates, predicted wind data, takeoff data, and position reports to be sent over the ACARS network.

The ACARS ground system is made up of two parts (see Figure 10-2). The first part is the radio and message handling network, which is controlled in the United States by Aeronautical Radio Incorporated (ARINC). The service provider operates the remote radio sites, the ACARS front end processing system and the electronic switching system act like a post office and ensure that messages are routed to the correct addressee.

All ACARS messages originated in the United States are relayed from the remote sites at which they are received to the message handling center in Chicago. The ground systems in other parts of the world work in a similar way to the US system.

The third part of the network is an airline's operations or message center. The ARINC network is connected to the airline operations center by a land-line. At the airline, the message handling is performed by a computer

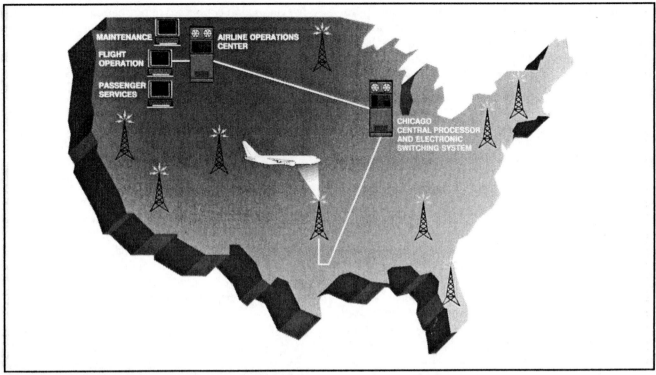

Figure 10-2. Components of the ACARS network. (Boeing)

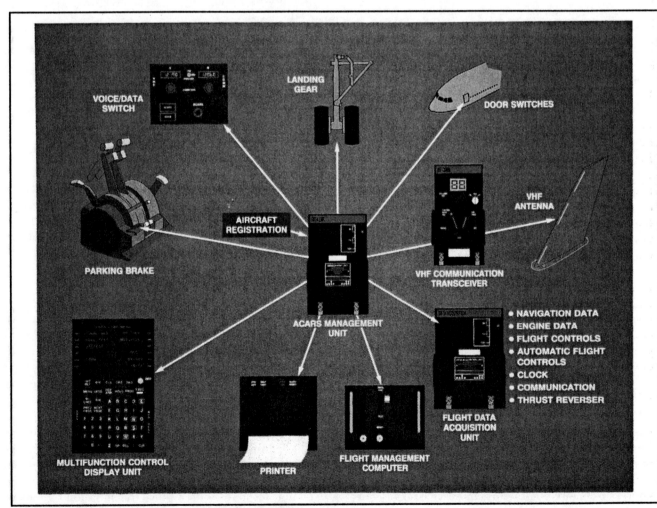

Figure 10-3. Typical ACARS airplane installation. (Boeing)

system which sends received messages to the appropriate department (operations, engineering, maintenance, customer services) for the appropriate action. Messages from an airline department, such as a request from engineering for engine data, follow the same route in reverse.

The ACARS in use vary greatly from one airline to another and are tailored to meet each airline's operational needs. When satellite communication systems are adopted in the near future, ACARS will take on a truly global aspect.

SELCAL

The SELCAL decoder is designed to relieve the flight crew from continuously monitoring the aircraft radio receivers. The SELCAL decoder is in effect an automatic monitor which listens for a particular combination of tones which are assigned to the individual aircraft by ARINC. Whenever a properly coded transmission is received from a ground ARINC station, the signal is decoded by the SELCAL unit, which then gives a signal to the flight crew indicating that a radio transmission is being directed to the aircraft. The flight crew can then listen to the appropriate receiver and hear the message.

ARINC ground stations equipped with tone-transmitting equipment call individual aircraft by transmitting two pairs of tones which will key only an airborne decoder set to respond to the particular combination of tones. When the proper tones are received, the decoder operates an external alarm circuit to produce a chime, light, buzz, or a combination of such signals.

A ground operator who wishes to contact a particular aircraft by means of the SELCAL unit selects the four-tone code which has been assigned to the aircraft. The tone code is transmitted by a radio-frequency wave, and the signal can be picked up by all receivers tuned to the frequency used by the transmitter. The only receiver which will respond to the signal and produce the alert signal for the flight crew is the SELCAL decoder system which has been set for the particular combination of tone frequencies generated by the ground operator.

NAVIGATION EQUIPMENT

"Airborne navigation equipment" is a phrase which describes many different systems. The VHF VOR (omnidirectional range) is an electronic navigation system. As the name implies, the omnidirectional, or all-directional range station, provides the pilot with courses from any point within its service range. It produces 360 usable radials or courses, any one of which

is a radio path connected to the station. The radials can be considered as lines that extend from the transmitter antenna like spokes of a wheel.

Operation is in the VHF portion of the radio spectrum (frequency range of 108.0 MHz - 117.95 MHz) with the result that interference from atmospheric and precipitation static is negligible. The navigational information is visually displayed on an instrument in the cockpit.

INSTRUMENT LANDING SYSTEM

The ILS (instrument landing system) can be visualized as a slide made of radio signals on which the aircraft can be brought safely to the runway. The entire system consists of a runway localizer, a glide slope signal, and marker beacons for position location. The localizer equipment produces a radio course aligned with the center of an airport runway.

The glide slope is a radio beam which provides vertical guidance to the pilot, assisting him in making the correct angle of descent to the runway. Glide slope signals are radiated from two antennas located adjacent to the touchdown point of the runway, as shown in Figure 10-4.

Two antennas are usually required for ILS operation. One for the localizer receiver, also used for VOR navigation, and one for the glide slope. The glide slope antenna is generally located on the nose area of the aircraft.

MARKER BEACONS AND DISTANCE-MEASURING EQUIPMENT

Marker beacons are used in connection with the instrument landing system. The markers are signals which indicate the position of the aircraft along the approach to the runway. Two markers are used in each installation. The location of each marker is identified by both an aural tone and a signal light.

The purpose of DME (distance-measuring equipment) is to provide a constant visual indication of the distance the aircraft is from a ground station. The aircraft is equipped with a DME transceiver which is tuned to a selected DME ground station. Usually DME ground stations are located in conjunction with a VOR facility (called VORTAC).

The airborne transceiver transmits a pair of spaced pulses to the ground station. The pulse spacing serves to identify the signal as a valid DME interrogation. After reception of the challenging pulses, the ground station responds with a pulse transmission on a separate frequency to send a reply to the aircraft. Upon

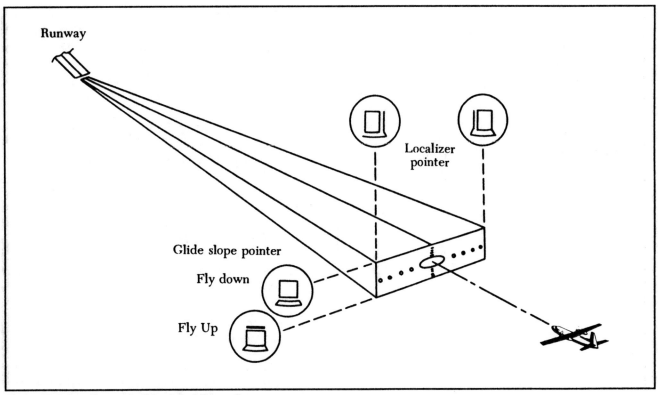

Figure 10-4. Localizer and glide slope information.

reception of the signal by the airborne transceiver, the elapsed time between the challenges and the reply is measured. This time interval is a measure of the distance separating the aircraft and the ground station. This distance is indicated in nautical miles.

AUTOMATIC DIRECTION FINDERS

ADF (automatic direction finders) are radio receivers equipped with directional antennas which are used to determine the direction from which signals are received. Most ADF receivers provide controls for manual operation in addition to automatic direction finding.

When an aircraft is within reception range of a radio station, the ADF equipment provides a means of fixing the position with reasonable accuracy. The ADF operates in the low and medium frequency spectrum from 190 kHz through 1,750 kHz. The direction to the station is displayed on an indicator as a relative bearing to the station.

RADAR BEACON TRANSPONDER (ATC TRANSPONDER)

The radar beacon transponder system is used in conjunction with a ground base surveillance radar to provide positive aircraft identification and location directly on the controller's radar scope.

The airborne equipment, or transponder, receives a ground radar interrogation for each sweep of the surveillance radar antenna and automatically dispatches a coded response. The flight identification code, a four-digit number, is assigned during the flight planning procedure, or by air traffic control.

Most large aircraft transponders are equipped with an altitude encoding feature. The aircraft's altitude is transmitted to the ground station through the transponder.

INERTIAL NAVIGATION SYSTEM

The inertial navigation system is presently being used on large aircraft as a long-range navigation aid. It is a self-contained system and does not require signal inputs from ground navigational facilities. The system derives attitude, velocity, and heading information from measurement of the aircraft's accelerations.

Two accelerometers are required, one referenced to north and the other to east. The accelerometers are mounted on a gyrostabilized unit, called the stable platform, to avert the introduction of errors resulting from the acceleration due to gravity.

LORAN

The word LORAN is formed from the words LOng RAnge Navigation. LORAN is a navigational system

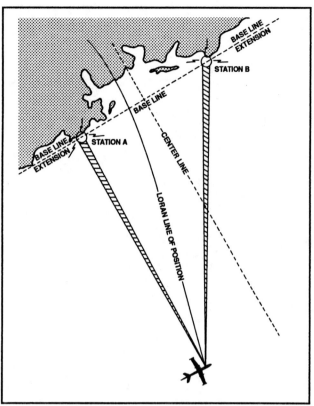

Figure 10-5. The principal of LORAN.

developed primarily to provide a means for making geographical fixes by the use of long range radio signals. The system is a valuable aid to navigation, since LORAN fixes can be made quickly and accurately, both by night and day. A LORAN airborne unit simply receives radio pulses broadcast from ground stations.

The basic principle of the system is a measurement of time difference, as illustrated in Figure 10-5. Two stations are necessary to establish a LORAN line of position. The master station, A, emits a continuous series of uniformly spaced pulses at a stable pulse recurrence rate. The slave station, B, sends out a similar series of pulses which are synchronized with the master pulses. The difference in the time of arrival of the pulses corresponds to the difference in distance from the stations, and can be accurately calculated and plotted on a chart.

Selected line of position curves may be drawn by connecting points of equal computed time or distance values. Each curve so constructed has the shape of a hyperbola, which is the mathematical name for a curve consisting of points whose difference in distance from two fixed points (in this case, A and B) remains con-

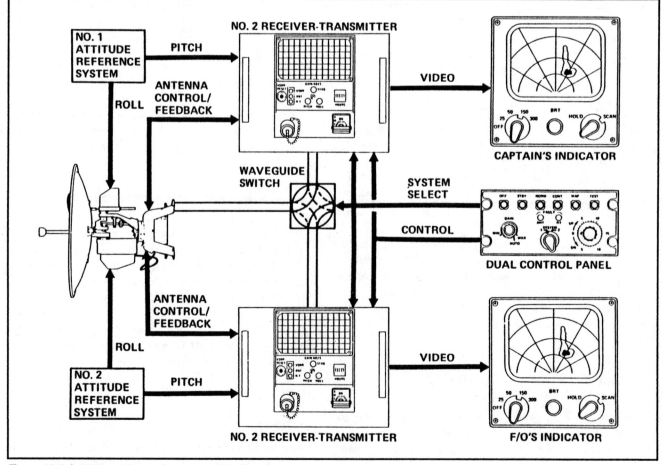

Figure 10-6. L-1011 weather radar system. (Lockheed)

stant. Thus, LORAN is called a hyperbolic system of navigation.

AIRBORNE WEATHER RADAR SYSTEM

Radar (radio detection and ranging) is a device used to see certain objects in darkness, fog, or storms, as well as in clear weather. In addition to the appearance of these objects on the radar scope, their range and relative position are also indicated.

Radar is an electronic system using a pulse transmission of radio energy to receive a reflected signal from a target. The received signal is known as an echo, the time between the transmitted pulse and received echo is computed electronically and is displayed on the radar scope in terms of nautical miles. An L-1011 radar system is shown in Figure 10-6.

The weather radar increases safety in flight by enabling the operator to detect storms in the flight path and chart a course around them.

The terrain-mapping facilities of the radar show shorelines, islands, and other topographical features along the flight path. These indications are presented on the visual indicator in range and azimuth relative to the heading of the aircraft.

RADIO ALTIMETER

Radio altimeters are used to measure the distance from the aircraft to the ground. The indicating instrument (see Figure 10-7) will indicate the true altitude of the aircraft, which is its height above water, mountains, buildings, or other objects on the surface of the earth.

Radio altimeters are primarily used during landing. The altimeter provides the pilot with the altitude of the aircraft during approach. Altimeter indications determine the decision height. This is the height, or point, that the pilot flying the aircraft makes a decision whether to continue to land, execute a climb-out, or go-around.

EMERGENCY LOCATOR TRANSMITTER (ELT)

Emergency locator transmitters are self-contained, self-powered radio transmitters designed to transmit a signal on the international distress frequencies. Operation is automatic on impact. The transmitter may also be activated by a remote switch in the cockpit, or a switch integral with the unit.

If the "G" force switch in the transmitter is activated from impact, it can be turned off only with the switch on the case.

Batteries are the power supply for emergency locator transmitters. When activated, the battery must be capable of furnishing power for signal transmission for at least 48 hours.

Testing of ELT's should be coordinated with the nearest FAA Tower or Flight Service Station and establish coordination for the test. Tests should be conducted only during the first five minutes of any hour and should be restricted to 3 audio sweeps.

Any time maintenance is performed in the vicinity of the ELT, the VHF communication receiver should be tuned to 121.5 MHz and listened to for ELT audio sweeps. If it is determined the ELT is operating, it must be turned off immediately.

BOEING 737-300 AVIONICS

COMMUNICATION

Short-range communications capability is provided in the very high frequency (VHF) range by two independent radios. Transmitting and receiving are controlled at the respective audio selector panels. The VHF-1 antenna is located on the upper fuselage; VHF-2 on the lower fuselage.

An audio selector panel (ASP) is installed at the captain, first officer, and observer stations. Each panel controls an independent crew station audio system and allows the crewmember to select the desired radios, navigation aids, interphones, and PA system for monitoring and transmission.

Transmitter selectors on each ASP select one radio or system for transmission by that crewmember. Any microphone at that crew station may then be keyed to transmit on the selected system.

Receiver switches select the systems to be monitored. A combination of systems may be selected. Receiver switches also control the volume for the headset and speaker at the respective crew stations.

Speaker and headset audio for each crew station come from a remote electronics unit located in the E & E compartment. It is controlled by the audio selector panels, and has separate independent circuits for each crew station. Audio warnings for altitude alert, the

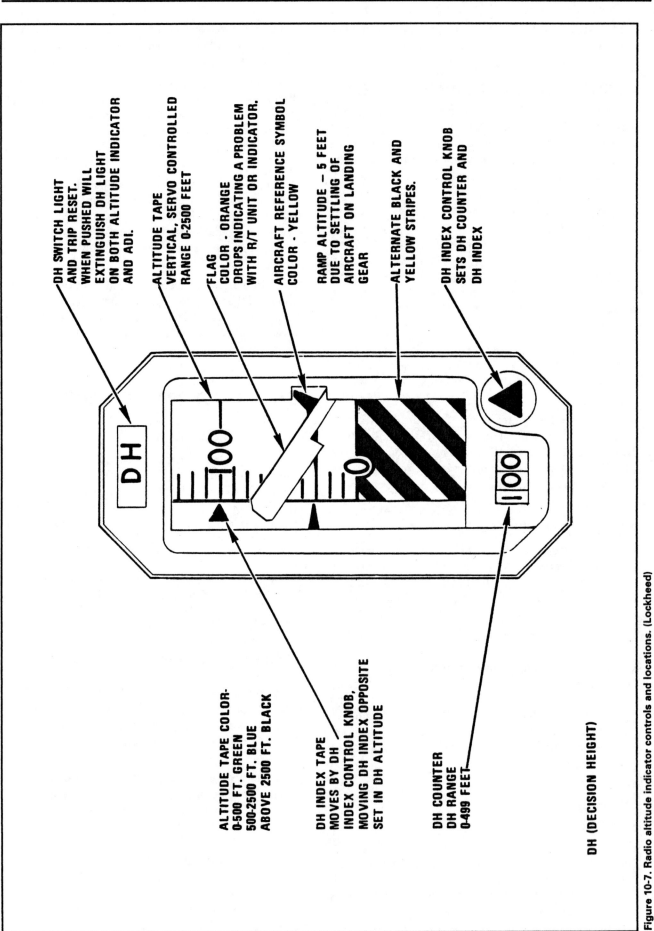

DH SWITCH LIGHT AND TRIP RESET. WHEN PUSHED WILL EXTINGUISH DH LIGHT ON BOTH ALTITUDE INDICATOR AND ADI.

ALTITUDE TAPE VERTICAL, SERVO CONTROLLED RANGE 0-2500 FEET

FLAG COLOR - ORANGE DROPS INDICATING A PROBLEM WITH R/T UNIT OR INDICATOR.

AIRCRAFT REFERENCE SYMBOL COLOR - YELLOW

RAMP ALTITUDE — 5 FEET DUE TO SETTLING OF AIRCRAFT ON LANDING GEAR

ALTERNATE BLACK AND YELLOW STRIPES.

DH INDEX CONTROL KNOB SETS DH COUNTER AND DH INDEX

ALTITUDE TAPE COLOR-
0-500 FT. GREEN
500-2500 FT. BLUE
ABOVE 2500 FT. BLACK

DH INDEX TAPE MOVES BY DH INDEX CONTROL KNOB, MOVING DH INDEX OPPOSITE SET IN DH ALTITUDE

DH COUNTER DH RANGE 0-499 FEET

DH (DECISION HEIGHT)

Figure 10-7. Radio altitude indicator controls and locations. (Lockheed)

ground proximity warning system and windshear are also heard through the speakers and headsets at preset volumes.

Each crew station has a headset, headphone jack, and speakers on the ceiling above each pilot's seat. Hand microphones and boom microphones may be plugged into the respective jacks at the cockpit crew stations, as shown in Figure 10-8. Each oxygen mask also has an integral microphone. Each hand microphone has a push-to-talk switch to key the selected audio system. The push-to-talk switches on the control wheel or ASP are used to key the oxygen mask or boom microphone, as selected by the MASK-BOOM switch.

FLIGHT INTERPHONE SYSTEM

The flight interphone system, Figure 10-9, is an independent communications network. Its primary pur-

pose is to provide private communication between cockpit crewmembers without intrusion from the service interphone system. The ground crew may also use flight interphone through a jack at the external power receptacle.

SERVICE INTERPHONE SYSTEM

The service interphone system, Figure 10-10, provides intercommunication between the cockpit, flight attendants, and ground personnel. Cockpit crewmembers communicate using either a separate handset (if installed) or their respective audio selector panel and any standard microphone.

The flight attendants communicate between flight attendant stations or the cockpit using any of the attendant handsets. The system is a party line, in that anyone who picks up a handset/microphone is auto-

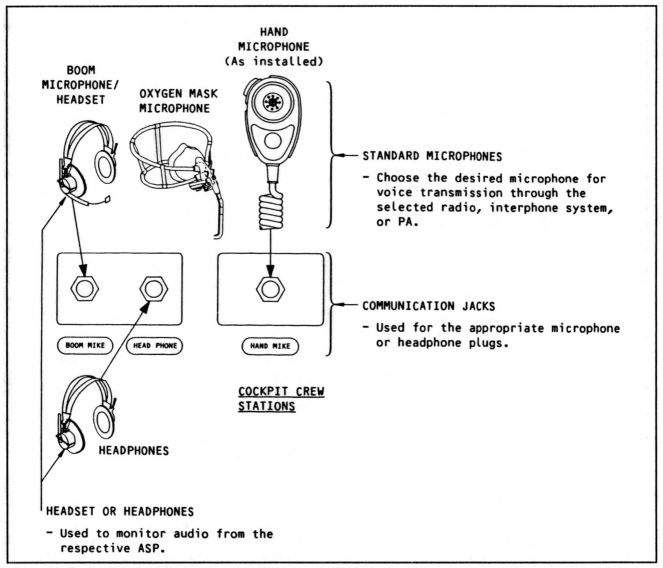

Figure 10-8. Boeing 737 miscellaneous communications controls. (Boeing)

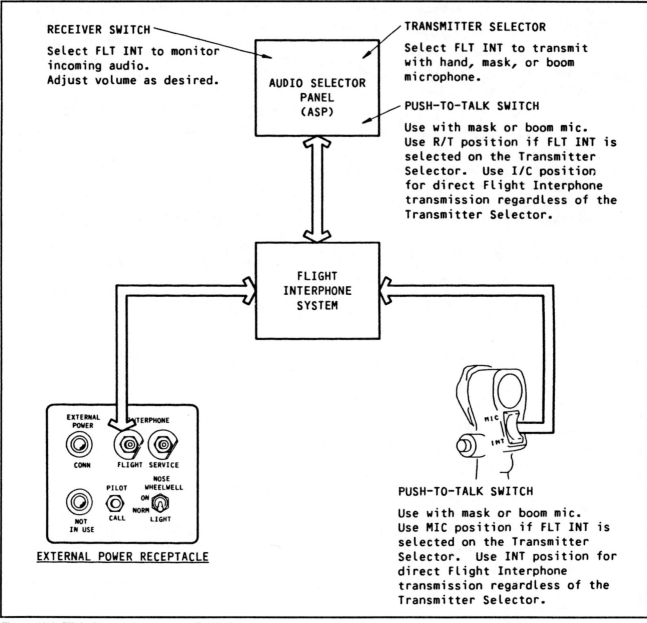

RECEIVER SWITCH

Select FLT INT to monitor
incoming audio.
Adjust volume as desired.

TRANSMITTER SELECTOR

Select FLT INT to transmit
with hand, mask, or boom
microphone.

PUSH-TO-TALK SWITCH

Use with mask or boom mic.
Use R/T position if FLT INT is
selected on the Transmitter
Selector. Use I/C position
for direct Flight Interphone
transmission regardless of the
Transmitter Selector.

AUDIO SELECTOR
PANEL
(ASP)

FLIGHT
INTERPHONE
SYSTEM

EXTERNAL POWER RECEPTACLE

PUSH-TO-TALK SWITCH

Use with mask or boom mic.
Use MIC position if FLT INT is
selected on the Transmitter
Selector. Use INT position for
direct Flight Interphone
transmission regardless of the
Transmitter Selector.

Figure 10-9. Flight interphone system. (Boeing)

matically connected to the system. External jacks for use by maintenance or service personnel can be added to the system by use of the service interphone switch.

PASSENGER ADDRESS SYSTEM

The passenger address (PA) system, Figure 10-11, allows cockpit crewmembers and flight attendants to make announcements to the passengers. Announcements are heard through speakers located in the cabin and in the lavatories.

The cockpit crewmembers can make announcements using a PA hand microphone or by using any standard

microphone and the respective audio selector panel. Flight attendants make announcements using PA hand microphones located at their stations. The attendants can also use the PA system to play recorded music for passenger entertainment.

CALL SYSTEM

The call system is used as a means for various crewmembers to gain the attention of other crewmembers and to indicate that interphone communication is desired. Attention is gained through the use of lights and aural signals (chimes or horn). The system can be activated from the cockpit, either flight attendant station, or from the external power receptacle.

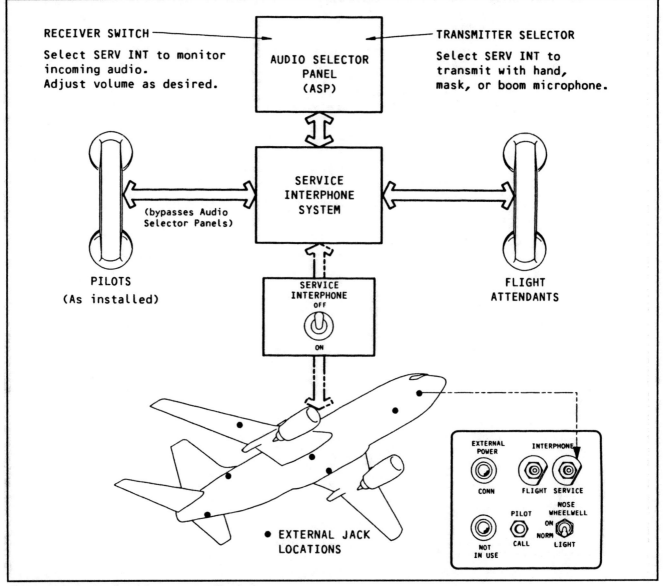

Figure 10-10. Service interphone system. (Boeing)

Passengers may also use the system to summon an attendant, through the use of individual call switches at each seat.

The cockpit may be called by either flight attendant station, or by the ground crew. The ground crew may only be called by the cockpit. Flight attendants may be called by the cockpit, the other attendant station, or by any passenger seat or lavatory. Master call lights in the passenger cabin identify the source of incoming calls to the attendants.

COCKPIT VOICE RECORDER

The cockpit voice recorder uses four independent channels to record cockpit audio on a 30 minute continuous-loop tape. Recordings older than 30 minutes are automatically erased. One channel records cockpit area conversations using the area microphone. The other channels record any individual audio and transmissions from the pilots and first observer.

ELECTRONIC FLIGHT INSTRUMENT SYSTEM

The electronic flight instrument system (EFIS) consists of two symbol generators (SGs), two control panels (CPs), two electronic attitude director indicators (EADIs or ADIs), two electronic horizontal situation indicators (EHSIs or HSIs) and ambient light sensing units.

The EFIS utilizes information provided by a variety of aircraft systems to generate the appropriate visual presentations on the EHSI and EADI.

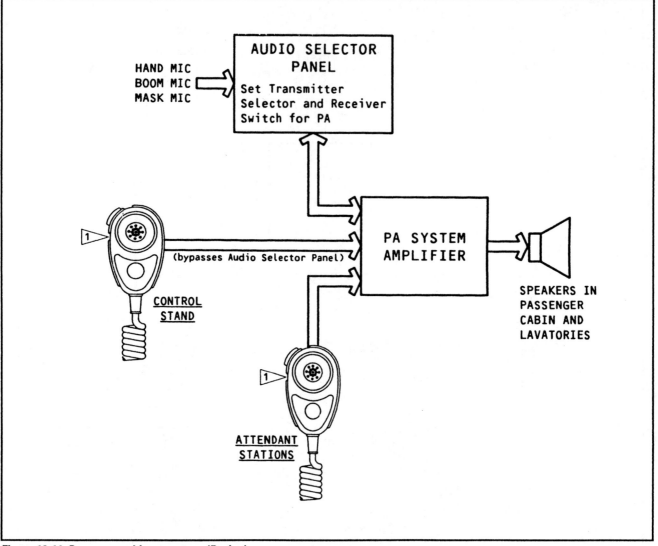

Figure 10-11. Passenger address system. (Boeing)

Data relating primarily to navigation is provided by aircraft systems such as the navigation radios, flight management computer (FMC), and the inertial reference systems (IRSs).

Automatic flight data is provided by the flight control computers (FCCs), the autothrottle (A/T), and the FMC.

Data which is used to display current aircraft status information is provided by the air data computers (ADCs) and the IRSs.

Automatic adjustment of the display intensity for each display unit is provided by the ambient light sensing units. Flight crew control of the EFIS displays is accomplished by positioning the various controls on the respective EFIS control panels to the desired settings.

Two symbol generators form the heart of the EFIS. The SGs receive inputs from various aircraft systems. The SGs respond to these inputs and then generate the proper visual displays for the respective EADI and EHSI, as shown in Figure 10-12.

Each SG is connected to an EFIS control panel. Using the respective EFIS control panel, a flight crewmember can select several EHSI display modes. The EFIS control panels also allow the flight crew to adjust the EADI, EHSI, and weather radar display brightness levels.

The EADI, shown in Figure 10-13, presents conventional EADI displays for attitude (pitch and roll), flight director commands, localizer deviation and glideslope deviation. In addition, the EADI displays information relating to the autoflight system mode annunciations, such as airplane speed (fast/slow display), pitch limit,

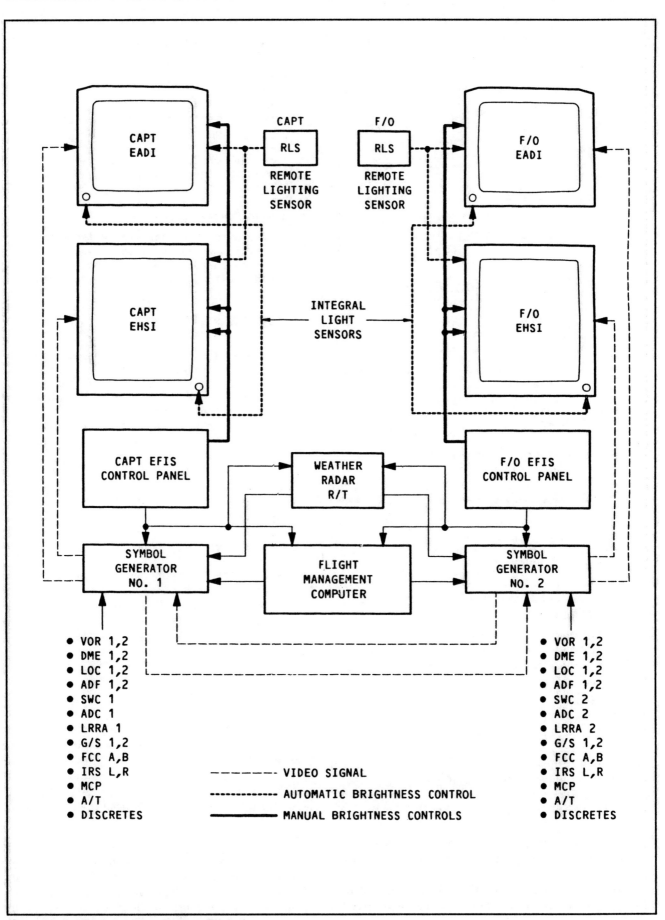

Figure 10-12. EFIS integration diagram. (Boeing)

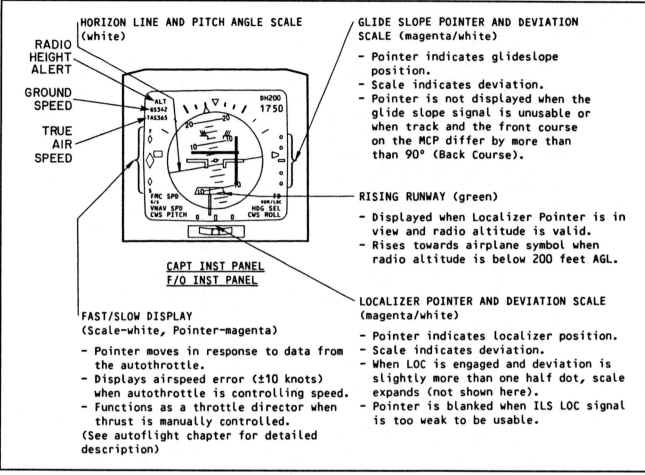

Figure 10-13. Electronic attitude director indicator (EADI) display. (Boeing)

true airspeed, ground speed, radio height alert, decision height, and radio altitude.

ELECTRONIC HORIZONTAL SITUATION INDICATOR (EHSI)

Each EHSI presents an electronically generated color display of conventional HSI navigation data (VOR/ILS and NAV modes). Each EHSI is also capable of displaying the airplane's flight progress on a plan view map, as seen in Figure 10-14. Each EHSI also serves as a weather radar display when the weather radar switch on the respective EFIS control panel is on.

During normal operation, each EHSI receives information from its own symbol generator. Each symbol generator receives data from a variety of aircraft systems to support the EHSI displays.

The EFIS control panels provide selection of the EHSI display modes. The selectable display modes are FULL rose NAVIGATION (FULL NAV), FULL rose VOR/ILS, EXPANDED rose NAVIGATION (EXP NAV), EXPANDED rose VOR/ILS, MAP, CENTER MAP (CTR MAP), and PLAN.

BOEING 757 AVIONICS SYSTEMS

Avionics on the 757 airplane consist of communication, navigation, instrument, and autoflight systems. These systems allow the flight crew to communicate, navigate, control the airplane and manage the flight profile in the most efficient and effective manner possible.

COMMUNICATION

Communication equipment aboard the airplane allows the crew members to communicate with other aircraft, ground stations, other crew members, maintenance crews, and the passengers. The selective call system advises pilots of radio communication from another aircraft or a ground station, and a voice recorder maintains a record of flight communication as mentioned earlier.

Three VHF communications radios are installed; designated L (left), C (center) and R (right). Control panels for the left and right are provided in the cockpit. Each panel allows the selection of two independent frequencies, the desired frequency being selected with

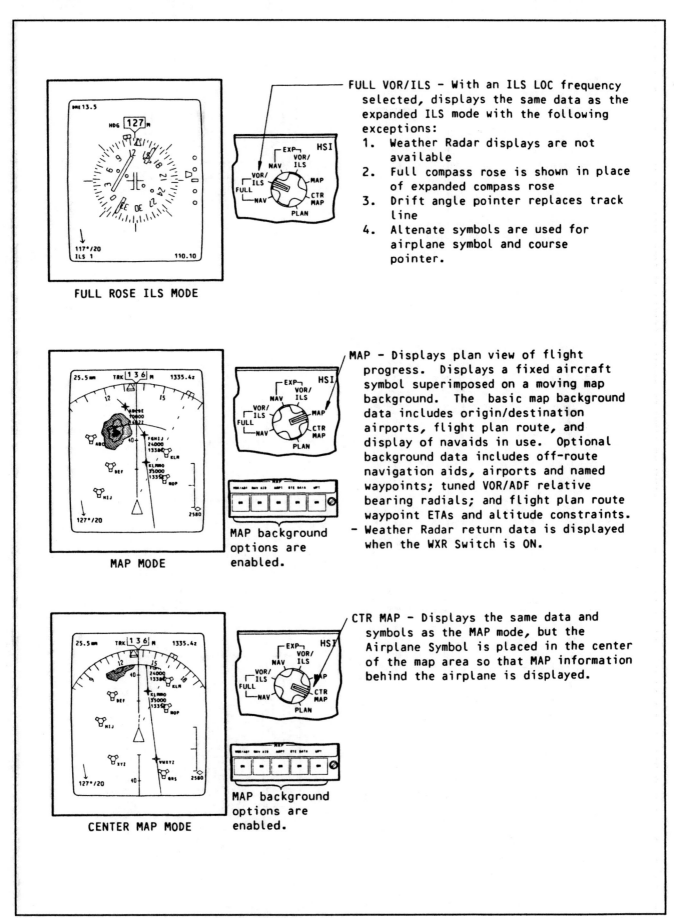

FULL VOR/ILS – With an ILS LOC frequency selected, displays the same data as the expanded ILS mode with the following exceptions:
1. Weather Radar displays are not available
2. Full compass rose is shown in place of expanded compass rose
3. Drift angle pointer replaces track line
4. Altenate symbols are used for airplane symbol and course pointer.

FULL ROSE ILS MODE

MAP – Displays plan view of flight progress. Displays a fixed aircraft symbol superimposed on a moving map background. The basic map background data includes origin/destination airports, flight plan route, and display of navaids in use. Optional background data includes off-route navigation aids, airports and named waypoints; tuned VOR/ADF relative bearing radials; and flight plan route waypoint ETAs and altitude constraints.
- Weather Radar return data is displayed when the WXR Switch is ON.

MAP MODE

MAP background options are enabled.

CTR MAP – Displays the same data and symbols as the MAP mode, but the Airplane Symbol is placed in the center of the map area so that MAP information behind the airplane is displayed.

CENTER MAP MODE

MAP background options are enabled.

Figure 10-14. EHSI mode selection and typical displays. (Boeing)

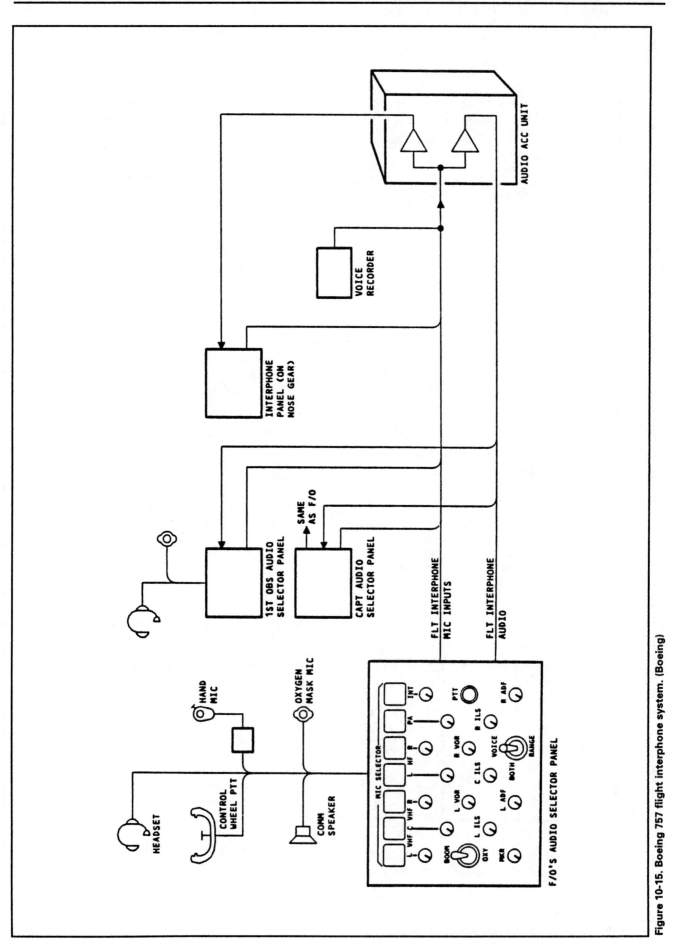

Figure 10-15. Boeing 757 flight interphone system. (Boeing)

the frequency transfer switch. Individual transmit and audio control is provided through the respective ASP (audio select panel).

An audio selector panel (ASP) is installed at the captain, first officer, and first observer stations. The panel allows each crew member to manage his own communications requirements.

The ASP permits two way (transmit and receive) communication capability from the flight interphone, cabin/service interphone, passenger address, and VHF radio systems. It provides voice and identification monitoring of selected navigation aids. Receiver volumes and microphone selections are also controlled from this panel. A cockpit loudspeaker and volume control is provided adjacent to each pilot seat.

INTERPHONE SYSTEMS

There are two independent interphone systems in the aircraft, the flight interphone system and the cabin/service interphone system.

The flight interphone system (FIS) permits intercommunication between cockpit crew members without intrusion from the other phone system. Ground personnel are able to communicate on the FIS through a jack located on the APU ground control panel, shown in Figure 10-15.

The cabin interphone system (CIS) permits intercommunication between the cockpit and flight attendant stations. Cockpit crewmembers communicate on the CIS through their audio select panel. The flight attendants communicate between flight attendant stations or with the cockpit using any of the handsets in the cabin. The system is a party line similar to the 737 system. The service interphone system consists of additional internal and external jacks connected to the cabin interphone system for use by maintenance personnel.

The call system, illustrated in Figure 10-16, allows the cockpit crew, flight attendants and ground personnel to indicate that interphone communication is desired. The cockpit crew can initiate calls through the pilots' call panel and are alerted through call lights and chimes.

The SELCAL alerts the flight crew that a ground station is calling the airplane on VHF or HF radio. The SELCAL lights, shown in Figure 10-17, on the pilots' call panel come on whenever the SELCAL decoder receives a properly coded signal via the corresponding communications system. A high chime sounds repetitively and the light illuminates. The decoder is reset by pressing the corresponding alert lamp/switch, or by the microphone push-to-talk.

The passenger address (PA) system, shown in Figure 10-18, allows cockpit crew and cabin attendants to make announcements throughout the cabin. Cockpit

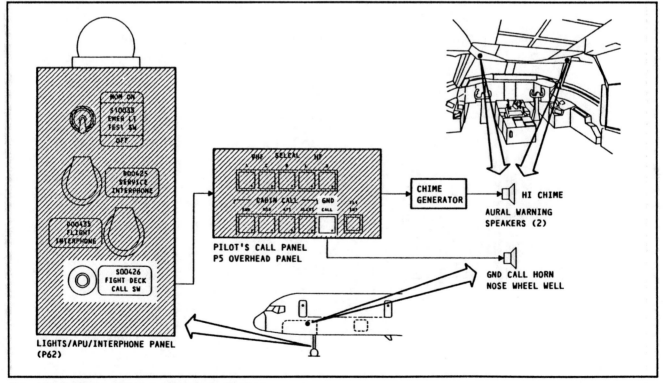

Figure 10-16. Boeing 757 crew call system. (Boeing)

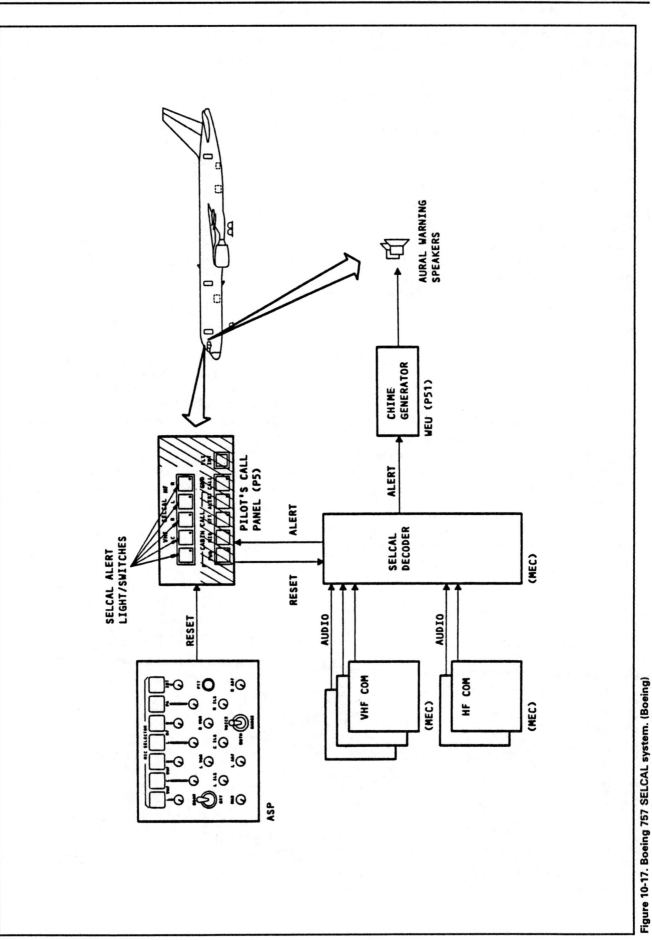

Figure 10-17. Boeing 757 SELCAL system. (Boeing)

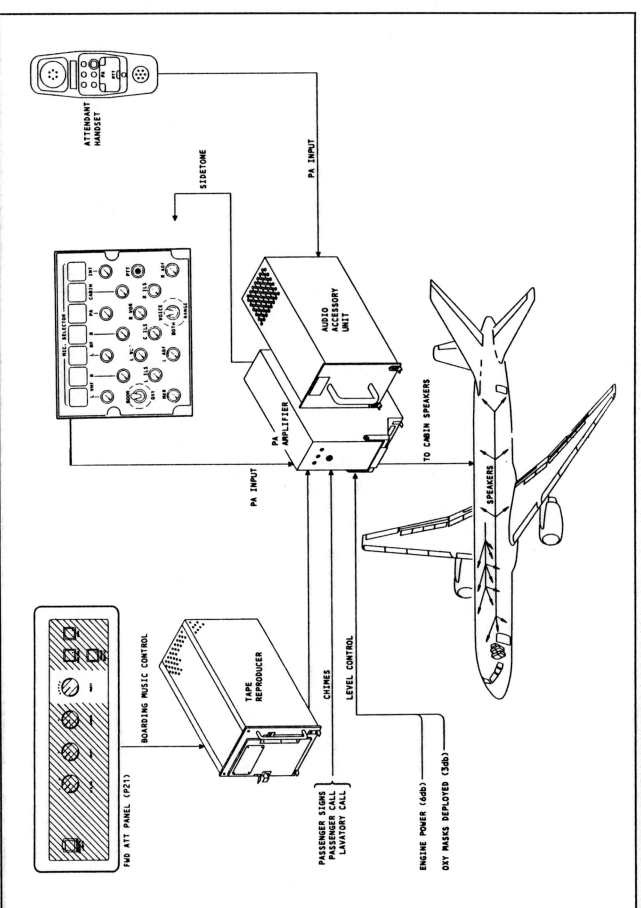

Figure 10-18. Boeing 757 passenger address system. (Boeing)

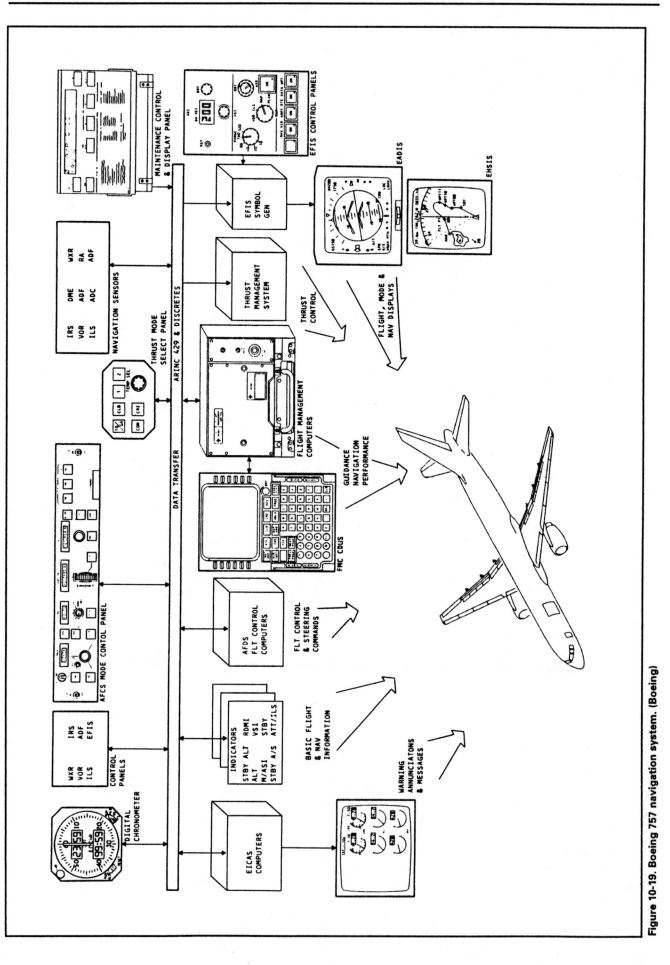

Figure 10-19. Boeing 757 navigation system. (Boeing)

crewmembers can make announcements through any microphone and respective ASP.

The passenger entertainment system (PES) consists of a multi-track tape player providing boarding music. PA announcements from any station override all tape player outputs.

VOICE RECORDER

The cockpit voice recorder records any transmissions from the cockpit made through the audio selector panels. It also records cockpit area conversations using an area microphone.

NAVIGATIONAL AND ELECTRONIC INSTRUMENT SYSTEMS

Navigation equipment aboard the airplane provides the pilot information on flight conditions, aircraft position, performance, guidance, and flight profile. This information may be displayed directly or may be used as inputs to the flight management system, which then calculates a 3 dimensional flight path and steers the airplane along a selected route.

The navigation equipment is integrated with computer, display and cautionary systems into a flight management system, illustrated in Figure 10-19. The

majority of the units are digital, with microprocessors and software programs replacing many of the discrete components of previous units.

The instrument systems provide the pilot with primary flight information, selectable navigation displays, system mode annunciations, advisory, caution, and warning messages.

The pitot-static system, shown in Figure 10-20, senses both dynamic and static air pressures and supplies these pressures to the left and right air data computers, to the standby instruments, and to other airplane systems as required.

The pitot probes are located on the right and left sides of the forward fuselage body. The static ports are located on each side of the forward body. The pitot probes sense total air pressure while the static ports sense ambient static air pressure. These pressures are used by the air data computer to determine the airplane's altitude, airspeed, and other related parameters.

The air data computer system monitors the airspace adjacent to the airplane and provides a single point source for altitude, airspeed, pressure, angle of attack and temperature data.

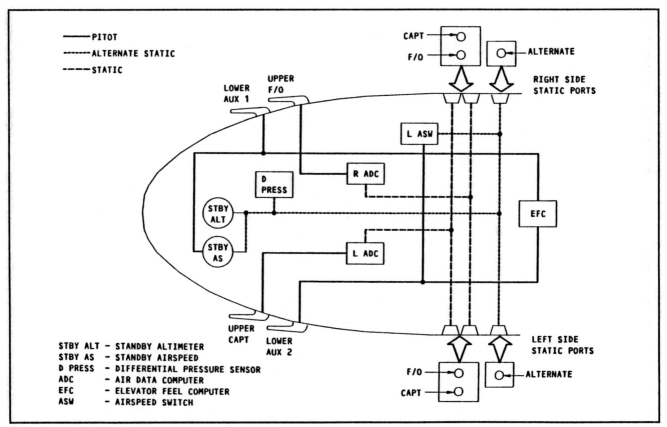

Figure 10-20. Boeing 757 pitot-static system. (Boeing)

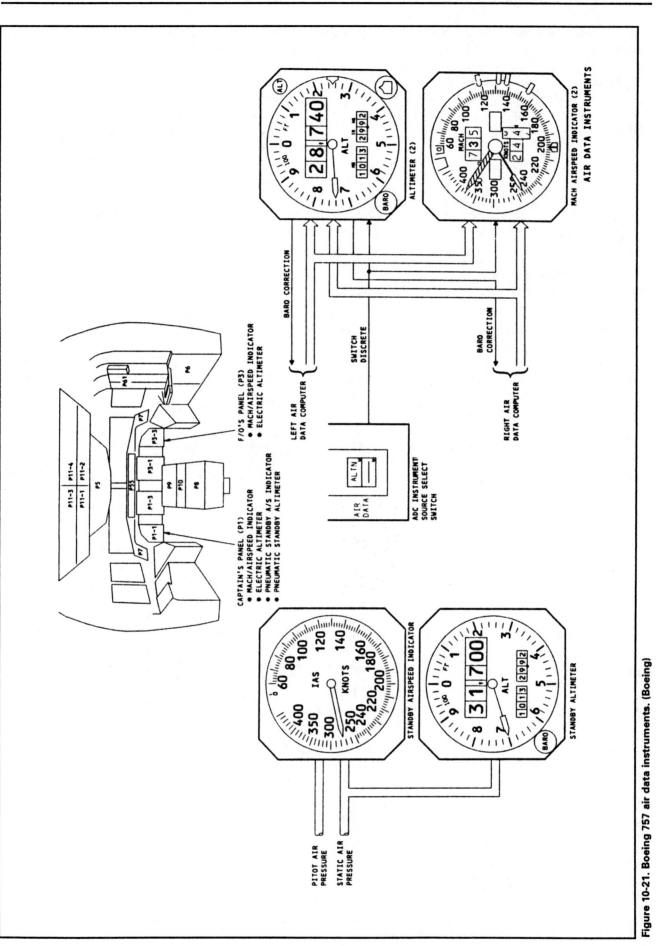

Figure 10-21. Boeing 757 air data instruments. (Boeing)

Inputs to the air data computers are total and ambient air pressures from the pitot-static system, and barometric correction from the altimeters. Other inputs include total air temperature (TAT) from the TAT probe and angle of attack (AOA) from the AOA sensors.

The air data computers convert these analog inputs to digital signals and uses them to determine output values. The computer output signals are transmitted on four digital data buses which supply data to the air data instruments, engine and flight controls, navigation, warning, flight management, and autoflight systems.

The air data instruments, shown in Figure 10-21, provide flight deck displays of altitude and airspeed. The standby airspeed indicator and altimeter are pneumatic instruments supplied with static and pitot air pressures from the pitot-static system. The electric altimeters and mach airspeed indicators are supplied data from both the left and right air data computers.

The standby attitude reference system (see Figure 10-22) provides pitch and roll attitude information to the pilot in the event of failure of the two primary attitude displays. Localizer and glideslope information from the center ILS receiver is also displayed on the standby attitude indicator for use in the event of failure of the

primary indicating systems. The attitude information is independent of other aircraft systems and requires only standby power.

The inertial reference system (IRS) senses airplane displacement about 3 axes to provide primary attitude, true and magnetic heading, vertical speed, navigation position, accelerations and angular rates, wind velocity and direction, and ground track. Each IRS contains 3 laser gyros, 3 accelerometers, power supplies, a microprocessor, BITE, and output circuitry. Each of the three inertial reference systems operates independently of the other two systems.

The IRSs receive barometric altitude, altitude rate, and true airspeed data from the air data computers. This information is used along with gyro and accelerometer data to determine the airplane's vertical speed and calculate wind parameters.

The air traffic control system (transponder) allows ground stations to monitor the aircraft's position continuously, by providing altitude and identity information.

Two separate systems (left and right) are installed. Each system consists of an antenna and transponder (transmitter/receiver) and are controlled from a single

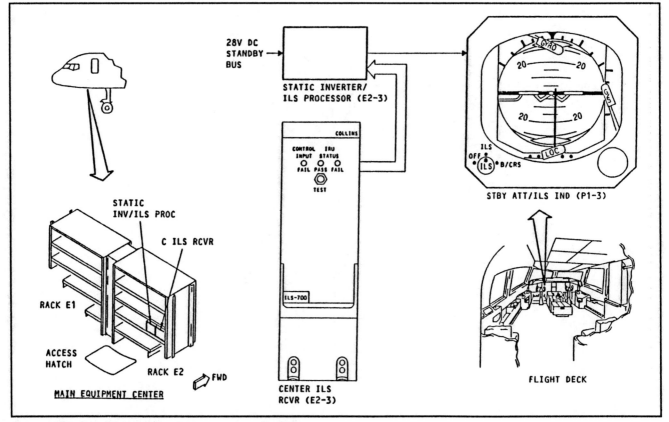

Figure 10-22. Standby attitude reference system. (Boeing)

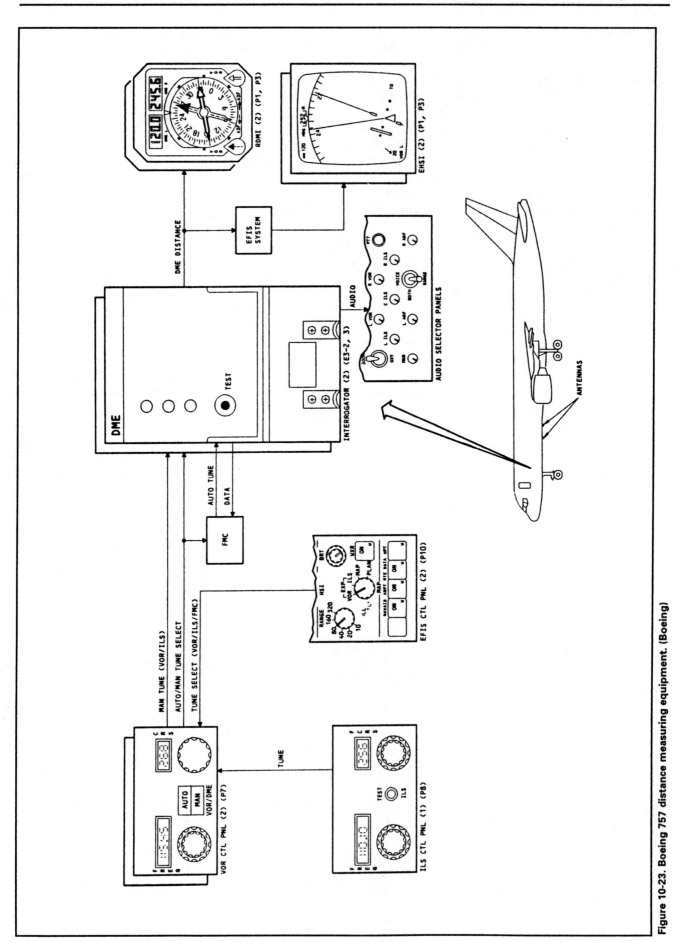

Figure 10-23. Boeing 757 distance measuring equipment. (Boeing)

control panel. The control panel is used to set the assigned code, select the left or right system, select altitude reporting, and initiate an identity pulse.

The distance measuring equipment (DME), see Figure 10-23, measures slant range (DME distance) from the aircraft to selected DME ground stations and provides data for DME distance displays and continuous distance information to the flight management computers (FMCs).

Two separate systems are installed, with each system consisting of one antenna and one interrogator. Three control panels are shared with the VOR and ILS receivers. The interrogator sends out interrogation pulse pairs to the selected ground station, which are then returned to the aircraft. The slant range is computed and displayed on the RDMIs and EHSIs, and is also routed to other navigation data users.

The automatic direction finder (ADF) provides the relative bearing of ground stations with respect to the airplane's heading. Standard broadcast stations and non-directional homing beacons are normally used with the ADF system.

The VOR navigation system, illustrated in Figure 10-24, provides magnetic bearing to or from a ground VOR transmitter. Two separate systems use a dual port, omni-directional loop antenna which feeds two independent receivers that are controlled by two control panels.

Bearing information is displayed on the RDMIs. Selection of VOR on the EFIS control panel provides an EHSI display of course, deviation, source (L/R VOR), and to/from information. A bearing angle relative to the transmitter is displayed on the RDMI and EHSI. Bearing, frequency, and course selection data are transferred in a digital format to the flight management computer system and to EFIS. Tuning can be done manually from the control panel, or it can be accomplished by commands from the flight management computer system. Audio goes directly to the interphone system.

The purpose of the weather radar system is to provide airborne weather detection, ranging and analysis. It can also be used to provide ground mapping as an aid to navigation by displaying significant ground objects and land contours.

The major components of this single system consist of an antenna, a transceiver and a control panel. The weather data is displayed on the two EHSIs. The weather radar system operates in the X-band with a

peak power output of 125 Watts and a maximum range displayed of 320NM.

The received return signals are processed in the transceiver and the detected weather conditions and ground mapping information are sent to the EFIS symbol generators which control the displays on the left and right EHSIs. The EHSIs display green, yellow, and red for weather precipitation and magenta for turbulence.

The instrument landing system (ILS), see Figure 10-25, provides information showing deviation from the established glideslope and runway centerline (localizer). Three complete systems are installed, left, center, and right. Two dual antennas are provided for glideslope and two for localizer. One control panel has three channels, one for each system. Displays are shared with other navigation systems.

The marker beacon system is used to provide positive position checks enroute and during landing approaches. The marker beacon system consists of an antenna, a receiver module located in the left VOR receiver, and display lights located on the pilots' instrument panels.

Marker transmitters located in standard flight paths transmit a narrow vertical beam. As the aircraft flies over a given beam, the receiver detects the beam and lights the appropriate panel light.

During runway approaches, three different types of markers can be utilized, with different panel lights illuminating and different tones supplied through the audio selector panels to the pilots.

The radio altimeter (RA) system is designed to provide terrain clearance data (radio altitude) up to 2500 ft., warning signals, and decision height information. This information is displayed primarily on the captain's and first officer's electronic attitude director indicators (EADI). Terrain clearance data is also used by the autopilot flight director system, ground proximity warning system, and EICAS.

The ground proximity warning system provides visual and aural warnings whenever the airplane is in danger of approaching terrain.

Below 2,500 feet, the system continuously monitors terrain clearance, descent rates, terrain closure rates, glide slope deviations, and flap/gear configuration so that alerts and warnings can be generated whenever the airplane is in an unsafe condition due to terrain proximity.

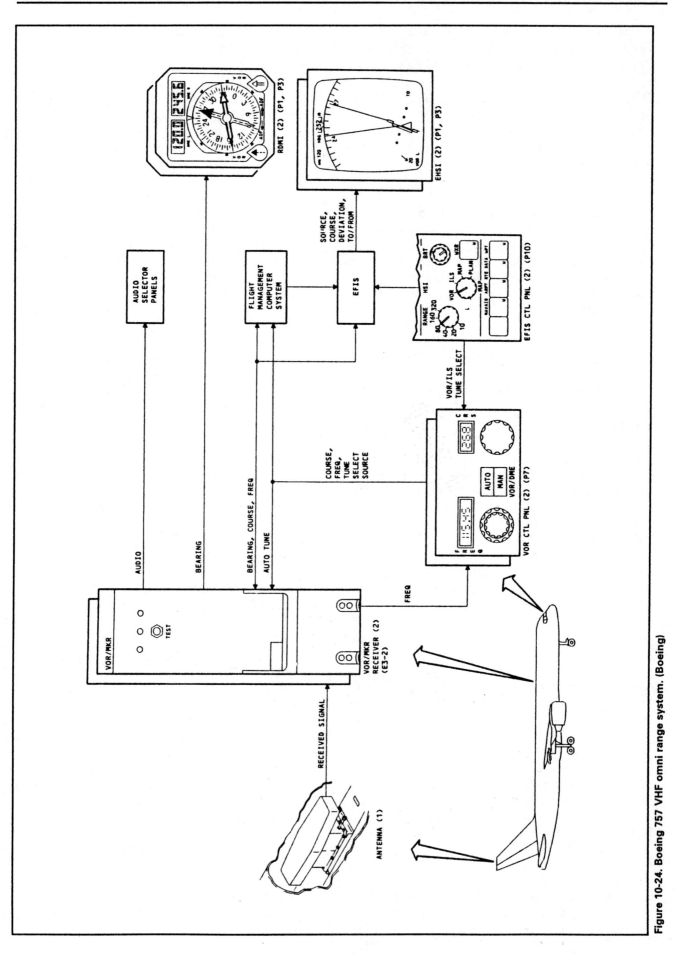

Figure 10-24. Boeing 757 VHF omni range system. (Boeing)

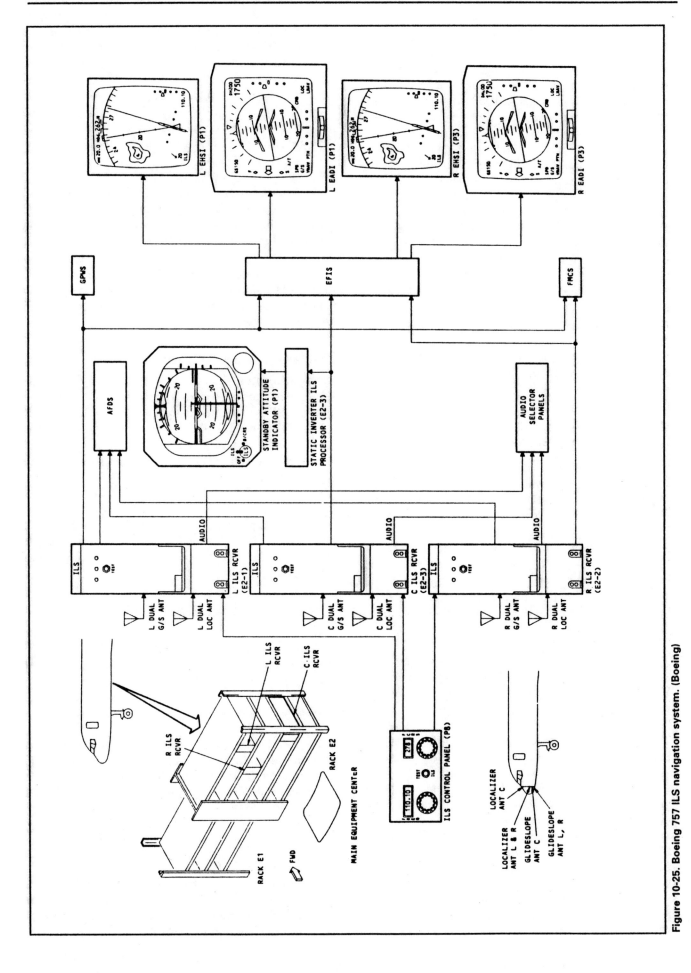

Figure 10-25. Boeing 757 ILS navigation system. (Boeing)

FLIGHT INSTRUMENT SYSTEM

The flight instrument system (FIS) (Figure 10-26) provides airplane attitude, heading, vertical speed, DME distance, VOR and ADF bearing, flight director and ILS commands, flight management computer displays, and weather radar displays.

The flight instruments are located on both pilots' instrument panels. Each pilot's instruments consist of an electronic attitude director indicator (EADI), an electronic horizontal situation indicator (EHSI), a radio distance magnetic indicator (RDMI), and a vertical speed indicator (VSI). The two electronic flight instrument control panels are located on left and right edges of the throttle quadrant stand.

The electronic flight instrument system (EFIS) operates as part of the flight management system to provide the EADIs with attitude and navigation information, and the EHSIs with ILS, VOR, or MAP displays both in a form suitable for accurate and rapid interpretation by both pilots. The EFIS also provides visual indications of failure warnings.

FLIGHT MANAGEMENT COMPUTER SYSTEM

The autoflight system controls the airplane by operating the control surfaces in response to inputs from the pilot, primary navigation sensors, or steering commands from the flight management system.

The flight management computer system (FMCS), see Figure 10-27, uses inputs from navigation, engine, fuel system, and flight environment sensors along with stored and entered data to provide navigation performance and guidance control to the pilot and autopilot flight director system (AFDS).

The FMCS contains two flight management computers and two FMC control display units. The computers are located in the main equipment center and control display units are located in the flight compartment.

Two flight management computers (FMC) receive inputs and provide outputs according to the mode selected on the FMC control display unit (CDU). The pilot may enter, retrieve or modify data, or select modes from the FMC CDU. The flight management computer system may be used in two ways. The FMC may provide advisory data to the pilot enabling him to fly a selected course or profile, or the pilot may couple FMC inputs directly into the automatic flight director system, causing the airplane to automatically follow a predetermined route. Armed and operational modes are displayed on the EADI with the autopilot, flight director or thrust management system engaged.

The flight management computer also provides both lateral and vertical navigation (LNAV and VNAV) based on a route specified by the flight crew and performance and navigation parameters stored within its memory. The crew monitors flight path parameters on the control display units (CDU) as well as on map and plan displays on the electronic horizontal situation indicators (EHSI). The CDU is also used to modify the route.

The autopilot flight director system (AFDS) provides pilot command and automatic modes for flight path control. Three flight control computers are installed. All functions for three axis control of the airplane are contained in each computer.

Each computer drives a set of dedicated servos to move the flight control surfaces and provides input to the stabilizer/elevator asymmetry module (SAM) for automatic stabilizer trim.

YAW DAMPER SYSTEM

The yaw damper modules use inputs from the air data computers and the inertial reference computers to derive rudder commands appropriate to flight conditions. These commands go to the yaw damper servos. Additionally, the modules monitor system operation and provide both manually initiated and automatic system testing.

The yaw damper servos use electrical commands from the yaw damper modules to control hydraulic flow to an actuator piston. This motion is linked in series with manual and autopilot inputs to the rudder power control actuators.

THRUST MANAGEMENT SYSTEM

The thrust management system performs thrust limit calculations and controls the throttles for full flight regime autothrottle operation. One thrust management computer moves the throttles and drives the displays on the EICAS display. Thrust limits are calculated based on selected mode and operating conditions.

Autothrottle functions control thrust, mach/airspeed, rate of altitude change or throttle retard rate as selected. A fast-slow command indicator reflects speed error in mach/airspeed mode. Limit functions operate in all modes to prevent overboost or overspeed.

DIGITAL FLIGHT DATA RECORDER SYSTEM

The digital flight data recorder system (DFDRS) provides the capability of recording the most recent 25 hours of flight parameters on magnetic tape, housed in a crash proof container.

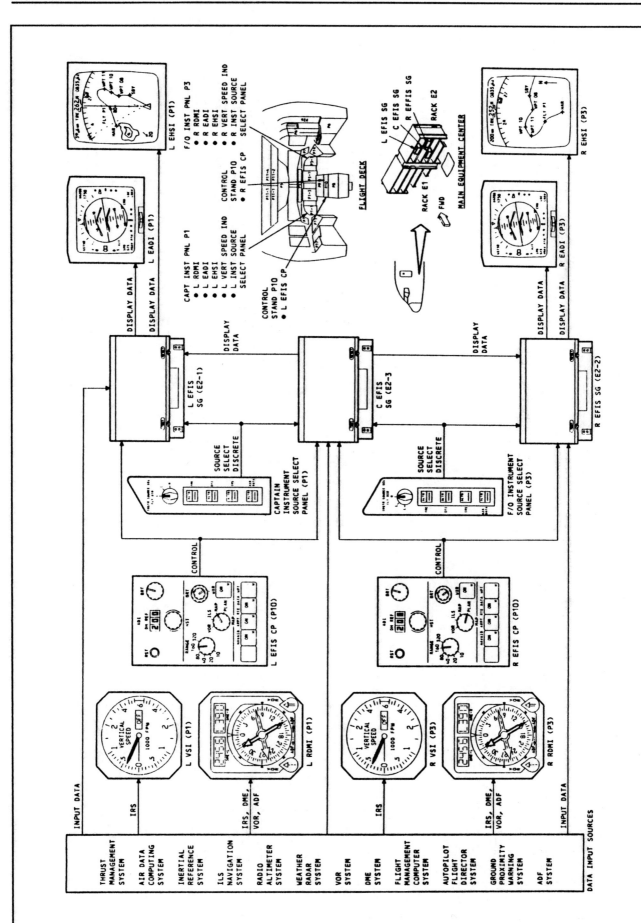

Figure 10-26. Boeing 757 EFIS flight instrument system. (Boeing)

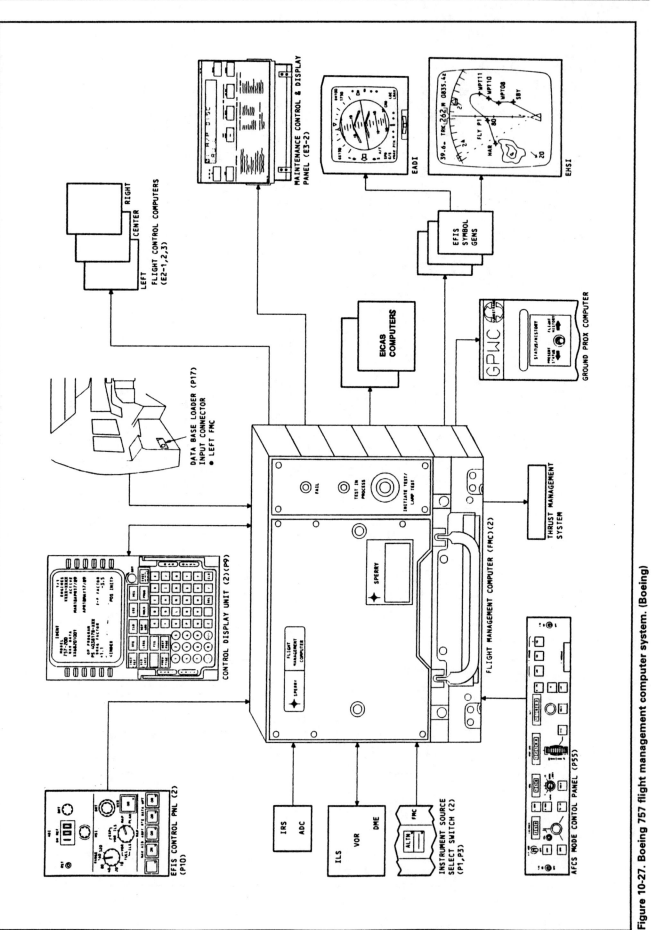

Figure 10-27. Boeing 757 flight management computer system. (Boeing)

The flight parameters that must be recorded as required by the FAA are: GMT-time, pressure altitude, computer airspeed, acceleration, compass heading, pitch and roll altitudes, control surface positions, engine status and performance, and VHF and HF radio transmissions. An underwater locator beacon is installed on the front face of the DFDR.

BOEING 767 FLIGHT MANAGEMENT SYSTEM

The flight management system, shown in Figure 10-28, is an integrated digital computer system which provides performance management, navigation and guidance, automatic flight control, flight instrument displays, and advisory, caution, and warning functions. Energy management flight profiles, flight planning data, navigation/guidance functions, and data base storage capability are also provided.

In addition, optional capabilities allow programming and storage of departures, arrivals, approaches, and company routes.

These functions are provided by the integration and interconnection of major subsystems including inertial reference units, flight management computers, flight control computers, a thrust management computer, air data computers, navigation sensors, and engine indication and crew alerting system (EICAS) computers.

The laser inertial reference units provide attitude, heading, acceleration, and angular rate data for displays and automatic controls. The flight management computers provide performance management, navigation, guidance, and display data for the electronic horizontal situation indicator map displays.

The flight control computers and thrust management computers provide automatic flight capability and thrust management functions. A maintenance control-display panel in the main equipment center provides maintenance personnel with a means to identify line replaceable units (LRUs) which may have failed in flight.

BOEING 777 AVIONICS SYSTEMS

FLIGHT AND SERVICE INTERPHONE SYSTEM

The flight interphone system permits the flight crew members on the flight deck to communicate with each other and with audio communications systems and ground crew members. The service interphone permits communication between the pilots, ground crew, and

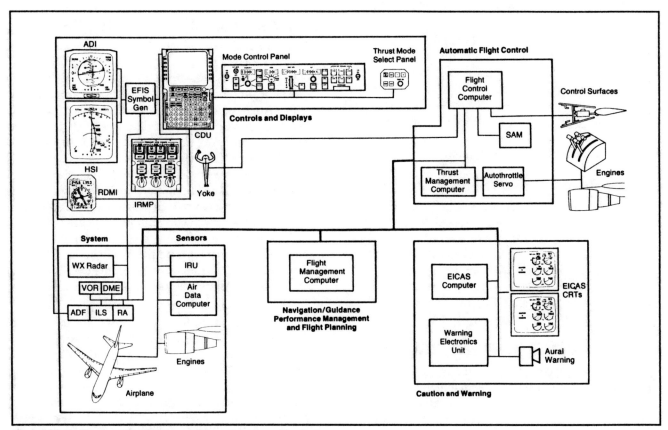

Figure 10-28. Boeing 767 flight management system. (Boeing)

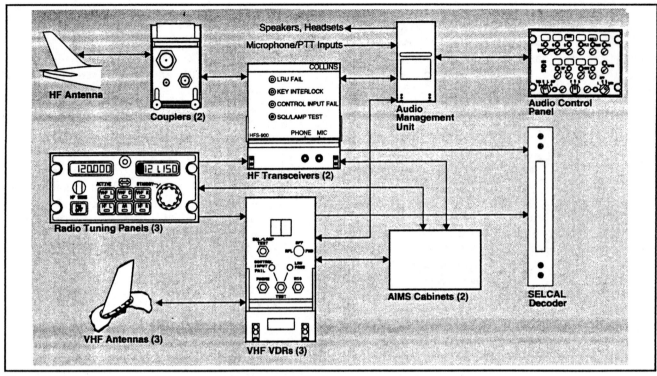

Figure 10-29. Boeing 777 VHF/HF communications systems. (Boeing)

maintenance personnel. Jacks for plug-in microphone and headsets are at various locations on the airplane. When the service interphone switch is ON, the service and flight interphone systems are connected together.

GROUND CREW CALL SYSTEM

The flight crew and the ground crew use the ground call system to alert each other. The system supplies aural and visual signals in the flight deck and in the nose wheel well area. The flight crew can select a call code which will sound a horn in the nose wheel well or the ground crew can call the pilots by using the switch on the APU shutdown panel.

VOICE RECORDER SYSTEM

A four-channel voice recorder with flight deck area microphone records the most recent 30 minutes of flight crew communications. It erases automatically so that only the last 30 minutes are on the tape. Inputs from the voice recorder are from the area microphone that picks up any conversations on the flight deck, the captains, first officers, and first observer's audio panel and their hot microphones (oxygen mask).

CABIN MANAGEMENT SYSTEM

The cabin management system (CMS) is an integrated system that combines many cabin and passenger functions. It controls the cabin interphone, passenger address, passenger entertainment, passenger service, and cabin lighting functions. It also provides for mon-

itor and control of many cabin functions. The integration of these functions permits control, monitoring, and test of the system from a central location.

VHF/HF COMMUNICATIONS SYSTEMS

The very high frequency (VHF) communications system, see Figure 10-29, supplies line-of-sight voice and data communication from air-to-ground or air-to-air. The short to medium range of VHF keeps interference with distant stations at the same frequency to a minimum. Each VHF communications system includes a voice/data radio (VDR) and a dedicated antenna. The high frequency (HF) system permits voice communication over distances much farther than line-of-sight radio systems. Communication from aircraft to ground stations, or to other aircraft, is provided during long over water flights. Each HF communications system includes a transceiver, an antenna coupler, and a common antenna. The antenna is on the leading edge of the vertical stabilizer. The antenna coupler matches the impedance of the transmission line to that of the transceiver.

Frequency selection for each transceiver is from any of the three radio tuning panels (RTPs). Any RTP can provide tuning data to any of the VHF VDRs or HF transceivers. A radio selector switch selects one of the five transceivers. The frequency-selector knobs select the desired frequency which is displayed on the liquid crystal display STANDBY indicator. The transfer switch toggles between active and STANDBY fre-

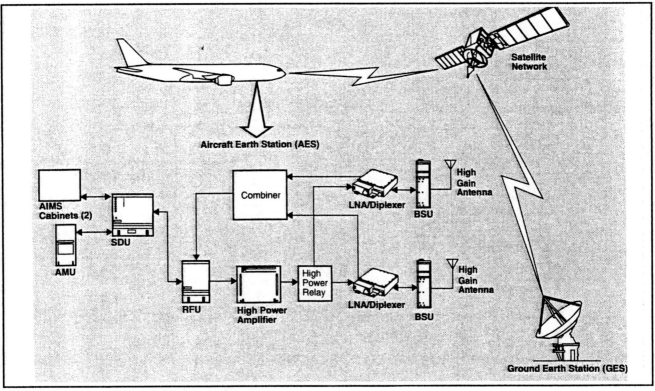

Figure 10-30. Boeing 777 SATCOM system. (Boeing)

quencies. The VHF radios interface with the AIMS data communication management function (DCMF). The DCMF supplies tuning data to the RTPs. The audio control panels supply microphone selection and headset monitoring functions. The central maintenance computing function (CMCF) of the AIMS tests and monitors the VHF and HF communications systems. The digital flight data acquisition function (DFDAF) of the AIMS receives microphone keying information.

The selective calling system (SELCAL) monitors all communication radios in the airplane. The system alerts the flight crew when it receives a ground call with the correct airplane code. This removes the need for continuous monitoring of the communication radios by the flight crew.

SATELLITE COMMUNICATION

The 777 has a satellite communications system, shown in Figure 10-30, as standard equipment. SATCOM supplies reliable long range voice or data communications. The system can transmit and receive information which includes flight crew and passenger voice, data communications, telex, and facsimile services. The system uses satellites as relay stations to cover long distances. SATCOM is more reliable than the HF communication system because it is not affected by atmospheric interference.

The system consists of the satellite network, the ground earth stations (GES), and the aircraft earth stations (AES). The satellite network relays radio signals between the AES and the GES. Each GES is a fixed radio station that interfaces with communication networks through ground links, and the airborne earth stations through the satellite. The AES is the SATCOM system on board the airplane that interfaces with various onboard communication systems and the ground earth stations.

ARNIC 629 DATA BUS SYSTEM

The 777 airplane uses ARNIC 629 data busses, which can be seen in Figure 10-31. ARNIC 629 data busses permit faster transfer of data between LRUs than ARNIC 429 data busses. It supports data communication between many terminals over a common bus. There are eleven ARNIC 629 busses on the 777. The primary flight control system has three dedicated ARNIC 629 flight control data busses, which connect with 26 line replaceable units (LRUs). Four ARNIC 629 system data busses supply the main communication path between the avionics, electrical, electro-mechanical, environmental control, and propulsion systems. The ARNIC 629 system data buses connect with 59 LRUs. These buses are independent from the primary flight control system data buses.

Four ARNIC 629 airplane information management system (AIMS) intercabinet buses connect with the

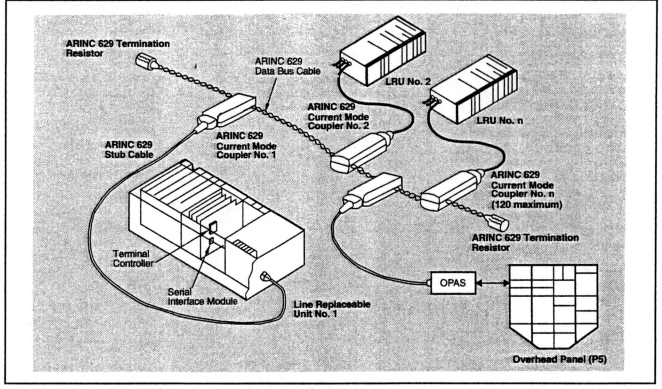

Figure 10-31. Boeing 777 ARINC 629 communication system. (Boeing)

two AIMS cabinets and the three control display units (CDU). ARNIC 629 components include terminal controllers and serial interface modules. These components are internal to the LRUs. In addition to the LRU ARNIC 629 components and the eleven ARNIC 629 data bus cable assemblies, the ARNIC 629 communication system includes stub cables and current mode couplers. The LRUs use a coupler and terminal (terminal controller and serial interface module) to communicate with the bus. Each terminal listens to the bus and waits for a quiet period before it transmits. Only one terminal on a bus transmits at a time. After a terminal transmits, three separate timers make sure that it does not transmit again until all of the other terminals on the bus have had a chance to transmit. The overhead panel ARNIC system (OPAS) multiplexes overhead panel switch positions for transmission on the ARNIC 629 system buses.

777 NAVIGATION SYSTEMS

The 777 uses navigation systems such as air data inertial reference systems along with more conventional systems. Also the 777 uses satellite navigation systems such as global positioning systems which provides greater accuracy along the flight path. The air data inertial reference unit (ADIRU) sends primary, secondary, and standby air data and inertial reference information to the flight deck displays, flight controls, autopilot, and other airplane systems. The navigation

radios, see Figure 10-32, supply reference data for instrument navigation using the flight management computing function (FMCF) of the aircraft information management system. Most of the conventional navigation systems which were described earlier in this chapter are shown with their interfaces in Figure 10-32.

GLOBAL POSITIONING SYSTEM

The global positioning system (GPS) uses navigation satellites to supply accurate airplane position to the FMCF, ADIRU, and the flight crew. GPS can supply information such as airplane latitude, longitude, altitude, and exact time. The ADIRU supplies inertial reference position and air data parameters, through the data conversion gateway function of the AIMS, to the global positioning system sensing units (GPSSUs). The FMCF uses GPS data to aid in the calculation of aircraft position.

TRAFFIC ALERT AND COLLISION AVOIDANCE SYSTEM

The ATC/mode S system allows ground facilities to track the airplane's movement through controlled airspace by monitoring airplane location and altitude. The traffic alert and collision avoidance system (TCAS) alerts the flight crew to possible collisions with other transponder airplanes in the same airspace. TCAS uses the ATC/mode S system to send TCAS data

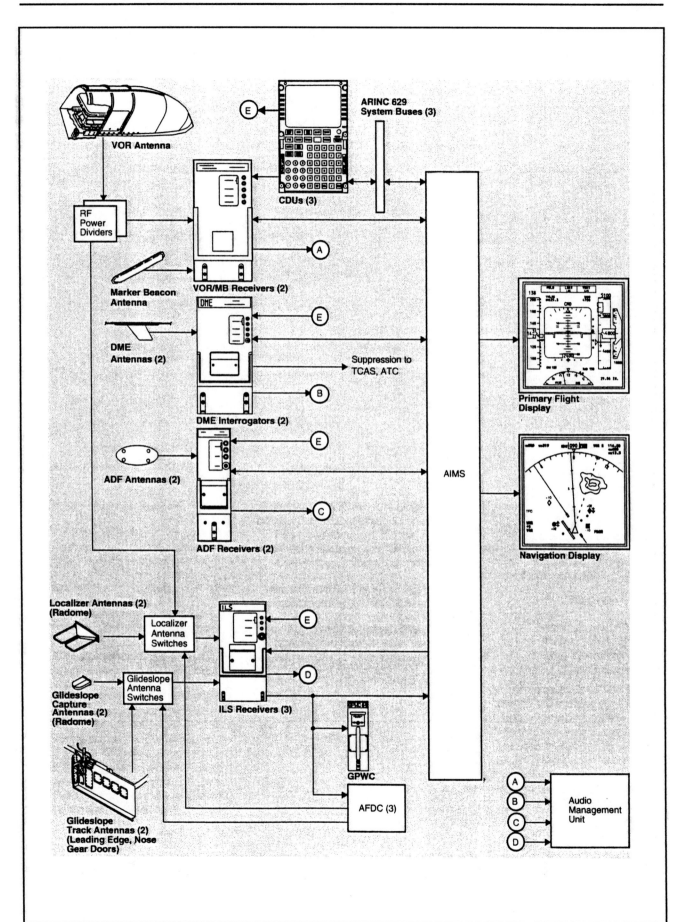

Figure 10-32. Boeing 777 navigation radios. (Boeing)

to other TCAS equipped airplanes. TCAS provides the flight crew with two types of advisories, traffic advisory (TA) and a resolution advisory (RA). The TA makes the flight crew aware of other traffic in the area, while the RA provides direction in avoiding a possible collision.

WEATHER RADAR SYSTEM

The weather radar system shows the flight crew weather conditions along the flight path. This allows them to change the flight path to fly around severe weather conditions. The flight crew also uses the weather radar system as a navigational aid. The

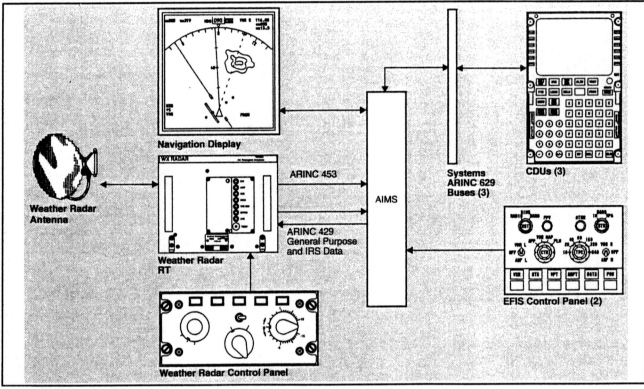

Figure 10-33. Boeing777 weather radar system and displays. (Boeing)

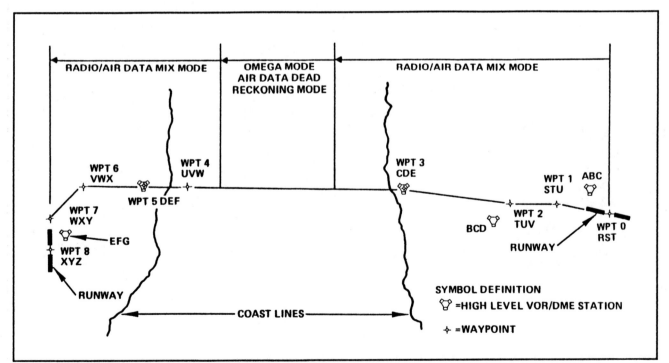

Figure 10-34. L-1011 Flight management system, route navigation. (Lockheed)

weather radar control system selects the operational mode, receiver gain, and antenna tilt angle. When the flight crew selects the weather mode on the radar control panel a four-color weather display is shown on the navigational displays, as shown in Figure 10-33. Heavy rainfall is shown in red, with moderate rainfall in yellow, and light rainfall in green. In the turbulence mode, turbulence associated with heavy rainfall shows in magenta. The radar map mode can show coastlines or large bodies of water.

L-1011 FLIGHT MANAGEMENT SYSTEM

The L-1011 flight management system (FMS) for international aircraft consists of two flight management computers (FMCs), two FMS control display units (CDU), and an accessory unit. Domestic aircraft have only one FMC.

The CDUs, used to insert data into the computer and to display flight information, are installed in the center console, forward of the throttles. The inertial NAV accessory unit provides an interface between the flight management computers and AFCS system.

FMS routes consist of a series of waypoints (positions to be overflown) that define the flight plans, including the DME stations or non-navaid points along the route.

The data necessary for assembling a flight plan for operation over a route is stored in the FMC's data bank. Prior to takeoff, the flight crew selects the route desired by manual insertion of a series of waypoints using the control display unit's keyboard.

The flight plan, shown in Figure 10-34, consists of nine waypoints, of which two are VOR/DME stations. All waypoints and VOR/DME stations have a three-digit alphanumeric identifier. In this example, the point of departure, WPT, is RST. The terminal waypoint, WPT/ 8, is XYZ. Along the route, two waypoints are also VOR/DME stations. These are WPT 3, station CDE, and WPT 5, station DEF.

To calculate the aircraft's position, the FMC automatically selects the navigational sensors to be used during flight. The normal mode of operation is the radio/air data mix mode, which is selected if at least one air data system and one VOR/DME system are furnishing valid data.

The OMEGA mode is used by the computer for navigation when VOR/DME information is not available. In this mode, position data is provided from the OMEGA system.

The system (Figure 10-35) consists of a receiver-processor unit, antenna, and the control display unit

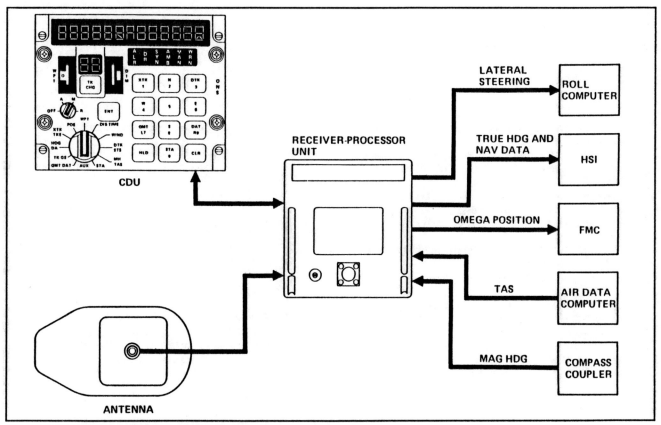

Figure 10-35. OMEGA navigation system. (Lockheed)

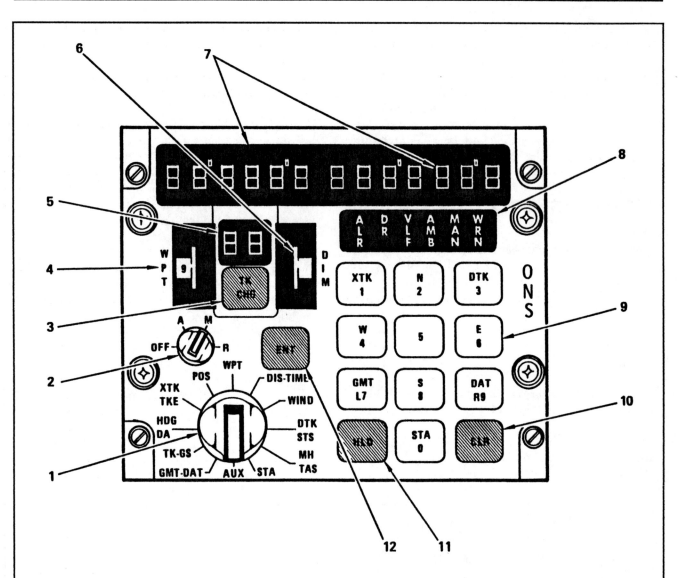

LEGEND

1. **Display Selector** — Selects data for presentation on the left and right displays.

2. **Mode Switch** — Applies power to the system and enables the automatic (A), manual (M), and remote (R) modes of system operation.

3. **TK CHG** — Allows initiation of manual track leg change.

4. **WPT Selector Switch** — With the display selector switch set to WPT, permits insertion of latitude and longitude data in waypoints 1 through 9.

5. **From/To and Waypoint Display** — Displays from and to waypoint numbers of track leg being navigated.

6. **DIM Control** — Controls light intensity of numerical and waypoint displays.

7. **Left and Right Numerical Displays** — Displays data selected via the display selector switch setting.

8. **Annunciators**

   A. **ALR (Alert)** — Comes on within 2 minutes of the selected waypoint and goes off when a track leg change is made automatically, or flashes 0.5 minutes before reaching

waypoint to indicate that track leg change must be made manually.

   B. **DR (Déad Reckoning)** — Comes on at system turn-on following entry of present position, remains on until system is in navigate mode.

   C. **VLF (Very low frequency)** — Comes on when the system reverts to VLF mode of operation.

   D. **AMB (Ambiguity)** — Comes on whenever an Omega position ambiguity is detected.

   E. **MAN (Manual)** — Comes on whenever a manual entry is made.

   F. **WRN (Warn)** — Comes on to indicate that an Omega system failure has been detected by the integrity monitoring function.

9. **Data Keyboard** — Provides 10 keys (0 through 9) for insertion of data.

10. **CLR Pushbutton** — Clears display data if not yet entered.

11. **HLD Pushbutton** — Permits position check and update display of action/malfunction codes and waypoint editing.

12. **ENT Pushbutton** — Transfers data entered via the keyboard into the system computer.

Figure 10-36. OMEGA navigation system CDU. (Lockheed)

(CDU) shown in Figure 10-36. The OMEGA is a low frequency radio system, whose primary function is to determine aircraft position. Other information that may be displayed is as follows: GMT and date, heading and drift angle, desired track and system internal status, cross track distance and track angle error, waypoint data, track angle and ground speed, distance to go and time to go, wind direction and speed, magnetic heading and TAS, and OMEGA station status.

The OMEGA system can be used to supply aircraft position to the flight management system (FMS), lateral steering commands to roll computers, and navigation data to horizontal situation indications (HSI). If the VOR/DME and OMEGA/ data is invalid or not available, the FMC uses the dead reckoning mode.

The air data computers (ADC) and the magnetic heading reference system are used in dead reckoning. If the

air data computers fail, the system will use last-remembered quantities to solve the navigation problem.

FMS control of flight phases improves the overall efficiency of the flight. The basic control phases are: climb, cruise, and descent. In climb, the FMS controls aircraft speed through the pitch axis, and engine pressure ratio (EPR) via the throttles. In cruise, short term variations in aircraft speed are corrected using the pitch axis; long term drifts are corrected via the throttles. The basic descent control is effected by pulling back the throttles and controlling aircraft speed via the pitch axis as the aircraft descends.

The flight management systems computer obtains various inputs which are shown in Figure 10-37. The flight management computer provides output information for lateral steering, pitch commands, and thrust management.

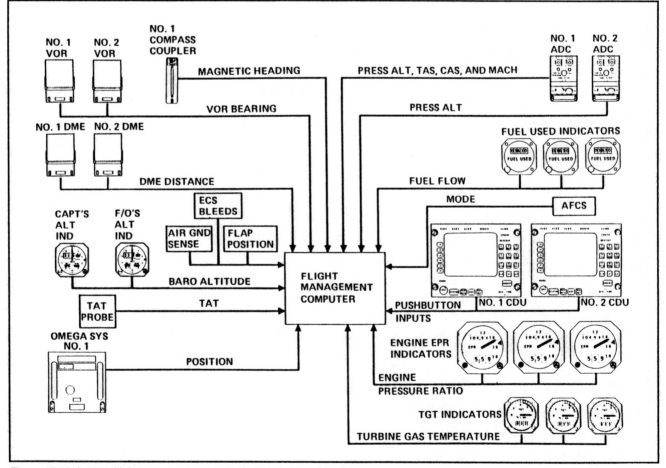

Figure 10-37. L-1011 flight management systems inputs. (Lockheed)

CHAPTER 10 STUDY QUESTIONS

1. What does the abbreviation ACARS stand for?

    _____

2. List the communication applications of ACARS as they pertain to most airlines.

    _____

    _____

3. Describe the function and operation of the ACARS and SELCAL systems.

    _____

    _____

    _____

4. What type of voice communication systems are generally used on large aircraft?

    _____

    _____

5. List the different types of navigation systems or equipment and their functions.

    _____

    _____

    _____

6. List the types of communication systems and their functions on the Boeing 737-300 aircraft.

    _____

    _____

    _____

    _____

7. List the basic instruments that make up an electronic flight control system.

    _____

    _____

8. What is the function of a cockpit voice recorder?

    _____

    _____

9. What flight parameter must be recorded on a flight data recorder?

    _____

    _____

10. What is the basic function of a flight management system?

    _____

    _____

11. The OMEGA navigation system supplies information about the aircrafts

    _____

    _____

12.   The Boeing 777 has a traffic alert and collision avoidance system which can provide the flight crew with what two types of advisories?

_____

_____

13.   What type of communication systems are used on the Boeing 777?

_____

_____

14.   List the main function of the ARINC 629 communications bus.

_____

_____

15.   The primary flight control system on the Boeing 777 has how many dedicated ARINC 629 data busses?

_____

INFORMATION AND AUXILIARY SYSTEMS

BOEING 777 AIRPLANE INFORMATION MANAGEMENT SYSTEMS

The airplane information management system (AIMS) integrates the avionic computing functions that require large quantities of data collection, integration, and calculation. The AIMS system consist of two cabinets with each cabinet containing eight line replaceable modules (LRMs). These cabinets operate as the main computer for eight avionic systems. The AIMS cabinets interface with approximately 130 LRUs, sensors, switches and indicators, as shown in Figure 11-1. These interfaces permit the AIMS to integrate the information from a majority of airplane systems in one place. It is efficient to integrate this information for central maintenance computing flight data recording, airplane condition monitoring and displays.

PRIMARY DISPLAY SYSTEM

The primary display system supplies information to the flight crew on the six flat panel liquid crystal display units. The primary displays can show the primary flight display (electronic flight indicating system EFIS), navigation display, engine indicating and crew alerting system (EICAS) and the multi-function display. The multi-function display includes the engine secondary, status, synoptic, maintenance page, checklist, and flight deck communication function (FDCF) formats. The display system, shown in Figure 11-2, has three basic control panels. These are the general controls, EFIS controls, and the EICAS controls. The captain and first officer have a primary flight display (PFD). The PFD display is normally on the outboard display units which communicates to the pilots the primary state of the airplane as well as autoflight, flight management, and thrust management command information. Some of the items shown on the primary flight display are the aircraft's attitude, airspeed, barometric altitude, vertical speed, heading, flight modes, radio altitude, ILS data, and TCAS resolution advisory information. The navigation displays provides flight and navigation information in one of several formats. The navigation display shows information in four display modes; VOR, approach, map, and plan. The plan mode is used to create, view, or change a flight plan.

FLIGHT MANAGEMENT COMPUTING SYSTEM

The flight management computing system (FMCS) reduces flight crew workload. This system provides vertical and lateral guidance for all phases of flight except takeoff. The FMCS also gives navigation information to the flight crew on the forward displays and auto-tunes the navigation radios. The primary crew interface for the flight management computing system are three CDUs. The flight crew enters data on either the left or right CDU. The center CDU operates as a back-up, if the left or right CDU fails. The FMCS has four basic functions; Navigation, flight planning, performance management, and navigation radio tuning. The navigation function calculates airplane position and velocity. The flight planning function uses flight crew entries to create the lateral flight plan. Memory in the FMCS contains an aerodynamic model of the airplane. The performance management function uses this model and flight crew entries to calculate the most economical fuel burn for the vertical flight path.

THRUST MANAGEMENT COMPUTING SYSTEM

The thrust management computing system (TMCS) moves the thrust levers, gives the thrust limit displays and autothrottle modes during takeoff and all flight phases. The TMCS also supplies trim commands to the engines. Both AIMS cabinets do the same thrust management computing function (TMCF). The master TMCF sends autothrottle commands to the autothrottle servo modules (ASMs) and the trim commands to the engine electronic controllers (EECs). The other TMCF operates as a standby. The TMCF calculates autothrottle commands with crew entries from the flight deck, FMCF and external sensor inputs. The TMCF sends the throttle position commands to the ASMs. The TMCF calculates and sends the EECs engine trim commands by looking at engine thrust differences.

DATA COMMUNICATIONS MANAGEMENT SYSTEM

The data communication management system (DCMS) supplies three functions, print driver, planenet inter-

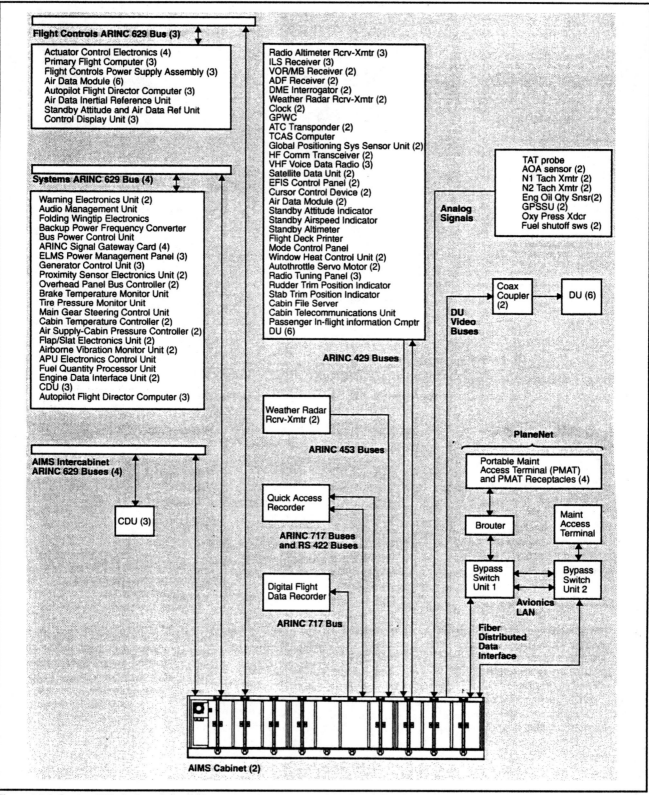

Figure 11-1. Boeing 777 airplane information management system interfaces. (Boeing)

face, and ACARS datalink. The planenet interface supplies software protocols to manage communications between the AIMS functions and the systems on the Avionics local area network (AVLAN) portion of the planenet. The aircraft communications addressing and reporting system (ACARS) datalink function provides a data communications link between the airplane and the ground.

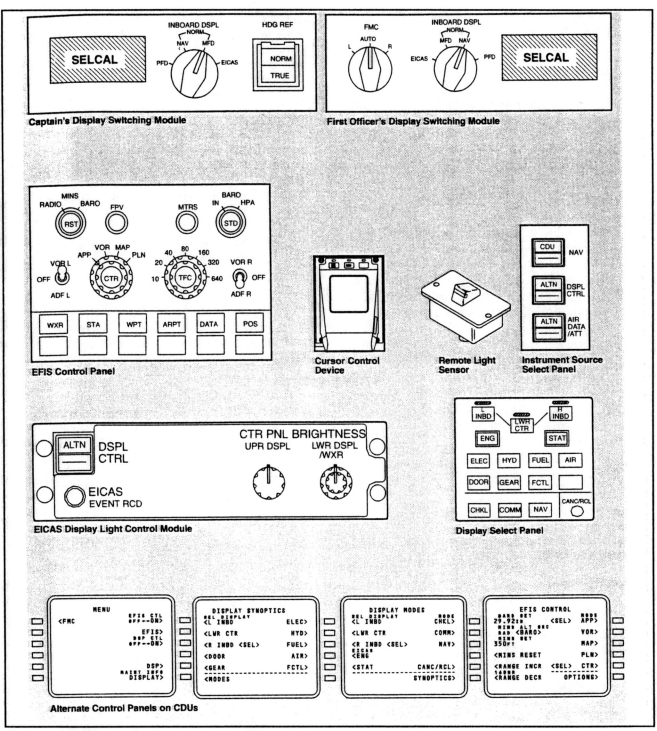

Figure 11-2. Boeing 777 display control panels AIMS. (Boeing)

DIGITAL FLIGHT DATA RECORDER SYSTEM

The digital flight data recorder (DFDR) system records mandatory and optional flight data for the most recent 25 hours of operation. The digital flight data acquisition function (DFDAF) in the AIMS collects and formats the data and sends it to the DFDR. The DFDAF receives data in ARINC 429, ARINC 629, analog, and discrete formats. The DFDAF changes this data into one digital format to send to the DFDR.

AIRPLANE CONDITION MONITORING SYSTEM AND MAINTENANCE INTERFACE

The purpose of the airplane condition monitoring system (ACMS) is to monitor, record and give reports for selected airplane data including, maintenance, performance, troubling, and trend monitoring data.

The central maintenance computer system uses the AIMS cabinets for the computing function. The maintenance crew uses a maintenance access terminal (MAT) to control and access the central maintenance computing system (CMCS). The MAT is a station with a display module, disk drive module, keyboard, and cursor controller/power supply module in the second observers position on the flight deck. The crew uses a maintenance access terminal (MAT) in the flight deck or a portable MAT (PMAT) in the main equipment center to operate the central maintenance computing system. There are three other locations on the airplane that permit the use of a PMAT; the nose and right wheel well, and the jack screw area. The MAT and PMAT communicate with the CMCS in the AIMS cabinet through two fiber distributed data interfaces (FDDI). The FDDIs supply a dual connection to the avionics local area network (LAN). The FDDI and the avionics LAN are elements of a Planenet. The MAT is connected directly to the avionics LAN. The MAT receptacles are connected to a network which provides a bridging function. There is a CMCS in each AIMS cabinet, but only one CMCS operates at a time, the other is a backup.

BOEING 747-400 CENTRAL MAINTENANCE COMPUTER SYSTEM

Many of the new generation Boeing aircraft, including the 747-400 and the Boeing 777, have the capability to troubleshoot themselves and report the trouble to the technicians on the ground.

The aircraft's systems and their flight operational status are continually monitored by the central maintenance computer system. The central maintenance computer system (CMCS) provides a centralized location for access to maintenance data from all major avionic, electrical and electromechanical systems. Virtually all components that have an electrical/electronic interface will be monitored by the CMCS.

The functions of the central maintenance computer are to collect, display, and store information on failed components. It can also initiate component and system tests, and monitor the integrity of input systems.

The integrated display system (IDS), shown in Figure 11-3, displays flight, navigation, and engine information from data transmitted from the airplane systems. The same data is also transmitted to the CMCS, through

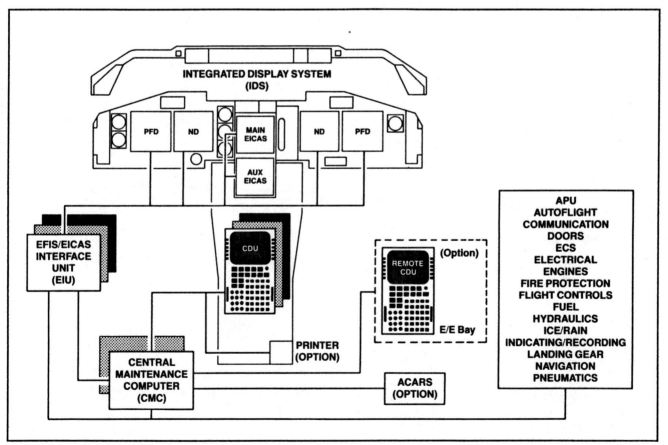

Figure 11-3. Boeing 747-400 integrated display system. (Boeing)

electrical connections from the integrated display system to the central maintenance computer system.

System failures, faults, parameter exceedances, engine indicating, and crew alerting system (EICAS) messages appear on the integrated display system and are called flight deck effects. An example of a flight deck effect could be an engine malfunction. The IDS in turn reports these flight deck effects through the electronic flight instrument system (EFIS/EICAS). A description of a flight deck effect and a description of the fault correlated to the flight deck effect are presented on a CMCS maintenance message. Maintenance messages are displayed on any one of the flight deck control display units (CDU), as shown in Figure 11-4.

Several airplane systems transmit data to the CMCS without transmitting the data to the IDS. The IDS, therefore, will not report flight deck effects to the CMCS for these systems, although it will isolate faults in these systems and provide a description on a CMCS maintenance message.

Two CMCs are provided for redundancy, with either one of the CMCs being capable of providing a complete CMCS function. Both CMCs, which are connected in parallel, continuously process all inputs and generate all outputs.

The outputs of the right CMC are connected to the selection relay in the left CMC. This relay normally selects the left CMC as a source of output data to the airplane systems. However, if the left CMC fails, the relay will then connect the outputs of the right CMC to the airplane systems. Crosstalk between the two computers ensures both CMCs record valid information simultaneously.

The integrated display system is responsible for displaying system faults, from which the flight crew or maintenance technicians may interrogate the CMCs to investigate the cause of the fault.

If needed, maintenance data can be transmitted through ACARS (aircraft communication addressing and reporting systems) to alert technicians on the ground of the problem. Technicians equipped with information on which components have failed and replacement parts, can meet the aircraft at the gate and still have time to review the maintenance instructions for the maintenance operation to be performed.

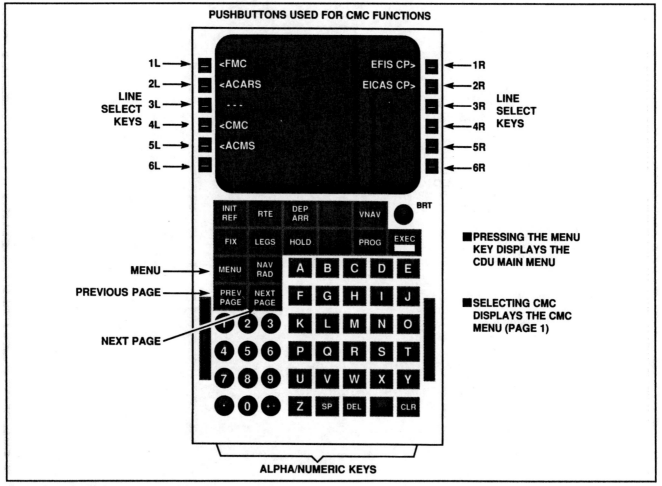

Figure 11-4. Control display unit. (Boeing)

To acquaint the maintenance technician with the operation of the central maintenance computer system, the control display unit's (CDU) function must be understood. Maintenance information is accessed by means of the push-buttons on the control display unit.

These push-buttons, shown in Figure 11-4, are used with the CMC in the following manner:

1. MENU key to display the CDU menu

2. LINE SELECT keys to select functions/data from CMC menus (Active keys are identified by a caret (^) on the screen)

3. NEXT and PREV (previous) page keys to advance (NEXT or backup (PREV) in multiple page menus

4. ALPHA/NUMERIC keys for making alphabetic/numeric entries.

The CMC menu consists of two pages which displays all of the CMC sub-menu functions. Page 1 is primarily used to support line maintenance. Page 2 is primarily used for extended troubleshooting. To go from one page to another, press the NEXT PAGE or PREV PAGE key on the CDU as desired. To select one of the sub-menus, press the LINE SELECT key (LSK) next to the desired sub-menu. The sub-menus that can be selected are: PRESENT LEG FAULTS; CONFIDENCE

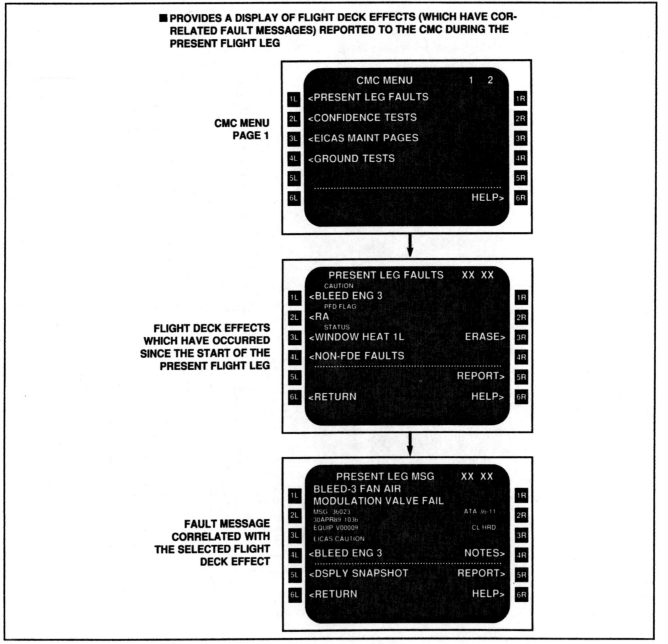

Figure 11-5. Present leg faults. (Boeing)

TESTS; EICAS MAINT PAGES; GROUND TESTS; EXISTING FAULTS; FAULT HISTORY; OTHER FUNCTIONS. An example of the CMC menu is shown in Figure 11-5.

As an example of information that can be accessed, the present leg faults function is displayed in Figure 11-5. The purpose of the present leg faults function is to display any faults, along with any associated flight deck effects that were reported to the CMC during the present flight leg. Pressing the line select key next to PRESENT LEG FAULTS on the CMC menu causes the CDU to display present leg flight deck effects (FDEs) which have a correlated CMC fault message. In this example, the flight deck effect is a EICAS caution; bleed eng 3, which is also displayed as a fault message; bleed 3 fan air modulation valve fail. It can also be determined from the fault message that this was a hard fault, not an intermittent one.

To display CMC fault messages that do not have correlated FDEs, press the line select key next to non-flight deck effects faults on the present leg faults page. This causes the most recent CMC fault message to be displayed. If there is more than one non-flight deck effect fault, then the next most recent fault is displayed on the next page, and so on.

Another basic function of the CMCS is the confidence test. This test can be used to check the status of individual aircraft systems. A test is initiated by pressing the line select key next to the system displayed. When a test is selected, the CMC provides digital and/or analog discrete signals to the appropriate system, which then performs the test. While the test is in progress, an IN PROGRESS message will be displayed above the selected system.

If for any reason a confidence test should not be performed, the word INHIBITED will be displayed. After the system test, the words PASS or FAIL will be displayed next to the system being tested. When the EICAS MAINT pages are selected, five ATA chapters (systems) are displayed at a time, one of these ATA chapters (systems) can be selected from the EICAS maintenance pages. The EICAS maintenance pages function allows selection of real time maintenance page displays.

The ground test function is to provide for initiating system tests and displaying the results on the CDU. Pressing the line select key next to GROUND TESTS on the CMC menu causes the CDU to display the ground tests menu. The CMC can initiate two types of ground tests. One type of ground test actually causes the line replaceable unit (LRU) to run its built in test equipment (BITE) routine once the CMC initiates the command. The other type only displays the BITE data from the LRU once the CMC initiates the command. The BITE for those types of LRUs are run continuously.

There are several other types of fault messages which can be displayed, such as existing faults, fault history, and shop faults. The purpose of the existing faults function is to display current system faults and any associated flight deck effects.

The existing faults menu displays a list of systems which have active fault messages. The systems are listed in ATA chapter order beginning with the lowest ATA chapter number. If there are existing faults for more than five ATA chapters, then the higher numbered chapters are displayed on subsequent pages.

The fault history pages, shown in Figure 11-6, are very similar to the existing fault messages, but as the name

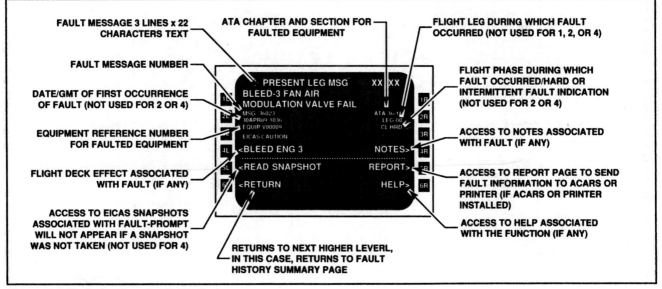

Figure 11-6. Fault message detail. (Boeing)

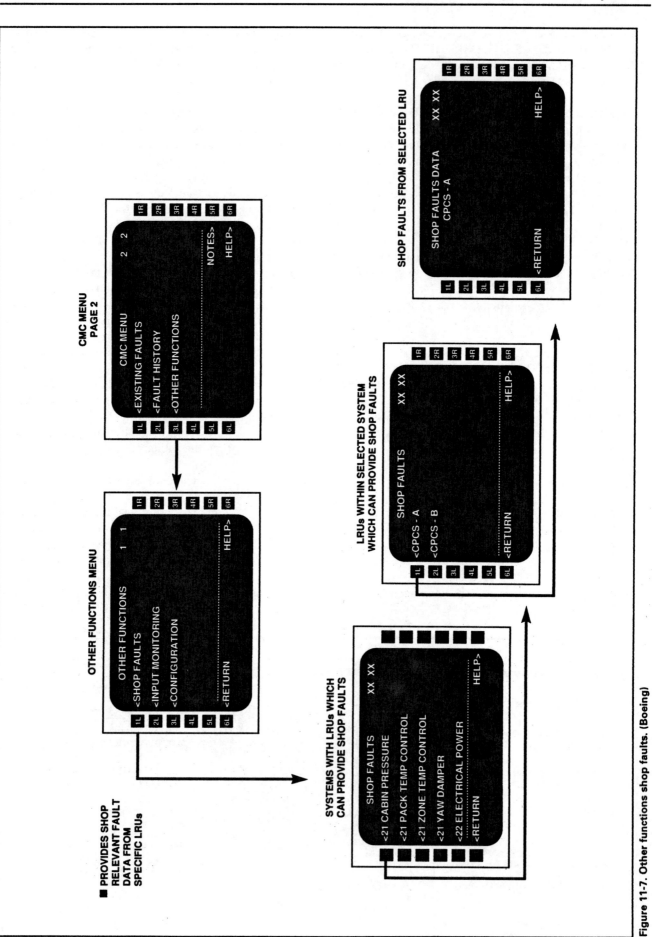

Figure 11-7. Other functions shop faults. (Boeing)

states, the history pages provide a summary of the fault messages, by aircraft system, stored in the CMC memory.

On the CMC menu under the heading of Other Functions is the shop faults function which displays specific line replaceable unit (LRU) internal fault data. This information can identify which components may have failed on certain line replaceable units as illustrated in Figure 11-7.

It is certainly beyond the scope of this discussion to totally familiarize the reader with the 747-400 central maintenance computer system. Although this system was designed in a very logical and easily understood manner, the users of the CMCS will need to be very familiar with all aspects of the system.

The centralized location for maintenance data should aid in performing maintenance more quickly and accurately. Central maintenance computer systems will certainly change the manner in which maintenance is accomplished.

AUXILIARY SYSTEMS

LOCKHEED L-1011 POTABLE WATER SYSTEM

The potable water system, shown in Figure 11-8, distributes drinkable water to lavatory sinks, drinking fountains and coffee makers in the galleys. Chlorinated potable water is stored in a fiberglass 150 gallon tank located in the lower galley sidewall area. Tank quantity, which varies between airlines, is determined by the length of a standpipe in the overflow line, as shown in Figure 11-9.

The air space above the water level is pressurized through the air supply port by two on-board compressors, illustrated in Figure 11-10, or by a ground air source connected at the service panel. Compressor output passes through position indicating check valves, which monitor the output pressure and cause annunciators at the flight station to illuminate if a 5 psi differential is sensed. Air then enters the tank through a screen filter, relief valve, and check valve. The filter contains a red indicator which is displayed when the filter is 80% clogged.

Compressor control switches monitor pressure in the tank to turn on the associated compressor when tank pressure is less than 30 psi, and turn off the compressor when tank pressure reaches 35 psi. The air is directed to the tank through a 35 psi regulator and a check valve.

If both compressors are inoperative, water can be made available to the user system by half filling the tank

with water, and pressurizing the remaining air space from a ground source. On demand, water under pressure exits the tank through an outlet at the lower center which is plumbed to all using facilities.

The material composition of most distribution lines is corrosion-resistant steel; however, titanium, monel, and flexible Teflon® hoses are used in some areas.

To prevent freezing, some distribution lines are heated by wrap-around heater blankets; heater jackets protect the fill/overflow valve and the drain valve. Two manually-operated shutoff valves are located in the distribution lines to permit isolation of galley facilities for maintenance purposes.

A 3/4" fill connection at the water service panel provides for attachment of a water supply line from ground servicing equipment. Water enters the tank through the open fill/overflow valve, which can be operated remotely at the service panel through a remote control cable, or directly at the valve by the valve handle. When the tank water level reaches the standpipe, overflow water returns to the service cart via the overflow line. When closed, the fill/overflow valve enables pressurization by interconnecting the fill port/line with the standpipe/overflow line.

The normally closed drain valve can be opened by operating its handle at the service panel. When the drain valve and supply shutoff valves are open, the entire system can be drained to a holding cart attached to the overflow/drain connection. The system must be drained if the aircraft is going to be parked without electrical power in below freezing weather for any length of time.

BOEING 757 POTABLE WATER SYSTEM

The major sub-systems of the potable water system are distribution, stowage, pressurization, quantity indication and fill/drain (servicing). The distribution system consists of lines that extend from the stowage tank to all the lavatories and galleys.

The water tank, shown in Figure 11-11, is filled with potable water from a ground cart through an exterior service panel. The tank is pressurized by an electric driven compressor or the engine bleed pneumatic manifold.

Once pressurized, the water is forced from the tank through distribution lines to the galleys and lavatories.

In the lavatories, some of the water is diverted through an electric water heater before being delivered to the hot water faucets.

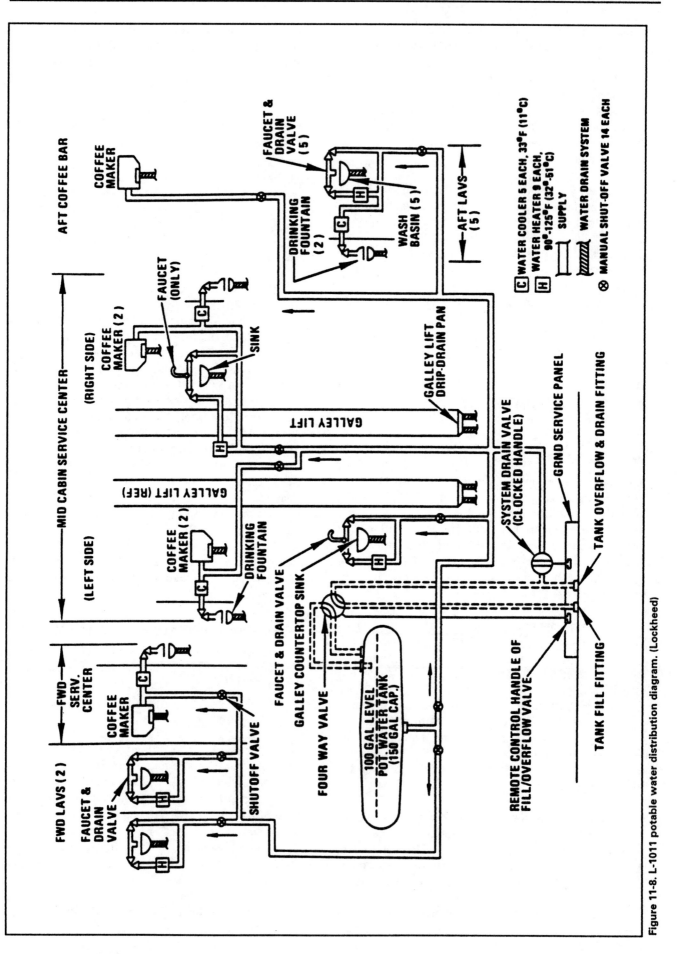

Figure 11-8. L-1011 potable water distribution diagram. (Lockheed)

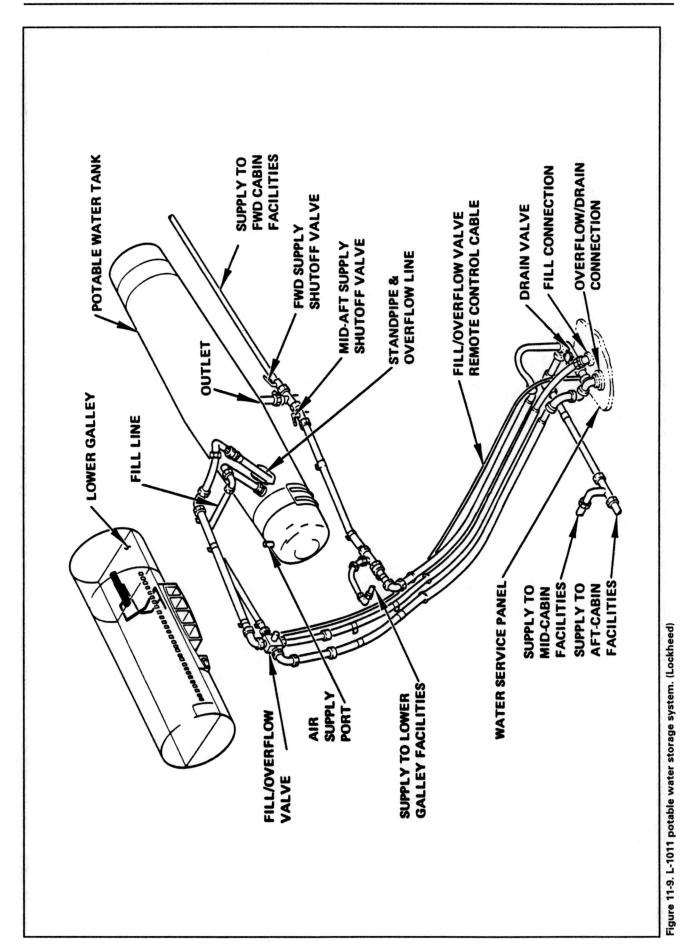

Figure 11-9. L-1011 potable water storage system. (Lockheed)

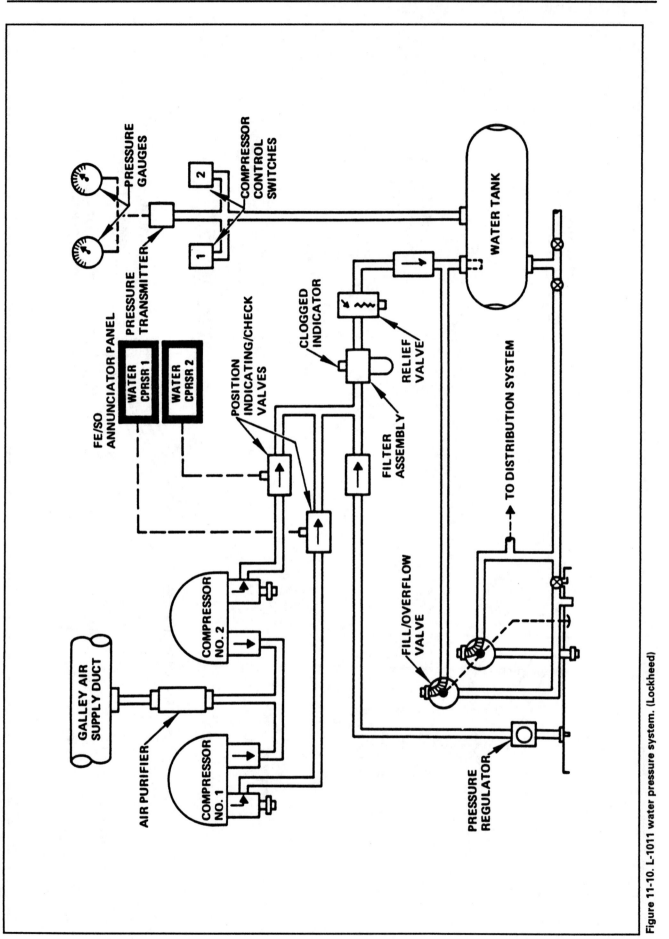

Figure 11-10. L-1011 water pressure system. (Lockheed)

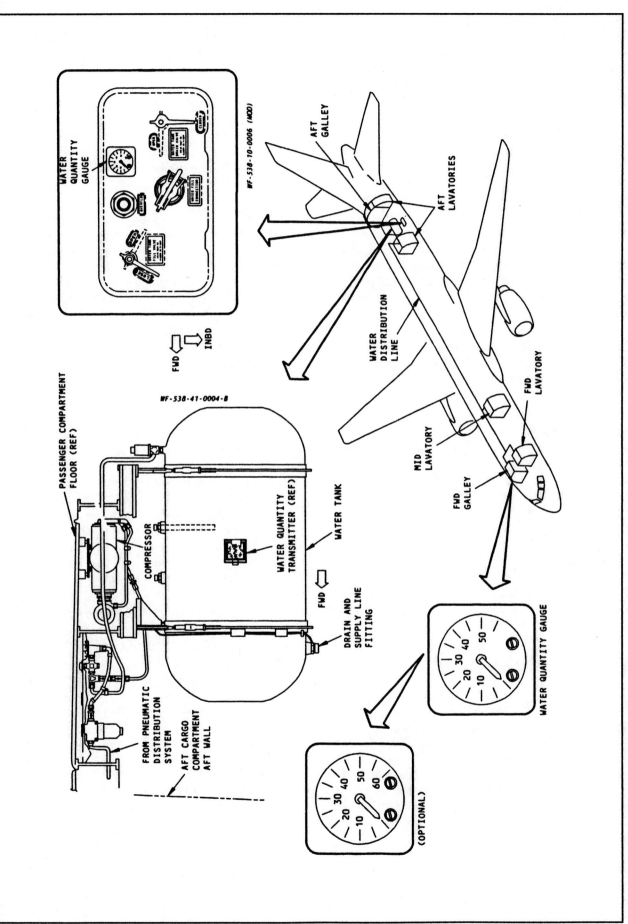

Figure 11-11. 757 potable water system. (Boeing)

The water heater, located under the wash basin in each lavatory, consists of a one and one-half quart cylindrical tank containing three 140 watt heating elements to heat the water, and a cycling thermal switch which regulates the water temperature to approximately 125°F. (52°C).

The water distribution system shown in Figure 11-12, is located below the passenger compartment floor for the aft galley complex and above the passenger compartment ceiling for all the lavatories and forward galley complex.

Waste water from the galleys and from the lavatory sinks is directed overboard through forward and aft drain masts. All supply and drain lines below the level of the passenger floor are protected from freezing by the use of heater tape. The drain masts are also electrically heated.

The quantity indication system uses a transmitter located on the tank and indicators located on the servicing panel and in the forward galley area.

All components of the water system are constructed of corrosion resistant materials suitable for use with superchlorinated water. Although some of the distribution lines are heated, they are fabricated of materials that will sustain freezing without rupture or permanent distortion. System pressure is maintained automatically and is designed so that system pressure shall not drop below 10 psig with one lavatory faucet open for full flow.

The water pressurization system interfaces with the left pneumatic distribution system. When pressurized, the left pneumatic distribution system provides air to pressurize the water system.

WASTE SYSTEMS

L-1011 WASTE SYSTEM

The waste system, Figure 11-13, consists of independent forward and aft subsystems which are functionally the same and physically similar. Both installations are self-contained, recirculating liquid chemical systems which process and store lavatory toilet waste products. Forward lavatory toilets are served by a 40-gallon waste tank; aft lavatory toilets, by an 80-gallon tank.

Forward and aft service panels contain provisions for draining, flushing and pre-charging the associated tank. The service panels also contain indicating lights for tank liquid level indication.

Each tank is pre-charged prior to flight with a dye-deodorant-disinfectant chemical flushing liquid; the forward tank with 15 gallons, the aft with 20 gallons.

In each system, pressure for toilet flushing is supplied by three tank-mounted motor/pump/filter assemblies, which operate one at a time in selective rotational sequence. One pump develops sufficient pressure to flush all subsystem toilets simultaneously. The pumps are controlled by solid-state circuitry in a logic control box mounted near the tank.

A flush valve on each toilet in the system is also controlled by the logic box. Flush signals are initiated at each toilet by a flush control lever/switch assembly. The logic control boxes are identical; each contains line-replaceable printed circuit cards, including a separate 12-second flush timer card for each toilet in the subsystem and space for spare timer card storage. Each logic box also contains externally-accessible switches and indicator lights for testing motor/pump/filter assemblies.

The waste water panel, shown in Figure 11-14, at the flight engineer station, contains forward and aft pump dial lights for annunciation of pump failure in the associated subsystem.

A flush signal is generated when a flush control lever is momentarily pressed. Logic box circuitry opens the associated flush valve and activates the next pump in rotational sequence. At the end of 12 seconds the flush valve is closed and the pump is shut off, unless its operating time is extended through activation of other timers by concurrent flush signals.

Waste tank odors are ducted overboard through a vent line which terminates near the service panel. Air pressure for tank venting can be supplied from one of three sources: cabin pressure, the pneumatic system, or ground air. When the aircraft is pressurized, cabin air passes through the toilets into the waste tank and exhausts overboard through the vent line and outflow control valve. If the cabin is not pressurized, odors are drawn from the tank by a vent air jet pump in the vent line, which can be operated from air pressure supplied by the pneumatic system, or from a ground source through the ground vent air valve at the service panel.

The waste tank is drained, flushed and filled at the waste service panel (Figure 11-13). It is gravity-drained to a suitable ground holding cart through a manually-operated drain valve, and is pressure-flushed/filled through a self-sealing fill/flush port. Fill or flush liquid enters the tank through a fill/flush

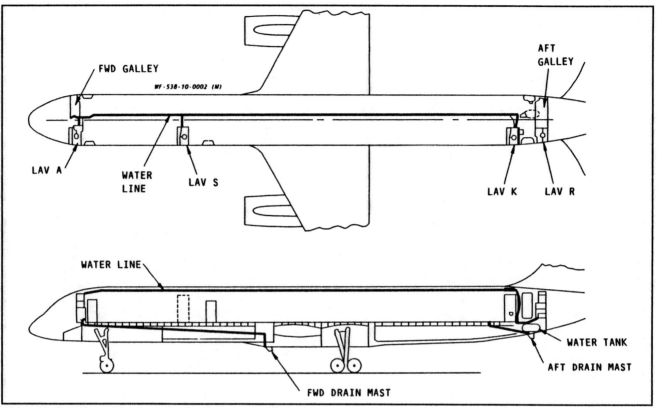

Figure 11-12. 757 potable water distribution system. (Boeing)

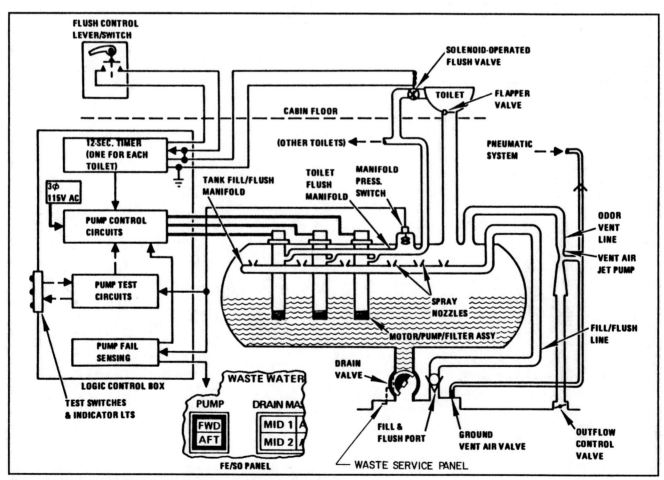

Figure 11-13. L-1011 waste disposal functional diagram. (Lockheed)

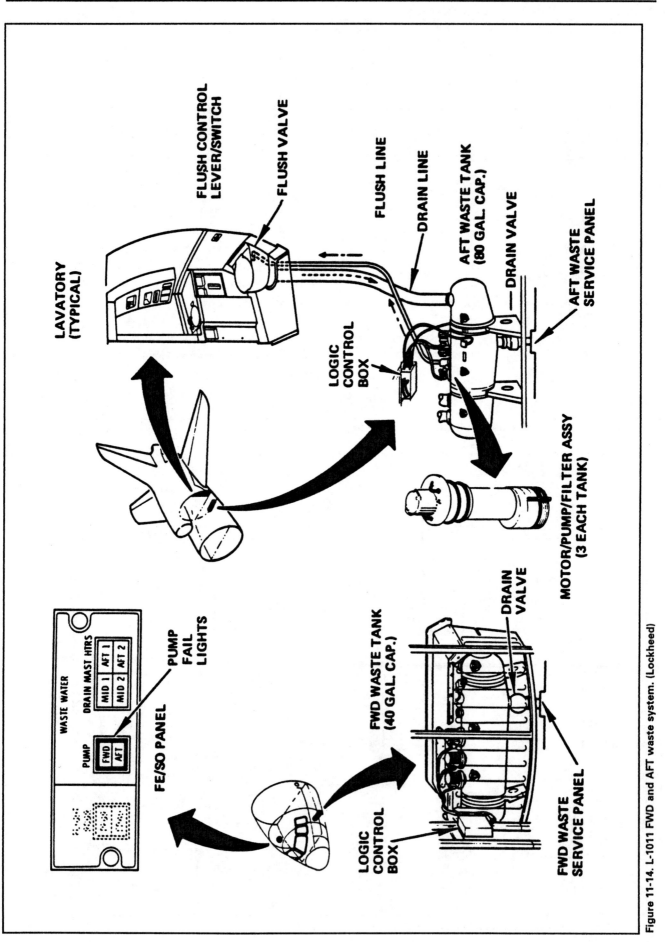

Figure 11-14. L-1011 FWD and AFT waste system. (Lockheed)

manifold which contains six spray nozzles. The noz-zles direct flush liquid spray to assure complete cleaning action.

With the drain valve closed, the tank is pre-charged through the fill/flush port and spray nozzles with a dye-deodorant-disinfectant liquid chemical. The service panel also contains indicating lights for determining the quantity of accumulated waste in the tank.

757 WASTE SYSTEM

The waste system shown in Figure 11-15 provides toilet facilities in each lavatory. The system consists of a toilet assembly in each lavatory, airplane exterior-mounted servicing panels, and the necessary plumbing and hardware for system control, operation and servicing.

Each toilet consists of a waste tank and flushing equipment. The lavatory compartments, toilet bowls and waste tanks are vented by the lavatory/galley ventilation system. Servicing is accomplished externally through three service panels.

The toilet/waste assembly, shown in Figure 11-16, is a self-contained unit installed in each lavatory. It is installed above the floor of the lavatory and attached to

airplane structure with two tie bolts. Initiation of the flush cycle is through a switch and timer located on the lavatory wall. The toilets are serviced from exterior service panels.

The toilet tank is constructed of molded Kevlar® and the various components required for operation of the toilet are mounted on the top. These components consist of the toilet bowl with separator, the motor-pump-filter assembly, the tank drain valve assembly, the motor driven shutoff valve assembly, fluid level sensor and the tank and toilet bowl vents. The entire unit is covered with an easily removable decorative shroud.

The toilet-timer is a self contained unit mounted with four screws behind the lavatory wall at the back of the toilet. A shaft on the unit extends though the wall and an operating handle is attached to this shaft with a self locking set screw. Each time the handle is pressed, power is applied to the control circuitry, starting a solid state timer and energizing a relay. This will supply 115 VAC power to the flush motor for a period of 10 seconds after which the relay will open.

747-400 TOILET WASTE SYSTEM

The 747-400 toilet waste system uses a vacuum system to collect, transport and store toilet waste. The waste sys-

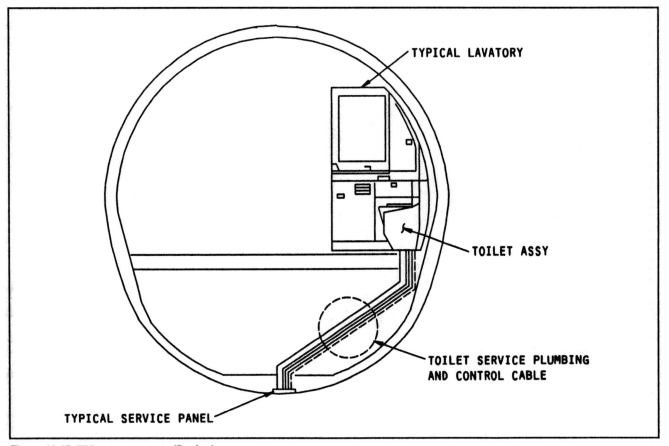

Figure 11-15. 757 waste system. (Boeing)

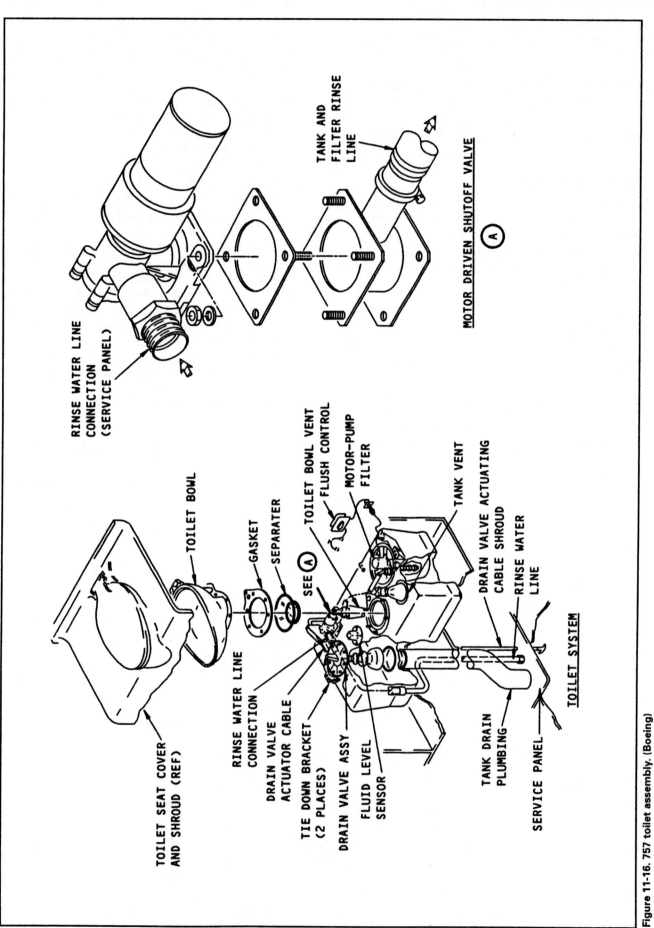

Figure 11-16. 757 toilet assembly. (Boeing)

tem, shown in Figure 11-17, provides toilets throughout the main deck and upper deck passenger cabin.

The system uses potable water to flush the toilet bowls, and vacuum (differential pressure) to transport the waste through toilet drain lines to waste tanks in the bulk cargo compartment. The toilet flushing cycle is controlled by a flush control unit. This unit sequences and times the cycle including the rinse water valve, flush valve, and vacuum blower operation.

The vacuum (differential) is created by a vacuum blower at lower altitudes and differential pressure at high altitudes. At altitudes below 16,000 feet (12,000 feet on descent) the vacuum blower is not operating, and the blower shutoff valve is closed. At high altitudes, the differential pressure between the cabin and ambient provides the vacuum.

All air leaving the waste tanks passes through a liquid separator. Waste tank level is monitored by two level sensors in each waste tank. the sensors are connected to a sensor and logic control module.

When a waste tank reaches capacity, the level monitoring system prevents the associated toilets from flushing, and illuminates a LAV INOP light on the attendant's panel. All waste tanks are serviced from

one waste service panel, shown in Figure 11-18. The panel contains a waste drain cap and rinse fittings. The drain cap is opened to provide a connection for ground service equipment. When the drain valves are opened, waste tank contents flow out this connection.

After draining, the tanks are rinsed with flushing liquid through the rinse fitting on the service panel. The liquid passes through a filter before entering the rinse housing assemblies in the tank. After rinsing, a wet pre-charge may be added to the tanks.

LIGHTING SYSTEMS

BOEING 757 AIRCRAFT LIGHTING SYSTEMS

Aircraft lighting systems provide illumination of several different areas of the aircraft. Some areas that require lights are the flight, passenger, cargo, and service compartments. In addition to compartment lights, exterior and emergency lighting systems also provide light in critical areas in and around the aircraft.

The exterior lights provide illumination of the ground during landing and taxi operations. The landing lights can also be used to make the aircraft more visible to air traffic controllers and other aircraft in flight.

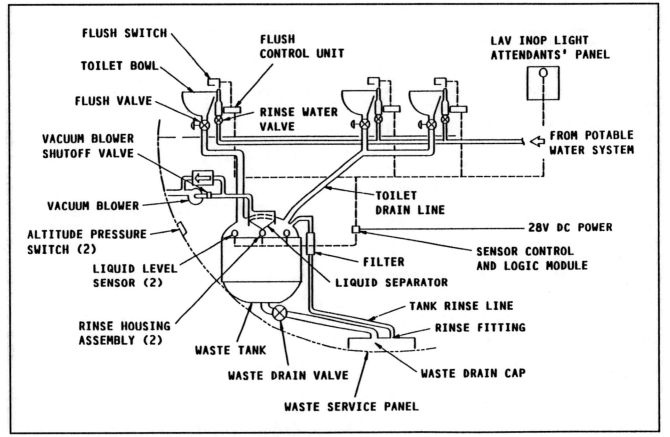

Figure 11-17. 747-400 toilet waste system summary. (Boeing)

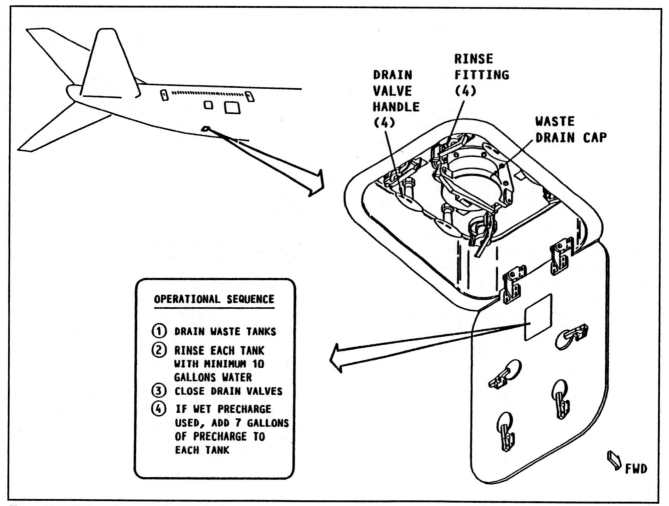

Figure 11-18. 747 waste service panel. (Boeing)

The 757 has four landing lights (see Figure 11-19); two in the wing roots and two on the nose landing gear. The wing root lights shine horizontally and the nose gear lights are aimed downward on a typical glide slope angle.

Other exterior lights include wing illumination lights mounted on each side of the fuselage to light up the leading edge of the wing and the engine nacelles.

The runway turnoff lights are mounted on the nose landing gear and illuminate the area to either side of the aircraft.

Anti-collision lights (strobe lights) are mounted on the top and bottom of the fuselage and on each wing tip. The fuselage lights are covered with a red lens and the wing lights are covered with a clear lens.

There are two position lights mounted on each wing tip facing forward and aft, as shown in Figure 11-19. The aft facing lights are covered with a clear lens while

the forward facing lights have a red lens on the left wing and a green lens on the right wing.

Two quartz halogen logo lights are positioned on the top surface of each horizontal stabilizer to illuminate the vertical stabilizer.

FLIGHT COMPARTMENT LIGHTING

The main instrument panel floodlights are controlled from switches on the P7 lighting panels, see Figure 11-20. These lights are fluorescent tubes and vary the length of time they are switched on to provide variable intensity.

The glare shield and aisle stand floodlights are controlled from rheostats located on the P5 overhead panel. There are three dome lights in the 757 which are controlled by a rheostat. Lighting for all the instrument and circuit breaker panels is controlled from the lighting control panels. The bulbs used for faceplate illumination are soldered on a circuit strip attached to the rear of the faceplate.

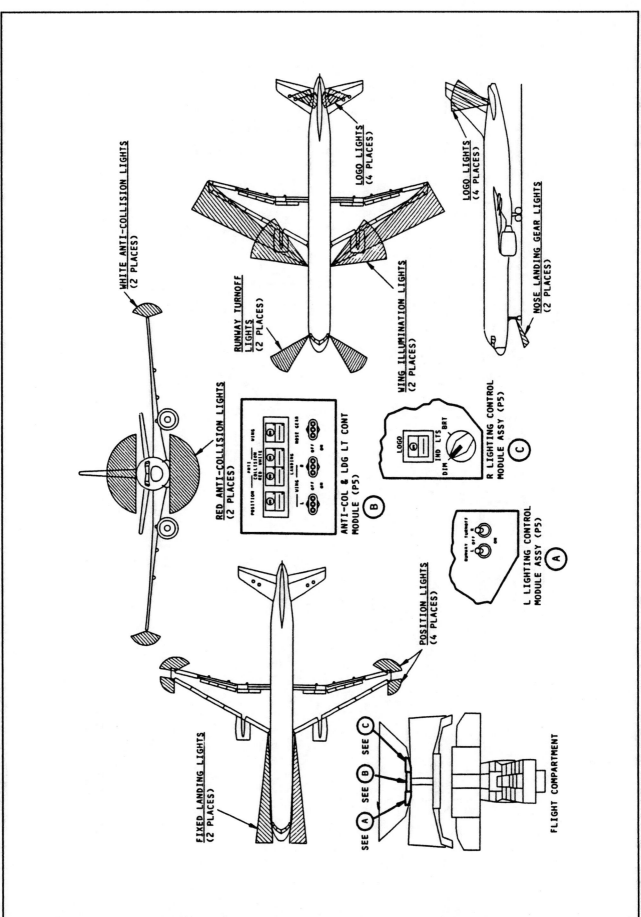

Figure 11-19. 757 exterior lights. (Boeing)

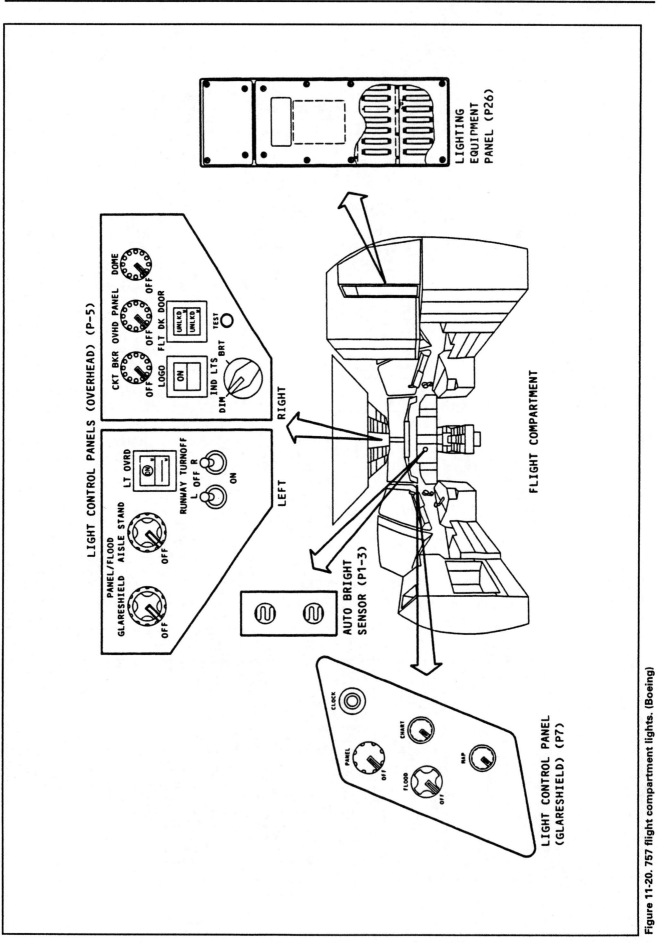

Figure 11-20. 757 flight compartment lights. (Boeing)

Map lights and chart lights controlled from the P7 panels illuminate the pilot's letdown chart holders and lap area. The flight compartment also includes utility (kit) lights which are moveable and two colored spot lights for miscellaneous use. The override light switch shown on the P5 panel in Figure 11-20 can be used as a means of turning on all of the instrument panel floodlights and dome lights from one switch.

PASSENGER COMPARTMENT LIGHTS

General illumination of the passenger cabin is with dual intensity fluorescent ceiling and sidewall lights operated with switches on the forward attendant's panel to the bright or dim mode, as shown in Figure 11-21. Incandescent lighting is used for additional spot lighting of work and access areas. A passenger reading light and switch is provided for each passenger seat.

A FASTEN SEAT BELT and a NO SMOKING sign is installed in each passenger service unit. Lavatory signs are located at each lavatory location and an occupied sign is installed as part of each lavatory sign to indicate when lavatories are in use. Exit signs mark each exit and also support the passenger, lavatory and crew call lights.

Laboratories have fluorescent mirror lights for general illumination and incandescent dome lights for dim illumination. Inflight, the mirror lights are turned on and off by operation of the lavatory door latch switches. They illuminate when the door is closed and locked and go out when unlocked.

CARGO COMPARTMENT LIGHTS

Forward and aft cargo compartment lighting is provided for the interior and exterior of each compartment. The forward cargo compartment lights are powered by 115 VAC and are enabled when the cargo door is not fully closed. The lower hinge proximity switch provides a ground which energizes the forward cargo compartment lights.

The forward cargo compartment light switch controls the five lights in the ceiling and the five lights in the door. The light switch is located just aft of the door. The aft cargo compartment light switch controls the eight lights in the ceiling and the five lights in the door.

SERVICE COMPARTMENT LIGHTS

Service compartment lighting is provided in the main and nose wheel wells and in the E/E equipment compartments. Service compartment lighting is also provided in the air conditioning, APU, and tail cone compartments. Service lighting is generally used to inspect or perform work in these service compart-ments. Cargo and service compartment lighting is shown in Figure 11-22.

EMERGENCY EQUIPMENT

BOEING 757 EMERGENCY LIGHTS

The emergency lights provide illumination of the passenger cabin and escape slide routes, using battery packs as the power source. The lights can be turned on manually or set to come on automatically in the event of failure of the primary lighting power.

The lights, illustrated in Figure 11-23, consist of EXIT sign modules over each door, exit indicators near the floor at each exit and over the main aisle between doors, area lights on ceiling and floor, in the cross aisles between doors, main aisle lights evenly spaced along the main aisle, floor mounted lights at 20" intervals on the left hand side of the aisle and slide lights externally mounted aft of each door and directed to illuminate the slide path.

Ten battery packs mounted in the passenger cabin ceiling area are used as the power source for these lights. These battery packs are mounted in pairs in the area of each door. Each pair of packs provides emergency power for the illumination of the adjacent lights.

The primary operational control for the emergency lights is a three position guarded switch on the pilot's overhead panel. The switch has an ON, an OFF, and a guarded ARMED position. Whenever this switch is in other than the ARMED position, the amber UNARMED caution light will illuminate, and an EMER LIGHTS alert message will be sent to the EICAS system. If aircraft power is lost and the emergency light switch is in the ARMED position, the emergency lights will be illuminated automatically, powered by the battery packs described earlier. The normal emergency light switch position when passengers are onboard the aircraft is the armed position.

BOEING 737-300 EMERGENCY EQUIPMENT

Clearly marked exit lights are located throughout the passenger cabin to indicate the approved emergency exit routes. All of the lights are powered by individual nickel cadmium batteries with a charging, monitoring and voltage regulator circuit.

Floor proximity emergency escape path lighting consists of locator lights spaced at approximately 40-inch intervals down the left-hand side of the aisle. Lighted arrows point to overwing exits and a lighted EXIT indicator is near the floor by each door and overwing exit. Escape path markings are provided for

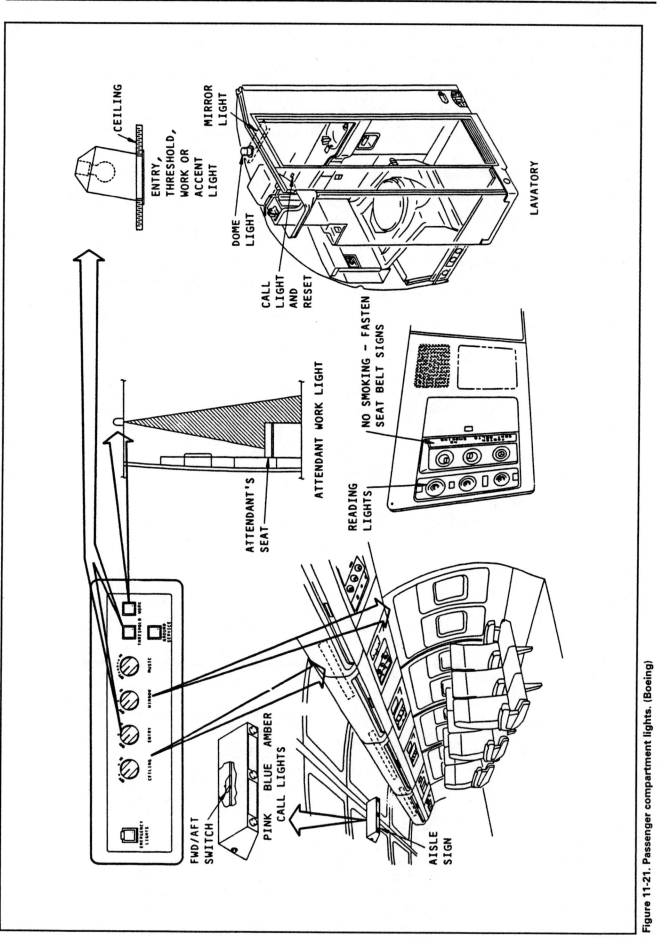

Figure 11-21. Passenger compartment lights. (Boeing)

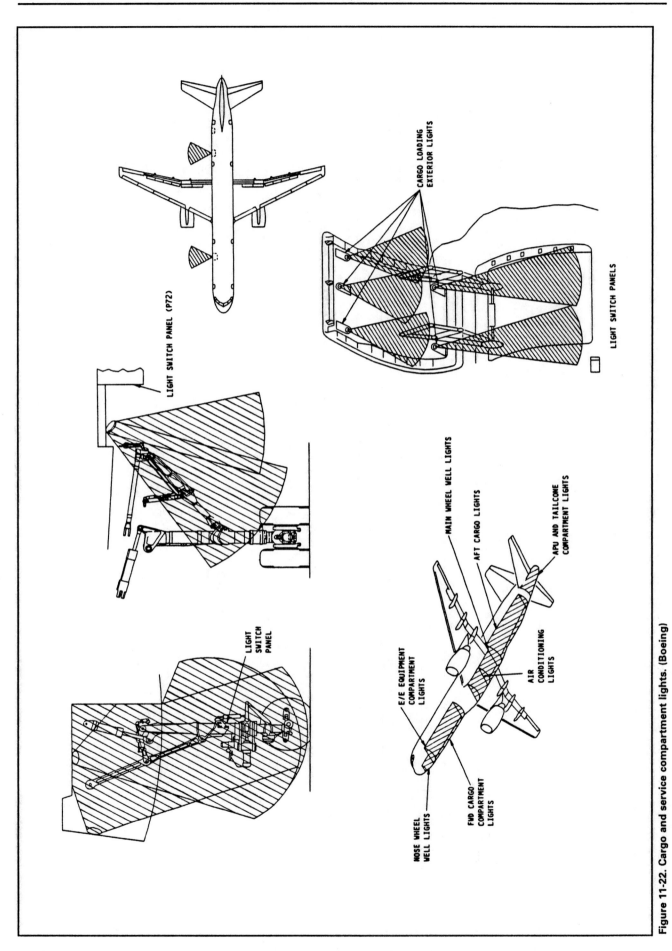

Figure 11-22. Cargo and service compartment lights. (Boeing)

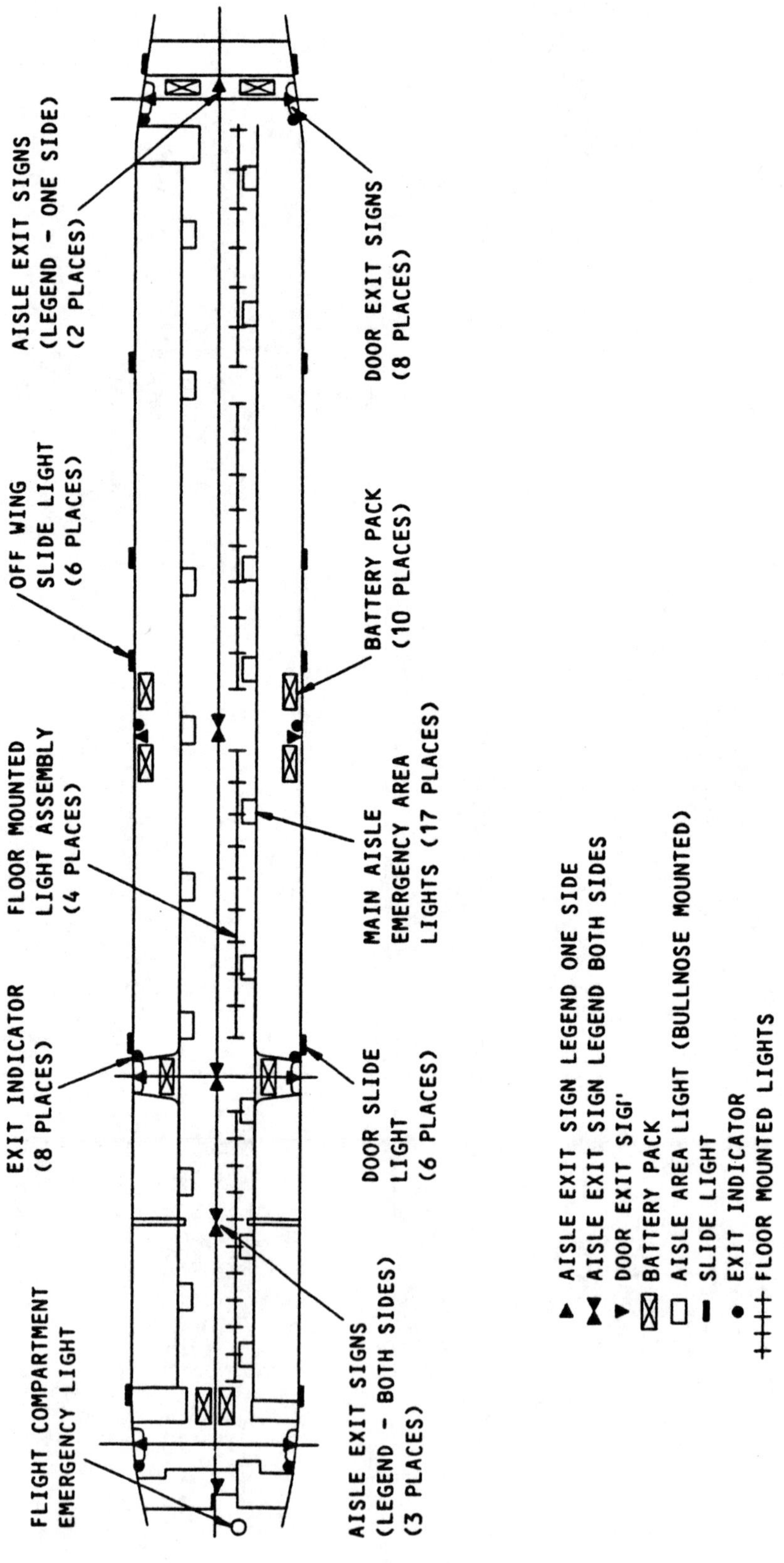

AISLE EXIT SIGNS (LEGEND - ONE SIDE) (2 PLACES)

DOOR EXIT SIGNS (8 PLACES)

OFF WING SLIDE LIGHT (6 PLACES)

BATTERY PACK (10 PLACES)

FLOOR MOUNTED LIGHT ASSEMBLY (4 PLACES)

MAIN AISLE EMERGENCY AREA LIGHTS (17 PLACES)

EXIT INDICATOR (8 PLACES)

DOOR SLIDE LIGHT (6 PLACES)

FLIGHT COMPARTMENT EMERGENCY LIGHT

AISLE EXIT SIGNS (LEGEND - BOTH SIDES) (3 PLACES)

▲ AISLE EXIT SIGN LEGEND ONE SIDE
⧖ AISLE EXIT SIGN LEGEND BOTH SIDES
▶ DOOR EXIT SIGI'
⊠ BATTERY PACK
▢ AISLE AREA LIGHT (BULLNOSE MOUNTED)
❙ SLIDE LIGHT
● EXIT INDICATOR
+++ FLOOR MOUNTED LIGHTS

Figure 11-23. 757 emergency lights layout. (Boeing)

visual guidance for emergency cabin evacuation when all sources of cabin lighting more than four feet above the aisle floor are totally obscured by smoke.

Exterior emergency lights illuminate the escape slides, as shown in Figure 11-24. The fuselage installed escape slide lights are adjacent to the forward and aft service and entry doors. Two lights are also installed on the fuselage to illuminate the overwing escape routes and ground contact area.

Emergency evacuation may be accomplished through four entry/service doors and two overwing escape hatches. Cockpit crewmembers may evacuate the airplane through two sliding cockpit windows.

The emergency evacuation routes are shown in Figure 11-25. Two escape hatches are located in the passenger cabin over the wings. These are plug-type hatches and are held in place by mechanical locks and airplane cabin pressure. The hatches can be opened from the inside or from outside of the airplane by a spring-loaded handle at the top of the hatch.

ESCAPE SLIDES

When an emergency dictates rapid evacuation of the airplane on the ground, it may be necessary to activate and use the emergency escape slides shown in Figure 11-25. The slides are inflatable rubber/nylon units which are stored in compartments on the bottom inner face of the forward entry, aft entry, and galley service doors.

The slide incorporates a retainer (girt) bar, illustrated in Figure 11-26, which is normally stowed in special stowage clips on the compartment cover. Before taxiing, this bar is removed from the hooks and fastened to brackets located on the floor of the airplane. It remains there throughout the flight.

If an emergency evacuation is needed upon landing and the door is opened, tension on the girt bar will cause the compartment latch to separate, allowing the compartment to open and the slide to automatically deploy outboard of the door opening.

For normal door operation, the girt bar is stowed in the spring loaded retaining clips at the bottom of the door. These clips require the girt bar to be snapped into position and not just laid on top of the clips. Improper stowage of the girt bar could result in inadvertent deployment of the slide. The slide cover has a viewing window for checking the pressure in the escape slide inflation bottle.

Inflation will begin during slide deployment. Automatic inflation requires approximately 5 seconds.

Should the automatic inflation system fail, the manual inflation handle must be pulled completely clear of the slide to effect proper inflation. The manual inflation handle is labeled PULL and is visible when the slide is ejected from its container.

EQUIPMENT COOLING SYSTEMS

BOEING 737-300 COOLING SYSTEM

EFIS equipment, circuit breaker panels in the cockpit, and electronic equipment in the E & E compartment are cooled by the equipment cooling system shown in Figure 11-27. Warm air, caused by the heat generated by the aircraft's electrical components, is ducted away by the selected AC powered fan.

On the ground, or with the cabin differential pressure less than 2.5 psi, the exhaust fan air is blown through a flow control valve and exhausted out the bottom of the airplane.

With increasing airflow at greater cabin differential pressures, the flow control valve closes. This action will occur when the aircraft is pressurized at altitude and has a cabin pressure differential of more than 2.5 psi. At this point, the cabin air to outside air pressure differential is sufficient to supply the equipment cooling system. Warm air from the electronic equipment cooling system is then diffused around the forward cargo compartment and out the forward outflow valve. This insures adequate heating of the forward cargo at high (colder) altitudes.

The no-airflow detectors in the ducting just forward of the equipment cooling fans consists of a thermal switch. Loss of airflow due to failure of an equipment cooling fan causes increasing heat to activate the thermal switch, illuminating the respective equipment cooling OFF light. Selecting the alternate fan should restore airflow passing the switch, and extinguish the OFF light.

Additional thermal switches are located in the E & E compartment. If an over-temperature occurs on the ground, alerting is also provided through the ground crew call horn in the nose wheel well.

L-1011 INSTRUMENT AND ELECTRONICS COOLING SYSTEM

The instrument cooling system, shown in Figure 11-28, uses a fan which runs all the time the aircraft is

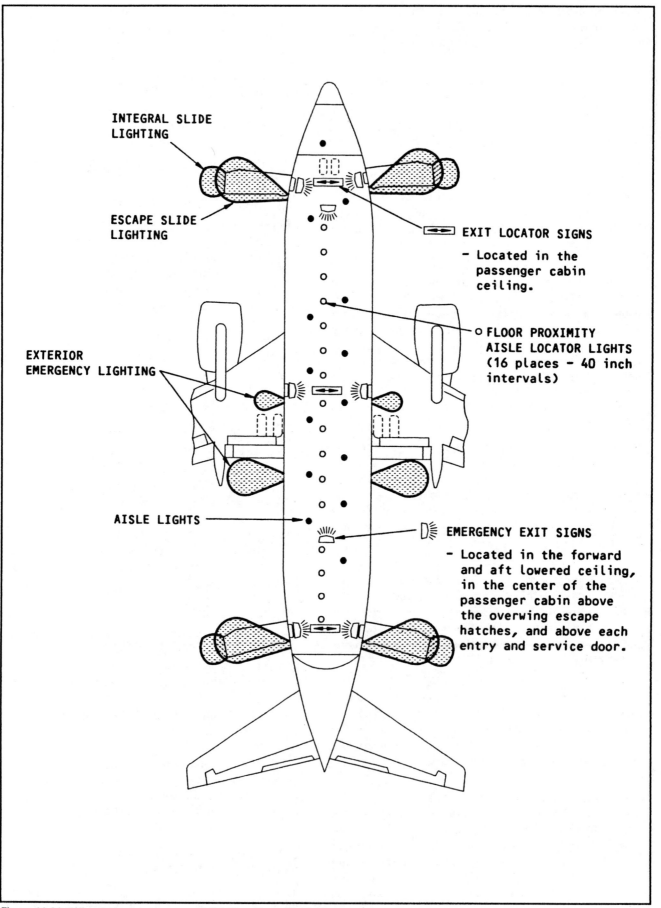

Figure 11-24. 737 exterior emergency exit light locations. (Boeing)

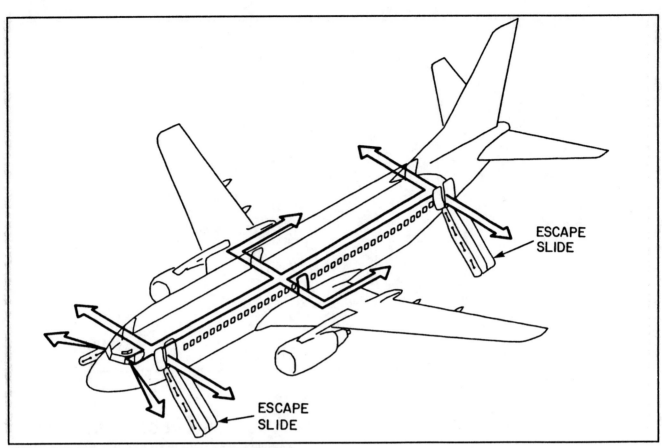

ESCAPE
SLIDE

ESCAPE
SLIDE

Figure 11-25. 737 emergency evacuation routes. (Boeing)

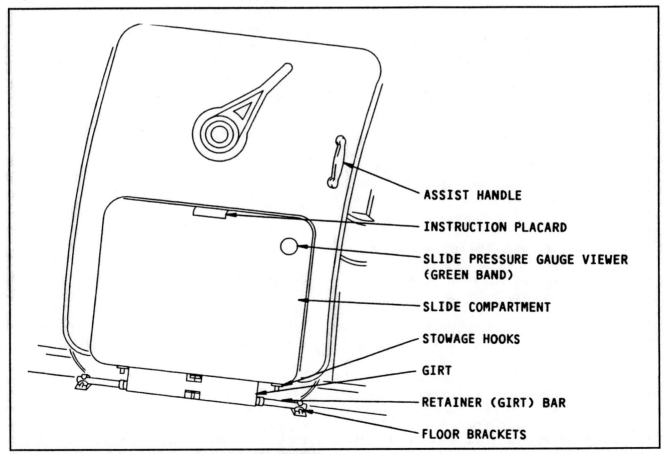

ASSIST HANDLE

INSTRUCTION PLACARD

SLIDE PRESSURE GAUGE VIEWER
(GREEN BAND)

SLIDE COMPARTMENT

STOWAGE HOOKS

GIRT

RETAINER (GIRT) BAR

FLOOR BRACKETS

Figure 11-26. Escape slide compartment and girt bar. (Boeing)

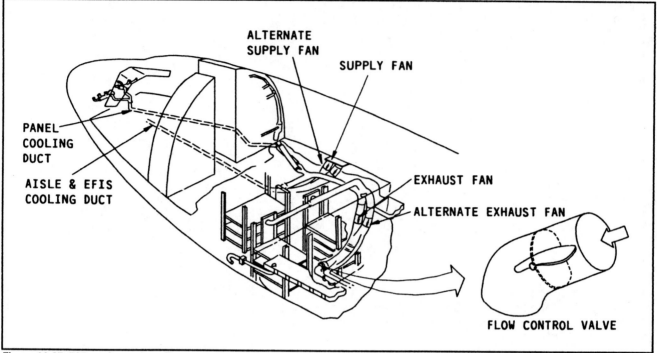

Figure 11-27. 737 equipment cooling components diagram. (Boeing)

using AC power. The fan draws air from below the flight engineer panel and supplies it to three nozzles behind the flight engineer panel, to one nozzle behind the engine instrument panel, and to two manifolds behind the pilots' instrument panels. From the manifolds, the air is directed at the cases of the horizontal situation indicator (HSI) and the attitude director indicator (ADI), and to the surrounding areas for cooling. Behind the flight engineer panel, the air is generally directed to all instruments.

When insufficient airflow is available for adequate instrument cooling, an airflow sensor, mounted on the fan supply duct behind the flight engineer panel, will provide a signal to illuminate the PILOTS INSTR COOL FAN light on the flight engineer annunciator panel.

A filter is installed in front of the grille to keep dirt and debris in the flight station from being drawn through the fan. The filter is held in place with Velcro® tape, so that when the filter becomes dirty, it is easy to remove and wash.

The forward electronics system, shown in Figure 11-29, uses a fan to draw air through the equipment and passes it under the floor of the forward cargo compartment where it vents overboard through the forward pressurization outflow valve. When the aircraft is on the ground, the exhaust flow control valve will open, even though the fan is still running. This exhausts the cooling air directly overboard.

757 EQUIPMENT COOLING SYSTEM

The Boeing 757 equipment cooling system is divided into a forward and an aft system. The forward system, illustrated in Figure 11-30, cools the equipment by using blow through and draw through air cooling. The forward system also incorporates an air cleaner, an overheat, a low flow, and a smoke detection system.

The low flow sensor installed in a branch of the exhaust ducting monitors airflow in the system and a smoke detector monitors the exhaust air for the presence of smoke. The overboard exhaust valve, connected to the ducting downstream from the left recirculation fan, serves as a back-up source for forward exhaust system airflow during flight and allows a major portion of the forward exhaust air to be discharged overboard during ground operation.

The aft equipment cooling system uses only draw through air to provide cooling for the equipment in the electrical racks. There is no smoke or low flow detection installed in the aft system. Both systems normally operate automatically through the use of relays.

The EICAS computers monitor the equipment cooling system for proper operation and provide messages to indicate malfunctions or normal operation. Indications will also be provided on the equipment cooling control panel, the air conditioning control panel and through the ground crew call system.

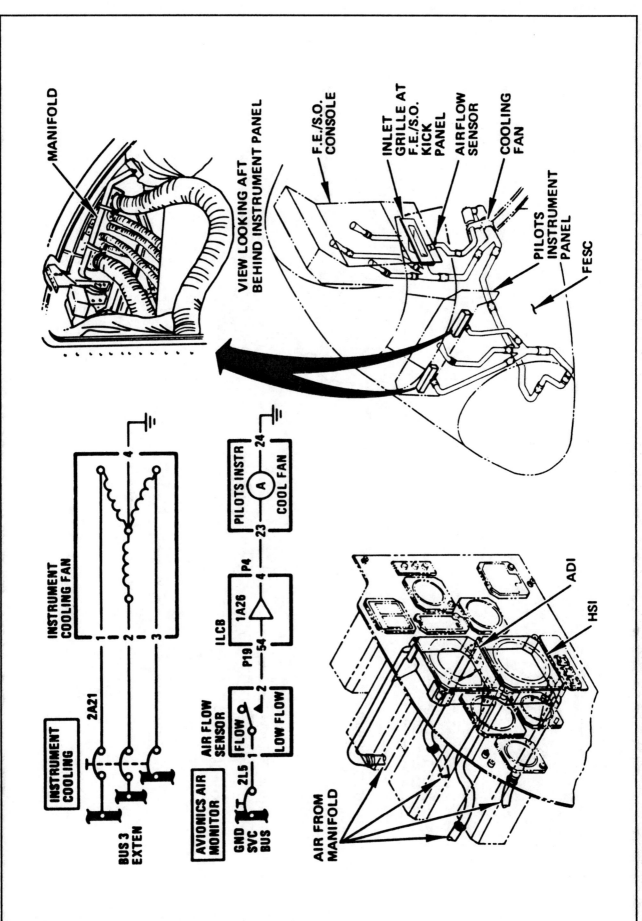

Figure 11-28. L-1011 instrument cooling system. (Lockheed)

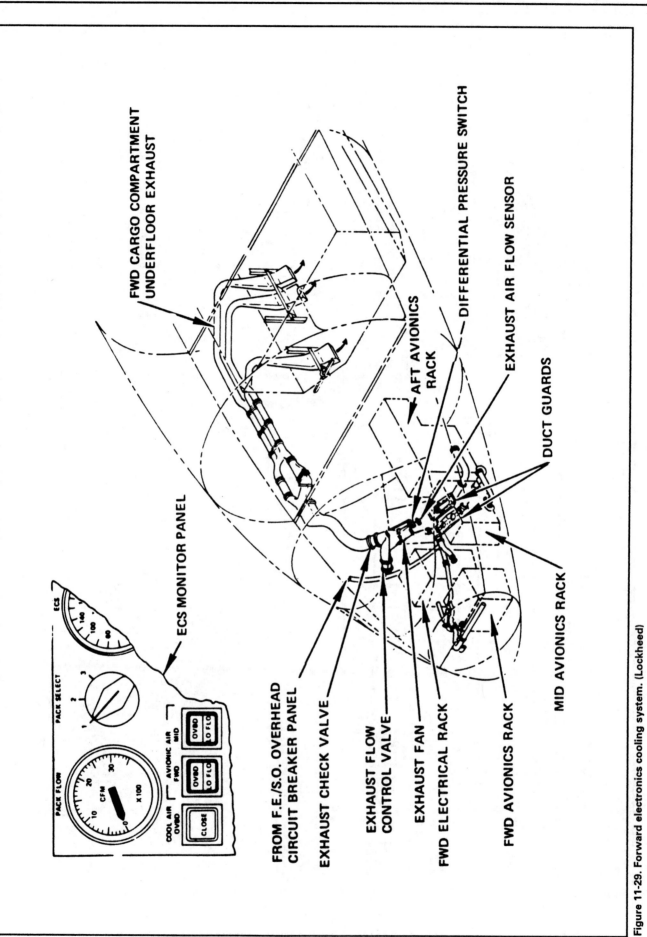

FWD CARGO COMPARTMENT UNDERFLOOR EXHAUST

DIFFERENTIAL PRESSURE SWITCH

EXHAUST AIR FLOW SENSOR

AFT AVIONICS RACK

DUCT GUARDS

ECS MONITOR PANEL

FROM F.E./S.O. OVERHEAD CIRCUIT BREAKER PANEL

EXHAUST CHECK VALVE

EXHAUST FLOW CONTROL VALVE

EXHAUST FAN

FWD ELECTRICAL RACK

FWD AVIONICS RACK

MID AVIONICS RACK

Figure 11-29. Forward electronics cooling system. (Lockheed)

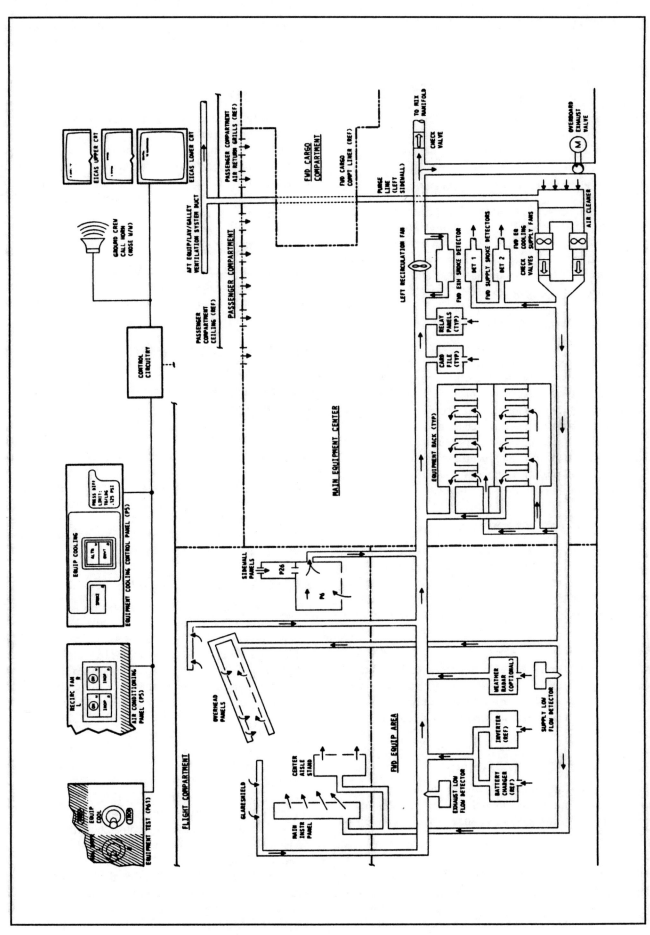

Figure 11-30. 757 forward equipment cooling system. (Boeing)

MAINTENANCE INFORMATION

MAINTENANCE MANUALS

The maintenance manual provides information which enables a technician to perform servicing functions, to locate and identify faults, to repair all systems and subsystems, and to replace any unit normally requiring such action on the flight line or in the hangar.

ILLUSTRATED PARTS CATALOG (IPC)

The IPC, customized for each airline, presents information for provisioning and requisitioning of replacement parts and assemblies. The IPC identifies current and superseded parts. It also identifies small replaceable parts such as filters, seals, bearings, and connectors which are components of a line replaceable unit (LRU).

WIRING DIAGRAM MANUAL

The wiring diagram manual contains four types of information: maintenance instructions on electrical connectors, customized wiring diagrams, various lists and charts of electrical data produced by the automated wiring data system, and electrical equipment location illustrations. These lists and illustrations, which reflect such data as equipment and wire numbers, wiring and connector locations by zone and station, and hookup information, are organized according to ATA numbering format and chapters.

STRUCTURAL REPAIR MANUAL

The structural repair manual contains descriptive information and repair procedures for primary and secondary structure of aircraft. The manual also includes damage classification, fastener substitution, and other information to facilitate repair operations.

OVERHAUL MANUAL

Most manufacturers provide separate and self-supporting overhaul instructions and illustrated parts lists for each repairable unit. The instructions provide complete information for repair, replacement, and bench testing.

TOOL AND EQUIPMENT LIST

The tool and equipment lists present tools and equipment recommended for servicing, line maintenance, and overhaul of the systems, subsystems, and components.

WEIGHT AND BALANCE MANUAL

The weight and balance manual presents data in sufficient depth for the airline to analyze and establish operating weights, center of gravity positions, and balance criteria. The manual contains all weight and balance material required by government regulations for commercial aircraft.

NONDESTRUCTIVE TESTING MANUAL

The nondestructive testing manual contains all pertinent data on the inspection and testing of structure by nondestructive means. Such methods as dye-penetrant, magnetic particle, eddy current, ultrasonic, and radiographic are discussed. Specific conditions are detailed for the inspection of particular structural areas and components.

SERVICE BULLETINS

These are issued to affect modifications to the aircraft, engine, or accessories, authorize critical or urgent parts substitution, and transmit special instructions to maintain the aircraft.

AIRWORTHINESS DIRECTIVES (AD NOTES)

Airworthiness Directives are issued by the Federal Aviation Administration (FAA) for an aircraft, engine, or part thereof when an unsafe condition exists with regard to the operation of the aircraft. ADs are also issued if the unsafe condition is likely to exist or develop in other products of the same type design. An aircraft may not be operated if an airworthiness directive applies to it, except in accordance with the requirements of the AD. Generally, an AD will require inspection of the aircraft with the necessary repair or replacement of aircraft components.

ATA SPECIFICATION 100

Most transport aircraft manuals use the Air Transport Association of America Specification Number 100, "Specification for Manufacturers' Technical Data." The subject matter is divided into chapters and groups of chapters to facilitate the location of information. This chapterization provides a functional breakdown of the entire airplane, as shown in Table 1-1. Information on all units comprising a system will be found in the chapter identified by the name of that system, or by a general name indicative of the several systems which may be covered in that chapter. Thus, all units relating to the generation and distribution of electrical power are covered in Chapter 24, ELECTRICAL POWER, while electrically driven pumps and valves serving the fuel system are covered in Chapter 28, FUEL. Also, all units of the elevator control system, hydraulic, mechanical and electrical units, are included in Chapter 27, FLIGHT CONTROLS. Each chapter begins with a chapter Table of Contents which shows the chapter divided into sections and the assigned subject numbers within that chapter.

CHAPTER NUMBERS

AIRCRAFT GENERAL

Time Limits/Maintenance Checks....................5
Dimensions & Chart 6
Lifting & Shoring 7
Leveling & Weighing............................8
Towing & Taxing 9
Parking & Mooring 10
Required Placards............................11
Servicing 12
Standard Practices—Airframe 20

AIRPLANE SYSTEMS

Air Conditioning 21
Auto Flight............................22
Communication 23
Electrical Power 24
Equipment/Furnishings............................25
Fire Protection............................26
Flight Controls 27
Fuel 28
Hydraulic Power 29
Ice & Rain Protection............................30
Instruments 31
Landing Gear 32
Lights 33
Navigation 34
Oxygen 35

Pneumatic 36
Water/Waste 38
Airborne Auxiliary Power 49

STRUCTURE

Structures-General 51
Doors 52
Fuselage 53
Nacelles/Pylons............................54
Stabilizers............................55
Windows 56
Wings............................57

POWERPLANT

Standard Practices-Engines............................70
Powerplant 71
Engine............................72
Engine Fuel & Control............................73
Ignition 74
Air Engine Controls............................76
Engine Indicating 77
Exhaust 78
Oil............................79
Starting 80
Water Injection 82
Charts 91

Table 11-1. ATA chapter numbers.

SUBJECT NUMBERING

The chapters of maintenance manuals are broken down into sections, each of which is numbered in a three-part subject-numbering system. (See Table 1-2.) The first number in the three-part subject number is the chapter number and serves to identify the major functional system to which the subject pertains. The middle number is the section number and serves to group all of the coverage pertaining to a system, subsystem, or group of related assemblies, including all units or components that are functionally part of the system or group of related assemblies. The last number identifies a specific subject and serves to identify and group all pages containing information relative to a specific unit, minor assembly, simple system, or simple circuit.

PAGE NUMBERING

In order to have each subject as independent as possible of the other subjects, each subject is page numbered within itself. The identification of pages, then, is by both the subject number and the subject page number.

The ATA Specification No. 100 provides for covering subjects under three main topics: Description and Operation, Troubleshooting, and Maintenance Practices. As a means for readily locating specific types of information within the subject, page number blocks are assigned as follows:

Description and Operation .. Pages 1 thru 100
Trouble Shooting.......... Pages 101 thru 200
Maintenance Practices...... Pages 201 thru 300

The Maintenance Practices coverage of a system or individual component is a combination of the following subtopics:

- Servicing
- Removal/Installation
- Adjustment/Test
- Inspection/Check
- Cleaning/Painting

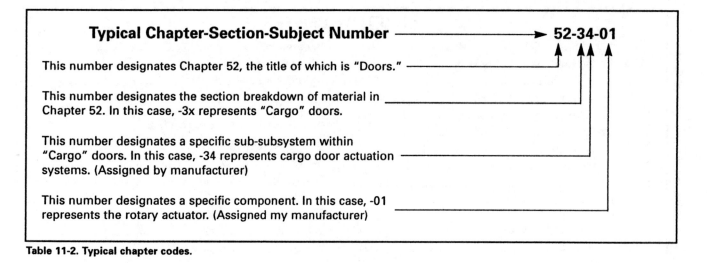

Typical Chapter-Section-Subject Number ———————➤ 52-34-01

This number designates Chapter 52, the title of which is "Doors." ———

This number designates the section breakdown of material in Chapter 52. In this case, -3x represents "Cargo" doors.

This number designates a specific sub-subsystem within "Cargo" doors. In this case, -34 represents cargo door actuation systems. (Assigned by manufacturer)

This number designates a specific component. In this case, -01 represents the rotary actuator. (Assigned my manufacturer)

Table 11-2. Typical chapter codes.

APPROVED REPAIRS

When the maintenance practice is covering only a single subtopic, or when the combination of subtopics would exceed approximately eight pages, each subtopic is treated as a separate topic and the following page number blocks are assigned.

Servicing . . . . Pages 301 thru 400

Removal/Installation . . . . Pages 401 thru 500

Adjustment/Test . . . . Pages 501 thru 600

Inspection/Check. . . . . Pages 601 thru 700

Cleaning/Painting . . . . Pages 701 thru 800

Approved Repairs . . . . Pages 801 thru 900

When covering general maintenance instructions which do not definitely fall within one of the subtopic categories as listed above, the Maintenance Practices topic (201 thru 300 page block) is used for these general instructions. The applicable subtopic page blocks are used for the other maintenance procedures required for the subject.

REVISION

Revisions to maintenance manuals are issued frequently. Sections or pages which are revised will generally be so indicated. These revisions keep the maintenance manuals up to date with current changes in maintenance practices and airplane design.

CHAPTER 11 STUDY QUESTIONS

1. Explain the function of the central maintenance computer on a Boeing 747-400.

   _____

   _____

   _____

2. What types of messages appear on the integrated display system of the central maintenance computer?

   _____

   _____

   _____

3. What are the flight deck effects and how are they reported?

   _____

   _____

   _____

4. What is the basic function of a potable water system on board a large aircraft?

   _____

   _____

   _____

5. Describe the method of heating water for use in the lavatory sink in a Boeing 757.

   _____

   _____

   _____

   _____

6. What is used to force the potable water to flow from a faucet?

   _____

   _____

   _____

7. Explain the operation of the waste system on an L-1011 aircraft.

   _____

   _____

   _____

8. What is meant by a vacuum waste system on a 747-400 aircraft?

   _____

   _____

   _____

9. List the areas of an aircraft that have provisions for illumination (lighting).

   _____

   _____

10. When would the emergency lights come on automatically?

_____

_____

_____

11. What is the power source for the emergency light?

_____

_____

_____

12. Explain the operation of an emergency escape slide.

_____

_____

_____

13. Describe the operation of the Boeing 757 equipment cooling system.

_____

_____

_____

14. List the types of manuals used during maintenance on large aircraft.

_____

_____

_____

15. What is ATA Code 100, and how is it used?

_____

_____

_____

APPENDIX A

McDONNELL DOUGLAS MD-80 FAMILY SPECIFICATIONS

McDonnell Douglas Corporation, Douglas Aircraft Company, Long Beach, California

		MD-81	MD-82/-88	MD-83	MD-87
CAPACITY					
Crew:		2, plus cabin attendants			
Passengers (Typical, All Economy)		155	155	155	130
Passengers (Maximum)		172	172	172	139
Cargo holds	Cu Ft	1253	1253	1013	937
	Cu M	35.5	35.5	28.7	26.5

DIMENSIONS (ALL MODELS):

Span	Ft	107.8	
	M	32.86	
Length overall	Ft	147.9 ....130.4	
	M	45.08 ....39.7	
Height overall	Ft	29.6 ....30.5	
	M	9.05 ....9.29	
Wing Area	Sq Ft	1209	
	Sq M	112	
Sweep Back		24.5 Degrees at 25% chord	

LANDING GEAR (TYPE): Fully retractable tricycle steerable nose wheel

Tread of main wheels	Ft	16.7	
	M	5.09	
Wheel base (fore & aft)	Ft	72.4 ....62.9	
	M	22.07 ....19.18	
Flaps (type):		Double slotted	
Slats (type):		Full span leading edge, three position	
Speed brake (type):		Wing mounted spoilers	
Reversers (type):		Target, ground operation only..	

ENGINES: Two Pratt & Whitney Aircraft Turbofan

	JT8D-209	JT8D-217A/-217C	JT8D-219	JT8D-217C
Takeoff thrust, Lb Static, sea level	18,500/77°F	20,000/84°F	21,000/84°F	20,000/84°F
Reserve thrust	19,250	20,850	1,700	20,850
Takeoff thrust, Kg Static, sea level	8,391/25°C	9,072/29°C	9,525/29°C	9,072/29°C
Reserve thrust	8,731	9,458	9,843	9,458

McDONNELL DOUGLAS
MD-80 FAMILY SPECIFICATIONS

		MD-81	MD-82/-88	MD-83	MD-87
WEIGHTS:					
Max Ramp	Lb	141,000	150,500	161,000	141,000
	Kg	63,958	68,267	73,030	63,958
Max Takeoff	Lb	140,000	149,500	160,000	140,000 (Opt 149,500 67,813)
	Kg	63,503	67,813	72,576	63,503
Max Landing	Lb	128,000	130,000	139,500	128,000
	Kg	58,060	58,968	63,277	58,060
Max Zero Fuel	Lb	118,000	122,000	122,000	118,000
	Kg	53,524	55,339	55,339	53,524
FUEL CAPACITY (6.7 Lb/Gal)					
	Gal	5,840	5,840	7,000[1]	5,840
	Lb	22,106	22,104	26,495	22,106 7,000[1] 26,495
PERFORMANCE					
Cruise Speed (35,000 Ft. ISA) standard day		M = 0.76, 504 MPH (811 Km/Hr)			
SPACE LIMITED PAYLOAD	Lb	38,105	38,105	35,705	30,820
	Kg	17,284	17,284	16,196	13,980
RANGE [2,3] (Domestic Reserves)	S Mi	1,800	2,360	2,880	2,730
	Km	2,897	3,798	4,635	4,395
FAA Landing Field at MTOGW SL Std Day	Ft	7,250	7,450	8,375	6,100
	M	2,210	2,271	2,553	1,859
FAA Landing Field at MLW SL Std Day	Ft	4,850	4,920	5,200	4,690
	M	1,478	1,500	1,585	1,430

[1] with auxiliary fuel tanks
[2] MD-81, 82, 83, 88; 155 passengers and baggage payload
[3] MD-87; 130 passengers and baggage payload

McDONNELL DOUGLAS
MD-90 FAMILY SPECIFICATIONS

McDonnell Douglas Corporation
Douglas Aircraft Company, Long Beach, California

		MD-90-10	MD-90-30	MD-90-40
CAPACITY:				
Crew:		2, plus cabin attendants		
Passengers				
Typical, Mixed Class)		114	153	170-180
Passengers (Maximum)		139	172	217
Cargo holds Cu Ft		938	1343	1609
Cu M		26.6	38.0	45.6
DIMENSIONS (ALL MODELS):				
Span	Ft	107.8		
	M	32.86		
Length overall	Ft	130.4	152.6	171.6
	M	39.7	46.5	52.3
Height overall	Ft	30.5	30.9	30.9
	M	9.29	9.4	9.4
Wing Area	Sq Ft	1209		
	Sq M	112		
Sweep Back		24.5 degrees at 25% chord...............		
LANDING GEAR (TYPE):		Full retractable tricycle steerable nose wheel............		
Tread of main wheels	Ft	16.7		
	M	5.09		
Wheel base (fore & aft)	Ft	62.9	77.2	88.3
	M	19.18	23.52	26.90
Flaps (type):		Double slotted		
Slats (type):		Full span leading edge, three position		
Speed brake (type):		Wing mounted spoilers.......................		
Reversers (type):		Cascade, ground operation only		
ENGINES:		International Aero Engines		
		V2500-D2	**V2500-D1**	**V2500-D5**
Takeoff thrust, Lb Static, sea level		22,000/86°F	25,000/86°F	28,000/86°F
Takeoff thrust, Kg Static, sea level		97.86/30°C	111.2/30°C	124.6/30°C

McDONNELL DOUGLAS
MD-90 FAMILY SPECIFICATIONS

		MD-90-10	MD-90-30	MD-90-40
WEIGHTS:				
Max Ramp	Lb	140,000	157,000	164,500
	Kg	63,492	71,202	74,603
Max Takeoff	Lb	139,000	156,000	163,500
	Kg	63,039	70,748	74,150
Max Landing	Lb	122,000	142,000	157,000
	Kg	55,329	64,399	21,202
Max Zero Fuel	Lb	114,000	130,000	149,000
	Kg	51,701	58,957	67,594
FUEL CAPACITY (6.7 Lb/Gal)				
	Gal	5,840	5,840	5,840
	Lb	22,104	22,104	22,104
PERFORMANCE				
Cruise Speed (35,000 Ft. ISA standard day)		M = 0.76, 504 MPH (811 Km/Hr)		
SPACE LIMITED PAYLOAD	Lb	28,190	38,675	45,860
	Kg	12,785	17,539	20,798
RANGE (Domestic Reserves)	S Mi	2,779	2,760	2,005
	Km	4,470	4,441	3,226
FAA Takeoff Field at MTOGW SL Std Day	Ft	5,910	6,880	6,900
	M	1,801	2,097	2,103
FAA Landing Field at MLW SL Std Day	Ft	4,565	5,090	5,545
	M	1,391	1,551	1,690

McDONNELL DOUGLAS DC-10
Technical Description

	SERIES 10	SERIES 15
CAPACITY		
Passengers	250-380	250-380
Cargo Holds:		
lower galley aircraft	3017 cu ft (85.4 cu m)	3017 cu ft (85.4 cu m)
upper galley aircraft	4618 cu ft (130.7 cu m)	4618 cu ft (130.7 cu m)
DIMENSIONS		
Wingspan:	155 ft 4 in (47.3 m)	155 ft 4 in (47.3 m)
Length overall:	182 ft 3 in (55.5 m)	180 ft 8 in (55 m)
Height overall:	58 ft 1 in (17.7 m)	58 ft 1 in (17.7 m)
WING AREA		
Including aileron:	3550 sq ft (329.8 sq m)	3550 sq ft (329.8 sq m)
Sweepback:	35 degrees	35 degrees
LANDING GEAR		
Tread (main wheels):	35 ft (10.6 m)	35 ft (10.6 m)
Wheel base (fore & aft):	72 ft 5 in (22 m)	72 ft 5 in (22 m)
ENGINES		
Takeoff thrust:	Three G.E. CF6-6D	Three G.E. CF6-50C2F
	40,000 lbs (18,144 kg)	46,500 lbs (21.092 kg)
STANDARD DELIVERY WEIGHTS		
Design gross weight (ramp)	443,000 lbs (200,945 kg)	458,000 lbs (207,746 kg)
Maximum takeoff weight:	440,000 lbs (199,584 kg)	455,000 lbs (206,385 kg)
Design landing weight:[1]	363,500 lbs (164,854 kg)	363,600 lbs (164,854 kg)
Max. zero fuel weight:	335,000 lbs (151,956 kg)	335,000 lbs (151,956 kg)
Operator's empty weight:	244,193 lbs (110,764 kg)	248,496 lbs (112,716 kg)
Fuel Capacity:	21,700 U.S. gal. (82,134 L)	26,647 U.S. gal (100,858 L)
	145,810 lbs (66,139 kg)	178,537 lbs (80,983 kg)
PERFORMANCE		
Weight limited payload:	98,807 lbs (41,189 kg)	86,504 lbs (39,238 kg)
Level flight speed:	600+ MPH (965 km/hr)	600+ MPH (965 km/hr)
FAA takeoff field length Standard weight	8900 ft (2,625 m)	7500 ft (2,212 m)
FAA landing field length Standard weight	5830 ft (1,720 m)	5830 ft (1,720 m)
Design range (277 pass. & bag.) (Domestic Reserves	3800 st. mi. (6,114 km)	4350 st. mi. (7,000 km)

[1]Higher weights are available

McDONNELL DOUGLAS DC-10
Technical Description

	SERIES 30	SERIES 40
CAPACITY		
Passengers	250-380	250-380
Cargo Holds:		
lower galley aircraft	3017 cu ft (85.4 cu m)	3017 cu ft (85.4 cu m)
upper galley aircraft	4618 cu ft (130.7 cu m)	4618 cu ft (130.7 cu m)
DIMENSIONS		
Wingspan:	165 ft 4 in (50.4 m)	165 ft 4 in (50.4 m)
Length overall:	180 ft 8 in (55 m)	180 ft 7 in (55 m)
Height overall:	58 ft 1 in (17.7 m)	58 ft 1 in (17.7 m)
WING AREA		
Including aileron:	3647 sq ft (338.8 sq m)	3647 sq ft (338.8 sq m)
Sweepback:	35 degrees	35 degrees
LANDING GEAR		
Tread (main wheels):	35 ft (10.6 m)	35 ft (10.6 m)
Wheel base (fore & aft):	72 ft 5 in (22 m)	72 ft 5 in (22 m)
ENGINES		
Takeoff thrust:	Three G.E. CF6-50C2 52,500 lbs (23,814 kg)	Three P&WA JT9D-59A (with short primary nozzle) 52,500 lbs (23,814 kg)
STANDARD DELIVERY WEIGHTS		
Design gross weight (ramp)	575,000 lbs (260,820 kg)	558,000 lbs (253,061 kg)
Maximum takeoff weight:	572,000 lbs (259,459 kg)	555,000 lbs (251,701 kg)
Design landing weight:[1]	403,000 lbs (182,766 kg)	403,000 lbs (182,766 kg)
Max. zero fuel weight:	368,000 lbs (166,924 kg)	368,000 lbs (166,924 kg)
Operator's empty weight:	267,191 lbs (121,197 kg)	272,368 lbs (123,544 kg)
Fuel Capacity:	36,650 U.S. gal (138,731 L) 245,566 lbs (111,388 kg)	36,650 U.S. gal (138,153 L) 245,579 lbs (111,394 kg)
PERFORMANCE		
Weight limited payload:	100,809 lbs (45,726 kg)	95,632 lbs (43,378 kg)
Level flight speed:	600+ MPH (965 km/hr)	600+ MPH (965 km/hr)
FAA takeoff field length Standard weight	9650 ft (2,847 m)	9550 ft (2,817 m)
FAA landing field length Standard weight	5960 ft (1,758 m)	5840 ft (1,723 m)
Design range (277 pass. & bag.) (Domestic Reserves	5860 st mi (9,429 km)	5750 st m (9,252 km)

[1]Higher weights are available

THE DC-10 FAMILY

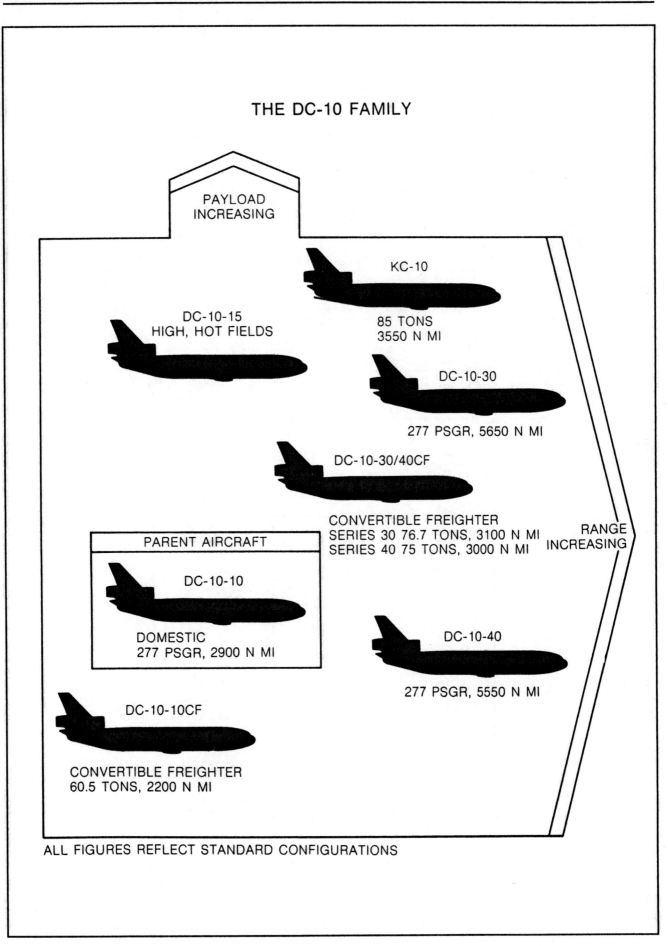

PAYLOAD
INCREASING

KC-10

85 TONS
3550 N MI

DC-10-15
HIGH, HOT FIELDS

DC-10-30

277 PSGR, 5650 N MI

DC-10-30/40CF

CONVERTIBLE FREIGHTER
SERIES 30 76.7 TONS, 3100 N MI
SERIES 40 75 TONS, 3000 N MI

RANGE
INCREASING

PARENT AIRCRAFT

DC-10-10

DOMESTIC
277 PSGR, 2900 N MI

DC-10-40

277 PSGR, 5550 N MI

DC-10-10CF

CONVERTIBLE FREIGHTER
60.5 TONS, 2200 N MI

ALL FIGURES REFLECT STANDARD CONFIGURATIONS

DC-10 ENGINE CHARACTERISTICS
GENERAL ELECTRIC CF6 FAMILY OF ENGINES

		-6D	-6D1	-6D1A	-50C	-50C1	-50C2	-50C2B	-50C2F
TAKEOFF THRUST IDEAL NOZZLE	(LB) *(N)	40,000 177,920	41,000 182,368	41,500 184,592	51,000 226,848	52,500 233,520	52,500 233,520	54,000 240,192	46,500 206,832
TAKEOFF FLAT RATED TEMP	(°F) (°C)	88 31	88 31	88 31	86 30	86 30	86 30	79 27	110 43
MAX CRUISE THRUST (M 0.85)	(LB) (N)	9,060 40,298	9,200 40,921	9,200 40,921	10,800 48,038	11,300 50,262	11,300 50,262	11,300 50,262	11,300 50,262
ENGINE SPECIFICATION WEIGHT	(LB) (kg)	8,111 3,679	8,111 3,679	8,111 3,679	8,936 4,053	8,936 4,053	8,936 4,053	8,936 4,053	8,936 4,053
CRUISE SPECIFIC FUEL CONSUMPTION (Δ FROM BASE)		BASE	SAME	SAME	BASE	SAME	—2%	—2%	—2%
DIFFERENCES FROM BASE CONFIGURATION		-6D, -6D1, AND -6D1A HAVE IDENTICAL PARTS			BASE	REVISED FUEL CONTROL SYSTEM	NEW FAN, STIFFENED FAN CASE, RESCHEDULED VARIABLE STATOR VANES		

*N (NEWTON)

DC-10 ENGINE CHARACTERISTICS
PRATT & WHITNEY JT9D FAMILY OF ENGINES

		-20	-59A
TAKEOFF THRUST IDEAL NOZZLE	(LB) (N)	45,700 203,273	53,000 235,744
TAKEOFF FLAT RATED TEMP	(°F) (°C)	84 29	86 30
MAX CRUISE THRUST (M 0.85, 35,000 FT)	(LB) (N)	10,680 47,504	11,950 53,153
CRUISE FLAT RATED TEMP	(°F)	STD + 18	STD + 18
CRUISE SPECIFIC FUEL CONSUMPTION		BASE	—1.8%
ENGINE SPEC WEIGHT	(LB) (KG)	8450 3832.9	9140 4145.9
DIFFERENCES FROM BASE CONFIGURATION		BASE	ALL NEW ENGINE EXCEPT HIGH-PRESSURE COMBUSTION IS SAME

DC-10 POPULATION
AS OF 1 JANUARY 1984

DC-10-10

MTOW	CF6-6D
410,000	84
430,000	24
440,000	5
455,000	6

DC-10-10CF

MTOW	CF6-6D
440,000	8

DC-10-15

MTOW	CF6-50C2
455,000	7

DC-10-30

MTOW	CF6-50C	CF6-50C1	CF6-50C2
555,000	50	0	34
558,000	3	0	1
565,000	7	0	13
572,000	8	9	16
580,000	0	0	15

DC-10-30CF

MTOW	CF6-50C	CF6-50C1	CF6-50C2
555,000	4	0	5
565,000	3	0	0
572,000	0	5	4
580,000	0	0	3

DC-10-40

MTOW	JT8D-20	JT8D-59A
530,000	22	
572,000		20

In addition to the above fleet, the U.S. Air Force has 20 KC-10's which are DC-10-30CF's with inflight refueling equipment.

AIRCRAFT CONFIGURATION SUMMARY

The following summary is based on data obtained from the "DC-9 Configuration Summary," detail type specifications and various other sources. The configurations shown are considered representative of each particular model. A more detailed definition of any specific aircraft may be found in the "DC-9 Configuration Summary."

Series Number	Model Number	Engine Type	Wing Configuration	Maximum Weights (Lb)			Reference Page
				Takeoff	Landing	Zero Fuel	
10	14	JT8D-1	1	85,700	81,700	71,400	3.3.1
	14	JT8D-1	1	86,300	81,700	71,800	3.3.2
	14/15	JT8D-1/-7	1	90,700	81,700	74,000	3.3.3
	15RC,MC	JT8D-7	1	90,700	81,700	74,000	3.3.4
20	21	JT8D-11	2	98,000	95,300	84,000	4.3.1
30	31	JT8D-7	2	98,000/103,000	93,400	82,000	5.3.1
	31	JT8D-7	2	100,000/108,000	95,300	87,000	5.3.2
	31	JT8D-7	2	100,000/103,000	95,300	84,000	5.3.3
	31	JT8D-9	2	103,000/105,000	98,100	87,000	5.3.4
	32	JT8D-7	2	108,000	98,100	87,000	5.3.5
	32	JT8D-9	2	108,000	98,100	87,000	5.3.6
	32	JT8D-9	2	110,000	102,000	92,000	5.3.7
	32	JT8D-15	2	110,000	101,000	92,000	5.3.8
	32	JT8D-15/-17	2	108,000	98,100	87,000	5.3.9
	33RC	JT8D-9	3	114,000	102,000	95,500	5.3.10
	33F	JT8D-11	3	114,000	102,000	95,500	5.3.11
	34	JT8D-15/-17	3	121,000	110,000	98,500	5.3.12

AIRCRAFT CONFIGURATION SUMMARY
(Continued)

Series Number	Model Number	Engine Type	Wing Configuration	Maximum Weights (Lb)			Reference Page
				Takeoff	Landing	Zero Fuel	
40	41	JT8D-11	3	114,000	102,000	93,000	6.3.1
	41	JT8D-15	3	114,000	102,000	93,000	6.3.2
50	51	JT8D-15	3	121,000	110,000	98,500	7.3.1
	51	JT8D-17	3	115,000	104,000	98,500	7.3.2
	51	JT8D-17	3	121,000	110,000	98,500	7.3.3
80	81	JT8D-209	4	140,000	128,000	118,000	8.3.1
	82	JT8D-217/217A	4	147,000	128,000	118,000	8.3.2

Wing Configuration:

1. Basic wing with double slotted flap (wing area = 934 Ft²)

2. Double slotted flap, leading edge slats, 6% chord extension, modified leading edge (wing area = 1,001 Ft²)

3. Wing configuration 2 with an incidence increase of 1.25°

4. Wing configuration 3 with 14.5 Ft increase in wing span (wing area = 1,270 Ft²) and 3- position leading edge slats

BOEING—U.S. STANDARD JET TRANSPORT CHARACTERISTICS

*Airplanes no longer in production

Characteristic	707-120*	707-120B*	707-320*	707-320B*	Advanced* 707-320B	Advanced* 707-320C Stripped Convertible	Advanced* 707-320C Convertible All-Passenger	All-Cargo
WING SPAN	130'10"	↑	142'5"	145'9"	↑	↑	↑	↑
WING AREA (SQ FT)	2,433	↑	2,892	↑	↑	↑	↑	↑
WING SWEEP (DEG)	35	↑	↑	↑	↑	↑	↑	↑
LENGTH	144'6"	145'1"(C)	152'11"	↑	↑	↑	↑	↑
HEIGHT	42'	↑	42'5"	↑	↑	↑	↑	↑
TREAD	22'1"	↑	↑	↑	↑	↑	↑	↑
WHEEL BASE	52'4"	↑	59'	↑	↑	↑	↑	↑
CABIN LENGTH	104'10"	↑	111'4"	↑	↑	↑	↑	↑
VOLUME (CU FT)	7,484	↑	7,983	↑	↑	↑	↑	↑
MAXIMUM WIDTH	140"	↑	↑	↑	↑	↑	↑	↑
FLOOR WIDTH	128"	↑	↑	↑	↑	↑	↑	↑
TYPICAL SEATING CAPACITY (FC/B/T)	181 (tourist)	30/95	14/135	14/133	14/133	—	14/133	—
CARGO VOLUME (CU FT) ALL-PASSENGER	1,665	↑	1,770	↑	—	—	1,700	—
CARGO VOLUME (CU FT) ALL-CARGO	—	—	—	—	—	7,020	—	6,749
ENGINE—QUAN. & MANUFACTURER(A)	4 P&W(B)	4 P&W	↑	↑	↑	↑	↑	↑
MODEL DESIGNATION	JT3C-6	JT3D-3B	JT4A-3/5/11/12	JT3D-3	JT3D-3B/7	JT3D-7A/3B	↑	↑
TAKEOFF THRUST (LB)	13,500	18,000	15,800/17,500	18,000	18,000/19,000	↑	↑	↑
ENGINE WEIGHT (LB)	4,234	4,300	5,100	4,300	↑	↑	↑	↑
FUEL CAPACITY (U.S. GAL)	15,456	17,300	23,855	23,855	↑	↑	↑	↑
OPTIONAL CAPACITY (U.S. GAL)	—	—	—	—	—	—	—	—
MAXIMUM TAXI WEIGHT (LB)	258,000	260,000	316,000	328,000	336,000	↑	↑	↑
TAKEOFF WEIGHT (LB)	257,340(E)	258,000(E)	312,000(E)	322,000(E)	333,600(E)	331,600(E)	333,600(E)	↑
LANDING WEIGHT (LB)	190,000	190,000	207,000	↑	247,000	↑	↑	↑
ZERO-FUEL WEIGHT (LB)	170,000	↑	190,000	↑	195,000	230,000	↑	↑
TYPICAL AIRLINE OEW (LB)	118,370	129,300	143,370	138,518	144,140	—	147,200	141,100
PAYLOAD (LB)	51,630	40,700	46,630	51,482	50,860	85,860	82,800	88,900
FIRST FLIGHT	12/20/57	6/22/60	1/11/59	1/31/62	6/63(D)	—	2/19/63(D)	↑
INITIAL SERVICE	10/26/58	6/61	8/26/59	6/1/62	—	5/67	6/3/63	↑

NOTES

(A) Where optional engine models are indiciated, the corresponding optional engine thrusts are shown. Engine weights are shown for the first engine indicated. Other engine weights correspondingly would affect OEW and payload.

(B) -220 version engine: JT4A-3, 15,800-lb thrust

(C) -138B version; length—135 ft 1 in

(D) A707-CFM-56 re-engine demonstrator flight test program began in November 1979 and ended in April 1980.

(E) Flight weight, flaps up

*Airplanes no longer in production

	707-420	720	720B
WING SPAN	142'5"	130'10"	→
WING AREA (SQ FT)	2,892	2,433	→
WING SWEEP (DEG)	35	→	→
LENGTH	152'11"	136'2"	136'9"
HEIGHT	42'5"	41'7"	→
TREAD	22'1"	21'11"	→
WHEEL BASE	59'	50'8"	→
CABIN LENGTH	111'4"	96'6"	
VOLUME (CU FT)	7,983	6,860	
MAXIMUM WIDTH	140"	→	→
FLOOR WIDTH	128"	→	→
TYPICAL SEATING CAPACITY (FC/B/T)	14/133	167 (tourist)	26/98
CARGO VOLUME (CU FT) ALL-PASSENGER	1,700	1,378	1,375
CARGO VOLUME (CU FT) ALL-CARGO	—	—	—
ENGINES—QUAN. & MANUFACTURER(A)	4 RR	4 P&W	→
MODEL DESIGNATION	508 Conway	JT3C-7/C-12	JT3D-1/3B
TAKEOFF THRUST (LB)	17,500	12,000/13,000	17,000/18,000
ENGINE WEIGHT (LB)	4,542	3,495/3,550	4,150
FUEL CAPACITY (U.S. GAL)	23,833	11,924	14,880
OPTIONAL CAPACITY (U.S. GAL)	—	13,574	16,151
MAXIMUM TAXI WEIGHT (LB)	316,000	203,000/230,000	235,000
TAKEOFF WEIGHT (LB)	312,000(E)	202,000/229,340(E)	234,340
LANDING WEIGHT (LB)	207,000	175,000/185,000	185,000
ZERO-FUEL WEIGHT (LB)	190,000	142,000/149,000	156,000
TYPICAL AIRLINE OEW (LB)	143,370	107,400/111,500	119,050
PAYLOAD (LB)	46,630	34,600/37,500	36,950
FIRST FLIGHT	5/19/59	11/23/59	10/6/60
INITIAL SERVICE	3/17/60	7/5/60	3/12/61

*Airplanes no longer in production

	727-100*		727-100C* Convertible All Passengers	All Cargo	727-200*
WING SPAN	108'	→	→	→	→
WING AREA (SQ FT)	1,560	→	→	→	→
WING SWEEP (DEG)	32	→	→	→	→
LENGTH	133'2"	→	→	→	153'2"
HEIGHT	34'	→	→	→	→
TREAD	18'9"	→	→	→	→
WHEEL BASE	53'3"	→	→	→	63'3"
CABIN LENGTH	72'8"	→	→	→	92'8"
VOLUME (CU FT)	5,133	→	5,150	→	6,561
MAXIMUM WIDTH	140"	→	→	→	→
FLOOR WIDTH	128"	→	→	→	→
TYPICAL SEATING CAPACITY (FC/B/T)	28/66	→	125 (tourist)	—	20/114
CARGO VOLUME (CU FT) ALL-PASSENGER	900	→	890	—	1,450
CARGO VOLUME (CU FT) ALL-CARGO	—	—	—	4,300	—
ENGINES—QUAN. & MANUFACTURER(A)	3 P&W	→	→	→	→
MODEL DESIGNATION	JT8D-1/7/9	→	→	→	JT8D-7/9/11
TAKEOFF THRUST (LB)	14,000/14,000 14,500	→	→	→	14,000/14,500 15,000
ENGINE WEIGHT (LB)	3,155	→	→	→	→
FUEL CAPACITY (U.S. GAL)	7,680	→	7,780	→	7,680
OPTIONAL CAPACITY (U.S. GAL)	—	—	—	—	—
MAXIMUM TAXI WEIGHT (LB)	161,000	175,000	178,000	→	173,000
TAKEOFF WEIGHT (LB)	160,000(B)	174,000(B)	177,000	→	172,000
LANDING WEIGHT (LB)	137,500	142,500	→	→	154,500
ZERO-FUEL WEIGHT (LB)	118,000	123,500	132,000	→	138,000
TYPICAL AIRLINE OEW (LB)	88,900	89,000	92,500	88,500	96,900
PAYLOAD (LB)	30,500	34,500	39,500	43,500	41,100
FIRST FLIGHT	2/9/6	—	12/30/65	→	7/27/67
INITIAL SERVICE	2/1/64	—	4/23/66	→	12/14/67

NOTES

(A) Where optional engine models are indicated, the corresponding optional engine thrusts are shown. Engine weights are shown for the first engine indicated. Other engine weights correspondingly would affect OEW and payload.

(B) Flight weight, flaps up

(C) JT8D-15A, -17A, -17AR are alternate options where -15, -17, and -17R are shown

*Airplanes no longer in production

	Advanced 727-200*	Advanced 727-200*	Advanced 727-200*	Advanced 727-200* Freighter
WING SPAN	→	→	→	108'
WING AREA (SQ FT)	→	→	→	1,560
WING SWEEP (DEG)	→	→	→	32
LENGTH	→	→	→	153'2"
HEIGHT	→	→	→	34'
TREAD	→	→	→	18'9"
WHEEL BASE	→	→	→	63'3"
CABIN LENGTH	→	→	→	92'8"
VOLUME (CU FT)	6,510			6,824
MAXIMUM WIDTH	→	→	→	140'
FLOOR WIDTH	→	→	→	128'
TYPICAL SEATING CAPACITY (FC/B/T)	14/131		189 (tourist)	—
CARGO VOLUME (CU FT) ALL-PASSENGER	1,525		1,130	—
CARGO VOLUME (CU FT) ALL-CARGO	—	—	—	6,365
ENGINES—QUAN. & MANUFACTURER(A)	3 P&W	→	→	→
MODEL DESIGNATION	JT8D-9A/15/17/17R(C)	JT8D-15/17/17R(C)	JT8D-17/17R(C)	JT8D-17A
TAKEOFF THRUST (LB)	14,000/15,500 16,000/17,400	15,500/16,000 17,400	16,000/17,400 →	16,000 →
ENGINE WEIGHT (LB)	3,352	3,414	3,430	3,495
FUEL CAPACITY (U.S. GAL)	8,090	→	8,105	8,105
OPTIONAL CAPACITY (U.S. GAL)	8,950/9,760	→	8,965/9,760/10,585	—
MAXIMUM TAXI WEIGHT (LB)	191,000	195,500	210,000	204,000
TAKEOFF WEIGHT (LB)	190,500	194,800	209,500	203,100
LANDING WEIGHT (LB)	160,000	160,000	161,000	166,000
ZERO-FUEL WEIGHT (LB)	141,000	141,000	147,000	155,000
TYPICAL AIRLINE OEW (LB)	101,200	102,300	104,100	91,898
PAYLOAD (LB)	39,800	37,700	42,900	63,102
FIRST FLIGHT	3/3/72	1/12/76	7/26/73	5/83
INITIAL SERVICE	7/72	4/1/76	11/15/73	8/83

*Airplanes no longer in production

	737-100*	737-200*	737-200* Convertible All-Passenger	737-200* Convertible All-Cargo	Advanced* 737-200	Advanced* 737-200 Convertible All-Passenger	Advanced* 737-200 Convertible All-Cargo	Advanced* 737-200 High Gross Wt/Passenger & Convertible
WING SPAN	93'	↑	↑	↑	↑	↑	↑	↑
WING AREA (SQ FT)	980	↑	↑	↑	↑	↑	↑	↑
WING SWEEP (DEG)	25	↑	↑	↑	↑	↑	↑	↑
LENGTH	94'	100'2"	↑	↑	↑	↑	↑	↑
HEIGHT	37'	↑	↑	↑	↑	↑	↑	↑
TREAD	17'2"	↑	↑	↑	↑	↑	↑	↑
WHEEL BASE	34'4"	37'4"	↑	↑	↑	↑	↑	↑
CABIN LENGTH	62'2"	68'6"	↑	↑	↑	↑	↑	↑
VOLUME (CU FT)	4,187	4,636	↑	↑	↑	↑	↑	↑
MAXIMUM WIDTH	139"	↑	↑	↑	↑	↑	↑	↑
FLOOR WIDTH	128"	↑	↑	↑	↑	↑	↑	↑
TYPICAL SEATING CAPACITY (FC/B/T)	103 (tourist)	115 (tourist)	↑	—	8/102	↑	—	8/102
CARGO VOLUME (CU FT) ALL-PASSENGER	650	875	↑	—	875	↑	—	875/740/640
CARGO VOLUME (CU FT) ALL-CARGO	—	—	—	3,605	—	—	3,605	3,605/3,475/3,370
ENGINES—QUAN. & MANUFACTURER(A)	2 P&W	↑	↑	↑	↑	↑	↑	↑
MODEL DESIGNATION	JT8D-7/9/9A	↑	↑	↑	JT8D-9A/15A/17A/17AR	↑	↑	JT8D-15A/17A/17AR
TAKEOFF THRUST (LB)	14,500 →	↑	↑	↑	14,500/15,000, 16,000/17,400(C)	↑	↑	15,500/16,000
ENGINE WEIGHT (LB)	3,166	↑	↑	↑	3,341	↑	↑	3,389
FUEL CAPACITY (U.S. GAL)	2,850	↑	↑	↑	5,160	↑	↑	↑
OPTIONAL CAPACITY (U.S. GAL)	4,209/4,774	4,209	4,726	↑	5,550/5,970	↑	↑	↑
MAXIMUM TAXI WEIGHT (LB)	97,800/111,000	110,000	116,000	↑	116,000/120,000(D)	↑	↑	125,000/128,600
TAKEOFF WEIGHT (LB)	97,000/110,000	109,000	115,500	↑	115,500/119,500(E)	↑	↑	124,500/128,100
LANDING WEIGHT (LB)	89,700/99,000	98,000	103,000	↑	103,000/107,000(F)	↑	↑	107,000/107,000(B)
ZERO-FUEL WEIGHT (LB)	81,700/92,000	88,000	95,000	↑	→	95,000/96,500	95,000/96,500(B)	95,000/99,000(B)
TYPICAL AIRLINE OEW (LB)	58,600/62,000	61,000	64,000	60,500	61,000	64,000	60,500	61,500/64,500
PAYLOAD (LB)	23,100/30,000	27,000	31,000	34,500	34,000	31,000/32,500	34,500/36,000	33,500/34,500
FIRST FLIGHT	4/9/67	8/8/67	9/18/68	↑	4/15/71	7/71	↑	3/79
INITIAL SERVICE	2/10/68	4/28/68	11/5/68	↑	6/71	8/71	↑	5/79

*Airplanes no longer in production

	737-300 Basic	737-300 Option			737-400 Basic	737-400 Option	737-400HGW High Gross Weight Option
WING SPAN	94'9"	↑	↑	↑	↑	↑	↑
WING AREA (SQ FT)	980	↑	↑	↑	↑	↑	↑
WING SWEEP (DEG)	25	↑	↑	↑	↑	↑	↑
LENGTH	109'7"	↑	↑	↑	119'7"	↑	↑
HEIGHT	36'6"	↑	↑	↑	↑	↑	↑
TREAD	17'2"	↑	↑	↑	↑	↑	↑
WHEEL BASE	40'10"	↑	↑	↑	46'10"	↑	↑
CABIN LENGTH	79'2"	↑	↑	↑	89'2"	↑	↑
VOLUME (CU FT)	5,250	↑	↑	↑	5,959	↑	↑
MAXIMUM WIDTH	139"	↑	↑	↑	↑	↑	↑
FLOOR WIDTH	128"	↑	↑	↑	↑	↑	↑
TYPICAL SEATING CAPACITY (FC/B/T)	8/120	↑	↑	↑	8/138	↑	↑
CARGO VOLUME (CU FT) ALL-PASSENGER	1,068	↑	↑	↑	1,373	↑	↑
CARGO VOLUME (CU FT) ALL-CARGO	—	—	—	—	—	—	—
ENGINES—QUAN. & MANUFACTURER(A)	2 CFMI	↑	↑	↑	↑	↑	↑
MODEL DESIGNATION	CFM56-3-B1	CFM56-3B-2	↑	↑	↑	CFM56-3C-1	↑
TAKEOFF THRUST (LB)	20,000	22,000	↑	↑	↑	23,500	↑
ENGINE WEIGHT (LB)	4,276	4,301	↑	↑	↑	↑	↑
FUEL CAPACITY (U.S. GAL)	5,311	↑	↑	↑	↑	↑	↑
OPTIONAL CAPACITY (U.S. GAL)	5,811/6,311	↑	↑	↑	↑	↑	↑
MAXIMUM TAXI WEIGHT (LB)	125,000	130,500	135,500	137,500/139,000	139,000	143,000	150,500
TAKEOFF WEIGHT (LB)	124,500	130,000	135,000	137,000/138,500	138,500	142,500	150,000
LANDING WEIGHT (LB)	114,000	↑	↑	↑	121,000	↑	124,000
ZERO-FUEL WEIGHT (LB)	105,000	105,000	106,500	↑	113,000	↑	117,000
TYPICAL AIRLINE OEW (LB)	70,300	70,350	↑	↑	73,500	73,600	74,000
PAYLOAD (LB)	34,700	34,650	36,150	↑	39,500	39,400	43,000
FIRST FLIGHT	2/84	↑	4/87	↑	3/88	↑	2/89
INITIAL SERVICE	12/84	↑	5/87	↑	9/88	↑	3/89

NOTES

(A) Where optional engine models are indicated, the corresponding optional engine thrusts are shown. Engine weights are shown for the first engine indicated. Other engine weights correspondingly would affect OEW and payload.

(B) 96,500-lb and 99,000-lb zero-fuel-weight options for cargo configurations (except for 120,000-lb gross weight)

(C) With APR

(D) Maximum taxi weight of 117,500 lb available

(E) Takeoff weight of 117,000 lb available

(F) Landing weight of 105,000 lb available

*Airplanes no longer in production

	737-500 Basic	Option
WING SPAN	94'9"	→
WING AREA (SQ FT)	980	→
WING SWEEP (DEG)	25	→
LENGTH	101'9"	→
HEIGHT	36'6"	→
TREAD	17'2"	→
WHEEL BASE	36'4"	→
CABIN LENGTH	71'4"	→
VOLUME (CU FT)	4,695	→
MAXIMUM WIDTH	139"	→
FLOOR WIDTH	128"	→
TYPICAL SEATING CAPACITY (FC/B/T)	8/100	→
CARGO VOLUME (CU FT) ALL-PASSENGER	822	→
CARGO VOLUME (CU FT) ALL-CARGO	—	—
ENGINES—QUAN. & MANUFACTURER(A)	2 CFMI	→
MODEL DESIGNATION	CFM56-3-B1	→
TAKEOFF THRUST (LB)	18,500	20,000
ENGINE WEIGHT (LB)	4,276	→
FUEL CAPACITY (U.S. GAL)	5,311	→
OPTIONAL CAPACITY (U.S. GAL)	5,811/6,311	→
MAXIMUM TAXI WEIGHT (LB)	116,000	125,000/134,000
TAKEOFF WEIGHT (LB)	115,500	124,500/133,500
LANDING WEIGHT (LB)	110,000	→
ZERO-FUEL WEIGHT (LB)	102,500	→
TYPICAL AIRLINE OEW (LB)	68,000	→
PAYLOAD (LB)	34,500	→
FIRST FLIGHT	6/89	→
INITIAL SERVICE	3/90	→

*Airplanes no longer in production

	747-100* (B) (C)	747-100B*	SR Option	747SP*	747-200B*	747-300
WING SPAN	195'8"	→	→	→	→	→
WING AREA (SQ FT)	5,500	→	→	→	→	→
WING SWEEP (DEG)	37.5	→	→	→	→	→
LENGTH	231'10"	→	→	184'9"	231'10"	→
HEIGHT	63'5"	→	→	65'5"	63'5"	→
TREAD	36'1"	→	→	→	→	→
WHEEL BASE	84'	→	→	67'4"	84"	→
CABIN LENGTH	187'	→	→	138'8"	187'	→
VOLUME (CU FT)	29,570	29,775	→	22,370	29,776	31,285
MAXIMUM WIDTH	241.5"	→	→	→	→	→
FLOOR WIDTH	233"	→	→	→	→	→
TYPICAL SEATING CAPACITY (FC/B/T)	48/337	→	550 (tourist)	28/303	32/74/260	34/76/290
CARGO VOLUME (CU FT) ALL-PASSENGER	6,250(E)	32,420	1,875(S)	3,335(F)	5,525(Q)	→
CARGO VOLUME (CU FT) ALL-CARGO	—	—	—	—	—	—
ENGINES—QUAN. & MANUFACTURER(A)	4 P&W	4 GE	→	4 RR	4 P&W	→
MODEL DESIGNATION	JT9D-7A	CF6-45A2(K)	→	RB211-524B2(L)	JT9D-7R4G2(M)	→
TAKEOFF THRUST (LB)	46,960	46,500	→	50,100	54,750	→
ENGINE WEIGHT (LB)	8,880	8,840	→	9,840	9,130	→
FUEL CAPACITY (U.S. GAL)	47,331	48,071	→	48,783	52,409	→
OPTIONAL CAPACITY (U.S. GAL)	—	—	—	50,359	53,985	→
MAXIMUM TAXI WEIGHT (LB)	713,000/738,000	713,000/753,000(N)	523,000/603,000	636,000/703,000(O)	778,000/836,000(P)	→
TAKEOFF WEIGHT (LB)	710,000/735,000	710,000/750,000	520,000/600,000	620,000/700,000	775,000/833,000	→
LANDING WEIGHT (LB)	564,000	→	505,000/525,000	450,000	564,000/630,000	574,000/630,000
ZERO-FUEL WEIGHT (LB)	526,500	→	475,000/485,000	410,000	526,500	535,000
TYPICAL AIRLINE OEW (LB)	356,900/357,100	368,700/370,000	359,300/359,300	330,400/331,000	372,920/374,100	381,820/383,000
PAYLOAD (LB)	169,600/169,400	147,800/156,500	115,700/125,700	79,600/79,000	153,580/152,400	153,180/152,000
FIRST FLIGHT	2/9/69	6/21/79	9/4/73	7/4/75	10/11/70	1/83
INITIAL SERVICE	1/22/70	9/79	9/6/73	3/15/76	11/25/71	2/83

*Airplanes no longer in production

	747-200B* COMBI All-Passenger	747-300* COMBI All-Passenger	747-400	747-400	747-400	747-400 COMBI All-Passenger	747-400 SR/LR Short-Range	Long-Range
WING SPAN	195'8"	↑	211'			211'	195'8"	211'
WING AREA (SQ FT)	5,500	↑	5,650			5,650	5,500	5,650
WING SWEEP (DEG)	37.5	↑	↑	↑	↑	↑	↑	↑
LENGTH	231'10"	↑	↑	↑	↑	↑	↑	↑
HEIGHT	63'5"	↑	↑	↑	↑	↑	↑	↑
TREAD	36'1"	↑	↑	↑	↑	↑	↑	↑
WHEEL BASE	84'	↑	↑	↑	↑	↑	↑	↑
CABIN LENGTH	187'	↑	↑					
VOLUME (CU FT)	29,775	31,285	31,285			↑	↑	↑
MAXIMUM WIDTH	241.5"	↑	↑	↑	↑	↑	↑	↑
FLOOR WIDTH	233"	↑	↑	↑	↑	↑	↑	↑
TYPICAL SEATING CAPACITY (FC/B/T)	32/74/260	34/76/290	34/76/90			24/542	34/76/290	
CARGO VOLUME (CU FT) ALL-PASSENGER	5,325(G)	↑	5,360(R)			5,235	5,360	
CARGO VOLUME (CU FT) ALL-CARGO	(I)	(I)	—	—	—	(I)	—	
ENGINES—QUAN. & MANUFACTURER(A)	4 P&W	4 GE	4 P&W	4 GE	4 RR	4GE		↑
MODEL DESIGNATION	JT9D-7R4G2(M)	CF6-80C2-B1	PW4056	CF6-80C2-B1F	RB211-524G	CF6-80C2-B1F(T)		↑
TAKEOFF THRUST (LB)	54,750	56,700	56,750	57,900	58,000	57,900		↑
ENGINE WEIGHT (LB)	9,130	9,385	9,250	9,485	9,739	9,485		↑
FUEL CAPACITY (U.S. GAL)	52,409	52,035	53,986	↑	↑	57,011		↑
OPTIONAL CAPACITY (U.S. GAL)	53,985	53,611	57,285	↑	↑	57,011		↑
MAXIMUM TAXI WEIGHT (LB)	778,000/836,000(P)	↑	803,000/873,000	↑	↑	803,000/873,000	603,000	673,000
TAKEOFF WEIGHT (LB)	775,000/833,000	↑	800,000/870,000	↑	↑	800,000/870,000	600,000	870,000
LANDING WEIGHT (LB)	585,000	605,000	574,000/630,000	↑	↑	↑	574,000	630,000
ZERO-FUEL WEIGHT (LB)	526,500	545,000	535,000	↑	↑	565,000	535,000	535,000
TYPICAL AIRLINE OEW (LB)	383,560/385,000	398,260/399,700	398,000/398,700	397,500/398,200	400,500/401,200	407,800/408,800	384,800	TBD
PAYLOAD (LB)	142,940/141,500	146,740/145,300	137,000/136,300	137,500/136,800	134,500/133,800	157,200/156,200	150,200	TBD
FIRST FLIGHT	11/18/74	10/14/82	4/88	6/88	8/88	6/89	TBD	TBD
INITIAL SERVICE	3/75	3/83	2/89	6/89	6/89	9/89	TBD	TBD

	747-200C* All-Passenger	All-Cargo	747-200F
*Airplanes no longer in production			
WING SPAN	195'8"	→	→
WING AREA (SQ FT)	5,500	→	→
WING SWEEP (DEG)	37.5	→	→
LENGTH	231'10"	→	→
HEIGHT	63'5"	→	→
TREAD	36'1"	→	→
WHEEL BASE	84'	→	→
CABIN LENGTH	187'	→	→
VOLUME (CU FT)	29,570	→	33,435
MAXIMUM WIDTH	241.5"	→	→
FLOOR WIDTH	233"	→	→
TYPICAL SEATING CAPACITY (FC/B/T)	32/420	19(D)	—
CARGO VOLUME (CU FT) ALL-PASSENGER	5,325	—	—
CARGO VOLUME (CU FT) ALL-CARGO	—	22,175(J)	22,810(H)
ENGINES—QUAN. & MANUFACTURER(A)	4 P&W	→	→
MODEL DESIGNATION	JT9D-7R4G2(M)	→	→
TAKEOFF THRUST (LB)	54,750	→	→
ENGINE WEIGHT (LB)	9,130	→	→
FUEL CAPACITY (U.S. GAL)	52,409	→	→
OPTIONAL CAPACITY (U.S. GAL)	53,985	→	→
MAXIMUM TAXI WEIGHT (LB)	778,000/836,000(P)	→	778,000/836,000
TAKEOFF WEIGHT (LB)	775,000/833,000	→	→
LANDING WEIGHT (LB)	630,000	→	→
ZERO-FUEL WEIGHT (LB)	590,000	→	→
TYPICAL AIRLINE OEW (LB)	385,560/387,000	358,260/359,700	338,960/340,400
PAYLOAD (LB)	204,440/203,000	231,740/230,300	251,040/249,600
FIRST FLIGHT	3/23/73	→	11/30/71
INITIAL SERVICE	5/12/73	→	4/19/72

NOTES

(A) OEW, payload, and weights are shown only for engines indicated. Other engines would correspondingly affect OEW and payload.

(B) Some in-service airplanes were modified with the installation of a side cargo door into eigher a Combi configuration or an all-cargo configuration.

(C) Side-cargo-door-modified 747-100SF redelivered with 713,000-, 738,000-, or 753,000-lb maximum taxi weights. All 100 Special Freighter mods had 585,000-lb maximum zero-fuel weight and 545,000-lb maximum landing weight.

(D) 32 seats on upper deck. Up to 19 passengers can be carried on upper deck in all-cargo mode.

(E) 30 LD-1 containers plus 1,000 cu ft bulk in lower lobe (pallet options available).

(F) 10 LD-1 containers and (3) 96 × 125 × 64-in. pallets plus 340 cu ft bulk in lower lobe.

(G) 14 LD-1 containers and (5) 96 × 125 × 64-in. pallets plus 800 cu ft bulk in lower lobe.

(H) (29) 8 × 8 × 10-ft pallets at 630 cu ft each plus lower lobe volume (optional installation of side cargo door will allow 10 ft high pallets at 745 cu ft in aft 21 positions).

(I) In the 6-pallet mode, six 8 high pallets at 630 cu ft each plus lower lobe volume total 8,315 cu ft. In the 12-pallet mode, (12) 8 ft high pallets at 630 cu ft each plus lower lobe volume total 12,100 cu ft. (10 ft high pallet/container capability available in aft positions.) 12-pallet configuration not available on 747-400 Combi.

(J) (28) 8 × 8 × 10-ft pallets at 630 cu ft each plus lower lobe volume.

(K) Optional engines include: General Electric CF-6-50E2-F (46,500-lb thrust) and Rolls-Royce RB211-524B2/-524C2.

(L) Optional engines: General Electric CF6-45A2/-45E2-F (46,500-lb thrust) and Rolls-Royce RB211-524C2/-524D4 (-524D4 derated on the SP to 51,600-lb thrust.)

(M) Optional engines include: General Electric CF6-50E2/-80C2/-80C2-B1 (52,500- to 56,700-lb thrust); Rolls-Royce RB211-524D4 (53,100-lb thrust).

(N) Maximum taxi weight of 738,000 lb available.

(O) Maximum taxi weight of 666,000, 676,000, and 696,000 lb available.

(P) Maximum taxi weight of 788,000, 803,000, and 823,000 lb available.

(Q) 14 LD-1 containers and (5) 96 × 125 × 64-in. pallets plus 1,000 cu ft bulk in lower lobe.

(R) 14 LD-1 containers and (5) 96 × 125 × 64-in. pallets plus 835 cu ft bulk in lower lobe.

(S) 5 LD-1 containers plus 1,000 cu ft bulk in lower lobe. Space available for 25 additonal LD-1/LD-3 containers.

(T) Optional engines include: Pratt & Whitney PW4056 (56,750-lb thrust) and Rolls-Royce RB211-524G (58,000-lb thrust).

*Airplanes no longer in production

	757-200*	757-200						
WING SPAN	124'10"	↑	↑	↑	↑	↑	↑	↑
WING AREA (SQ FT)	1,951	↑	↑	↑	↑	↑	↑	↑
WING SWEEP (DEG)	25	↑	↑	↑	↑	↑	↑	↑
LENGTH	155'3"	↑	↑	↑	↑	↑	↑	↑
HEIGHT	44'6"	↑	↑	↑	↑	↑	↑	↑
TREAD	24'	↑	↑	↑	↑	↑	↑	↑
WHEEL BASE	60'	↑	↑	↑	↑	↑	↑	↑
CABIN LENGTH	118'5"	↑	↑	↑	↑	↑	↑	↑
VOLUME (CU FT)	8,140	↑	↑	↑	↑	↑	↑	↑
MAXIMUM WIDTH	140"	↑	↑	↑	↑	↑	↑	↑
FLOOR WIDTH	128"	↑	↑	↑	↑	↑	↑	↑
TYPICAL SEATING CAPACITY (FC/B/T)	16/170(B)	↑	↑	↑	↑	↑	↑	↑
CARGO VOLUME (CU FT) ALL-PASSENGER	1,790	↑	↑	↑	↑	↑	↑	↑
CARGO VOLUME (CU FT) ALL-CARGO	—	—	—	—	—	—	—	—
ENGINES—QUAN. & MANUFACTURER(A)	2 RR	→	2 P&W	→	→	2 RR	→	2 P&W
MODEL DESIGNATION	RB211-535C	RB211-535E4(D)	PW2037(C)	→	→	RB211-535E4(D)	RB211-535E4(D)	PW2037(C)
TAKEOFF THRUST (LB)	37,400	40,100	38,200	→	→	40,100	40,100	38,200
ENGINE WEIGHT (LB)	7,350	7,360	7,180	→	→	7,360	7,360	7,180
FUEL CAPACITY (U.S. GAL)	11,253	11,276	↑	↑	↑	↑	↑	↑
OPTIONAL CAPACITY (U.S. GAL)	—	—	—	—	—	—	—	—
MAXIMUM TAXI WEIGHT (LB)	221,000	221,000/231,000	231,000/241,000	↑	241,000	↑	251,000/256,000	↑
TAKEOFF WEIGHT (LB)	220,000	220,000/230,000	230,000/240,000	↑	240,000	↑	250,000/255,000	↑
LANDING WEIGHT (LB)	198,000	↑	↑	↑	↑	↑	↑	↑
ZERO-FUEL WEIGHT (LB)	184,000	↑	↑	↑	↑	↑	↑	↑
TYPICAL AIRLINE OEW (LB)	125,810	126,060	125,750	125,750	125,750	126,060	126,210	125,900
PAYLOAD (LB)	58,190	57,940	58,250	58,250	58,250	57,940	57,790	58,100
FIRST FLIGHT	2/82	2/84	1/84	3/84	6/86	2/85	—	—
INITIAL SERVICE	1/83	10/84	4/84	11/84	7/86	3/85	—	—

NOTES

*Airplanes no longer in production

(B) Represents an overwing exit configuration. An optional pair of type I exits aft of the wing in lieu of the overwing exits is available.

(C) Optional engine: PW2040 (41,700-lb thrust).

(D) Optional engine: RB211-53524-B (43,100-lb thrust).

	757-200 Combi Passengers & 2 Pallets	747-200 Package Freighter
WING SPAN	124'10"	→
WING AREA (SQ FT)	1,951	→
WING SWEEP (DEG)	25	→
LENGTH	155'3"	→
HEIGHT	44'6"	→
TREAD	24'	→
WHEEL BASE	60'	→
CABIN LENGTH	118'5"	→
VOLUME (CU FT)	8,140	→
MAXIMUM WIDTH	140"	→
FLOOR WIDTH	128"	→
TYPICAL SEATING CAPACITY (FC/B/T)	12/138	—
CARGO VOLUME (CU FT) ALL-PASSENGER	—	—
CARGO VOLUME (CU FT) ALL-CARGO	2,540	8,430
ENGINES—QUAN. & MANUFACTURER(A)	2 RR	2 P&W
MODEL DESIGNATION	RB211-535E4(D)	PW2037(C)
TAKEOFF THRUST (LB)	40,100	38,200
ENGINE WEIGHT (LB)	7,360	7,180
FUEL CAPACITY (U.S. GAL)	11,276	→
OPTIONAL CAPACITY (U.S. GAL)	—	—
MAXIMUM TAXI WEIGHT (LB)	241,000	251,256,000
TAKEOFF WEIGHT (LB)	240	250,000/255,000
LANDING WEIGHT (LB)	198,000	210,000
ZERO-FUEL WEIGHT (LB)	184,000	200,000
TYPICAL AIRLINE OEW (LB)	127,520	112,500
PAYLOAD (LB)	56,480	87,500
FIRST FLIGHT	7/88	8/87
INITIAL SERVICE	9/88	10/87

*Airplanes no longer in production

	767-200				767-200ER Extended Range			
WING SPAN	156'1"	↑	↑	↑	↑	↑	↑	↑
WING AREA (SQ FT)	3,050	↑	↑	↑	↑	↑	↑	↑
WING SWEEP (DEG)	31.5	↑	↑	↑	↑	↑	↑	↑
LENGTH	159'2"	↑	↑	↑	↑	↑	↑	↑
HEIGHT	52'	↑	↑	↑	↑	↑	↑	↑
TREAD	30'6"	↑	↑	↑	↑	↑	↑	↑
WHEEL BASE	64'7"	↑	↑	↑	↑	↑	↑	↑
CABIN LENGTH	116'	↑	↑	↑	↑	↑	↑	↑
VOLUME (CU FT)	12,876	↑	↑	↑	↑	↑	↑	↑
MAXIMUM WIDTH	186"	↑	↑	↑	↑	↑	↑	↑
FLOOR WIDTH	178"	↑	↑	↑	↑	↑	↑	↑
TYPICAL SEATING CAPACITY (FC/B/T)	18/198	↑	↑	↑	15/40/119	↑	↑	↑
CARGO VOLUME (CU FT) ALL-PASSENGER	3,070(B)	↑	↑	↑	2,875(C)	↑	↑	↑
CARGO VOLUME (CU FT) ALL-CARGO	—	—	—	—	—	—	—	—
ENGINES—QUAN. & MANUFACTURER(A)	2 P&W	2 GE	2 P&W	2 GE	2 P&W	2 GE	2 P&W	2 GE
MODEL DESIGNATION	JT9D-7R4D/E	CF6-80A/A2	PW4050	CF6-80C2-B2F	JT9D-7R4D/E	CFG-80A/A2	PW4050/52/56	CF6-80C2-B2F/BFF
TAKEOFF THRUST (LB)	48,000/50,000	↑	50,200	52,500	48,000/50,000	↑	50,200/52,000/56,750	52,500/57,900
ENGINE WEIGHT (LB)	8,965	8,699	9,294	9,517	8,965	8,699	9,294	9,517
FUEL CAPACITY (U.S. GAL)	16,700	↑	↑	↑	16,700/20,450	↑	20,450/24,140	↑
OPTIONAL CAPACITY (U.S. GAL)	—	—	—	—	—	—	—	—
MAXIMUM TAXI WEIGHT (LB)	302,000/317,000	↑	↑	↑	337,000/352,200	↑	352,200/388,000	↑
TAKEOFF WEIGHT (LB)	300,000/315,000	↑	↑	↑	335,000/351,000	↑	351,000/387,000	↑
LANDING WEIGHT (LB)	270,000/272,000	↑	↑	↑	278,000	↑	278,000/285,000	↑
ZERO-FUEL WEIGHT (LB)	248,000/250,000	↑	↑	↑	253,000	↑	253,000/260,000	↑
TYPICAL AIRLINE OEW (LB)	178,400	177,500	179,900	180,100	183,800	183,000	184,400/184,600	184,500/184,800
PAYLOAD (LB)	69,600/71,600	70,500/72,500	68,100/70,100	67,900/69,900	69,200	70,000	68,600/75,400	68,400/75,200
FIRST FLIGHT	9/81 - 6/83	2/82 - 1/84	TBD	↑	3/84 - 5/85	8/85 - 5/85	1-90-3/88-10-89	TBD - TBD
INITIAL SERVICE	9/81 - 7/83	11/82 - 2/84	(D)	↑	3/84 - 7/85	9/85 - 7/85	TBD-6/88-TBD	TBD - (D)

*Airplanes no longer in production

	767-300				
WING SPAN	156'1"	↑	↑	↑	↑
WING AREA (SQ FT)	3,050	↑	↑	↑	↑
WING SWEEP (DEG)	31.5	↑	↑	↑	↑
LENGTH	180'3"	↑	↑	↑	↑
HEIGHT	52'	↑	↑	↑	↑
TREAD	30'6"	↑	↑	↑	↑
WHEEL BASE	74'8"	↑	↑	↑	↑
CABIN LENGTH	137'1"	↑	↑	↑	↑
VOLUME (CU FT)	15,588	↑	↑	↑	↑
MAXIMUM WIDTH	186"	↑	↑	↑	↑
FLOOR WIDTH	178"	↑	↑	↑	↑
TYPICAL SEATING CAPACITY (FC/B/T)	24/237	↑	↑	↑	↑
CARGO VOLUME (CU FT) ALL-PASSENGER	4,030(B)	↑	↑	↑	↑
CARGO VOLUME (CU FT) ALL-CARGO	—	—	—	—	—
ENGINES—QUAN. & MANUFACTURER(A)	2 P&W	2 GE	2 P&W	2 GE	2 RR
MODEL DESIGNATION	JT9D-7R4D/E	CF6-80A/A2	PW4050	CF6-80C2-B2F	RB211-524G
TAKEOFF THRUST (LB)	48,000/50,000	→	50,200	52,500	58,000
ENGINE WEIGHT (LB)	8,965	8,699	9,294	9,517	9,832
FUEL CAPACITY (U.S. GAL)	16,700	—	—	—	↑
OPTIONAL CAPACITY (U.S. GAL)	—		—	—	—
MAXIMUM TAXI WEIGHT (LB)	347,000/352,000	↑	352,000	↑	↑
TAKEOFF WEIGHT (LB)	345,000/351,000	↑	351,000	↑	↑
LANDING WEIGHT (LB)	300,000	↑	↑	↑	↑
ZERO-FUEL WEIGHT (LB)	278,000	↑	↑	↑	↑
TYPICAL AIRLINE OEW (LB)	191,100	190,200	193,600	193,800	196,900
PAYLOAD (LB)	86,900	87,800	84,400	84,200	81,100
FIRST FLIGHT	1/86 - TBD	2/86 - TBD	TBD	3/89	TBD
INITIAL SERVICE	9/86 - TBD	10/86 - TBD	(D)	4/89	(D)

NOTES

(B) Includes LD-2 con6ainers fwd and aft, and 430 cu ft bulk.
(C) Includes 125 × 96 × 64-in. pallets fwd, LD-2 containers aft and 430 cu ft bulk
(D) Availability subject to customer order.

*Airplanes no longer in production

	767-300ER Extended Range		
WING SPAN	156'1"	→	→
WING AREA (SQ FT)	3,050	→	→
WING SWEEP (DEG)	31.5	→	→
LENGTH	180'3"	→	→
HEIGHT	52'	→	→
TREAD	30'6"	→	→
WHEEL BASE	74'8"	→	→
CABIN LENGTH	137'1"	→	→
VOLUME (CU FT)	15,588	→	→
MAXIMUM WIDTH	186"	→	→
FLOOR WIDTH	178"	→	→
TYPICAL SEATING CAPACITY (FC/B/T)	18/42/150	18/42/150	18/42/150
CARGO VOLUME (CU FT) ALL-PASSENGER	3,770(C)	→	→
CARGO VOLUME (CU FT) ALL-CARGO	—	—	—
ENGINES—QUAN. & MANUFACTURER(A)	2 P&W	2 GE	2 RR
MODEL DESIGNATION	PW4056/60	CF6-80C2-B4F/B6F	RB211-524G/H
TAKEOFF THRUST (LB)	56,750/60,000	57,900/61,500	58,000/60,000
ENGINE WEIGHT (LB)	9,294/9,344	9,317/9,367	9,832
FUEL CAPACITY (U.S. GAL)	24,050	→	→
OPTIONAL CAPACITY (U.S. GAL)	—	—	—
MAXIMUM TAXI WEIGHT (LB)	381,000/409,000	→	388,000/409,000
TAKEOFF WEIGHT (LB)	380,000/407,000	→	387,000/407,000
LANDING WEIGHT (LB)	300,000/320,000	→	300,000/320,000
ZERO-FUEL WEIGHT (LB)	278,000/288,000	→	278,000/288,000
TYPICAL AIRLINE OEW (LB)	196,900/197,600	197,100/197,800	200,200/200,900
PAYLOAD (LB)	81,100/90,400	80,900/90,200	77,800/87,100
FIRST FLIGHT	2/87 - TBD	12/86 - 1/88	TBD - 5/89
INITIAL SERVICE	4/88 - (D)	6/88 - 3/88	(D) - 3/90

BOEING 777 PRINCIPAL CHARACTERISTICS

	777-200 Domestic Market A		777-200 International Market B	777 Domestic Stretch Market A	777 International Stretch Market B
Maximum Weight, Lb (Kg)					
Taxi	508,000 (230,400)	537,000 (243,600)	632,000 (286,700)	632,000 (286,700)	Future
Takeoff	506,000 (229,500)	535,000 (242,700)	630,000 (285,800)	630,000 (285,800)	
Landing	445,000 (201,800)	445,000 (201,800)	460,000 (208,700)	460,000 (208,700)	
Zero Fuel	420,000 (190,500)	420,000 (190,500)	430,000 (195,000)	430,000 (195,000)	
Engines Thrust, Lb					
Pratt & Whitney					Future
PW4073A	← 73,500				
PW4077	←	77,200			
PW4084	←		84,600	84,600	
General Electric					
GE90-B3	← 74,500				
GE90-B5	←	76,400			
GE90-B4	←		84,700	84,700	
Rolls Royce					
RB211-Trent-870	← 71,200				
RB211-Trent-877	←	76,900			
RB211-Trent-884	←		84,300	84,300	
Fuel Capacity					
US.Gal (L)	31,000 (117,300)	31,000 (117,300)	44,700 (169,200)	31,000 (117,300)	Future
Seating					
Three Class	305	305	305	368	Future
Two Class	375	375	375	451	
All Economy	440	440	440	550	
Lower Hold Volume					
Cubic Feet (Cubic Meters) Future	5,656 (160)	5,656 (160)	5,656 (160)	552 (214)	552 (214)
Maximum Operating Speed Knots CAS (Mach)	330 (0.87)				

GENERAL COMMON ABBREVIATIONS

ABNORM	Abnormal
ABS	Absolute
AC	Alternating Current
A/C	Air Conditioning
ACARS	Aircraft Communications Addressing & Reporting System
ACCEL	Acceleration, Accelerate(d)
ACE	Actuator Control Electronics
ACESS	Advanced Cabin Entertainment And Service System
ACM	Air Cycle Machine
ACMF	Airplane Condition Monitoring Function
ACMS	Aircraft Condition Monitoring System
ACP	Audio Control Panel
ACQ	Acquisition
A/D	Analog To Digital
ADC	Air Data Computer
ADF	Automatic Direction Finder
ADIRS	Air Data Inertial Reference System
ADIRU	Air Data Inertial Reference Unit
ADM	Air Data Module
ADP	Air Driven Pump/Air Driven Demand Hydraulic Pump
AEM	Audio Entertainment Multiplexer
AES	Aircraft Earth Station
AFDS	Automatic Flight Director System
AFOLTS	Automatic Fire Overheat Logic Test System
AFM	Airplane Flight Manual
AFS	Autoflight System
A/G	Air/Ground
AGB	Accessory Gear Box
AGIS	Air Ground Indication System
AGL	Above Ground Level
AIDS	Aircraft Integrated Data System
AIL	Aileron
AIMS	Aircraft Information Management System
ALT	Altitude
ALT HOLD	Altitude Hold
ALTM	Altimeter
ALTN	Alternate
AM	Amplitude Modulation
AMB	Ambient
AMP	Amperes
AMU	Audio Management Unit
ANNUNC	Annunciator
ANS	Ambient Noise Sensors
ANT	Antenna
AOA	Angle Of Attack
A/P, AP	Autopilot
APB	Auxiliary Power Breaker
APD	Approach Progress Display
APL	Airplane
APP, APPR	Approach
APPROX	Approximately
APU	Auxiliary Power Unit
ARINC	Aeronautical Radio Incorporated
ARPT, APRT	Airport
ASC	Aural Synthesizer Card
ASCPC	Air Supply Control and Cabin Pressure
ASM	Autothrottle Servo Motor
ASP	Audio Selector Panel
ASSY	Assembly
ASYM	Asymmetrical
A/S	Airspeed
A/T	Autothrottle, Adjustment/Test
ATC	Air Traffic Control
ATE	Automatic Test Equipment
ATS	Access Test System
ATT	Attitude
ATTND	Attendant
AUG	Augmentation
AUTO	Automatic
AUX	Auxiliary
AVAIL	Available
AVM	Airborne Vibration Monitor
AVS	Audio Visual System
&	And
B/A	Bank Angle
BAL	Balance
BARO	Barometric
BAT/BATT	Battery
BCD	Binary Coded Decimal
B/CRS	Back Course
B/D	Bottom Of Descent
BFE	Buyer Furnished Equipment
BFO	Beat Frequency Oscillator
BIFUR	Bifurcation
BIT	Built In Test

BITE	Built In Test Equipment	CMD	Command
BK, BRK	Brake	CMPTR	Computer
BKGRD	Background	CMS	Cabin Management System
BLD	Bleed	CMU	Central Management Unit
BMV	Brake Metering Valve	CNX	Cancelled
BNR	Binary Numerical Representation	CO	Company
BPCU	Bus Power Control Unit	COMM	Communication
BRG	Bearing	COMP	Compressor
BRKR(S)	Breaker(s)	COMPT	Compartment
BRKT	Bracket	CON	Continuous
BRT	Bright	COND	Condition
BTB(S)	Bus Tie Breaker(s)	CONFIG	Configuration
BTL	Bottle	CONN	Connection
BU	Back Up	CONT	Control
		CORR	Correction
C, CTR	Center	CP	Control Panel
°C	Degrees Centigrade	CPCS	Cabin Pressure Control System
CAA	Civil Aviation Authority (UK)	CRS	Course
CAB	Cabin	CRT	Cathode Ray Tube
CACP	Cabin Area Control Panel	CRZ	Cruise
CACTCS	Cabin Air Conditioning and Temperature Control System	CSD	Constant Speed Drive
		CSM	Cabin System Module
CANC	Cancel	CSMU	Cabin System Management Unit
CAP	Capture	CTAI	Cowl Thermal Anti-icing
CAPT	Captain	CTC	Cabin Temperature Controllers
CAR	Cargo	CTR	Center
CAS	Calibrated Airspeed	CU	Control Unit
CB(S), C/B	Circuit Breaker(s)	CW	Clockwise
CCA	Central Control Actuator	CWS	Control Wheel Steering
CCD	Cursor Control Device		
CCS	Cabin Configuration System	D/A	Digital To Analog
CCTM	Cabin Configuration/Test Module	DA	Drift Angle
CCW	Counterclockwise	DAC	Digital Audio Control
CDG	Configuration Database Generator	DADC	Digital Air Data Computer
CDU	Control Display Unit	DATR	Digital Audio Tape Reproducer
CFM	Cubic Feet Per Minute	DC	Direct Current
CG	Center Of Gravity	DCAS	Digital Controlled Audio System
CH, CHAN	Channel	DCGF	Data Conversion Gateway Function
CHG	Change	DCMF	Data Communication Management Function
CHR	Chronograph		
CHGR	Charger	DCMS	Data Communication Management System
CIC	Cabin Interphone Controller		
CIH	Cabin Interphone Handset	DCV	Directional Control Valve
CIS	Cabin Interphone System	DECEL	Decelerate(d)
CIT	Compressor Inlet Temperature	DEC	Decrease
CK	Check	DED	Dedicated
CKT	Circuit	DEG	Degree
C/L	Center Line	DEL	Delete
CL	Close	DEM	Demand
CLB	Climb	DEP	Depressurize
CLNG	Cooling	DEPT	Departure
CLR	Clear	DEST	Destination
CLS	Cabin Lighting System	DET	Detector
CLSD	Closed	DEV	Deviation
CMC	Central Maintenance Computer	DFDAC	Digital Flight Data Acquisition Card
CMCF	Central Maintenance Computer Function	DFDAF	Digital Flight Data Acquisition Function

DFDR	Digital Flight Data Recorder		ERP	Eye Reference Point
DH	Decision Height		ESC	Entertainment/Service Controller
DIFF	Difference/Differential		ET	Elapsed Time
DIR	Direct, Director		ETOPS	Extended Twin Engine Operations
DISC	Disconnect		EVAC	Evacuation
DISCH	Discharge		EVBC	Engine Vane & Bleed Control
DISCONT	Discontinued		EXH	Exhaust
DISP	Dispatch		EXT	External
DISPL	Display		EXTIN	Extinguish(ed)
DIST	Distance		EXTING	Extinguishing
DK	Deck			
DLS	Data Load System		°F	Degrees Fahrenheit
DME	Distance Measuring Equipment		F/A	Flight Attendant
DMM	Data Memory Module		FAA	Federal Aviation Administration
DN	Down		FADEC	Full Authority Digital Electronic
DNA	Does Not Apply			Engine Control
DNTKFX	Down Track Fix		FCC	Flight Control Computer
DPCU	Digital Passenger Control Unit		FCU	Fuel Control Unit
DR	Door, Drain		FD, F/D	Flight Director
DSF	Display System Function		FDAF	Flight Data Acquisition Function
DSP	Display Select Panel		FDAU	Flight Data Acquisition Unit
DTK	Desired Track		FDDI	Fiber Distributed Data Interface
			FDEP	Flight Data Entry Panel
EBU	Engine Build Up		FDH	Flight Deck Handset
ECS	Environmental Control System		FDR	Flight Data Recorder
ECU	Electronic Control Unit		FDS	Flight Director System
E/D	End Of Descent		FEXT	Fire Extinguisher
EDI	Engine Data Interface		F/F, FF	Fuel Flow
EDIU	Engine Data Interface Unit		FFR	Fuel Flow Regulator
EDT	Engine Driven Pump/Engine		FGN	Foreign
	Primary Hydraulic Pump		FIG	Figure
E/E	Electrical/Electronic		FIM	Fault Isolation Manual
EEC	Electronic Engine Control		FL	Flight Level
EES	Emergency Evaluation Signal		FL CH, FL CHG	Flight Level Change
EFI	Electronic Flight Instruments		FLD	Field
EFIS	Electronic Flight Instrument System		FLT	Flight
EGT	Exhaust Gas Temperature		FLT DIR	Flight Director
EICAS	Engine Indicating And Crew		FLTR	Filter
	Alerting System		FLUOR	Fluorescent
EIU	EFIS/EICAS Interface Unit		FM	Frequency Modulation
ELEC	Electrical		FMC	Flight Management Computer
ELECT	Electronic		FMCS	Flight Management Computer
ELEV	Elevator			System
ELMS	Electrical Load Management System		FMS	Flight Management System
EMC	Entertainment Multiplexer		FMU	Fuel Metering Unit
	Controller		F/O	First Officer
EMER	Emergency		FOD	Foreign Object Damage
EMI	Electromagnetic Interference		FPM	Feet Per Minute
ENG(S)	Engine(s)		FPV	Flight Path Vector
ENT	Entry		FQIS	Fuel Quantity Indicating System
ENTMT	Entertainment		FREQ	Frequency
EPC	External Power Contactor		FRM	Fault Reporting Manual
EPCS	Electronic Propulsion Control		F/S	Fast/Slow
	System		FSEU	Flap Slat Electronic Unit
EPR	Engine Pressure Ratio		FT	Feet, Foot
EPRL	Engine Pressure Ratio Limit		FTG	Fitting
EQUIP	Equipment		FWD	Forward

FWT	Folding Wing Tip		**IGV**	Inlet Guide Vanes
			ILLUM	Illuminate(d)
G	One Gravitational Unit		**ILS**	Instrument Landing System
GA	Go Around		**IM**	Inner Marker
GAL	Gallon		**IMBAL**	Imbalance
GB(S)	Generator Breaker(s)		**IMP**	Imperial
GBST	Ground Based Software Tool		**IN**	Inch, Inches
GCB	Generator Circuit Beaker		**INBD**	Inboard
GCU	Generator Control Unit		**INC**	Incorporated
GE	General Electric		**INCR**	Increase
GEN	Generator		**IND**	Indicator
GES	Ground Earth Station		**INFLT**	Inflight
GG	Graphics Generator		**INFO**	Information
GMT	Greenwich Mean Time		**INHB**	Inhibit
GP	Group		**INIT**	Initialize, Initialization
GPM	Gallon Per Minute		**INOP**	Inoperative
GPS	Global Positioning System		**INPH,INT**	Interphone
GPSSU	Global Positioning System Sensor Unit		**INSP**	Inspection
GPWS	Ground Proximity Warning System		**INST(S)**	Instrument(s)
GR	Gear		**INSTR**	Instrument(s)
GND, GRD	Ground		**INTLKS**	Interlocks
G/S	Glideslope		**INV**	Static Inverter, Invalid
GS	Ground Speed		**IP**	Intermediate Pressure
GW	Gross Weight		**IRS**	Inertial Reference System
			IRU	Inertial Reference Unit
H	Altitude		**ISA**	International Standard Atmosphere
HDG	Heading		**ISLN**	Isolation
HDG HOLD	Heading Hold		**IVSI**	Instantaneous Vertical Speed Indicator
HDG SEL	Heading Select			
HF	High Frequency		**JETT, JTSN**	Jettison
HG	Mercury		**KTS**	Knots
HI	High		**KEAS**	Knots, Equivalent Airspeed
HMU	Hydromechanical Control Unit		**KG(S)**	Kilogram(s)
HOR/HORIZ	Horizontal		**KGH**	Kilograms Per Hour
HORZ	Horizon		**KHZ**	Kilohertz (Kilocycles)
HP	High Pressure		**KIAS**	Knots Indicated Airspeed
HPA	Hecto Pascal		**KPA**	Kilopascal
HPC	High Pressure Compressor		**KVA**	Kilovolt - Ampere
HPSOV	High Pressure Shut Off Valve		**KVARS**	Kilovars
HPT	High Pressure Turbine		**KW(S)**	Kilowatt(s)
HR	Hour			
HT	Heat		**L**	Left
HTR	Heater		**LAC**	Local Area Controller
HYD	Hydraulic		**LAT**	Lateral
HYDQUIM	Hydraulic Digital Quantity Interface Module		**LAV**	Lavatory
			LB(S)	Pound(s)
HZ	Hertz (Cycles Per Second)		**LCD**	Liquid Crystal Display
			LCL	Local
IAS	Indicated Airspeed		**LCN**	Load Classification Number
ICU	Instrument Comparator Unit		**LDG**	Landing
IDENT	Identification		**LDG GR**	Landing Gear
I/C	Inspection/Check		**LE**	Leading Edge
IDG	Integrated Drive Generator		**LED**	Light Emitting Diode
IDS	Integrated Display System		**LF**	Left Front
IFR	Instrument Flight Rules		**LGW**	Landing Gross Weight
IGN	Ignition, Igniter		**LH**	Left Hand

LIM	Limit		MKR	Marker
LK	Lock		MLS	Microwave Landing System
LKD	Locked		MM	Middle Marker, Maintenance
LMM	Localizer Middle Marker			Manual
LN	Left Nose		MMO	Maximum Operating Speed In Mach
L NAV, LNAV	Lateral Navigation			Number
LO	Low		MN	Main
LOC	Localizer		MOD, MDL	Module
LOGO	Logographic		MON	Monitor
LOM	Localizer Outer Marker		MPH	Miles Per Hour
LONG	Longitudinal		MSB	Most Significant Bit
LP	Loop, Low Pressure		MSEC	Millisecond
LPC	Low Pressure Compressor		MSG	Message
LPM	Liters Per Minute		MSL	Mean Sea Level
LPT	Low Pressure Turbine		M-SPD	Manual Speed
LR	Left Rear		MSTR	Master
LRC	Long Range Cruise		MSU	Mode Selector Unit
LRM	Line Replaceable Module		MT	Mach Trim
LRRA	Low Range Radio Altimeter		MTG	Miles To Go
LRU	Line Replaceable Unit		MTOW	Maximum Takeoff Weight
LSB	Lower Side Band		MTS	Mach Trim System
LSU	Lavatory Service Unit		MTW	Maximum Taxi Weight
LT(S)	Light(s)		MU	Management Unit
LVDT	Linear Variable Differential		MUX	Multiplex
	Transducer		MZFW	Maximum Zero Fuel Weight
LVL	Level			
LW	Left Wing		N_1	Low Pressure Rotor
LWR	Lower		N_2	High/Intermediate Pressure Rotor
			N_3	High Pressure Rotor
M	Mach		N/A	Not Applicable
MAC	Mean Aerodynamic Chord		NAC	Nacelle
MAG	Magnetic		NAV	Navigation
MAINT	Maintenance		NCD	No Computed Data
MALF	Malfunction		ND	Navigation Display
MAN	Manual		NEUT	Neutral
MAST	Mach Airspeed Indicator		NEG	Negative
MAT	Maintenance Access Terminal		NLG	Nose Landing Gear
MAWEA	Modular Avionic Warning And		NO.	Number
	Electronic Assembly		NORM	Normal
MAX	Maximum		NOZ	Nozzle
MBS	Millibars		NM	Nautical Mile(s)
MCD	Magnetic Chip Detector			
MCP	Mode Control Panel		OAT	Outside Air Temperature
MCT	Maximum Continuous Thrust		OBS	Observer
MCU	Modular Concept Unit		OC, O/C	On Course
MDA	Minimum Descent Altitude		OEW	Operating Empty Weight
MEA	Minimum Enroute Altitude		OFST	Offset
MEC	Main Equipment Center		OK	Okay
MED	Medium		OM	Outer Marker
MEM	Memory		OP	Open
MEW	Manufacturer's Empty Weight		OPAS	Overhead Panel ARINC 629 System
MFD	Multi-function Display		OPR	Operate
MHZ	Megahertz		OPRN	Operation
MI	Miles		OUTBD	Outboard
MIC	Microphone		OVBD	Overboard
MIN	Minimum		OVHD	Overhead
MISC	Miscellaneous		OVHT	Overheat

OVPRESS	Overpressure		PSU	Passenger Service Unit
OVRD	Override		PT$_2$	Engine Inlet Temperature
OVSP	Overspeed		PTH	Pitch
OVU	Overhead Electronic Unit		PTT	Push To Talk
OXY, O$_2$	Oxygen		PVD	Paravisual Display
			PW	Pratt-Whitney
P	Pressure Change (Delta Pressure)		PWR	Power
PA	Passenger Address		P6	Panel 6
PAC	Passenger Address Controller		P11	Panel 11
PALCS	Passenger Address Level Control Sensor		%	Percent
PAS	Passenger Address System		QAD	Quick Attach Detach
PASS	Passenger		QAR	Quick Access Recorder
PB	Push-button		QEC	Quick Engine Change
PC	Personal Computer		QFE	Local Station Pressure
PCA	Power Control Actuator		QNH	Altimeter Setting
PCP	Pilot Call Panel		QTY	Quantity
PCU	Passenger Control Unit, Power Control Unit		R	Right
PDI	Pictorial Deviation Indicator		RA	Radio Altitude
PDS	Primary Display System		RABS	Reverse Actuated Bleed System
PES	Passenger Entertainment System		RAM	Random Access Memory
PF	Pilot Flying		RAT	Ram Air Turbine
PFCS	Primary Flight Control System		RCL	Recall
PFD	Primary Flight Display		RCP	Radio Communication Panel
PG	Page		RCVR	Receiver
PGM	Program		RCDR	Recorder
PIREP	Pilot Report		RDRMI	Radio Digital Distance Magnetic Indicator
PLI	Pitch Limit Indicator		RDMI	Radio Distance Magnetic Indicator
PLT(S)	Pilot(s)		RDR	Radar
PMA	Permanent Magnet Alternator		RECD	Recorded
PMAT	Portable Maintenance Access Terminal		RECIRC	Recirculate
PMG	Permanent Magnet Generator		REF	Reference
PMP	Pump		REFRIG	Refrigeration
PNF	Pilot Not Flying		REG	Regulator
PNL	Panel		REL	Release
PO	Outside Air Pressure		REPEL, REP	Repellant
POS	Position		REQ	Required
POT	Potentiometer		RES	Reserve
PPH	Pounds Per Hour		REU	Remote Electronics Unit
PRESS	Pressure		REV	Reverser, Revision
PRGM	Program		RF	Radio Frequency
PRIM	Primary		RFL	Reflected
PROC	Procedure		RH	Right Hand
PROG	Progress		R/I	Remove/Install
PROT	Protection		RLY	Relay
PROX	Proximity		RMI	Radio Magnetic Indicator
PRSOV	Pressure Regulating/Shutoff Valve		RN	Right Nose
P/RST	Push To Reset		ROM	Read Only Memory
PRV	Pressure Regulating Valve		ROT	Rotation
P/S	Pitot/Static		RPTG, RPIG	Reporting
PSC	Preset Course		RPM	Revolutions Per Minute
PSH	Pre-set Heading		RR	Right Rear, Rolls Royce
PSI	Pounds Per Square Inch		RST	Reset
PSIG	Pounds Per Square Inch Gage		RSVR	Reservoir
PSS	Passenger Service System		RT, R/T	Receiver-Transmitter, Rate Of Turn

RTE	Route		**TAI**	Thermal Anti-ice
RTO	Rejected Takeoff		**TAS**	True Airspeed
RTP	Radio Tuning Panel		**TAT**	Total Air Temperature
RUD	Rudder		**TBF**	To Be Furnished
RVDT	Rotary Variable Differential Transducer		**T/C**	Top Of Climb
			TC	Time Constant
RVR	Runway Visual Range		**TCC**	Turbine Case Cooling
RVSR	Reverser		**T/D**	Top Of Descent
RW	Right Wing		**TE**	Trailing Edge
RWY	Runway		**TEMP**	Temperature
			TGT	Target
SAARU	Secondary Attitude Air Data Reference Unit		**THR**	Thrust
			THROT	Throttle
SAT	Static Air Temperature		**THRSH**	Threshold
SATCOM	Satellite Communications		**THRU**	Through
SCID	Signal Collection/Tail ID Card		**TLA**	Throttle Lever Angle
SCU	Signal Conditioning Unit		**TMS**	Thrust Management System
SDU	Satellite Data Unit		**TMSP**	Thrust Mode Select Panel
SEC	Second		**TO, T/O**	Takeoff
SEL	Select, Selector		**TOL**	Tolerance
SELCAL	Selective Calling		**TOT**	Total
SEN	Sensor		**T/R**	Thrust Reverser
SENS	Sensitivity		**TRC**	Thermatic Rotor Control
SERV, SVC	Service		**TRK**	Track
SEU	Seat Electronic Unit		**TRU**	Transformer Rectifier(s)
SFE	Seller Furnished Equipment		**TT2**	Engine Inlet Temperature
SG	Symbol Generator		**TURB**	Turbine
SIS	Service Interphone System		**TURBL**	Turbulence
SLCTD	Selected		**TVOR**	Terminal VOR
SLCTR	Selector			
SLST	Sea Level Static Thrust		**U/D**	Upper Deck
SOL	Solenoid		**ULB**	Underwater Locator Beacon
SOP	Standard Option Pin		**UNLKD**	Unlocked
SOV	Shut Off Valve		**UNSHD**	Unscheduled
SP, SPD	Speed		**ULC**	Universal Logic Card
SPDBRK	Speedbrake		**UPR**	Upper
SPM	Surface Position Monitor		**USB**	Upper Side Band
SQL	Squelch		**UTC**	Coordinated Universal Time
SS	Single Shot		**UTIL**	Utility
SSB	Single Side Band			
SSM	Sign Status Matrix		**V**	Volt
STA	Station		**VBS**	Vertical Beam Sensor
STAB	Stabilizer		**VBV(S)**	Variable Bleed Valve(s)
STAT	Status		**VDR**	VHF Data Radio
STBY	Standby		**VEF**	Critical Engine Failure Speed
STC	Sensitivity Time Control		**VERT**	Vertical
STRG	Steering		**VFR**	Visual Flight Rules
STS	System Status		**VG**	Vertical Gyro
SUP	Supply		**VHF**	Very High Frequency (30-300 MHZ)
S/W	Software		**VIB**	Vibration
SW	Switch		**VIU**	Video Interface Unit
SYN	Synchronize		**VLV**	Valve
SYNC	Synchronous		**VMCG**	Ground Minimum Control Speed
SYS	System		**VMO**	Maximum Operating Speed
			V NAV, VNAV	Vertical Navigation
TACAN	Tactical Air Navigation		**VOL**	Volume
TACH	Tachometer		**VOLT**	Voltage

VOR	VHF Omnidirectional Range		WOW	Weight On Wheels
VORTAC	VOR And TACAN Co-located		WS	Windshear
VOX	Voice		WSHLD	Windshield
VR	Rotation Speed		WTAI	Wing Thermal Anti-icing
VREF	Reference Speed		W/W	Wheel Well
V/S	Vertical Speed		WX	Weather
V_1	Takeoff Decision Speed		WXR	Weather Radar
V_2	Scheduled Target Speed (T.O.)			
VSCF	Variable Speed Constant Frequency		XCVR	Transceiver
VSI	Vertical Speed Indicator		XDCR, XDUCER	Transducer
VSV(S)	Variable Stator Vane(s)		X-FEED	Crossfeed
VTK	Vertical Track		XFER	Transfer
			XFMR	Transformer
W	Warm		XMISSION	Transmission
WARN	Warning		XMIT	Transmit
WES	Warning Electronics System		XMTR	Transmitter
WEU	Warning Electronics Unit		XPNDR	Transponder
WPT	Waypoint		XTK	Cross Track
WDM	Wiring Diagram Manual			
WG	Wing		Y/D	Yaw Damper
WGT, WT	Weight			
WHCU	Window Heat Control Unit		ZFW	Zero Fuel Weight
WHL(S)	Wheel(s)		ZMU	Zone Management Unit
W/O	Without		ZPC	Zone Power Converter

GLOSSARY

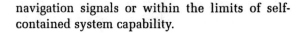

Absolute Altimeter — An altimeter that reads accurate indications in absolute altitude.

Absolute Altitude — The altitude above the surface of the earth.

Actuator — A hydraulic, electric, or pneumatic device used to move an object.

Air Carrier — A person who undertakes directly by lease, or other arrangement, to engage in air transportation.

Air Commerce — Interstate, overseas, or foreign air commerce or the transportation of mail by aircraft or any operation or navigation of aircraft within the limits of any Federal airway, or any operation or navigation of aircraft which directly affects, or which may endanger safety in interstate, overseas, or foreign air commerce.

Air Cycle Machine — Used in an air conditioning package to absorb mechanical energy (compressed air) and to cool cabin air for air conditioning through expansion cooling.

Airframe — The fuselage, booms, nacelles, cowlings, fairings, airfoil surfaces (including rotors but excluding propellers and rotating airfoils of engines), and landing gear of an aircraft and their accessories and controls.

Airliner — A large transport type aircraft that is used for air commerce for the transportation of passengers or cargo.

Air Transportation — Interstate, overseas, or foreign air transportation or the transportation of mail by aircraft.

Ambient Pressure — The pressure of the air that surrounds the aircraft on the outside.

Area Navigation (RNAV) — A method of navigation that permits aircraft operations on any desired course within the coverage of station-referenced navigation signals or within the limits of self-contained system capability.

Arm — Distance in inches to the CG of an object.

Auxiliary Power Unit (APU) — A small turbine engine used to provide electrical power and bleed air for ground operations only.

Azimuth — Horizontal direction or bearing, measured in degrees from zero reference point.

Balance Tab — It operates in such a manner as to move in the opposite direction of the main control surface. It will assist in moving the main control surface.

Basic Weight — Sum of the empty weight and certain equipment (that which is specified by owner).

Bleed Trip — Closing of the bleed valve due to an overheat.

Bus — A conductive surface used to transmit or carry electrical power to various user circuits.

Bus Tie Breaker (BTB) — Used to connect a numbered load bus to the "sync" bus.

Category — As used with respect to the certification of aircraft, means a grouping of aircraft based upon intended use of operating limitations. Examples include transport, normal, utility, acrobatic, limited, restricted, and provisional.

Category III Operations — With respect to the operation of aircraft, means an ILS approach to, and landing on, the runway of an airport using a Category III ILS instrument approach procedure issued by the Administrator or other appropriate authority.

Category A — with respect to transport category rotorcraft, means multiengine rotorcraft designed with engine and system isolation features specified in Part 29 and utilizing scheduled takeoff and landing operations under critical engine failure concept which assures adequate designated surface area and adequate performance capability for continued safe flight in the event of engine failure.

Category B — with respect to transport category rotorcraft, means single-engine or multiengine rotorcraft which do not fully meet all Category A standards. Category B rotorcraft have no guaranteed stay-up ability in the event of engine failure and unscheduled landing is assumed.

Class — As used with respect to the certification of aircraft, means a broad grouping of aircraft having similar characteristics of propulsion, flight, or landing. Examples include airplane, rotorcraft, glider, balloon, landplane, and seaplane.

Commercial Operator — A person who, for compensation or hire, engages in the carriage by aircraft in air commerce of persons or property, other than as an air carrier or foreign air carrier or under the authority of Part 375 of this Title. Where it is doubtful that an operation is for "compensation or hire," the test applied is whether the carriage by air is merely incidental to the person's other business or is, in itself, a major enterprise for profit.

Composite Material — A type of aircraft structure that generally uses plastic materials with a strengthening agent, such as epoxy (i.e. Carbon-graphite/Kevlar®/fiberglass).

Computer (aircraft) — An electronic unit that receives information (data) from sensors, processes the information, then performs the function it was programmed to do. Generally, this function is in the form of an output or command.

Constant Speed Drive (CSD) — A hydromechanical unit mounted on each engine used to drive its generator at a constant speed for constant frequency.

Course Deviation Indicator (CDI) — Provides VHF radio navigation information.

Crewmember — A person assigned to perform duty in an aircraft during flight time.

Datum — Imaginary line from which all measurement of arms are taken.

Decision Height — With respect to the operation of aircraft, means the height at which a decision must be made, during an ILS or PAR instrument approach, to either continue the approach or to execute a missed approach.

Design Landing Weight (DLW) — The maximum weight at landing touchdown authorized by applicable government regulations to maintain structural capability.

Empty Weight — The weight of the airplane structure, powerplant, fixed equipment (that which is required by FAA), unusable fuel, undrainable oil, and total hydraulic fluid.

Equipment — Those things which an individual aircraft owner may specify above the minimum required to meet FAA requirements for certification.

Field Relay (FR) — Used to control the generator through its field circuit.

Fireproof — (1) With respect to materials and parts used to confine fire in a designated fire zone, means the capacity to withstand, at least as well as steel, in dimensions appropriate for the purpose for which they are used, the heat produced when there is a severe fire of extended duration in that zone; and

(2) With respect to other materials and parts, means the capacity to withstand the heat associated with fire, at least as well as steel, in dimension appropriate for the purpose for which they are used.

Fire Resistant — (1) With respect to sheet or structural members, means the capacity to withstand the heat associated with fire, at least as well as aluminum alloy, in dimensions appropriate for the purpose for which they are used; and

(2) With respect to fluid-carrying lines, fluid system parts, wiring, air ducts, fittings, and powerplant controls, means the capacity to perform the intended functions under the heat and other conditions likely to occur when there is a fire at the place concerned.

Flame Resistant — Not susceptible to combustion to the point of propagating a flame, beyond safe limits, after the ignition source is removed.

Flammable — With respect to a fluid or gas, means susceptible to igniting readily or to exploding.

Flap Extended Speed — The highest speed permissible with wing flaps in a prescribed extended position.

Flash Resistant — Not susceptible to burning violently when ignited.

Flight Crewmember — A pilot, flight engineer, or flight navigator assigned to duty in an aircraft during flight time.

Flight Deck — Cockpit; the area where the aircraft is controlled from.

Flight Level — A level of constant atmospheric pressure related to a reference datum of 29.92 inches of mercury. Each is stated in three digits that represent hundreds of feet. For example, flight level 250 represents a barometric altimeter indication of 25,000 feet; flight 255, an indication of 25,500 feet.

Flight Time — The time from the moment the aircraft first moves under its own power for the purpose of flight until the moment it comes to rest at the next point of landing. ("Block-to-block" time.)

Foreign Air Carrier — Any person other than a citizen of the United States, who undertakes directly, by lease or other arrangement, to engage in air transportation.

Foreign Air Transportation — The carriage by aircraft of persons or property as a common carrier for compensation or hire, or the carriage of mail by aircraft, in commerce between a place in the United States and any place outside of the United States, whether that commerce moves wholly by aircraft or partly by aircraft and partly by other forms of transportation.

Freighter — An aircraft whose main purpose is to carry freight, not passengers.

Generator Breaker (GB) — Used to connect an operating generator to its load bus.

GPWS — Ground Proximity Warning System

Gross Weight — Total weight of an airplane at any given moment.

Ground Power Unit (GPU) — Used to provide onboard electrical aircraft power on the ground only.

Heat Exchanger — A device used to transfer heat from one substance to another. Heat exchangers can be air to air, air to liquid, or almost any combination.

Horizon Director Indicator (HDI) — Provides artificial horizon information in conjunction with radio navigation and ILS glide slope functions.

Idle Thrust — The jet thrust obtained with the engine power control lever set at the stop for the least thrust position at which it can be placed.

IFR Conditions — Weather conditions below the minimum for flight under visual flight rules.

Indicated Airspeed — The speed of an aircraft as shown on its pitot static airspeed indicator calibrated to reflect standard atmosphere adiabatic compressible flow at sea level uncorrected for airspeed system errors.

Instrument — A device using an internal mechanism to show visually or aurally the attitude, altitude, or operation of an aircraft or aircraft part. It includes electronic devices for automatically controlling an aircraft in flight.

Interstate Air Transportation — The carriage by aircraft of persons or property as a common carrier for compensation or hire, or the carriage of mail by aircraft in commerce—

(1) Between a place in a State or the District of Columbia and another place in another State or the District of Columbia;

(2) Between places in the same State through the airspace of any place outside that State; or

(3) Between places in the same possession of the United States; whether that commerce moves wholly by aircraft or partly by aircraft and partly by other forms of transportation.

Intrastate Air Transportation — the carriage of persons or property as a common carrier for compensation or hire, by turbojet-powered aircraft capable of carrying thirty or more persons, wholly within the same State of the United States.

Landing Gear Extended Speed — The maximum speed at which an aircraft can be safely flown with the landing gear extended.

Landing Gear Operating Speed — The maximum speed at which the landing gear can be safely extended or retracted.

Large Aircraft — Aircraft of more than 12,500 pounds, maximum certificated takeoff weight.

Leading Edge Device (LED) — Slats or flaps along the wing leading edge to improve airplane control during slow flight (takeoff, approach, and landing).

Mach Number — The ratio of true airspeed to the speed of sound.

Maintenance — Inspection, overhaul, repair, preservation, and the replacement of part, but excludes preventive maintenance.

Manual Reversion — A term used to describe aileron and elevator operation, following a complete loss of hydraulic power, by use of tabs on the inboard ailerons and the elevators.

Manufacturer's Empty Weight (MEW) — The weight of the airplane, as delivered to the operator, without the operator's equipment items.

Minimum Descent Altitude — The lowest altitude, expressed in feet above mean sea level, to which descent is authorized on final approach or during circle-to-land maneuvering in execution of a standard instrument approach procedure, where no electronic glide slope is provided.

Maximum Gross Taxi Weight (MGTW) — The maximum weight authorized for ground maneuvering by the applicable government regulations. Also designated as the maximum structural design taxi weight.

Maximum Take-off Gross Weight (MTOGW) — The maximum taxi gross weight less the fuel burn off weight for starting, taxiing, engine run-up, and holding.

Moment — Weight of object × its arm.

Operating Empty Weight (OEW) — Manufacturer's empty weight plus the operator's items, such as crew and weight, crew baggage, cargo containers, oil, *unusable* fuel, food and beverages, galley equipment, passenger service equipment, emergency equipment, potable water, and entertainment systems. It is the airplane ready to fly, except for usable fuel and payload.

Operating Weight — Basic weight, crew and their baggage, stewardess equipment, emergency and extra equipment that may be required. This does not include fuel, cargo, or anything that cannot be disposed of in flight. To summarize: includes everything but *fuel, passengers, and cargo*.

Pack — A combination of heat exchangers and air cycle machines (compressor and turbine) used to condition the air in the airplane.

Pack Trip — Closing of the pack valve due to an overheat.

Parallel Electrical System — A system in which all generators normally share the total electrical load.

PDCS — Performance Data Computer System.

"Pickle" Switch — Switches on the Captain's and F/O's control wheel used to electrically trim the horizontal stabilizer.

Pilot In Command — Means the pilot responsible for the operation and safety of an aircraft during flight time.

Pylons — Used to support and attach the engines to the aircraft.

Radio Magnetic Direction Indicator (RMDI) — Provides compass heading information together with VHF radio and ADF bearing information.

Range — The distance, in miles, an aircraft is designed to fly without refueling.

Recirculating Fan — A fan which draws air from the aircraft cabin to recirculate air from the conditioned air manifold.

S Duct — Air duct to the number two engine intake on a 727 and an L-1011.

Second In Command — A pilot who is designated to be second in command of an aircraft during flight time.

Selsyn — A self-synchronizing unit or a synchro.

Series — A specific family of one type of aircraft (i.e. DC-9-33). DC-9 is the type. 30 is the series. This specific aircraft is a 33 model.

Servo Tab (Control Tab) — Is operated directly from the cockpit to move the primary control surface.

Small Aircraft — Aircraft of 12,500 pounds or less, maximum certificated takeoff weight.

Split Bus Power Distribution System — An electrical system which uses two isolated bus bars under normal conditions.

Standard Atmosphere — The atmosphere defined in *U.S. Standard Atmosphere, 1962*. Sea level, 59°, 29.92 in. Hg.

Stopway — An area beyond the take-off runway, no less wide than the runway and centered upon the extended centerline of the runway, able to support the airplane during an aborted takeoff, without causing structural damage to the airplane, and designated by the airport authorities for use in decelerating the airplane during an aborted takeoff.

"Sync" Bus — An AC bus used to tie the three main AC buses and generators together for equal load sharing (known as parallel operation).

Takeoff Thrust — With respect to turbine engines, means the jet thrust that is developed under static conditions at a specific altitude and atmospheric temperature under the maximum conditions of rotorshaft rotational speed and gas temperature approved for the normal takeoff, and limited in continuous use to the period of time shown in the approved engine specification.

Tare Weight — Items included on scale reading when weighing aircraft that are necessary for procedure of weighing but must be deducted for actual aircraft weight.

Time In Service — With respect to maintenance time records, means the time from the moment an aircraft leaves the surface of the earth until it touches it at the next point of landing.

Transformer/Rectifier (TR) — Unit used to convert AC power to DC power.

Turbofan Engine — An aircraft gas turbine engine that produces much of its thrust through the use of a fan that bypasses air around the core of the engine.

Type — As used with respect to the certification of aircraft, means those aircraft which are similar in design. Examples include: 727, DC-9, 747.

VR (Rotation Speed) — Speed at which rotation is started to attain V_2 at 35 feet above the runway; must not be less that 105% V_{MCA}.

Vortex Generators — Devices on the vertical stabilizer used to improve boundary layer control.

Zero Fuel Weight (ZFW) — The payload (weight limited) plus the operating empty weight. Also, the maximum airplane weight less the weight of *usable* fuel and engine injection fluid (if any).

INDEX

A

AC, 2-4, 4-17

ACARS, 11-5

ACCELEROMETERS, 10-5, 10-23, 5-29

ACTUATING CYLINDERS, 5-2

ACTUATORS
Actuator Control Electronics
(ACEs), 5-30
Jack-screw type, 5-19
Servojack, 5-22, 5-25

AERONAUTICAL RADIO
INCORPORATED (ARINC), 10-2

AFT EQUIPMENT COOLING, 11-30

AILERON, 5-1

AILERONS
All speed, 5-34
Inboard, 5-10, 5-13
Master, 5-10
Outboard, 5-4, 5-6

AIR CYCLE MACHINES, 2-11, 2-13

AIR DATA COMPUTER, 10-23, 10-31,
10-39

AIR DATA COMPUTER (ADC), 10-12,
2-19

AIR DATA INERTIAL REFERENCE
SYSTEM, 10-34

AIR DATA INERTIAL REFERENCE
UNIT (ADIRU), 1-7, 5-31

AIR DATA INSTRUMENTS, 10-23

AIR DATA SENSORS, 3-6

AIR MIXING VALVE, 2-11

AIR SUPPLY AND CABIN PRESSURE
CONTROLLER (ASCPC), 2-23

AIR SUPPLY CONTROL, 2-23

AIR TRAFFIC CONTROL SYSTEMS, 1-15

AIRBORNE NAVIGATION EQUIPMENT,
10-4

AIRBUS INDUSTRIE, 1-34
A300/A310, 1-34
A320, 1-34
A330/A340, 1-34

AIRCRAFT COMMUNICATION
ADDRESSING AND REPORTING
SYSTEM (ACARS), 10-1

AIRGATE FAIRINGS, 1-31

AIRPLANE CONDITION MONITORING
SYSTEM (ACMS), 11-3

AIRPLANE INFORMATION
MANAGEMENT SYSTEM (AIMS),
1-18, 5-31, 11-1

AIRWORTHINESS DIRECTIVE (AD),
11-34

ALLIEDSIGNAL, 2-2
GTCP 85-98 APU, 2-2
GTCP85-129 series, 2-2
GTCP85-129(H), 2-2

ALTERNATING CURRENT (AC), 2-4, 4-17

ALTITUDE ALERT, 1-25, 10-7

ANTENNAS, 10-1, 10-37, 3-1

ANTI-ICE SYSTEM, 3-1, 3-6
Antenna, 3-6
Anti-fogging, 3-5
EICAS, 3-5
Engine, 3-1, 3-5
EPR corrections, 3-5
Heating elements, 3-1
Inlet guide vanes, 3-2
Pneumatic, 3-6
Stall warning, 3-2
Wing, 3-1, 3-6

APU, 1-31, 4-17

AREA NAVIGATION SYSTEMS, 10-1

ARINC, 10-2

ARINC 429, 11-3

ARINC 629, 1-18, 11-3, 2-25
Buses, 5-30
Data bus, 10-33

ARINC 700, 1-7

ASYMMETRY
Brake, 5-19
Comparator, 5-19
Condition, 5-19
Transducers, 5-19

ATA CHAPTER, 11-7
Number, 11-7

ATC, 10-34
Mode S, 10-34

ATTITUDE AIR DATA REFERENCE
UNIT (SAARU), 5-31

AUDIO SELECTOR PANEL (ASP), 10-7,
10-17

AUTOFLIGHT SYSTEM, 10-12, 10-23,
10-28

AUTOMATIC DIRECTION FINDER
(ADF), 10-5, 10-25

AUTOMATIC FLIGHT MANAGEMENT
SYSTEM, 1-15

AUTOMATIC PILOT, 1-25

AUTOMATIC SYSTEM CONTROLLERS
(ASC), 1-30

AUTOMATIC TERMINAL
INFORMATION SERVICE (ATIS), 10-1

AUTOPILOT, 10-1, 10-25, 5-2, 5-25, 5-28
Load Alleviation Function (LAF),
5-25

AUTOPILOT FLIGHT DIRECTOR
COMPUTER (AFDC), 5-31

AUTOPILOT FLIGHT DIRECTOR
SYSTEM (AFDS), 10-28

AUTOTHROTTLE, 1-7, 10-28

AUXILIARY POWER UNIT (APU), 1-31,
2-1, 4-17

AVIONICS, 1-7

AVIONICS LOCAL AREA NETWORK
(AVLAN), 11-2

AXIAL-FLOW, 1-22

B

BATTERY
Charger, 4-7, 4-11, 4-17
Nickel cadmium, 4-1, 4-11
Power system, 4-7

BATTERY CHARGER, 2-2

BITE, 10-23, 4-15, 7-17

BOEING, 1-4
737-100, 1-4
737-200, 1-4
737-300, 1-4
737-400, 1-4, 1-6
737-500, 1-4, 1-6
737-600, 1-7
737-700, 1-7
737-800, 1-7
747, 1-7
757, 1-9
767, 1-13
767-200ER, 1-13
767-300, 1-13
777, 1-15

BOEING 737-300 FIRE WARNING
SYSTEM
APU bottle discharge, 9-14
APU inlet door, 9-14
Bleed air valve, 9-12
Engine fire extinguisher, 9-12
Freon, 9-12
Kidde sensor element, 9-12
Lavatory smoke detection, 9-12
MASTER CAUTION light, 9-12
Squib, 9-12
Temperature-indicator, 9-15
WARNING horn, 9-12
WARNING lights, 9-12

BOEING 737-300 HYDRAULIC SYSTEM
    Alternate flaps, 7-7
    Boeing 737-300 quantity
        indications, 7-7
    Case drain, 7-5
    Check valves, 7-7
    Flight control, 7-7
    Heat exchanger, 7-5
    Standby reservoir, 7-5
    Standby system, 7-4, 7-7
    System A, 7-4
    System B, 7-4
    Trailing edge flaps, 7-7
BOEING 737-300 OXYGEN SYSTEM
    Chemical oxygen generator, 8-8
    Flow indicator, 8-10
    Overhead panel, 8-8
    Passenger emergency oxygen, 8-8
    Quick-donning diluter demand
        mask/regulators, 8-8
BOEING 747, 1-7
    -100, 1-8
    -200, 1-8
    -300, 1-8
    -400, 1-8
    747F, 1-8
    747SP, 1-8
    747SR, 1-8
    Air conditioning system, 2-13
BOEING 747 FUEL SYSTEM, 6-21
    ATA chapter, 6-27
    Boost pump, 6-25
    Central Maintenance Computer
        (CMC), 6-26
    Control Display Units (CDU), 6-26
    Crossfeed valve, 6-25
    Flight deck, 6-28
    Fuel management panel, 6-25
    Fuel Quantity Indicating System
        (FQIS), 6-24
    Fuel Storage Tank, 6-23
    Fuel synoptic display, 6-27
    Fuel system circuit cards, 6-25
    Fuel system management, 6-26
    Horizontal Stabilizer Tank (HST),
        6-21, 6-24
    Low pressure indication, 6-26
    Overhead panel, 6-26
    Pressure switch, 6-26
BOEING 747-400 HYDRAULIC
    SYSTEM, 7-23
    AC motor-driven demand pump,
        7-23
    Air-driven demand pump, 7-25
    Case drain, 7-25
    EICAS, 7-27
    Engine-driven pump, 7-25
    Reservoir, 7-25
BOEING 747-400 LANDING GEAR, 7-27
    Centering cam, 7-27
    Landing gear tillers, 7-27
    Proximity switch, 7-27
BOEING 747-400 OXYGEN SYSTEM
    Frangible disc, 8-10
    High pressure cylinders, 8-10
BOEING 757
    Accumulator, 7-20

Air conditioning system, 2-13
Air/ground relay, 7-20
Alternate Brake Selector Valve
    (ABSV), 7-20
Alternate brake system, 7-20
Alternate extension, 7-15
ANTISKID light, 7-20
Antiskid valve modules, 7-23
AUTOBRAKE light, 7-23
Brake overheat, 7-20
Brake system, 7-20
Brake system alternate antiskid
    valves, 7-20
Brake system antiskid valves, 7-20
Brake system, antiskid/autobrake,
    7-20
Brake temperature, 7-17
Built-In Test Equipment (BITE), 7-
    17
Bungee, 7-17
Downlock link, 7-13
Hydraulic brake assemblies, 7-17
Inertial Reference System (IRS),
    7-20
Landing gear centering cams, 7-17
Landing gear drag brace, 7-17
Landing gear lever position, 7-20
Landing gear tillers, 7-17
Landing gear torsion link, 7-17
Landing gear truck beam, 7-17
Logic cards, 7-17
Main landing gear, 7-13, 7-17, 7-20
Nose gear, 7-13, 7-15
Nosewheel steering, 7-17
Proximity switch, 7-15, 7-17, 7-20
Reserve brake system, 7-17, 7-20
Struts, 7-20
Uplock, 7-13
BOEING 757 FIRE EXTINGUISHING
SYSTEM
    Bottle discharge indication, 9-25
    Engine fire extinguishing, 9-25
    Flight deck, 9-25
    Handle, 9-25
    Squib, 9-25
BOEING 757 FIRE WARNING SYSTEM
    Detector, 9-23
    Systron Donner, 9-22
BOEING 757 HYDRAULIC SYSTEM, 7-7
    Case drain (CD), 7-10
    Color code, 7-10
    EICAS, 7-10
    Engine-driven pump (EDP), 7-10
    Heat exchanger, 7-10, 7-13
    Overhead panel, 7-10
    Power Transfer Unit (PTU), 7-10
    Ram air turbine, 7-10
BREAKOUT MECHANISM, 5-15
BUILT-IN-TEST, 2-23
BULK CARGO, 1-15, 1-31
BUNGEES, 5-15, 7-17
    Over-ride, 5-10
BUS
    Bus Tie Breaker (BTB), 4-14
    Essential AC, 4-7
    Essential DC, 4-7
    Ground handling bus, 4-14

Split, 4-2, 4-7
Split System Breaker (SSB), 4-3,
    4-14, 4-15
Split system parallel, 4-2, 4-11
Transformer Rectifier Unit (TRU),
    4-14

C

CABIN AIR CONDITIONING
    TEMPERATURE CONTROL SYSTEM
    (CACTCS), 2-23
CABIN DIFFERENTIAL PRESSURES,
    11-27
CABIN INTERPHONE SYSTEM (CIS),
    10-17
CABIN MANAGEMENT SYSTEM, 10-32
    Cabin interphone, 10-32
    Cabin lighting, 10-32
    Passenger address, 10-32
    Passenger entertainment, 10-32
    Passenger service, 10-32
CABIN PRESSURE SELECTOR, 2-18
CABIN TEMPERATURE CONTROLLER
    (CTC), 2-23
CABLE BREAK DETECTORS, 5-19
CALL SYSTEM, 10-10
    External power receptacle, 10-10
CARBON DIOXIDE 9-3
CARBON FIBERS, 1-18
CARGO SYSTEM, 1-15
CATHODE RAY TUBE, 1-15
CDU, 11-1
CENTRAL MAINTENANCE
    COMPUTER, 11-4
CENTRAL MAINTENANCE COMPUT-
    ING SYSTEM (CMCS), 4-11, 11-4
CENTRIFUGAL SWITCH, 2-3
CHECK VALVE, 2-9
CHECKLIST, 1-29
CHORD, 1-7, 5-34
CMC, 11-5
    Menu, 11-6
    Shop faults function, 11-9
COCKPIT VOICE RECORDER, 10-11,
    10-21
COMBI INTERIOR, 1-29
COMPOSITE, 1-34
COMPRESSOR
    Bleed, 2-1
    Load, 2-1, 2-5, 2-8
CONFIDENCE TEST, 11-7
CONSTANT SPEED DRIVE (CSD), 4-1,
    4-4, 4-15
CONTROL DISPLAY UNIT (CDU), 10-28,
    10-34, 11-6
CONTROL PATH, 5-10
CONTROL SURFACE DAMPERS, 5-12
CONTROL SYSTEM
    Artificial feel, 5-26
    Cable tension regulator, 5-15
    Control laws, 5-28

Crosshead, 5-15
Feedback mechanism, 5-19
Feel computer, 5-7
Feel system, 5-7
Load alleviation, 5-29
Pressurization, 5-15
Surface Position Indicator (SPI), 5-13
Torque limiter, 5-10
CONTROL THERMOSTAT, 2-3
COOLING DOOR, 2-13
CROSS-CREW QUALIFICATION, 1-34
CRT, 1-29, 1, 9-29
CRUISE SPEED, 1-22, 1-26

D

DARK COCKPIT, 1-29
DASH NUMBERS, 1-1
DATA COMMUNICATION MANAGE-
MENT SYSTEM (DCMS), 11-1
DC, 2-3, 4-1, 4-17
DC-9
Fueling, 6-21
DC-9 HYDRAULIC SYSTEM, 7-30
Landing gear, 7-31
Multiple disc brake, 7-31
Power transfer unit, 7-30
Steering cylinders, 7-31
DC-10 HYDRAULIC SYSTEM, 7-31
DEFUELING, 6-6, 6-11
DIGITAL, 1-5, 1-15, 1-25, 1-29, 5-29, 9-29
DIGITAL DATA BUS, 10-23
DIGITAL ELECTRONICS, 1-15
DIGITAL FLIGHT DATA ACQUISITION
UNIT (DFDAU), 10-2
DIGITAL FLIGHT DATA RECORDER
(DFDR), 11-3
DIHEDRAL, 1-9
DIRECT CURRENT (DC), 2-3, 2-18, 4-1,
4-17
DIRECT LIFT CONTROL SERVO (DLCS),
5-13
DIRECT LIFT CONTROL SERVOS, 5-10
DISTANCE MEASURING EQUIPMENT
(DME), 10-25, 10-37
DOUGLAS AIRCRAFT COMPANY (*see
McDonnell Douglas*)

E

EDUCTOR COOLING SYSTEM, 1-7
EFIS, 1-25, 1, 10-28, 11-1, 11-5
EICAS, 1-15, 11-1, 11-5, 11-30, 3-5, 4-11,
6-26, 7-10, 7-27, 9-1, 9-29
EICAS MAINTENANCE PAGES, 11-7
ELECTRICAL MANAGEMENT SYSTEM
(ELMS), 2-25
ELECTRICAL SYSTEM, 2-2, 4-1, 4-7, 4-17
Automatic load shedding system,
4-19
Backup converter, 4-17
External power, 4-19

Transformer Rectifier Unit (TRU),
4-2
ELECTRICAL SYSTEM
Power management panels, 4-17
ELECTRONIC ATTITUDE DIRECTOR
INDICATOR (EADI), 10-11, 10-28
ELECTRONIC CONTROL UNIT (ECU),
2-8
ELECTRONIC FLIGHT INSTRUMENTA-
TION SYSTEM (EFIS), 1-25
ELECTRONIC HORIZONTAL SITUA-
TION INDICATOR (EHSI), 10-28
ELEVATORS, 5-1, 5-10, 5-15
Flutter, 5-15
EMERGENCY, 11-23
Automatic slide inflation, 11-27
Escape hatches, 11-27
Escape path lighting, 11-23
Escape slides, 11-27
Evacuation, 11-27
EMERGENCY LOCATOR
TRANSMITTER (ELT), 10-7
EMERGENCY POWER, 4-1
EMPENNAGE, 1-31
ENGINE ANTI-ICE, 2-8
ENGINE BLEED AIR, 2-9
ENGINE BLEED AIR VALVE, 2-9
ENGINE INDICATING AND CREW
ALERTING SYSTEM (EICAS), 1-15,
9-29, 10-31, 11-1, 11-5, 11-30
ENVIRONMENTAL CONTROL SYSTEM
(ECS), 1-31, 2-11
EQUIPMENT COOLING SYSTEM, 11-27
EXTENDED RANGE TWIN ENGINE
OPERATIONS (ETOPS), 1-20
EXTERNAL POWER, 4-1, 4-11, 4-19
Carts, 4-14
Receptacle, 10-9, 10-10

F

FEEDBACK LINKAGE, 5-15
FILTERS, 2-2, 2-9
FIRE
Class A fire, 9-3
Class B fire, 9-3
Class C fire, 9-3
Class D fire, 9-3
Class E fire, 9-3
Detection, 9-5
FIRE DETECTION SYSTEM, 9-1
Bimetallic thermoswitch, 9-1
Cabin pressurization, 9-2
Continuous-loop detector system,
9-1
Labyrinth, 9-2
Photoelectric cell, 9-2
Smoke detection system, 9-2
Thermal switch, 9-1
FIRE EXTINGUISHING AGENTS, 9-3
Carbon dioxide, 9-3
Halogenated hydrocarbon, 9-3
Inert cold gas, 9-3
Nitrogen, 9-4

FIRE EXTINGUISHING SYSTEM
Boeing 757, 9-25
Discharge valves, 9-4
High-rate-of-discharge (HRD), 9-4
Red indicating disk, 9-5
FIRE PROTECTION SYSTEM, 9-1
Extinguishing system, 9-1
Lockheed L-1011, 9-5
Nacelles, 9-1
Wheel wells, 9-1
FLAPS, 1-7
Asymmetrical flap condition, 5-19
Asymmetry, 5-19
Double slotted, 1-7
Flap/Slat Electronic Unit (FSEU),
5-33
Fowler, 5-10
Krueger, 5-33
Outboard trailing edge, 5-7
Power Drive Unit (PDU), 5-19
Retracted, 5-4, 5-7
Slotted, 5-34
Trailing edge, 5-34, 7-7
Triple slotted, 1-7
Triple slotted trailing edge, 1-4, 5-6
Wing, 5-4
FLAT PANEL DISPLAY, 1-18
FLIGHT CONTROL COMPUTER (FCC),
1-30, 5-22, 5-29, 10-31
FLIGHT CONTROL DATA
CONCENTRATOR (FCDC), 5-24
FLIGHT CREW, 1-31
FLIGHT DECK, 1-1, 1-15, 1-29, 2-13, 4-15
FLIGHT DECK COMMUNICATION
FUNCTION (FDCF), 11-1
FLIGHT DECK EFFECT, 11-5
FLIGHT DIRECTOR, 1-25, 10-1, 10-12,
10-25
FLIGHT ENVELOPE, 1-13, 1-34, 5-28
FLIGHT INSTRUMENT SYSTEM (FIS),
10-28
FLIGHT INTERPHONE SYSTEM (FIS),
10-17, 10-31
FLIGHT MANAGEMENT, 11-1
FLIGHT MANAGEMENT COMPUTER
(FMC), 2-19, 10-2, 10-25, 10-28, 10-37
FLIGHT MANAGEMENT SYSTEM, 10-37
FLY-BY-WIRE, 1-18, 1-42, 4-17, 5-22, 5-30
FORWARD ELECTRONICS SERVICE
CENTER (FESC), 1-31
FORWARD ELECTRONICS SYSTEM,
11-30
FREON, 9-12
FREQUENCY, 10-1, 10-14, 3-2, 4-4, 4-11,
4-14, 4-15
FUEL
Capacity, 1-3, 1-22
Clear and bright, 6-1
Contamination, 6-1
Efficiency, 1-11
Flow, 2-8
Gasoline, 6-1
Hydrocarbons, 6-1
Icing, 6-1

Jet A, 6-1
Jet B, 6-1
Kerosene, 6-1
Micro-organisms, 6-1
Tanks, 1-25, 1-31
Viscosity, 6-1
Water, dissolved, 6-1
Water, entrained, 6-1
FUEL PUMP
    AC-powered, 6-6
    Boost, 6-6
    Centrifugal booster, 6-3
    Engine-driven, 6-3, 6-6
FUEL SOLENOID VALVE, 2-3
FUEL SYSTEM
    Boeing 747, 6-21, 6-24-6-25, 6-27
    Boost pump screens, 6-1
    Capacitance indicators, 6-4
    Central refueling system, 6-6
    Check valves, 6-6
    Crossfeed system, 6-5
    Defueling, 6-6, 6-11
    Differential pressure switch, 6-3
    Fire switch, 6-6
    Flow indicators, 6-2
    Flow transmitter, 6-4
    Heat, 6-3
    Jettison, 6-3, 6-6
    Lockheed L-1011, 6-10-6-12, 6-17,
        6-20
    McDonnell Douglas DC-9, 6-21
    Micro-organisms, 6-17
    Pressure gauge, 6-5
    Pressure indicator, 6-2
    Pressure warning, 6-5
    Quantity indicating system, 6-4
    Screens, 6-1
    Selector valves, 6-3
    Shutoff valves, 6-6
    Starvation, 6-6
    Strainers, 6-3
    Tanks, 6-2-6-3
    Valve-in-transit indicator light, 6-5
    Vent system, 6-6
    Water, 6-17
FUEL TANK, 1-27
    Temperature indicator, 6-5
FUJI HEAVY INDUSTRIES, 1-20
FULL AUTHORITY DIGITAL ENGINE
    CONTROL (FADEC), 1-7, 1-42

G

G FORCE SWITCH, 10-7
GASPER AIR, 2-13
GENERAL ELECTRIC, 1-5
    CF6, 1-13
    CF6-50, 1-27
    CF6-50E2, 1-8
    CF6-80C2, 1-29
    CFM56-3, 1-5
    CFM56-3-B1, 1-6
    CFM56-5A1, 1-42
    CFM56-5B, 1-7
    GE-90, 1-17

GENERATOR, 4-2
    Auxiliary power breaker (APB), 4-14
    Backup, 4-17
    Bus tie breaker (BTB), 4-3
    Constant Speed Drive (CSD), 4-4,
        4-15
    Control, 4-2
    Control units, 4-15
    Frequency, 4-4, 4-11, 4-15
    Generator Circuit Breaker (GCB),
        4-14
    Generator Control Current
        Transformer (GCCT), 4-3
    Generator drive oil temperature
        indicator, 4-11
    Heat exchanger, 4-4, 4-15
    Integrated Drive Generator (IDG),
        4-11
    Overhead panel, 4-2
    Permanent Magnet Generator
        (PMG), 4-17
    Voltage regulator, 4-2, 4-4, 4-11
GLASS COCKPIT, 1-34
GLIDESLOPE, 10-12, 10-23
GLOBAL POSITIONING SYSTEM
    (GPS), 10-34
GLOBAL POSITIONING SYSTEM
    SENSING UNIT (GPSSU), 10-34
GROSS WEIGHT, 1-3, 1-26
GROUND CALL SYSTEM, 10-32
GROUND POWER EQUIPMENT, 2-1
GROUND PROXIMITY WARNING
    SYSTEM (GPWS), 9-19, 10-25
GUST SUPPRESSION FUNCTION, 5-32

H

HEAT EXCHANGER, 2-9, 2-13, 4-4, 4-15,
    7-5, 7-10, 7-13
HEATING ELEMENTS, 3-9
HIGH BYPASS RATIO, 1-13
HIGH FREQUENCY SYSTEM (HF), 10-1,
    10-32
HIGH LIFT AUGMENTATION, 5-29
HIGH LIFT CONTROL SYSTEM
    (HLCS), 5-30
HORIZONTAL SITUATION INDICATOR
    (EHSI OR HSI), 10-11
HOT SECTION, 2-2
HYDRAULIC
    Accumulators, 5-29
    Fuses, 5-10
    Priority valves, 5-10
    Ram Air Turbine (RAT), 5-24
    Systems, 5-24
HYDRAULIC FLUIDS, 7-1
HYDRAULIC PUMPS, 7-2
    Constant-delivery, 7-2
    Electric motor-driven, 7-3
    Piston-type, 7-3
    Ram air turbine, 7-3
    Variable-delivery, 7-2
HYDRAULIC SYSTEM, 7-1
    Accumulator, 7-4

    Actuating cylinder, 7-4
    Boeing 737-300, 7-4-7-5, 7-7
    Boeing 747-400, 7-23
    Boeing 757, 7-7, 7-10
    DC-9, 7-30
    DC-10, 7-31
    Double-action cylinder, 7-4
    Filters, 7-2
    Landing gear, 7-1
    Leading edge devices, 7-1
    Lockheed L-1011, 7-29
    Pressure relief valve, 7-3
    Pumps, 7-2
    Ram air turbine, 7-10
    Reservoirs, 7-2
    Selector valve, 7-2
    Speed brakes, 7-1
    Valves, 7-2
HYDRAULIC SYSTEM LIQUIDS, 7-1
    Chemical stability, 7-1
    Fire point, 7-1
    First aid treatment, 7-2
    Flash point, 7-1
    Seals, 7-1
    Skydrol® 500B, 7-1
    Viscosity, 7-1
HYDROCARBONS, 6-1
HYPOXIA, 8-1

I

INERTIAL NAVIGATION SYSTEM, 10-5
INERTIAL REFERENCE SYSTEM (IRS),
    10-23
INFORMATION MANAGEMENT
    SYSTEM (AIMS), 10-33
INLET DOOR, 2-3
INLET GUIDE VANES, 2-6, 2-8
INLET PLENUM, 2-5
INSTRUMENT COOLING SYSTEM,
    11-27
INSTRUMENT LANDING SYSTEM
    (ILS), 10-1, 10-4, 10-25
INTEGRATED DISPLAY SYSTEM (IDS),
    11-4
INTEGRATED DRIVE GENERATOR
    (IDG), 4-1, 4-11
INTERCOMMUNICATION, 10-17
INTERPHONE SYSTEM, 10-9

K

KAWASAKI HEAVY INDUSTRIES, 1-20
KILOVOLT-AMPS-REACTIVE (KVAR),
    4-4
KILOWATTS (KW), 4-4
KVA, 1-7

L

LATERAL AXIS, 5-1
LD3 CONTAINERS, 1-29
LEADING EDGE DEVICES, 5-6

LIFT-TO-DRAG RATIO, 5-33

LIGHTING SYSTEM, 11-19
    Anti-collision, 11-20
    Cargo compartment, 11-23
    Emergency, 11-23
    EXIT, 11-23
    Exterior, 11-19
    FASTEN SEAT BELT, 11-23
    Incandescent, 11-23
    Instrument panel floodlights, 11-20
    Landing, 11-19
    Main aisle, 11-23
    Map lights, 11-23
    NO SMOKING, 11-23
    Passenger cabin, 11-23
    Runway turnoff, 11-20
    Service compartment, 11-23

LINE REPLACEABLE UNIT (LRU), 10-31, 6-25

LIQUID CRYSTAL DISPLAY (LCD), 1-7, 1-18

LOAD CONTROL VALVE, 2-3

LOCALIZER, 10-23

LOCKHEED
    L-1011, 1-31, 6-6

LOCKHEED L-1011 FIRE SYSTEM, 9-5
    Bottles, 9-7
    Extinguisher test panel, 9-10
    Extinguishing, 9-5
    Labyrinth, 9-5
    Monobromotrifluoromethane, 9-7
    Red thermal discharge disk, 9-9
    Smoke detection, 9-5
    Squib, 9-9

LOCKHEED L-1011 FUEL SYSTEM, 6-6
    Defueling, 6-11
    Defueling, boost pump, 6-12
    Defueling, manifold isolation valve, 6-12
    Fire, engine, 6-15
    Fuel pump, boost, 6-15
    Fuel system, bypass check valve, 6-17
    Fuel system, crossfeed valves, 6-15
    Fuel system, dripless stick, 6-20
    Fuel system, flame arrestor, 6-12
    Fuel system, flow equalizer, 6-15
    Fuel system, jet ejector pumps, 6-17
    Fuel system, jettison, 6-20
    Fuel system, level sight gauge, 6-20
    Fuel system, low level warning, 6-18
    Fuel system, quantity tank probe, 6-18
    Fuel system, surge box, 6-15
    Fuel system, surge tank, 6-12
    Fuel system, tank quantity measurements, 6-17
    Fuel system, vent system, 6-12
    Fueling manifold, 6-10
    Manifold isolation valve, 6-10
    Nozzle adapters, 6-10
    Poppet check valve, 6-12
    Scavenge system, 6-10
    Seepage, 6-12
    ShutOff Valve (SOV), 6-10
    Surge boxes, 6-10

    Surge tank, 6-10

LOCKHEED L-1011 HYDRAULIC SYSTEM, 7-29
    Air turbine motor, 7-29
    System A, 7-29
    System B, 7-29
    System C, 7-29
    System D, 7-29

LOCKHEED L-1011 OXYGEN SYSTEM
    Chemical oxygen generators, 8-6
    Diluter-demand regulators, 8-2
    Flow indicator, 8-2
    Mask, 8-4
    Overpressure relief fitting, 8-2
    Overpressure safety plug, 8-6
    Passenger oxygen controller, 8-6
    Passenger service module (PSM), 8-7
    Pressure reducer, 8-2

LONGITUDINAL AXIS, 5-1

LONGITUDINAL STABILITY AUG-MENTATION SYSTEM (LSAS), 1-30

LORAN, 10-5

LOW FLOW SENSOR, 11-30

LOW FREQUENCY, 10-39

LOW OIL PRESSURE LIGHT, 2-3

LRU, 11-1

M

MACH, 1-7, 5-33

MAIN ENGINE START (MES), 2-2

MAIN LANDING GEAR, 2-21

MAINTENANCE ACCESS TERMINAL (MAT), 11-4

MAINTENANCE INFORMATION
    Air Transport Association of America Specification Number 100, 11-34
    Airworthiness Directives, 11-34
    ATA Specification No. 100, 11-35
    Illustrated Parts Catalog (IPC), 11-34
    Maintenance manual, 11-34
    Nondestructive testing manual, 11-34
    Overhaul manual, 11-34
    Revisions to maintenance manuals, 11-36
    Service instructions, 11-34
    Structural repair manual, 11-34
    Tool and equipment lists, 11-34
    Weight and balance manual, 11-34
    Wiring diagram manual, 11-34

MAINTENANCE PRACTICE, 11-36

MARKER BEACON, 10-1, 10-4, 10-25

MAXIMUM PRESSURE DIFFERENTIAL, 2-16, 2-23

MAXIMUM RANGE, 1-8, 1-27

MAXIMUM TAKEOFF WEIGHT, 1-6, 1-22

MCDONNELL DOUGLAS, 1-20
    DC-10, 1-20, 4-19
    DC-3, 1-20
    DC-6, 1-20
    DC-9, 1-20, 1-22, 4-3, 4-17, 6-21, 7-30
    MD-11, 1-20, 1-29

    MD-80, 1-20, 1-22, 1-25
    MD-81, 1-22
    MD-82, 1-22
    MD-83, 1-22
    MD-87, 1-22
    MD-88, 1-22
    MD-90, 1-20

MICROPHONE, 10-9
    Boom, 10-9
    Hand, 10-9
    Integral, 10-9

MID ELECTRICAL SERVICE CENTER (MESC), 1-31

MITSUBISHI HEAVY INDUSTRIES, 1-20

MONITORING CHANNEL, 5-26

MONOBROMOTRIFLUOROMETHANE, 9-7

MULTI-FUNCTION DISPLAY, 11-1

N

N_1, 1-13, 1-34

N_2, 1-13, 1-34

N_3, 1-34

NACELLES, 1-1, 1-4, 3-1, 9-1

NAVIGATION EQUIPMENT, 10-21

NAVIGATIONAL AIDS, 10-1

NEGATIVE PRESSURE RELIEF VALVE, 2-19

NOSE GEAR, 2-21

O

OMEGA, 10-37

OMNIDIRECTIONAL RADIO RECEIVERS, 10-1

OPERATIONAL FLEXIBILITY, 1-13

OUTFLOW VALVE, 2-16, 2-18

OUTSIDE AIR TEMPERATURE (OAT), 3-1

OVERHEAD PANEL, 1-29, 3-10, 5-24, 7-10

OVERHEAD PANEL AVIONICS SYSTEM (OPAS), 2-25

OXYGEN SYSTEM, 8-1
    Boeing 737-300, 8-8
    Boeing 747-400, 8-10
    Chemical oxygen generator, 8-1
    Emergency, 8-1
    Explosive or rapid decompression, 8-1
    Flight crew oxygen, 8-1
    Flight deck environment, 8-1
    Generator chemical core, 8-1
    Hypoxia, 8-1
    Lockheed L-1011, 8-2
    Partial pressure, 8-1
    Pressure-demand, 8-1
    Pressurization, 8-1
    Sodium Chlorate, 8-1
    Squib, 8-2

P

PACK VALVES, 2-11, 2-13
PARAMETER EXCEEDANCES, 11-5
PASSENGER ADDRESS (PA) SYSTEM,
    10-1, 10-10, 10-17
PASSENGER ENTERTAINMENT
    SYSTEM (PES), 10-21
PITCH, 1-30, 10-31, 5-1, 5-13, 5-28
PITCH TRIM, 5-2, 5-26
PITOT-STATIC SYSTEM, 10-21
PLANENET, 11-2, 11-4
PNEUMATIC DUCT PRESSURE
    INDICATOR, 2-11
PNEUMATIC SYSTEM, 2-1, 2-9, 2-13,
    2-18
POSITION TRANSDUCERS, 5-30
POWER CONTROL UNITS (PCUS), 5-31
PRATT & WHITNEY
    2037, 1-13
    4460, 1-29
    JT8D, 1-1, 1-22
    JT8D-200, 1-22, 1-25
    PW4000, 1-17
    V2500, 1-25
    V2500-A1, 1-42
PRECOOLER, 2-18
PRESSURE RELIEF VALVE, 2-18, 2-23
PRESSURIZATION, 1-28, 2-8, 2-11, 2-13,
    2-18
PRIMARY FLIGHT COMPUTERS
    (PFCS), 5-30
PRIMARY FLIGHT DISPLAY (PFD), 11-1
PYLONS, 1-1, 1-42

R

RADAR, 10-7
    Display, 10-14
    Display brightness, 10-12
    Echo, 10-7
    Pulse transmission, 10-7
    RAdio Detection And Ranging, 10-7
    Weather, 10-7, 10-36
RADAR BEACON TRANSPONDER, 10-5
RADIO ALTIMETER (RA), 10-7, 10-25
RADIO DISTANCE MAGNETIC
    INDICATOR (RDMI), 10-28
RADIO TUNING PANEL (RTP), 10-32
RAIN, 3-2
    Overhead panel, 3-5
    Repellent, 3-2, 3-5
    Sight gauge, 3-5
    Windshield wipers, 3-2, 3-5
RAM AIR TURBINE (RAT), 4-1
RESERVOIRS, 2-11, 3-10
ROLL, 10-31, 5-1, 5-13
ROLLS-ROYCE, 1-8, 1-26
    RB-211, 1-31, 1-34
    RB211, 1-8
    RB211-524L, 1-29

RB211535, 1-13
    Trent 800, 1-17
RUDDER, 5-1

S

S DUCT, 1-34
SATELLITE COMMUNICATIONS
    SYSTEM, 10-33
    Airborne earth station (AES), 10-33
    Ground Earth Stations (GES), 10-33
    Relay stations, 10-33
    SATCOM, 10-33
SATELLITE NAVIGATION, 10-34
SELCAL, 10-4, 10-33
    Decoder, 10-4, 10-17
    System, 10-17
SELECTIVE CALLING SYSTEMS
    (SELCAL), 10-1
SEMI-MONOCOQUE, 1-31
SERVICE CENTER, 1-31, 2-21, 5-19
SIDESTICK CONTROLLER, 5-24, 5-28
SIX-WHEEL TRUCKS, 1-19
SKYDROL®, 7-1
SLATS, 1-4, 1-22, 3-5, 5-4, 5-6, 5-10, 5-29
    Fully extended, 5-22
    Leading edge, 5-7, 5-19
    Position indicator, 5-22
    Proximity switches, 5-22
    Retracted, 5-22
SNECMA, 1-5
SPEED BRAKES, 5-6, 5-13, 5-26
SPOILERS, 5-4, 5-10, 5-13
    Flight, 5-4, 5-6
    Roll, 5-26
STABILITY
    Dutch roll, 5-29
    Neutral static, 5-29
    Short term attitude, 5-29
STABILIZER BRAKE, 5-2
STABILIZERS
    Stabilizer Trim Control Module
        (STCM), 5-32
    Trimmable Horizontal Stabilizer
        (THS), 5-22, 5-25
STALL WARNING, 5-34
STANDBY HYDRAULIC SYSTEM, 5-3
STANDBY POWER, 4-1
STARTER DUTY CYCLE, 2-3
STATUS MESSAGES, 9-33
STRUTS, 1-5, 1-9
SWEPT BACK, 1-9, 1-31, 5-3
SYMBOL GENERATORS (SGS), 10-11
SYSTEM STATUS, 9-33

T

T-TAIL CONFIGURATION, 1-22
TAKEOFF THRUST, 1-3, 1-25
THERMAL SWITCHES, 11-27
THREE PHASE AC POWER, 4-15

THRUST MANAGEMENT COMPUTING
    SYSTEM (TMCS), 10-28, 10-31, 11-1
THRUST RATINGS, 1-9
TIMED ACCELERATION FUEL
    CONTROL UNIT (TAFCU), 2-2
TITANIUM, 1-7
TOTAL AIR TEMPERATURE (TAT),
    10-23, 3-1, 3-6
TRAFFIC ADVISORY (TA), 10-36
TRAFFIC ALERT AND COLLISION
    AVOIDANCE SYSTEM (TCAS), 10-34
TRANSPONDERS, 10-5
TRI-JET, 1-1
TRIM AIR, 2-13
TRIM SYSTEMS, 5-7
TRIM TAB, 5-7
TROUBLESHOOT, 11-4
TWIN SPOOL AXIAL-FLOW, 1-4

U

UNDERWATER LOCATOR BEACON,
    10-31
UNIT LOAD DEVICES (LD), 1-19
UNITED TECHNOLOGIES, DIVISION
    OF P&W, 1-26

V

VARIABLE PITCH STATOR VANES, 1-13
VERTICAL AXIS, 5-1
VERTICAL FIN, 1-31
VERY HIGH FREQUENCY (VHF), 10-1,
    10-7
VHF COMMUNICATIONS RADIOS,
    10-14
VHF COMMUNICATIONS SYSTEM,
    10-32
VISCOSITY, 3-3, 6-1
VOICE RECORDER, 10-32
VOLTAGE REGULATOR, 4-2, 4-4, 4-11
VOR NAVIGATION SYSTEM, 10-25

W

WARNING SYSTEM, 9-10
    Aircraft overspeed, 9-10
    Altitude alert, 9-1
    Aural, 9-19
    Aural warnings, 9-15
    Auto-pilot disconnect, 9-1
    Boeing 737-300, 9-12
    Boeing 757, 9-22
    Cabin pressure, 9-1
    Clacker, 9-15, 9-18
    Digital computers, 9-19
    Doors, 9-1
    Engine Indicating and Crew
        Alerting System (EICAS), 9-1
    Fire, 9-1
    Fire and overheat, 9-1

Fire warning bell, 9-15
Flight controls, 9-1
Gear lever position, 9-17
Ground proximity, 9-1, 9-19
Horn, 9-17
Horn cutout switch, 9-17
Landing gear indication, 9-17
Mach/airspeed, 9-18
On-board, 9-1
Overspeed, 9-1
Positive rate of climb, 9-20
Slat position, 9-1
Stall, 9-18
Stick shaker, 9-18
Tactile signals, 9-15
Takeoff configuration, 9-17
Unsafe landing, 9-1, 9-10
Unsafe takeoff, 9-1, 9-10
Visual warnings, 9-15
Windshear, 9-19

WASTE, 11-14
    Drain valve, 11-17
    Flush valve, 11-14
    Level monitoring system, 11-19
    Motor-pump-filter, 11-17
    Service panels, 11-14
    Tank odors, 11-14
    Toilet flushing, 11-14
    Vacuum, 11-19
    Water panel, 11-14
WATER, 11-9, 2-11, 3-2–3-3
    Chlorinated, 11-9
    Distribution system, 11-14
    Heater, 11-14
    Heater blankets, 11-9
    Potable, 11-9
    Service panel, 11-9
WATER SEPARATOR, 2-11
WAYPOINTS, 10-37

WIND SHEAR DETECTION, 1-25, 1-29
WINDOW HEATING SYSTEMS, 3-9
WINDSHIELD HEAT, 3-9
WINDSHIELD WASHER FLUID, 3-10
WING FLAPS, 5-6
WINGLETS, 1-9, 1-29

Y

YAW, 5-1, 5-13, 5-26
    Dampening, 5-26
    Damper unit, 5-32
    Stability, 5-26
YAW DAMPER, 10-28, 5-3